PRINCIPLES of ISLAMIC JURISPRUDENCE

Mohammad Hashim Kamali

PRINCIPLES of ISLAMIC JURISPRUDENCE

Revised Edition

ISLAMIC TEXTS SOCIETY

This edition published 1991 by The Islamic Texts Society
22a Brooklands Avenue, Cambridge CB2 2DQ, UK

Reprinted 1997

A catalogue record of this book is available
from the British Library

ISBN 0 946621 23 3 *cased*
ISBN 0 946621 24 1 *paper*

Typeset by Goodfellow & Egan, Cambridge
Printed in Malta by Interprint Limited

Publication of this volume has been
made possible by the generous support
of Dar al-Maal al-Islami, Geneva.

ABOUT THE AUTHOR

Dr. Mohammad Hashim Kamali is currently Professor of Law at the International Islamic University of Malaysia, where he has been teaching Islamic law and jurisprudence since 1985. Born in Afghanistan in 1944, he studied law in Kabul University, where he was later appointed Assistant Professor. Following this he worked as Public Attorney with the Ministry of Justice in Afghanistan.The author then went to England where he completed his LL.M., and then his doctoral studies in London University where he specialised in Islamic law and Middle Eastern Studies. Dr. Kamali then held a post of Assistant Professor at the Institute of Islamic Studies at McGill University in Montreal, and later worked as Research Associate with the Social Science and Humanities Research Council of Canada. He is the author of *Law in Afghanistan, A Study of the Constitutions, Matrimonial Law and the Judiciary* (Leiden: E.J. Brill, 1985), and *Freedom of Expression in Islam* (forthcoming). The author has published a number of articles in learned international journals. He comes from a family with long-standing legal and judicial service in Afghanistan and his knowledge of Islamic law is an interesting blend of the theory and practice of this discipline in Afghanistan and then of studying and teaching this subject in England, Canada and Malaysia.

Foreword

Uṣūl al-fiqh has always occupied a prominent place in the teaching curricula of Islamic institutions of legal learning. As a discipline of *Sharīʿah*, *uṣūl al-fiqh* embodies the study of the sources of Islamic law and the methodology for its development. But even beyond its specific frame of reference one might say that *uṣūl al-fiqh* provides a set of criteria for the correct evaluation and understanding of almost any branch of Islamic learning. The teaching programmes of Islamic law which are conducted in English are in many ways hampered by the shortage of adequate reading materials in this language, and this is particularly the case with regard to *uṣūl al-fiqh*. The need for a comprehensive text on *uṣūl al-fiqh* has long been felt by students and readers in this University. Dr. Hashim Kamali's contribution is therefore well received and appreciated by all those who are concerned with studying or teaching *uṣūl al-fiqh* in this University. Since the initial publication of this book in 1989 in Kuala Lumpur, it has already become a well-acknowledged and widely read work of reference on the subject. The style of Professor Kamali's writing is refreshingly unconventional and yet his work remains well-founded and in close contact with the Arabic sources of his discipline. The author's personal experience of training in both Islamic and modern legal disciplines has been well reflected in his work as he makes frequent comparisons with the concepts and principles of Western jurisprudence.

I take this opportunity to express my appreciation of Professor Kamali's valuable contribution. I also welcome the decision of the Islamic Texts Society of Cambridge, U.K., to bring out a new and more refined edition of this book. Students and readers of Islamic jurisprudence in English-speaking institutions of higher learning who do not read Arabic will find this book a significant contribution in the depth and detail of information that it provides along the lines one would expect to find in the Arabic sources of its origin. In his Preface the author himself has explained the approach he has taken to the writing of this book and has made comments on how the existing literature on *uṣūl al-fiqh* in

English tends to be generic and therefore insufficient for purposes of undertaking a full course of study in this subject.

I wish Professor Mohammad Hashim Kamali great success in his continued efforts to write and add to our fund of knowledge and understanding.

Prof. Tan Sri Datuk Ahmad Ibrahim
Dean/Shaikh
Kulliyyah of Laws
International Islamic University
Malaysia

بسم الله الرحمن الرحيم

Contents

Preface

I. Apart from the fact that the existing works on Islamic Jurisprudence in the English language do not offer an exclusive treatment of *uṣūl al-fiqh*, there is also a need to pay greater attention to the source materials, namely the Qur'ān and *sunnah*, in the study of this science. In the English works, the doctrines of *uṣūl al-fiqh* are often discussed in relative isolation from the authorities in which they are founded. Furthermore, these works tend to exhibit a certain difference of style and perspective when they are compared to the Arabic works on the subject. The *uṣūl al-fiqh* as a whole and all of the various other branches of the Sharīᶜah bear testimony to the recognition, as the most authoritative influence and source, of divine revelation (*waḥy*) over and above that of rationality and man-made legislation. This aspect of Islamic law is generally acknowledged, and yet the relevance of *waḥy* to the detailed formulations of Islamic law is not highlighted in the English works in the same way as one would expect to find in the works of Arabic origin. I have therefore made an attempt to convey not only the contents of *uṣūl al-fiqh* as I found them in Arabic sources but also the tone and spirit of the source materials which I have consulted. I have given frequent illustrations from the Qur'ān, the *Sunnah* and the well-recognised works of authority to substantiate the theoretical exposition of ideas and doctrines. The works of the *madhāhib*, in other words, are treated in conjunction with the authority in which they are founded.

II. The idea to write this book occurred to me in early 1980 when I was teaching this subject to postgraduate students at the Institute of Islamic Studies at McGill University in Montreal. But it was only after 1985 when I started a teaching post at the International Islamic University, Selangor, Malaysia, that I was able to write the work I had intended. I was prompted to this decision primarily by the shortage of English textbooks on Islamic jurisprudence for students who seek to acquire an intermediate to advanced level of proficiency in this subject. Works that are currently available in English on Islamic law and jurisprudence are on the whole generic in that they tend to treat a whole range of topics both on *uṣūl al-fiqh* and the various branches of *fiqh* (i.e. *furū*ᶜ *al-fiqh*), often within the scope of a single volume. The information that such works contain on *uṣūl al-fiqh* is on the whole insufficient for purposes of pursuing a full course of study on this subject. The only exception to note here, perhaps, is the area of personal law, that is, the law of marriage, divorce, inheritance, etc., which has been treated exclusively, and there are a number of English texts currently available on the subject. Works of Arabic origin on *uṣūl al-fiqh* are, on the whole, exclusive in the treatment of this discipline. There is a selection of textbooks in Arabic, both classical and modern, at present available on this subject, ranging from the fairly concise to the more elaborate and advanced. Works such as ᶜAbd al-Wahhāb Khallāf's *ᶜIlm Uṣūl al-Fiqh*, Abū Zahrah's *Uṣūl al-Fiqh*, Muḥammad al-Khuḍarī's *Uṣūl al-Fiqh*, and Badrān's *Uṣūl al-Fiqh al-Islāmī* are but some of the well-known modern works in the field. Classical works on *uṣūl al-fiqh*, of which there are many, are, broadly speaking, all fairly elaborate, sometimes running into several volumes. I have relied, in addition to the foregoing, on al-Ghazālī's *Al-Mustaṣfā min ᶜIlm al-uṣūl*, al-Āmidī's *Al-Iḥkām fī Uṣūl al-Aḥkām*, al-Shāṭibī's *Al-Muwāfaqāt fī Uṣūl al-Aḥkām* and al-Shawkānī's *Irshād al-Fuḥūl fī Taḥqīq al-Ḥaqq min ᶜIlm al-Uṣūl*. These are all devoted, almost exclusively, to the juridical subject-matter of *uṣūl al-fiqh*, and rarely, if ever, address the historical development of this discipline beyond such introductory and incidental references as the context may require. Arabic writers tend to treat the historical development of jurisprudence separately from the *uṣūl al-fiqh* itself. There are several Arabic works of modern origin currently available on the history of jurisprudence and its various phases of development, namely the Prophetic period, the era of the Companions, the early schools of law in the Ḥijāz and Iraq, the emergence of the *madhāhib*, the era of imitation (*taqlīd*), and the call for a return to *ijtihād*. This discipline is generally known as '*tārīkh al-tashrī*ᶜ' which, as the title suggests, is primarily concerned with the history of juristic thought and institutions.[1] The Arabic texts on *uṣūl al-fiqh* itself are on the whole devoted to a treatment of the sources and methodology of the law, and tend to leave out its history of development.

The reverse of this is true with regard to works that are currently available on the general subject of Islamic jurisprudence in the English language. Works of Western authorship on this subject are, broadly speaking, primarily concerned with the history of jurisprudence, whereas the juridical subject-matter of *uṣūl al-fiqh* does not receive the same level of attention as is given to its historical development. Bearing in mind the nature of the existing English literature on the subject, and the fact that there is adequate information available on the history of Islamic jurisprudence in English, the present work does not attempt to address the historical developments and instead focuses on *uṣūl al-fiqh* itself.

Another point to be noted regarding works on Islamic jurisprudence in English by both Muslim and non-Muslim authors is that they are somewhat selective in their treatment of the relevant topics, and certain subjects tend to be ignored or treated only briefly. Consequently, information on some topics, such as the rules of interpretation, classification of words, commands and prohibitions, and textual implications (*al-dalālāt*) is particularly brief and often non-existent in these works. Even some of the more familiar topics such as *qiyās, istiḥsān, istiṣlāḥ, istiṣḥāb* and *sadd al-dharā'i*ᶜ are treated superficially in most of the English books that are currently in use. The reasons for such omissions are not always clear. The authors might have considered some of these topics to be somewhat technical and involved for English readers whose interest in *uṣūl al-fiqh* has for a long time remained confined to general and introductory information on the subject. Some of these topics, such as the rules of interpretation, *al-dalālāt* and the technicalities of *qiyās* which draw somewhat heavily on the use of Arabic terminology, might have been viewed in this light. The English-speaking student of Islamic studies has been perceived as someone who would have little use for technical detail on *uṣūl al-fiqh*. This might at best offer a plausible explanation, but it is one which carries little weight, especially in view of the greater interest that has been more recently taken in Islamic legal studies in the West, as well as some of the English speaking institutions of higher learning that have emerged in Islamic countries themselves.[2] Moreover, the fact that Islamic countries have in recent decades shown a fresh interest in developing greater harmony between the *Sharī*ᶜ*ah* and statutory laws has also meant that practicing lawyers and judges in these countries are increasingly encouraged to enhance their expertise in the *Sharī*ᶜ*ah* disciplines.

Modern Arabic writings on *uṣūl al-fiqh* tend to differ from the older works on the subject in that the former take cognizance of recent developments both in the Muslim communities and beyond. Thus the reader of many a modern work often comes across comments and comparisons which seek to explain the application and relevance of the *Sharī*ᶜ*ah* doctrines to modern legislation, and to the principles of Western jurisprudence. Much to their credit, some ulema and writers of modern works have attempted to relate the classical formulations and doctrines of *uṣūl al-fiqh* to the contemporary socio-legal conditions of their communities. There exists a level of concern over the gap that has gradually developed between the *Sharī*ᶜ*ah* and modern law and over the fact that the problem still remains to be tackled. There have also been attempts, be them in the form of individual reform proposals, a call for fresh *ijtihād* over particular issues, or formal resolutions adopted at national and international gatherings of scholars, which seek to tap the resources of *uṣūl al-fiqh* in bridging the gap between the *Sharīᶜah* and modern conditions of society. A full account of such developments would fall well beyond the scope and objective of the present work.[3] But in discussing certain doctrines such as *ijtihād, ijmāᶜ, istiḥsān* and *maṣlaḥah*, I have attempted to present the modern current of opinion, and occasionally my own views, as to how these principles could be utilised in contemporary legal and judicial processes. I have taken this liberty despite the awareness that it might fall beyond the brief of a work which seeks to be an exposition of the existing doctrines and institutions as they are. I wish to add here that I alone bear full responsibility for the propriety or otherwise of my views.

Furthermore, the recent Arabic texts on *uṣūl al-fiqh* tend to treat their subject-matter in a more consolidated and simplified form which makes it manageable to the modern student of law. These works are on the whole more concise by comparison with the earlier authorities on the subject. It is primarily in matters of format and style in which they differ from the older works. As for substantive matters, the modern works are normally expected to preserve the continuity of the earlier authorities, and the two are basically indistinguishable in this regard. Having said this, one might add further that the modern works tend to differ from their predecessors in one other respect, namely that the former tend to offer a more even-handed treatment of the views and doctrines of such schools of thought as the Muᶜtazilah, the Shīᶜah and the Ẓāhiriyyah, etc., and tend to treat ideas on merit rather than their formal acceptance and recognition by the established *madhāhib*. In addition to the textbook materials on *uṣūl al-fiqh*, a number of legal encyclopedias have emerged in recent decades in Egypt and elsewhere, usually bearing the title '*al-Mawsūᶜah al-Fiqhiyyah*' with the express purpose of offering a balanced treatment of the views and contributions of all the prominent schools of law. As a result, the relatively stronger orientation toward particular schools that is noticeable in the earlier works on *uṣūl al-fiqh*, especially those that were authored after the crystallisation of the *madhāhib*, is not a prominent feature of the modern works. A more open attitude has in fact emerged which seeks to move away from the sectarian bias that can be found in some earlier works, and it is no longer unusual for a Sunnī scholar to write on Shīᶜī thought, scholars and institutions, with a view to highlighting their contributions to Islamic law and jurisprudence. The present writer welcomes this development, but if his own work fails to offer adequate coverage of the doctrines of the various schools, it is due solely to considerations of brevity and space which may be expected of a handbook of this size.

III. It is perhaps true to say that Islamic jurisprudence exhibits greater stability and continuity of values, thought and institutions when compared to Western jurisprudence. This could perhaps be partially explained by reference to the respective sources of law in the two legal systems. Whereas rationality, custom, judicial precedent, morality and religion constitute the basic sources of Western law, the last two acquire greater prominence in Islamic Law. The values that must be upheld and defended by law and society in Islam are not always validated on rationalist grounds alone. Notwithstanding the fact that human reason always played an important role in the development of *Sharīᶜah* through the medium of *ijtihād*, the *Sharīᶜah* itself is primarily founded in divine revelation.

A certain measure of fluidity and overlap with other disciplines such as philosophy and sociology is perhaps true of both Islamic and Western jurisprudence. But it is the latter which exhibits the greater measure of uncertainty over its scope and content. Thus according to one observer, books that bear the title 'jurisprudence' vary widely in subject-matter and treatment, because 'the nature of the subject is such that no distinction of its scope and content can be clearly determined,'[4] and in Julius Stone's somewhat dramatic phrase, jurisprudence is described as 'a chaos of approaches to a chaos of topics, chaotically delimited'.[5]

Uṣūl al-fiqh, on the other hand, has a fairly well-defined structure, and the ulema had little difficulty in treating it as a separate discipline of Islamic learning. Textbooks on *uṣūl al-fiqh* almost invariably deal with a range of familiar topics and their contents are on the whole fairly predictable. This is perhaps reflective of the relative stability that the *Sharīᶜah* in general and the *uṣūl al-fiqh* in particular has exhibited through its history of development, almost independently of government and its legislative organs. This factor has, however, also meant that *uṣūl al-fiqh* has for the most part been developed by individual jurists who exerted themselves in their private capacity away from the government machinery and involvement in the development of juristic thought. Consequently, *uṣūl al-fiqh* has to some extent remained a theoretical discipline and has not been internalised by the legislative machinery of government. The history of Islamic jurisprudence is marred by a polarisation of interests and values between the government and the ulema. The ulema's disaffection with the government did not encourage the latter's participation and involvement in the development of juristic thought and institutions, and this has to some extent discouraged flexibility and pragmatism in Islamic jurisprudence. Note, for example, the doctrinal requirements of *ijmāʿ*, especially the universal consensus of the entire body of the *mujtahidūn* of the Muslim community that is required for its conclusion, a condition which does not concede to considerations of feasibility and convenience. There is also no recognition whatsoever of any role for the government in the doctrine of *ijmāʿ* as a whole. The government for its part also did not encourage the ulema's involvement and participation in its hierarchy, and isolated itself from the currents of juristic thought and the scholastic expositions of the ulema. The schools of jurisprudence continued to grow, and succeeded in generating a body of doctrine, which, however valuable, was by itself not enough to harness the widening gap between the theory and practice of law in government. One might, for example, know about *qiyās* and *maṣlaḥah*, etc., and the conditions which must be fulfilled for their valid operation. But the benefit of having such knowledge would be severely limited if neither the jurist nor the judge had a recognised role or power to apply it. One might add here also the point that no quick solutions are expected to the problem over the application of the *Sharīʿah* in modern jurisdictions. The issue is a long-standing one and is likely to continue over a period of time. It would appear that a combination of factors would need to be simultaneously at work to facilitate the necessary solutions to the problem under discussion. One such factor is the realisation of a degree of consensus and cooperation between the various sectors of society, including the ulema and the government, and the willingness of the latter, to take the necessary steps to bring internal harmony to its laws. To merge and to unify the *Sharīʿah* and modern law into an organic unity would hopefully mean that the duality and the internal tension between the two divergent systems of law could gradually be minimised and removed.

Bearing in mind the myriad and rapidly increasing influences to which modern society is exposed, the possibility of consensus over values becomes ever more difficult to obtain. To come to grips with the fluctuation of attitude and outlook on basic values that the law must seek to uphold has perhaps become the most challenging task of the science of jurisprudence in general. To provide a set of criteria with which to determine the propriety or otherwise of law and of effective government under the rule of law, is the primary concern of jurisprudence.

The Muslim jurist is being criticised for having lost contact with the changing conditions of contemporary life in that he has been unable to relate the resources of *Sharīʿah* to modern government processes in the fields of legislation and judicial practice. A part of the same criticism is also levelled against the government in Islamic countries in that it has failed to internalise the *uṣūl al-fiqh* in its legislative practices. The alleged closure of the door of *ijtihād* is one of the factors which is held accountable for the gap that has developed between the law and its sources on the one hand and the changing conditions of society on the other. The introduction of statutory legislation which has already become a common practice in Islamic countries has also affected the role and function of *ijtihād*. Apart from circumventing the traditional role of the jurist/*mujtahid*, the self-contained statutory code and the formal procedures that are laid down for its ratification have eroded the incentive to his effective participation in legislative construction. Furthermore, the wholesale importation of foreign legal concepts and institutions to Islamic countries and the uneasy combinations that this has brought about in legal education and judicial practice are among the sources of general discontent. These and many other factors are in turn accountable for the Islamic revivalism/resurgence which many Muslim societies are currently experiencing.

In view of the diverse influences and the rapid pace of social change visible in modern society it is perhaps inevitable to encounter a measure of uncertainty in identifying the correct balance of values. But the quest to minimise this uncertainty must remain the central concern of the science of jurisprudence. The quest for better solutions and more refined alternatives lies at the very heart of *ijtihād*, which must, according to the classical formulations of *uṣūl al-fiqh*, never be allowed to discontinue. For *ijtihād* is *wājib kafā'ī*, a collective obligation of the Muslim community and its scholars to exert themselves in order to find solutions to new problems and to provide the necessary guidance in matters of law and religion. But even so, to make an error in *ijtihād* is not only tolerated but is worthy of reward given the sincerity and earnestness of the *mujtahid* who attempts it. And it is often through such errors that the best solution can ultimately be reached. One can have different solutions to a particular problem, and sometimes the best solution may be known and yet unattainable given the feasibility and practical considerations that might limit one's range of choice. In such situations one must surely do that which is possible under the circumstances. But it is imperative not to abandon *ijtihād* completely. It is a common and grave error to say that *ijtihād* is unattainable and that the conditions for its exercise are too exacting to fulfil. To regulate *ijtihād* is indeed the primary objective of *uṣūl al-fiqh* and of whatever it has to teach regarding the sources of law and the methods of interpretation and deduction. A grasp of the concepts and doctrines of *uṣūl al-fiqh* is not only helpful but necessary to *ijtihād* so as to enable the Muslim jurist and legislator to contribute to the on-going search for better solutions to social issues, and hopefully also toward the development of the outlook that the *Sharīʿah*, despite its restraints, also possesses considerable flexibility and resources to accommodate social change.

IV. With regard to the translation of technical Arabic terms, I have to some extent followed the existing works, especially Abdur Rahim's *Principles of Muhammadan Jurisprudence*. But in the absence of any precedent, or when I was able to find a better alternative, I have improvised the equivalent English terms myself. Most of the Arabic terms are easily convertible into English without engaging in technicalities, but there are occasions where this is not the case, and at times the choice of terms is determined on grounds of consistency and style rather than semantic accuracy. To give an example, one of the chapters in this book is devoted to the discussion of textual implications (*al-dalālāt*). The five varieties of textual implications, namely *ʿibārah al-naṣṣ, ishārah al-naṣṣ, dalālah al-naṣṣ, iqtiḍāʾ al-naṣṣ* and *mafhūm al-mukhālafah*, each signify a different concept for which an exact English equivalent is difficult to find. I have always tried to give priority to semantic accuracy, but as can be seen this is not the only factor which has determined my choice of 'explicit meaning', 'alluded meaning', 'implied meaning', 'required meaning' and 'divergent meaning' for the foregoing terms respectively. For at times like this, it becomes difficult to be semantically exact as the shades of meaning and concepts tend to be somewhat overlapping. A measure of technicality and arbitrariness in the choice of terms is perhaps inevitable in dealing with certain topics of *uṣūl al-fiqh* such as the classification of words and the rules of interpretation. On such occasions, I thought it helpful not to isolate the English terms from their Arabic originals. I have therefore repeated the Arabic terms frequently enough to relate them to their English equivalents in the text. But when the reader is not sure of the meaning of technical terms a look at the glossary which appears at the end of the text might prove useful.

The translation of the Qur'ānic passages which occur in the text is generally based on Abdullah Yusuf Ali's translation of the Holy Qur'ān. On occasion, however, I have substituted elements in this translation for easier and more simplified alternatives. But whenever I have done so, it is usually the result of my having checked more than one translation. The reader will also notice that I have not given the original of the Qur'ānic passages in Arabic, as this is not difficult to find. Besides, the Qur'ānic text is uniform and there is no variation in the wording of its text in all of its numerous printings that are commonly used. But when it comes to the Ḥadīth, although the main authorites on Ḥadīth are inclined to maintain consistency in both the concept and wording of the Ḥadīth, it is nevertheless not unusual to come across inconsistency or variation in the exact wording of a particular Ḥadīth in various sources. Partly for this reason, but also for the sake of accuracy and convenience, I have given both the Arabic original and the English translation of the Ḥadīth on first occurrence in the text. The English rendering of the Ḥadīth consists for the most part of my own translation of the Arabic original, otherwise I have used the English translation as and when it was available.

A word may also be in order here regarding the English rendering of the terms *fiqh* and *uṣūl al-fiqh*. The difference between them is fairly obvious in their respective Arabic usages: *uṣūl al-fiqh* is unequivocal in its reference to the 'roots of *fiqh*'. This is, however, not so clear in the equivalent English terms which are currently in use. The terms 'Muhammadan Law' and 'Islamic Law' have often been used in a generic sense and applied both to *fiqh* and *uṣūl al-fiqh*. The same is true of its familiar alternative, 'Islamic jurisprudence'. None of these convey the clarity which is found in their Arabic equivalents. There are, for example, books currently available in English bearing one or the other of the these titles, although their contents do not seek to distinguish the two disciplines from one another.

The term 'Muhammadan Law' seems to be already falling out of use, and it has almost become an established practice to reserve 'Islamic Law' for *fiqh*, and 'Islamic jurisprudence' for *uṣūl al-fiqh*. This use of terminology should be retained. A similar distinction between the terms 'source' and 'proof' would seem advisable. The former should, as far as possible, be reserved for the Qur'ān and *Sunnah*, and the latter for other proofs.

My transliteration of Arabic words is essentially the same as that of the *Encyclopedia of Islam* (New Edition), with two exceptions which have become standard practice: q for ḳ and j for <u>dj</u>.

And finally, I would like to take this opportunity to thank most warmly my colleagues and students at the Faculty of Law, International Islamic University, with whom I have frequently raised and discussed matters of mutual interest. I have often benefited from their views which I have taken into account in writing the present work. I would also like to thank the secretarial staff of the faculty for their unfailing willingness to type for me whenever I have approached them. And last but not least, I wish to thank the library staff of the I.I.U. for their assistance, and for being courteous and helpful.

V. Since the publication of the first edition of this book in April 1989, the comments, observations and responses that I have received from scholars, students, and readers have been very positive and encouraging. The changes that I have carried out for the present edition of the book relate to both its content and format, although the overall approach to these changes was to leave the bulk of the original work intact. The changes that I have made are on the whole confined to particular parts and they do not entail a recomposition of the original text. I have thus added fresh information and elaborated parts of the chapters on abrogation (*naskh*), analogical reasoning (*qiyās*), and presumption of continuity (*istiṣḥāb*). The new information either consists of the elaboration of concepts or insertion of additional illustrations for purposes of clarity and relevance to contemporary concerns over the themes of Islamic jurisprudence. The addition to the chapter on *naskh* thus reflects the results of a discussion over a paper entitled 'The Nature, Sources and Objective of the Sharīʿah' which I presented to a symposium organised by the International Islamic University in Kuala Lumpur in September 1989. The additions to some of the other chapters consist mainly of fresh research and expert opinion on the potential contribution of some of the neglected principles of *uṣūl al-fiqh* such as *istiṣḥāb* to modern jurisprudence. I have also refined minor portions of the text in the interest of clarity and precision.

As for the changes of format these were carried out as a result of my consultation with the editorial staff of the Islamic Texts Society, particularly Mohsen al-Najjar and T.J. Winter. It was thus agreed at the outset to re-set the whole of the original text so as to implement the standard practice of the Islamic Texts Society concerning transliteration, footnotes and minor editorial changes in the text. It is thus hoped that these changes have assured the production of a smoother and more familiar text for its readers in Europe and America.

Professor Ahmad Ibrahim, Professor Emeritus and Dean of the Faculty of Law, International Islamic University, Malaysia, has contributed a new Foreword for the second edition. He was kind enough to do so despite his numerous other commitments, and preoccupation with his own writings. I take this opportunity to thank him most warmly for his valuable contribution, and the fact that he wrote a Foreword to both the first and the present editions of my book. He has taken a keen interest in my research and has been most helpful and understanding in relieving me from other commitments so as to be able to concentrate on writing and research.

Students and colleagues at the International Islamic University have been generous and supportive of my endeavours. I take this opportunity to thank them once again for their thoughtful appreciation. A tangible result of all this is that this book has now become a recommended text in a number of courses not only in the Faculty of Law but also in other faculties and departments of this University.

Mohammad Hashim Kamali
International Islamic University, Malaysia.
March 1991.

NOTES

1. Note for example al-Khuḍarī's, *Tārīkh al-Tashrī^{c} al-Islāmī*; al-Ṣābūnī et al., *Al-Madkhal al-Fiqhī wa Tārīkh al-Tashrī^{c} al-Islāmī*; al-Qaṭṭān's *Al-Tashrī^{c} wa al-Fiqh fī al-Islām: Tārīkhān wa Manhajān*, and al-Nabhān's *Al-Madkhal li al-Tashrī^{c} al-Islāmī: Nish'atuh, Adwāruh al-Tārīkhiyyah, Mustaqbaluh*. For full publication data see my Bibliography.

2. Note for example the International Islamic University of Malaysia, and that of Islamabad, Pakistan, where *uṣūl al-fiqh* is offered as a core subject both in the LL.B and the masters degree programmes.

3. For an account of the recent trends and developments in scholarly publications, conference resolutions, and the various periodicals and encyclopedias which are designed to promote such tendencies, the reader is referred to Muḥammad Fārūq al-Nabhān, *Al-Madkhal li al-Tashrī^{c} al-Islāmī*, pp. 342–407 and Mannā^{c} al-Qaṭṭān, *Al-Tashrī^{c} wa al-Fiqh fī al-Islām*, pp. 331–355.

4. Dias, *Jurisprudence*, p. 1.

5. See this and other statements by Bentham, Dicey and Arnold in Curzon, *Jurisprudence*, p. 13.

CHAPTER ONE

Introduction to *Uṣūl al-Fiqh*

1. Definition and Scope

Uṣūl al-fiqh, or the roots of Islamic law, expound the indications and methods by which the rules of *fiqh* are deduced from their sources. These indications are found mainly in the Qur'ān and *Sunnah*, which are the principal sources of the *Sharīʿah*. The rules of *fiqh* are thus derived from the Qurān and *Sunnah* in conformity with a body of principles and methods which are collectively known as *uṣūl al-fiqh*. Some writers have described *uṣūl al-fiqh* as the methodology of law, a description which is accurate but incomplete. Although the methods of interpretation and deduction are of primary concern to *uṣūl al-fiqh*, the latter is not exclusively devoted to methodology. To say that *uṣūl al-fiqh* is the science of the sources and methodology of the law is accurate in the sense that the Qur'ān and *Sunnah* constitute the sources as well as the subject matter to which the methodology of *uṣūl al-fiqh* is applied. The Qur'ān and *Sunnah* themselves, however, contain very little by way of methodology, but rather provide the indications from which the rules of *Sharīʿah* can be deduced. The methodology of *uṣūl al-fiqh* really refers to methods of reasoning such as analogy (*qiyās*), juristic preference (*istiḥsān*), presumption of continuity (*istiṣḥāb*) and the rules of interpretation and deduction. These are designed to serve as an aid to the correct understanding of the sources and *ijtihād*.

To deduce the rules of *fiqh* from the indications that are provided in the sources is the expressed purpose of *uṣūl al-fiqh*. *Fiqh* as such is the end product of *uṣūl al-fiqh*; and yet the two are separate disciplines. The main difference between *fiqh* and *uṣūl al-fiqh* is that the former is concerned with the knowledge of the detailed rules of Islamic law in its various branches, and the latter with the methods that are applied in the deduction of such rules from their sources. *Fiqh*, in other words, is the law itself whereas *uṣūl al-fiqh* is the methodology of the law. The relationship between the two disciplines resembles that of the rules of grammar to a language, or of logic (*manṭiq*) to philosophy. *Uṣūl al-fiqh* in this sense provides standard criteria for the correct deduction of the rules of *fiqh* from the sources of *Sharīᶜah*. An adequate knowledge of *fiqh* necessitates close familiarity with its sources. This is borne out in the definition of *fiqh*, which is 'knowledge of the practical rules of *Sharīᶜah* acquired from the detailed evidence in the sources'.[1] The knowledge of the rules of *fiqh*, in other words, must be acquired directly from the sources, a requirement which implies that the *faqīh* must be in contact with the sources of *fiqh*. Consequently a person who learns the *fiqh* in isolation from its sources is not a *faqīh*.[2] The *faqīh* must know not only the rule that misappropriating the property of others is forbidden but also the detailed evidence for it in the source, that is, the Qur'ānic *āyah* (2:188) which provides: 'Devour not each other's property in defiance of the law.' This is the detailed evidence, as opposed to saying merely that 'theft is forbidden in the Qur'ān'.

Knowledge of the rules of interpretation is essential to the proper understanding of a legal text. Unless the text of the Qur'ān or the *Sunnah* is correctly understood, no rules can be deduced from it, especially in cases where the text in question is not self-evident. Hence rules by which one is to distinguish a speculative text from the definitive, the manifest (*ẓāhir*) from the explicit (*naṣṣ*), the general (*ᶜāmm*) from the specific (*khāṣṣ*), the literal (*ḥaqīqī*) from the metaphorical (*majāzī*) etc., and how to understand the implications (*dalālāt*) of a given text are among the subjects which warrant attention in the study of *uṣūl al-fiqh*. An adequate grasp of the methodology and rules of interpretation also ensures the proper use of human reasoning in a system of law which originates in divine revelation. For instance, analogy (*qiyās*) is an approved method of reasoning for the deduction of new rules from the sources of *Sharīᶜah*. How analogy should be constructed, what are its limits, and what authority would it command in conjunction, or in conflict, with the other recognised proofs are questions which are of primary concern to *uṣūl al-fiqh*. Juristic preference, or *istiḥsān*, is another rationalist doctrine and a recognised proof of Islamic law. It consists essentially of giving preference to one of the many conceivable solutions to a particular problem. The choice of one or the other of these solutions is mainly determined by the jurist in the light of considerations of equity and fairness. Which of these solutions is to be preferred and why, and what are the limits of personal preference and opinion in a particular case, is largely a question of methodology and interpretation and therefore forms part of the subject matter of *uṣūl al-fiqh*.

The principal objective of *uṣūl al-fiqh* is to regulate *ijtihād* and to guide the jurist in his effort at deducing the law from its sources. The need for the methodology of *uṣūl al-fiqh* became prominent when unqualified persons attempted to carry out *ijtihād*, and the risk of error and confusion in the development of *Sharīᶜah* became a source of anxiety for the ulema. The purpose of *uṣūl al-fiqh* is to help the jurist to obtain an adequate knowledge of the sources of *Sharīᶜah* and of the methods of juristic deduction and inference. *Uṣūl al-fiqh* also regulates the application of *qiyās, istiḥsān, istiṣḥāb, istiṣlāḥ*, etc., whose knowledge helps the jurist to distinguish as to which method of deduction is best suited to obtaining the *ḥukm sharᶜī* of a particular problem. Furthermore, *uṣūl al-fiqh* enables the jurist to ascertain and compare strength and weakness in *ijtihād* and to give preference to that ruling of *ijtihād* which is in close harmony with the *nuṣūṣ*.

It may be added here that knowledge of the rules of interpretation, the *ᶜĀmm*, the *Khāṣṣ*, the *Muṭlaq*, the *Muqayyad*, etc., is equally relevant to modern statutory law. When the jurist and the judge, whether a specialist in the *Sharīᶜah* or in secular law, fails to find any guidance in the clear text of the statute on a particular issue, he is likely to resort to judicial construction or to analogy. The skill, therefore, to interpret a legal text and to render judicial decisions is indispensable for a jurist regardless as to whether he sits in a *Sharīᶜah* court or in a court of statutory jurisdiction. A specialist in *uṣūl al-fiqh* will thus find his skill of considerable assistance to the understanding and interpretation of any legal text.[3]

To what extent is it justified to say that al-Shāfiᶜī was the founder of *uṣūl al-fiqh*? One theory has it that *uṣūl al-fiqh* has existed for as long as the *fiqh* has been known to exist. For *fiqh* could not have come into being in the absence of its sources, and of methods with which to utilise the source materials.[4] This would in turn, imply that *uṣūl al-fiqh* had existed long before al-Shāfiᶜī. Numerous examples could be cited to explain how in early Islam, the Companions deduced the rules of *fiqh* from their sources. *Uṣūl al-fiqh*, in other words, had substantially existed before the period which saw the emergence of the leading imams of jurisprudence. But it was through the works of these imams, especially al-Shāfiᶜī, that *uṣūl al-fiqh* was articulated into a coherent body of knowledge. Even before al-Shāfiᶜī, we know that Abū Ḥanīfah resorted to the use of analogy and *istiḥsān* while Imām Mālik is known for his doctrine of the Madinese *ijmāᶜ*, subjects to which we shall have occasion to return. When al-Shāfiᶜī came on the scene, he found a wealth of juristic thought and advanced levels of argumentation on methodological issues. But the existing works were not entirely free of discordance and diversity which had to be sifted through by the standards which al-Shāfiᶜī articulated in his legal theory of the *uṣūl*. He devoted his *Risālah* exclusively to this subject, and this is widely acknowledged to be the first work of authority on *uṣūl al-fiqh*.

It is nevertheless accurate to say that *fiqh* precedes the *uṣūl al-fiqh* and that it was only during the second Islamic century that important developments took place in the field of *uṣūl al-fiqh*.[5] For during the first century there was no pressing need for *uṣūl al-fiqh*. When the Prophet was alive, the necessary guidance and solutions to problems were obtained either through divine revelation, or his direct ruling. Similarly, during the period following the demise of the Prophet, the Companions remained in close contact with the teachings of the Prophet and their decisions were mainly inspired by his precedent. Their proximity to the source and intimate knowledge of the events provided them with the authority to rule on practical problems without there being a pressing need for methodology.[6] However, with the expansion of the territorial domain of Islam, the Companions were dispersed and direct access to them became increasingly difficult. With this, the possibility of confusion and error in the understanding of the textual sources became more prominent. Disputation and diversity of juristic thought in different quarters accentuated the need for clear guidelines, and the time was ripe for al-Shāfiᶜī to articulate the methodology of *uṣūl al-fiqh*. Al-Shāfiᶜī came on the scene when juristic controversy had become prevalent between the jurists of Madinah and Iraq, respectively known as Ahl al-Ḥadīth and Ahl al-Ra'y. This was also a time when the ulema of Ḥadīth had succeeded in their efforts to collect and document the Ḥadīth. Once the *fuqahā'* were assured of the subject-matter of the *Sunnah*, they began to elaborate the law, and hence the need for methodology to regulate *itjihād* became increasingly apparent. The consolidation of *uṣūl al-fiqh* as a *Sharīᶜah* discipline was, in other words, a logical conclusion of the compilation of the vast literature of Ḥadīth.[7]

And finally among the factors which prompted al-Shāfiᶜī into refining the legal theory of *uṣūl al-fiqh* was the extensive influx of non-Arabs into Islamic territories and the disconcerting influence that this brought on the legal and cultural traditions of Islam. Al-Shāfiᶜī was anxious to preserve the purity of the *Sharīᶜah* and of the language of the Qur'ān. In his *Risālah*, al-Shāfiᶜī enacted guidelines for *ijtihād* and expounded the rules governing the *Khāṣṣ* and the *ᶜĀmm*, the *nāsikh* and the *mansūkh*, and articulated the principles governing *ijmāᶜ* and *qiyās*. He expounded the rules of relying on the solitary Ḥadīth (*khabar al-wāḥid*) and its value in the determination of the *aḥkām*. Al-Shāfiʿī refuted the validity of *istiḥsān* and considered it to be no more than an arbitrary exercise in law-making. Admittedly al-Shāfiʿī was not the first to address these matters, but it is widely acknowledged that he brought a coherence to *uṣūl al-fiqh*, which had hitherto remained scattered and unconsolidated.[8]

It will be noted in this connection that the Shīʿī ulema have claimed that their fifth Imam, Muḥammad al-Bāqir, and his son and successor, Jaʿfar al-Ṣādiq, were the first to write on the subject of *uṣūl*. According to Abū Zahrah, who has written extensively on the lives and works of the early Imams, the Shīʿī Imams have written, like many others, on the subject, but neither of the two Imams have written anything of an equivalent order to that of the *Risālah*. Hence al-Shāfiʿī's position and contribution to *uṣūl al-fiqh* remains unique, and he is rightly regarded as the founder of *uṣūl al-fiqh*.[9]

The basic outline of the four principal sources of the law that al-Shāfiʿī spelled out was subsequently accepted by the generality of ulema, although each of the various schools of jurisprudence has contributed towards its further development. The Ḥanafīs, for example, added *istiḥsān*, and custom (*ʿurf*) to the *uṣūl al-fiqh*, and the Mālikīs reduced the concept of consensus (*ijmāʿ*) to the Madinese consensus only, while the Ḥanbalī approach to the subject closely resembled that of the Mālikīs. But even so, none departed significantly from the basic principles which al-Shāfiʿī had articulated.[10]

Broadly speaking, the so-called closure of the gate of *ijtihād* at around the fourth Islamic century did not affect the *uṣūl al-fiqh* in the same way as it might have affected the *fiqh* itself. The era of imitation (*taqlīd*) which followed might even have added to the strength and prominence of *uṣūl al-fiqh* in the sense that the imitators observed, and relied on, the methodology of the *uṣūl* as a yardstick of validity for their arguments. Consequently *uṣūl al-fiqh* gained universal acceptance and was, in a way, utilised as a means with which to justify *taqlīd*.[11]

A brief word may be added here regarding the difference between the *uṣūl*, and the maxims of *fiqh* (*al-qawāʿid al-fiqhiyyah*), as the two are sometimes confused with one another. The maxims of *fiqh* refer to a body of abstract rules which are derived from the detailed study of the *fiqh* itself. They consist of theoretical guidelines in the different areas of *fiqh* such as evidence, transactions, matrimonial law, etc. As such they are an integral part of *fiqh* and are totally separate from *uṣūl al-fiqh*. Over 200 legal maxims have been collected and compiled in works known as *al-ashbāh wa al-naẓā'ir*;[12] one hundred of these have been adopted in the introductory section (i.e. the first 100 articles) of the Ottoman *Majallah*. The name '*al-qawāʿid al-fiqhiyyah*' may resemble the expression *uṣūl al-fiqh*, but the former is not a part of the latter and the two are totally different from one another.

A comparison between *uṣūl al-fiqh* and *uṣūl al-qānūn* will indicate that these two disciplines have much in common with one another, although they are different in other respects. They resemble one another in that both are concerned with the methodology of the law and the rules of deduction and interpretation; they are not concerned with the detailed rules of the law itself. In the case of the law of property, for example, both *uṣūl al-fiqh* and *uṣūl al-qānūn* are concerned with the sources of the law of property and not with the detailed rules governing transfer of ownership or regulating the contract of sale. These are subjects which fall within the scope of the law of property, not the methodology of law.

Although the general objectives of *uṣūl al-fiqh* and *uṣūl al-qānūn* are similar, the former is mainly concerned with the Qur'ān, *Sunnah*, consensus, and analogy. The sources of *Sharīʿah* are, on the whole, well-defined and almost exclusive in the sense that a rule of law or a *ḥukm sharʿī* may not be originated outside the general scope of its authoritative sources on grounds, for example, of rationality (*ʿaql*) alone. For *ʿaql* is not an independent source of law in Islam. *Uṣūl al-fiqh* is thus founded in divine ordinances and the acknowledgement of God's authority over the conduct of man.

Uṣūl al-qānūn, on the other hand, consist mainly of rationalist doctrines, and reason alone may constitute the source of many a secular law. Some of these are historical sources such as Roman Law or British Common Law whose principles are upheld or overruled in light of the prevailing socio-economic conditions of society. The sources of *Sharīʿah* on the other hand, are permanent in character and may not be overruled on grounds of either rationality or the requirement of social conditions. There is, admittedly, a measure of flexibility in *uṣūl al-fiqh* which allows for necessary adjustments in the law to accommodate social change. But in principle the *Sharīʿah* and its sources can neither be abrogated nor subjected to limitations of time and circumstance. The role of the jurist and the *mujtahid* in *uṣūl al-fiqh* is basically one of deduction and inference of rules which are already indicated on the sources, while this is not necessarily the case with regard to *uṣūl al-qānūn*. The Parliament or the legislative assembly of a Western state, being the sovereign authority, can abrogate an existing statute or introduce a new law as it may deem fit. The legislative organ of an Islamic state, on the other hand, cannot abrogate the Qur'ān or the *Sunnah*, although it may abrogate a law which is based on *maṣlaḥah* or *istiḥsān*, etc. Abrogation is, on the whole, of a limited application to the definite rulings of divine revelation and has basically come to an end with the demise of the Prophet.[13]

Sovereignty in Islam is the prerogative of Almighty God alone. He is the absolute arbiter of values and it is His will that determines good and evil, right and wrong. It is neither the will of the ruler nor of any assembly of men, not even the community as a whole, which determines the values and the laws which uphold those values. In its capacity as the vicegerent of God, the Muslim community is entrusted with the authority to implement the *Sharīᶜah*, to administer justice and to take all necessary measures in the interest of good government. The sovereignty of the people, if the use of the word 'sovereignty' is at all appropriate, is a delegated, or executive sovereignty (*sulṭān tanfīdhī*) only.[14] Although the consensus or *ijmāᶜ* of the community, or of its learned members, is a recognised source of law in Islam, in the final analysis, *ijmāᶜ* is subservient to divine revelation and can never overrule the explicit injunctions of the Qur'ān and *Sunnah*. The role of the ballot box and the sovereignty of the people are thus seen in a different light in Islamic law to that of Western jurisprudence.

And lastly, unlike its Western counterpart, Islamic jurisprudence is not confined to commands and prohibitions, and far less to commands which originate in a court of law. Its scope is much wider, as it is concerned not only with what a man must do or must not do, but also with what he ought to do or ought not to do, and the much larger area where his decision to do or to avoid doing something is his own prerogative. *Uṣūl al-fiqh* provides guidance in all these areas, most of which remain outside the scope of Western jurisprudence.

II. Two Approaches to the Study of *Uṣūl al-fiqh*

Following the establishment of the *madhāhib* the ulema of the various schools adopted two different approaches to the study of *uṣūl al-fiqh*, one of which is theoretical and the other deductive. The main difference between these approaches is one of orientation rather than substance. Whereas the former is primarily concerned with the exposition of theoretical doctrines, the latter is pragmatic in the sense that theory is formulated in light of its application to relevant issues. The difference between the two approaches resembles the work of a legal draftsman when it is compared to the work of a judge. The former is mainly concerned with the exposition of principles whereas the latter tends to develop a synthesis between the principle and the requirements of a particular case. The theoretical approach to the study of *uṣūl al-fiqh* is adopted by the Shāfiᶜī school and the Mutakallimūn, that is the ulema of *kalām* and the Muᶜtazilah. The deductive approach is, on the other hand, mainly attributed to the Ḥanafīs. The former is known as *uṣūl al-Shāfiʿiyyah* or *ṭarīqah al-Mutakallimīn*, whereas the latter is known as *uṣūl al-Ḥanafiyyah*, or *ṭarīqah al-fuqahā'*.

Al-Shāfiʿī was mainly concerned with articulating the theoretical principles of *uṣūl al-fiqh* without necessarily attempting to relate these to the *fiqh* itself. As a methodologist *par excellence*, he enacted a set of standard criteria which he expected to be followed in the detailed formulation of the rules of *fiqh*. His theoretical exposition of *uṣūl al-fiqh*, in other words, did not take into consideration their practical application in the area of the *furūʿ*. In addition, the Shāfiʿīs and the Mutakallimūn are inclined to engage in complex issues of a philosophical character which may or may not contribute to the development of the practical rules of *fiqh*. In this way subjects such as the *ʿiṣmah* of the prophets prior to their prophetic mission, and matters pertaining to the status of the individual or his duties prior to the revelation of the *Sharīʿah*, and also logical and linguistic matters of remote relevance to the practical rules of *fiqh* tend to feature more prominently in the works of the Shāfiʿīs and Mutakallimūn than those of the Ḥanafīs. The Ḥanafīs have on the other hand attempted to expound the principles of *uṣūl al-fiqh* in conjunction with the *fiqh* itself and tend to be more pragmatic in their approach to the subject. In short, the theoretical approach tends to envisage *uṣūl al-fiqh* as an independent discipline to which the *fiqh* must conform, whereas the deductive approach attempts to relate the *uṣūl al-fiqh* more closely to the detailed issues of the *furūʿ al-fiqh*. When, for example, the Ḥanafīs find a principle of *uṣūl* to be in conflict with an established principle of *fiqh*, they are inclined to adjust the theory to the extent that the conflict in question is removed, or else they try to make the necessary exception so as to reach a compromise. Three of the most important works which adopt the theoretical approach to *uṣūl al-fiqh* are *Al-Muʿtamad fi Uṣūl al-Fiqh* by the Muʿtazilī scholar, Abū al-Husayn al-Baṣrī (d. 436), *Kitāb al-Burhān* of the Shāfiʿī scholar, Imām al-Ḥaramayn al-Juwaynī (d. 487) and *Al-Mustaṣfā* of Imam Abū Ḥāmid al-Ghazālī (d. 505). These three works were later summarised by Fakhr al-Dīn al-Rāzī (d. 606) in his work entitled *Al-Maḥṣūl*. Sayf al-Dīn al-Āmidī's larger work, *Al-Iḥkām fī uṣūl al-Aḥkām* is an annotated summary of the three pioneering works referred to above.

The earliest Ḥanafī work on *uṣūl al-fiqh* is *Kitāb fī al-Uṣūl* by Abū al-Ḥasan al-Karkhī (d. 340) which was followed by *Uṣūl al-Jaṣṣāṣ* of Abū Bakr al-Rāzī al-Jaṣṣāṣ (d. 370). Fakhr al-Islām al-Bazdawī's (d. 483) well-known work, *Uṣūl al-Bazdawī*, is also written in conformity with the Ḥanafī approach to the study of this discipline. This was followed by an equally outstanding contribution by Shams al-Dīn al-Sarakhsī (d. 490) bearing the title, *Uṣūl al-Sarakhsī*. A number of other ulema have contributed to the literature in both camps. But a difference of format which marked a new stage of development was the writing of handbooks in the form of *mukhtaṣars* with a view to summarise the existing works for didactic purposes.

The next phase in the development of literature on *uṣūl al-fiqh* is marked by the attempt to combine the theoretical and deductive approaches into an integrated whole which is reflected in the works of both the Shāfiᶜī and Ḥanafī ulema of later periods. One such work which attempted to combine al-Bazdawī's *Uṣūl* and al-Āmidī's *Al-Iḥkām* was completed by Muẓaffar al-Dīn al-Sāᶜātī (d. 694) whose title *Badīᶜ al-Niẓām al-Jāmiᶜ Bayn Uṣūl al-Bazdawī wa al-Iḥkām* is self-explanatory as to the approach the author has taken to the writing of this work. Another equally significant work which combined the two approaches was completed by Ṣadr al-Sharīᶜah, ᶜAbd Allah b. Masᶜūd al-Bukhārī (d. 747) bearing the title *Al-Tawḍīh*, which is, in turn, a summary of *Uṣūl al-Bazdawī, Al-Maḥṣūl*, and the *Mukhtaṣar al-Muntaḥā* of the Mālikī jurist, Abū ᶜUmar ᶜUthmān b. al-Ḥājib (d. 646). Three other well-known works which have combined the two approaches to *uṣūl al-fiqh* are *Jamᶜ al-Jawāmiᶜ* of the Shāfiᶜī jurist Tāj al-Din al-Subkī (d. 771), *Al-Taḥrīr* of Kamāl al-Din b. al-Humām al-Ḥanafī (d. 860), and *Musallam al-Thubūt* of the Ḥanafī jurist Muḥibb al-Dīn b. ᶜAbd al-Shakūr (d. 1119). And finally, this list would be deficient without mentioning Abū Isḥāq Ibrāhīm al-Shāṭibī's *Al-Muwāfaqāt*, which is comprehensive and perhaps unique in its attention to the philosophy (*ḥikmah*) of *tashrīᶜ* and the objectives that are pursued by the detailed rulings of the *Sharīᶜah*.[15]

III. Proofs of Sharīᶜah *(Al-Adillah Al-Sharᶜiyyah)*

The *adillah sharᶜiyyah*, and the *aḥkām*, that is, laws or values that regulate the conduct of the *mukallaf*, are the two principal themes of *uṣūl al-fiqh*. Of these two, however, the former is by far the more important as, according to some ulema, the *aḥkām* are derived from the *adillah* and are therefore subsidiary to them. It is perhaps in view of the central importance of these two topics to *uṣūl al-fiqh* that al-Āmidī defines the latter as the science of the 'Proofs of *fiqh (adillah al-fiqh)* and the indications that they provide in regard to the *aḥkām* of the *Sharīᶜah*.'[16]

Literally, *dalīl* means proof, indication or evidence. Technically it is an indication in the sources from which a practical rule of *Sharīᶜah*, or a *ḥukm* is deduced. The *ḥukm* so obtained may be definitive (*qaṭᶜī*) or it may be speculative (*ẓannī*) depending on the nature of the subject, clarity of the text, and the value which it seeks to establish.[17] In the terminology of *uṣūl al-fiqh, adillah sharᶜiyyah* refer to four principal proofs, or sources of the *Sharīᶜah*, namely the Qur'ān, *Sunnah*, consensus and analogy. *Dalīl* in this sense is synonymous with *aṣl*, hence the four sources of *Sharīᶜah* are known both as *adillah* and *uṣūl*. There are a number of *āyāt* in the Qur'ān which identify the sources of *Sharīᶜah* and the order of priority between them. But one passage in which all the principal sources are indicated occurs in Sūra al-Nisā' (4:58–59) which is as follows: 'O you believers! Obey God and obey the Messenger and those of you who are in charge of affairs. If you have a dispute concerning any matter, refer it to God and to the Messenger,' 'Obey God' in this *āyah* refers to the Qur'ān, and 'Obey the Messenger' refers to the *Sunnah*. Obedience to 'those who are in charge of affairs' is held to be a reference to *ijmāᶜ*, and the last portion of the *āyah* which requires the referral of disputes to God and to the Messenger authorises *qiyās*. For *qiyās* is essentially an extension of the injunctions of the Qur'ān and *Sunnah*. The rationale or the effective cause of *qiyās* may be clearly indicated in these sources or it may be identified by way of inference (*istinbāṭ*). In either case, *qiyās* essentially consists of the discovery of a *ḥukm* which is already indicated in the divine sources.[18]

Some *fuqahā'* have drawn a distinction between *dalīl* and *amārah* (lit. sign or allusion) and apply *dalīl* to the kind of evidence which leads to a definitive ruling or that which leads to positive knowledge (*ᶜilm*). *Amārah* on the other hand is reserved for evidence or indication which only leads to a speculative ruling.[19] In this way, the term '*dalīl*' would only apply to the definitive proofs, namely the Qur'ān, *Sunnah* and *ijmāᶜ*, and the remaining proofs which comprise a measure of speculation, such as *qiyās* and *istiḥsān*, etc., would fall under the category of *amārāt*.

The proofs of *Sharīᶜah* have been further divided into transmitted proofs (*adillah naqliyyah*) and rational proofs (*adillah ᶜaqliyyah*). The authority of the transmitted proofs is independent of their conformity or otherwise with the dictates of reason, although as we shall later elaborate, most of the transmitted proofs can also be rationally justified. However, the authority and the binding force of the Qur'ān, *Sunnah* and *ijmāᶜ* are independent of any rational justification that might exist in their favour. To these are added two other transmitted proofs, namely the ruling of the Companions, and the laws revealed prior to the advent of Islam (*sharā'iᶜ man qablanā*)[20]

The rational proofs are, on the other hand, founded in reason and need to be rationally justified. They can only be accepted by virtue of their rationality. *Qiyās*, *istiḥsān*, *istiṣlāḥ* and *istiṣḥāb* are basically all rationalist doctrines although they are in many ways dependent on the transmitted proofs. Rationality alone is not an independent proof in Islam, which is why the rational proofs cannot be totally separated from the transmitted proofs. *Qiyās*, for example, is a rational proof, but it also partakes in the transmitted proofs to the extent that *qiyās* in order to be valid must be founded on an established *ḥukm* of the Qur'ān, *Sunnah* or *ijmāᶜ*. However the issue to which *qiyās* is applied (i.e. the *farᶜ*) must have a *ᶜillah* in common with the original *ḥukm*. To establish the commonality of the *ᶜillah* in *qiyās* is largely a matter of opinion and *ijtihād*. *Qiyās* is therefore classified under the category of *adillah ᶜaqliyyah*.

As noted above, the *adillah sharᶜiyyah* are on the whole in harmony with reason. This will be clear from the fact that the *Sharīᶜah* in all of its parts is addressed to the *mukallaf*, that is, the competent person who is in possession of his faculty of reasoning. The *Sharīᶜah* as a whole does not impose any obligation that would contradict the requirements of *ᶜaql*. Since the criterion of obligation (*taklīf*) is *ᶜaql*, and without it all legal obligations fall to the ground, it would follow that a *ḥukm sharᶜī* which is abhorrent to *ᶜaql* is of no consequence.[21]

The *adillah sharᶜiyyah* have been further classified into *mustaqill* and *muqayyad*, that is independent and dependent proofs respectively. The first three sources of the *Sharīᶜah* are each an independent *aṣl*, or *dalīl mustaqill*, that is, a proof in its own right. *Qiyās* on the other hand is an *aṣl* or *dalīl muqayyad* in the sense, as indicated above, that its authority is derived from one or the other of the three independent sources. The question may arise as to why *ijmāᶜ* has been classified as an independent proof despite the fact that it is often in need of a basis (*sanad*) in the Qur'ān or the *Sunnah*. The answer to this is that *ijmāᶜ* is in need of a *sanad* in the divine sources for its formulation in the first place. However, once the *ijmāᶜ* is concluded, it is no longer dependent on its *sanad* and it becomes an independent proof. Unlike *qiyās*, which continues to be in need of justification in the form of a *ᶜillah*, a conclusive *ijmāᶜ* is not in need of justification and is therefore an independent *aṣl*.[22]

The only other classification of *adillah* which needs to be mentioned is their division into definitive (*qaṭᶜī*) and speculative (*ẓannī*) proofs. This division of *dalīl sharᶜī* contemplates the proofs of *Sharīᶜah* not only in their entirety but also in respect of the detailed rules which they contain. In this way, the Qur'ān, *Sunnah* and *ijmāᶜ* are definitive proofs in the sense that they are decisive and binding. However each of these sources contains speculative rules which are open to interpretation. A *dalīl* in this sense is synonymous with *ḥukm*. A *dalīl* may be *qaṭᶜī* in regards to both transmission (*riwāyah*) and meaning (*dalālah*). The clear injunctions of the Qur'ān and *Ḥadīth Mutawātir* are all *qaṭᶜī* in respect of both transmission and meaning. We shall have occasion later to elaborate on this subject in the context of the characteristic features of Qur'ānic legislation. Suffice it here to say that the Qur'ān is authentic in all of its parts, and therefore of proven authenticity (*qaṭ*ᶜ*ī al-thubūt*). The solitary, or *āḥād*, Ḥadīth on the other hand is of speculative authenticity and therefore falls under the category of speculative proofs.[23] Similarly, a ruling of *ijmā*ᶜ may have reached us by continuous testimony (*tawātur*) in which case it would be definitely proven (*qaṭ*ᶜ*ī al-thubūt*). But when *ijmā*ᶜ is transmitted through solitary reports, its authenticity would be open to doubt and therefore *ẓannī al-thubūt*.

The text of the Qur'ān or the Ḥadīth may convey a command or a prohibition. According to the general rule, a command (*amr*) conveys obligation (*wujūb*), and prohibition (*nahy*) conveys *taḥrīm* unless there is evidence to suggest otherwise. It is in the light of the wording of the text, its subject-matter and other supportive evidence that the precise *shar*ᶜ*ī* value of a textual ruling can be determined. A command may thus imply a recommendation (*nadb*) or a mere permissibility (*ibāḥah*) and not *wujūb*. Likewise a prohibition (*nahy*) in the Qur'ān or the *Sunnah* may be held to imply abomination (*karāhah*) and not necessarily *taḥrīm*. Consequently, when the precise value of the *qaṭ*ᶜ*ī* and the *ẓannī* on the scale of five values is not self-evident, it is determined by supportive evidence that may be available in the sources or by *ijtihād. The qaṭ*ᶜ*ī* of the Qur'ān and *Sunnah* is basically not open to interpretation. The scope of interpretation and *ijtihād* is consequently confined to the *ẓannī* proofs alone.[24]

NOTES

1. Āmidī, *Iḥkām*, 1, 6; Shawkānī, *Irshād*, p. 3.
2. Cf. Abū Zahrah, *Uṣūl*, p. 6.
3. Cf. Badrān, *Uṣūl*, pp. 37–38.
4. Cf. Abū Zahrah, *Uṣūl*. p. 8ff.
5. Khallāf, ᶜ*Ilm*, p. 16; Abū Zahrah, *Uṣūl*, p. 10.
6. Ibid., pp. 16–17.
7. Cf. Badrān, *Uṣūl*, p. 12.
8. Ibid., p. 14.
9. Abū Zahrah, *Uṣūl*, p. 13. Badrān, *Uṣūl*, p. 14.
10. Ibid., p. 14.
11. Ibid., p. 14.
12. Two well known works both bearing the title *Al-Ashbāh wa al-Naẓā'ir* are authored by Jalāl al-Dīn al-Suyūṭī and Ibn Nujaym al-Ḥanafī respectively.
13. Cf. Badrān, *Uṣūl*., pp. 41–43.
14. Cf. Zaydān, *Al-Fard wa al-Dawlah*, p. 29.
15. Abū Zahrah, *Uṣūl*, pp. 14–20; Hītū, *Wajīz*, pp. 13–24; Zuhayr, *Uṣūl*, I, 4.
16. Āmidī, *Iḥkām*, I, 7; Badrān, *Uṣūl*, p. 36.
17. Ibid., I. 9; Badrān, *Uṣūl*, p. 46, Hītū, *Wajīz*, p. 99.

18. Cf. Badrān, *Uṣūl*, pp. 51–52.
19. Āmidī, *Iḥkām*, I, 9.
20. Cf. Badrān, *Uṣūl*, pp. 54–55.
21. Āmidī, *Iḥkām*, III, 180; Badrān, *Uṣūl*, p. 50.
22. Āmidī, *Iḥkām*, I, 260.
23. Shawkānī, *Irshād*, p. 47; Badrān, *Uṣūl*, p. 53; Hītū, *Wajīz*, p. 305.
24. Khallāf, *ʿIlm*, p. 35, Abū Zahrah, *Uṣūl*, p. 71; Shaltūt, *Al-Islām*, p. 498.

CHAPTER TWO

The First Source of *Sharīʿah*: The Qur'ān

Being the verbal noun of the root word *qara'a* (to read), 'Qur'ān' literally means 'reading' or 'recitation'. It may be defined as 'the book containing the speech of God revealed to the Prophet Muḥammad in Arabic and transmitted to us by continuous testimony, or *tawātur*'.[1] It is a proof of the prophecy of Muḥammad, the most authoritative guide for Muslims, and the first source of the *Sharīʿah*. The ulema are unanimous on this, and some even say that it is the only source and that all other sources are explanatory to the Qur'ān. The revelation of the Qur'ān began with the Sūra al-ʿAlaq (96:1) starting with the words 'Read in the name of your Lord' and ending with the *āyah* in sūra al-Mā'idah (5:3): 'Today I have perfected your religion for you and completed my favour toward you, and chosen Islam as your religion.'[2] Learning and religious guidance, being the first and the last themes of the Qur'ānic revelation, are thus the favour of God upon mankind.

There are 114 sūras and 6235 *āyāt* of unequal length in the Qur'ān. The shortest of the sūras consist of four and the longest of 286 *āyāt*. Each chapter has a separate title. The longest sūras appear first and the sūras become shorter as the text proceeds. Both the order of the *āyāt* within each sūra, and the sequence of the sūras, were re-arranged and finally determined by the Prophet in the year of his demise. According to this arrangement, the Qur'ān begins with sūra al-Fātiḥah and ends with sūra al-Nās.[3]

The contents of the Qur'ān are not classified subject-wise. The *āyāt* on various topics appear in unexpected places, and no particular order can be ascertained in the sequence of its text. To give just a few examples, the command concerning *ṣalāh* appears in the second sūra, in the midst of other *āyāt* which relate to the subject of divorce (al-Baqarah, 2:228–248). In the same sūra, we find rules which relate to wine-drinking, apostasy and war, followed by passages concerning the treatment of orphans and the marriage of unbelieving women (al-Baqarah, 216–211). Similarly the *āyāt* relating to the pilgrimage of *ḥajj* occur both in sūra al-Baqarah (196–203) and sūra al-Ḥajj (22:26–27). Rules on marriage, divorce and revocation (*rijʿah*) are found in the sūras al-Baqarah, al-Ṭalāq, and al-Nisā'. From this a conclusion has been drawn that the Qur'ān is an indivisible whole and a guide for belief and action which must be accepted and followed in its entirety. Hence any attempt to follow some parts of the Qur'ān and abandon others will be totally invalid. This is in fact the purport of the Qur'ānic text (al-Mā'idah, 5:52) where the Prophet has been warned: 'Beware of them (i.e. the disbelievers) lest they seduce you away from a part of that which God has sent down to you.'[4]

The Qur'ān consists of manifest revelation (*waḥy ẓāhir*), which is defined as communication from God to the Prophet Muḥammad, conveyed by the angel Gabriel, in the very words of God. Manifest revelation differs from internal revelation (*waḥy bāṭin*) in that the latter consists of the inspiration (*ilhām*) of concepts only: God inspired the Prophet and the latter conveyed the concepts in his own words. All the sayings, or *aḥādīth*, of the Prophets fall under the category of internal revelation, and as such they are not included in the Qur'ān. A brief word may be added here concerning *Ḥadīth Qudsī*. In this variety of Ḥadīth, the Prophet narrates a concept directly from God. *Ḥadīth Qudsī* differs from the other varieties of Ḥadīth in form only. The Prophet himself has not distinguished *Ḥadīth Qudsī* from other *aḥādīth*: it was in fact introduced as a separate category by the ulema of Ḥadīth at around the fifth century Hijrah. Ḥadīth in all of its varieties consists of divine inspiration which is communicated in the words of the Prophet. No Ḥadīth may be ranked on equal footing with the Qur'ān. The *ṣalāh* cannot be performed by reciting the Ḥadīth, nor is the recitation of Ḥadīth considered as of the same spiritual merit as the Qur'ān.[5]

The Qur'ān explicitly states that it is all communicated in pure and clear Arabic (al- Naḥl, 16:30). Although the ulema are in agreemeent that words of non-Arabic origin occur in the Qur'ān, they are, nevertheless, words which were admitted and integrated into the language of the Arabs before the revelation of the Qur'ān. To give just a few examples, words such as *qisṭās* (scales – occurring in the sūra al-Isrā', 17:35), *ghassāq* (intense cold) in sūra al-Naba' (78:25) and *sijjīl* (baked clay – in al-Ḥijr, 15:74) are of Greek, Turkish and Persian origins respectively.[6]

But this usage is confined to odd words; a phrase or a sentence of non-Arabic origin does not occur in the Qur'ān.[7] Since the Qur'ān consists of manifest revelation in Arabic, a translation of the Qur'ān into another language, or its commentary whether in Arabic or other languages, are not a part of the Qur'ān. However, Imām Abū Ḥanīfah has held the view that the Qur'ān is the name for a meaning only, and as such, *ṣalāh* may be performed in its Persian translation. But the disciples of Abū Ḥanīfah have disagreed with this view and it is reported that Abū Ḥanīfah himself reversed his initial ruling, and this is now considered to be the correct view of the Ḥanafī school.[8]

The Prophet himself memorised the Qur'ān, and so did his Companions. This was, to a large extent, facilitated by the fact that the Qur'ān was revealed piecemeal over a period of twenty-three years in relation to particular events. The Qur'ān itself explains the rationale of graduality (*tanjīm*) in its revelation as follows: 'The unbelievers say, why has not the Qur'ān been sent down to him [Muḥammad] all at once. Thus [it is revealed] that your hearts may be strengthened, and We rehearse it to you gradually, and well-arranged' [al-Furqān, 23:32].

Elsewhere we read in the text: 'It is a Qur'ān We have divided into parts in order that you may recite it to people at intervals: We have revealed it by stages' (Banī Isrā'īl, 17:106). In yet another passage, Almighty God addresses the Prophet: 'By degrees shall We teach you to declare [the message] so that you do not forget' (al-Aʿlā, 87:6).

Graduality in the revelation of Qur'ān afforded the believers the opportunity to reflect over it and to retain it in their memories. Revelation over a period of time also facilitated continuous contact and renewal of spiritual strength so that the hostility of the unbelievers toward the new faith did not weaken the hearts of the Muslims. Furthermore, in view of the widespread illiteracy of the Arabs at the time, had the Qur'ān been revealed all at once, they would have found it difficult to understand. The Qur'ānic legislation concerning matters which touched the lives of the people was therefore not imposed all at once. It was revealed piecemeal so as to avoid hardship to the believers.[9] The ban on the consumption of alcohol affords an interesting example of the Qur'ānic method of graduality in legislation, and throws light on the attitude of the Qur'ān to the nature and function of legislation itself. Consumption of alcohol was apparently, subject to no restriction in the early years. Later, the following Qur'ānic passage was revealed in the form of a moral advice: 'They ask you about alcohol and gambling, say: in these there is great harm and also benefit for the people, but their harm far outweighs their benefit' (al-Baqarah; 2:219). Then offering prayers while under the influence of alcohol was prohibited (al-Nisā', 4:43).

Finally a total ban on wine drinking was imposed (al-Mā'idah, 5:93) and both alcohol and gambling were declared to be 'works of the devil . . . the devil wants to sow enmity and rancour among you'. This shows the gradual tackling of problems as and when they arose.

The ulema are in agreement to the effect that the entire text of the Qur'ān is *Mutawātir*, that is, its authenticity is proven by universally accepted testimony. It has been retained both in memory and in written record throughout the generations. Hence nothing less that *tawātur* is accepted in evidence to establish the authenticity of the variant readings of the Qur'ān. Thus the variant reading of some words in a few *āyāt*, attributed to 'Abdullāh ibn Masᶜūd, for example, which is not established by *tawātur* is not a part of the Qur'ān. In the context of penance (*kaffārah*) of a false oath, for example, the standard text provides this to be three days of fasting. But Ibn Masᶜūd's version has it as three consecutive days of fasting. Since the additional element (i.e. consecutive) in the relevant *āyah* in sūra al-Mā'idah (5:92) is not established by *tawātur*, it is not a part of the Qur'ān and is therefore of no effect.[10]

During the lifetime of the Prophet, the text of the Qur'ān was preserved not only in memories, but also in inscriptions on such available materials as flat stones, wood and bones, which would explain why it could not have been compiled in a bound volume. Initially the first Caliph, Abū Bakr, collected the Qur'ān soon after the battle of Yamāmah which led to the death of at least seventy of the memorisers of the Qur'ān. Zayd b. Thābit, the scribe of the Prophet, was employed on the task of compiling the text which he accomplished between 11 and 14 Hijrah. But several versions and readings of this edition soon crept into use. Hence the third Caliph, ᶜUthmān, once again utilised the services of Zayd to verify the accuracy of the text and compiled it in a single volume. All the remaining variations were then destroyed. As a result only one authentic text has remained in use to this day.[11]

The Qur'ān was revealed in two distinct periods of the Prophet's mission in Mecca and Madinah respectively. The larger part of the Qur'ān, that is nineteen out of the total of thirty parts, was received during the first twelve and a half years of the Prophet's residence in Mecca. The remainder of the Qur'ān was received after the Prophet's migration to Madinah over a period of just over nine and a half years.[12] The Meccan part of the Qur'ān is mainly devoted to matters of belief, the Oneness of God (*Tawḥīd*), the necessity of the prophethood of Muḥammad, the hereafter, disputation with the unbelievers and their invitation to Islam. But the Madinese part of the Qur'ān also comprised legal rules and regulated the various aspects of life in the new environment of Madinah. Since the Madinese period signified the formation of the *ummah* and of the nascent Islamic state, the Qur'ānic emphasis was shifted to principles regulating the political, legal, social and economic life of the new community. During this period Islam expanded to other parts of Arabia, and the Qur'ānic response to the need for rules to regulate matters of war and peace, the status and rights of the conquered people as well as the organisation of the family and principles of government feature prominently in the Madinese part of the Qur'ān.[13] The knowledge of the Meccan and the Madinese contents of the Qur'ān gives one an insight into the context and circumstances in which the *āyāt* were revealed; it is particularly relevant to the understanding of the incidence of abrogation (*naskh*) in the Qur'ān. To distinguish the abrogating (*al-nāsikh*) from the abrogated (*al-mansūkh*) portions of the text depends on determining the chronological order in the revelation of the relevant *āyāt*. Similarly, most of the general (*ᶜĀmm*) rulings of the text have been qualified either by the text itself or by the Ḥadīth. Thus the knowledge of the Makkī and Madanī parts of the revelation facilitates a better understanding of some of the characteristic features of the Qur'ānic legislation.

A sūra is considered to be Makkī if its revelation had begun in Mecca, even if it contained *āyāt* that were later revealed in Madinah. The Qur'ān consists of eighty-five Meccan and twenty-nine Madinan sūras. The differences of content and style that are observed in each are reflective of the prevailing circumstances of each period. Since Muslims were in the minority in Mecca the Meccan *āyāt* may thus be especially meaningful to Muslims living in a dominantly un-Islamic environment, whereas the Madinese *āyāt* may take for granted the presence of the sovereign authority of the Islamic state. The Meccan sūras are generally short but rhythmical and intense in their emotional appeal to the pagan Arabs, whereas the Madinan sūras are detailed and convey a sense of serenity that marks a difference of style in the revelation of the Qur'ān.[14]

The distinction between the Meccan and Madinan parts of the Qur'ān is based on the information that is provided mainly by the Companions and the following generation of the 'successors': the Prophet himself has said nothing on the subject. The distinction is also facilitated considerably by internal evidence in the Qur'ān, such as the theme itself: *āyāt* about warfare were, for example, revealed only after the Hijrah, but references to Abū Lahab in sūra 111 and to the battle of Badr (3:123) indicate the Meccan origin of the sūras in which they occur. Similarly the form of address is often different in the two parts. The frequent address, 'O you who believe' and 'O people of the Book' indicates a Madinan origin, while 'O people' or 'O mankind' are typically Meccan. There are nineteen sūras in the Qur'ān which begin with abbreviated letters (*al-muqaṭṭaʿāt*); all of them are known to be Meccan except two, namely al-Baqarah, and Āl-ʿImrān. All references to the *munāfiqūn* (hypocrites) are Madinan and all sūras that contain a *sajdah*, that is, an order to prostrate, are Meccan. The distinction between the Makkī and Madinese portions of the text is on the whole a well-established feature of the Qur'ān, which is normally indicated next to the title of each sūra, and the best evidence of such distinction is internal evidence in the Qur'ān itself.[15]

With regard to distinguishing the Makkī from the Madanī contents of the Qur'ān, the ulema have applied three different criteria: 1) The time of revelation, meaning that the part of the Qur'ān which was revealed prior to the Prophet's migration to Madinah is classified as Makkī and the remaining part which was revealed after this occasion is identified as Madanī regardless of the locality in which they were received. In this way the *āyāt* which were actually revealed in Mecca after the Year of Victory (*ʿām al-fatḥ*) or during the Farewell Pilgrimage (*ḥajjah al-widāʿ*) are accounted as Madanī. This is considered to be the most preferred of the three methods under discussion. 2) The place of revelation, which means that all the *āyāt* that were revealed while the Prophet was in Mecca, or its neighbouring areas, are classified as Makkī, and *āyāt* that were actually revealed in Madinah or its surrounding areas are classified as Madanī. This criterion is, however, not conclusive in that it leaves out the *āyāt* which were received while the Prophet was travelling to places such as Jerusalem or Tabūk. 3) The nature of the audience, which means that all the parts of the Qur'ān which are addressed to the people of Makkah are classified as Makkī and those which are addressed to the people of Madinah are classified as Madanī. In this way all the passages which begin with phrases such as 'O mankind' or 'O people' are Makkī and those which open with phrases such as 'O believers' are typically Madanī.[16]

In the sense that legal material occupies only a small portion of the bulk of its text, the Qur'ān is not a legal or a constitutional document. The Qur'ān calls itself *hudā*, or guidance, not a code of law. Out of over 6,200 *āyāt*, less than one-tenth relate to law and jurisprudence, while the remainder are largely concerned with matters of belief and morality, the five pillars of the faith and a variety of other themes. Its ideas of economic and social justice, including its legal contents, are on the whole subsidiary to its religious call.

The legal or practical contents of the Qur'ān (*al-aḥkām al-ʿamaliyyah*) constitute the basis of what is known as *fiqh al-Qur'ān*, or the *juris corpus* of the Qur'ān. There are close to 350 legal *āyāt* in the Qur'ān, most of which were revealed in response to problems that were actually encountered. Some were revealed with the aim of repealing objectionable customs such as infanticide, usury, gambling and unlimited polygamy. Others laid down penalties with which to enforce the reforms that the Qur'ān had introduced. But on the whole, the Qur'ān confirmed and upheld the existing customs and institutions of Arab society and only introduced changes that were deemed necessary.[17] There are an estimated 140 *āyāt* in the Qur'ān on devotional matters such as *ṣalāh*, legal alms (*zakāh*), *ṣiyām* (fasting), the Pilgrimage of *ḥajj*, *jihād*, charities, the taking of oaths and penances (*kaffārāt*). Another seventy *āyāt* are devoted to marriage, divorce, the waiting period of *ᶜiddah*, revocation (*rijᶜah*), dower, maintenance, custody of children, fosterage, paternity, inheritance and bequest. Rules concerning commercial transactions (*muᶜāmalāt*) such as sale, lease, loan and mortgage, constitute the subject of another seventy *āyāt*. There are about thirty *āyāt* on crimes and penalties such as murder, highway robbery (*ḥirābah*), adultery and false accusation (*qadhf*). Another thirty *āyāt* speak of justice, equality, evidence, consultation, and the rights and obligations of citizens. There are about ten *āyāt* relating to economic matters regulating relations between the poor and the rich, workers' rights and so on.[18] It will be noted, however, that the *fuqahā'* are not in agreement over these figures, as calculations of this nature tend to differ according to one's understanding of, and approach to, the contents of the Qur'ān.[19]

Characteristics of Qur'ānic Legislation

We have already described the phenomenon of graduality (*tanjīm*) in Qur'ānic legislation, its division into Makkī and Madanī, and also the fact that the Qur'ān has been revealed entirely in pure Arabic. In the discussion below, I have also included ratiocination (*taᶜlīl*) among the characteristic features of Qur'ānic legislation despite the fact that the Qur'ān specifies the effective cause or the rationale of only some of its laws. The Qur'ān is nevertheless quite expressive of the purpose, reason, objective, benefit, reward and advantage of its injunctions. Since the Qur'ān addresses the conscience of the individual with a view to persuading and convincing him of the truth and divine origin of its message, it is often combined with an allusion to the benefit that may accrue by the observance of its commands or the harm that is prevented by its prohibitions. This is a feature of the Qur'ānic legislation which is closely associated with ratiocination (*taᶜlīl*) and provides the *mujtahid* with a basis on which to conduct further enquiry into *taᶜlīl*. However, of all the characteristic features of Qur'ānic legislation, its division into *qaṭᶜī* and *ẓannī* is perhaps the most significant and far-reaching, as it relates to almost any aspect of enquiry into the Qur'ānic legislation. I shall therefore take up this subject first.

I. The Definitive (*qaṭᶜī*) and the Speculative (*ẓannī*)

A ruling of the Qur'ān may be conveyed in a text which is either unequivocal and clear, or in language that is open to different interpretations. A definitive text is one which is clear and specific; it has only one meaning and admits of no other interpretations. An example of this is the text on the entitlement of the husband in the estate of his deceased wife, as follows: 'In what your wives leave, your share is a half, if they leave no child' (al-Nisā', 4:12). Other examples are 'The adulterer, whether a man or a woman, flog them each a hundred stripes' (al-Baqarah, 2:196), and 'Those who accuse chaste women of adultery and fail to bring four witnesses [to prove it], flog them eighty stripes' (al-Nūr, 24:4). The quantitative aspects of these rulings, namely one half, one hundred, and eighty are self-evident and therefore not open to interpretation. The rulings of the Qur'ān on the essentials of the faith such as *ṣalāh* and fasting, the specified shares in inheritance and the prescribed penalties, are all *qaṭᶜī*: their validity may not be disputed by anyone; everyone is bound to follow them, and they are not open to *ijtihād*.

The speculative *āyāt* of the Qur'ān are, on the other hand, open to interpretation and *ijtihād*. The best interpretation is that which can be obtained from the Qur'ān itself, that is, by looking at the Qur'ān as a whole and finding the necessary elaboration elsewhere in a similar or even a different context. The *Sunnah* is another source which supplements the Qur'ān and interprets its rulings. When the necessary interpretation can be found in an authentic Ḥadīth, it becomes an integral part of the Qur'ān and both together carry a binding force. Next in this order comes the Companions who are particularly well-qualified to interpret the Qur'ān in light of their close familiarity with its text, the surrounding circumstances, and the teachings of the Prophet.[20]

An example of the *ẓannī* in the Qur'ān is the text which reads, 'Prohibited to you are your mothers and your daughters' (al-Nisā'. 4:23). The text is definitive in regard to the prohibition of marriage with one's mother and daughter and there is no disagreement on this point. However, the word *banātukum* ('your daughters') could be taken for its literal meaning, which would be a female child born to a person either through marriage or through *zinā*, or for its juridical meaning. In the latter sense '*banātukum*' can only mean a legitimate daughter.

The jurists are in disagreement as to which of these meanings should be read into the text. The Ḥanafīs have upheld the first of the two meanings and have ruled on the prohibition of marriage to one's illegitimate daughter, whereas the Shāfiᶜīs have upheld the second. According to this interpretation, marriage with one's illegitimate daughter is not forbidden as the text only refers to a daughter through marriage. It would follow from this that the illegitimate daughter has no right to inheritance, and the rules of guardianship and custody would not apply to her.[21]

In a similar vein, the ulema have differed on the definition of futile, as opposed to deliberate, oaths, which occur in sūra al-Mā'idah (5:92): 'God will not call you to account for what is futile (*al-laghw*) in your oaths, but He will call you to account for your deliberate oaths . . .' The text then continues to spell out the expiation, or *kaffārah*, for deliberate oaths, which consists of either feeding ten hungry persons who are in need, or setting a slave free, or fasting for three days. According to the Ḥanafīs, a futile oath is one which is taken on the truth of something that is suspected to be true but the opposite emerges to be the case. The majority have, on the other hand, held it to mean taking an oath which is not intended, that is, when taken in jest without any intention. Similar differences have arisen concerning the precise definition of what may be considered as a deliberate oath (*yamīn al-muᶜaqqadah*).[22] There is also disagreement as to whether the three days of fasting should be consecutive or could be three separate days. Hence the text of this *āyah*, although definitive on the basic requirement of *kaffārah* for futile oaths, is speculative as to the precise terms of the *kaffārah* and the manner of its implementation.

To give another example of *ẓannī* in the Qur'ān, we may refer to the phrase *yunfaw min al-arḍ* ('to be banished from the earth') which occurs in sūra al-Mā'idah (5:33). The phrase spells out the penalty for highway robbery (*ḥirābah*), or according to an alternative but similar interpretation, for waging war on the community and its legitimate leadership. Banishment (*nafy*) in this *āyah* can mean exile from the place the offence is committed in the first place. This is, in fact, the obvious meaning of the phrase, and the one which has been adopted by the majority of the ulema. But the Ḥanafī jurists maintain that the phrase means imprisonment, not exile. According to the Ḥanafīs, a literal approach to the interpretation of this phrase does not prove to be satisfactory: if one is to be literal, then how can one be banished from the face of the earth by any method but death? *Nafy*, or exile, on the other hand, is a penalty other than killing. Furthermore, if the offender is to be banished from one place to another within the Muslim territories, the harm is not likely to be prevented as he may commit further offences. The Ḥanafīs have further argued that banishing a Muslim outside the territory of Islam is not legally permissible. The only proper meaning of the phrase which would achieve the *Sharīʿah* purpose behind the penalty, is, therefore, imprisonment.

And lastly, the whole *āyah* of *muḥārabah* in which the phrase *yunfaw min al-arḍ* occurs is open to divergent interpretations. The *āyah* in question reads:

> The punishment of those who wage war against God and His Messenger and strive to make mischief in the land is that they should be killed or crucified or their hands and their feet should be cut off on opposite sides, or they should be banished from the earth.

In this passage, confusion arises from the combination of phrases which contain differential penalties for *ḥirābah*. This is mainly due to the use of the article *aw*, meaning 'and' between the three phrases which provide three different penalties for the offence in question. It is thus not known for certain as to which of the three penalties are to be applied to the offender, that is, the *muḥārib*. The majority view is that the *muḥārib* is liable to execution when he actually robs and kills his victim, but if he only robs him, the offender is liable to the mutilation of hands. And finally, if there be no killing involved and no robbery, then the penalty is banishment. In the more intensified cases where the offender kills and robs his victim, the former is to be killed and crucified. Acccording to an alternative juristic opinion, it is for the ruler to determine one or the other, or a combination of these penalties, in individual cases.

A Qur'ānic injunction may simultaneously possess a definitive and a speculative meaning, in which case each of the two meanings will convey a ruling independently of the other. An example of this is the injunction concerning the requirement of ablution for prayers which reads in part '. . . and wipe your heads' (al-Mā'idah, 5:6). This text is definitive on the requirement of wiping (*masḥ*) of the head in *wuḍū'*, but since it does not specify the precise area of the head to be wiped, it is speculative in regard to this point. Hence we find that the jurists are unanimous in regard to the first, but have differed in regard to the second aspect of this injunction.[23]

There are sometime instances where the scope of disagreement over the interpretation of the Qur'ān is fairly extensive. Maḥmūd Shaltūt, for example, underlines this point by noting that at times seven or eight different juristic conclusions have been arrived at on one and the same issue. And he goes on to say that not all of these views can be said to be part of the religion, nor could they be legally binding. These are *ijtihādī* opinions; *ijtihād* is not only permissible but is encouraged. For the *Sharīʿah* does not restrict the liberty of the individual to investigate and express an opinion. They may be right or they may be wrong, and in either case, the diversity of opinion offers the political authority a range of choice from which to select the view it deems to be most beneficial to the community. When the ruler authorises a particular interpretation of the Qur'ān and enacts it into law, it becomes obligatory for everyone to follow only the authorised version.[24]

The ulema are in agreement that the specific (*Khāṣṣ*) of the Qur'ān (and of *Sunnah*) is definitive, but they are in disagreement as to whether the general (*ᶜĀmm*) is definitive or speculative. The Ḥanafīs maintain that the *ᶜĀmm* is definitive and binding: but the Mālikīs, Shāfiᶜīs and Ḥanbalīs hold that the *ᶜĀmm* by itself is speculative and open to qualification and specification. We need not, at this point, go into the details of the *ᶜĀmm* and the *Khāṣṣ* as we shall have occasion to return to this subject later. Suffice it here to explain how the *ᶜĀmm* and *Khāṣṣ* may be related to *qaṭᶜī* and *ẓannī*.

First we may highlight the *ẓannī* content of the *ᶜĀmm* by referring to the Qur'ānic ruling which provides: 'Forbidden to you (in marriage) are your mothers, your daughters, your sisters, your father's sisters and your mother's sisters' (al-Nisā', 4:23). This is a general ruling in that mothers, daughters, sisters, etc. are all *ᶜĀmm* as they include, in the case of 'mother' not only the real mother but also the step-mother and even the grandmother. Similarly, 'daughters' can include real daughters, step-daughters, grand-daughters and even illegitimate daughters. The application of these terms to all of their various meanings is *qaṭᶜī* according to the Ḥanafīs, but is *ẓannī* according to the majority of ulema. Whenever the *ẓannī* of the Qur'ān is explained and clarified by the Qur'ān itself or by the *Sunnah*, it may become *qaṭᶜī*, in which case the clarification becomes an integral part of the original ruling. On the subject of prohibited degrees in marriage, there is ample evidence both in the Qur'ān and the *Sunnah* to specify and elaborate the *ᶜĀmm* of the Qur'ān on this subject. Similarly, when the Qur'ān or the *Sunnah* specifies a general ruling of the Qur'ān, the part which is so specified becomes *qaṭᶜī*.

To give another example of the *ᶜĀmm* which can be clearly seen in its capacity as *ẓannī* we refer to the Qur'ānic proclamation that 'God has permitted sale but prohibited usury' (al-Baqarah, 2:275). This is a general ruling in the sense that sale, that is any sale, is made lawful. But there are certain varieties of sale which are specifically forbidden by the *Sunnah*. Consequently, the *ᶜĀmm* of this *āyah* is specified by the *Sunnah* to the extent that some varieties of sale, such as sale of unripened fruit on a tree, were forbidden and therefore excluded from the scope of this *āyah*. The ulema are all in agreement to the effect that once the *ᶜĀmm* has been specified even in a narrow and limited sense, the part which still remains unspecified is reduced to *ẓannī* and will be treated as such.

Broadly speaking, the *Khāṣṣ* is definitive. When, for example, the Qur'ān (al-Nūr, 24:4) prescribes the punishment of eighty lashes for slanderous accusation (*qadhf*), the quantitative aspect of this punishment is specific (*Khāṣṣ*) and not susceptible to any speculation. But then we find that the same passage (al-Nūr, 24:4) prescribes a supplementary penalty for the slanderous accuser (*qādhif*) where it reads: 'Never accept their testimony, for they are evildoers (*fāsiqūn*), except for those who repent afterwards and make amends.' This text is clear and definitive on the point that the *qādhif* is to be disqualified as a witness, but then an element of doubt is introduced by the latter portion of the text which tends to render ambiguous the precise scope of its application. Having enacted both the principal and the supplementary penalties for slanderous accusers and *fāsiqūn* it becomes questionable whether the *qādhif* should qualify as a witness after repentance. Does the text under discussion mean that the concession is only to be extended to the *fāsiqūn* and not necessarily to slanderous accusers? If the answer is in the affirmative, then once the *qādhif* is convicted of the offence, no amount of repentance will qualify him as an upright witness again. The whole confusion is due to uncertainty in the meaning of a pronoun, namely *al-ladhīna* (i.e. 'those') which is not known to refer to all or only part of the preceding elements in the text. The Ḥanafīs disqualify the *qādhif* permanently from being a witness, whereas the Shāfiᶜīs would admit him as a witness after repentance. This example also serves to show that it is not always self-evident whether a text is *qaṭᶜī* or *ẓannī* as this too may be open to interpretation. But the main point of citing this example is to show that although the *Khāṣṣ* is *qaṭᶜī*, an aspect thereof may be *ẓannī* in a way that might affect the definitive character of the *Khāṣṣ* as a whole.

Although in principle the *Khāṣṣ* is *qaṭᶜī* and, as such, is not open to speculative interpretation, there may be exceptions to this general rule. For example, the penance (*kaffārah*) of a false oath according to a textual ruling of the Qur'ān (al-Mā'idah, 5:92) is of three types, one of which is to feed ten poor persons. This is a specific ruling in the sense that 'ten poor persons' has only one meaning. But even so, the Ḥanafīs have given this text an alternative interpretation, which is that instead of feeding ten poor persons, one such person may be fed ten times. The majority of ulema, however, do not agree with the Ḥanafīs on this point. Be that as it may, this example will serve to show that the scope of *ijtihād* is not always confined to the *ᶜĀmm* but that even the *Khāṣṣ* and definitive rulings may require elaboration which might be based on speculative reasoning.

Furthermore, the *Khāṣṣ* of the Qur'ān normally occurs in the form of a command or a prohibition which, as discussed below in a separate chapter, can either be *qaṭʿī* or *ẓannī*. The *ẓannī* component of a command or a prohibition is readily identified by the fact that a command in the Qur'ān may amount either to *wājib* or to *mandūb* or even to a mere *mubāḥ*. Similarly, it is not always certain whether a prohibition in the Qur'ān amounts to a total ban (*taḥrīm*) or to a mere abomination (*karāhah*).

The absolute (*Muṭlaq*) and the qualified (*Muqayyad*) are also classified as the sub-varieties of *Khāṣṣ*. But these too can be related to the *qaṭʿī-ẓannī* division in at least two ways. Firstly, that somewhat like the *ʿĀmm*, the absolute is speculative in regard to the precise scope of its application. Secondly, the qualification of the absolute, the grounds on which it is qualified and the nature of the relationship between the qualified and the qualifier are not always a matter of certain knowledge. The absolute in the Qur'ān is sometimes qualified on speculative grounds, which is why the jurists are not in agreement over the various aspects of qualifying the *Muṭlaq*. Further detail on the subject of *Muṭlaq* and *Muqayyad* and juristic disagreements over its various aspects can be found in a separate chapter below. Suffice it here to give an illustration: there are two separate rulings on the subject of witnesses in the Qur'ān, one of which is absolute and the other qualified in regard to the attributes of the witness. First it is provided with regard to the transaction of sale to 'bring witnesses when you conclude a sale – *wa-shhidū idhā tabāyaʿtum*' (al-Baqarah, 2:282). In this *āyah*, the witness is not qualified in any way whatsoever. But elsewhere we find in a reference to the subject of revocation in divorce (*rijʿah*), the command to 'bring two just witnesses' (al-Ṭalāq, 65:2). The ulema have on the whole related these two *āyāt* to one another and the conclusion is drawn that the qualified terms of the second *āyah* must also be applied to the first, which would mean that witnesses must be upright and just whether it be a case of a commercial transaction or of revocation in divorce. This is the settled law, but to relate this to our discussion over the *qaṭʿī* and the *ẓannī*, it will be noted that determining the precise scope of the first *āyah* is open to speculation. Does the requirement of witnesses apply only to sale or to all commercial transactions? To enter a detailed discussion on this point might seem out of place in the face of the fact that notwithstanding the clear terms of the Qur'ānic injunction, the rules of *fiqh* as developed by the majority of ulema, with the exception of the Ẓāhirīs, do not require any witnesses either in sale or in the revocation of divorce. The ulema have, of course, found reasons in support of their rulings both from within and outside the Qur'ān. But even the bare facts we have discussed so far are enough to show that the *Muṭlaq* and *Muqayyad* are susceptible to speculative reasoning. But to discuss the foregoing example a little further, it will be noted that the juxtaposition of the two *āyāt* and the conclusion that the one is qualified by the other is to a large extent based on speculative reasoning. And then the qualified terms of the second of the two *āyāt* may be taken a step further, and the question is bound to be asked, as indeed it has been, as to the precise meaning of a just witness. The ulema of the various schools have differed on the attribute of *ᶜadālah* in a witness and their conclusions are based largely on speculative *ijtihād*.

We need not perhaps discuss in detail the point that the binary division of words into the literal (*Ḥaqīqī*) amd metaphorical (*Majāzī*) which we shall elsewhere elaborate can also be related to the *qaṭᶜī* and *ẓannī*. Although relying on the literal meaning of a word is the norm and a requirement of certainty in the enforcement of a legal text, it may be necessary at times to depart from the literal in favour of adopting the metaphorical meaning of a word. To give an example, *ṭalāq* literally means release or setting free, but as a technical term, it has acquired a specific meaning, and it is the metaphorical meaning of *ṭalāq* which is normally applied. The ulema have identified a large variety of grounds on which the *Ḥaqīqī* and the *Majāzī* can be related to one another. The *Majāzī* is to a large extent speculative and unreal. Some ulema have even equated the *Majāzī* with falsehood, and, as such, it has no place in the Qur'ān. It is thus suggested that the *Majāzī* is not to be relied upon in interpreting the practical injunctions of the Qur'ān. Be this as it may, the point is clear that speculative reasoning has a wide scope in determining the meaning and application of *Ḥaqīqī* and *Majāzī* in the Qur'ān, and indeed in any other source of *Sharīᶜah*.

Furthermore, the ulema have deduced the rules of *Sharīᶜah* not only from the explicit words of the Qur'ān, which is referred to as the *manṭūq*, but also from the implicit meanings of the text through inference and logical construction, which is referred to as the implied meaning, or *mafhūm*. Once again, this subject has been discussed in a separate chapter under *al-dalālāt*, that is, textual implications. The only purpose of referring to this subject here is to point out that the deduction of the rules of *Sharīᶜah* by way of inference from the implied meaning of a text partakes in speculative reasoning and *ijtihād*. Naturally, not all the *aḥkām* deduced in this way can be classified as *ẓannī*. The implied meaning of a text can often command the same degree of authority as the explicit ruling of the same text. Having said this, however, to extend, for example, the requirement of expiation (*kaffārah*) for erroneous killing which is releasing a slave, or feeding sixty poor persons, or fasting for two months – to the case of intentional killing on the analysis that the purpose of *kaffārah* is compensation for a sin and that this is true of all types of homicide – is basically no more than speculative *ijtihād*. This is the implied meaning of the text in sūra al-Nisā', 4:92, which is explicit on the *kaffārah* of erroneous killing. But the implied meaning of this text does not command the same degree of certainty as the clear words thereof, which is why the ulema are not in agreement on it.

In the discussion of the *qaṭʿī* and *ẓannī*, the Qur'ān and *Sunnah* are seen as complementary and integral to one another. The reason is that the speculative of the Qur'ān can be made definitive by the *Sunnah* and vice versa. The *ẓannī* of the Qur'ān may be elevated into *qaṭʿī* by means of corroborative evidence in the Qur'ān itself or in the *Sunnah*. Similarly, the *ẓannī* of the *Sunnah* may be elevated into *qaṭʿī* by means of corroborative evidence in the *Sunnah* itself or in the Qur'ān. And then the *ẓannī* of both the Qur'ān and *Sunnah* may be elevated into *qaṭʿī* by means of a conclusive *ijmāʿ*, especially the *ijmāʿ* of Companions.

As stated above, a speculative indication in the text of the Qur'ān or Ḥadīth may be supported by a definitive evidence in either, in which case it is as valid as one which was definitive in the first place. To illustrate this, all the solitary (*Āḥād*) *aḥādīth* which elaborate the definitive Qur'ānic prohibition of usury (*ribā*) in sūra 2:275 are speculative by virtue of being *Āḥād*. But since their substance is supported by the definitive text of the Qur'ān, they become definitive despite any doubt that may exist in respect of their authenticity. Thus as a general rule, all solitary *aḥādīth* whose authenticity is open to speculation are elevated to the rank of *qaṭʿī* if they can be substantiated by clear evidence in the Qur'ān.[25] However, if the *ẓannī* cannot be so substantiated by the *qaṭʿī*, it is not binding unless it can be validated by some evidence which may lead to one of the following two possibilities. Firstly, the *ẓannī* is found to be in conflict with a *qaṭʿī* of the Qur'ān, in which case it must be rejected. To illustrate this, it is reported that the widow of the Prophet, ʿĀ'ishah, rejected the alleged Ḥadīth that the (soul of the) deceased is tortured by the weeping of his relatives over his death,[26] the reason being that this was contrary to the definitive text of the Qur'ān (al-Anʿām, 6:164) which provides that 'no soul may be burdened with the burden of another soul'. And secondly, the speculative indication may be such that it cannot be related to a definitive evidence in any way. The ulema have differed on this; some would advise suspension while others would apply the presumption of permissibility (*ibāḥah*), but the best view is that the matter is open to *ijtihād*.[27]

The *qaṭʿī* of the Qur'ān is an integral part of the dogma, and anyone who rejects or denies its validity automatically renounces Islam. But denying a particular interpretation of the *ẓannī* does not amount to transgression. The *mujtahid* is entitled to give it an interpretation, and so is the ruler who may select one of the various interpretations for purposes of enforcement.[28]

II. Brevity and Detail (*al-ijmāl wa'l-tafṣīl*)

By far the larger part of the Qur'ānic legislation consists of an enunciation of general principles, although in certain areas, the Qur'ān also provides specific details. Being the principal source of the *Sharīᶜah*, the Qur'ān lays down general guidelines on almost every major topic of Islamic law. While commenting on this point, Abū Zahrah concurs with Ibn Ḥazm's assessment that 'every single chapter of *fiqh* finds its origin in the Qur'ān, which is then explained and elaborated by the *Sunnah*'.[29] On a similar note, al-Shāṭibī makes the following observation: Experience shows that every *ᶜālim* who has resorted to the Qur'ān in search of the solution to a problem has found in the Qur'ān a principle that has provided him with some guidance on the subject.[30]

The often-quoted declaration that 'We have neglected nothing in the Book' (al-Anᶜām, 6:38) is held to mean that the *ru'ūs al-aḥkām*, that is, the general principles of law and religion, are exhaustively treated in the Qur'ān.[31] That the Qur'ān is mainly concerned with general principles is borne out by the fact that its contents require a great deal of elaboration, which is often provided, although not exhaustively, by the *Sunnah*. To give an example, the following Qur'ānic *āyah* provides the textual authority for all the material sources of the *Sharīᶜah*, namely the Qur'ān, the *Sunnah*, consensus and analogy. The *āyah* reads: 'O you who believe, obey God and obey the Messenger, and those of you who are in authority; and if you have a dispute concerning any matter refer it to God and to the Messenger . . .' (al-Nisā', 4:58). 'Obey God' in this *āyah* refers to the Qur'ān as the first source, 'and obey the Messenger' refers to the *Sunnah* of the Prophet, 'and those of you who are in authority' authorises the consensus of the ulema. The last portion of the *āyah* ('and if you have a dispute . . .') validates *qiyās*. For a dispute can only be referrd to God and to the Messenger by extending the rulings of the Qur'ān and *Sunnah* through analogy to similar cases. In this sense one might say that the whole body of *uṣūl al-fiqh* is a commentary on this single Qur'ānic *āyah*.[32] Al-Shāṭibī further observes that wherever the Qur'ān provides specific details it is related to the exposition and better understanding of its general principles.[33] Most of the legal contents of the Qur'ān consist of general rules, although it contains specific injunctions on a number of topics. Broadly speaking, the Qur'ān is specific on matters which are deemed to be unchangeable, but in matters which are liable to change, it merely lays down general guidelines.

The Qur'ānic legislation on civil, economic, constitutional and international affairs is, on the whole, confined to an exposition of the general principles and objectives of the law. With regard to civil transactions, for example, the *nuṣūṣ* of the Qur'ān on the fulfilment of contracts, the legality of sale, the prohibition of usury, respect for the property of others, the documentation of loans and other forms of deferred payments are all concerned with general principles. Thus in the area of contracts, the Qur'ānic legislation is confined to the bare minimum of detail,[34] and in the area of civil transactions and property, the believers are enjoined to 'devour not the properties of one another unlawfully, but let there be lawful trade by mutual consent' (al-Nisā, 4:29). Elsewhere we read in sūrah al-Baqarah (2:275) that 'God has permitted sale and prohibited usury'. The detailed varieties of lawful trade, the forms of unlawful interference with the property of others, and the varieties of usurious transactions, are matters which the Qur'ān has not elaborated. Some of these have been explained and elaborated by the *Sunnah*. As for the rest, it is for the scholars and the *mujtahidūn* of every age to specify them in the light of the general principles of the *Sharīᶜah* and the needs and interests of the people.[35]

In the sphere of crimes and penalties, the Qur'ānic legislation is specific with regard to only five offences, namely murder, theft, highway robbery, *zinā* and slanderous accusation. As for the rest, the Qur'ān authorises the community and those who are in charge of their affairs (i.e. the *ulū al-amr*) to determine them in the light of the general principles of *Sharīᶜah* and the prevailing conditions of society. Once again the Qur'ān lays down the broad principles of penal law when it provides that 'the punishment of an evil is an evil like it' (al-Shūrā, 42:40), and 'when you decide to punish then punish in proportion to the offence committed against you' (al-Naḥl, 16:126).

In the area of international relations, the Qur'ān lays down rules which regulate war with the unbelievers and expound the circumstances in which their property may be possessed in the form of booty. But the general principle on which relations between Muslims and non-Muslims are to be regulated is stated in the following passage:

> God does not forbid you to act considerately towards those who have never fought you over religion nor evicted you from your homes, nor [does he forbid you] to act fairly towards them. God loves the fairminded. He only forbids you to be friendly with the ones who have fought you over [your] religion and evicted you from your homes and have abetted others in your eviction. Those who befriend them are wrongdoers (al-Mumtaḥinah, 60:8–9).

Similarly, the Qur'ānic commandments to do justice are confined to general guidelines and no details are provided regarding the duties of the judge or the manner in which testimony should be given.[36] On the principles of government, such as consultation, equality and the rights of citizens, the Qur'ān does not provide any details. The general principles are laid down, and it is for the community, the ulema and leaders to organise their government in the light of the changing conditions of society.[37] The Qur'ān itself warns the believers against seeking the regulation of everything by the express terms of divine revelation, as this is likely to lead to rigidity and cumbersome restrictions: 'O you believers, do not keep asking about things which, if they were expounded to you, would become troublesome for you . . .' (5:104). In this way, the Qur'ān discourages the development of an over-regulated society. Besides, what the Qur'ān has left unregulated is meant to be devised, in accord with the general objectives of the Lawgiver, through mutual consultation and *ijtihād*. A careful reading of the Qur'ān further reveals that on matters pertaining to belief, the basic principles of morality, man's relationship with his Creator, and what are referred to as *ghaybiyyāt*, that is transcendental matters which are characteristically unchangeable, the Qur'ān is clear and detailed, as clarity and certainty are the necessary requirements of belief. In the area of ritual performances (*ᶜibādāt*) such as *ṣalāh*, fasting and *ḥajj*, on the other hand, although these too are meant to be unchangeable, the Qur'ān is nevertheless brief, and most of the necessary details have been supplied by the *Sunnah*. An explanation for this is that ritual performances are all of a practical, or *ᶜamalī*, nature and require clear instructions which are best provided through practical methods and illustration. With regard to *ṣalāh*, legal alms (*zakāt*) and *ḥajj*, for example, the Qur'ān simply commands the believers to 'perform the *ṣalāh*, and pay the *zakāt*' and states that 'pilgrimage to the house is a duty that God has imposed on mankind' (al-Naḥl, 16:44 and Āl-ᶜImrān, 3:97 respectively). With regard to *ṣalāh*, the Prophet has ordered his followers to 'perform *ṣalāh* the way you see me performing it',

صلّوا كما رأيتموني أُصلّي

and regarding the *ḥajj* he similarly instructed people to 'take from me the rituals of the *ḥajj*'.[38]

خذوا عنّي مناسككم

The details of *zakāt* such as the quorum, the amount to be given and its numerous other conditions have been supplied by the *Sunnah*.

The Qur'ān also contains detailed rules on family matters, the prohibited degrees of relationship in marriage, inheritance and specific punishments for certain crimes. These are, for the most part, associated with human nature and regulate the manner in which man's natural needs may be fulfilled. The basic objectives of the law regarding these matters are permanent. They are, however, matters which lead to disputes. The purpose of regulating them in detail is to prevent conflict among people. The specific rulings of the Qur'ān in these areas also took into consideration the prevalence of certain entrenched social customs of Arabia which were overruled and abolished. The Qur'ānic reforms concerning the status of women, and its rules on the just distribution of property within the family could, in view of such customs, only be effective if couched in clear and specific detail.[39]

The Qur'ān frequently provides general guidelines on matters of law and religion, which are often specified by the Qur'ān itself; otherwise the *Sunnah* specifies the general in the Qur'ān and elaborates its brief and apparently ambiguous provisions. By far the larger part of Qur'ānic legislation is conveyed in general terms which need to be specified in relation to particular issues. This is partly why we find that the study of the *ᶜĀmm* (general) and *Khāṣṣ* (particular) acquires a special significance in the extraction of substantive legal rules from the general provisions of the Qur'ān. Once again the fact that legislation in the Qur'ān mainly occurs in brief and general terms has to a large extent determined the nature of the relationship between the Qur'ān and *Sunnah*. Since the general, the ambiguous and the difficult portions of the Qur'ān were in need of elaboration and *takhṣīṣ* (specification), the Prophet was expected to provide the necessary details and determine the particular focus of the general rulings of the Qur'ān. It was due to these and other such factors that a unique relationship was forged between the *Sunnah* and the Qur'ān in that the two are often integral to one another and inseparable. By specifying the general and by clarifying the *mujmal* in the Qur'ān, the *Sunnah* has undoubtedly played a crucial role in the development of *Sharīᶜah*. It is the clear and the specific (*Khāṣṣ*) in the Qur'ān and *Sunnah* which provides the core and kernel of the *Sharīᶜah* in the sense that no law can be said to have any reality if all or most of it were to consist of brief and general provisions. To that extent, the specifying role of the *Sunnah* in its relationship to the Qur'ān is of central importance to *Sharīᶜah*. And yet the general in the Qur'ān has a value of its own. In it lies the essence of comprehensive guidance and of the permanent validity of the Qur'ān. It is also the *ᶜĀmm* of the Qur'ān which has provided scope and substance for an ever-continuing series of commentaries and interpretations. The ulema and commentators throughout the centuries have attempted to derive a fresh message, a new lesson or a new principle from the Qur'ān that was more suitable to the realities of their times and the different phases of development in the life of the community. This was to a large extent facilitated by the fact that the Qur'ān consisted for the most part of broad principles which could be related to a variety of circumstances. To give one example, on the subject of consultation (*shūrā*) the Qur'ān contains only two *āyāt*, both of which are general. One of these commands the Prophet to 'consult them [the community] in their affairs' (Āl-ʿImrān, 3:159) and the other occurs in the form of praise to the Muslim community on account of the fact that 'they conduct their affairs by consultation among them' (Al-Shūrā, 42:38). The fact that both of these are general proclamations has made it possible to relate them to almost any stage of development in the socio-political life of the community. The Qur'ān has not specified the manner as to how the principle of *shūrā* should be interpreted; it has not specified any subject on which consultation must take place, nor even any person or authority who should be consulted. These are all left to the discretion of the community. In its capacity as the vicegerent of God and the locus of political authority, the community is at liberty to determine the manner in which the principle of *shūrā* should be interpreted and enforced.[40]

III. The Five Values

As a characteristic feature of Qur'ānic legislation, it may be stated here that commands and prohibitions in the Qur'ān are expressed in a variety of forms which are often open to interpretation and *ijtihād*. The question as to whether a particular injunction in the Qur'ān amounts to a binding command or to a mere recommendation or even permissibility cannot always be determined from the words and sentences of its text. The subject of commands and prohibitions need not be elaborated here as this is the theme of a separate chapter of this work. It will suffice here to note the diversity of the Qur'ānic language on legislation. Broadly speaking, when God commands or praises something, or recommends a certain form of conduct, or refers to the positive quality of something, or when it is expressed that God loves such-and-such, or when God identifies something as a cause of bounty and reward, all such expressions are indicative of the legality (*mashrūʿiyyah*) of the conduct in question which partakes in the obligatory and commendable. If the language of the text is inclined on the side of obligation (*wujūb*), such as when there is a definite demand or a clear emphasis on doing something, the conduct is question in obligatory (*wājib*), otherwise it is commendable (*mandūb*).

Similarly, when God explicitly declares something permissible (*ḥalāl*) or grants a permission (*idhn*) in respect of doing something, or when it is said that there is 'no blame' or 'no sin' accrued from doing something, or when God denies the prohibition of something, or when the believers are reminded of the bounty of God in respect of things that are created for their benefit,[41] all such expressions are indicative of permissibility (*ibāḥah*) and option (*takhyīr*) in respect of the conduct or the object in question.

Whenever God demands the avoidance of a certain conduct, or when He denounces a certain act, or identifies it as a cause for punishment, or when a certain conduct is cursed and regarded as the work of Satan, or when its harmful effects are emphasised, or when something is proclaimed unclean, a sin or a deviation (*ithm, fisq*) – all such expressions are indicative of prohibition which partakes in abomination (*karāhah*). If the language is explicit and emphatic in regard to prohibition, the conduct/object in question becomes *ḥarām*, otherwise it is reprehensible, or *makrūh*. It is for the *mujtahid* to determine the precise value of such injunctions in the light of both the language of the text as well as the general objectives and principles of the *Sharīʿah*.[42]

This style of Qur'ānic legislation, and the fact that it leaves room for flexibility in the evaluation of its injunctions, is once again in harmony with the timeless validity of its laws. The Qur'ān is not specific on the precise value of its injunctions, and it leaves open the possibility that a command in the Qur'ān may sometimes imply an obligation, a recommendation or a mere permissibility. The Qur'ān does not employ the categories known as the five values (*al-aḥkām al-khamsah*) which the *fuqahā'* have attempted to specify in juristic manuals. When an act is evaluated as obligatory, it is labelled *farḍ* or *wājib*; when it is absolutely forbidden, it is evaluated as *ḥarām*. The shades of values which occur between these two extremes are primarily religious in character and provide a yardstick which can be applied to any type of human conduct. But only the two extremes, namely the *wājib* and *ḥarām*, incorporate legal commands and prohibitions. The rest are largely non-legal and non-justiciable in a court of law. The Qur'ān thus leaves open the possibility, although not without reservations, of enacting into *ḥarām* what may have been classified by the *fuqahā'* of one age as merely reprehensible, or *makrūh*. Similarly, the recommendable, or *mandūb*, may be elevated into a *wājib* if this is deemed to be in the interest of the community in a different stage of its experience and development.

IV. Ratiocination (*taʿlīl*) in the Qur'ān

Literally *taʿlīl* means 'causation', or 'search for the causes', and refers to the logical relationship between the cause and effect. But the ulema of jurisprudence tend to use *taʿlīl* and its derivative *ʿillah*, for different purposes. In its juridical usage, *ʿillah* (i.e. effective cause) does not exactly refer to a causal relationship between two phenomena; it rather means the *ratio* of the law, its value and its purpose. Broadly speaking, *ʿillah* refers to the rationale of an injunction, and in this sense, it is synonymous with *ḥikmah*, that is, the purpose and the objective of the law. But there is a difference between *ʿillah* and *ḥikmah* which I shall discuss in a subsequent chapter on analogical deduction (*qiyās*). There is another Arabic word, namely *sabab*, which is synonymous with *ʿillah*, and the two are often used interchangeably. Yet the ulema of *uṣūl* tend to use *sabab* in reference to devotional matters (*ʿibādāt*) but use *ʿillah* in all other contexts. Thus it is said that the arrival of Ramadan is the cause (*sabab*) of fasting but that intoxication is the *ʿillah* of the prohibition in wine-drinking.[43]

The authority of the Qur'ān as the principal source of the *Sharīʿah* is basically independent of ratiocination. The believers are supposed to accept its rulings regardless of whether they can be rationally explained. Having said this, however, there are instances where the Qur'ān justifies its rulings with a reference to the benefits that accrue from them, or the objectives which they may serve. Such explanatons are often designed to make the Qur'ān easier to understand. To give an example in the context of encounters between members of the opposite sex, the believers are enjoined in sūra al-Nūr (24:30) 'to avert their glances and to guard their private parts'. The text then goes on to provide that in doing so they will attain greater chastity of character and conduct. To give another example, in sūra al-Ḥashr (59:7) the Qur'ān regulates the distribution of booty among the needy, the orphans and the wayfarers 'so that wealth does not merely circulate among the wealthy'. In the first *āyah*, averting the glance is justified as it obstructs the means to promiscuity and *zinā*. The ruling in the second *āyah* is justified as it prevents the accumulation of wealth in a few hands. Whereas the foregoing are instances in which the text explicitly states the *ʿillah* of the injunctions concerned, on numerous other occasions the jurists have identified the *ʿillah* through reasoning and *ijtihād*. The identification of *ʿillah* in many of the following cases, for example, is based on speculative reasoning on which the ulema are not unanimous: that arrival of the specified time is the cause (*sabab* or *ʿillah*) of the prayer, that the month of Ramadan is the cause of fasting, that the existence of the Kaʿbah is the cause of *ḥajj*; that owning property is the cause of *zakāt*, that theft is the cause of amputation of the hand, that travelling is the cause of shortening the prayer and that intentional killing is the cause of retaliation. These and other similar conclusions with regard to the assignment of *ʿillah* have been drawn in the light of supportive evidence in the Qur'ān and *Sunnah*, but even so many of them are disputed by the ulema. These examples will in the meantime serve to show the difference between the literal/logical meaning of '*ᶜillah*' and its juridical usage among the ulema of jurisprudence.[44]

The question arises as to whether the incidence of *taᶜlīl* in the Qur'ān gives the *mujtahid* the green light to enquire into the causes and reasons behind its injunctions, or whether it exists simply to facilitate a better understanding of the text. The ulema have held different views on this issue. The opponents of *taᶜlīl* maintain that divine injunctions embodied in the clear text have no causes unless the Lawgiver provides us with clear indications to the contrary. Thus it would not only be presumptuous on the part of the *mujtahid* to adopt an inquisitive approach to divine injunctions, but searching for the cause (*ᶜīllah*) or the objective *ḥikmah* of the Qur'ānic rules amounts to no more than an exercise in speculation. Besides, the opponents of *taᶜlīl* have argued that the believer should surrender himself to the will of God, which can best be done by unquestioning acceptance of God's injunctions. To look into the motive, purpose and rationale of such injunctions, and worse still, to accept them on their rational merit, is repugnant to sincerity in submission to God. Furthermore, in his attempt to identify the rationale of an injunction, the *mujtahid* can only make a reasonable guess which cannot eliminate the possibility of error. There may even be more than one cause or explanation to a particular ruling of the Qur'ān, in which case one cannot be certain which of the several causes might be the correct one. This is the view of the Ẓāhirīs. The majority of ulema have, however, held that the *aḥkām* of the *Sharīᶜah* contemplate certain objectives, and when such can be identified, it is not only permissible to pursue them but it is our duty to make an effort to identify and to implement them. Since the realisation of the objectives (*maqāṣid*) of the *Sharīᶜah* necessitates identification of the cause/rationale of the *aḥkām*, it becomes our duty to discover these in order to be able to pursue the general objectives of the Lawgiver.[45] Thus it is the duty of the *mujtahid* to identify the proper causes of divine injunctions, especially in the event where more than one *ᶜillah* can be attributed to a particular injunction. The majority view on *taᶜlīl* takes into account the analysis that the rules of *Sharīᶜah* have been introduced in order to realise certain objectives and that the Lawgiver has enacted the detailed rules of *Sharīᶜah*, not as an end in themselves, but as a means to realising those objectives. In this way, any attempt to implement the law should take into account not only the externalities of the law but also the rationale and the intent behind it. Thus when a man utters the credo of Islam to achieve worldy gain or to attain social prestige, his confession is not valid. The reason is that the true purpose of confession to the faith is the exaltation and worship of God, and if this is violated, a formal confession is of no value. Similarly, if a man says a prayer for the sake of display and self-commendation, it is not valid. The real purpose and value of the law is therefore of primary importance, and indeed it is necessary that the *mujtahid* identifies it so as to be able to implement the law in accordance with its purpose. The Qur'ān admittedly requires unquestioning obedience to God and to His Messenger, but at the same time, it exhorts men to understand the spirit and purpose of God's injunctions. Time and time again, the Qur'ān invites the believers to rational enquiry, as opposed to blind imitation, in the acceptance of its messages.[46]

Taʿlīl acquires a special significance in the context of analogical deduction. *ʿIllah* is an essential requirement, indeed the *sine qua non* of analogy. To enable the extension of an existing rule of the *Sharīʿah* to similar cases, the *mujtahid* must establish a common *ʿillah* between the original and the new case. Without the identification of a common *ʿillah* between two parallel cases, no analogy can be constructed. To this it may be added that there is a variety of *qiyās*, known as *qiyās manṣūṣ al-ʿillah*, or *qiyās* whose *ʿillah* is indicated in the *naṣṣ*, in which the *ʿillah* of the law is already identified in the text. When the *ʿillah* is so identified, there remains no need for the *mujtahid* to establish the effective cause of the injunction by recourse to reasoning or *ijtihād*. However, this variety of *qiyās* is limited in scope when it is compared to *qiyās* whose *ʿillah* is not so indicated on the *nuṣūṣ*. It thus remains true to say that *taʿlīl*, that is, the search to identify the effective cause of the *Sharīʿah* rules, is of central importance to *qiyās*. Further discussion on the *ʿillah* of analogy, the manner of its identification, and rules which govern the propriety of *taʿlīl* in *qiyās* can be found in our discussion of *qiyās* in a separate chapter below.

There seems to be a confusion on the part of the opponents of *taʿlīl* as to the purpose and nature of *taʿlīl*. The opponents of *taʿlīl* seem to have perceived this phenomenon as a sign of impudence and impropriety in belief. In reality, however, this need not be the case. One may attempt *taʿlīl* while remaining totally faithful to the divine origin and essence of the Qur'ān. To exercise *taʿlīl* does not lessen either the binding power or the holiness of the divine injunctions. We may, for example, offer various interpretations of the cause of performing the *ṣalāh* or of giving *zakāh*; but whether we can understand the reason or not, *ṣalāh* and *zakāh* are still obligatory upon Muslims.

V. Inimitability (*iʿjāz*) of the Qur'ān

This is reflected in at least four aspects of the Qur'ān. First, in its linguistic excellence: many scholars have pointed out that there exists no piece of literature that can match the literary excellence of the Qur'ān with respect to both content and form.[47] It is neither poetry nor prose; its rhythm and its genre and word structure are unique. It is the spiritual miracle of the prophethood of Muḥammad, who never learned to read or write, and it is considered to have been far beyond his own ability to produce a linguistic artefact of this kind. In more than one place, the Qur'ān challenges those who deny its divine origin by asking them to produce anything to match it.[48]

The second aspect of *iʿjāz* in the Qur'ān is its narration of events which took place centuries ago. The accuracy of the Qur'ānic narratives concerning such events is generally confirmed by historical evidence.[49]

The third aspect of *iʿjāz* in the Qur'ān is its accurate prediction of future events, such as the victory of the Muslims in the battle of Badr (al-Anfāl, 8:7), the conquest of Mecca (al-Fatḥ, 48:27) and the eventual defeat of the Persians by the Roman empire: 'The Romans were defeated in a land near-by, but even after this defeat, they will be victorious in a few years (*fī biḍʿi sinīn*; literally in a period lasting up to ten years)' (al-Rūm, 30:2). The Romans were defeated by the Persians when the latter took Jerusalem in 614 A.D. But seven years later the Persians were defeated when the Romans won the battle of Issus in 622.[50]

The fourth aspect of *iʿjāz* in the Qur'ān is manifested in its scientific truth concerning the creation of man, the earth and the planetary system. The tenets thus inform us:

— 'We created man from an extract of clay, then We placed him as a drop of semen in a secure resting-place. Then We turned the drop into a clot; next We turned the clot into tissue; and then We turned the tissue into bones and clothed the bones with flesh' (al-Mu'minūn, 23:12–14).

— That the earth was previously a part of the sun, and only after it was separated from the sun did it become suitable for human habitation (al-Anbiyā', 21:30).

— That all life originated in water (al-Anbiyā', 21:30).

— That originally the universe consisted of fiery gas (Ḥā-mīm, 41:11).

— That matter is made up of minute particles (Yūnus, 10:62).

— That fertilisation of certain plants is facilitated by the wind (al-Ḥijr, 15:22).

Another manifestation of *iʿjāz* in the Qur'ān is to be seen in its humanitarian, legal and cultural reforms that were unprecedented in the history of nations. Thus in the sphere of government, the ruler and the ruled were both equally subjected to adjudication under the rule of law.[51] In the area of civil transactions and commerce, the Qur'ān established mutual agreement as the norm and essence of all contracts. The principal Qur'ānic reform in the area of property was the introduction of the doctrine of *istikhlāf*: the Qur'ān declares that all property belongs to God, and that man, in his capacity as the vicegerent of God, is a mere trustee whose exercise of the right of ownership is subjected to the *maṣlaḥah* of society to be supervised by the government. In the sphere of international relations, treaty relations, the conduct of war, and treatment of prisoners of war; all were regulated by a set of principles which aimed at the realisation of justice and respect for human dignity. Relations among individuals were to be governed by the principles of freedom and equality, and the state was equally subjected to the observance, and indeed the protection, of these values.[52]

VI. Occasions of Revelation (*asbāb al-nuzūl*)

Asbāb al-nuzūl deal with the phenomenology of the Qur'ān, and explain the events which are related to the revelation of its particular passages. The well-known *asbāb al-nuzūl* have been related to us by reliable Companions. It is a condition for the reliability of such reports that the person relating it should have been present at the time or the occasion which is relevant to a particular passage. The authenticity of such reports is subject to the same rules as are applied to Ḥadīth in general. In this way, reports from the Successors (*tābiʿūn*) only which do not go back to the Prophet and his Companions are considered to be weak (*ḍaʿīf*).[53]

The knowledge of *asbāb al-nuzūl* is necessary for anyone who wishes to acquire more than a superficial knowledge of the Qur'ān, and there are at least two main reasons to explain this. One of these is that knowledge of words and concepts is incomplete without the knowledge of the context and the nature of the audience. For a form of speech – a question for example – may also convey other meanings such as elucidation, surprise, or reprimand, etc. Similarly, a command may mean a mere permissibility, a recommendation, or a threat, etc., depending on the circumstances in which it is issued and the nature of the audience. An incidental meaning or a shade of expression may at times reflect the main purpose of a particular text and this cannot be known without the knowledge of the *asbāb al-nuzūl*. Ignorance of the *asbāb al-nuzūl* may thus lead to the omission or misunderstanding of a part or even the whole of an injunction.[54] Secondly, ignorance of *asbāb al-nuzūl* may lead to unwarranted disagreement and even conflict. For the Qur'ān comprises passages which are in the nature of probability (*ẓāhir*) and ambiguity (*mujmal*). Such instances in the text can be clarified by reference to the circumstances in which they were received. It is reported that in a conversation with ᶜAbd Allāh ibn ᶜAbbās, ᶜUmar ibn al-Khaṭṭāb asked him: 'Why should there be disagreement among this *ummah*, all of whom follow the same Prophet and pray in the direction of the same *qiblah*?' To this Ibn ᶜAbbās replied, 'O Commander of the Faithful, the Qur'ān was sent down to us, we read it and we know the circumstances in which it was revealed. But there may be people after us who will read the Qur'ān without knowing the occasions of its revelation. Thus they will form their own opinion, which might lead to conflict and even bloodshed among them.'

ᶜUmar disagreed with Ibn ᶜAbbās for saying so at first but, when the latter departed, ᶜUmar pondered over what he had said. He then sent for Ibn ᶜAbbās only to tell him that he agreed with his view.[55] It has been observed that by making this remark, Ibn ᶜAbbās was referring to certain misinterpretations of the Qur'ān which had occurred owing to ignorance of the *asbāb al-nuzūl*. In particular, some of the Qur'ānic passages had been revealed concerning the unbelievers, but were taken by some commentators to be of general application to Muslims and non-Muslims alike. There were also passages in the Qur'ān which were revealed in reference to the conduct of people who had died before the revelation of certain rulings, and yet these were taken by some commentators to be of general application.[56]

Furthermore, the knowledge of *asbāb al-nuzūl* is informative of the conditions of the Arab society at the time. Their customary and linguistic usages and their nuances of expression were naturally reflected in the Qur'ān. The peculiarities of Arab social customs often gave exegesis of the Qur'ānic text a perspective and offered solutions to some of the doubts/ambiguities which would otherwise be difficult to understand. The *asbāb al-nuzūl* take full cognizance of the customary practices of Arabian society and the relationship, if any, of such practices to Qur'ānic legislation. To give an example, the Qur'ānic *āyah* 'Our Lord punish us not, if we forget or make a mistake' (al-Baqarah, 2:286), is held to be referring to unbelief, that is, when words which partake in unbelief are uttered inadvertently. This is forgiven just as are words of unbelief that are expressed under duress. However, the exemption here is not extended to similar pronouncements, such as statements of divorce, freeing of a slave, or sale and purchase, for freeing a slave was not known in the custom of the Arabs nor were the inhibitions over oath-taking (*aymān*). The general support of this *āyah* is thus given a concrete application in the light of the prevailing custom.[57]

NOTES

1. The Qur'ān also calls itself by alternative names, such as *kitāb, hudā, furqān*, and *dhikr* (book, guide, distinguisher, and remembrance respectively). When the definite article, *al*, is prefixed to the Qur'ān, it refers to the whole of the Book; but without this prefix, the Qur'ān can mean either the whole or a part of the Book. Thus one may refer to a singular sūra or *āyah* thereof as the Qur'ān, but not as al-Qur'ān.

2. Some disagree on this point, saying that the last *āyah* of the Qur'ān was al-Baqarah 2:281 as follows: 'Fear the day when you will be brought back to God; then every soul will be paid in full according to whatever it has earned, and they will not be treated unjustly.'

3. Hughes, *Dictionary*, p. 485ff; von Denffer, *ʿUlūm*, p. 68ff.

4. Shaltūt, *Al-Islām*, pp. 499–500; Qaṭṭān, *Tashrīʿ*, p. 83; Badrān, *Uṣūl*, p. 72.

5. Khallāf, *ʿIlm*, p. 23; Abdur Rahim, *Jurisprudence*, p. 69; Abū Zahrah, *Uṣūl*, p. 59.

6. For an exclusive treatment of words of foreign origin in the Qur'ān see Shawkānī, *Irshād*, p. 22ff. See also Ghazālī, *Mustaṣfā*, I, 68.

7. Shaltūt, *Al-Islām*, p. 486; von Denffer, *ʿUlūm*, p. 73.

8. This report is attributed to a Nūḥ b. Maryam who has confirmed that Abū Ḥanīfah changed his initial ruling. See Abū Zahrah, *Uṣūl*, p. 60; Shaltūt, *Al-Islām*, p. 478; Ṣābūnī, *Madkhal*, p. 4.

9. Ṣābūnī, *Madkhal*, pp. 41–42; Abū Zahrah, *Uṣūl*, p. 61; Qaṭṭān, *Tashrīʿ*, p. 57ff.

10. Ghazālī, *Mustaṣfā*, I. 64; Shawkānī, *Irshād*, p. 30; Shaltūt, *Al-Islām*, p. 440. The same would apply to the two other instances of variant readings which are attributed to ʿAbdullāh ibn Masʿūd concerning the punishment of theft, and the form of divorce known as *īlā'* in sūra al-Mā'idah (5: 38) and al-Baqarah (2: 226) respectively. Since these are only supported by solitary reports (*Āḥād*) they do not constitute a part of the Qur'ān.

11. Abū Zahrah, *Uṣūl*, p. 62; Abdur Rahim, *Jurisprudence*, p. 71.

12. To be precise, the Meccan period lasted twelve years, five months and thirteen days, and the Madinan period, nine years, seven months and seven days.

13. Cf. Ṣābūnī, *Madkhal*, pp. 41–44; Khallāf, *ʿIlm*, p. 24.

14. Cf. von Denffer, *ʿUlūm*, p. 90.

15. Ibid., p. 91.

16. Cf. Qaṭṭān, *Tashrīʿ*, 69–70.

17. Cf. Abdur Rahim, *Jurisprudence*, p. 71.

18. Shaltūt, *Al-Islām*, p. 494; Khallāf *ʿIlm*, pp. 32–33.

19. Note, for example, Ghazālī, who estimates the *āyāt al-aḥkām* at 500. While commenting on Ghazālī's estimate, Shawkānī on the other hand observes that any such calculation can only amount to a rough estimate (*Mustaṣfā*, II, 101, and Shawkānī, *Irshād*, p. 250).

20. Khallāf, *ʿIlm*, p. 35; Abū Zahrah, *Uṣūl*, p. 71.

21. Shaʿbān, 'Manhaj', p. 31.

22. A typical form of a sinful oath is when a person takes an oath on the truth of something which he knows to be untrue; this is called *yamīn al-ghamūs*, which is a variety of *yamīn al-muʿaqqadah*. However the Ḥanafīs maintain that the latter only refers to the situation where a person pledges to do something in the future but then refuses to fulfil it. He is then liable to pay the *kaffārah*.

23. Badrān, *Uṣūl*, p. 66.
24. Shaltūt, *Al-Islām*, p. 498.
25. Shāṭibī, *Muwāfaqāt*, III, 9; Qaṭṭān, *Tashrīᶜ*, p. 82.
26. Shāṭibī, *Muwāfaqāt*, III, 9.
27. Ibid., III, 12.
28. Shaltūt, *Al-Islām*, pp. 498–99, Abū Zahrah, *Uṣūl*, p. 71; Khallāf, *ᶜIlm*, p. 35; Badrān. *Uṣūl*, p. 67.
29. Abū Zahrah, *Uṣūl*, p. 80, where he quotes Ibn Ḥazm in support of his own view.
30. Shāṭibī, *Muwāfaqāt*, III, 219.
31. Abū Zahrah, *Uṣūl*, p. 70.
32. Ṣābūnī, *Muḥāḍarāt*, p. 31. For a further discussion of this *āyah* see below in the sections of this work on the *ḥujjiyyah* of *Sunnah*, *ijmāᶜ* and *qiyās* respectively.
33. Shāṭibī, *Muwāfaqāt*, III, 217.
34. Of the two *āyāt* on the subject of contracts, one is in the form of a command and the other in the form of a question, as follows: 'O you believers, fulfil your contracts' (al-Mā'idah, 5:1), and 'O you believers, why do you say things which you do not carry through?' (al-Ṣaff, 61 : 2). These are, in turn, confirmed by another *āyah* (al-Nisā', 4 : 58) where an emphasis is laid on the fulfilment of trusts and the principle of fair treatment: 'God commands you to turn over trusts to those to whom they belong, and when you judge among people, judge righteously.' Contracts must therefore not amount to a violation of justice, a breach of trust, or a departure from the moral ideals of the law.
35. Cf. Badrān, *Bayān*, pp. 2–3.
36. Shaltūt, *Al-Islām*, p. 501.
37. Ṣābūnī, *Madkhal*, p. 73.
38. Shāṭibī, *Muwāfaqāt*, III, 178; Abū Zahrah, *Uṣūl*, p. 122; Khallāf, *ᶜIlm*, p. 167.
39. Cf. Ṣābūnī, *Madkhal*, p. 72; Badrān, *Bayān*, p. 4.
40. Cf. Shaᶜbān, 'Manhaj', p. 29.
41. Note, e.g., 'and He created for you ships and cattle on which you ride' (al-Zukhruf, 43 : 12), and 'He created cattle from which you derive warmth . . . and you eat of their meat' (al-Naḥl, 16 : 5), and 'say, who has forbidden the beautiful gifts of God which He has produced for His servants, and the clean food for their sustenance' (al-Aᶜrāf, 7 : 32).
42. Cf. Shaᶜbān, 'Manhaj', pp. 22–23.
43. Cf. Ahmad Hasan, 'Rationality', p. 101.
44. Ibid., p. 104.
45. Ibn Ḥazm, *Iḥkam*, VIII, 76ff; Ṣābūnī, *Madkhal*, p. 75. For further discussion on *taᶜlīl* in the Qur'ān see the section on *qiyās* below where *taᶜlīl* is discussed in connection with the *ᶜillah* of *qiyās*.
46. Cf. Ahmad Hasan, 'Rationality', 102.
47. Note for example sūra al-Baqarah (2:23) which reads: 'If you are in any doubt about what We have sent to Our servant, then bring a chapter like it and call in your witnesses besides God, if you are truthful.'
48. Abū Zahrah, *Uṣūl*, p. 65; Ṣābūnī, *Madkhal*, p. 45.
49. von Denffer, *ᶜUlūm*, p. 152.
50. For further details on *iᶜjāz* see von Denffer, *ᶜUlūm*, pp. 152–57; Abū Zahrah, *Uṣūl*, pp. 65–66; Khallāf, *ᶜIlm*, pp. 25–27.
51. For further details on the principles of government under the rule of law – also referred to as the principle of legality – see my article 'The Citizen and State', p. 30ff.
52. Cf. Ṣābūnī, *Madkhal*, p. 46; Abū Zahrah, *Uṣūl*, p. 67; Kamali, 'The Citizen', 15ff.
53. von Denffer, *ᶜUlūm*, p. 93ff.
54. Shāṭibī, *Muwāfaqāt*, III, 201.

55. Ibid., p. 202.

56. Khuḍarī, *Uṣūl*, pp. 209–210. Thus when Qudāmah b. Maẓᶜūn was charged with the offence of wine-drinking, ᶜUmar b. al-Khaṭṭāb decided to punish him, but the defendant cited the Qur'ānic *āyah* in sūra al-Mā'idah (5:95) in his own defence. This *āyah* reads 'there is no blame on those who believe and do good deeds for what they consume provided they are God-fearing believers . . .' Ibn Maẓᶜūn claimed that he was one of them. ᶜAbd Allah b. ᶜAbbās refuted this view and explained that this particular *āyah* had been revealed concerning people who died before wine-drinking was definitively forbidden.

57. Ibid., p. 211.

CHAPTER THREE

The Sunnah

Introduction

Literally, *Sunnah* means a clear path or a beaten track but it has also been used to imply normative practice, or an established course of conduct. It may be a good example or a bad, and it may be set by an individual, a sect or a community.[1] In pre-Islamic Arabia, the Arabs used the word '*Sunnah*' in reference to the ancient and continuous practice of the community which they inherited from their forefathers. Thus it is said that the pre-Islamic tribes of Arabia had each their own *sunnah* which they considered as a basis of their identity and pride.[2] The opposite of *Sunnah* is *bidᶜah*, or innovation, which is characterised by lack of precedent and continuity with the past. In the Qur'ān, the word '*Sunnah*' and its plural, *sunan*, have been used on a number of occasions (16 times to be precise). In all these instances, *sunnah* has been used to imply an established practice or course of conduct. To the ulema of Ḥadīth, *Sunnah* refers to all that is narrated from the Prophet, his acts, his sayings and whatever he has tacitly approved, plus all the reports which describe his physical attributes and character. The ulema of jurisprudence, however, exclude the description of the physical features of the Prophet from the definition of *Sunnah*.[3] *Sunnah al-Nabī* (or *Sunnah al-Rasūl*), that is, the Prophetic *Sunnah*, does not occur in the Qur'ān as such. But the phrase *uswah ḥasanah* (excellent conduct) which occurs in sūra al-Aḥzāb (33:21) in reference to the exemplary conduct of the Prophet is the nearest Qur'ānic equivalent of *Sunnah al-Nabī*.[4] The *uswah*, or example of the Prophet, was later interpreted to be a reference to his *Sunnah*. The Qur'ān also uses the word '*ḥikmah*' (lit. wisdom) as a source of guidance that accompanies the Qur'ān itself. Al-Shāfiᶜī quotes at least seven instances in the Qur'ān where '*ḥikmah*' occurs next to *al-kitāb* (the Book). In one of these passages, which occurs in sūra al-Jumᶜah (62:2), for example, we read that God Almighty sent a Messenger to educate and to purify the people by 'teaching them the Book and the *ḥikmah*'. According to al-Shāfiᶜī's interpretation, which also represents the view of the majority, the word '*ḥikmah*' in this context means the *Sunnah* of the Prophet.[5] Both the terms '*Sunnah*' and '*Sunnah Rasūl Allāh*' have been used by the Prophet himself and his Companions. Thus when the Prophet sent Muᶜādh b. Jabal as judge to the Yemen, he was asked as to the sources on which he would rely in making decisions. In reply Muᶜādh referred first to the 'Book of Allah' and then to the '*Sunnah* of the Messenger of Allah'.[6]

لما أراد رسول الله ﷺ ان يبعث معاذ بن جبل إلى اليمن قال له : كيف تقضي إذا عرض لك قضاء ؟ قال أقضي بما في كتاب الله ، قال فان لم تجد في كتاب الله قال : فبسنة رسول الله قال : فان لم يكن في سنة رسول الله قال : اجتهد رأيي ولا آلو

In another Ḥadīth, the Prophet is reported to have said, 'I left two things among you. You shall not go astray so long as you hold on to them: the Book of Allah and my *Sunnah* (*sunnatī*).'[7]

تركت فيكم اثنين لن تضلّوا ما تمسكتم بهما كتاب الله وسنتي

There is evidence to suggest that the *Sunnah* of the Prophet was introduced into the legal theory by the jurists of Iraq towards the end of the first century. The term '*Sunnah* of the Prophet' occurs, for example, in two letters which are addressed to the Umayyad ruler, ᶜAbd al-Malik b. Marwān (d. 86) by the Khārijite leader ᶜAbd Allāh b. Ibāḍ, and al-Ḥasan al-Baṣrī. But this might mean that the earliest available record on the establishment of terminology dates back to the late first century. This evidence does not necessarily prove that the terminology was not in use before then.[8]

Initially the use of the term '*Sunnah*' was not restricted to the *Sunnah* of the Prophet but was used to imply the practice of the community and precedent of the Companions. This usage of '*Sunnah*' seems to have continued till the late second century when al-Shāfiʿī tried to restrict it to the *Sunnah* of the Prophet alone. Sometimes the Arabic definite article '*al*' was prefixed to *Sunnah* to denote the *Sunnah* of the Prophet while the general usage of *Sunnah* as a reference to the practice of the community, or its living tradition, continued. By the end of the second century Hijrah, the technical/juristic meaning of *Sunnah* appears to have become dominant, until the ulema used it exclusively to imply the normative conduct of the Prophet.[9] The ulema thus discouraged the use of such expressions as the *Sunnah* of Abū Bakr or ʿUmar. In their view, the proper usages of *Sunnah* were to be confined to *Sunnah Allāh*, and *Sunnah Rasūl Allāh*, that is the *Sunnah* of God, or His way of doing things, and the *Sunnah* of His Messenger. But there were variant opinions among the ulema which disputed the foregoing, especially in view of the Ḥadīth in which the Prophet is reported to have said, 'You are to follow my *Sunnah* and the *Sunnah* of the Rightly-Guided caliphs.'

عليكم بسنتي وسنة الخلفاء الراشدين من بعدي

But again, as al-Shawkānī points out, it is possible that in this Ḥadīth, the Prophet had used '*Sunnah*' as a substitute for '*ṭarīqah*' or the way that his Companions had shown.[10] Al-Shawkānī's interpretation might suggest that the Prophet may not have used '*Sunnah*' in the exclusive sense that the ulema later attempted to attach to this term.

In its juristic usage, '*Sunnah*' has meant different things. To the ulema of *uṣūl al-fiqh*, *Sunnah* refers to a source of the *Sharīʿah* and a legal proof next to the Qur'ān. But to the ulema of *fiqh*, '*Sunnah*' primarily refers to a *sharʿī* value which falls under the general category of *mandūb*. Although in this sense, *Sunnah* is used almost synonymously with *mandūb*, it does not necessarily mean that *Sunnah* is confined to the *Mandūb*. For in its other usage, namely as a source of *Sharīʿah*, *Sunnah* may authorise and create not only a *mandūb* but also any of the following: *wājib, ḥarām, makrūh* and *mubāḥ*. Thus in the usage of *uṣūl al-fiqh*, one might say that this or that ruling has been validated by the Qur'ān or by the *Sunnah*, whereas a *faqīh* would be inclined to say that this or that act is *Sunnah*, which means that it is neither *farḍ* nor *wājib*; it is one of the five values which falls under the category of *mandūb*.[11]

Notwithstanding the fact that the ulema have used *Sunnah* and Ḥadīth almost interchangeably, the two terms have meanings of their own. Literally, *Ḥadīth* means a narrative, communication or news consisting of the factual account of an event. The word occurs frequently in the

Qur'ān (23 times to be precise) and in all cases it carries the meaning of a narrative or communication. In none of these instances has *Ḥadīth* been used in its technical sense, that is, the exclusive saying of the Prophet. In the early days of Islam following the demise of the Prophet, stories relating to the life and activities of the Prophet dominated all other kinds of narratives, so the word began to be used almost exclusively to a narrative from, or a saying of, the Prophet.[12]

Ḥadīth differs from *Sunnah* in the sense that Ḥadīth is a narration of the conduct of the Prophet whereas *Sunnah* is the example or the law that is deduced from it. Ḥadīth in this sense is the vehicle or the carrier of *Sunnah*, although *Sunnah* is a wider concept and used to be so especially before its literal meaning gave way to its juristic usage. *Sunnah* thus referred not only to the Ḥadīth of the Prophet but also to the established practice of the community. But once the literal meanings of Ḥadīth and *Sunnah* gave way to their technical usages and were both exclusively used in reference to the conduct of the Prophet, the two became synonymous. This was largely a result of al-Shāfiʿī's efforts, who insisted that the *Sunnah* must always be derived from a genuine Ḥadīth and that there was no *Sunnah* outside the Ḥadīth. In the pre-Shāfiʿī period, 'Ḥadīth' was also applied to the statements of the Companions and their Successors, the *tābiʿūn*. It thus appears that 'Ḥadīth' began to be used exclusively for the acts and sayings of the Prophet only after the distinction between the *Sunnah* and Ḥadīth was set aside.[13]

There are two other terms, namely *khabar* and *athar*, which have often been used as alternatives to 'Ḥadīth'. Literally, *khabar* means 'news or report', and *athar*, 'impression, vestige or impact'. The word '*khabar*' in the phrase '*khabar al-wāḥid*' for example, means a solitary Ḥadīth. The majority of ulema have used Ḥadīth, *khabar* and *athar* synonymously, whereas others have distinguished *khabar* from *athar*. While the former is used synonymously with Ḥadīth, *athar* (and sometimes *ʿamal*) is used to imply the precedent of the Companions.[14]

The majority of ulema have upheld the precedent of the Companions as one of the transmitted (*naqlī*) proofs. The jurists of the early schools of law are known to have based opinions on *athar*. Imām Mālik even went so far as to set aside the Prophetic Ḥadīth in its favour on the strength of the argument that *athar* represented the genuine *Sunnah*, as the Companions were in a better position to ascertain the authentic *Sunnah* of the Prophet. There were indeed, among the Companions, many distinguished figures whose legal acumen and intimate knowledge of the sources equipped them with a special authority to issue *fatwās*. Sometimes they met in groups to discuss the problems they encountered, and their agreement or collective judgment is also known as *athar*. For al-Shāfiʿī (d. 204/819) however, *athar* does not necessarily represent the *Sunnah* of the Prophet. In the absence of a Ḥadīth from the Prophet, al-Shāfiʿī followed the precedent of Companions, and in cases where a difference of opinion existed among the Companions, al-Shāfiʿī preferred the opinion of the first four caliphs over others, or one which was in greater harmony with the Qur'ān.[15] According to al-Shāfiʿī, the *Sunnah* coming direct from the Prophet in the form of Ḥadīth through a reliable chain of narrators is a source of law irrespective of whether it was accepted by the community or not. He emphasised the authority of the Ḥadīth from the Prophet in preference to the opinion or practice of the Companions. Al-Shāfiʿī contended that Ḥadīth from the Prophet, even a solitary Ḥadīth, must take priority over the practice and opinion of the community, the Companions and the Successors.[16] Al-Shāfiʿī directed his efforts mainly against the then prevailing practice among jurists which gave preference to the practice of the community and the decisions of the Companions, over the Ḥadīth. Al-Shāfiʿī attempted to overrule the argument, advanced by Imām Mālik, for example, that the Madinese practice was more authoritative than Ḥadīth. In his *Muwaṭṭa'*, for example, Mālik (d. 179/795) generally opens every legal chapter with a Ḥadīth from the Prophet, but in determining the detailed legal issues, he does not consistently adhere to the principle of the priority of Ḥadīth over *athar*. It is interesting to note that the *Muwaṭṭa'* contains 1,720 Ḥadīths, out of which 822 are from the Prophet and the remainder from the Companions, Successors and others. This would suggest that Imām Mālik was not overly concerned with the distinction between Ḥadīth and *athar* which was to become the main theme of al-Shāfiʿī's endeavour to establish the overriding authority of the Prophetic Ḥadīth.[17]

Proof-Value (*Ḥujjiyyah*) of *Sunnah*

The ulema are unanimous to the effect that *Sunnah* is a source of *Sharīʿah* and that in its rulings with regard to *ḥalāl* and *ḥarām* it stands on the same footing as the Qur'ān.[18] The *Sunnah* of the Prophet is a proof (*ḥujjah*) for the Qur'ān, testifies to its authority and enjoins the Muslim to comply with it. The words of the Prophet, as the Qur'ān tells us, are divinely inspired (al-Najm, 53:3). His acts and teachings that are meant to establish a rule of *Sharīʿah* constitute a binding proof.[19] While commenting on the Qur'ānic *āyah* which states of the Prophet that 'he does not speak of his own desire, it is none other than *waḥy* sent to him', Al-Ghazālī writes that some of the divine revelation which the Prophet received constitutes the Qur'ān, whereas the remainder is *Sunnah*. The words of the Prophet are *ḥujjah* on anyone who heard the Prophet saying them. As for us and the generality of Muslims who have received them through the verbal and written reports of narrators, we need to ascertain their authenticity.[20] The proof of authenticity may be definitive (*qaṭᶜī*), or it may amount to a preferable conjecture (*al-ẓann al-rājiḥ*); in either case, the *Sunnah* commands obedience of the *mukallaf*. All the rulings of the Prophet, especially those which correspond with the Qur'ān and corroborate its contents, constitute binding law.[21]

In more than one place, the Qur'ān enjoins obedience to the Prophet and makes it a duty of the believers to submit to his judgment and his authority without question. The following *āyāt* are all explicit on this theme, all of which are quoted by al-Shāfiᶜī, in his renowned work, *Al-Risālah* (p. 47ff):

> And whatever the Messenger gives you, take it, and whatever he forbids you, abstain from it (al-Ḥashr, 59:7).
> Obey God and obey the Messenger and those who are in charge of affairs among you. Should you happen to dispute over something, then refer it to God and to the Messenger (al-Nisā', 4:58–59).

To refer the judgement of a dispute to God means recourse to the Qur'ān, and referring it to the Messenger means recourse to the *Sunnah*.[22] In another passage, the Qur'ān emphasises: 'Whoever obeys the Messenger verily obeys God' (al-Nisā', 4:80). And finally, the Qur'ān is categorical to the effect that the definitive rulings of the Qur'ān and *Sunnah* are binding on the believers in that they are no longer at liberty to differ with the dictates of the divine will or to follow a course of their own choice: 'Whenever God and His Messenger have decided a matter, it is not for a faithful man or woman to follow another course of his or her own choice' (al-Aḥzāb, 33:36). In yet another place the Qur'ān stresses that submission to the authority of the Prophet is not a matter of mere formalistic legality but is an integral part of the Muslim faith: 'By thy Lord, they will not believe till they make thee a judge regarding disagreements between them and find in themselves no resistance against accepting your verdict in full submission' (al-Nisā', 4:65). It is concluded from these and other similar passages in the Qur'ān that the *Sunnah* is a proof next to the Qur'ān in all *sharᶜī* matters and that conformity to the terms of Prophetic legislation is a Qur'ānic obligation on all Muslims. The Companions have reached a consensus on this point: Both during the lifetime of the Prophet and following his demise, they eagerly obeyed the Prophet's instructions and followed his examples regardless as to whether his commands or prohibitions originated in the Qur'ān or otherwise. The first two caliphs, Abū Bakr and ᶜUmar; resorted to the *Sunnah* of the Prophet whenever they knew of it. In cases when they did not know, they would ascertain if other Companions had any knowledge of the Prophetic *Sunnah* in connection with particular issues. The Caliph ᶜUmar is also on record as having issued written instruction to his judges in which he asked them to follow the *Sunnah* of the Prophet whenever they could not find the necessary guidance in the Qur'ān.[23]

Classification and Value: I

Sunnah has been classified in various ways, depending, of course, on the purpose of classification and the perspective of the investigator. However, two of the most commonly accepted criteria for such classifications are the subject matter (*matn*) of *Sunnah* and the manner of its transmission (*isnād*). This section is primarily concerned with the classification of *Sunnah* from the viewpoint of its subject matter.

To begin with, the *Sunnah* is divided into three types, namely verbal (*qawlī*), actual (*fiᶜlī*) and tacitly approved (*taqrīrī*). The other division of the *Sunnah* which will concern us here is its division into legal and non-legal *Sunnah*.

The verbal *Sunnah* consist of the sayings of the Prophet on any subject, such as the Ḥadīth '*fī al-sā'imah zakāh*': livestock is liable to *zakāh*.[24] The Actual *Sunnah* of the Prophet consists of his deeds and actual instructions, such as the way he performed the *ṣalāh*, the fasting, the rituals of *ḥajj*, or the transactions he concluded such as sale and giving loans, etc. Similarly, the fact that the Prophet authorised mutilation of the hand of the thief from the wrist illustrated, in actual terms, how the Qur'ānic *āyah* (al-Mā'idah, 5:38) should be implemented. This *āyah* simply provides that the hand should be cut without specifying exactly from which part. The tacitly approved *Sunnah* consists of the acts and sayings of the Companions which came to the knowledge of the Prophet and of which he approved. The tacit approval of the Prophet may be inferred from his silence and lack of disapproval, or from his express approval and verbal confirmation.[25] An example of such a *Sunnah* is the report that two of the Companions went on a journey, and when they failed to find water for ablution, they both performed the obligatory prayers with *tayammum*, that is, wiping the hands, face and feet with clean sand. Later, when they found water, one of them performed the prayers again whereas the other did not. Upon their return, they related their experience to the Prophet, who is reported to have approved both courses of action. Hence it became *Sunnah taqrīrīya*.[26] Another example of this is the report that one of the prominent Companions, ᶜAmr b. al-ᶜĀṣ, said that in the campaign of Dhāt al-Salāsil he had had a wet dream in the night, but owing to extreme cold he did not take a bath but instead performed the morning *ṣalāh* with *tayammum*. He then related this to the Prophet, who laughed but said nothing, which would imply that the act in question is permissible in similar circumstances, that is, when extreme cold proves to be hazardous to health.[27]

The sayings of Companions such as, 'we used to do such and such during the lifetime of the Prophet' constitute a part of *Sunnah taqrīrīya* only if the subject is such that it could not have failed to attract the attention of the Prophet. An example of this is the saying of Abū Saᶜīd al-Khudrī that 'for the charity of ᶜīd al-Fiṭr, we used to give a *ṣāᶜ* of dates or of barley'. This is a matter that could not have remained hidden and therefore constitutes *Sunnah taqrīrīya*. However, the statement of a Companion which refers to matters of an obscure type, or when the statement itself is vague and does not specify whether the issue had arisen while the Prophet was alive — such statements do not constitute *Sunnah taqrīrīya*.[28]

The entire bulk of the *Sunnah*, that is, the sayings, acts and tacit enactments of the Prophet, may be once again divided into two types: non-legal and legal *Sunnah*.

Non-legal *Sunnah* (*Sunnah ghayr tashrīᶜiyyah*) mainly consists of the natural activities of the Prophet (*al-afᶜāl al-jibilliyyah*) such as the manner in which he ate, slept, dressed, and such other activities as do not seek to constitute a part of the *Sharīᶜah*. Activities of this nature are not of primary importance to the Prophetic mission and therefore do not constitute legal norms. According to the majority of ulema, the Prophet's preferences in these areas, such as his favourite colours, or the fact that he slept on his right side in the first place, etc., only indicate the permissibility (*ibāḥah*) of the acts in question.[29] The reason given is that such acts could be either *wājib, mandūb* or merely *mubāḥ*. The first two can only be established by means of positive evidence: *wājib* and *mandūb* are normally held to be absent unless they are proved to exist. Since there is no such evidence to establish that the natural activities of the Prophet fall into either of these two categories, there remains the category of *mubāḥ* and they fall in this category for which no positive evidence is necessary.[30]

On a similar note, *Sunnah* which partakes in specialised or technical knowledge, such as medicine, commerce and agriculture, is once again held to be peripheral to the main function of the Prophetic mission and is therefore not a part of the *Sharīᶜah*. As for acts and sayings of the Prophet that related to particular circumstances such as the strategy of war, including such devices that misled the enemy forces, timing of attack, siege or withdrawal, these too are considered to be situational and not a part of the *Sharīᶜah*.[31]

There are certain matters which are peculiar to the person of the Prophet so that his example concerning them does not constitute general law. For instance, polygamy above the limit of four, marriage without a dower, prohibition of remarriage for the widows of the Prophet, connected fasting (*ṣawm al-wiṣāl*) and the fact that the Prophet admitted the testimony of Khuzaymah b. Thābit as legal proof. The rules of *Sharīʿah* concerning these matters are as stated in the Qur'ān, and remain the legal norm for the generality of Muslims.[32] According to the majority opinion, the position in regard to such matters is partly determined by reference to the relevant text of the Qur'ān and the manner in which the Prophet is addressed. When, for example, the Qur'ān addresses the Prophet in such terms as 'O you Messenger', or 'O you folded up in garments' (al-Muzzammil, 73:1; al-Muddaththir, 74:1), it is implied that the address is to the Prophet alone unless there is conclusive evidence to suggest otherwise.[33]

Certain activities of the Prophet may fall in between the two categories of legal and non-legal *Sunnah* as they combine the attributes of both. Thus it may be difficult to determine whether an act was strictly personal or was intended to set an example for others to follow. It is also known that at times the Prophet acted in a certain way which was in accord with the then prevaling custom of the community. For instance, the Prophet kept his beard at a certain length and trimmed his moustache. The majority of ulema have viewed this not as a mere observance of the familiar usage at the time but as an example for the believers to follow. Others have held the opposite view by saying that it was a part of the social practice of the Arabs which was designed to prevent resemblance to the Jews and some non-Arabs who used to shave the beard and grow the moustache. Such practices were, in other words, a part of the current usage and basically optional. Similarly, it is known that the Prophet used to go to the *ʿīd* prayers (*ṣalāt al-ʿīd*) by one route and return from the mosque by a different route, and that the Prophet at times performed the *ḥajj* pilgrimage while riding a camel. The Shāfiʿī jurists are inclined to prefer the commendable (*mandūb*) in such acts to mere permissibility whereas the Ḥanafīs consider them as merely permissible, or *mubāḥ*.[34]

The legal *Sunnah* (*Sunnah tashrīʿiyya*) consists of the exemplary conduct of the Prophet, be it an act, saying, or a tacit approval, which incorporates the rules and principles of *Sharīʿah*. This variety of *Sunnah* may be divided into three types, namely the *Sunnah* which the Prophet laid down in his capacities as Messenger of God, as the Head of State or Imām, or in his capacity as a judge. We shall discuss each of these separately, as follows:

(a) In his capacity as Messenger of God, the Prophet has laid down rules which are, on the whole complementary to the Qur'ān, but also established rules on which the Qur'ān is silent. In this capacity, the *Sunnah* may consist of a clarification of the ambiguous (*mujmal*) parts of the Qur'ān or specifying and qualifying the general and the absolute contents of the Qur'ān. Whatever the Prophet has authorised pertaining to the principles of religion, especially in the area of devotional matters (*ᶜibādāt*) and rules expounding the lawful and the unlawful, that is, the *ḥalāl* and *ḥarām*, constitutes general legislation (*tashrīᶜ ᶜāmm*) whose validity is not restricted to the limitations of time and circumstance. All commands and prohibitions that are imposed by the *Sunnah* are binding on every Muslim regardless of individual circumstances, social status, or political office. In acting upon these laws, the individual normally does not need any prior authorisation by a religious leader or the government.[35]

The question arises as to how it is determined that the Prophet acted in one or the other of his three capacities as mentioned above. It is not always easy to answer this question in categorical terms. The uncertainty which has arisen in answering this question in particular cases is, in fact, one of the main causes of juristic disagreement (*ikhtilāf*) among the *fuqahā'*. The ulema have on the whole attempted to ascertain the main thrust, or the direction (*jihah*) of the particular acts and saying of the Prophet. An enquiry of this nature helps to provide an indication as to the value of the *Sunnah* in question: whether it constitutes an obligation, commendation, or *ibāḥah* on the one hand, or a prohibition or abomination (*karāhah*) on the other.

When the direction of an act is known from the evidence in the sources, there remains no doubt as to its value. If, for example, the Prophet attempts to explain an ambiguous ruling of the Qur'ān, the explanation so provided would fall in the same category of values as the original ruling itself. According to the majority of ulema, if the ambiguous of the Qur'ān is known to be obligatory, or commendable, the explanatory *Sunnah* would carry the same value. For example, all the practical instructions of the Prophet which explained and illustrated the obligatory *ṣalāh* would be *wājib* and his acts pertaining to the supererogatory prayers such as *ṣalāh* on the occasion of lunar and solar eclipse (*ṣalāt al-khusūf wa al-kusūf*) would be *mandūb*.[36] Alternatively, the *Sunnah* may itself provide a clear indication as to whether a particular rule which it prescribes is *wājib, mandūb*, or merely permissible. Another method of ascertaining the value of a particular act is to draw an analogy between an undefined act and an act or saying whose value is known. Additionally, the subject-matter of the *Sunnah* may provide a sign or an indication as to its value. With regard to prayers, for example, the call to prayers, or *adhān*, and the call which immediately precedes the standing to congregational prayer (i.e. the *iqāmah*) are indications as to the obligatory nature of the prayer. For it is known from the rules of *Sharīʿah* that *adhān* and *iqāmah* precede the obligatory *ṣalāh* only. A *ṣalāh* which is not obligatory such as the *ʿīd* prayer, or *ṣalāt al-istisqāʾ* ('prayers offered at the time of drought'), are not preceded by the preliminaries of *adhān* or *iqāmah*. Another method of evaluating an act is by looking at its opposite, that is, its absence. If it is concluded that the act in question would have been in the nature of a prohibition had it not been authorised by the Prophet, then this would imply that it is obligatory. For example, circumcision is evaluated to be an obligation. Since it consists essentially of the infliction of injury for no obvious cause, had it not been made into an obligation, then it would presumably be unlawful. Its validation by the *Sharīʿah*, in other words, is taken as an indication of its *wujūb*. This explanation is basically applicable to all penalties that the *Sharīʿah* has prescribed, although in most cases the value of the prescribed punishment is understood from the direct rulings of the relevant texts. And lastly, an act may require the belated performance (*qaḍāʾ*) of a *wājib* or a *mandūb*, and as such its value would correspond to that of its prompt performance (*adāʾ*).[37]

The foregoing are the categories of acts whose direction and value can be ascertained. However, if no such verification is possible, then one must look at the intention behind its enactment. If a Prophetic act is intended as a means of seeking the pleasure of God, then it is classified as *mandūb*; and according to a variant view, as *wājib*. However, if the intention behind a particular act could not be detected either, then it is classified as *wājib*, and according to a variant view as *mandūb*; but the matter is subject to interpretation and *ijtihād*.[38]

(b) All the rulings of *Sunnah* which originate from the Prophet in his capacity as Imām or the Head of State, such as allocations and expenditure of public funds, decisions pertaining to military strategy and war, appointment of state officials, distribution of booty, signing of treaties, etc., partake in the legal *Sunnah* which, however, does not constitute general legislation (*tashrīʿ ʿāmm*). *Sunnahs* of this type may not be practiced by individuals without obtaining the permission of the competent government authorities first. The mere fact that the Prophet acted in a certain way, or said something relating to these matters, does not bind individuals directly, and does not entitle them to act on their own initiative without the express permission of the lawful authority.[39] To give an example, according to a Ḥadīth, 'whoever kills a warrior [in battle] may take his belongings'.[40]

من قتل قتيلاً فله سلبه

The ulema have differed as to the precise import of this Ḥadīth. According to one view, the Prophet uttered this Ḥadīth in his capacity as Imām, in which case no-one is entitled to the belongings of his victim in the battlefield without the express authorisation of the Imām. Others have held the view that this Ḥadīth lays down a general law which entitles the soldier to the belongings of the deceased even without the permission of the Imām.[41]

It has been observed that the Prophet might have uttered this Ḥadīth in order to encourage the Companions to do *jihād* in the light of the then prevailing circumstances. The circumstances may have been such that an incentive of this kind was required; or it may be that it was intended to lay down a general law without any regard for particular situations. According to Imām Shāfiʿī, the Ḥadīth under consideration lays down a general rule of *Sharīʿah*. For this is the general norm in regards to the *Sunnah*. The main purpose of the Prophet's mission was to lay down the foundations of the *Sharīʿah*, and unless there is an indication to the contrary, one must assume that the purpose of the Ḥadīth in general is to lay down general law.[42]

(c) *Sunnah* which originates from the Prophet in his capacity as a judge in particular disputes usually consists of two parts: the part which relates to claims, evidence and factual proof and the judgment which is issued as a result. The first part is situational and does not constitute general law, whereas the second part lays down general law, with the proviso, however, that it does not bind the individual directly, and no-one may act upon it without the prior authorisation of a competent judge. Since the Prophet himself acted in a judicial capacity, the rules that he has enacted must therefore be implemented by the office of the *qāḍī*.[43] Hence when a person has a claim over another which the latter denies, but the claimant knows of a similar dispute which the Prophet has adjudicated in a certain way, this would not entitle the claimant to take the law into his own hands. He must follow proper procedures to prove his claim and to obtain a judicial decision.[44]

To distinguish the legal from non-legal *Sunnah*, it is necessary for the *mujtahid* to ascertain the original purpose and context in which a particular ruling of the *Sunnah* has been issued and whether it was designed to establish a general rule of law. The Ḥadīth literature does not always provide clear information as to the different capacities in which the Prophet might have acted in particular situations, although the *mujtahid* may find indications that assist him to some extent. The absence of adequate information and criteria on which to determine the circumstantial and non-legal *Sunnah* from that which constitutes general law dates back to the time of the Companions. The difficulty has persisted ever since, and it is due mainly to the shortage of adequate information that disagreement has arisen among the ulema over the understanding and interpretation of the *Sunnah*.[45]

To give another example, juristic disagreement has arisen concerning a Ḥadīth on the reclamation of barren land which reads, 'whoever reclaims barren land becomes its owner.'[46]

من أحيى أرضاً ميتة فهي له

The ulema have differed as to whether the Prophet uttered this Ḥadīth in his Prophetic capacity or in his capacity as head of state. If the former is established to be the case then the Ḥadīth lays down a binding rule of law. Anyone who reclaims barren land becomes its owner and need not obtain any permission from the Imām or anyone else. For the Ḥadīth would provide the necessary authority and there would be no need for official permission. If on the other hand it is established that the Prophet uttered this Ḥadīth in his capacity as Imām, then it would imply that anyone who wishes to reclaim barren land must obtain the prior permission of the Imām. The Ḥadīth in other words, only entitles the Imām to grant the citizen the right to reclaim barren land. The majority of jurists have adopted the first view whereas the Ḥanafīs have held the second. The majority of jurists, including Abū Ḥanīfah's disciple, Abū Yūsuf, have held that the consent of the State is not necessary for anyone to commence reclaiming barren land. But it appears that jurists and scholars of the later ages prefer the Ḥanafī view which stipulates that reclaiming barren land requires the consent of the State. The Ḥanafī view is based on the rationale of preventing disputes among people. The Mālikīs on the other hand only require government consent when the land is close to a human settlement, and the Ḥanbalīs only when it has previously been alienated by another person.[47]

Disagreement has also arisen with regard to the Ḥadīth that adjudicated the case of Hind, the wife of Abū Sufyān. This woman complained to the Prophet that her husband was a tight-fisted man and that despite his affluence, he refused to give adequate maintenance to her and her child. The Prophet instructed her to 'take [of her husband's property] what is sufficient for yourself and your child according to custom'.[48]

خُذي ما يكفيك وولدك بالمعروف

The ulema have disagreed as to whether the Prophet uttered this Ḥadīth so as to enact a general rule of law, or whether he was acting in the capacity of a judge. If it be admitted that the Ḥadīth consists of a judgment addressing a particular case, then it would only authorise the judge to issue a corresponding order. Thus it would be unlawful for a creditor to take his entitlement from the property of his debtor without a judicial order. If it be established, on the other hand, that the Ḥadīth lays down a general rule of law, then no adjudication would be required to entitle the wife or the creditor to the property of the defaulting debtor. For the Ḥadīth itself would provide the necessary authority. If any official permission is to be required then it would have to be in the nature of a declaration or clearance only.[49]

The Ḥanafīs, Shāfiʿīs and Ḥanbalīs have held that when a man who is able to support his wife wilfully refuses to do so, it is for the wife to take action and for the *qāḍī* to grant a judgement in her favour. If the husband still refuses to fulfil his duty, the *qāḍī* may order the sale of his property from whose proceeds the wife may obtain her maintenance. The court may even imprison a persistently neglectful husband. The wife is, however, not entitled to a divorce, the reason being that when the Prophet instructed Hind to take her maintenance from her husband's property, she was not granted the right to ask for a divorce. The Mālikīs are basically in agreement with the majority view, with the only difference that in the event of the husband's persistent refusal, the Mālikīs entitle the wife to ask for a divorce. Notwithstanding some disagreement as to whether the court should determine the quantity of maintenance on the basis of the financial status of the husband, the wife, or both, according to the majority view, the husband's standards of living should be the basis of the court decision. Thus the ulema have generally considered the Ḥadīth under consideration to consist of a judicial decision of the Prophet, and as such it only authorises the judge to adjudicate the wife's complaint and to specify the quantity of maintenance and the method of its payment.[50]

Sunnah which consists of general legislation often has the quality of permanence and universal application to all Muslims. *Sunnah* of this type usually consists of commands and prohibitions which are related to the Qur'ān in the sense of endorsing, elaborating or qualifying the general provisions of the Holy Book.[51]

Qur'ān and *Sunnah* Distinguished

The Qur'ān was recorded in writing from beginning to end during the lifetime of the Prophet, who ascertained that the Qur'ān was preserved as he received it through divine revelation. The Prophet clearly expressed the concern that nothing of his own *Sunnah* should be confused with the text of the Qur'ān. This was, in fact, the main reason why he discouraged his Companions, at the early stage of his mission in any case,[52] from reducing the *Sunnah* into writing lest it be confused with the Qur'ān. The *Sunnah* on the other hand was mainly retained in memory by the Companions who did not, on the whole, keep a written record of the teachings of the Prophet. There were perhaps some exceptions as the relevant literature suggests that some, though a small number, of the Companions held collections of the Ḥadīth of the Prophet which they wrote and kept in their private collections. The overall impression obtained is, however, that this was done on a fairly limited scale.

The Companions used to verify instances of doubt concerning the text of the Qur'ān with the Prophet himself, who would often clarify them through clear instruction. This manner of verification is, however, unknown with regard to the *Sunnah*.[53]

The entire text of the Qur'ān has come down to us through continuous testimony (*tawātur*) whereas the *Sunnah* has in the most part been narrated and transmitted in the form of solitary, or *Āḥād*, reports. Only a small portion of the *Sunnah* has been transmitted in the form of *Mutawātir*.

The Qur'ān in none of its parts consists of conceptual transmission, that is, transmission in the words of the narrator himself. Both the concepts and words of the Qur'ān have been recorded and transmitted as the Prophet received them. The *Sunnah* on the other hand consists, in the most part, of the transmission of concepts in words and sentences that belong to the narrators. This is why one often finds that different versions of the one and the same Ḥadīth are reported by people whose understanding or interpretation of a particular Ḥadīth is not identical.

The scope of *ikhtilāf*, or disagreement, over the *Sunnah* is more extensive than that which may exist regarding the Qur'ān. Whereas the ulema have differed in their understanding/interpretation of the text of the Qur'ān, there is no problem to speak of concerning the authenticity of the contents of the Qur'ān. But disagreement over the *Sunnah* extends not only to questions of interpretation but also to authenticity and proof, issues which we shall further elaborate as our discussion proceeds.[54]

Priority of the Qur'ān over the *Sunnah*

As *Sunnah* is the second source of the *Sharīʿah* next to the Qur'ān, the *mujtahid* is bound to observe an order of priority between the Qur'ān and *Sunnah*. Hence in his search for a solution to a particular problem, the jurist must resort to the *Sunnah* only when he fails to find any guidance in the Qur'ān. Should there be a clear text in the Qur'ān, it must be followed and be given priority over any ruling of the *Sunnah* which may happen to be in conflict with the Qur'ān. The priority of the Qur'ān over the *Sunnah* is partly a result of the fact that the Qur'ān consists wholly of manifest revelation (*waḥy ẓāhir*) whereas the *Sunnah* mainly consists of internal revelation (*waḥy bāṭin*) and is largely transmitted in the words of the narrators themselves. The other reason for this order of priority relates to the question of authenticity. The authenticity of the Qur'ān is not open to doubt, it is, in other words, *qaṭʿī*, or decisive, in respect of authenticity and must therefore take priority over the *Sunnah*, or at least that part of *Sunnah* which is speculative (*ẓannī*) in respect of authenticity. The third point in favour of establishing an order of priority between the Qur'ān and the *Sunnah* is that the latter is explanatory to the former. Explanation or commentary should naturally occupy a secondary place in relationship to the source.[55] Furthermore, the order of priority between the Qur'ān and *Sunnah* is clearly established in the Ḥadīth of Muʿādh b. Jabal which has already been quoted. The purport of this Ḥadīth was also adopted and communicated in writing by ʿUmar b. al-Khaṭṭāb to two judges, Shurayḥ b. Ḥārith and Abū Mūsā al-Ashʿarī, who were ordered to resort to the Qur'ān first and to the *Sunnah* only when they could find no guidance in the Qur'ān.[56]

A practical consequence of this order of priority may be seen in the Ḥanafī distinction between *farḍ* and *wājib*. The former is founded in the definitive authority of the Qur'ān, whereas the latter is founded in the definitive *Sunnah*, but is one degree weaker because of a possible doubt in its transmission and accuracy of content. These are some of the factors which would explain the general agreement of the ulema to the effect that the authority of Qur'ān overrides that of the *Sunnah*.[57]

There should in principle be no conflict between the Qur'ān and the authentic *Sunnah*. If, however, a conflict is seen to exist between them, they must be reconciled as far as possible and both should be retained. If this is not possible, the *Sunnah* in question is likely to be of doubtful authenticity and must therefore give way to the Qur'ān. No genuine conflict is known to exist between the *Mutawātir* Ḥadīth and the Qur'ān. All instances of conflict between the *Sunnah* and the Qur'ān, in fact, originate in the solitary, or *Āḥād*, Ḥadīth, which is in any case of doubtful authenticity and subordinate to the overriding authority of the Qur'ān.[58]

It has, however, been suggested that establishing such an order of priority is anomalous and contrary to the basic role that the *Sunnah* plays in relation to the Qur'ān. As the familiar Arabic phrase, *al-Sunnah qāḍiyah ʿalā al-kitāb* (*Sunnah* is the arbiter of the Qur'ān) suggests, it is normally the *Sunnah* which explains the Qur'ān, not vice versa. The fact that the *Sunnah* explains and determines the precise meaning of the Qur'ān means that the Qur'ān is more dependent on the *Sunnah* than the *Sunnah* is on the Qur'ān.[59] In the event, for example, where the text of the Qur'ān imparts more than one meaning or when it is conveyed in general terms, it is the *Sunnah* which specifies the meaning that must prevail. Again, the manifest (*ẓāhir*) of the Qur'ān may be abandoned by the authority of the *Sunnah*, just as the *Sunnah* may qualify the absolute (*muṭlaq*) in the Qur'ān. The Qur'ān on the other hand does not play the same role with regard to the *Sunnah*. It is not the declared purpose of the Qur'ān to explain or clarify the *Sunnah*, as this was done by the Prophet himself. Since the *Sunnah* explains, qualifies, and determines the purport of the Qur'ān, it must take priority over the Qur'ān. If this is admitted, it would follow that incidents of conflict between the Qur'ān and *Sunnah* must be resolved in favour of the latter. Some ulema have even advanced the view that the Ḥadīth of Muʿādh b. Jabal (which clearly confirms the Qur'ān's priority over the *Sunnah*) is anomalous in that not everything in the Qur'ān is given priority over the *Sunnah*.[60] For one thing, the *Mutawātir* Ḥadīth stands on the same footing as the Qur'ān itself. Likewise, the manifest (*ẓāhir*) of the Qur'ān is open to interpretation and *ijtihād* in the same way as the solitary, or *Āḥād*, Ḥadīth; which means that they are more or less equal in these respects. Furthermore, according to the majority opinion, before implementing a Qur'ānic rule one must resort to the *Sunnah* and ascertain that the ruling in question has not been qualified in any way or given an interpretation on which the text of the Qur'ān is not self-evident.[61]

In response to the assertion that the *Sunnah* is the arbiter of the Qur'ān, it will be noted, as al-Shāṭibī points out, that this need not interfere with the order of priority in favour of the Qur'ān. For in all cases where the *Sunnah* specifies or qualifies the general or the absolute terms of the Qur'ān, the *Sunnah* in effect explains and interprets the Qur'ān. In none of such instances is the Qur'ān abandoned in favour of the *Sunnah*. The word *qāḍiyah* (arbiter) in the expression quoted above therefore means *mubayyinah* (explanatory) and does not imply the priority of the *Sunnah* over the Qur'ān. The textual rulings of the Qur'ān concerning theft and the obligation of *zakāh* have, for example, been qualified by the *Sunnah*. However, it is only proper to say that in both these cases, the *Sunnah* elaborates the general rulings of the Qur'ān, and it would hardly be accurate to suggest that the *Sunnah* has introduced anything new or that it seeks to overrule the Qur'ān. When an interpreter explains a particular legal text to us, it would hardly be correct to say that we act upon the words of the interpreter without referring to the legal text itself.[62]

Furthermore, the explanatory role of the *Sunnah* in relationship to the Qur'ān has been determined by the Qur'ān itself, where we read in an address to the Prophet in sūra al-Naḥl (16:44): 'We have sent down to you the Remembrance so that you may explain to the people what has been revealed to them.' The correct conclusion drawn from this and similar Qur'ānic passages is that the *Sunnah*, being explanatory to the Qur'ān, is subordinate to it.[63]

Is *Sunnah* an Independent Source?

An adequate answer to the question as to whether the *Sunnah* is a mere supplement to the Qur'ān or a source in its own right necessitates an elaboration of the relationship of the *Sunnah* to the Qur'ān in the following three capacities:

Firstly, the *Sunnah* may consist of rules that merely confirm and reiterate the Qur'ān, in which case the rules concerned originate in the Qur'ān and are merely corroborated by the *Sunnah*. The question as to whether the *Sunnah* is an independent source is basically redundant with regard to matters on which the *Sunnah* merely confirms the Qur'ān, as it is obvious that in such cases the *Sunnah* is not an independent source. A substantial part of the *Sunnah* is, in fact, of this variety: all *aḥādīth* pertaining to the five pillars of the faith and other such matters like the rights of one's parents, respect for the property of others, and *aḥādīth* which regulate homicide, theft and false testimony, etc., basically reaffirm the Qur'ānic principles on these subjects.[64] To be more specific, the Ḥadīth that "it is unlawful to take the property of a Muslim without his express consent",[65]

لا يحلّ مال امرىء مسلم الا بطيب عن نفسه

merely confirms the Qur'ānic *āyah* which orders the Muslims to "devour not each other's properties unlawfully unless it is through trade by your consent" (al-Nisā', 4:19). The origin of this rule is Qur'ānic, and since the foregoing Ḥadīth merely reaffirms the Qur'ān, there is no room for saying that it constitutes an independent authority in its own right.

Secondly, the *Sunnah* may consist of an explanation or clarification to the Qur'ān; it may clarify the ambivalent (*mujmal*) of the Qur'ān, qualify its absolute statements, or specify the general terms of the Qur'ān. This is once again the proper role that the *Sunnah* plays in relationship to the Qur'ān: it explains it. Once again a substantial part of the *Sunnah* falls under this category. It is, for example, through this type of *Sunnah* that Qur'ānic expressions like *ṣalāh, zakāh, ḥajj* and *ribā*, etc., have acquired their juridical (*sharʿī*) meanings. To give another example, with regard to the contract of sale the Qur'ān merely declares sale to be lawful as opposed to *ribā*, which is forbidden. This general principle has later been elaborated by the *Sunnah* which expounded the detailed rules of *Sharīʿah* concerning sale, including its conditions, varieties, and sales which might amount to *ribā*. The same could be said of the lawful and unlawful vareties of food, a subject on which the Qur'ān contains only general guidelines while the *Sunnah* provides the details.[66] Again, on the subject of bequest, the Qur'ān provides for the basic legality of bequest and the rule that it must be implemented prior to the distribution of the estate among the heirs (al-Nisā', 4:12). The *Sunnah* supplements these principles by enacting additional rules which facilitate a proper implementation of the general principles of the Qur'ān.[67]

The foregoing two varieties of *Sunnah* between them comprise the largest bulk of *Sunnah*, and the ulema are in agreement that these two types of *Sunnah* are integral to the Qur'ān and constitute a logical whole with it. The two cannot be separated or taken independently from one another. It is considered that the *Sunnah* which qualifies or elaborates the general provisions of the Qur'ān on devotional matters (*ʿibādāt*), on the punishment of theft, on the duty of *zakāh*, and on the subject of bequest, could only have originated in divine inspiration (*ilhām*), for these cannot be determined by means of rationality and *ijtihād* alone.[68]

Thirdly, the *Sunnah* may consist of rulings on which the Qur'ān is silent, in which case the ruling in question originates in the *Sunnah* itself. This variety of *Sunnah*, referred to as *al-Sunnah al-mu'assisah*, or 'founding *Sunnah*', neither confirms nor opposes the Qur'ān, and its contents cannot be traced back to the Holy Book. It is only this variety of *Sunnah* which lies in the centre of the debate as to whether the *Sunnah* is an independent source of law. To give some examples: the prohibition regarding simultaneous marriage to the maternal and paternal aunt of one's wife (often referred to as 'unlawful conjunction'), the right of pre-emption (*shufʿ*), the grandmother's entitlement to a share in inheritance, the punishment of *rajm*, that is, death by stoning for adultery when committed by a married Muslim – all originate in the *Sunnah* as the Qur'ān itself is silent on these matters.[69]

There is some disagreement among jurists as to whether the *Sunnah*, or this last variety of it at any rate, constitutes an independent source of *Sharīʿah*. Some ulema of the later ages (*al-muta'akhkhirūn*), including al-Shāṭibī and al-Shawkānī, have held the view that the *Sunnah* is an independent source.[70] They have further maintained that the Qur'ānic *āyah* in sūra al-Naḥl (16:44 – quoted above) is inconclusive and that despite its being clear on the point that the Prophet interprets the Qur'ān, it does not overrule the recognition of the *Sunnah* as an independent source. On the contrary, it is argued that there is evidence in the Qur'ān which substantiates the independent status of *Sunnah*. The Qur'ān, for example, in more than one place requires the believers to 'obey God and obey His Messenger, (al-Nisā', 4:58; 4:80; al-Mā'idah, 5:92). The fact that obedience to the Prophet is specifically enjoined next to obeying God warrants the conclusion that obedience to the Prophet means obeying him whenever he orders or prohibits something on which the Qur'ān might be silent. For if the purpose of obedience to the Prophet were to obey him only when he explained the Qur'ān, then 'obey God' would be sufficient and there would have been no need to add the phrase 'obey the Messenger'.[71] Elsewhere the Qur'ān clearly places submission and obedience to the Prophet at the very heart of the faith as a test of one's acceptance of Islam. This is the purport of the *āyah* which reads: 'By thy Lord, they will not believe till they make thee the judge regarding disagreements between them, and find in themselves no resistance against the verdict, but accept it in full submission' (al-Nisā, 4:65). Furthermore, the proponents of the independent status of the *Sunnah* have quoted the Ḥadīth of Muᶜādh b. Jabal in support of their argument. The Ḥadīth is clear on the point that the *Sunnah* is authoritative in cases on which no guidance can be found in the Qur'ān. The *Sunnah*, in other words, stands on its own feet regardless of whether it is substantiated by the Qur'ān or not.[72]

According to the majority of ulema, however, the *Sunnah*, in all its parts, even when it enacts original legislation, is explanatory and integral to the Qur'ān.[73] Al-Shāfiᶜī's views on this matter are representative of the majority position. In his *Risālah*, al-Shāfiᶜī states:

> I do not know anyone among the ulema to oppose [the doctrine] that the *Sunnah* of the Prophet is of three types: first is the *Sunnah* which prescribes the like of what God has revealed in His Book; next is the *Sunnah* which explains the general principles of the Qur'ān and clarifies the will of God; and last is the *Sunnah* where the Messenger of God has ruled on matters on which nothing can be found in the Book of God. The first two varieties are integral to the Qur'ān, but the ulema have differed as to the third.[74]

Al-Shāfiᶜī goes on to explain the views that the ulema have advanced concerning the relationship of *Sunnah* to the Qur'ān. One of these views, which receives strong support from al-Shāfiᶜī himself, is that God has explicitly rendered obedience to the Prophet an obligatory duty (*farḍ*). In his capacity as Messenger of God, the Prophet has introduced laws some of which originate in the Qur'ān while others do not. But all Prophetic legislation emanates in divine authority. The *Sunnah* and the Qur'ān are of the same provenance, and all must be upheld and obeyed. Others have held the view that the Prophetic mission itself, that is the fact that the Prophet is the chosen Messenger of God, is sufficient proof for the authority of the *Sunnah*. For it is through the *Sunnah* that the Prophet fulfilled his divine mission. According to yet another view there is no *Sunnah* whose origin cannot be traced back to the Qur'ān. This view maintains that even the *Sunnah* which explains the number and content of *ṣalāh* and the quantities of *zakāh* as well as the lawful and forbidden varieties of food and trade merely elaborates general principles of the Qur'ān.[75] More specifically, all the *aḥādīth* which provide details on the lawful and unlawful varieties of food merely elaborate the Qur'ānic declaration that God has permitted wholesome food and prohibited that which is unclean (al-Aᶜrāf: 7:157).[76]

The majority view, which seeks to establish an almost total identity between the *Sunnah* and the Qur'ān, further refers to the saying of the Prophet's widow, ᶜĀ'ishah, when she attempted to interpret the Qur'ānic epithet *wa innaka la ᶜalā khuluqin ᶜaẓīm* ('and you possess an excellent character') (al-Qalam, 68:4). ᶜĀ'ishah is quoted to have said that 'his (the Prophet's) *khuluq* was the Qur'ān'. *Khuluq* in this context means the conduct of the Prophet, his acts, sayings, and all that he has approved. Thus it is concluded that the *Sunnah* is not separate from the Qur'ān.[77]

Furthermore, the majority view seeks to establish an identity between the general objectives of the Qur'ān and *Sunnah*: The *Sunnah* and the Qur'ān are unanimous in their pursuit of the three-fold objectives of protecting the necessities (*ḍarūriyyāt*), complementary requirements (*ḥājiyyāt*) and the 'embellishments' (*taḥsīniyyāt*).[78] It is then argued that even when the *Sunnah* broaches new ground, it is with the purpose of giving effect to one or the other of the objectives that have been validated in the Qur'ān. Thus the identity between the Qur'ān and *Sunnah* is transferred, from one of theme and subject, to that of the main purpose and spirit that is common to both.[79]

And finally, the majority explain that some of the rulings of the *Sunnah* consist of an analogy to the Qur'ān. For example, the Qur'ān has decreed that no one may marry two sisters simultaneously. The Ḥadīth (cited below on page 71) which prohibits simultaneous marriage to the maternal and paternal aunt of one's wife is based on the same effective cause (*ᶜillah*), which is to avoid the severance of close ties of kinship (*qaṭᶜ al-arḥām*). In short, the *Sunnah* as a whole is no more than a supplement to the Qur'ān. The Qur'ān is indeed more than comprehensive and provides complete guidance on the broad outline of the entire body of the *Sharīᶜah*.[80]

In conclusion, it may be said that both sides are essentially in agreement on the authority of *Sunnah* as a source of law and its principal role in relationship to the Qur'ān. They both acknowledge that the *Sunnah* contains legislation which is not found in the Qur'ān.[81] The difference between them seems to be one of interpretation rather than substance. The Qur'ānic *āyāt* on the duty of obedience to the Prophet, and those which assign to him the role of the interpreter of the Qur'ān, are open to variant interpretations. These passages have been quoted in support of both the views, that the *Sunnah* is supplementary to the Qur'ān, and that it is an independent source. The point which is basic to both these views is the authority of the Prophet and the duty of adherence to his *Sunnah*. In the meantime, both sides acknowledge the fact that the *Sunnah* contains legislation which is additional to the Qur'ān. When this is recognised, the rest of the debate becomes largely redundant. For what else is there to be achieved by the argument that the *Sunnah* is an independent source? The partisans of the two views have, in effect, resolved their differences without perhaps declaring this to be the case. Since the Qur'ān provides ample evidence to the effect that the Prophet explains the Qur'ān and that he must be obeyed, there is no need to advance a theoretical conflict between the two facets of a basic unity. Both views can be admitted without the risk of running into a logical contradiction. The two views should therefore be seen not as contradictory but as logical extensions of one another.

Distortion and Forgery

There is no dispute over the occurrence of extensive forgery in the Ḥadīth literature. The ulema of Ḥadīth are unanimous on this, and some have gone so far as to affirm that in no other branch of Islamic sciences has there been so much forgery as in the Ḥadīth. The very existence of a bulk of literature and works by prominent ulema bearing the title *al-Mawḍūᶜāt*, or 'fabricated Ḥadīth', bears witness to extensive forgery in this area.[82]

There is some disagreement over determining the historical origins of forgery in Ḥadīth. While some observers have given the caliphate of ᶜUthmān as a starting point, others have dated it a little later, at around the year 40 Hijrah, when political differences between the fourth caliph, ᶜAlī, and Muᶜāwiyah led to military confrontation and the division of the Muslims into various factions. According to a third view, forgery in Ḥadīth started even earlier, that is, during the caliphate of Abū Bakr when he waged the War of Apostasy (*riddah*) against the refusers of *zakāh*. But the year 40 is considered the more likely starting point for the development of serious and persistent differences in the community, which is marked by the emergence of the Khārijites and the Shīᶜah. Muslims were thenceforth divided, and hostility between them acquired a religious dimension when they began to use the Qur'ān and *Sunnah* in support of their claims. When the misguided elements among them failed to find any authority in the sources for their views, they either imposed a distorted interpretation on the source materials, or embarked on outright fabrication.[83]

The attribution of false statements to the Prophet may be divided into two types: (1) deliberate forgery, which is usually referred to as *ḥadīth mawḍūᶜ*; (2) unintentional fabrication, which is known as *ḥadīth bāṭil* and is due mainly to error and recklessness in reporting. For example, in certain cases it is noted that the chain of narrators ended with a Companion or a Successor only but the transmitter instead extended it directly to the Prophet. The result is all the same, and fabrication whether deliberate or otherwise must in all cases be abandoned.[84] Our present discussion is, however, mainly concerned with deliberate fabrication in Ḥadīth.

The initial forgery in Ḥadīth is believed to have occurred in the context of personality cult literature (*faḍā'il al-ashkhāṣ*) which aimed at crediting (or discrediting) leading political figures with exaggerated claims. The earliest forgery in this context, according to the Sunnīs, was committed by the Shīᶜah. This is illustrated by the Ḥadīth of Ghadīr Khumm in which the Prophet is quoted to have said that "ᶜAlī is my brother, executor and successor. Listen to him and obey him'. A similar statement attributed to the Prophet is as follows: 'Whoever wishes to behold Adam for his knowledge, Noah for his piety, Ibrahim for his gentleness, Moses for his commanding presence and Jesus for his devotion to worship – let him behold ᶜAlī.'[85]

There are numerous fabricated *aḥādīth* condemning Muᶜāwiyah, including, for example, the one in which the Prophet is quoted to have ordered the Muslims, 'When you see Muᶜāwiyah on my pulpit, kill him.' The fanatic supporters of Muᶜāwiyah and the Umayyad dynasty are, on the other hand, known to have fabricated Ḥadīth such as 'The trusted ones are three: I, Gabriel and Muᶜāwiyah.'[86]

The Khārijites are on the whole considered to have avoided fabricating Ḥadīth, which is due mainly to their belief that the perpetrator of a grave sin is no longer a Muslim. Since they saw the fabrication of Ḥadīth in this light, they avoided indulgence in forgery as a matter of principle and a requirement of their doctrine.[87]

A group of heretic factions known as *al-Zanādiqah* (pl. of *Zindīq*), owing to their hatred of Islam, fabricated Ḥadīth which discredited Islam in the view of its followers. Included among such are: 'eggplants are a cure for every illness'; and 'beholding a good-looking face is a form of *ᶜibādah*'. It is reported that just before his execution, one of the notorious fabricators of Ḥadīth, ᶜAbd al-Karīm b. Abū al-ᶜAwja', confessed that he had fabricated 4,000 *aḥādīth* in which *ḥalāl* was rendered *ḥarām* and *ḥarām* was rendered *ḥalāl.* It has been further reported that the *Zanādiqah* fabricated a total of 14,000 *aḥādīth*,[88] a report which may or may not be credible. For a statement of this nature tends to arouse suspicion as to its veracity: even in fabricated matters, it is not a facile task to invent such a vast number of Ḥadīth on the subject of *ḥalāl* and *ḥarām*. Could it be that exaggerated figures of this order were quoted mainly for their subversive value?

Racial, tribal and linguistic fanaticism was yet another context in which Ḥadīth were fabricated. Note for example the following: 'Whenever God was angry, He sent down revelation in Arabic, but when contented, He chose Persian for this purpose.' The Arab fanatic too has matched this anathema by claiming that 'Whenever God was angry he sent down revelation in Persian, but when contented He chose to speak in Arabic.'[89] These and other similar forgeries relating to the virtues or superiority of certain tribes, cities, and periods of time over others have been isolated by the ulema of Ḥadīth and placed in the category of *al-Mawḍūᶜāt*.[90]

Known among the classes of forgers are also professional story-tellers and preachers (*al-quṣṣāṣ wa'l-wāᶜiẓūn*), whose urge for popularity through arousing an emotional response in their audience led them to indulge in forgery. They made up stories and attributed them to the Prophet. It is reported that once a story-teller cited a Ḥadīth to an audience in the mosque on the authority of Aḥmad b. Ḥanbal and Yaḥyā b. Maᶜīn which runs as follows: 'Whoever says 'there is no God but Allah', Allah will reward him, for each word uttered, with a bird in Paradise, with a beak of gold and feathers of pearls.' At the end of his sermon, the speaker was confronted by Aḥmad b. Ḥanbal and Yaḥyā b. Maᶜīn who were present on the occasion and told the speaker that they had never related any Ḥadīth of this kind.[91]

Juristic and theological differences constitute another theme of forgery in Ḥadīth. This is illustrated by the following statement attributed to the Prophet: 'Whoever raises his hands during the performance of *ṣalāh*, his *ṣalāh* is null and void.' In yet another statement, we read: 'Whoever says that the Qur'ān is the created speech of God becomes an infidel [. . .] and his wife stands divorced from him as of that moment.'

Another category of fabricated Ḥadīth is associated with the religious zeal of individuals whose devotion to Islam led them to the careless ascription of Ḥadīth to the Prophet. This is illustrated by the forgeries committed by one Nūḥ b. Abū Maryam on the virtues of the various sūras of the Qur'ān. He is said to have later regretted what he did and explained that he fabricated such Ḥadīth because he saw people who were turning away from the Qur'ān and occupying themselves with the *fiqh* of Abū Ḥanīfah and the battle stories of Muḥammad b. Isḥāq. Numerous other names occur in the relevant literature, including those of Ghulām Khalīl and Ibn Abī ᶜAyyāsh of Baghdad, who were both known as pious individuals, but who invented Ḥadīth on the virtues of certain words of praise (*adhkār wa-awrād*) and other devotional matters.[92]

Without wishing to go into details, other themes on which Ḥadīth forgery has taken place included the urge on the part of courtiers who distorted an existing Ḥadīth so as to please and flatter their overlords. Similarly, the desire to establish the permissibility or virtue of certain varieties of food, beverages, clothes and customary practices led individuals to introduce exaggerations and arbitrary changes in the Ḥadīth.[93]

Classification and Value: II

From the viewpoint of the continuity and completeness of their chains of transmitters, the Ḥadīth are once again classified into two categories: continuous (*muttaṣil*) and discontinued (*ghayr muttaṣil*). A continuous Ḥadīth is one which has a complete chain of transmission from the last narrator all the way back to the prophet. A discontinued Ḥadīth, also known as *Mursal*, is a Ḥadīth whose chain of transmitters is broken and incomplete. The majority of ulema have divided the continuous Ḥadīth into the two main varieties of *Mutawātir* and *Āḥād*. To this the Ḥanafīs have added an intermediate category, namely the 'well-known', or *Mashhūr*.

I. The Continuous Ḥadīth

1. *The Mutawātir*

Literally, *Mutawātir* means 'continuously recurrent'. In the present context, it means a report by an indefinite number of people related in such a way as to preclude the possibility of their agreement to perpetuate a lie. Such a possibility is inconceivable owing to their large number, diversity of residence, and reliability.[94] A report would not be called *Mutawātir* if its contents were believed on other grounds, such as the rationality of its content, or that it is deemed to be a matter of axiomatic knowledge.[95] A report is classified as *Mutawātir* only when it fulfills the following conditions:

a) The number of reporters in every period or generation must be large enough to preclude their collusion in propagating falsehood. Should the number of reporters in any period fall short of a reliable multitude, their report does not establish positive knowledge and is therefore not *Mutawātir*.[96] Some ulema have attempted to specify a minimum, varying from as low as four to as many as twenty, forty and seventy up into the hundreds. All of these figures are based on analogies: the requirement of four is based on the similar number of witnesses which constitute legal proof; twenty is analogous to the Qur'ānic *āyah* in sūra al-Anfāl (8:65) which reads: 'If there are twenty steadfast men among you, they will overcome two hundred [fighters].' The next number, that is seventy, represents an analogy to another Qur'ānic passage where we read that 'Moses chose seventy men among his people for an appointment with Us' (al-Aᶜrāf, 7:155). Some have drawn an analogy from the number of participants in the battle of Badr. However, al-Ghazālī is representative of the majority opinion when he observes that all of these analogies are arbitrary and have no bearing on the point. For certainty is not necessarily a question of numbers; it is corroborative evidence, the knowledge and trustworthiness of reporters, that must be credited even in cases where the actual number of reporters is not very large.[97] Thus when a reasonable number of persons report something which is supported by other evidence, their report may amount to positive knowledge.[98]
b) The reporters must base their report on sense perception. If, therefore, a large number of people report that the universe is created, their report would not be *Mutāwatir*. The report must also be based on certain knowledge, not mere speculation. If, for example, the people of Islamabad inform us of a person they thought was Zayd, or a bird they thought was a pigeon, neither would amount to certainty.[99]
c) Some ulema have advanced the view that the reporters must be upright persons (*ᶜudūl*), which means that they must neither be infidels nor profligates (*kuffār wa-fussāq*). The correct view, however, is that neither of these conditions are necessary. What is essential in *Mutawātir* is the attainment of certainty, and this can be obtained through the reports of non-Muslims, profligates and even children who have reached the age of discernment, that is, between seven and fifteen. The position is, of course, entirely different with regard to solitary Ḥadīth, which will be discussed later.[100]
d) That the reporters are not biased in their cause and are not associated with one another through a political or sectarian movement. And finally, all of these conditions must be met from the origin of the report to the very end.[101]

What is the value (*ḥukm*) of the *Mutawātir*? According to the majority of ulema, the authority of a *Mutawātir* Ḥadīth is equivalent to that of the Qur'ān. Universal continuous testimony (*tawātur*) engenders certainty (*yaqīn*) and the knowledge that it creates is equivalent to knowledge that is acquired through sense-perception. Most people, it is said, know their forefathers by means of *Mutawātir* reports just as they know their children through sense-perception. Similarly, no one is likely to deny that Baghdad was the seat of the caliphate for centuries, despite their lack of direct knowledge to that effect. When the reports of a large number of the transmitters of Ḥadīth concur in their purport but differ in wording or in form, only their common meaning is considered *Mutawātir*. This is called *Mutawātir bi'l-maᶜnā*, or conceptual *Mutawātir*. Examples of this kind of *Mutawātir* are numerous in the Ḥadīth. Thus the verbal and actual *Sunnah* which explain the manner of performing the obligatory prayers, the rituals of *ḥajj*, fasting, the quantities of *zakāh*, rules relating to retaliation (*qiṣāṣ*) and the implementation of *ḥudūd*, etc., all constitute conceptual *Mutawātir*. For a large number of the Companions witnessed the acts and sayings of the Prophet on these matters, and their reports have been transmitted by multitudes of people throughout the ages.[102] The other variety of *Mutawātir*, which is of rare occurrence compared to the conceptual *Mutawātir*, is called *Mutawātir bi'l-lafẓ*, or verbal *Mutawātir*. In this type of *Mutawātir*, all the reports must be identical on the exact wording of the Ḥadīth as they were uttered by the Prophet himself. For example the Ḥadīth which reads: 'Whoever lies about me deliberately must prepare himself for a place in Hell-fire.'[103]

من كذب عليّ متعمداً فليتبوأ مقعده من
النّار .

The exact number of the verbal *mutawātir* is a subject of disagreement, but it is suggested that it does not exceed ten *aḥādīth*.[104]

2. *The Mashhūr (Well-Known) Ḥadīth*

The *Mashhūr* is defined as a Ḥadīth which is originally reported by one, two or more Companions from the Prophet or from another Companion but has later become well-known and transmitted by an indefinite number of people. It is necessary that the diffusion of the report should have taken place during the first or the second generation following the demise of the Prophet, not later. This would mean that the Ḥadīth became widely known during the period of the Companions or the Successors. For it is argued that after this period, all the Ḥadīth became well-known, in which case there will be no grounds for distinguishing the *Mashhūr* from the general body of Ḥadith.[105]

For Abū Ḥanīfah and his disciples, the *Mashhūr* Ḥadīth imparts positive knowledge, albeit of a lesser degree of certainty than *Mutawātir*. But the majority of non-Ḥanafī jurists consider *Mashhūr* to be included in the category of solitary Ḥadīth, and that it engenders speculative knowledge only. According to the Ḥanafīs, acting upon the *Mashhūr* is obligatory but its denial does not amount to disbelief.[106] The difference between the *Mutawātir* and *Mashhūr* lies mainly in the fact that every link in the chain of transmitters of the *Mutawātir* consists of a plurality of reporters, whereas the first link in the case of *Mashhūr* consists of one or two Companions only. As for the remaining links in the chain of transmitters, there is no difference between the *Mutawātir* and *Mashhūr*. Examples of the *Mashhūr* Ḥadīth are those which are reported from the Prophet by a prominent Companion and then transmitted by a large number of narrators whose agreement upon a lie is inconceivable.[107] The *Mashhūr*, according to the Ḥanafīs, may qualify the 'general' of the Qur'ān. Two such *aḥādīth* which have so qualified the Qur'ān are as follows: 'The killer shall not inherit',

لا يرث القاتل

is a *Mashhūr* Ḥadīth which qualifies the general provisions of the Qur'ān on inheritance in sūra al-Nisā' (4:11). Similarly the *Mashhūr* Ḥadīth which provides: 'No woman shall be married simultaneously with her paternal or maternal aunt . . .'

لا تنكح المرأة على عمتها ولا على خالتها

has qualified the general provisions of the Qur'ān on marriage where the text spells out the prohibited degrees of marriage and then declares 'it is lawful for you to marry outside these prohibitions' (al-Nisā', 4:24).[108] The list of prohibitions provided in this *āyah* does not include simultaneous marriage with the maternal or paternal aunt of one's wife; this is supplied by the Ḥadīth.

3. *The Āḥād (Solitary Ḥadīth)*

The *Āḥād*, or solitary Ḥadīth (also known as *Khabar al-Wāḥid*), is a Ḥadīth which is reported by a single person or by odd individuals from the Prophet. Imām Shāfiʿī refers to it as *Khabar al-Khāṣṣah*, which applies to every report narrated by one, two or more persons from the Prophet but which fails to fulfil the requirements of either the *Mutawātir* or the

Mashhūr.[109] It is a Ḥadīth which does not impart positive knowledge on its own unless it is supported by extraneous or circumstantial evidence. This is the view of the majority, but according to Imām Aḥmad b. Ḥanbal and others, *Āḥād* can engender positive knowledge. [110] Some ulema have rejected it on the basis of an analogy they have drawn with a provision of the law of evidence, namely that the testimony of one witness falls short of legal proof. Those who unquestioningly accept the authority of *Āḥād*, such as the Ẓāhirī school, maintain that when the Prophet wanted to deliver a ruling in regard to a particular matter he did not invite all the citizens of Madinah to attend. The majority of jurists, however, agree that *Āḥād* may establish a rule of law provided that it is related by a reliable narrator and the contents of the report are not repugnant to reason.[111] Many ulema have held that *Āḥād* engenders speculative knowledge acting upon which is preferable only. In the event where other supportive evidence can be found in its favour or when there is nothing to oppose its contents, then acting upon *Āḥād* is obligatory.[112] But *Āḥād* may not, according to the majority of ulema, be relied upon as the basis of belief (*ʿaqīdah*). For matters of belief must be founded in certainty even if a conjecture (*ẓann*) may at time seem preferable.[113] As the Qur'ān tells us, 'verily conjecture avails nothing against the truth' (al-Najm, 53:28) *Āḥād*, being conjectural, does not establish the truth.

According to the majority of the ulema of the four Sunnī schools, acting upon *Āḥād* is obligatory even if *Āḥād* fails to engender positive knowledge. Thus in practical legal matters, a preferable *ẓann* is sufficient as a basis of obligation. It is only in matters of belief where conjecture 'avails nothing against the truth'.[114] Having said this, however, *Āḥād* may only form the basis of obligation if it fulfills the following requirements:

a) That the transmitter is a competent person, which means that reports communicated by a child or a lunatic of whatever age are unacceptable. Women, blind persons and slaves are considered competent for purposes of reporting the Ḥadīth; it is only in regard to being a witness that they suffer some disability.[115]
b) The transmitter of *Āḥād* must be a Muslim, which means that a report by a non-Muslim is unacceptable. However, the reporter must fulfil this condition only at the time of reporting the Ḥadīth, but not necessarily at the time when he received the information. There are instances of Ḥadīth, for example, reported by Companions pertaining to the acts of the Prophet which they observed before they had professed Islam.[116]
c) The transmitter must be an upright person (*ʿadl*) at the time of

reporting the Ḥadīth. The minimum requirement of this condition is that the person has not committed a major sin and does not persist in committing minor ones; nor is he known for persistence in degrading profanities such as eating in the public thoroughfare, associating with persons of ill-repute and indulgence in humiliating jokes. Although the ulema are unanimous on the requirement of uprightness of character (*ᶜadālah*), they are not in agreement as to what it precisely means. According to the Ḥanafīs, a Muslim who is not a sinner (*fāsiq*) is presumed to be upright. The Shāfiᶜīs are more specific on the avoidance of sins, both major and minor, as well as indulgence in profane *mubāḥāt*. To the Mālikī jurist, Ibn al-Ḥājib, *ᶜadālah* refers to piety, observance of religious duties and propriety of conduct. There is also some disagreement among the ulema on the definition of, and distinction between, major and minor sins.[117]

The *ᶜadālah* of a transmitter must be established by positive proof. Hence when the *ᶜadālah* of a transmitter is unknown, his report is unacceptable. Similarly, a report by an anonymous person (*riwāyah al-majhūl*) such as when the chain of transmitters reads in part that 'a man' reported such-and-such is unacceptable. The *ᶜadālah* of a narrator may be established by various means including *tazkiyah*, that is when at least one upright person confirms it, or when the transmitter is known to have been admitted as a witness in court, or when a *faqīh* or a learned person is known to have relied or acted on his report. But there must be positive evidence that the *faqīh* did not do so due to additional factors such as a desire on his part merely to be cautious.[118]

The qualification of *ᶜadālah* is established for all the Companions regardless of their juristic or political views. This conclusion is based on the Qur'ān which declares in a reference to the Companions that 'God is well pleased with them, as they are with Him' (al-Tawbah, 9:100). A person's reputation for being upright and trustworthy also serves as a proof of his reliability. According to some ulema of Ḥadīth, such a reputation is even more credible than confirmation by one or two individuals.[119] With regard to certain figures such as Imām Mālik, Sufyān al-Thawrī, Sufyān b. ᶜUyaynah, al-Layth b. Saᶜd, etc., their reputation for *ᶜadālah* is proof of reliability above the technicalities of *tazkiyah*.[120]

d) The narrator of *Āḥād* must possess a retentive memory so that his report may be trusted. If he is known for committing frequent errors and inconsistencies, his report is unacceptable. The faculty of retention, or *ḍabṭ*, is the ability of a person to listen to an utterance, to comprehend its meaning as it was originally intended and then to retain it and take all necessary precautions to safeguard its accuracy. In cases of doubt in the retentiveness of a transmitter, if his report can be confirmed by the action of his predecessors, it may be accepted. But in the absence of such verification, reports by persons who are totally obscure and whose retentiveness cannot be established are unacceptable.[121]

e) That the narrator is not implicated in any form of distortion (*tadlīs*) either in the textual contents (*matn*) of a Ḥadīth or in its chain of transmitters (*isnād*). Distortion in the text is to add to the saying of the Prophet elements which did not exist, or to detract from its original content so as to distort its purport and mislead the listener. *Tadlīs* in the *isnād* is to tamper with the names and identity of narrators, which is, essentially, not very different from outright forgery.[122] One form of *tadlīs* is to omit a link in the chain of narrators. The motive for such omission is immaterial. Sometimes it is observed, for example, that a single weak link in an otherwise reliable chain of transmitters is omitted with a view to showing the *isnād* reliable in every part. Whatever the motive may be, a *tadlīs* of this kind is, for all intents and purposes, equivalent to forgery. However, if the narrator is a prominent scholar of irreproachable reputation, his report is normally accepted notwithstanding a minor omission in the chain of *isnād*.[123]

f) The transmitter of *Āḥād* must, in addition, have met with and heard the Ḥadīth directly from his immediate source. The contents of the Ḥadīth must not be outlandish (*shādhdh*) in the sense of being contrary to the established norms of the Qur'ān and other principles of *Sharīʿah*. In addition, the report must be free of subtle errors such as rendering *ab* as *ibn* ('father' as 'son') or other such words that are similar in appearance but differ in meaning.[124]

The three Imāms, Abū Ḥanifah, al-Shāfiʿī and Aḥmad b. Ḥanbal rely on *Āḥād* when it fulfills the foregoing conditions. Abū Ḥanīfah, however, has laid down certain additional conditions, one of which is that the narrator's action must not contradict his narration. It is on this ground, for example, that Abū Ḥanīfah does not rely on the following Ḥadīth, narrated by Abū Hurayrah: 'When a dog licks a dish, wash it seven times, one of which must be with clean sand.'[125]

إذا ولغ الكلب في إناء أحدكم فليغسله سبعا
احداهن بالتراب الطاهر .

Abū Ḥanīfah has explained this by saying that Abū Hurayrah did not act upon it himself. Since the requirement of washing is normally three times, the report is considered weak, including its attribution to Abū Hurayrah.[126] The majority, on the other hand, take the view that discrepancies between the action and the report of a narrator may be due to forgetfulness or some other unknown factor. Discrepancies of this kind do not, by themselves, provide conclusive evidence to render the report unreliable.

The Ḥanafīs further require that the subject matter of *Āḥād* is not such that would necessitate the knowledge of a vast number of people. If, for example, we are informed, by means of a solitary report, of an act or saying of the Prophet which was supposed to be known by hundreds or thousands of people and yet only one or two have reported it, such a Ḥadīth would not be reliable. The Ḥadīth, for example, that 'Anyone who touches his sexual organ must take a fresh ablution',[127]

إذا مسّ أحدكم ذكره فليتوضّأ

is not accepted by the Ḥanafīs. The Ḥanafīs have explained: had this Ḥadīth been authentic, it would have become an established practice among all Muslims, which is not the case. The Ḥadīth is therefore not reliable. The majority of ulema, however, do not insist on this requirement on the analysis that people who witness or observe an incident do not necessarily report it. We know, for example, that countless numbers of people saw the prophet performing the pilgrimage of *ḥajj*, and yet not many reported their observations.[128]

And finally, the Ḥanafīs maintain that when the narrator of *Āḥād* is not a *faqīh*, his report is accepted only if it agrees with *qiyās*, otherwise *qiyās* would be given priority over *Āḥād*. However, if the narrator is known to be a *faqīh*, then his report would be preferred over *qiyās*. It is on this ground, for example, that the Ḥanafīs have rejected the Ḥadīth of *muṣarrāt*, that is the animal whose milk is retained in its udders so as to impress the buyer. The Ḥadīth is as follows: 'Do not retain milk in the udders of a she-camel or goat so as to exaggerate its yield. Anyone who buys a *muṣarrāt* has the choice, for three days after having milked it, either to keep it, or to return it with a quantity [i.e. a *ṣāʿ*] of dates.'[129]

لا تُصرّوا في الابل والغنم ، من ابتاع شاة مصرّاة
فهو فيها بالخيار ثلاثة أيام ، إن شاء أمسكها وان
شاء ردها وردّ معها صاعاً من تمر

The Ḥanafīs regard this Ḥadīth to be contrary to *qiyās*, that is, to analogy with the rule of equality between indemnity and loss. Abū Ḥanīfah has held the view that the *ṣāᶜ* of dates may not be equal in value to the amount of milk the buyer has consumed. Hence if the buyer wishes to return the beast, he must return it with the cost of milk which was in its udders at the time of purchase, not with a fixed quantity of dates. The majority of ulema, including Mālik, Shāfiᶜī, Ibn Ḥanbal and the disciples of Abū Ḥanīfah, (Abū Yūsuf and Ẓufar), have on the other hand accepted this Ḥadīth and have given it priority over *qiyās*. According to the majority view, the compensation may consist of a *ṣāᶜ* of dates or of its monetary value. Dates were specified in the Ḥadīth as it used to be the staple food in those days, which may not be the case any more.[130]

Imām Mālik would rely on a solitary Ḥadīth on condition that it does not disagree with the practice of the Madinese (*ᶜamal ahl al-Madīnah*). For he considers the standard practice of the people of Madinah to be more representative of the conduct of the Prophet than the isolated report of one or two individuals. In his opinion, the Madinese practice represents the narration of thousands upon thousands of people from, ultimately, the Prophet. It is, in other words, equivalent to a *Mashhūr*, or even *Mutawātir*. When an *Āḥād* report contradicts the practice of the Madinese, the latter is, according to the Mālikī view, given priority over the former. The Mālikīs have thus refused to follow the Ḥadīth regarding the option of cancellation (*khiyār al-majlis*) which provides that 'the parties to a sale are free to change their minds so long as they have not left the meeting of the contract'.

إذا تبايع الرجلان فكل واحـد منهما بالخيـار ما لم يتفرّقا

The reason being that this Ḥadīth is contrary to the practice of the people of Madinah.[131] The Madinese practice on this point subscribed to the view that a contract is complete when the parties express their agreement through a valid offer and acceptance. The contract is binding as of that moment regardless as to whether the 'meeting of contract' continues or not.

All the four Imāms of jurisprudence have considered *Āḥād* to be authoritative in principle, and none reject it unless there is evidence to suggest a weakness in its attribution to the Prophet, or which may contradict some other evidence that is more authoritative in their view.

The majority of ulema do not insist that the *Āḥād* should consist of a verbatim transmission of what the narrator heard in the first place, although this is the most authoritative form of transmission in any kind of Ḥadīth. They would instead accept the conceptual transmission of an *Āḥād*, on condition, however, that the narrator understands the language and purport of the Ḥadīth in full. Only then would the rendering of the Ḥadīth in the narrator's own words, which conveys an equivalent meaning, be acceptable. However if the narrator does not possess this degree of knowledge and is unable to transmit the Ḥadīth in its original form, all the four Sunnī schools are in agreement that his own rendering of the concept of the Ḥadīth is unacceptable.[132]

Some ulema of the Ḥanafī and other schools have held that conceptual transmission is totally forbidden, a view which is refuted by the majority, who say that the Companions often transmitted one and the same Ḥadīth in varying words, and no-one can deny this. One of the most prominent Companions, ᶜAbd Allāh b. Masᶜūd, is noted for having reported many *aḥādīth* from the Prophet and made it known that 'the Prophet (ﷺ) said this, or something like this, or something very close to this'. No one has challenged the validity of this manner of reporting; hence the permissibility of conceptual transmission is confirmed by the practice of the Companions, and their consensus is quoted in its support. Having said this, however, accuracy in the transmission of Ḥadīth and retaining its original version is highly recommended.[133] This is, in fact, the purport of a Ḥadīth from the Prophet which reads: 'May God bless with success one who heard me saying something, and who conveys it to others as he heard it; and may the next transmitter be even more retentive than the one from whom he received it.'[134]

نضّر الله امرأ سمع منّا شيئاً فبلغه كما سمعه ،
فربّ مبلّغ أوعى له من سامع

Sometimes the transmitter reports a Ḥadīth but omits a part of it. The question then arises as to whether this form of transmission is permissible at all. In principle, the narrator of Ḥadīth, of any type of Ḥadīth, must not omit any part which is integral to its meaning. For instance: when the omitted part consists of a condition, or an exception to the main theme of the Ḥadīth, or which makes a reference to the scope of its application. However, the narrator may omit a part of the Ḥadīth which does not affect the meaning of the remaining part. For in this case, the Ḥadīth at issue will be regarded, for all intents and purposes, as two *aḥādīth*. It has been a familiar practice among the ulema to omit a part of the Ḥadīth which does not have a bearing on its main theme. But if the omission is such that it would bring the quoted part into conflict with its full version, then the issue will be determined, not under the foregoing, but under the rules of conflict and preference (*al-taʿāruḍ wa'l-tarjīḥ*). In any case, the preferred practice is not to omit any part of the Ḥadīth, as the omitted part may well contain valuable information on some point and serve a purpose that may not have occurred to the narrator himself.[135]

In certain *aḥādīth* which are reported by a number of transmitters, there is sometimes an addition to the text of a Ḥadīth by one transmitter which is absent in the reports of the same Ḥadīth by others. The first point to ascertain in a discrepancy of this nature is to find out whether the Ḥadīth in question was originally uttered in one and the same meeting/occasion or on different occasions. If the latter is the case, then there is no conflict and both versions may be accepted as they are. But if it is established that the different versions all originated in one and the same meeting, then normally the version which is transmitted by more narrators will prevail over that which is variantly transmitted by one, provided that the former are not known for errors and oversight in reporting. Consequently, the additional part of the Ḥadīth which is reported by a single transmitter will be isolated and rejected for the simple reason that error by one person is more likely in this case than by a multitude. But if the single narrator who has reported the addition is an eminently reliable person and the rest are known for careless reporting, then his version will be preferred, although some ulema of Ḥadīth do not agree with this. Additions and discrepancies that might be observed in the *isnād*, such as when a group of narrators report a Ḥadīth as a *Mursal* whereas one person has reported it as a *Musnad* (that is, a *Muttaṣil*, or continous) – will be determined by the same method which applies to discrepancy in the text. However, sometimes the preference of one over the other version may be determined on different grounds. To give an example, according to one Ḥadīth, 'Whoever buys foodstuff is not to sell the same before it is delivered to him.'

من ابتاع طعاماً فلا يبعه حتى يستوفيه

However, according to another report the Prophet has issued a more general instruction according to which the Muslims are forbidden from selling that which they do not have in their possession.

لا تبع ما ليس عندك

The Ḥanafīs have preferred the second version, as it is conveyed in broader terms which comprise foodstuffs as well as other commodities.[136]

II. The Discontinued Ḥadīth (*al-Ḥadīth Ghayr al-Muttaṣil*)

This is a Ḥadīth whose chain of transmitters does not extend all the way back to the Prophet. It occurs in three varieties: *Mursal, Muᶜḍal* and *Munqaṭiᶜ*. The *Mursal*, which is the main variety of discontinued Ḥadīth, is sometimes also referred to as *Munqaṭiᶜ*. The *Mursal* is defined as a Ḥadīth which a Successor (*tābiᶜī*) has directly attributed to the Prophet without mentioning the last link, namely the Companion who might have narrated it from the Prophet. This is the majority definition. The Ḥanafīs, however, have defined *Mursal* as a Ḥadīth that a reliable narrator has attributed to the Prophet while omitting a part of its *isnād*. The missing link may be a Companion or even a Successor, according to the majority, but it may be a narrator among the second generation of Successors according to the Ḥanafīs. Since the identity of the missing link is not known, it is possible that he might have been an upright person, or not. Because of these and other similar doubts in its transmission, in principle, the ulema of Ḥadīth do not accept the *Mursal*.[137] According to al-Shawkānī, 'The majority of ulema of *uṣūl* have defined *Mursal* as a Ḥadīth transmitted by one who has not met with the Prophet, (ﷺ) and yet quotes the Prophet, (ﷺ) directly. The transmitter may be a Successor or a follower (*tābiᶜ al-tābiᶜī*) or anyone after that.' Imām Aḥmad b. Ḥanbal does not rely on it, nor does Imām Shāfiᶜī unless it is reported by a famous Successor who is known to have met with a number of Companions. Thus a *Mursal* transmitted by prominent Successors such as Saᶜīd b. al-Musayyib, al-Zuhrī, ᶜAlqamah, Masrūq, al-Shaᶜbī, Ḥasan al-Baṣrī, Qatādah, etc., is accepted, provided that it fulfills the following conditions.[138]

Firstly, that the *Mursal* is supported by another and more reliable Ḥadīth with a continuous chain of transmitters, in which case it is the latter that would represent the stronger evidence.

Secondly, that one *Mursal* is supported by another *Mursal*, and the latter is accepted and relied upon by the ulema.

Thirdly, that the *Mursal* is in harmony with the precedent of the Companions, in which case it is elevated and attributed to the Prophet. The process here is called *rafᶜ*, and the Ḥadīth is called *Marfūᶜ*.

Fourthly, that the *Mursal* has been approved by the ulema, and a number of them are known to have relied on it.

Fifthly, that the transmitter of *Mursal* has a reputation not to have reported weak and doubtful Ḥadīth. For instance the *Mursal* transmitted by Saᶜīd b. al-Musayyib or any one of the prominent Successors mentioned above is normally acceptable.[139]

When a *Mursal* is strengthened in any of these ways, especially when the Successor who has reported it is a leading figure and has met with the Companions, Imām Shāfiʿī would accept it. But even so, if the *Mursal* in question is contradicted by another Ḥadīth which is more reliable, the latter will take priority.

The foregoing basically explains al-Shāfiʿī's approach to the *Mursal*. Imām Abū Ḥanīfah and Imām Mālik, on the other hand, are less stringent in their acceptance of the *Mursal*. They accept not only the *Mursal* which is transmitted by a Successor, but also one which is transmitted by the second generation of Followers, known as *tābiʿ al-tābiʿī*. In support of this they quote the Ḥadīth in which the Prophet is reported to have said, 'Honour my Companions, for they are the best among you, then those who follow them and then the next generation; and then lying will proliferate.'[140]

اكــرمـوا أصحــابي فانهم خياركم ، ثـم الـذين
يلونهم ، ثم الذين يلونهم ، ثم يظهر الكذب

However, both Imāms Abū Ḥanīfah and Mālik add the proviso that the narrator of a *Mursal* must be a leading transmitter of Ḥadīth, failing which his report will be unacceptable. They rely on it only when they are assured of the trustworthiness of the narrator. They have held the view that when an upright and learned man is convinced about the truth and reliability of a report, he tends to link it directly to the Prophet, saying that the Prophet said such-and-such, but when he is not so convinced, he refers to the person from whom he received it. Examples of such *Mursals* are those that are transmitted by Muḥammad b. Ḥasan al-Shaybānī who is a *tābiʿ al-tābiʿī* but considered to be reliable. The majority of ulema are of the view that acting upon a *Mursal* Ḥadīth is not obligatory.[141]

The differential approaches that the leading Imāms have taken toward the reliability of the *Mursal* may be partially explained by the fact that Shāfiʿī and Aḥmad b. Ḥanbal lived at a time when the distance to the Prophet was further extended. Hence they felt the need of continuity in transmission more strongly than their predecessors, Abū Ḥanīfah and Mālik.

The remaining two varieties of disconnected Ḥadīth that need only briefly to be mentioned are the *Munqaṭiʿ* and the *Muʿḍal*. The former refers to a Ḥadīth whose chain of narrators has a single missing link somewhere in the middle. The *Muʿḍal* on the other hand is a Ḥadīth in which two consecutive links are missing in the chain of its narrators. Neither of them are acceptable; and the ulema are in agreement on this.[142]

Ṣaḥīḥ, *Ḥasan* and *Ḍaʿīf*

From the viewpoint of their reliability, the narrators of Ḥadīth have been graded into the following categories: (1) the Companions who are generally accepted to be reliable; (2) *thiqāt thābitūn*, or those who rank highest in respect of reliability next to the Companions; (3) *thiqāt*, or trustworthy but of a lesser degree than the first two; (4) *ṣadūq*, or truthful, that is one who is not known to have committed a forgery or serious errors; (5) *ṣadūq yahīm*, that is truthful but committing errors; (6) *maqbūl* or accepted, which implies that there is no proof to the effect that his report is unreliable; (7) *majhūl*, or a narrator of unknown identity. These are followed by lower classes of persons who are classified as sinners (*fussāq*), those suspected of lying, and outright liars.[143]

Ḥadīth is classified as *Ṣaḥīḥ* or authentic when its narrators belong to the first three categories.[144] It is defined as a Ḥadīth with a continuous *isnād* all the way back to the Prophet consisting of upright persons who also possess retentive memories and whose narration is free both of obvious and of subtle defects.[145]

The *Ḥasan* Ḥadīth differs from the *Ṣaḥīḥ* in that it may include among its narrators a person or persons who belong to the fourth, fifth or sixth grades on the foregoing scale. It is a Ḥadīth that falls between *Ṣaḥīḥ* and *Ḍaʿīf*, and although its narrators are known for truthfulness, they have not attained the highest degree of reliability and prominence.[146]

The weak, or *Ḍaʿīf*, is a Ḥadīth whose narrators do not possess the qualifications required in *Ṣaḥīḥ* or *Ḥasan*. It is called weak owing to a weakness that exists in its chain of narrators or in its textual contents. Its narrator is known to have had a bad memory, or his integrity and piety has been subjected to serious doubt.[147] There are several varieties of *Ḍaʿīf; Mursal* is one of them. The ulema of Ḥadīth, including Imām Muslim, do not consider *Mursal* to amount to a *sharʿī* proof (*ḥujjah*). There are other categories of *Ḍaʿīf*, including *Shādhdh, Munkar* and *Muḍṭarib* which need not be elaborated here. Briefly, *Shādhdh* is a Ḥadīth with a poor *isnād* which is at odds with a more reliable Ḥadīth. *Munkar* is a Ḥadīth whose narrator cannot be classified to be upright and retentive of memory; and *Muḍṭarib* is a Ḥadīth whose contents are inconsistent with a number of other reports, none of which can be preferred over the others.[148]

According to the general rule, the overall acceptability of a Ḥadīth is determined on the weakest element in its proof. Thus the presence of a single weak narrator in the chain of *isnād* would result in weakening the Ḥadīth altogether. If one of the narrators is suspected of lying whereas all the rest are classified as trustworthy (*thiqāt*) and the Ḥadīth is not known through other channels, then it will be graded as weak. In scrutinising the reliability of Ḥadīth, the ulema of Ḥadīth are guided by the rule that every Ḥadīth must be traced back to the Prophet through a continuous chain of narrators whose piety and reputation are beyond reproach. A Ḥadīth which does not fulfil these requirements is not accepted. A weak or *Ḍaʿīf* Ḥadīth does not constitute a *sharʿī* proof (*ḥujjah*) and is generally rejected.

NOTES

1. Thus we read in a Ḥadīth, 'Whoever sets a good example – *man sanna sunnatan ḥasanatan* – he and all those who act upon it shall be rewarded till the day of resurrection; and whoever sets a bad example – *man sanna sunnatan sayyi'atan* – he and all those who follow it will carry the burden of its blame till the day of resurrection.' For details see Isnawī, *Nihāyah*, II, 170; Shawkānī, *Irshād*, p. 33.
2. For details see Guraya, *Origins*, p. 8ff; Ahmad Hasan, *Early Development*, p. 85.
3. Sibāʿī, *Al-Sunnah*, p. 47; Azami, *Studies*, p. 3.
4. The *āyah* in question addresses the believers in the following terms: 'Certainly you have, in the Messenger of God, an excellent example' (al-Aḥzāb, 33 : 21).
5. Shāfiʿī, *Risālah*, pp. 44–45; Sibāʿī, *Al-Sunnah*, p. 50.
6. Abū Dāwud, *Sunan* (Hasan's trans.), III, 1019, Ḥadīth no. 3585.
7. Shāṭibī, *Muwāfaqāt*, III, 197; Ibn Qayyim, *Iʿlām*, 1, 222.
8. For details see Guraya, *Origins*, p. 5.
9. Cf. Azami, *Studies*, p. 4.
10. Abū Dāwud, *Sunan*, III, 1294, Ḥadīth no. 4590; Shawkānī, *Irshād*, p. 33.
11. Isnāwī, *Nihāyah*, II, 170; Shawkānī, *Irshād*, p. 33; Hitu, *Wajīz*, p. 264.
12. Cf. Azami, *Studies*, pp. 1–3.
13. Cf. Ahmad Hasan, *Early Development*, p. 48; Shabir, *Authority of Ḥadīth*, pp. 2–3.
14. Cf. Azami, *Studies, p. 3*.
15. Shāfiʿī, *Risālah*, pp. 128–130.
16. Ibid., p. 177; Guraya, *Origins*, p.29; Ahmad Hasan, *Early Development*, pp. 49–51.
17. Guraya, *Origins*, pp. 29–34.
18. Shawkānī, *Irshād*, p. 33.
19. Khallāf, *ʿIlm*, p. 37.
20. Ghazālī, *Mustaṣfā*, I, 83.
21. Khallāf, *ʿIlm*, p. 37.
22. Shāṭibī, *Muwāfaqāt*, IV, 7.
23. Shawkānī, *Irshād*, p. 36; Khallāf, *ʿIlm*, p. 38; Badrān, *Uṣūl* p. 81.
24. Abū Dāwud, *Sunan*, II, 406, Ḥadīth no. 1562; Āmidī, *Iḥkām*, III, 170.
25. Khallāf, *ʿIlm*, p. 36; Abū Zahrah, *Uṣūl*, p. 89.
26. Tabrīzī, *Mishkāt*, I, 166, Ḥadīth no. 533; Shawkānī, *Irshād*, p. 41; Khallāf, *ʿIlm*, p. 36.
27. Abū Dāwud, *Sunan*, I, 88, Ḥadīth no. 334; Badrān, *Uṣūl*, pp. 69–70.
28. Shawkānī, *Irshād*, p. 61; Badrān, *Bayān*, p. 74.
29. Shaltūt, *Al-Islām*, p. 512; Khallāf, *ʿIlm*, p. 43.

30. Isnawī, *Nihāyah*, II, 171; Hitu, *Wajīz*, p. 272. As for the report that the prominent Companion, ʿAbd Allāh b. ʿUmar used to imitate the Prophet in his natural activities too, it is held that he did so, not because it was recommended (*mandūb*), but because of his devotion and affection for the Prophet.

31. Shaltūt, *Al-Islām*, p. 512; Khallāf, *ʿIlm*, p. 43.

32. In particular note sūras al-Nisā' (4 : 3), al-Baqarah (2 : 282) and al-Ṭalāq (65 : 2).

33. Hitu, *Wajīz*, p. 273; Khallāf, *ʿIlm*, p. 44.

34. Shawkānī, *Irshād*, p. 35ff; Abū Zahrah, *Uṣūl*, p. 90; Hitu, *Wajīz*, p. 273.

35. Shaltūt, *Al-Islām*, p. 513.

36. Hitu, *Wajīz*, p. 274; Badrān, *Bayān*, p. 41.

37. Hitu, p. 275.

38. Ibid., p. 276.

39. Shaltūt, *Al-Islām*, p. 513.

40. Abū Dāwud, *Sunan*, II, 758, Ḥadīth no. 2715; Ibn Qayyim, *Iʿlām*, II, 223.

41. Shaltūt, *Al-Islām*, p. 515.

42. Ibid., 516.

43. Shawkānī, *Irshād*, p. 36; Khallāf, *ʿIlm*, p. 44.

44. Shaltūt, *Al-Islām*, p. 514.

45. Ghazālī, *Mustaṣfā*, II, 51; Badrān, *Bayān*, pp. 41–42; Mutawallī, *Mabādi'*, p. 38.

46. Abū Dāwud, *Sunan* (Hasan's trans.), II, 873, Ḥadīth no. 3067; Tabrīzī, *Mishkāt*, II, 889, Ḥadīth no. 2945.

47. Abū Dāwud, footnote 2534 at p. 873; Al-Marghinānī, *Hedaya* (Hamilton's trans.), p. 610.

48. Tabrīzī, *Mishkāt*, II, 1000, Ḥadīth no. 3342.

49. Shaltūt, *Al-Islām*, p. 515.

50. Al-Khaṭīb, *Mughnī al-Muḥtāj*, III, 442; Dīn, *Al-Nafaqah*, pp. 20–23.

51. Shaltūt, *Al-Islām*, p. 516.

52. The Prophet had initially ordered his Companions not to write anything other than the Qur'ān from him. This was, however, later amended and the Prophet permitted the writing of his *Sunnah*. Badrān (*Uṣūl*, pp. 83–84) refers to at least two instances where the Prophet allowed his instructions to be reduced into writing.

53. Shaltūt, *Al-Islām*, p. 511.

54. Ibid., p. 512.

55. Cf. Shāṭibī, *Muwāfaqāt*, IV, 3; Badrān, *Uṣūl*, p. 101.

56. Shāṭibī, IV, 4; Sibāʿī, *Sunnah*, p. 377; Badrān, *Uṣūl*, p. 82. Shāṭibī adds that two other prominent Companions, ʿAbd Allāh b. Masʿūd, and ʿAbd Allāh b. ʿAbbās are on record as having confirmed the priority of the Qur'ān over the *Sunnah*.

57. Shāṭibī, IV, 4.

58. Cf. Badrān, *Uṣūl*, p. 102.

59. While quoting Awzāʿī on this point, Shawkānī (*Irshād*, p. 33) concurs with the view that the *Sunnah* is an independent source of *Sharīʿah*, and not necessarily, as it were, a commentary on the Qur'ān only. See also Shāṭibī, *Muwāfaqāt*, IV, 4.

60. See Shaṭibī, *Muwāfaqāt*, IV, 5.

61. Ibid., see also Sibāʿī, *Al-Sunnah*, pp. 378–79.

62. Shaṭibī, *Muwafaqāt*, IV, 5.

63. Ibid., IV, 6.

64. Sibāʿī, *Al-Sunnah*, p. 379; Khallāf, *ʿIlm*, p. 39; Badrān, *Uṣūl*, p. 102.

65. Bayhaqī, *Al-Sunan al-Kubrā*, III, 10.

66. Ibn Qayyim, *Iʿlām*, II, 238; Sibāʿī, *Al-Sunnah*, p. 380; Badrān, *Uṣūl*, pp. 103–105.

67. Badrān, *Bayān*, p. 6.

68. Ibid., p. 7.
69. Ibn Qayyim, *Iʿlām*, II, 233; Khallāf, *ʿIlm*, p. 40; Sibāʿī, *Al-Sunnah*, p. 380.
70. Cf. Shawkānī, *Irshād*, p. 33; Sibāʿī, *Al-Sunnah*, p. 380.
71. Shāṭibī, *Muwāfaqāt*, IV, 7.
72. Ibid., IV, 8; Sibāʿī, *Al-Sunnah*, p. 383.
73. Cf. Abū Zahrah, *Uṣūl*, p. 82.
74. Shāfiʿī, *Risālah*, pp. 52–53.
75. Ibid.
76. Cf. Sibāʿī, *Al-Sunnah*, p. 388.
77. Qurṭubī, *Tafsīr*, XVIII, 227.
78. For further discussion see Chapter xiii on *maṣlaḥah mursalah*.
79. Cf. Sibāʿī, *Al-Sunnah*, p. 388–90.
80. Ibid.
81. Ibid., p. 385.
82. Cf. Shabir, *Authority of Ḥadīth*, p. 50.
83. Sibāʿī, *Al-Sunnah*, p. 75; Shabir, *Authority of Ḥadīth*, p. 51.
84. Azami, *Studies*, pp. 68–70; Hitu, *Wajīz*, p. 292.
85. For details see Sibāʿī, *Al-Sunnah*, pp. 76–80; Azami, *Studies*, pp.68–73.
86. Sibāʿī, p. 81.
87. Ibid., p. 82.
88. Ibid., pp. 84–85; Azami, *Studies*, p. 68; Hitu, *Wajīz*, p. 290.
89. For these and more examples see Sibāʿī, *Al-Sunnah*, p. 85ff.
90. Note e.g. Jalāl al-Dīn al-Suyūṭī's (d. 911 A.H.) *Al-La'ālī al-Maṣnūʿah fī al-Aḥādīth al-Mawḍūʿah*; Shaykh ʿAlī al-Qārī al-Ḥanafī (d. 1014), *Al-Mawḍūʿāt al-Kabīr*, and Yaḥyā b. ʿAlī al-Shawkānī (d. 1250), *Al-Fawā'id al-Majmūʿah fi'l-Aḥādīth al-Mawḍūʿah*.
91. Sibāʿī, *Al-Sunnah*, pp. 86–87; Azami, *Studies*, p. 69; Hitu, *Wajīz*, p. 291.
92. Ibid.
93. See for details Sibāʿī, *Al-Sunnah*, p. 88; Hitu, *Wajīz*, p. 291.
94. Shawkānī, *Irshād*, p. 46; Abū Zahrah, *Uṣūl*, p. 84; Mahmassani, *Falsafah* (Ziadeh's trans.), p. 74.
95. Khuḍarī, *Uṣūl*, p. 214; Aghnides, *Muhammedan Theories*, p. 40.
96. Shawkānī, *Irshād*, p. 47; Hitu, *Wajīz*, p. 294.
97. Ghazālī, *Mustaṣfā*, I, 88; Shawkānī, *Irshād*, p. 47; Hitu, *Wajīz*, p. 295.
98. Ghazālī (*Mustaṣfā*), I, 87–88) illustrates this as follows: supposing that five or six persons report the death of another, this does not amount to certainty, but when this is confirmed by seeing the father of the deceased coming out of the house while obviously grief-stricken and exhibiting signs of disturbance that are unusual for a man of his stature, then the two combined amount to positive knowledge.
99. Ghazālī, *Mustaṣfā*, I, 86; Khuḍarī, *Uṣūl*, p. 214.
100. Shawkānī, *Irshād*, p. 48; Hitu, *Wajīz*, p. 295.
101. Ghazālī, *Mustaṣfā*, I, 86; Shawkānī, *Irshād*, p. 48.
102. Isnāwī, *Nihāyah*, II, 185; Abū Zahrah *Uṣūl*, p. 84; Khallāf, *ʿIlm*, p. 41.
103. Abū Dāwud, *Sunan* (Hasan's trans.), III, 1036, Ḥadīth no. 3643.
104. Badrān, *Uṣūl*, p. 78.
105. Abū Zahrah, *Uṣūl*, p. 84; Aghnides, *Muhammadan Theories*, p. 44. Shawkānī's (*Irshād*, p. 49) definition of *Mashhūr*, however, includes *aḥādīth* which became well-known as late as the second or even the third century Hijrah.
106. Abū Zahrah, *Uṣūl*, p. 84; Badrān, *Uṣūl*, p. 85.
107. Khallāf, *ʿIlm*, p. 41.
108. Dārimī, *Sunan*, Kitāb al-farā'iḍ, II, 384; Ibn Mājah, *Sunan*, II, 913, Ḥadīth no. 2735; Muslim, *Ṣaḥīḥ*, p. 212; Ḥadīth no. 817; Badrān, *Uṣūl*, p. 85.

109. Shāfiʿī, *Risālah*, p. 159ff; Abū Zahrah, *Uṣūl*, p.84; Mahmassani, *Falsafah*, p. 74.
110. Shawkānī, *Irshād*, pp. 48–49.
111. Āmidī, *Iḥkām*, I, 161; Mahmassani, *Falsafah*, p. 74.
112. Shawkānī, *Irshād*, p. 47; Abū Zahrah, *Uṣūl*, p. 85.
113. Abū Zahrah, *Uṣūl*, p. 85; Hitu, *Wajīz*, p. 305. As for the *Āḥād* pertaining to subsidiary matters which are not essential to dogma such as the torture of the grave (*ʿadhāb al-qabr*), intercession (*shafāʿah*), etc., these must be accepted and believed. Anyone who denies them is a sinner (*fāsiq*) but not a *kāfir*, as he denies something which is not decisively proven.
114. Badrān, *Uṣūl*, p. 91; Khuḍarī, *Uṣūl*, p. 227.
115. Khuḍarī, *Uṣūl*, p. 217.
116. Ibid., p. 216.
117. For details on the conditions of *Āḥād* see Shawkānī, *Irshād*, pp. 48–52; Hitu, *Wajīz*, p. 307ff; Abū Zahrah, *Uṣūl*, p. 86; Mahmassani *Falsafah*, p. 74.
118. Khuḍarī, *Uṣūl*, p. 217.
119. Shawkānī, *Irshād*, p. 67; Badrān, *Uṣūl*, p. 92.
120. Khuḍarī, *Uṣūl*, p. 217.
121. Shawkānī, *Irshād*, p. 52; Abū Zahrah, *Uṣūl*, p. 86; Badrān, *Uṣūl*, p. 93; Khuḍarī, *Uṣūl*, p. 218.
122. Shawkānī, *Irshād*, p. 55.
123. Khuḍarī, *Uṣūl*, pp. 218–219.
124. Abū Zahrah, *Uṣūl*, p. 85.
125. Muslim, *Ṣaḥīḥ Muslim*, p. 41, Ḥadīth no. 119.
126. Abū Zahrah, *Uṣūl*, p. 85.
127. Tabrīzī, *Mishkāt*, I, 104, Ḥadīth no. 319.
128. Hitu, *Wajīz*, p. 302; Badrān, *Uṣūl*, p. 95.
129. Muslim, *Ṣaḥīḥ Muslim*, p. 248, Ḥadīth no. 928.
130. Hitu, *Wajīz*, p. 304; Badrān, *Uṣūl*, pp. 97–98.
131. Shāfiʿī, *Risālah*, p. 140; Muslim, *Ṣaḥīh Muslim*, p. 251, Ḥadīth no. 944; Abū Zahrah, *Uṣūl*, p. 85.
132. Hitu, *Wajīz*, pp. 317ff; Badrān, *Uṣūl*, pp. 93–94.
133. Khuḍarī, *Uṣūl*, p. 229.
134. Tabrīzī, *Mishkāt*, I, 78, Ḥadīth no. 230; Khuḍarī, *Uṣūl*, p. 229.
135. Khuḍarī, *Uṣūl*, p. 227; Hitu, *Wajīz*, pp. 319–320.
136. Tabrīzī, *Mishkāt*, II, 863, Ḥadīth no. 2844; Ibn Mājah, *Sunan*, II, 737, Ḥadīth no. 2187; Khuḍarī, *Uṣūl*, p. 233; Hitu, *Wajīz* pp. 318–319.
137. Hitu, *Wajīz*, p. 316; Khuḍarī, *Uṣūl*, p. 229; Abū Zahrah, *Uṣūl*, p. 86.
138. Shawkānī, *Irshād*, p. 64; Abū Zahrah, *Uṣūl*, p. 87.
139. Badrān, *Uṣūl*, p. 100; Khuḍarī, *Uṣūl*, p. 231; Khīn, *Athar*, p.399.
140. Shāfiʿī, *Risālah*, p. 904; Isnawī, *Nihāyah*, II, 223; Tabrīzī, *Mishkāt*, III, 1695, Ḥadīth no. 6003.
141. Ibid., p. 64; Abū Zahrah, *Uṣūl*, p. 87; Khīn, *Athar*, p. 401.
142. Azami, *Studies*, p. 43; Hitu, *Wajīz*, p. 316.
143. Ibid., p. 60.
144. Ibid., p. 62.
145. Shawkānī, *Irshād*; p. 64; Sibāʿī, *Al-Sunnah*, p. 94; Hitu, *Wajīz* p. 321.
146. Sibāʿī, *Al-Sunnah*, p. 95; Azami, *Studies*, p. 62.
147. Sibāʿī, *Sunnah*, loc. cit.
148. Ibid., p. 96.

CHAPTER FOUR

Rules of Interpretation I: Deducing the Law from its Sources

Introductory Remarks

To interpret the Qur'ān or the *Sunnah* with a view to deducing legal rules from the indications that they provide, it is necessary that the language of the Qur'ān and the *Sunnah* be clearly understood. To be able to utilise these sources, the *mujtahid* must obtain a firm grasp of the words of the text and their precise implications. For this purpose, the ulema of *uṣūl* include the classification of words and their usages in the methodology of *uṣūl al-fiqh*. The rules which govern the origin of words, their usages and classification are primarily determined on linguistic grounds and, as such, they are not an integral part of the law or religion. But they are instrumental as an aid to the correct understanding of the *Sharīʿah*.

Normally the *mujtahid* will not resort to interpretation when the text itself is self-evident and clear. But by far the greater part of *fiqh* consists of rules which are derived through interpretation and *ijtihād*. As will be discussed later, *ijtihād* can take a variety of forms, and interpretation which aims at the correct understanding of the words and sentences of a legal text is of crucial significance to all forms of *ijtihād*.

The function of interpretion is to discover the intention of the Lawgiver – or of any person for that matter – from his speech and actions. Interpretation is primarily concerned with the discovery of that which is not self-evident. Thus the object of interpretation in Islamic Law, as in any other law, is to ascertain the intention of the Lawgiver with regard to what has been left unexpressed as a matter of necessary inference from the surrounding circumstances.[1]

From the viewpoints of their clarity, scope, and capacity to convey a certain meaning, words have been classified into various types. With reference to their conceptual clarity, the ulema of *uṣūl* have classified words into the two main categories of 'clear' and 'unclear' words. The main purpose of this division is to identify the extent to which the meaning of a word is made clear or left ambiguous and doubtful. The significance of this classification can be readily observed in the linguistic forms and implications of commands and prohibitions. The task of evaluating the precise purport of a command is greatly facilitated if one is able to ascertain the degree of clarity (or of ambiguity) in which it is conveyed. Thus the manifest (*Ẓāhir*) and explicit (*Naṣṣ*) are 'clear' words, and yet the jurist may abandon their primary meaning in favour of a different meaning as the context and circumstances may require. Words are also classified, from the viewpoint of their scope, into homonym, general, specific, absolute and qualified. This classification basically explains the grammatical application of words to concepts: whether a word imparts one or more than one meaning, whether a word is of a specific or general import, and whether the absolute application of a word to its subject matter can be qualified and limited in scope.

From the viewpoint of their actual use, such as whether a word is used in its primary, secondary, literal, technical or customary sense, words are once again divided into the two main categories of literal (*Ḥaqīqī*) and metaphorical (*Majāzī*). The methodology of *uṣūl al-fiqh* tells us, for example, that commands and prohibitions may not be issued in metaphorical terms as this would introduce uncertainty in their application. And yet there are exceptions to this, such as when the metaphorical becomes the dominant meaning of a word to the point that the literal or original meaning is no longer in use.

The strength of a legal rule is to a large extent determined by the language in which it is communicated. To distinguish the clear from the ambiguous and to determine the degrees of clarity/ambiguity in words also helps the jurist in his efforts at resolving instances of conflict in the law. When the *mujtahid* is engaged in the deduction of rules from indications which often amount to no more than probabilities, some of his conclusions may turn out to be at odds with others. *Ijtihād* is therefore not only in need of comprehending the language of the law, but also needs a methodology and guidelines with which to resolve instances of conflict in its conclusions.

We shall be taking up each of these topics in the following pages, but it will be useful to start this section with a discussion of *ta'wīl*.

Ta'wīl (Allegorical Interpretation)

It should be noted at the outset that in Arabic there are two common words for 'interpretation', namely *tafsīr* and *ta'wīl*. The latter is perhaps closer to 'interpretation', whereas *tafsīr* literally means 'explanation'. The English equivalents of these terms do not convey the same difference between them which is indicated in their Arabic usage. 'Allegorical interpretation' is an acceptable equivalent of *ta'wīl*, but I prefer the original Arabic to its English equivalent. I propose therefore to explain the difference between *tafsīr* and *ta'wīl* and then to use '*ta'wīl*' as it is.

Tafsīr basically aims at explaining the meaning of a given text and deducing a *ḥukm* from it within the confines of its words and sentences.[2] The explanation so provided is, in other words, borne out by the content and linguistic composition of the text.

Ta'wīl, on the other hand, goes beyond the literal meaning of words and sentences and reads into them a hidden meaning which is often based on speculative reasoning and *ijtihād*. The norm in regard to words is that they impart their obvious meaning. *Ta'wīl* is a departure from this norm, and is presumed to be absent unless there is reason to justify its application.[3] *Ta'wīl* may operate in various capacities, such as specifying the general, or qualifying the absolute terms of a given text. All words are presumed to convey their absolute, general, and unqualified meanings unless there is reason to warrant a departure to an alternative meaning.

From a juridical perspective, *ta'wīl* and *tafsīr* share the same basic purpose, which is to clarify the law and to discover the intention of the Lawgiver in the light of the indications, some of which may be definite and others more remote. Both are primarily concerned with speech that is not self-evident and requires clarification. Sometimes the Lawgiver or the proper legislative authority provides the necessary explanation to a legal text. This variety of explanation, known as *tafsīr tashrīʿī*, is an integral part of the law. To this may be added *tafsīr* which is based on definitive indications in the text and constitutes a necessary and logical part of it. Beyond this, all other explanations, whether in the form of *tafsīr* or of *ta'wīl*, partake in the nature of opinion and *ijtihād* and as such do not constitute an integral part of the law. The distinction between *tafsīr* and *ta'wīl* is not always clear-cut and obvious. An explanation or commentary on a legal text may partake in both, and the two may converge at certain points. It is nevertheless useful to be aware of the basic distinction between *tafsīr* and *ta'wīl*. We should also bear in mind that in the context of *uṣūl al-fiqh*, especially in our discussion of the rules of interpretation, it is *ta'wīl* rather than *tafsīr* with which we are primarily concerned.

The ulema of *uṣūl* have defined *ta'wīl* as departure from the manifest

(*Ẓāhir*) meaning of a text in favour of another meaning where there is evidence to justify the departure.[4] *Ta'wīl* which is attempted in accordance with the conditions that ensure its propriety is generally accepted, and the ulema of all ages, including the Companions, have applied it in their efforts at deducing legal rules from the Qur'ān and *Sunnah*. *Ta'wīl* which is properly constructed constitutes a valid basis for judicial decisions. But to ensure the propriety of *ta'wīl*, it must fulfil certain conditions, which are as follows: (1) That there is some evidence to warrant the application of *ta'wīl*, and that it is not founded on mere inclination or personal opinion. (2) That the word or words of a given text are amenable to *ta'wīl*. In this way only certain types of words, including for example the manifest (*Ẓāhir*) and explicit (*Naṣṣ*), are open to *ta'wīl*, but not the unequivocal (*Mufassar*) and the perspicuous (*Muḥkam*). Similarly, the general (*ʿĀmm*) and the absolute (*Muṭlaq*) are susceptible to *ta'wīl* but not the specific (*Khāṣṣ*) and the qualified (*Muqayyad*), although there are cases where these too have been subjected to *ta'wīl*. (3) That the word which is given an allegorical interpretation has a propensity, even if only a weak one, in favour of that interpretation. This condition would preclude a far-fetched interpretation that goes beyond the capacity of the words of a given text. (4) That the person who attempts *ta'wīl* is qualified to do so and that his interpretation is in harmony with the rules of the language and customary or juridical usage. Thus it would be unacceptable if the word *qur'* in the Qur'ānic text (al-Baqarah, 2:228) were to be given a meaning other than the two meanings which it bears, namely menstruation (*ḥayḍ*) and the clean period between menstruations (*ṭuhr*). For *qur'* cannot carry an additional meaning, and any attempt to give it one would violate the rules of the language. But *ta'wīl* in the sense of a shift from the literal to the metaphorical and from the general to the specific is not a peculiarity of Arabic, in that words in any language are, in fact, amenable to these possibilities.[5]

There are two types of *ta'wīl*, namely *ta'wīl* which is remote and far-fetched, and 'relevant' *ta'wīl* which is within the scope of what might be thought of as correct understanding. An example of the first type is the Ḥanafī interpretation of a Ḥadīth which instructed a Companion, Fīrūz al-Daylamī, who professed Islam while he was married to two sisters, to 'retain [*amsik*] one of the two, whichever you wish, and separate from the other'.[6]

امسك ايّتهما شئت وفارق الأخرى

The Ḥanafīs have interpreted this Ḥadīth to the effect that al-Daylamī was asked to contract a new marriage with one of the sisters, if they happened to have been married in a single contract of marriage, but that if they had been married in two separate contracts, to retain the one whom he married first, without a contract. The Ḥanafīs have resorted to this *ta'wīl* apparently because of the *Sharīʿah* rule which does not permit two women to be married in a single contract. If this were to be the case, then a new contract would be necessary with the one who is to be retained.

But this is regarded as a remote interpretation, one which is not supported by the wording of the Ḥadīth. Besides, al-Daylamī was a new con[illegible]t to Islam who could not be presumed to be knowledgeable of the rule [illegible] *Sharīʿah*. Had the Prophet intended the meaning that the Ḥanafīs have given to the Ḥadīth, the Prophet would have clarified it himself. As it is, the Ḥanafī interpretation cannot be sustained by the contents of the Ḥadīth, which is why it is regarded as far-fetched.[7]

Ta'wīl is relevant and correct if it can be accepted without recourse to forced and far-fetched arguments. The interpretation, for example, which the majority of ulema have given to the phrase '*idhā qumtum ila'l-ṣalāh*' ('when you stand for prayers') in the Qur'anic text concerning the requirement of ablution for *ṣalāh* (al-Mā'idah, 5:7) to mean 'when you intend to pray' is relevant and correct; for without it, there would be some irregularity in the understanding of the text. The passage under discussion reads, in the relevant part: 'O believers, when you stand for *ṣalāh*, wash your faces, and your hands up to the elbows . . .' 'When you stand for *ṣalāh*' here is understood to mean 'when you intend to perform *ṣalāh*'. The fact that ablution is required before entering the *ṣalāh* is the proper interpretation of the text, as the Lawgiver could not be said to have required the faithful to perform the ablution after having started the *ṣalāh*.[8]

To set a total ban on *ta'wīl*, and always to try to follow the literal meaning of the Qur'ān and *Sunnah*, which is what the Ẓāhirīs have tended to do, is likely to lead to a departure from the spirit of the law and its general purpose. It is, on the other hand, equally valid to say that interpretation must be attempted carefully and only when it is necessary and justified, for otherwise the law could be subjected to arbitrariness and abuse. A correct interpretation is one for which support could be found in the *nuṣūṣ*, in analogy (*qiyās*), or in the general principles of the law. Normally a correct interpretation does not conflict with the explicit injunction of the law, and its accuracy is borne out by the contents of the text itself.[9]

Classification I: Clear and Unclear Words

From the viewpoint of clarity (*wuḍūḥ*), words are divided into the two main categories of clear and unclear words. A clear word conveys a concept which is intelligible without recourse to interpretation. A ruling which is communicated in clear words constitutes the basis of obligation, without any recourse to *ta'wīl*. A word is unclear, on the other hand, when it lacks the foregoing qualities: the meaning which it conveys is ambiguous/incomplete, and requires clarification. An ambiguous text which is in need of clarification cannot constitute the basis of action. The clarification so required can only be supplied through extraneous evidence, for the text itself is deficient and fails to convey a complete meaning without recourse to evidence outside its contents. A clear text, on the other hand, is self-contained, and needs no recourse to extraneous evidence.

From the viewpoint of the degree of clarity and conceptual strength, clear words are divided into four types in a ranking which starts with the least clear, namely the manifest (*Ẓāhir*) and then the explicit (*Naṣṣ*), which commands greater clarity than the *Ẓāhir*. This is followed by the unequivocal (*Mufassar*) and finally the perspicuous (*Muḥkam*), which ranks highest in respect of clarity. And then from the viewpoint of the degree of ambiguity in their meaning, words are classified, once again, into four types which start with the least ambigious and end by the most ambiguous in the range. We shall begin with an exposition of the clear words.

I. 1 & 2 The *Ẓāhir* and the *Naṣṣ*

The manifest (*Ẓāhir*) is a word which has a clear meaning and yet is open to *ta'wīl*, primarily because the meaning that it conveys is not in harmony with the context in which it occurs. It is a word which has a literal/original meaning of its own but which leaves open the possibility of an alternative interpretation. For example, the word 'lion' in the sentence 'I saw a lion' is clear enough, but it is possible, although less likely, that the speaker might have meant a brave man. *Ẓāhir* has been defined as a word or words which convey a clear meaning, while this meaning is not the principal theme of the text in which they appear.[10]

When a word conveys a clear meaning that is also in harmony with the context in which it appears, and yet is still open to *ta'wīl*, it is classified as *Naṣṣ*. The distinction between the *Ẓāhir* and *Naṣṣ* mainly depends on their relationship with the context in which they occur. *Ẓāhir* and *Naṣṣ* both denote clear words, but the two differ in that the former does not constitute the dominant theme of the text whereas the *Naṣṣ* does. These may be illustrated in the Qur'ānic text concerning polygamy, as follows:

> And if you fear that you cannot treat the orphans justly, then marry the women who seem good to you, two, three or four (al-Nisā, 4:3).

Two points consitute the principal theme of this *āyah*, one of which is that polygamy is permissible, and the other that it must be limited to the maximum of four. We may therefore say that these are the explicit rulings (*Naṣṣ*) of this text. But this text also establishes the legality of marriage between men and women, especially in the part where it reads 'marry of the women who seem good to you'. However, legalising marriage is not the principal theme of this text, but only a subsidiary point. The main theme is the *Naṣṣ* and the incidental point is the *Ẓāhir*.[11]

The effect of the *Ẓāhir* and the *Naṣṣ* is that their obvious meanings must be followed and action upon them is obligatory unless there is evidence to warrant recourse to *ta'wīl*, that is, to a different interpretation which might be in greater harmony with the intention of the Lawgiver. For the basic rules of interpretation require that the obvious meaning of words should be accepted and followed unless there is a compelling reason for abandoning the obvious meaning. When we say that the *Ẓāhir* is open to *ta'wīl*, it means that when the *Ẓāhir* is general, it may be specified, and when it is absolute, it may be restricted and qualified. Similarly the literal meaning of the *Ẓāhir* may be abandoned in favour of a metaphorical meaning. And finally, the *Ẓāhir* is susceptible to abrogation which, in the case of the Qur'ān and *Sunnah*, could only occur during the lifetime of the Prophet. An example of the *Ẓāhir* which is initially conveyed in absolute terms but has subsequently been qualified is the Qur'ānic text (al-Nisā', 4:24) which spells out the prohibited degrees of relationship in marriage. The text then continues, 'and lawful to you are women other than these, provided you seek them by means of your wealth and marry them properly . . .' The passage preceding this *āyah* refers to a number of female relatives with whom marriage is forbidden, but there is no reference anywhere in this passage either to polygamy or to marriage with the paternal and maternal aunt of one's wife. The apparent or *Ẓāhir* meaning of this passage, especially in the part where it reads 'and lawful to you are women other than these' would seem to validate polygamy beyond the limit of four, and also marriage to the paternal and maternal aunt of one's wife. However, the absolute terms of this *āyah* have geen qualified by another ruling of the Qur'ān (al-Nisā', 4:3) quoted earlier which limits polygamy to four. The other qualification to the text under discussion is provided by the *Mashhūr* Ḥadīth which forbids simultaneous marriage with the maternal and paternal aunt of one's wife.[12] This illustration also serves to show an instance of conflict between the *Ẓāhir* and the *Naṣṣ*. Since the second of the two *āyāt* under discussion is a *Naṣṣ*, it is one degree stronger than the *Ẓāhir* and would therefore prevail. This question of conflicts between the *Ẓāhir* and *Naṣṣ* will be further discussed later.

It will be noted that *Naṣṣ*, in addition to the technical meaning which we shall presently elaborate, has a more general meaning which is commonly used by the *fuqahā'*. In the terminology of *fiqh*, *Naṣṣ* means a definitive text or ruling of the Qur'ān or the *Sunnah*. Thus it is said that this or that ruling is a *Naṣṣ*, which means that it is a definitive injunction of the Qur'ān or *Sunnah*. But *Naṣṣ* as opposed to *Ẓāhir* denotes a word or words that convey a clear meaning, and also represents the principal theme of the text in which it occurs. An example of *Naṣṣ* in the Qur'ān is the Qur'ānic text on the priority of debts and bequests over inheritance in the administration of an estate. The relevant *āyah* assigns specific shares to a number of heirs and then provides that the distribution of shares in all cases is to take place 'after the payment of legacies and debts' (al-Nisā', 4:11). Similarly, the Qur'ānic text which provides that 'unlawful to you are the dead carcass and blood' (al-Mā'idah, 5:3), is a *Naṣṣ* on the prohibition of these items for human consumption.[13] As already stated, the *Naṣṣ*, like the *Ẓāhir*, is open to *ta'wīl* and abrogation. For example, the absolute terms of the *āyah* which we just quoted on the prohibition of dead carcasses and blood have been qualified elsewhere in the Qur'ān where 'blood' has been qualified as 'blood shed forth' (al-Anᶜām, 6:145). Similarly, there is a Ḥadīth which permits consumption of two types of dead carcasses, namely fish and locust.[14] (See full version of this Ḥadīth on page 131.) Another example of the *Naṣṣ* which has been subjected to *ta'wīl* is the Ḥadīth concerning the legal alms (*zakāh*) of livestock, which simply provides that this shall be 'one in every forty sheep'.[15]

في أربعين شاة شاة

The obvious *Naṣṣ* of this Ḥadīth admittedly requires that the animal itself should be given in *zakāh*. But it would seem in harmony with the basic purpose of the law to say that either the sheep or their equivalent monetary value may be given. For the purpose of *zakāh* is to satisfy the needs of the poor, and this could equally be done by giving them the equivalent amount of money; it is even likely that they might prefer this.[16] The Ḥanafīs have offered a similar interpretation for two other Qur'ānic *āyāt*, one on the expiation of futile oaths,and the other on the expiation of deliberate breaking of the fast during Ramadan. The first is enacted at feeding ten poor persons (al-Mā'idah, 5:92), and the second at feeding sixty such persons (al-Mujādalah, 58:4). The Ḥanafīs have held that this text can be implemented either by feeding ten needy persons or by feeding one such person on ten occasions. Similarly, the provision in the second *āyah* may be understood, according to the Ḥanafīs, to mean feeding sixty poor persons, or one such person sixty times.[17]

As already stated, *Naṣṣ* is stronger than *Ẓāhir*, and should there be a conflict between them, the former prevails over the latter. This may be illustrated in the following two Qur'ānic passages, one of which is a *Naṣṣ* in regard to the prohibition of wine, and the other a *Ẓāhir* in regard to the permissibility of eating and drinking in general. The two passages are as follows:

> O believers! Intoxicants, games of chance and sacrificing to stones and arrows are the unclean works of Satan. So avoid them . . . (al-Mā'idah, 5:93).
>
> On those who believe and do good deeds, there is no blame for what they consume while they keep their duty and believe and do good deeds (al-Mā'idah, 5:96).

The *Naṣṣ* in the first *āyah* is the prohibition of wine, which is the main purpose and theme of the text. The *Ẓāhir* in the second *āyah* is the permissibility of eating and drinking without restriction. The main purpose of the second *āyah* is, however, to accentuate the virtue of piety (*taqwā*) in that *taqwā* is not a question of austerity with regard to food, it is rather a matter of God – consciousness and good deeds. There is an apparent conflict between the two *āyāt*, but since the prohibition of wine is established in the *Naṣṣ*, and the permissibility regarding food and drink is in the form of *Ẓāhir*, the *Naṣṣ* prevails over the *Ẓāhir*.[18]

To give an example of *Ẓāhir* in modern criminal law, we may refer to the word 'night' which occurs in many statutes in connection with theft. When theft is committed at night, it carries a heavier penalty. Now if one takes the manifest meaning of 'night', then it means the period between sunset and sunrise. However this meaning may not be totally harmonious with the purpose of the law. What is really meant by 'night' is the dark of the night, which is an accentuating circumstance in regard to theft. Here the meaning of the *Ẓāhir* is qualified with reference to the rational purpose of the law and the nature of the offence in question.[19]

I. 3 & 4 Unequivocal (*Mufassar*) and Perspicuous (*Muḥkam*)

Mufassar is a word or a text whose meaning is completely clear and is, in the meantime, in harmony with the context in which it appears. Because of this and the high level of clarity in the meaning of *Mufassar*, there is no need for recourse to *ta'wīl*. But the *Mufassar* may still be open to abrogation which might, in reference to the Qur'ān and *Sunnah*, have taken place during the lifetime of the Prophet. The idea of the *Mufassar*, as the word itself implies, is that the text explains itself. The Lawgiver has, in other words, explained His own intentions with complete clarity, and the occasion for *ta'wīl* does not arise. The *Mufassar* occurs in two varieties, one being the text which is self-explained, or *Mufassar bidhātih*, and the other is when the ambiguity in one text is clarified and explained by another. This is known as *Mufassar bighayrih*, in which case the two texts become an integral part of one another and the two combine to constitute a *Mufassar*.[20] An example of *Mufassar* in the Qur'ān is the text in sūra al-Tawbah (9:36) which addresses the believers to 'fight the pagans all together (*kāffah*) as they fight you all together'. The word '*kāffah*' which occurs twice in this text precludes the possibility of applying specification (*takhṣīṣ*) to the words preceding it, namely the pagans (*mushrikīn*). *Mufassar* occurs in many a modern statute with regard to specified crimes and their penalties, but also with regard to civil liabilities, the payment of damages, and debts. The words of the statute are often self-explained and definite so as to preclude *ta'wīl*. But the basic function of the explanation that the text itself provides is concerned with that part of the text which is ambivalent (*mujmal*) and needs to be clarified. When the necessary explanation is provided, the ambiguity is removed and the text becomes a *Mufassar*. An example of this is the phrase '*laylah al-qadr*' ('night of *qadr*') in the following Qur'ānic passage. The phrase is ambiguous to begin with, but is then explained:

> We sent it [the Qur'ān] down on the Night of Qadr. What will make you realise what the Night of Qadr is like? [. . .] It is the night in which angels and the spirit descend [. . .] (al-Qadr, 97:1–4).

The text thus explains the '*laylah al-qadr*' and as a result of the explanation so provided, the text becomes self-explained, or *Mufassar*. Hence there is no need for recourse to *ta'wīl*. Sometimes the ambiguous of the Qur'ān is clarified by the *Sunnah*, and when this is the case, the clarification given by the *Sunnah* becomes an integral part of the Qur'ān. There are numerous examples of this, such as the words *ṣalāh, zakāh, ḥajj, ribā*, which occur in the following *āyāt*:

> Perform the *ṣalāh* and pay the *zakāh* (al-Naḥl, 16:44).
> God has enacted upon people the pilgrimage of *ḥajj* to be performed by all who are capable of it (Āl-ʿImrān, 3:97).
> God permitted sale and prohibited usury (*ribā*) (al-Baqarah, 2:275).

The juridical meanings of *ṣalāh, zakāh, ḥajj* and *ribā* could not be known from the brief references that are made to them in these *āyāt*. Hence the

Prophet provided the necessary explanation in the form of both verbal and practical instructions. In this way the text which was initially ambivalent (*mujmal*) became *Mufassar*. With regard to *ṣalāh*, for example, the Prophet instructed his followers to 'perform the *ṣalāh* the way you see me performing it',

صلّوا كما رأيتموني أُصلّي

and regarding the *ḥajj* he ordered them to 'take from me the rituals of the *ḥajj*.'[21]

خذوا عني مناسككم

There are also many *aḥādīth* which explain the Qur'ānic prohibition of *ribā* in specific and elaborate detail.

The value (*ḥukm*) of the *Mufassar* is that acting upon it is obligatory. The clear meaning of a *Mufassar* is not open to interpretation and unless it has been abrogated, the obvious text must be followed. But since abrogation of the Qur'ān and *Sunnah* discontinued upon the demise of the Prophet, to all intents and purposes, the *Mufassar* is equivalent to the perspicuous (*Muḥkam*), which is the last in the range of clear words and is not open to any change.

Specific words (*al-alfāẓ al-khāṣṣah*) which are not open to *ta'wīl* or any change in their primary meanings are in the nature of *Mufassar*. Thus the Qur'ānic punishment of eighty lashes for slanderous accusation (*qadhf*) in sūra al-Nūr (24:4), or the *āyah* of inheritance (al-Nisā', 4:11) which prescribes specific shares for legal heirs, consist of fixed numbers which rule out the possibility of *ta'wīl*. They all partake in the qualities of *Mufassar*.[22]

Since *Mufassar* is one degree stronger than *Naṣṣ*, in the event of a conflict between them, the *Mufassar* prevails. This can be illustrated in the two ḥadīths concerning the ablution of a woman who experiences irregular menstruations that last longer than the expected three days or so: she is required to perform the *ṣalāh*; as for the ablution (*wuḍū'*) for *ṣalāh*, she is instructed, according to one Ḥadīth:

> A woman in prolonged menstruations must make a fresh *wuḍū'* for every *ṣalāh*:[23]

المستحاضة تتوضأ لكل صلاة

And according to another Ḥadīth

> A woman in prolonged menstruation must make a fresh *wuḍū'* at the time of every *ṣalāh*.[24]

المستحاضة تتوضأ وقت كل صلاة

The first Ḥadīth is a *Naṣṣ* on the requirement of a fresh *wuḍū'* for every *ṣalāh*, but the second Ḥadīth is a *Mufassar* which does not admit of any *ta'wīl*. The first Ḥadīth is not completely categorical as to whether 'every *ṣalāh*' applies to both obligatory and supererogatory (*farā'iḍ wa-nawāfil*) types of *ṣalāh*. Supposing that they are both performed at the same time, would a separate *wuḍū'* be required for each? But this ambiguity/question does not arise under the second Ḥadīth as the latter provides complete instruction: a *wuḍū'* is only required at the time of every *ṣalāh* and the same *wuḍū'* is sufficient for any number of *ṣalāhs* at that particular time.[25]

Words and sentences whose meaning is clear beyond doubt and are not open to *ta'wīl* and abrogation are called *Muḥkam*. An exanmple of this is the frequently occurring Qur'ānic statement that 'God knows all things'. This kind of statement cannot be abrogated, either in the lifetime of the Prophet, or after his demise.[26] The text may sometimes explain itself in terms that would preclude the possibility of abrogation. An example of this is the Qur'ānic address to the believers concerning the wives of the Prophet: 'It is not right for you to annoy the Messenger of God; nor should you ever marry his widows after him. For that is truly an enormity in God's sight' (al-Aḥzāb, 33:35). The prohibition here is emphasised by the word *abadan* (never, ever) which renders it *Muḥkam*, thereby precluding the possibility of abrogation. The *Muḥkam* is, in reality, nothing other than *Mufassar* with one difference, namely that *Muḥkam* is not open to abrogation. An example of *Muḥkam* in the *Sunnah* is the ruling concerning *jihād* which provides that '*jihād* (holy struggle) remains valid till the day of resurrection'.[27]

الجهاد ماضٍ إلى يوم القيامة

The ulema of *uṣūl* have given the Qur'ānic *āyah* on slanderous accusation as another example of *Muḥkam*, despite some differences of interpretation that have arisen over it among the Ḥanafī and Shāfiʿī jurists. The *āyah* provides, concerning persons who are convicted and punished for slanderous accusation (*qadhf*): 'And accept not their testimony ever, for such people are transgressors' (al-Nūr, 24:4). Once again the occurrence of *abadan* ('for ever') in this text renders it *Muḥkam* and precludes all possibility of abrogation. The Ḥanafīs have held that the express terms of this *āyah* admit of no exception. A *qādhif*, that is, a slanderous accuser, may never be admitted as a witness even if he repents. But according to the Shāfiʿīs, if the *qādhif* repents after punishment, he may be admitted as a witness. The reason for this exception, according to the Shāfiʿīs, is given in the subsequent portion of the same text, which reads: 'Unless they repent afterwards, and rectify themselves.' The grounds of these differential interpretations need not be elaborated here. Suffice it to point out that the differences are over the understanding of the pronouns in the text, whether they refer to the *qādhif* and transgressors both, or to the latter only. There is no difference of opinion over the basic punishment of *qadhf*, which is eighty lashes as the text provides, but only with regard to the additional penalty disqualifying them as witnesses forever. It would thus appear that these differences fall within the scope of *tafsīr* rather than that of *ta'wīl*.

The *Muḥkam* is not open to abrogation. This may be indicated in the text itself, as in the foregoing examples, or it may be due to the absence of an abrogating text. The former is known as *Muḥkam bidhātih*, or *Muḥkam* by itself, and the second as *Muḥkam bighayrih*, or *Muḥkam* because of another factor.[28]

The purpose of the foregoing distinction between the four types of clear words is to identify their propensity or otherwise to *ta'wīl*, that is, of admitting a meaning other than their obvious meaning, and whether or not they are open to abrogation. If a word is not open to either of these possibilities, it would follow that it retains its original or primary meaning and admits of no other interpretation. The present classification, in other words, contemplates the scope of *ta'wīl* in that the latter is applicable only to the *Ẓāhir* and *Naṣṣ* but not to the *Mufassar* and *Muḥkam*. The next purpose of this classifaction is to provide guidelines for resolving possible conflicts between the various categories of words. In this way an order of priority is established by which the *Muḥkam* prevails over the other three varieties of clear words and the *Mufassar* takes priority over the *Naṣṣ*, and so on. But this order of priority applies only when the two conflicting texts both occur in the Qur'ān. However, when a conflict arises between, say, the *Ẓāhir* of the Qur'ān and the *Naṣṣ* of the *Sunnah*, the former would prevail despite its being one degree weaker in the order of priority. This may be illustrated by the *āyah* of the Qur'ān concering guardianship in marriage, which is in the nature of *Ẓāhir*. The *āyah* provides: 'If he has divorced her, then she is not lawful to him until she marries (*ḥattā tankiḥa*) another man' (al-Baqarah, 2:229). This text is *Ẓāhir* in respect of guardianship as its principal theme is divorce, not guardianship. From the Arabic form of the word '*tankiḥa*' in this text, the Ḥanafīs have drawn the additional conclusion that an adult woman can contract her own marriage, without the presence of a guardian. However there is a Ḥadīth on the subject of guardianship which is in the nature of *Naṣṣ*, which provides that 'there shall be no marriage without a guardian (*walī*)'.[29]

لا نكاح الا بولي

This Ḥadīth is more specific on the point that a woman must be contracted in marriage by her guardian. Notwithstanding this, however, the *Ẓāhir* of the Qur'ān is given priority, by the Ḥanafīs at least, over the *Naṣṣ* of the Ḥadīth. The majority of ulema have, however, followed the ruling of the *Sunnah* on this point.[30]

II. Unclear Words (*al-Alfāẓ Ghayr al-Wāḍiḥah*)

These are words which do not by themselves convey a clear meaning without the aid of additional evidence that may be furnished by the Lawgiver Himself, or by the *mujtahid*. If the inherent ambiguity is clarified by means of research and *ijtihād*, the words are classified as *Khafī* (obscure) and *Mushkil* (difficult). But when the ambiguity could only be removed by an explanation which is furnished by the Lawgiver, the word is classified either as *Mujmal* (ambivalent) or *Mutashābih* (intricate), as follows.[31]

II.1 *The Obscure (Khafī)*

Khafī denotes a word which has a basic meaning but is partially ambiguous in respect of some of the individual cases to which it is applied: the word is consequently obscure with regard to these cases only. The ambiguity in *Khafī* needs to be clarified by extraneous evidence which is often a matter of research and *ijtihād*. An example of *Khafī* is the word 'thief' (*sāriq*) which has a basic meaning but which, when it is applied to cases such as that of a pickpocket, or a person who steals the shrouds of the dead, does not make it immediately clear whether 'thief' includes a pickpocket or not and whether the punishment of theft can be applied to the latter. The basic ingredients of theft are present in this activity, but the fact that the pickpocket uses a kind of skill in taking the assets of a person in wakefulness makes it somewhat different from theft. Similarly, it is not certain whether 'thief' includes a *nabbāsh*, that is, one who steals the shroud of the dead, since a shroud is not a guarded property (*māl muḥraz*). Imām Shāfiʿī and Abū Yūsuf would apply the prescribed penalty of theft to the *nabbāsh*, whereas the majority of ulema only make him liable to the discretionary punishment of *taʿzīr*. There is also an *ijtihādī* opinion which authorises the application of the *ḥadd* of theft to the pickpocket.[32]

The word '*qātil*' (killer) in the Ḥadīth that 'the killer shall not inherit',[33]

لا يرث القاتل

is also *Khafī* in respect of certain varieties of killing such as 'erroneous killing' (*qatl al-khaṭa'*). The Mālikīs have held that erroneous killing is not included in the meaning of this Ḥadīth, whereas according to the Ḥanafīs, it is in the interest of safeguarding the lives of the people to include erroneous killing within the meaning of this Ḥadīth.[34] To remove the ambiguity in *Khafī* is usually a matter of *ijtihād*, which would explain why there are divergent rulings on each of the foregoing examples. It is the duty of the *mujtahid* to exert himself so as to clarify the ambiguity in the *Khafī* before it can constitute the basis of a judicial order.

II.2 The Difficult (*Mushkil*)

Mushkil denotes a word which is inherently ambiguous, and whose ambiguity can only be removed by means of research and *ijtihād*. The *Mushkil* differs from the *Khafī* in that the latter has a basic meaning which is generally clear, whereas the *Mushkil* is inherently ambiguous. There are, for example, words which have more than one meaning, and when they occur in a text, the text is unclear with regard to one or the other of those meanings. Thus the word '*qur*'' which occurs in sūra al-Baqarah (2:228) is *Mushkil* as it has two distinct meanings: menstruation (*ḥayḍ*) and the clean period between two menstruations (*ṭuhr*). Whichever of these is taken, the ruling of the text will differ accordingly. Imām Shāfiʿī and a number of other jurists have adopted the latter, whereas the Ḥanafīs and others have adopted the former as the correct meaning of *qur'*.

Sometimes the difficulty arising in the text is caused by the existence of a conflicting text. Although each of the two texts may be fairly clear as they stand alone, they become difficult when one attempts to reconcile them. This may be illustrated in the following two *āyāt*, one of which provides:

> 'Whatever good that befalls you is from God, and whatever misfortune that happens to you, is from yourself' (al-Nisā', 4:79).

Elsewhere we read in sūra Āl-ᶜImrān (3:154): 'Say that the matter is all in God's hands.' A similar difficulty is noted in the following two passages. According to the first, 'Verily God does not command obscenity/evil' (al-Aᶜrāf, 7:28). And then we read in sūra Banī Isrā'īl (17:16), 'When We decide to destroy a population, We first send a definite order to their privileged ones, and when they transgress, the word is proven against them, then We destroy them with utter destruction.' Could it be said that total destruction is a form of evil? There is no certainty as to the correct meaning of *Mushkil*, as it is inherently ambiguous. Any explanation which is provided by the *mujtahid* is bound to be speculative. The *mujtahid* is nevertheless bound to exert himself in order to discover the correct meaning of *Mushkil* before it can be implemented and adopted as a basis of action.[35]

II.3 The Ambivalent (*Mujmal*)

Mujmal denotes a word or text which is inherently unclear and gives no indication as to its precise meaning. The cause of ambiguity in *Mujmal* is inherent in the locution itself. A word may be a homonym with more than one meaning, and there is no indication as to which might be the correct one, or alternatively the Lawgiver has given it a meaning other than its literal one, or the word may be totally unfamiliar. In any of these eventualities, there is no way of removing the ambiguity without recourse to the explanation that the Lawgiver has furnished Himself, for He introduced the ambiguous word in the first place. Words that have been used in a transferred sense, that is, for a meaning other than their literal one, in order to convey a technical or a juridical concept, fall under the category of *Mujmal*. For example, expressions such as *ṣalāh*, *ribā, ḥajj*, and *ṣiyām* have all lost their literal meanings due to the fact that the Lawgiver has used them for purposes other than those which they originally conveyed. Each of these words has a literal meaning, but since their technical meaning is so radically different from the literal, the link between them is lost and the technical meaning becomes totally dominant. A word of this type remains ambivalent until it is clarified by the Lawgiver Himself. The juridical meaning of all the Qur'ānic words cited above has been explained by the Prophet, in which case, they cease to be ambivalent. For when the Lawgiver provides the necessary explanation, the *Mujmal* is explained and turns into *Mufassar*.

The *Mujmal* may sometimes be an unfamiliar word which is inherently vague, but is clarified by the text where it occurs. For example '*al-qāriᶜah*' and '*halūᶜ*' which occur in the Qur'ān. The relevant passages are as follows:

> The stunning blow (*al-qāriᶜah*)! What is the stunning blow? What will make you realise what the stunning blow is? It is the Day on which the people will act like scattered moths; and the mountains will be like carded wool . . . (al-Qāriᶜah, 101:1–5).
>
> Truly man was created restless (*halūᶜan*); so he panics whenever any evil touches him; and withholds when some fortune befalls him (al-Maᶜārij, 70:20–23).

The ambivalent words in these passages have thus been explained and the text has as a result become self-explained, or *Mufassar*. The *Mujmal* turns into the *Mufassar* only when the clarification that the Lawgiver provides is complete; but when it is incomplete, or insufficient to remove the ambiguity, the *Mujmal* turns into a *Mushkil*, which is then open to research and *ijtihād*. An example of this is the word *ribā* which occurs in the Qur'ān (al-Baqarah, 2:275) in the form of a *Mujmal*, as when it reads: 'God permitted sale and prohibited *ribā*', the last word in this text literally meaning 'increase'. Since not every increase or profit is unlawful, the text remains ambivalent as to what type of increase it intends to forbid. The Prophet has clarified the basic concept of *ribā* in the Ḥadīth which specifies six items (gold, silver, wheat, barley, salt and dates) to which the prohibition applies. But this explanation is insufficient for detailed purposes in that it leaves room for reflection and enquiry as to the rationale of the text with a view to extending the same rule to similar commodities. The Ḥadīth thus opens the way to further *ijtihād* and analogy to the goods that it has specified.[36]

II.4 The Intricate (*Mutashābih*)

This denotes a word whose meaning is a total mystery. There are words in the Qur'ān whose meaning is not known at all. Neither the words themselves nor the text in which they occur provide any indication as to their meaning. The *Mutashābih* as such does not occur in the legal *nuṣūṣ*, but it does occur in other contexts. Some of the sūras of the Qur'ān begin with what is called *al-muqaṭṭaᶜāt*, that is, abbreviated letters whose meaning is a total mystery. Expressions such as *alif-lām-mīm, yā-sīn, ḥā-mīm* and many others which occur on 29 occasions in the Qur'ān, are all classified as *Mutashābih*. Some ulema have held the view that the *muqaṭṭaᶜāt* are meant to exemplify the inimitable qualities of the Qur'ān, while others maintain that they are not abbreviations but symbols and names of God; that they have numerical significance; and that they are used to attract the attention of the audience. According to yet another view, the *Mutashābih* in the Qur'ān is meant as a reminder of limitations in the knowledge of the believer, who is made to realise that the unseen realities are too vast to be comprehended by reason.[37]

Some ulema, including Ibn Ḥazm al-Ẓāhirī, have held the view that with the exception of the *muqaṭṭaʿāt* there is no *Mutashābih* in the Qur'ān. Others have maintained that the passages of the Qur'ān which draw resemblances between God and man are also in the nature of *Mutashābih*.[38] Thus the *āyāt* which provide: 'the hand of God is over their hands' (al-Fatḥ, 48:10); and in a reference to the Prophet Noah where we read: 'build a ship under Our eyes and Our inspiration' (Hūd, 11:37) and in sūra al-Raḥmān (55:27) where the text runs 'and the face of your Lord will abide forever', are instances of *Mutashābih* as their precise meaning cannot be known. One can of course draw an appropriate metaphorical meaning in each case, which is what the Muʿtazilah have attempted, but this is neither satisfactory nor certain. To say that 'hand' metaphorically means power, and 'eyes' means supervision is no more than a conjecture. For we do not know the subject of our comparison. The Qur'ān also tells us that 'there is nothing like Him' (al-Shūrā, 42:11). Since the Lawgiver has not explained these resemblances to us, they remain unintelligible.[39]

The existence of the *Mutashābih* in the Qur'ān is proven by the testimony of the Book itself, which is as follows:

> He it is who has sent down to you the Book. Some of it consist of *Muḥkamāt*, which are the Mother of the Book, while others are *Mutashābihāt*. Those who have swerving in their hearts, in their quest for sedition, follow the *Mutashābihāt* and search for its hidden meanings. But no one knows those meanings except God. And those who are firmly grounded in knowledge say: We believe in it, the whole is from our Lord. But only people of inner understanding really heed. (Āl-ʿImrān, 3:7).

The ulema have differed in their understanding of this *āyah*, particularly with regard to the definition of *Muḥkamāt* and *Mutashābihāt*. But the correct view is that *Muḥkam* is that part of the Qur'ān which is not open to conjecture and doubt, whereas the *Mutashābih* is. With regard to the letters which appear at the beginning of sūras, it has been suggested that they are the names of the sūras in which they occur. As for the question of whether acting upon the *Mutashābih* is permissible or not, there is disagreement, but the correct view is that no one may act upon it. This is so not because the *Mutashābih* has no meaning, but because the correct meaning is not known to any human being.[40] There is no doubt that all the *Mutashābihāt* have a meaning, but it is only known to God, and we must not impose our estimations on the words of God in areas where no indication is available to reveal the correct meaning to us.[41]

Classification II: The ᶜĀmm (General) and the *Khāṣṣ* (Specific).

From the viewpoint of their scope, words are classified into the 'general' and the 'specific'. This is basically a conceptual distinction which is not always obvious in the grammatical forms of words, although the ulema have identified certain linguistic patterns of words which assist us in differentiating the *ᶜĀmm* from the *Khāṣṣ*.

ᶜĀmm may be defined as a word which applies to many things, not limited in number, and includes everything to which it is applicable.[42] An example of this is the word '*insān*' (human being) in the Qur'ānic *āyah*, 'verily the human being is in loss' (al-ᶜAṣr, 103:1), or the command, 'whoever enters this house, give him a dirham'. In both examples the application of 'human being' and 'whoever' is general and includes every human being without any limitation. *ᶜĀmm* is basically a word that has a single meaning, but which applies to an unlimited number without any restrictions. All words, whether in Arabic or any other language, are basically general, and unless they are specified or qualified in some way, they retain their generality. According to the reported *ijmāᶜ* of the Companions and the accepted norms of Arabic, the words of the Qur'ān and *Sunnah* apply in their general capacity unless there is evidence to warrant a departure from the general to an alternative meaning.[43] To say that the *ᶜĀmm* has a single meaning differentiates the *ᶜĀmm* from the homonym (*Mushtarak*) which has more than one meaning. Similarly, the statement that the *ᶜĀmm* applies to an unlimited number precludes the *Khāṣṣ* from the definition of *ᶜĀmm*.[44] A word may be general either by its form, such as men, students, judges, etc., or by its meaning only, such as people, community, etc., or by way of substitution, such as by prefixing pronouns like all, every, entire, etc., to common nouns. Thus the Qur'ānic *āyah* which provides that 'every soul shall taste of death' (Āl-ᶜImrān, 3:185), or the statement that 'every contract consists of two parties' are both general in their import.

The *ᶜĀmm* must include everything to which it is applicable. Thus when a command is issued in the form of an *ᶜĀmm* it is essential that it is implemented as such. In this way, if A commands his servant to give a dirham to everyone who enters his house, the proper fulfilment of this command would require that the servant does not specify the purport of A's command to, say, A's relatives only. If the servant gives a dirham only to A's relatives with the explanation that he understood that this was what A had wanted, the explanation would be unacceptable and the servant would be at fault.

When a word is applied to a limited number of things, including everything to which it can be applied, say one or two or a hundred, it is referred to as 'specific' (*Khāṣṣ*). A word of this kind may denote a particular individual such as Aḥmad, or Zayd, or an individual belonging to a certain species such as a horse or a bird, or an individual belonging to a genus such as a human being.[45] As opposed to the general, the specific word applies to a limited number, be it a genus, or a species, or a particular individual. So long as it applies to a single subject, or a specified number thereof, it is *Khāṣṣ*. But if there is no such limitation to the scope of its application, it is classified as *ᶜĀmm*.

Legal rules which are conveyed in specific terms are definite in application and are normally not open to *ta'wīl*. Thus the Qur'ānic *āyah* which enacts the 'feeding of ten poor persons' as the expiation for futile oaths is specific and definite in that the number 'ten' does not admit of any *ta'wīl*. However, if there be exceptional reasons to warrant a recourse to *ta'wīl*, then the *Khāṣṣ* may be open to it. For example, the requirement to feed ten poor persons in the foregoing *āyah* has been interpreted by the Ḥanafīs as either feeding ten persons or one such person ten times. The Ḥanafīs have, however, been overruled by the majority on this point who say that the *Khāṣṣ*, as a rule, is not amenable to *ta'wīl*.

In determining the scope of the *ᶜĀmm*, reference is made not only to the rules of the language but also to the usage of the people, and should there be a conflict between the two priority is given to the latter. The Arabs normally use words in their general sense. But this statement must be qualified by saying that linguistic usage has many facets. Words are sometimes used in the form of *ᶜĀmm* but the purpose of the speaker may actually be less than *ᶜĀmm* or even *Khāṣṣ*. The precise scope of the *ᶜĀmm* has thus to be determined with reference to the conditions of the speaker and the context of the speech. When, for example, a person says that 'I honoured the people' or 'I fought the enemy forces', he must surely mean only those whom he met. *ᶜĀmm* as a rule applies to all that it includes, especially when it is used on its own. But when it is used in combination with other words, then there are two possibilities: either the *ᶜĀmm* remains as before, or it is specified by other words.[46]

It thus appears that there are three types of *ᶜĀmm*, which are as follows: Firstly, the *ᶜĀmm* which is absolutely general, which may be indicated by a prefix in the form of a pronoun. Note for example the Qur'ānic *āyāt*, 'there is no living creature on earth [*wa mā min dābbatin fi'l-arḍ*] that God does not provide for' (Hūd, 11:6); and 'We made everything [*kulla shay'in*] alive from water' (al-Anbiyā', 21:30). In the first *āyah*, the prefix '*mā min*' ('no one', 'no living creature'), and in the second *āyah*, the word '*kull*' (i.e. 'all' or 'every') are expressions which identify the ʿĀmm. Both of these *āyāt* consist of general propositions which preclude specification of any kind. Hence they remain absolutely general and include all to which they apply without any exception. Secondly, there is the ʿĀmm which is meant to imply a *Khāṣṣ*. This usage of ʿĀmm is also indicated by evidence which suggests that the ʿĀmm comprises some but not absolutely all the individuals to whom it could possibly apply. An example of this is the word '*al-nās*' ('the people') in the Qur'ānic *āyah*, 'pilgrimage to the House is a duty owed to God by all people who are able to undertake it' (Āl-ʿImrān, 3:97). Here the indictions provided by the text imply that children and lunatics or anyone who cannot afford to perform the required duty are not included in the scope of this *āyah* Thirdly, there is the ʿĀmm which is not accompanied by either of the foregoing two varieties of indications as to its scope. An example of this is the Qur'ānic word *al-muṭallaqāt* ('divorced women') in the text which provides that 'divorced women must observe three courses upon themselves' (al-Baqarah, 2:228). This type of ʿĀmm is *Ẓāhir* in respect of its generality, which means that it remains general unless there is evidence to justify specification (*takhṣīṣ*). In this instance, however, there is another Qur'ānic ruling which qualifies the general requirement of the waiting period, or ʿ*iddah*, that the divorced women must observe. This ruling occurs in sūra al-Aḥzāb (33:49) which is as follows: 'O believers! When you enter the contract of marriage with believing women and then divorce them before consummating the marriage, they do not have to observe any ʿ*iddah*'. In this way, women who are divorced prior to consummating the marriage are excluded from the general requirement of the first *āyah*. The second *āyah*, in other words, specifies the first.[47]

In grammatical terms, the ʿĀmm in its Arabic usage takes a variety of identifiable forms. The grammatical forms in which the ʿĀmm occurs are, however, numerous, and owing to the dominantly linguistic and Arabic nature of the subject, I shall only attempt to explain some of the well-known patterns of the ʿĀmm.

When a singular or a plural form of a noun is preceded by the definite article *al* it is identified as ʿĀmm. For example the Qur'ānic text which provides, 'the adulterer, whether a woman or a man, flog them one hundred lashes' (al-Nūr, 24:2). Here the article *al* preceding 'adulterer' (*al-zāniyah wa'l-zānī*) indicates that all adulterers must suffer the prescribed punishment. Similarly, when the plural form of a noun is preceded by *al*, it is identified as ʿĀmm. The example that we gave above relating to the waiting period of the divorced women (*al-muṭallaqāt*) is a case in point. The *āyah* in question begins by the word '*al-muṭallaqāt*', that is, 'the divorced women'[48] who are required to observe a waiting period of three courses before they can marry again. 'The divorced women' is an ᶜĀmm which comprises all to whom this expression can apply.

The Arabic expressions *jamīᶜ*, *kāffah* and *kull* ('all', 'entire'), are generic in their effect, and when they precede or succeed a word, the latter comprises all to which it is applicable. We have already illustrated the occurrence of '*kull*' in the Qur'ānic text where we read 'We made everything [*kulla shay'in*] alive from water'. The word *jamīᶜ* has a similar effect when it precedes or follows another word. Thus the Qur'ānic text which reads, 'He has created for you all that is in the earth' [*khalaqa lakum mā fi'l-arḍ jamīᶜā*] (al-Baqarah, 2:29) means that everything in the earth is created for the benefit of man. Similarly, when a word, usually a plural noun, is prefixed by a conjunctive such as *walladhīna* ('those men who') and *wallātī* ('those women who'), it becomes generic in its effect. An example of this in the Qur'ān occurs in sūra al-Nūr (24:21): 'Those who [*walladhīna*] accuse chaste women of adultery and fail to bring four witnesses, flog them eighty lashes.' This ruling is general as it applies to all those who can possibly be included in its scope, and it remains so unless there is evidence to warrant specification. As it happens, this ruling has, in so far as it relates to the proof of slanderous accusation, been specified by a subsequent *āyah* in the same passage. This second *āyah* makes an exception in the case of the husband who is allowed to prove a charge of adultery against his wife by taking four solemn oaths instead of four witnesses, but the wife can rebut the charge by taking four solemn oaths herself (al-Nūr, 24:6). The general ruling of the first *āyah* has thus been qualified insofar as it concerns a married couple.

An indefinite word (*al-nakirah*) when used to convey the negative is also generic in its effect. For instance the Ḥadīth *lā ḍarar wa lā ḍirār fi'l-Islām* ('no harm shall be inflicted or reciprocated in Islam') is general in its import, as '*lā ḍarar*' and '*lā ḍirār*' are both indefinite words which convey their concepts in the negative, thereby negating all to which they apply.

The word '*man*' ('he who') is specific in its application, but when used in a conditional speech, it has the effect of a general word. To illustrate this in the Qur'ān, we may refer to the text which provides: 'Whoever [*wa-man*] kills a believer in error, must release a believing slave' (al-Nisā', 4:92); and 'Whoever [*fa-man*] among you sees the new moon must observe the fast' (al-Baqarah, 2:185).

There is general agreement to the effect that the *Khāṣṣ* is definitive (*qaṭᶜī*) in its import, but the ulema have differed as to whether the ᶜĀmm is definitive or speculative (*ẓannī*). According to the Ḥanafīs, the application of ᶜĀmm to all that it includes is definitive, the reason being that the language of the law is usually general and if its application were to be confined to only a few of the cases covered by its words without a particular reason or authority to warrant such limited application, the intention of the Lawgiver would be frustrated.[49] The majority of ulema, including the Shāfiᶜīs, Mālikīs and Ḥanbalīs, maintain on the other hand that the application of *ᶜĀmm* to all that it includes is speculative as it is open to limitation and *ta'wīl*, and so long as there is such a possibility, it is not definitive. The result of this disagreement becomes obvious in the event of a conflict between the *ᶜĀmm* of the Qur'ān and the *Khāṣṣ* of the Ḥadīth, especially the weak or the solitary Ḥadīth. According to the majority view, a solitary Ḥadīth may specify a general provision of the Qur'ān, for the *ᶜĀmm* of Qur'ān is *ẓannī* and the *Khāṣṣ* of a solitary Ḥadīth, although definitive in meaning, is of speculative authenticity. A *ẓannī* may be specified by a *qaṯᶜī* or another *ẓannī*.[50] To the Ḥanafīs, however, the *ᶜĀmm* of Qur'ān is definite, and the solitary Ḥadīth, or *qiyās* for that matter, is speculative. A definitive may not be limited nor specified by a speculative. The two views may be illustrated with reference to the Qur'ānic text concerning the slaughter of animals, which provides 'eat not [of meat] on which God's name has not been pronounced' (al-Anᶜām, 6:121). In conjunction with this general ruling, there is a solitary Ḥadīth which provides that 'the believer slaughters in the name of God whether he pronounces the name of God or not'.[51]

ذبيحة المسلم حلال ذكر اسم الله أو لم يذكر

According to the majority, this Ḥadīth specifies the Qur'ānic *āyah*, with the result that slaughter by a Muslim, even without pronouncing the name of God, is lawful for consumption. But to the Ḥanafīs, it is not lawful, as the *ᶜĀmm* of the Qur'ān may not be specified by solitary (*Āḥād*) Ḥadīth. This disagreement between the juristic schools, however, arises in respect of the solitary Ḥadīth only. As for the *Mutawātir* (and the *Mashhūr*) there is no disagreement on the point that either of these may specify the general in the Qur'ān just as the Qur'ān itself sometimes specifies its own general provisions.[52]

A general proposition may be qualified either by a dependent clause, that is, a clause which occurs in the same text, or by an independent locution. The majority of ulema consider either of these eventualities as two varieties of *takhṣīṣ*. According to the Ḥanafīs, however, an independent locution can specify another locution only if it is established that the two locutions are chronologically parallel to one another. but if they are not so parallel, the later in time abrogates the former, and the case is one of abrogation rather than *takhṣīṣ*. In the event where the qualifying words relate to what has preceded and do not form a complete locution by themselves, they are not regarded as independent propositions. According to the majority, but not the Ḥanafīs, a dependent clause may qualify a general proposition by introducing an exception (*istithnā'*), a condition (*sharṭ*), a quality (*ṣifah*), or indicating the extent (*ghāyah*) of the original proposition. Each of such clauses will have the effect of limiting and specifying the operation of the general proposition. An example of specification in the form of *istithnā'* is the general ruling which prescribes documentation of commercial transactions that involve deferred payments in sūra al-Baqarah (2:282). This general provision is then followed, in the same *āyah*, by the exception 'unless it be a transaction handled on the spot that you pass around among yourselves in which case it will not be held against you if you did not reduce it into writing'. This second portion of the *āyah* thus embodies an exception to the first. Specification (*takhṣīṣ*) in the form of a condition (*sharṭ*) to a general proposition may be illustrated by reference to the Qur'ānic text which prescribes the share of the husband in the estate of his deceased wife. The text thus provides, 'in what your wives leave, you are entitled to one half if they have no children' (al-Nisā' , 4:12). The application of the general rule in the first portion of the *āyah* has thus been qualified by the condition which the text itself has provided in its latter part, namely the absence of children. And then to illustrate *takhṣīṣ* by way of providing a description or qualification (*ṣifah*) to a general proposition, we may refer to the Qur'ānic text regarding the prohibition of marriage with one's step-daughter where we read '[and forbidden to you are] your step-daughters under your guardianship from your wives with whom you have consummated the marriage' (al-Nisā', 4:23). Thus the general prohibition in the first part of the *āyah* has been qualified by the description that is provided in the latter part. And lastly, to illustrate *takhṣīṣ* in the form of *ghāyah*, or specifying the extent of application of a general proposition, we may refer to the Qur'ānic text on ablutions for *ṣalāh*. The text prescribes the 'washing of your hands up to the elbows' (al-Mā'idah, 5:6). Washing the hands, which is a general ruling, is thus specified in regard to the area which must be covered in washing. Similarly when it is said 'respect your fellow citizens unless they violate the law', the word 'citizens' includes all, but the succeeding phrase specifies the extent of the operation of the general ruling.[53]

When the application of a general proposition is narrowed down, not by a clause which is part of the general locution itself, but by an independent locution, the latter may consist of a separate text, or of a reference to the general requirements of reason, social custom, or the objectives of *Sharīᶜah* (*ḥikmah al-tashrīᶜ*). It is by virtue of reason, for example, that infants and lunatics are excluded from the scope of the Qur'ānic obligation of *ḥajj*, which occurs in sūra Āl-ᶜImrān (3:97). Similarly, the general text of the Qur'ān which reads that '[a wind] will destroy everything by the command of its Lord' (al-Aḥqāf, 46:25), customarily denotes everything which is capable of destruction. Similarly, in the area of commercial transactions, the general provisions of the law are often qualified in the light of the custom prevailing among people. We have already illustrated specification of one text by another in regard to the waiting period (*ᶜiddah*) of divorced women. The general provision that such women must observe a *ᶜiddah* consisting of three menstrual cycles occurs in sūra al-Baqarah (2:228). This has in turn been qualified by another text in sūra al-Aḥzāb (33:49) which removes the requirement of *ᶜiddah* in cases where divorce takes place prior to the consummation of marriage.[54] And lastly, the general provision of the Qur'ān concerning retaliation in injuries on an 'equal for equal' basis (al-Mā'dah, 5:48) is qualified in the light of the objectives of the Lawgiver in the sense that the offender is not to be physically wounded in the manner that he injured his victim, but is to be punished in proportion to the gravity of his offence.

Next, there arises the question of chronological order between the general and the specifying provisions. The specifying clause is either parallel in origin to the general, or is of later origin, or their chronological order is unknown. According to the Ḥanafīs, when the specifying clause is of a later origin than the general proposition, the former abrogates the latter and is no longer regarded as *takhṣīṣ*, but as a partial abrogation of one text by another. According to the Ḥanafīs, *takhṣīṣ* can only take place when the *ᶜĀmm* and the *Khāṣṣ* are chronologically parallel to one another; in cases where this order cannot be established between them, they are presumed to be parallel. The difference between abrogation and *takhṣīṣ* is that abrogation consists of a total or partial suspension of a ruling at a later date, whereas *takhṣīṣ* essentially limits the application of the *ᶜĀmm ab initio*. To the majority of ulema *takhṣīṣ* is a form of explanation (*bayān*) in all of its varieties, but to the Ḥanafīs it is a form of *bayān* only when the specifying clause is independent of the general proposition, chronologically parallel to it, and is of the same degree of strength as the *ᶜĀmm* in respect of being a *qaṭᶜī* or a *ẓannī*. But when the specifying clause is of a later origin than the general proposition, the effect which it has on the latter, according to the Ḥanafīs, is one of abrogation rather than *bayān*.[55] The majority view on *takhṣīṣ* thus differs from the Ḥanafīs in that *takhṣīṣ* according to the majority may be by means of both a dependent or an independent locution, and the specifying clause need not be chronologically parallel to the general proposition. This is because in the majority opinion, the specifying clause explains and does not abrogate or invalidate the general proposition.[56]

Notwithstanding the ulema's disagreement regarding the nature of *takhṣīṣ*, it would appear that *takhṣīṣ* is not a partial invalidation of the *ᶜĀmm*, but an explanation or qualification thereof. This is the majority view, and seems to be preferable to the Ḥanafī view which equates *takhṣīṣ* with partial abrogation.[57] Imām Ghazālī discusses the Ḥanafī position at some length, and refutes it by saying that a mere discrepancy in time does not justify the conclusion that *takhṣīṣ* changes its character into abrogation. Nor is it justified to say that a discrepancy in the strength of the indication (*dalīl*) determines the difference between *takhṣīṣ* and abrogation.[58]

The effect of *ᶜĀmm* is that it remains in force, and action upon it is required, unless there is a specifying clause which would limit its application. In the event where a general provision is partially specified, it still retains its legal authority in respect of the part which remains unspecified. According to the majority of ulema, the *ᶜĀmm* is speculative as a whole, whether before or after *takhṣīṣ*, and as such it is open to qualification and *ta'wīl* in either case. For the Ḥanafīs, however, the *ᶜĀmm* is definitive in the first place, but when it is partially specified, it becomes speculative in respect of the part which still remains unspecified; hence it will be treated as *ẓannī* and would be susceptible to further specification by another *ẓannī*.[59]

As for the question of whether the cause of a general ruling can operate as a limiting factor in its general application, it will be noted that the cause never specifies a general ruling. This is relevant, as far as the Qur'ān is concerned, to the question of *asbāb al-nuzūl*, or the occasions of its revelation. One often finds general rulings in the Qur'ān which were revealed with reference to specific issues. Whether the cause of the revelation contemplated a particular situation or not, it does not operate as a limiting factor on the application of the general ruling. Thus the occasion of the revelation of the *āyah* of imprecation (*liᶜān*) in sūra al-Nūr (24:6) was a complaint that a resident of Madinah, Hilāl ibn Umayyah, made to the Prophet about the difficulty experienced by the spouse in proving, by four eyewitnesses, the act of adultery on the part of the other spouse. The cause of the revelation was specific but the ruling remains general. Similarly, the Ḥadīth which provides that 'when any hide is tanned, it is purified'[60]

ايما أهاب دبغ فقد طهر

was, according to reports, uttered with reference to a sheepskin, but the ruling is nevertheless applicable to all types of skins. The actual wording of a general ruling is therefore to be taken into consideration regardless of its cause. If the ruling is conveyed in general terms, it must be applied as such even if the cause behind it happens to be specific.[61]

Conflict between *ᶜĀmm* and *Khāṣṣ*

Should there be two textual rulings on one and the same subject in the Qur'ān, one being *ᶜĀmm* and the other *Khāṣṣ*, there will be a case of conflict between them according to the Ḥanafīs, but not according to the majority. The reason is that to the Ḥanafīs, *ᶜĀmm* and *Khāṣṣ* are both definitive (*qaṭᶜī*) and as such a conflict between them is possible, whereas to the majority, only the *Khāṣṣ* is *qaṭᶜī* and it would always prevail over the *ᶜĀmm*, which is *ẓannī*.

The Ḥanafīs maintain that in the event of a conflict between the general and the specific in the Qur'ān, one must ascertain the chronological order between them first; whether, for example, they are both Makkī or Madanī *āyāt* or whether one is Makkī and the other Madanī. If the two happen to be parallel in time, the *Khāṣṣ* specifies the *ᶜĀmm*. If a different chronological sequence can be established between them, then if the *ᶜĀmm* is of a later origin, it abrogates the *Khāṣṣ*, but if the *Khāṣṣ* is later, it only partially abrogates the *ᶜĀmm*. This is because the Ḥanafīs maintain that the *Khāṣṣ* specifies the *ᶜĀmm* only when they are chronologically parallel, both are *qaṭᶜī*, and both are independent locutions.

The majority of ulema, as already noted, do not envisage the possibility of a conflict between the *ᶜĀmm* and the *Khāṣṣ*: when there are two rulings on the same point, one being *ᶜĀmm* and the other *Khāṣṣ*, the latter becomes explanatory to the former and both are retained. For the majority, the *ᶜĀmm* is like the *Ẓāhir* in that both are speculative and both are open to qualification and *ta'wīl*.[62]

The two foregoing approaches to *takhṣīṣ* may be illustrated by the conflict arising in the following two *aḥādīth* concerning legal alms (*ẓakāh*). One of these provides, 'whatever is watered by the sky is subject to a tithe'.

ما سقته السماء ففيه العشر

The second Ḥadīth provides that 'there is no charity in less than five *awsāq*'.[63]

ليس فيما دون خمسة أوساق صدقة .

A *wasaq* (sing. of *awsaq*) is a quantitative measure equivalent to about ten kilograms. The first Ḥadīth contains a general ruling in respect of any quantity of agricultural crops, but the second Ḥadīth is specific on this point. The majority of ulema (including the Shāfiʿīs) have held that the second Ḥadīth explains and qualifies the first. The first Ḥadīth lays down the general principle and the second enacts the quorum (*niṣāb*) of *ẓakāh*. For the Ḥanafīs, however, the first Ḥadīth abrogates the second, as they consider that the first Ḥadīth is of a later origin than the second. According to the Ḥanafīs, when the *ʿĀmm* is of a later origin than the *Khāṣṣ*, the former abrogates the latter completely. Hence there is no case for *takhṣīṣ* and the Ḥanafīs as a result impose no minimum quantitative limit with regard to *ẓakāh* on produce obtained through dry farming. The two views remain far apart, and there is no meeting ground between them. However, as already indicated, the majority opinion is sound, and recourse to abrogation in cases of conflict between the *ʿĀmm* and *Khāṣṣ* is often found to be unnecessary. In modern law too one often notices that the particular usually qualifies the general, and the two can co-exist. The *ʿĀmm* and the *Khāṣṣ* can thus each operate in their respective spheres with or without a discrepancy in their time of origin and the degree of their respective strength.[64]

Classification III: The Absolute (*Muṭlaq*)and the Qualified (*Muqayyad*)

Muṭlaq denotes a word which is neither qualified nor limited in its application. When we say, for example, a 'book', a 'bird' or a 'man', each one is a generic noun which applies to any book, bird or man without any restriction. In its original state, the *Muṭlaq* is unspecified and unqualified. The *Muṭlaq* differs from the *ʿĀmm*, however, in that the latter comprises all to which it applies whereas the former can apply to any one of a multitude, but not to all.[65] However, the ulema have differed regarding the *Muṭlaq* and the *Muqayyad*. To some ulema, including al-Bayḍāwī, the *Muṭlaq* resembles the *ʿĀmm*, and the *Muqayyad* resembles the *Khāṣṣ*. Hence anything which specifies the *ʿĀmm* can qualify the *Muṭlaq*. Both are open to *ta'wīl* and *Muṭlaq/Muqayyad* are complementary to *ʿĀmm/Khāṣṣ* respectively.[66] When the *Muṭlaq* is qualified by another word or words it becomes a *Muqayyad*, such as qualifying 'a book' as 'a green book', or 'a bird' as 'a huge bird' or 'a man' as 'a wise man'. The *Muqayyad* differs from the *Khāṣṣ* in that the former is a word which implies an unspecified individual/s who is merely distinguished by certain attributes and qualifications. An example of *Muṭlaq* in the Qur'ān is the expiation (*kaffārah*) of futile oaths, which is freeing a slave (*fa-taḥrīru raqabatin*) in sūra al-

Mā'idah, (5:92). The command in this text is not limited to any kind of slaves, whether Muslim or non-Muslim. Yet in another Qur'ānic passage the expiation of erroneous killing consists of 'freeing a Muslim slave' (*fa-taḥrīru raqabatin mu'minatin*) (al-Nisā', 4:92). In contrast to the first text which is conveyed in absolute terms, the command in the second *āyah* is qualified in that the slave to be released must be a Muslim.

The *Muṭlaq* remains absolute in its application unless there is a limitation to qualify it. Thus the Qur'ānic prohibition of marriage 'with your wives' mothers' in sūra al-Nisā' (4:23) is conveyed in absolute terms, and as such, marriage with one's mother-in-law is forbidden regardless as to whether the marriage with her daughter has been consummated or not. Since there is no indication to qualify the terms of the Qur'ānic command, it is to be implemented as it is. But when a *Muṭlaq* is qualified into a *Muqayyad*, the latter is to be given priority over the former. Thus if we have two texts on one and the same subject, and both convey the same ruling (*ḥukm*) as well as both having the same cause (*sabab*) but one is *Muṭlaq* and the other *Muqayyad*, the latter prevails over the former. To illustrate this in the Qur'ān, we refer to the two *āyāt* on the prohibition of blood for human consumption. The first of these, which occurs in absolute terms, provides, 'forbidden to you are the dead carcass and blood' (al-Mā'idah, 5:3). But elsewhere in the Qur'ān there is another text on the same subject which qualifies the word 'blood' as 'blood shed forth' (*daman masfūḥan*) (al-Anᶜām, 6:145). This second *āyah* is a *Muqayyad* whereas the first is *Muṭlaq*, hence the *Muqayyad* prevails. It will be noted here that the two texts convey the same ruling, namely prohibition, and that they have the same cause or subject in common (i.e. consumption of blood). When this is the case, the ulema are in agreement that the *Muqayyad* qualifies the *Muṭlaq* and prevails over it.[67]

However if there are two texts on the same issue, one absolute and the other qualified, but they differ with one another in their rulings and in their causes, or in both, then neither is qualified by the other and each will operate as it stands. This is the view of the Ḥanafī and Mālikī schools, and the Shāfiᶜīs concur insofar as it relates to two texts which differ both in their respective rulings and their causes. However the Shāfiᶜīs maintain the view that if the two texts vary in their ruling (*ḥukm*) but have the same cause in common, the *Muṭlaq* is qualified by the *Muqayyad*. This may be illustrated by referring to the two Qur'ānic *āyāt* concerning ablution, one of which reads, in an address to the believers, to 'wash your faces and your hands [*aydīkum*] up to the elbows' (al-Mā'idah, 5:7). The washing of hands in this *āyah* has been qualified by the succeeding phrase, that is 'up to the elbows'. The second Qur'ānic provision which we are about to quote occurs in regard to *tayammum*, that is, ablution with clean sand in the event where no water can be found, in which case the Qur'ān provides, 'take clean sand/earth and wipe your faces and your hands' (al-Nisā', 4:43). The word '*aydīkum*' (your hands) occurs as a *Muqayyad* in the first text but as a *Muṭlaq* in the second. However the two texts have the same cause in common, which is cleanliness for *ṣalāh*. There is admittedly a difference between the two rulings, in that the first requires washing, and the second wiping, of the hands, but this difference is of no consequence. The first is a *Muqayyad* in regard to the area of the hands to be washed whereas the second is conveyed in absolute terms. The second is therefore qualified by the first, and the *Muqayyad* prevails. Consequently in wiping the hands in *tayammum*, too, one is required to wipe them up to the elbows.

And lastly we give another illustration, again of two texts, one *Muṭlaq*, the other *Muqayyad*, both of which convey the same ruling but differ in respect of their causes. Here we refer to the two Qur'ānic *āyāt* on the subject of witnesses. One of these, which requires the testimony of two witness in all commercial transactions, is conveyed in absolute terms, whereas the second is qualified. The first of the two texts does not qualify the word 'men' when it provides 'and bring two witnesses from among your men' (al-Baqarah, 2:282). But the second text on same subject, that is, of witnesses, conveys a qualified command when it provides and bring two just witnesses [when you revoke a divorce]' (al-Ṭalāq, 65:2). The ruling in both of these texts is the same, namely the requirement of two witnesses, but the two rulings differ in respect of their causes. The cause of the first text, as already noted, is commercial transactions which must accordingly be testified to by two men; whereas the cause of the second ruling is the revocation of *ṭalāq*. In the first *āyah* witnesses are not qualified, but they are qualified in the second *āyah*. The latter prevails over the former. Consequently, witnesses in both commercial transactions and the revocation of *ṭalāq* must be upright and just.[68]

The foregoing basically represents the majority opinion. But the Ḥanafīs maintain that when the *Muqayyad* and the *Muṭlaq* differ in their causes, the one does not qualify the other and that each should be implemented independently. The Ḥanafīs basically recognise only one case where the *Muqayyad* qualifies the *Muṭlaq*, namely when both convey the same ruling and have the same cause in common. But when they differ in either of these respects or in both, then each must stand separately. In this way the Ḥanafīs do not agree with the majority in regard to the qualification of the area of the arms to be wiped in *tayammum* by the same terms which apply to ablution by water (*wuḍū'*). The Ḥanafīs argue that the *ḥukm* in regard to *tayammum* is conveyed in absolute terms and must operate as such. They contend that unlike *wuḍū'*, *tayammum* is a *sharʿī* concession, and the spirit of concession should prevail in the determination of its detailed requirements, including the area of the arm that is to be wiped.[69]

Classification IV: The Literal (*Ḥaqīqī*) and the Metaphorical (*Majāzī*)

A word may be used in its literal sense, that is, for its original or primary meaning, or it may be used in a secondary and metaphorical sense. When a word is applied literally, it keeps its original meaning, but when it is used in a metaphorical sense, it is transferred from its original to a secondary meaning on grounds of a relationship between the two meanings.[70] There is normally a logical connection between the literal and the metaphorical meanings of a word. The nature of this relationship varies and extends over a wide range of possibilities. There are at least thirty to forty variations in how the metaphorical usage of a word may relate to its literal meaning.[71] The metaphorical usage of a word thus consists of a transfer from the original to a connected meaning. Once such a transfer has taken place both the original and the metaphorical meanings of a word cannot be assigned to it at one and the same time.

Words are normally used in their literal sense, and in the language of the law it is the literal meaning which is relied upon most. Hence if a word is simultaneously used in both these senses, the literal will prevail. When, for example, a person says in his will that 'I bequeath my property to the memorisers of the Qur'ān' or to 'my offspring', those who might have memorised the Qur'ān but have forgotten it since will not be entitled. Similarly, 'offspring (*awlād*)' primarily means sons and daughters, not grandchildren. For applying '*awlād*' to 'grandchildren' is a metaphorical usage which is secondary to its original meaning.[72]

Both the *Ḥaqīqī* and the *Majāzī* occur in the Qur'ān, and they each convey their respective meanings. Thus when we read in the Qur'ān to 'kill not [*lā taqtulū*] the life which God has made sacrosanct', '*lā taqtulū*' carries its literal meaning. Similarly the *Majāzī* occurs frequently in the Qur'ān. When, for example, we read in the Qur'ān that 'God sends down your sustenance from the heavens' (Ghāfir, 40:13), this means rain which causes the production of food. Some ulema have observed that *Majāzī* is in the nature of a homonym which could comprise what may be termed as falsehood or that which has no reality and truth, and that falsehood has no place in the Qur'ān. Imām Ghazālī discusses this argument in some length and represents the majority view when he refutes it and acknowledges the existence of the *Majāzī* in the Qur'ān. The Qur'ānic expression, for example, that 'God is the light of the heavens and the earth' (al-Nūr, 24:35) and 'whenever they [the Jews] kindled the fire of war, God extinguished it' (al-Mā'idah, 5:67), God being 'the light of the universe', and God having 'extinguished the fire of war', are both metaphorical usages; and numerous other instances of the *Majāzī* can be found in the Qur'ān.[73] As already stated, the *Ḥaqīqī* and the *Majāzī* both occur in the Qur'ān, and they each convey their respective meanings. But this is only the case where the *Majāzī* does not represent the dominant usage. In the event where a word has both a literal and a metaphorical meaning and the latter is well-established and dominant, it is likely to prevail over the former. Some ulema have, however, held the opposite view, namely that the *Ḥaqīqī* would prevail in any case; and according to yet a third view, both are to be given equal weight. But the first of these views represents the view of the majority. To give an example, the word '*ṭalāq*' literally means 'release' or 'removal of restriction' (*izālah al-qayd*), be it from the tie of marriage, slavery, or ownership, etc. But since the juridical meaning of *ṭalāq*, which is dissolution of marriage, or divorce, has become totally dominant, it is this meaning that is most likely to prevail, unless there be evidence to suggest otherwise.[74]

The *Ḥaqīqī* is sub-divided, according to the context in which it occurs, into linguistic (*lughawī*), customary (*ʿurfī*) and juridical (*sharʿī*). The linguistic *Ḥaqīqī* is a word which is used in its dictionary meaning, such as 'lion' for that animal, and 'man' for the male gender of the human being. The customary *Ḥaqīqī* occurs in the two varieties of general and special: when a word is used in a customary sense and the custom is absolutely common among people, the customary *Ḥaqīqī* is classified as general, that is, in accord with the general custom. An example of this in Arabic is the word '*dābbah*' which in its dictionary meaning applies to all living beings that walk on the face of the earth, but which has been assigned a different meaning by general custom, that is, an animal walking on four legs. But when the customary *Ḥaqīqī* is used for a meaning that is common to a particular profession or group, the customary *Ḥaqīqī* is classified as special, that is, in accord with a special custom. For example the Arabic word *rafʿ* ('nominative') and *naṣb* ('accusative') have each acquired a technical meaning that is common among grammarians and experts in the language.

There is some disagreement as to the nature of the juridical *Ḥaqīqī*, as some ulema consider this to be a variety of the *Majāzī*, but having said this, the juridical *Ḥaqīqī* is defined as a word which is used for a juridical meaning that the Lawgiver has given it in the first place, such as '*ṣalāh*', which literally means 'supplication' but which, in its well-established juridical sense, is a particular form of worship. Similarly, the word '*zakāh* literally means 'purification', but in its juridical sense, denotes a particular form of charity whose details are specified in the *Sharīᶜah*.[75]

It would take us too far afield to describe the sub-divisions of the *Majāzī*, as we are not primarily concerned with technical linguistic detail. Suffice it to point out here that the *Majāzī* has also been divided into linguistic, customary and juridical varieties. However, there is one other classification which merits our attention. This is the division of the *Ḥaqīqī* and *Majāzī* into plain (*Ṣarīḥ*) and allusive (*Kināyah*).

If the application of a word is such that it clearly discloses the speaker's intention, it is plain, otherwise it is allusive. The highest degree of clarity in expression is achieved by the combination of the plain (*Ṣarīḥ*) and the literal (*Ḥaqīqī*) such as the sentence 'Aḥmad bought a house', or 'Fāṭimah married Aḥmad'. The plain may also be combined with the metaphorical, as in the sentence 'I ate from this tree', while it is intended to mean 'from the fruit of this tree'.

The 'allusive' or *Kināyah* denotes a form of speech which does not clearly disclose the intention of its speaker. It can occur in combination with the literal or the metaphorical. When a person wishes, for example, to confide in his colleague in front of others, he might say 'I met your friend and spoke to him about the matter that you know'. This is a combination of the literal and the allusive in which all the words used convey their literal meanings but where the whole sentence is allusive in that it does not disclose the purpose of the speaker with clarity. Supposing that a man addresses his wife and tells her in Arabic '*iᶜtaddī*' (start counting) while intending to divorce her. This utterance is allusive, as 'counting' literally means taking a record of numbers, but is used here in reference to counting the days of the waiting period of *ᶜiddah*. This speech is also metaphorical in that the *ᶜiddah* which is caused by divorce is used as a substitute for 'divorce'. It is a form of *Majāzī* in which the effect is used as a substitute for the cause.[76]

When a speech consists of plain words, the intention of the person using them is to be gathered from the words themselves, and there is no room for further enquiry as to the intention of the speaker. Thus when a man tells his wife 'you are divorced', the divorce is pronounced in plain words and occurs regardless of the husband's intention. But in the case of allusive words, one has to ascertain the intention behind them and the circumstances in which they were uttered. Thus when a man tells his wife 'you are forbidden to me', or when he asks her to 'join your relatives', no divorce will take place unless there is evidence to show that the husband intended a divorce.[77]

Legal matters which require certainty, such as offences entailing the *ḥadd* punishment, cannot be established by language which is not plain.

For example when a person confesses to such offences in allusive words, he is not liable to punishment.[78]

The jurists are in agreement that a word may be used metaphorically while still retaining its literal meaning, such as the word '*umm*' (mother) which the Arabs sometimes use metaphorically for 'grandmother' and yet still retains its literal meaning. But there is disagreement among the ulema of *uṣūl* as to whether both the literal and metaphorical meanings of a word can be applied simultaneously. When, for example, a man orders his servant to 'kill the lion', could this also include a brave person? The Ḥanafīs and the Muᶜtazilah have answered this question in the negative, saying that words normally carry their literal meanings unless there is evidence to warrant a departure to another meaning. The Shāfiᶜīs and the ulema of Ḥadīth have held, on the other hand, that the literal and the metaphorical meaning of a word can be simultaneously applied. They have thus validated either of the two meanings of the Qur'ānic provision 'or when you have touched women' (al-Nisā', 4:43), which could mean touching the women with the hand, or touching in the sense of having sexual intercourse. The text in which this *āyah* occurs spells out the circumstances that break the state of purity. Thus when a Muslim 'touches a woman' he must take a fresh ablution for the next *ṣalāh*. But according to the Ḥanafīs, the Qur'ānic *āyah* on this point only conveys the metaphorical meaning of 'touching', that is, sexual intercourse. Hence when a person is in the state of ablution, and then touches a woman by the hand, his ablution remains intact. For the Shāfiᶜīs, however, the key word in this *āyah* carries both its literal and metaphorical meanings simultaneously. Consequently the state of purity is broken, not only by sexual intercourse, but also by a mere touch such as a handshake with a woman who is not of one's family.[79]

The Homonym (*Mushtarak*)

A homonym is a word which has more than one meaning. Some ulema, including al-Shāfiᶜī, have held the view that the homonym is a variety of *ᶜĀmm*. The two are, however, different in that the homonym inherently possesses more than one meaning, which is not necessarily the case with the *ᶜĀmm*. An example of the *Mushtarak* in Arabic is the word '*ᶜayn*' which means several things, including eye, water-spring, gold, and spy. Similarly the word '*qur*'' has two meanings, namely menstruation, and the clean period between two menstruations. The Ḥanafīs, the Ḥanbalīs and the Zaydīs have upheld the first, while the Shāfiᶜīs, Mālikīs and Jaᶜfarīs have upheld the second meaning of *qur'*.[80]

The plurality of meanings in a homonym may be due to the usage of different Arab tribes and communities. Some used it for one meaning, others for the other. Otherwise a word may have acquired a metaphorical meaning which became literal in course of time. When *Mushtarak* occurs in the Qur'ān or *Sunnah*, it denotes one meaning alone, not more than one. For the Lawgiver does not intend more than one meaning for a word at any given time. The Shāfiʿīs and some Muʿtazilah have taken exception to this view as they maintain that in the absence of any indication in support of one of the two or more meanings of a *Mushtarak*, both or all may be upheld simultaneously provided that they do not contradict one another. According to a variant view, however, plurality of meanings on a simultaneous basis is permissible in negation or denial (*nafy*) but not in affirmation and proof (*ithbāt*). If, for example, Aḥmad says 'I did not see a *ʿayn* (*mā ra'aytu ʿaynan*)', *ʿayn* in this negative statement could comprise all of its various meanings. But if Aḥmad says 'I saw a *ʿayn*', than *ʿayn* in this statement must be used for only one of its several meanings.[81] This view, however, does not extend to commands and prohibitions which do not admit of affirmation or denial as such. The rule in regard to commands and prohibitions of the *Sharīʿah* is that the Lawgiver does not intend to uphold more than one of the different meanings of a homonym at any given time. An example of a homonym which occurs in the context of a Qur'ānic command is the word '*yad*' (hand) in 'as for the thief, male or female, cut off their hands' (al-Mā'idah, 5:38). 'Hand' in this *āyah* has not been qualified in any way, hence it can mean 'hand' from the tip of the fingers up to the wrist, or up to the elbow, or even up to the shoulder; it also means left or right hand. But the ulema have agreed on the first and the last of these meanings, that is, the right hand, up to the wrist.[82] To illustrate the homonym in the context of a prohibitory order in the Qur'ān we refer to the word '*nakaḥa*' in sura al-Nisā' (4:22) which reads, 'and marry not women whom your fathers had married (*mā nakaḥa ābā'ukum*)'. '*Nakaḥa*' is a homonym which means both marriage and sexual intercourse. The Ḥanafīs, the Ḥanbalīs, al-Awzāʿī and others have upheld the latter, whereas the Shāfiʿīs and the Mālikīs have upheld the former meaning of *nakaḥa*. According to the first view, a woman who has had sexual intercourse with a man is forbidden to his children and grandchildren; a mere contract of marriage, without consummation, would thus not amount to a prohibition in this case. The Shāfiʿīs and Mālikīs, however, maintain that the text under discussion only refers to the contract of marriage. Accordingly a woman who has entered a contract of marriage with one's father or grandfather is unlawful for one to marry regardless as to whether the marriage had been consummated or not.[83]

To determine which of the two or more meanings of the *Mushtarak* is to be upheld in a particular locution, reference is usually made to the context and circumstances in which it occurs. If it is a locution that pertains to the *Sharīᶜah*, then determining the precise purport of its words must also take into consideration the general principles and objectives of the *Sharīᶜah*. The *Mushtarak* is in the nature of *Mushkil* (difficult) and it is for the *Mujtahid* to determine its correct meaning by means of research and *ijtihād*; it is his duty to do so in the event where *Mushtarak* constitutes the basis of a judicial order.[84] The *mujtahid* will normally look into the context. When, for example, a homonym has two meanings, one literal and the other juridical, and it occurs in a juridical context, than as a rule the juridical meaning will prevail. With words such as *ṣalāh* and *ṭalāq*, for example, each possesses a literal meaning, that is 'supplication' and 'release' respectively, but when they occur in a juridical context, then their juridical meanings will take priority. As such, *ṣalāh* would be held to refer to a particular form of worship, and *ṭalāq* would mean 'dissolution of marriage'.

Finally it will be noted in passing that *Mushtarak* as a concept is not confined to nouns but also includes verbs. In our discussion of commands and prohibitions in a separate chapter, we have shown how a word in its imperative mood can impart more than one meaning. We have also discussed and illustrated the words of the Qur'ān that occur in the imperative mood, but the juridical value that they convey can either be an obligatory command, a recommendation, or mere permissibility.

NOTES

1. Cf. Abdur Rahim, *Jurisprudence*, p. 78.
2. Badrān, *Bayān*, p. 124 ff.
3. Khallāf, *ᶜIlm*, pp. 167–68.
4. Āmidī, *Iḥkām*, III, 53; Badrān, *Uṣūl*, p. 400.
5. Āmidī, *Iḥkām*, III, 54; Badrān, *Uṣūl*, pp. 400–401.
6. Tabrīzī, *Mishkāt*, III, 948, Ḥadīth no. 3178; Āmidī, *Iḥkām*, II, 54; Badrān, *Uṣūl*, p. 401.
7. Āmidī, *Iḥkām*, III, 56; Badrān, *Uṣūl*, p. 401. See for more examples of far-fetched interpretation, Āmidī, *Iḥkām* III, 55–64.
8. Badrān, *Uṣūl*, p. 402.
9. Khallāf, *ᶜIlm*, p. 166.
10. Ibid., p. 161; Badrān, *Uṣūl*, p. 403; Abū Zahrah, *Uṣūl*, p. 93.
11. Abū Zahrah, *Uṣūl*, p. 93; Badrān, *Uṣūl*, p. 402.
12. Abū Dāwud, *Sunan* (Hasan's trans.), II, 551, Ḥadīth no. 2060; Khallāf, *ᶜIlm*, p. 163; Abū Zahrah, *Uṣūl*, p. 94.
13. Badrān, *Uṣūl*, p. 403; Abū Zahrah, *Uṣūl*, p. 94.
14. Tabrīzī, *Mishkāt*, II, 1203, Ḥadīth no. 4132.
15. Abū Dāwud, *Sunan*, II, 410, Ḥadīth no. 1567.

16. Khallāf, ʿ*Ilm*, p. 165; Āmidī (*Iḥkām*, III, 57) considers this to be a *ta'wīl* which is far-fetched.
17. Khallāf, ʿ*Ilm* p. 166.
18. Abū Zahrah, *Uṣūl*, p. 95.
19. Cf. Khallāf, ʿ*Ilm*, p. 166.
20. Abū Zahrah, *Uṣūl*, p. 96; Badrān, *Uṣūl*, pp. 404–405.
21. Tabrīz, *Mishkāt*, I, 215, Ḥadīth no. 683; Shāṭibī, *Muwāfaqāt* III, 178; Khallāf, ʿ*Ilm*, p. 167; Badrān, *Uṣūl*, p. 405.
22. Badrān, *Uṣūl*, p. 404.
23. Abū Dāwud, *Sunan*, I, 76, Ḥadīth nos. 294, and 304 respectively.
24. Ibid.
25. Khallāf, ʿ*Ilm*, p. 169; Badrān, *Uṣūl*, p. 408.
26. Hughes, *Dictionary of Islam*, p. 518; Badrān, *Uṣūl*, p. 406; Abū Zahrah, *Uṣūl*, p. 96.
27. Abū Dāwud, *Sunan*, II, 702, Ḥadīth no. 2526; Abū Zahrah, *Uṣūl*, p. 96.
28. Abū Zahrah, *Uṣūl*, p. 96; Badrān, *Uṣūl*, p. 406.
29. Abū Dāwud, *Sunan* (Hasan's trans.), II, 555 Ḥadīth no. 2078; Badrān, *Uṣūl*, p. 408.
30. Badrān, *Uṣūl*, p. 409.
31. Khallāf, ʿ*Ilm*, p. 162; Badrān, *Uṣūl*, p. 409.
32. Khallāf, ʿ*Ilm*, p. 170; Badrān, *Uṣūl*, p. 410.
33. Shāfiʿī, *Al-Risālah*, p. 80.
34. Badrān, *Uṣūl*, p. 411.
35. Khallāf, ʿ*Ilm*, p. 173; Badrān, *Uṣūl*, p. 413.
36. Muslim, *Ṣāḥiḥ Muslim*, I, 252, Ḥadīth no 949; Khallāf, ʿ*Ilm*, pp. 173–175; Badrān, *Uṣūl*, pp. 414–415.
37. *The Holy Qur'ān* (Yusuf Ali's trans.) p. 118; Denffer, ʿ*Ulūm*, p. 84; Abdur Rahim, *Jurisprudence*, p. 100.
38. Badrān, *Uṣūl*, p. 416.
39. Khallāf, ʿ*Ilm*, p. 176.
40. Ghazālī, *Mustaṣfā*, I, 68.
41. Shawkānī, *Irshād*, pp. 31–32.
42. Ghazālī, *Mustaṣfā*, II, 12; Abdur Rahim, *Jurisprudence*, p. 79.
43. Khallāf, ʿ*Ilm*, p. 178; Badrān, *Uṣūl*, p. 375.
44. Badrān, *Uṣūl*, p. 370.
45. Abdur Rahim, *Jurisprudence*, p. 79.
46. Shāṭibī, *Muwāfaqāt*, III, 154.
47. Badrān, *Uṣūl*, pp. 386–387; Khallāf, ʿ*Ilm*, p. 185.
48. Khallāf, ʿ*Ilm* p. 182 ff; Badrān, *Uṣūl*, p. 371 ff; Abdur Rahim, *Jurisprudence*, p. 86 ff.
49. Shāṭibī, *Muwāfaqāt*, III, 153; Abū Zahrah, *Uṣūl*, p. 124; Abdur Rahim, *Jurisprudence*, p. 82.
50. Abū Zahrah, *Uṣūl*, p. 125; Badrān, *Uṣūl*, p. 381.
51. Bayhaqī, *Al-Sunan al-Kubrā*, VII, 240; Badrān, *Uṣūl*, p. 383.
52. Shawkānī, *Irshād*, p. 157; Abū Zahrah, *Uṣūl*, p. 125.
53. Abdur Rahim, *Jurisprudence*, pp. 83–84; Khallāf, ʿ*Ilm*, p. 187; Badrān, *Uṣūl*, pp. 375–378.
54. Abū Zahrah, *Uṣūl*, p. 128; Abdur Rahim, *Jurisprudence*, p. 84; Badrān, *Uṣūl*, p. 379.
55. Badrān, *Uṣūl*, p. 376.
56. Abū Zahrah, *Uṣūl*, pp. 128–129.
57. Ibid., p. 129.

58. Ghazālī, *Mustaṣfā*, II, 103–105.
59. Khallāf, *ᶜIlm* p. 183; Abū Zahrah, *Uṣūl*, p. 129.
60. Abū Dāwud, *Sunan* (Hasan's trans.), II, 1149; Ḥadīth no. 4111; Abū Zahrah, *Uṣūl*, p. 130.
61. Abū Zahrah, *Uṣūl*, p. 130; Khallāf, *ᶜIlm*, p. 189.
62. Ibid, p. 131; Badrān, *Uṣūl*, p. 383.
63. Al-Tabrīzī, *Mishkāt*, I, 563–65, Ḥadīth nos. 1794 & 1797; Abū Zahrah, *Uṣūl*, p. 131.
64. Cf. Abū Zahrah, *Uṣūl*, p. 132.
65. Khallāf, *ᶜIlm*, p. 192; Badrān, *Uṣūl*, pp. 351, 371.
66. Anṣārī, *Ghāyat al-Wuṣūl*, p. 84.
67. Khallāf, *ᶜIlm*, p. 193; Abdur Rahim, *Jurisprudence*, pp. 91–92.
68. Ibid., p. 194; Badrān, *Uṣūl*, p. 354.
69. Ibid., pp. 193–194.
70. Abdur Rahim, *Jurisprudence*, p. 93; Badrān, *Uṣūl*, p. 394.
71. See for details Shawkānī, *Irshād*, pp. 23–24.
72. Badrān, *Uṣūl*, p. 395; Hitu, *Wajīz*, p. 115.
73. Ghazālī, *Mustaṣfā*, I, 67–78.
74. Hitu, *Wajīz*, p. 115.
75. Badrān, *Uṣūl*, p. 394; Hitu, *Wajīz*, p. 112.
76. See for further detail on the various forms of the *Majāzī*, Abdur Rahim, *Jurisprudence*, pp. 94–97; Badrān, *Uṣūl*, p. 397 ff.
77. Badrān, *Uṣūl*, p. 398.
78. Abdur Rahim, *Jurisprudence*, p. 98.
79. Badrān, *Uṣūl*, p. 397.
80. Abū Zahrah, *Uṣūl*, p. 132; *EI*², IV, 101.
81. Shawkānī, *Irshād*, p. 21; Isnāwī, *Nihāyah*, I, 166; Abū Zahrah, *Uṣūl*, p. 133.
82. Khallāf, *ᶜIlm*, p. 180.
83. Badrān, *Bayān*, pp. 103–104.
84. Abū Zahrah, *Uṣūl*, p. 133; Khallāf, *ᶜIlm*, p. 179.

CHAPTER FIVE

Rules of Interpretation II: *Al-Dalālāt* (Textual Implications)

The law normally requires compliance not only with the obvious meaning of its text but also with its implied meaning, and indirect indications and inferences that could be drawn from it. With reference to the textual rulings of the Qur'ān and the *Sunnah*, the ulema of *uṣūl* have distinguished several shades of meaning that a *naṣṣ* may be capable of imparting. The Ḥanafī jurists have distinguished four levels of meaning in an order which begins with the explicit or immediate meaning of the text. Next in this order is the 'alluded' meaning which is followed by the 'inferred' meaning, and lastly by the 'required' meaning. There is yet a fifth variety of meaning, namely the 'divergent' meaning, which is somewhat controversial but has, in principle, been accepted, as our discussion will show. The explicit meaning (*ʿibārah al-naṣṣ*), which is based on the words and sentences of the text, is the dominant and most authoritative meaning which takes priority over the other levels of implied meanings that might be detectable in the text. In addition to its obvious meaning, a text may impart a meaning which is indicated by the signs and allusions that it might contain. This secondary meaning is referred to as *ishārah al-naṣṣ*, that is the alluded meaning. A legal text may also convey a meaning which may not have been indicated by the words or signs and yet is a complementary meaning which is warranted by the logical and juridical purport of the text. This is known as *dalālah al-naṣṣ*, or the inferred meaning, which is one degree below the alluded meaning by virtue of the fact that it is essentially extraneous to the text. But as will later be discussed, there is a difference of opinion between the Ḥanafī and the Shāfiʿī jurists as to whether the inferred meaning should necessarily be regarded as inferior to the alluded meaning. Next in this order is the *iqtiḍā' al-naṣṣ*, or the required meaning, which is once again a logical and necessary meaning without which the text would remain incomplete and would fail to achieve its desired purpose.[1] When there is a conflict between the first and the second meanings, priority is given to the first. Similarly, the second will take priority over the third and the third over the fourth, as we shall presently explain.

I. The Explicit Meaning (*ʿIbārah al-Naṣṣ*)

As already stated, this is the immediate meaning of the text which is derived from its obvious words and sentences. The explicit meaning represents the principal theme and purpose of the text, especially in cases where the text might impart more than one meaning and comprises in its scope a subsidiary theme or themes in addition to the one which is obvious. In its capacity as the obvious and dominant meaning, the *ʿibārah al-naṣṣ* is always given priority over the secondary and subsidiary themes or meanings of the text. To illustrate this, we refer to the Qur'ānic passage on the subject of polygamy, a text which conveys more than one meaning, as follows 'And if you fear that you may be unable to treat the orphans fairly, then marry of the women who seem good to you, two, three or four. But if you fear that you cannot treat [your co-wives] equitably, then marry only one . . .' (al-Nisā', 4:3). At least three or four meanings are distinguishable in this text which are: first, the legality of marriage, a meaning which is conveyed by the phrase *fankiḥū mā ṭāba lakum min al-nisā'* ('marry of the women who seem good to you'); second, limiting polygamy to the maximum of four; third, remaining monogamous if polygamy may be feared to lead to injustice; and fourth, the requirement that orphaned girls must be accorded fair treatment, a meaning which is indicated in the first part of the text. All of these are conveyed in the actual words and sentences of the text. But the first and the last are subsidiary and incidental whereas the second and the third represent the explicit themes and meanings of the text, that is, the *ʿibārah al-naṣṣ*. Limiting polygamy to the maximum of four is the explicit meaning which takes absolute priority over all the implied and incidental meanings that this text might convey.[2]

Most of the *nuṣūṣ* of *Sharīʿah* convey their rulings by way of *ʿibārah al-naṣṣ*. Thus the command to perform the obligatory prayers, to observe the fast during Ramadan, to enforce the prescribed penalties for certain offences, to give specified shares to the legal heirs in inheritance, etc., are all instances of *ʿibārah al-naṣṣ*. The effect of *ʿibārah al-naṣṣ* is that it conveys a definitive ruling *ḥukm qaṭʿī* on its own and is in no need of corroborative evidence. But if the text is conveyed in general terms, it may be susceptible to qualification, in which case it may not impart a definitive rule of law but a speculative (*ẓannī*) evidence only.[3]

II. The Alluded Meaning (*Ishārah al-Naṣṣ*)

The text itself may not be obvious with regard to its alluded meaning, but it imparts, nevertheless, a rationally concomitant meaning which is obtained through further investigation of the signs that might be detectable therein. Since the alluded meaning does not represent the principal theme of the text and yet embodies a necessary inference, it is called *ishārah al-naṣṣ*. The alluded meaning may be easily detectable in the text, or may be reached through deeper investigation and *ijtihād*. An example of the *ishārah al-naṣṣ* in the Qur'ān is the text concerning the maintenance of young children which provides: 'It is his [father's] duty to provide them with maintenance and clothing according to custom' (al-Baqarah, 2:233). The explicit meaning of this text obviously determines that it is the father's duty to support his child. It is also understood from the wording of the text, especially from the use of the pronoun '*lahu*' (his) that only the father and no-one else bears this obligation. This much is easily detectable and constitutes the explicit meaning of this text. But to say that the child's descent is solely attributed to the father and his identity is determined with reference to that of the father is a rational and concomitant meaning which is derived through further investigation of the signs that are detectable in the text.[4] Similarly, the rule that the father, when in dire need, may take what he needs of the property of his offspring without the latter's permission is yet another meaning which is derived by way of *ishārah al-naṣṣ*. This meaning is derived from the combination of the text under discussion and the Ḥadīth of the Prophet which proclaims that 'you and your property both belong to your father'.[5]

أنت ومالك لوالدك

Another example of a combination of the explicit and alluded meanings occurring in the same text is the Qur'ānic *āyah* on the permissibility of divorce which provides, in an address to the believers: 'There shall be no blame on you if you divorce your wives with whom you had no sexual intercourse, nor had you assigned for them a dower' (al-Baqarah, 2:236). The explicit meaning of this text is that divorce is permissible prior to the consummation of marriage and the assignment of a dower. The alluded meaning here is the legality of concluding a contract of marriage without the assignment of a dower (*mahr*). For a divorce can only occur when there is a subsisting marriage. The text implies this to be the case, and that a marriage can legally exist even without the assignment of a *mahr*[6].

To give yet another example of *ishārah al-naṣṣ* we may refer to the Qur'ānic text on consultation (*shūrā*) where we read, in an address to the Prophet, 'So pardon them [the Companions] and ask for [God's] forgiveness for them and consult them in affairs' (Āl-ʿImrān, 3:159). The *ʿibārah al-naṣṣ* in this text requires that community affairs must be conducted through consultation. The alluded meaning of this text requires the creation of a consultative body in the community to facilitate the consultation which is required in the obvious text.

The effect of *ishārah al-naṣṣ* is similar to that of *ʿibārah al-naṣṣ* in that both constitute the basis of obligation, unless there is evidence to suggest otherwise. To illustrate this, we may refer once again to the Qur'ānic text (al-Baqarah, 2:233) which laid down the rule that the child follows the descent of his father. This is a definitive ruling (*ḥukm qaṭʿī*) which has, however, been set aside by *ijmāʿ* in respect of slavery to the effect that the offspring of a slave does not necessarily acquire the status of his father. In this example, the *ishārah al-naṣṣ* initially laid down a definitive ruling but it has been set aside in respect of slavery by another definitive evidence, namely the *ijmāʿ*.[7]

III. The Inferred Meaning (*Dalālah al-Naṣṣ*)

This is a meaning which is derived from the spirit and rationale of a legal text even if it is not indicated in its words and sentences. Unlike the explicit meaning and the alluded meaning which are both indicated in the words and signs of the text, the inferred meaning is not so indicated. Instead, it is derived through analogy and the identification of an effective cause (*ʿillah*) which is in common between the explicit meaning and the meaning that is derived through inference. This might explain why some ulema have equated *dalālah al-naṣṣ* with analogical deduction, namely *qiyās jalī*. To illustrate this, we may refer to the Qur'ānic text on the obligation to respect one's parents. In particular, the text provides, 'and say not *uff* to them' (al-Isrā' 17:23), which obviously forbids the utterance of the slightest word of contempt to the parents. The effective cause of this prohibition is honouring the parents and avoiding offence to them. There are, of course, other forms of offensive behaviour, besides a mere contemptuous word such as *uff*, to which the effective cause of this prohibition would apply. The inferred meaning of this text is thus held to be that all forms of abusive words and acts which offend the parents are forbidden even if they are not specifically mentioned in the text under consideration.[8]

To give another example, the Qur'ān proclaims, concerning the property of orphans, that 'those who unjustly devour the property of the orphans only devour fire into their bodies' (al-Nisā', 4:10). The explicit meaning of this text forbids guardians and executors from devouring the property of their orphaned wards for their personal gain. But by way of inference the same prohibition is extended to other forms of destruction and waste which might have been caused, for example, through financial mismanagement that does not involve personal gain and yet leads to the loss and destruction of the property of the orphans. Although the text provides no indication as to the different ways in which destruction can be caused, they are nevertheless equally forbidden. As already stated, this kind of inference is equivalent to what is known as obvious analogy (*qiyās jalī*) which consists of identifying the effective cause of a textual ruling, and when this is identified the original ruling is analogically extended to all similar cases. The effective cause of the ruling in the foregoing *āyah* is protection of the orphans' property, and any act which causes destruction or loss of such property falls under the same prohibition.[9]

IV. The Required Meaning (*Iqtiḍā' al-Naṣṣ*)

This is a meaning on which the text itself is silent and yet which must be read into it if it is to fulfil its proper objective. To give an example, the Qur'ān proclaims concerning the prohibited degrees of relations in marriage: 'unlawful to you are your mothers and your daughters . . .' (al-Nisā', 4:22). This text does not mention the word 'marriage', but even so it must be read into the text to complete its meaning. Similarly we read elsewhere in the Qur'ān: 'unlawful to you are the dead carcass and blood' (al-Mā'idah, 5:3), without mentioning that these are unlawful 'for consumption'. But the text requires the missing element to be supplied in order that it may convey a complete meaning.

To give a slightly different example of *iqtiḍā' al-naṣṣ*, we may refer to the Ḥadīth which provides: "There is no fast (*lā ṣiyāma*) for anyone who has not intended it from the night before."

لا صيام لمن لم يفرضه من الليل

The missing element could either be that the fasting is 'invalid' or that it is 'incomplete'. The Ḥanafīs have upheld the latter whereas the Shāfiʿīs have read the former meaning into this Ḥadīth. Whichever meaning is upheld, the consequences that it may lead to will vary accordingly.[10]

To summarise, a legal text may be interpreted through the application of any one or more of the four varieties of textual implications. The meaning that is arrived at may be indicated in the words of the text, by the signs which occur therein, by inference, or by the supplementation of a missing element. These methods of legal construction may be applied individually or in combination with one another, and they are all designed to carry the text to its proper and logical conclusions.

As stated above, in the event of a conflict between the *ʿibārah al-naṣṣ* and the *ishārah al-naṣṣ*, the former prevails over the latter. This may be illustrated by a reference to the two Qur'ānic *āyāt* concerning the punishment of murder. One of these explicitly proclaims that 'retaliation is prescribed for you in cases of murder' (al-Baqarah, 2:178). But elsewhere in the Qur'ān, it is provided: 'Whoever deliberately kills a believer, his punishment will be permanent hellfire' (al-Nisā', 4:93). The explicit meaning of the first *āyah* provides that the murderer must be retaliated against; the explicit meaning of the second *āyah* is that the murderer is punished with permanent hellfire. The alluded meaning of the second *āyah* is that retaliation is not a required punishment for murder; instead the murderer will, according to the explicit terms of this *āyah* be punished in the hereafter. There is no conflict in the explicit meanings of the two texts, but only between the explicit meaning of the first and the alluded meaning of the second. A conflict thus arises as to which of the two punishments are to be upheld. But since the first ruling constitutes the explicit meaning of the text and the second is an alluded meaning, the former prevails over the latter.[11]

For another illustration of a conflict between the explicit and the alluded meanings, we refer to the Qur'ānic text which informs the believers of the dignified status of the martyrs, as follows: 'And think not of those who are slain in God's way as dead; they are alive, finding their sustenance in the presence of God' (Al-ʿImrān, 3:169). The explicit terms of this text obviously declare the martyrs to be alive and that anyone who thinks they are dead is mistaken. The alluded meaning of this text is held to be that no funeral prayer is necessary for the martyr as he is deemed to be still alive. However, this conclusion conflicts with the explicit meaning of another Qur'ānic text which orders, concerning the dead in general, to 'pray on their behalf [*ṣalli ʿalayhim*] as your prayers are a source of tranquillity for them' (al-Tawbah, 9:103). This text explicitly requires prayers for everyone, martyr or otherwise, as they are dead literally and juridically and their property may be inherited by their legal heirs, etc. This is the explicit meaning of this second text and it prevails over the alluded meaning of the first.[12]

To illustrate the conflict between the alluded meaning and the inferred meaning, we refer firstly to the Qur'ānic text on the expiation of erroneous homicide which provides: 'The expiation (*kaffārah*) of anyone who erroneously kills a believer is to set free a Muslim slave' (al-Nisā', 4:92). The explicit meaning of this *āyah* is that erroneous homicide must be expiated by releasing a Muslim slave. By way of inference, it is further understood that freeing a Muslim slave would also be required in intentional homicide. For the purpose of *kaffārah* is compensation and atonement for a sin. It is argued that the murderer is also a sinner and has committed a sin far greater then the one who kills as a result of error. The inferred meaning derived in this way is that the murderer is liable, at least, to the same *kaffārah* which is required in erroneous homicide. However, according to the next *āyah* in the same passage, to which reference has already been made: 'Whoever deliberately kills a believer, his punishment is permanent hellfire' (al-Nisā', 4:93). The alluded meaning of this text is that freeing a slave is not required in intentional killing. This meaning is understood from the explicit terms of this *āyah* which provide that the punishment of deliberate homicide is a permanent abode in hell. This would in turn imply that murder is an unpardonable sin, and as such there is no room for *kaffārah* in cases of murder. This is the alluded meaning of the second *āyah*; and a conflict arises between this and the inferred meaning of the first *āyah*. The alluded meaning, which is that the murderer is not required to pay a *kaffārah*, takes priority over the inferred meaning that renders him liable to payment.[13]

The Shāfiʿīs are in disagreement with the Ḥanafīs on the priority of the alluded meaning over the inferred meaning. According to the Shāfiʿīs, the inferred meaning takes priority over the alluded meaning. The reason given for this is that the former is founded in both the language and rationale of the text whereas the latter is not; that the alluded meaning is only derived from a sign which is basically weaker than the words and the rationale of the text, and that the inferred meaning is a closer meaning and should therefore be given priority over the alluded meaning. It is on the basis of this analysis that, in the foregoing example, the Shāfiʿīs have given priority to the inferred meaning of the text with the result that the murderer is also required to pay the *kaffārah*.[14]

V. Divergent Meaning (*Mafhūm al-Mukhālafah*) and the Shāfiʿī Classification of *al-Dalālāt*

The basic rule to be stated at the outset here is that a legal text never implies its opposite meaning, and that any interpretation which aims at reading a divergent meaning into a given text is unwarranted and untenable. If a legal text is at all capable of imparting a divergent meaning, then there needs to be a separate text to validate it. But any attempt to obtain two divergent meanings from one and the same text is bound to defy the very essence and purpose of interpretation. This argument has been more forcefully advanced by the Ḥanafīs, who are basically of the view that *mafhūm al-mukhālafah* is not a valid method of interpretation.[15] Having said this, however, *mafhūm al-mukhālafah* is upheld on a restrictive basis not only by the Shāfiᶜīs but even by the Ḥanafīs; they have both laid down certain conditions which must be fulfilled so as to ensure the proper use of this method.

Mafhūm al-mukhālafah may be defined as a meaning which is derived from the words of the text in such a way that it diverges from the explicit meaning thereof.[16] To give an example, the Qur'ān proclaims the general rule of permissibility (*ibāḥah*) of foodstuffs for human consumption with a few exceptions which are specified in the following text: 'Say, I find nothing in the message that is revealed to me forbidden for anyone who wishes to eat except the dead carcass and blood shed forth' (*daman masfūḥan*) (al-Anᶜām, 6:145). With reference to the latter part of this text, would it be valid to suggest that blood which is not shed forth (*dam ghayr masfūḥ*) is lawful for human consumption? The answer to this question is in the negative. For otherwise the text would be subjected to an interpretation which is most likely to oppose its obvious meaning. As for the permissibility of unspilt blood such as liver and spleen, which consist of clotted blood, this is established, not by the *āyah* under consideration, but by a separate text. Liver and spleen are lawful to eat by virtue of the Ḥadīth of the Prophet which proclaims that 'lawful to us are two types of corpses and two types of blood. These are the fish, the locust, the liver and the spleen.'[17]

أُحلّت لنا ميتتان ودمان : الميتتان : الحوت
والجراد والدمان : الكبد والطّحال

As already indicated, the Shāfiᶜīs have adopted a different approach to *mafhūm al-mukhālafah*. But to put this matter in its proper perspective, we would need to elaborate on the Shāfiᶜī approach to textual implications (*'al-dalālāt'*) as a whole, and in the course of this general discussion, we shall turn to *mafhūm al-mukhālafah* in particular.

Unlike the Ḥanafī classification of textual implications into four types, the Shāfiᶜīs have initially divided *al-dalālāt* into the two main varieties of *dalālah al-manṭūq* (pronounced meaning) and *dalālah al-mafhūm* (implied meaning). Both of these are derived from the words and sentences of the text. The former form the obvious text and the latter come through logical and juridical construction thereof. An example of *dalālah al-manṭūq* is the Qur'ānic *āyah* which proclaims that 'God has permitted sale and prohibited usury' (al-Baqarah, 2:275). This text clearly speaks of the legality of sale and the prohibition of usury. *Dalālah al-manṭūq* has in turn been subdivided into two types, namely *dalālah al-iqtiḍā'* (required meaning), and *dalālah al-ishārah* (alluded meaning). Both of these are either indicated in the words of the text or constitute a necessary and integral part of its meaning. As will be noted, even from this brief description, the difference between the Shāfiʿī and Ḥanafī approaches to the classification of *al-dalālāt* is more formal than real.[18] Abū Zahrah has aptly observed that essentially all of the four Ḥanafī varieties of *al-dalālāt* are, in one way or another, founded in the actual words and sentences of the text. Despite the technical differences that might exist between the four types of implications, they are basically all founded in the text. In this way all of the four-fold Ḥanafī divisions of *al-dalālāt* can be classified under *dalālah al-manṭūq*.[19]

Dalālah al-mafhūm is an implied meaning which is not indicated in the text but is arrived at by way of inference. This is to a large extent concurrent with what the Ḥanafīs have termed *dalālah al-naṣṣ*. But the Shāfiʿīs have more to say on *dalālah al-mafhūm* in that they sub-divide this into the two types of *mafhūm al-muwāfaqah* (harmonious meaning) and *mafhūm al-mukhālafah* (divergent meaning). The former is an implicit meaning on which the text may be silent but is nevertheless in harmony with its pronounced meaning. This harmonious meaning (*mafhūm al-muwāfaqah*) may be equivalent to the pronounced meaning (*dalālah al-manṭūq*), or may be superior to it. If it is the former, it is referred to as *laḥn al-khiṭāb* (parallel meaning) and if the latter, it is known as *faḥwā al-khiṭāb* (superior meaning). For example, to extend the Qur'ānic ruling in sūra al-Nisā' (4:10) which only forbids 'devouring the property of orphans' to other forms of mismanagement and waste, is a 'parallel' meaning (*laḥn al-khiṭāb*). But to extend the Qur'ānic text which forbids the utterance of '*uff*', that is the slightest word of contempt, to, for instance, physical abuse of one's parents, is a meaning which is 'superior' to the pronounced meaning of the text.[20] The validity of these forms of harmonious meanings is approved by the ulema of all schools (except the Ẓāhirīs) who are generally in agreement with the basic concept of *mafhūm al-muwāfaqah*. But this is not the case with regard to *mafhūm al-mukhālafah*, on which the ulema have disagreed.[21]

As noted above, *mafhūm al-mukhālafah* diverges from the pronounced meaning (*dalālah al-manṭūq*) of the text, which may, however, be either in harmony or in disharmony with it. It is only when *mafhūm al-mukhālafah* is in harmony with the pronounced meaning of the text that it is accepted as a valid form of interpretation, otherwise it is rejected. For an example of the divergent meaning which is in harmony with the pronounced meaning of the text, we may refer to the Ḥadīth which provides: 'When the water reaches the level of *qullatayn* [approximately two feet] it does not carry dirt.'[22]

إذا بلغ الماء قلتين لم يحمل الخبث

In this way when a polluting substance falls into water of this depth, it is still regarded as clean for purposes of ablution. This is the pronounced, or explicit, meaning of the text. By way of *mafhūm al-mukhālafah*, it is understood that water below this level is capable of 'retaining' dirt. This is an interpretation which is deemed to be in harmony with the pronounced meaning of the Ḥadīth.[23]

According to the Shāfiʿīs, deduction by way of *mafhūm al-mukhālafah* is acceptable only if it fulfills certain conditions, which are as follows: firstly, that the divergent meaning does not exceed the scope of the pronounced meaning. For example, the Qur'ānic *āyah* which prohibits 'saying *uff*' to one's parents may not be given a divergent meaning so as to make physical abuse of them permissible. Secondly, that the divergent meaning has not been left out in the first place for a reason such as fear or ignorance; for example, if a man orders his servant to 'distribute this charity among the Muslims', but by saying so he had actually intended people in need, whether Muslims or non-Muslims, and yet omitted to mention the latter for fear of being accused of disunity by his fellow Muslims. Should there be evidence as to the existence of such a fear, then no divergent meaning should be deduced. A similar case would be when a person says that 'maintenance is obligatory for ascendants and descendants', while he did not know that collaterals are also entitled to maintenance. Should there be evidence as to his ignorance on this point, then no divergent meaning should be attempted to the effect, for example, of saying that maintenance is not obligatory for collaterals. Thirdly, that the divergent meaning does not go against that which is dominant and customary in favour of something which is infrequent and rare. To give an example: the Qur'ān provides concerning the prohibited degrees of relationship in marriage: 'and forbidden to you are [. . .] your step-daughters who live with you, born of your wives with whom you have consummated the marriage; but there is no prohibition if you have not consummated the marriage' (al-Nisā', 4:23). This text is explicit on the point that marriage to a step-daughter who is under the guardianship of her step-father is forbidden to the latter. By way of *mafhūm al-mukhālafah*, this *āyah* might be taken to mean that a step-daughter who does not live in the house of her mother's husband may be lawfully married by the latter. But this would be a meaning which relies on what would be a rare situation. The probable and customary situation in this case would be that the step-daughter lives with her mother and her step-father, which is why the Qur'ān refers to this qualification, and not because it was meant to legalise marriage with the step-daughter who did not live with him.[24] Fourthly, that the original text is not formulated in response to a particular question or event. For instance, the Prophet was once asked if free-grazing livestock was liable to *zakāh*; and he answered in the affirmative. But this answer does not imply that the stall-fed livestock is not liable to *zakāh*. The answer was originally given to a question which specified the free-grazing livestock and not in order to exempt the stall-fed variety from *zakāh*. Fifthly, that the divergent meaning does not depart from the reality, or the particular state of affairs, which the text is known to have envisaged. For example the Qur'ān provides in a reference to relations between Muslims and non-Muslims: 'Let not the believers befriend the unbelievers to the exclusion of their fellow believers' (Āl-ᶜImrān, 3:28). This *āyah* apparently forbids friendship with the unbelievers, but this is not the purpose of the text. This *āyah* was, in fact, revealed in reference to a particular state of affairs, namely concerning a group of believers who exclusively befriended the unbelievers, and they were forbidden from doing this; it did not mean to impose a ban on friendship with unbelievers. The text, in other words, contemplated a particular situation and not the enactment of a general principle, and should therefore not be taken out of context by recourse to *mafhūm al-mukhālafah*.[25] Sixthly, that the divergent meaning does not lead to a conclusion that would oppose another textual ruling. To give an example, we refer to the Qur'ānic text on the requirement of retaliation which provides: 'Retaliation is prescribed for you in cases of murder: the free for the free, the slave for the slave, the woman for the woman [. . .]' (al-Baqarah, 2:178). This text may not be taken by way of *mafhūm al-mukhālafah* to mean that a man is not retaliated against for murdering a woman. For such a conclusion would violate the explicit ruling of another Qur'ānic text which requires retaliation for all intentional homicides on the broadest possible basis of 'life for life' (al-Ma'idah, 5:45).

The main restriction that the Ḥanafīs have imposed on *mafhūm al-mukhālafah* is that it must not be applied to a revealed text, namely the Qur'ān and the *Sunnah*. As a method of interpretation, *mafhūm al-mukhālafah* is thus validated only with regard to a non-revealed text. Only in this context, that is, in regard to rational proofs and man-made law, can it provide a valid basis of *ḥukm* and *ijtihād*. The main reason that the Ḥanafīs have given in support of this view is that the Qurᶜān itself discourages reliance on *mafhūm al-mukhālafah*, for there are many injunctions in the Qur'ān and *Sunnah* whose meaning will be distorted if they were to be given divergent interpretation. To give an example, we read in the Qur'ān, in a reference to the number of months that God enacted on the day He created the universe, that there shall be twelve months in a year. The text then continues to provide that 'four of them are sacred, so avoid committing acts of oppression [*ẓulm*] therein' (al-Tawbah, 9:36).[26] By way of *mafhūm al-mukhālafah*, this text could be taken to mean that acts of oppression are permissible during the rest of the year. This would obviously corrupt the purpose of this text, as oppression is always forbidden regardless of the time in which it is committed.[27] Similarly, there is a Ḥadīth which instructs the believers that 'none of you may urinate in permanently standing water nor may you take a bath therein to cleanse yourselves of major pollution (*janābah*)'.[28]

لا يبولن أحدكم في الماء الدائم ولا يغتسلن
فيه من الجنابة

By way of *mafhūm al-mukhālafah*, this text could be taken to mean that taking a bath other than the one specifically for *janābah* is permissible in such water, or that urinating is permissible in flowing water, neither of which would be correct. Bathing in small ponds below a certain depth is not permitted whether it be for *janābah* or otherwise.

The Ḥanafīs have further concluded that whenever necessary the Qur'ān itself has stated the divergent implications of its own rulings, and when this is the case, the divergent meaning becomes an integral part of the text and must be implemented accordingly. This style of the Qur'ānic legislation suggests that if recourse to *mafhūm al-mukhālafah* were generally valid, there would be no need for it to be explicitly spelled out in the Qur'ānic text. The Qur'ān, in other words, is self-contained and does not leave it to us to deduce the law from it by recourse to divergent interpretation. Note, for example, the text which instructs the husband to avoid sexual intercourse with his wife during her menstruation. The text then immediately follows on to specify its own divergent implication: 'And approach them not until they are clean. But when they have purified themselves, you may approach them' (al-Baqarah, 2:223). In the same sūra, there is another text, to which reference has already been made, concerning the prohibition of marriage between the step-daughter and her step-father who has consummated the marriage with her mother. The text then continues to specify its divergent meaning by providing that 'there is no prohibition if you have not consummated the marriage' (al-Baqarah, 2:23). The Ḥanafīs have thus concluded that *mafhūm al-mukhālafah* is not applicable to the *nuṣūṣ* of the Qur'ān and *Sunnah*. We only deduce from the *nuṣūṣ* such rules as are in harmony with their explicit terms.[29]

The Shāfiʿīs and the Mālikīs who validate the application of *mafhūm al-mukhālafah* to the *nuṣūṣ* have, in addition to the conditions that were earlier stated, imposed further restrictions which consist of specifying exactly what forms of linguistic expressions are amenable to this method of interpretation. For this purpose the Shāfiʿīs have sub-divided *mafhūm al-mukhālafah* into four types. The main purpose of this classification is to introduce greater accuracy into the use of *mafhūm al-mukhālafah*, specifying that it is an acceptable method of deduction only when it occurs in any of the following forms but not otherwise:

1. *Mafhūm al-Ṣifah* (Implication of the Attribute). When the ruling of a text is dependent on the fulfilment of a quality or an attribute then the ruling in question obtains only when that quality is present; otherwise it lapses. This can be shown in the Qur'ānic text on the prohibited degrees of relations in marriage which includes 'the wives of your sons proceeding from your loins' (al-Nisā' 4:23). The pronounced meaning of this text is the prohibition of the wife of one's own son in marriage. The son has thus been qualified in the text by the phrase 'proceeding from your loins'. By way of *mafhūm al-mukhālafah*, it is concluded from this qualification that the wife of an adopted son, or of a son by fosterage (*raḍāʿa*), that is a child who has suckled the breast of one's wife, is not prohibited.[30]
2. *Mafhūm al-Sharṭ* (Implication of the Condition). When the ruling of a text is contingent on a condition, then the ruling obtains only in the presence of that condition, and lapses otherwise. An example of this is the Qur'ānic text on the entitlement to maintenance of divorced women who are observing their waiting period (*ʿiddah*). The text proclaims: 'If they are pregnant, then provide them with maintenance until they deliver the child' (al-Ṭalāq, 65:6). The condition here is pregnancy and the *ḥukm* applies only when this condition is present. By way of *mafhūm al-mukhālafah*, it is concluded, by those who validate this method at least, that maintenance is not required if the divorced woman, who is finally divorced, is not pregnant. Similarly, the Qur'ānic test which provides for a concession in regard to fasting is conveyed in conditional terms. Having laid down the duty of fasting, the text then continues: 'but if any one is ill or travelling, the prescribed fasting should be observed later' (al-Baqarah, 2:185). By way of *mafhūm al-mukhālafah*, it is concluded that the concession to break the fast does not apply if one is neither ill nor travelling, which is a valid interpretation.[31]
3. *Mafhūm al-Ghāyah* (Implication of the Extent). When the text itself demarcates the extent or scope of the operation of its ruling, the latter will obtain only within the scope of the stated limits and will lapse when the

limit is surpassed. To illustrate this, the Qur'ānic text on the time of fasting provides the farthest limit beyond which one must stop eating and drinking during Ramadan: 'Eat and drink until you see the white streak [of dawn in the horizon] distinctly from the black' (al-Baqarah, 2:187). By way of *mafhūm al-mukhālafah*, it is concluded that when whiteness appears in the horizon, one may neither eat nor drink.[32]

4. *Mafhūm al-ᶜAdad* (Implication of the Stated Number). When the ruling of a text is conveyed in terms of a specified number, the number so stated must be carefully observed. Thus the Qur'ānic text on the punishment of adultery is clearly stated to be one hundred lashes (al-Nūr, 24:2). By way of *mafhūm al-mukhālafah* this text is taken to mean that it is not permissible either to increase or decrease the stated number of lashes.[33]

In conclusion, it may be said that the foregoing methods are generally designed to encourage rational enquiry in the deduction of the *aḥkām* from the divinely revealed sources. They provide the jurist and the *mujtahid* with guidelines so as to ensure the propriety of interpretation and *ijtihād*. The restrictions that are imposed on the liberty of the *mujtahid* are obvious enough in that the textual rulings of the Qur'ān and *Sunnah* must be treated carefully so that they are not stretched beyond the limits of their correct implications. Yet the main thrust of the guidelines that are provided is one of encouragement to the exercise of rational enquiry in the understanding and implementation of the *nuṣūṣ*. The rules of interpretation that are discussed under this and the preceding chapter are once again indicative of the primacy of revelation over reason, and yet they are, at the same time, an embodiment of the significant role that reason must play side by side with the revelation. The two are substantially concurrent and complementary to one another.

NOTES

1. Khallāf, *ᶜIlm*, p. 143; Badrān, *Uṣūl*, p. 417.
2. Khallāf, *'Ilm*, p. 145.
3. Badrān, *Uṣūl*, pp. 419–420; Khuḍarī, *Uṣūl*, p. 119.
4. Abū Zahrah, *Uṣūl*, p. 111; Khuḍarī, *Uṣūl*, p. 120.
5. Tabrīzī, *Mishkāt*, II, 1002, Ḥadīth no. 3354; Khallāf, *ᶜIlm*, p. 146.
6. Badrān, *Uṣūl*, p. 420.
7. Ibid., p. 421.
8. Abū Zahrah, *Uṣūl*, p. 112.
9. Khallāf, *ᶜIlm*, p. 150.
10. Ibn Mājah, *Sunan*, I, 542, Ḥadīth no. 1700; Badrān, *Uṣūl*, p. 424.
11. Abū Zahrah, *Uṣūl*, p. 115; Khallāf, *ᶜIlm*, p. 150.
12. Badrān, *Uṣūl*, p. 428.
13. Ibid., p. 429; Khallāf, *ᶜIlm*, p. 153.

14. Abū Zahrah, *Uṣūl*, p. 115.
15. Khallāf, *ᶜIlm*, p. 153.
16. Hitu, *Wajīz*, p. 125.
17. Tabrīzī, *Mishkāt*, II, 1203, Ḥadīth no. 4132; Khallāf, *ᶜIlm* p. 154.
18. Badrān, *Uṣūl*, p. 429; Khuḍarī, *Uṣūl*, pp. 121–122; Hitu, Wajīz, p. 120.
19. Abū Zahrah, *Uṣūl*, p. 116.
20. Hitu, *Wajīz*, p. 124; Ṣāliḥ, *Mabāḥith*, p. 301.
21. Badrān, *Uṣūl*, p. 430.
22. Ibn Mājah, *Sunan* I, 172, Ḥadīth no. 518.
23. Zuhayr, *Uṣūl*, II, 114.
24. Hitu, *Wajīz*, p. 125; Badrān, *Uṣūl*, p. 433.
25. Hitu, *Wajīz*, p. 126; Badrān, *Uṣūl*, p. 434.
26. These are the months of Muḥarram, Dhū al-Ḥijjah, Dhū al-Qiᶜdah and Rajab.
27. Badrān, *Uṣūl*, p. 435.
28. Tabrīzī, *Mishkāt*, I, 148; Ḥadīth no. 474.
29. Abū Zahrah, *Usūl*, pp. 117–118.
30. Badrān, *Uṣūl*, p. 432; Ṣāliḥ, *Mabāḥith*, p. 302; Khuḍarī, *Uṣūl*, p. 123.
31. Hitu, *Wajīz*, p. 127;
32. Khuḍarī, *Uṣūl*, p. 123.
33. Khuḍarī, *Uṣūl*, p. 123.

CHAPTER SIX

Commands and Prohibitions

The language of the Qur'ān (and the *Sunnah*) differs from that of modern statutes in that Qur'ānic legislation is not confined to commands and prohibitions and their consequences, but is often coupled with an appeal to the conscience of the individual. This moral appeal may consist of a persuasion or a warning, an allusion to the possible benefit or harm that may accrue from observing or violating an injunction, or a promise of reward/punishment in the hereafter. Modern laws are often devoid of such appeals, as they are usually confined to an exposition of imperative rules and their tangible results.[1]

Commands and prohibitions in the Qur'ān occur in a variety of forms. While an injunction is normally expected to be in the imperative mood, there are occasions where a simple past is used as a substitute. For example, the injunctions that 'retaliation is prescribed for you in cases of murder' and that 'fasting is prescribed for you' (al-Baqarah, 2:178 and 183) are both expressed in the past tense. Similarly, a Qur'ānic injunction may occur in the form of a moral condemnation of a certain form of conduct, such as the rule on the sanctity of private dwellings which provides: 'It is no virtue to enter houses from the back' (al-Baqarah, 2:189).[2] Also, a Qur'ānic command/prohibition may be conveyed in the form of an allusion to the consequences of a form of conduct, such as a promise of reward or punishment in the hereafter. For example, after expounding the rules of inheritance in sūra al-Nisā' (4:13–14) the text goes on to promise to those who observe them a reward, and warns violators of a punishment, in the hereafter.

I. Commands

A command proper (*amr*) is defined as a verbal demand to do something issued from a position of superiority over who is inferior.[3] Command in this sense differs from both supplication (*duʿā'*) and request (*iltimās*) in that the former is a demand from an inferior to one who is superior, whereas a request is a demand among people of equal or near-equal status. Since a verbal command can mean different things, namely an obligatory order, a mere recommendation, or even permissibility, the ulema have differed as to which of these is the primary and which the secondary meaning of a command. Some have held the view that *amr* is in the nature of a homonym (*mushtarak*) which imparts all of these meanings. Others have held that *amr* partakes in only two of these concepts, namely obligation and recommendation, but not permissibility. Still others have held that *amr* implies a permission to do something and that this is the widest meaning of *amr*, which is common to all three of the foregoing concepts.[4]

According to the majority opinion, however, a command by itself, that is, when it is not attended by clues or circumstances that might give it a particular meaning, implies obligation or an emphatic demand only. But this may change in the event of other indications being present, which might reduce a command to permissibility, recommendation, or indeed to a variety of other meanings. Thus when we read in the Qur'ān commands such as *kulū wa'shrabū* ('eat and drink') (al-Aʿrāf, 7:31), the indications are that they amount to no more than permissibility (*ibāḥah*). For eating and drinking are the necessities of human life, and a command in respect of them must logically amount to a permissibility only. Similarly the Qur'ānic permission in respect of hunting after the completion of the *ḥajj* ceremonies given in sūra al-Mā'idah (5:2 – *wa idhā ḥalaltum faṣṭādū*) and its address to the believers to 'scatter in the land' (*fa'ntashirū fi'l-arḍ*) after performing the Friday prayers (al-Jumuʿah, 62 : 10) are both in the imperative form. But in both cases the purpose is to render these activities permissible only.[5]

A command may likewise convey a recommendation should there be indications to warrant this conclusion. This is, for example, the case with regard to the Qur'ānic command which requires the documentation of loans: 'When you give or take a loan for a fixed period, reduce it into writing' (al-Baqarah, 2:282). However, from an indication which occurs in the next *āyah* in the same sūra, it is concluded that the command here implies a recommendation (*nadb*) only. This *āyah* reads: 'and if one of you deposit a thing on trust, let the trustee [faithfully] discharge his trust'. Here the use of the word 'trust' (*amānah*) signifies that the creditor may trust the debtor even without any writing.[6] The majority of ulema have held the same view regarding the requirement of witnesses in commercial contracts, which is the subject of another Qur'ānic command occurring in the same passage, known as the *āyah al-mudāyanah* (2:282): 'Whenever you enter a contract of sale, let it be witnessed and let neither the scribe nor the witness suffer harm.' The Ẓāhirī ulema have upheld the obvious meaning of these provisions and have made documentation a requirement of every loan, or any form of deferred payment, and have made witnesses a requirement of every contract of sale. This, in their view, is more conducive to the fulfilment of contracts and the prevention of disputes among people.[7]

A command may, according to the indications provided by the context and circumstances, imply a threat, such as the Qur'ānic address to the unbelievers: 'Do what you wish' (*iʿmalū mā shi'tum-al-Nūr*, 24:33) and to the devil: 'Lead to destruction those that you can' (*wastafziz man istaṭaʿta*) (Banī Isrā'īl, 17:64). A command may similarly imply contempt (*ihānah*) such as the Qur'ānic address to the unbelievers on the Day of Judgement: 'Taste [the torture], you mighty and honourable!' A command may sometimes imply supplication when someone says, for example, 'O Lord grant me forgiveness', and indeed a host of other meanings which may be understood in the light of the context and surrounding circumstances.[8] As already noted, the majority of ulema have held that a command normally conveys an obligation unless there are indications to suggest otherwise.

The Lawgiver may at times order something which has hitherto been prohibited. The question then arises as to the nature of a command which follows a prohibition (*al-amr baʿd al-ḥaẓar*); does it convey an obligation or a mere permissibility? The majority of ulema have held the view that a command following a prohibition means permissibility, not obligation. Two examples of such a command in the Qur'ān have already been given above in the context of the permission to hunt following its prohibition during the *ḥajj* ceremonies and the permission to conduct trade following its prohibition at the time of the Friday prayers (al-Mā'idah, 5:2; and al-Jumuʿah, 62:10 respectively).[9] An example of such a command in the *Sunnah* is the Ḥadīth in which the Prophet is reported to have said: 'I had forbidden you from visiting the graves. Nay, visit them, for it reminds you of the hereafter'.[10]

كنت نهيتكم عن زيارة القبور ، الا فزوروها فانّها
تُذكِّر الآخرة

The next question which arises in this connection is whether a command requires a single compliance or repetition. According to the majority view, this question can only be determined in the light of indications which might specify that repeated performance is required. However in the absence of such indications, a single instance of performance is the minimum requirement of a command. Among the indications which determine repetition is when a command is issued in conditional terms. For example, the Qur'ānic provision 'if you are impure then clean yourselves' (al-Mā'idah, 5:7), or the text which provides: 'The adulterer and adultress, flog them each one hundred lashes', that is, if they commit adultery (al-Nūr, 24:2). Since the command to take a bath in the first *āyah* is conditional on *janābah*, that is, on sexual intercourse, then a bath must be taken following every instance of sexual intercourse. Similarly when a command is dependent on a cause or an attribute, then it must be fulfilled whenever the cause or the attribute is present. The Qur'ānic command, for example, which reads: 'Perform the *ṣalāh* at the decline of the sun' (Banī Isrā'īl, 17:18), requires repeated performance at every instance when the cause for it is present, that is, when the specified time of *ṣalāh* arrives.[11]

As for the question whether a command requires immediate or delayed performance, it is once again observed that the command itself merely consists of a demand, and the manner of its performance must be determined in the light of indications and surrounding circumstances. When, for example, A tells B to 'do such and such now', or alternatively orders him to 'do such and such tomorrow', both orders are valid and there is no contradiction. However, if a command were to require immediate execution then the word 'now' in the first order would be superfluous just as the word 'tomorrow' in the second order would be contradictory. When a person commands another to 'bring me some water' while he is thirsty, then by virtue of this indication, the command requires immediate performance just as the order to 'collect the rent' when it is given, say, in the middle of the month while the rent is collected at the end of each month, must mean delayed performance.

It is thus obvious that the commandant may specify a particular time in which the command must be executed. The time limit may be strict or it may be flexible. If it is flexible, like the command to perform the obligatory *ṣalāh*, then performance may be delayed until the last segment of the prescribed time. But if the command itself specifies no time limit, such as the order to perform an expiation (*kaffārah*), then execution may be delayed indefinitely within the expected limits of one's lifetime. However, given the uncertainty of the time of one's death, an early performance is recommended in regard to *kaffārāt*.[12]

And lastly the question arises as to whether a command to do something implies the prohibition of its opposite. According to the majority view, a command to do something does imply the prohibition of its opposite regardless as to whether the opposite in question consists of a single act or of a plurality of acts. Thus when a person is ordered to move, he is in the meantime forbidden to remain still; or when a person is ordered to stand, he is forbidden from doing any of a number of opposing acts such as sitting, crouching, lying down, etc. However, some ulema, including al-Juwaynī, al-Ghazālī, Ibn al-Ḥājib and the Muᶜtazilah, have held that a command does not imply the prohibition of its opposite. A group of the Ḥanafī and Shāfiᶜī ulema have held that only one of the several opposing acts, whether known or unknown, is prohibited, but not all.[13] The result of such differences would obviously have a bearing on whether the person who commits the opposite of a command must be penalised, and if so, to what extent. Specific answers to such questions can obviously only be determined in the light of the surrounding circumstances and the state of mind of the individual concerned, as well as the general objectives of the Lawgiver/commander that can be ascertained in a given command.

II. Prohibitions

Prohibition (*nahy*), being the opposite of a command, is defined as a word or words which demand the avoidance of doing something addressed from a position of superiority to one who is inferior.[14] The typical form of a prohibitory order in Arabic is that of a negative command beginning with *lā* such as *lā tafᶜal* (do not), or the Qur'ānic prohibition which reads 'slay not [*lā taqtulū*] the life which God has made sacred' (al-Anᶜām, 6:151). A prohibition may be expounded in a statement (*jumlah khabariyyah*) such as occurs, for example, in the Qur'ān (al-Baqarah, 2:221): 'prohibited to you are the flesh of dead corpses and blood'. It may sometimes occur in the form of a command which requires the avoidance of something, such as the Qur'ānic phrase *wa dharū al-bayᶜ* ('abandon sale', that is during the time of Friday *ṣalāh* – al-Jumuᶜah, 62:100), or *wa'jtanibū qawl al-zūr* ('avoid lying') in sūra al-Ḥajj (22:30), or may occur in a variety of other forms that are found in the Qur'ān.

A prohibition, like a command, may convey a variety of meanings. Although the primary meaning of *nahy* is illegality, or *taḥrīm*, *nahy* is also used to imply a mere reprehension (*karāhiyyah*), or guidance (*irshād*), or reprimand (*ta'dīb*), or supplication (*duᶜā'*). An example of *nahy* which implies reprehension is the Qur'ānic *āyah* addressing the believers to 'prohibit not [*lā tuḥarrimū*] the clean foods that God has made lawful to you' (al-Mā'idah, 5:87). *Nahy* which conveys moral guidance may be illustrated by the Qur'ānic *āyah* addressing the believers to 'ask not questions about things which, if made plain to you, may cause you trouble' (al-Mā'idah, 5:104). An example of *nahy* which implies a threat is when a master tells his recalcitrant servant: 'Don't follow what I say and you will see.' An example of *nahy* which conveys supplication in the Qur'ān occurs in sūra al-Baqarah (2:286) which reads: 'Our Lord, condemn us not if we forget.' Since *nahy* can convey several meanings, the ulema have differed as to which of these is the primary (*ḥaqīqī*) as opposed to the secondary or metaphorical meanings of *nahy*. Some have held that illegality (*taḥrīm*) is the primary meaning of *nahy* while others consider reprehension (*karāhiyyah*) to be the original meaning of *nahy*. According to yet another view, *nahy* is a homonym in respect of both. The majority (*jumhūr*) of ulema have held the view that *nahy* primarily implies *taḥrīm*, a meaning which will be presumed to prevail unless there are indications to suggest otherwise. An example of *nahy* in the Qur'ān which has retained its primary meaning is the phrase '*lā taqtulū*' in the *āyah* which provides 'slay not life which God has made sacred'. There is no indication in this text to warrant a departure from the primary meaning of *lā taqtulū*, which must therefore prevail. The primary meaning of *nahy* may be abandoned for a figurative meaning if there is an indication to justify this. Hence the phrase *lā tu'ākhidhnā* ('condemn us not') implies supplication, as the demand here is addressed to Almighty God, and is hence a demand from a position of inferiority, which indicates that the correct meaning of *nahy* in this context is supplication, or *du*ʿ*ā*'.[15]

III. Value of Legal Injunctions

The object of a prohibition may be to prevent an act such as adultery (*zinā*), or it may be to prevent the utterance of words such as those purporting to effect the sale of dead corpses, or of a freeman, by means of offer and acceptance. In either case, the prohibition does not produce any rights or legal effects whatsoever. Hence no right of paternity is established through *zinā*; on the contrary the perpetrator is liable to punishment. Similarly, no contract is concluded and no right of ownership is proven as a result of the sale of a corpse.

If the object of prohibition is an act, and it is prohibited owing to an extraneous attribute rather than the essence of the act itself, such as fasting on the day of ʿ*īd*, then the act is null and void (*bāṭil*) according to the Shāfiʿīs but is irregular (*fāsid*) according to the Ḥanafīs. The act, in other words, can produce no legal result according to the Shāfiʿīs, but does create legal consequences according to the Ḥanafīs although it is basically sinful. The Ḥanafīs consider such acts to be defective and must be dissolved by means of annulment (*faskh*), or must be rectified if possible. If the prohibition consists of words such as concluding a contract of sale which partakes in usury, it is still *bāṭil* according to the Shāfiʿīs but *fāsid* according to the Ḥanafīs, which means that it should be either revoked or amended to the extent that it is purified of its usurious content.

The position is, however, different with regard to devotional matters (*ʿibādāt*) whose purpose is seeking the pleasure of God. The *fāsid* in this area is equivalent to *bāṭil*. Hence there is no merit to be gained by fasting on the day of *ʿīd*, nor will it be taken into account in compensation to the fasting owed by the *mukallaf*.

But if the prohibition is due to an external factor such as a sale concluded at the time of the Friday prayer, or when *ṣalāh* is performed in usurped land (*al-arḍ al-maghṣūbah*), the ulema are generally in agreement that all the legal consequences will follow from the prohibited act, although the perpetrator would have incurred a sin. Thus the sale so concluded will prove the right of ownership and the *ṣalāh* is valid and no compensatory performance of the same *ṣalāh* will be required.[16] Further detail on the *fāsid* and *bāṭil* can be found in our discussion of the *aḥkām*, which is the subject of a separate chapter.

As for the question of whether a prohibition requires both immediate as well as repeated compliance, the ulema are generally in agreement that it does and that this is the only way a prohibition can be observed. Unless the object of a prohibition is avoided at all times, the prohibition is basically not observed. It is therefore necessary to avoid the prohibited act as from the moment it is issued and whenever it is applicable. This is the case with regard to prohibitions that are not qualified in any way, such as the Qur'ānic text concerning the property of the orphans which provides: 'Do not approach [*lā taqrabū*] the property of the orphan except in the way that is best' (al-Anʿam, 6:152). However if a prohibition is qualified by a condition that overrules immediate compliance, then it has to be observed within the meaning of that condition. An example of this occurs in the Qur'ān (al-Mumtaḥinah, 60:10) which reads, in an address to the believers: 'When there come to you believing women refugees, examine [and test] them. God knows best as to their faith. If you find that they are believers, then send them not back to the unbelievers.' In this *āyah*, the prohibition (not to send them back) is conditional upon finding that they are believers, and until then the prohibition must remain in abeyance.[17] There is a difference between a command and a prohibition in that the purpose of the former is to create something or to establish the existence of something, and this is realised by a single instance of execution, and there is basically no need for repetition. A prohibition on the other hand aims at the absence of something, and this cannot be realised unless it is absent all the time. A single instance of absence is thus not enough to fulfil the purpose of a prohibition.[18]

As already stated, a command which succeeds a prohibition conveys permissibility only. The position is once again different with regard to a prohibition: whenever a prohibition succeeds a command, it conveys illegality or *taḥrīm*, not a mere permissibility.[19]

Injunctions, whether occurring in the Qur'ān or the *Sunnah*, are of two types: explicit (*ṣarīḥ*) and implicit (*ghayr ṣarīḥ*). Explicit commands and prohibitions require total obedience without any allowance for individual circumstances and regardless as to whether they are found to be rational or not. For it is in the essence of devotion (*ᶜibādah*) that obedience does not depend on the rationality or otherwise of an injunction. The question arises as to whether one should adopt a literal approach to the enforcement of commands and prohibitions, or should allow considerations of rationality and *maṣlaḥah* to play a part in the manner of their implementation. For example, the Ḥadīth which provides that the owners of livestock must give 'one in forty sheep' in *zakāh*[20]: should this provision be followed literally, or could we say that the equivalent price of one or many sheep could also be given in *zakāh*? Similarly, when the Qur'ān enjoins the Muslims concerning attendance at the Friday congregational prayers to 'rush to the remembrance of God and abandon sale' (al-Jumuᶜah, 62:9), should the word rush (*fa's ᶜaw*) be taken literally or in the sense of an emphasis on diligence at attending the Friday prayers? A similar question can be raised with regard to the second part of the same *āyah* which commands the Muslims to 'abandon sale' (*wa dharū'l-bayᶜ*). Should this be taken to imply that a sale which has occurred at the specified time is actually unlawful and void, or should it once again be taken as an order that requires perseverence and consistent observance? Should one follow the main objective of the Lawgiver or the literal requirements of the text which convey a command or a prohibition? These are but some of the questions which are asked concerning the correct understanding of Qur'ānic injunctions.[21]

The implicit injunctions are also divided into two types. The first of these is when a ruling of the Qur'ān is conveyed in implicit terms but has been substantiated by the explicit terms of the Ḥadīth, in which case it becomes equivalent to an explicit ruling.[22] The second type of implicit injunction is when a ruling of the Qur'ān occurs, not in the form of a command or a prohibition, but as praise or condemnation of a certain conduct. The precise import of such provisions cannot always be ascertained as to whether they convey an injunction or a mere warning or recommendation as the case may be. Note for example the text which reads that 'God does not love the prodigals (*al-musrifīn*)' (al-Aᶜrāf, 7:31). The text of this *āyah* does not indicate the precise legal or religious enormity of extravagance, and it cannot be ascertained whether extravagance is prohibited or merely disapproved.

Another question which merits attention in the study of commands and prohibitions is related to the means that lead to the performance of a command, or the avoidance of a prohibition. The question is whether the means should also be covered by the rules which regulate their ends. Briefly, the answer to this question is in the affirmative. The means which lead to the observance of commands and prohibitions are covered by the same ruling which applies to the command/prohibition in the first place.[23]

A *mujtahid* who deduces the law from a given text must be adequately familiar with the language of the Qur'ān, and must know that the *aḥkām* are not only expressed in the imperative but that a praise or a promise of reward may in effect be equivalent to a command. Similarly, a mere denunciation, a threat of punishment in the hereafter, or a reference to the adverse consequences of a form of conduct, may be equivalent to a prohibition.[24] The distinction as to whether a command in the Qur'ān conveys an obligation (*wujūb*), a recommendation (*nadb*) or mere permissibility (*ibāḥah*) must be determined in the light of the objectives of the *Sharīᶜah* as well as by looking at the meaning of the words of the Qur'ān. To determine the value (*ḥukm*) of a command, attention is paid not only to the grammatical form of the words in which it is conveyed, but also to the general objectives of the law. This is equally true of a prohibitory text. To determine whether a prohibition conveys actual *taḥrīm*, or mere reprehension (*karāhah*) is not always easily understood from the words of the *nuṣūṣ*. Only a portion of the *nuṣūṣ* convey a precise meaning by virtue of clarity of their language. In Shāṭibī's estimation, a much larger portion of the *nuṣūṣ* of the Qur'ān cannot be determined by reference only to the linguistic forms in which they are expressed. The *mujtahid* must therefore be fully informed of the general principles and objectives of the *Sharīᶜah* so as to be able to determine the precise values of the *nuṣūṣ* and the commands or prohibitions that they contain.[25]

NOTES

1. Cf. Shaltūt, *Islām*, p. 499.
2. This is one of the several *āyāt* which occur in the Qur'ān concerning the privacy of one's home.
3. Badrān, *Uṣūl*, p. 360.
4. Ibid., p. 361; Shawkānī, *Irshād*, p. 91.
5. Cf. Shāṭibī, *Muwāfaqāt*, III, 88.
6. Khallāf, *ᶜIlm*, p. 111.
7. Abū Zahrah, *Uṣūl*, p. 75; Badrān, *Usūl*, p. 362.
8. Badrān, *Uṣūl*, pp. 361–362; Hitu, *Wajīz*, pp. 134–138
9. Badrān, *Uṣūl*, p. 363; Hitu, *Wajīz*, p. 141.
10. Ghazālī, *Mustaṣfā*, I, 83; Āmidī, *Iḥkām*, IV, 211; Tabrīzī, *Mishkāt*, I, 554, Ḥadīth no. 1769.
11. Shawkānī, *Irshād*, pp. 98–99; Badrān, *Uṣul*, p. 364.
12. Shawkānī, *Irshād*, pp. 99–100; Badrān, *Uṣūl*, pp. 365–366.
13. Shawkānī, *Irshād*, pp. 101–102.
14. Badrān, *Uṣūl*, p. 366.
15. Shawkānī, *Irshād*, pp. 109–110; Badrān, *Uṣūl*, pp. 366–368; Hitu, *Wajīz*, p. 150.
16. Shawkānī, *Irshād*, p. 110; Badrān, *Uṣūl*, p. 369.
17. Badrān, *Uṣūl*, p. 370.
18. Hitu, *Wajīz*, p. 151.
19. Ibid.
20. Abū Dāwud, *Sunan*, II, 410, Ḥadīth no. 1567; Ghazālī, *Mustaṣfā*, I, 159.
21. For a detailed treatment of commands and prohibitions see Shāṭibī, *Muwāfaqāt*, III, 90–140
22. Ibid., III, 92.
23. Ibid., III, 93.
24. Abū Zahrah, *Uṣūl*, p. 72.
25. Shāṭibī, *Muwāfaqāt*, III, 90.

CHAPTER SEVEN

Naskh (Abrogation)

Literally, *naskh* means 'obliteration', such as in *nasakhat al-rīḥ athar al-mashy*, meaning 'the wind obliterated the footprint'. *Naskh* also means transcription or transfer (*al-naql wa al-taḥwīl*) of something from one state to another while its essence remains unchanged. In this sense, '*naskh*' has been used in the Qur'ānic *āyah* which reads: *innā kunnā nastansikhu mā kuntum taᶜmalūn*, that is, 'verily We write all that you do' (al-Jāthiyah, 45:29). This usage of *naskh* can also be seen in the familiar Arabic expressions, *tanāsukh al-arwāḥ* (reincarnation), and *tanāsukh al-mawārīth*, the transfer of inheritance from persons to persons. The ulema have differed as to which of these two meanings of *naskh* is the literal (*ḥaqīqī*) as opposed to that which might be metaphorical (*majāzī*). Some ulema, including Abū Bakr al-Bāqillānī and al-Ghazālī, have held that '*naskh*' is a homonym and applies equally to either of its two meanings. According to the majority view, however, obliteration (*al-rafᶜ wa al-izālah*) is the primary, and transcription/transfer is the secondary, meaning of *naskh*.[1]

Naskh may be defined as the suspension or replacement of one *Sharīᶜah* ruling by another, provided that the latter is of a subsequent origin, and that the two rulings are enacted separately from one another. According to this definition, *naskh* operates with regard to the rules of *Sharīᶜah* only, a proviso which precludes the application of *naskh* to rules that are founded in rationality (*ᶜaql*) alone. The *ḥukm*, or ruling, in this definition not only includes commands and prohibitions but also the three intermediate categories of recommended, reprehensible and *mubāḥ*. The requirement that the two rulings must be separate means that each must be enacted in a separate text. For when they both occur in one and the same passage, it is likely that one complements or qualifies the other, or that one may embody a condition or an exception to the other.[2]

Abrogation applies almost exclusively to the Qur'ān and the *Sunnah*; its application to *ijmā*ᶜ and *qiyās*, as will later be explained, has been generally overruled. And even then, the application of *naskh* to the Qur'ān and *Sunnah* is confined, in terms of time, to one period only, which is the lifetime of the Prophet. There is, in other words, no *naskh* after the demise of the Prophet. But during his lifetime, there were instances when some of the rulings of the Qur'ān and *Sunnah* were either totally or partially repealed by subsequent rulings. This was due mainly to the change of circumstances in the life of the community and the fact that the revelation of the Qur'ān spanned a period of twenty-three years. The ulema are unanimous on the occurrence of *naskh* in the *Sunnah*. It is, however, with regard to the occurrence of *naskh* in the Qur'ān on which there is some disagreement both in principle as well as on the number of instances in which *naskh* is said to have occurred.[3]

Abrogation is by and large a Madinese phenomenon which occurred as a result of the changes that the Muslim community encountered following the Prophet's migration to Madinah. Certain rules were introduced, at the early stage of the advent of Islam, which were designed to win over the hearts of the people. An example of this is the number of daily prayers which was initially fixed at two but was later increased to five. Similarly, *mut*ᶜ*ah*, or temporary marriage, was initially permitted but was subsequently prohibited when the Prophet migrated to Madinah.[4] These and similar changes were effected in the *nuṣūṣ* at a time when the Muslim community acquired sovereign authority and fresh legislation was deemed necessary to regulate its life in the new environment of Madinah.

Some Ḥanafī and Muᶜtazilī scholars have held the view that *ijmā*ᶜ can abrogate a ruling of the Qur'ān or the *Sunnah*. The proponents of this view have claimed that it was due to *ijmā*ᶜ that ᶜUmar b. al-Khaṭṭāb discontinued the share of the *mu'allafah al-qulūb* in the *zakāh*. These were persons of influence whose friendship and co-operation was deemed to be beneficial to Islam.[5] The Qur'ān assigned them a share in *zakāh* (al-Tawbah, 9:60), but this was discontinued apparently because the *mujtahidūn* of the time reached a unanimous agreement to that effect. The correct view, however, is that owing to differences of opinion that are recorded on this matter, no *ijmā*ᶜ could be claimed to have materialised.[6] Besides, the majority of ulema have held that *ijmā*ᶜ neither abrogates nor can be abrogated itself; and at any rate *ijmā*ᶜ cannot abrogate a *naṣṣ* of the Qur'ān or the *Sunnah*. For a valid *ijmā*ᶜ may never be concluded in contradiction to the Qur'ān or the *Sunnah* in the first place. Al-Āmidī elaborates this as follows: the *ḥukm* which the *ijmā*ᶜ seeks to repeal might be founded in a *naṣṣ*, another *ijmā*ᶜ, or *qiyās*. The first is not possible, for the *ijmā*ᶜ which seeks to abrogate the *naṣṣ* of Qur'ān or *Sunnah* is either based on an indication (*dalīl*) or not. If it is not based on any *dalīl*, then it is likely to be erroneous, and if it is based on a *dalīl* this could either be a *naṣṣ* or *qiyās*. If the basis (*sanad*) of *ijmā*ᶜ is a *qiyās*, then abrogation is not permissible (as we shall explain later); and if the *sanad* of *ijmā*ᶜ is a *naṣṣ*, then abrogation is by that *naṣṣ*, not by *ijmā*ᶜ. The share of the *mu'allafah al-qulūb* was discontinued by ᶜUmar b. al-Khaṭṭāb on the grounds of the *Sharīᶜah*-oriented policy (*al-siyāsah al-sharᶜiyyah*), which is explained in the caliph's widely-quoted phrase that 'God has exalted Islam, which is no longer in need of their favour.'[7]

According to the general rule a Qur'ānic *naṣṣ* or a *Mutawātir* Ḥadīth cannot be abrogated by a weaker Ḥadīth, by *ijmā*ᶜ or by *qiyās*. For they are not of equal authority to the *naṣṣ*. This is, in fact, the main argument in support of the rule, already referred to, that no abrogation of the *nuṣūṣ* is possible after the demise of the Prophet, for the Qur'ān and the *Sunnah* ceased to be revealed with his demise. Since nothing weaker than the Qur'ān and *Sunnah* can abrogate anything in either of these sources, abrogation, to all intents and purposes, came to an end with the death of the Prophet. *Ijmā*ᶜ, *qiyās* and *ijtihād*, being weaker in comparison to the *nuṣūṣ*, cannot abrogate the rules of divine revelation.[8]

It is in view of these and similar considerations that the ulema have arrived at the general rule that *ijmā*ᶜ can neither abrogate anything nor be abrogated itself. Abrogation in other words is generally not relevant to *ijmā*ᶜ. The preferable view, however, is that *ijmā*ᶜ cannot abrogate the rulings of the Qur'ān, the *Sunnah*, or of another *ijmā*ᶜ which is founded in the Qur'ān, *Sunnah*, or *qiyās*. However, a subsequent *ijmā*ᶜ may abrogate an existing *ijmā*ᶜ which might be founded in considerations of public interest, or *maṣlaḥah mursalah*. This would in theory appear to be the only situation in which *ijmā*ᶜ could operate as an abrogator.[9]

And finally, since the principal function of *qiyās* is to extend the rulings of the Qur'ān and *Sunnah* to similar cases, it may never operate in the opposite direction, namely, to repeal a text of the Qur'ān or *Sunnah*. Broadly speaking, *qiyās* has no place in the theory of *naskh: qiyās* cannot be an abrogator, basically because it is weaker than the *naṣṣ* and *ijmā*ᶜ and thus cannot abrogate either. Nor can *qiyās* itself be abrogated, for *qiyās* is normally based on a textual ruling and is bound to remain valid for as long as the original text remains valid. It is thus inconceivable that a *qiyās* be abrogated while the text in which it is founded remains in force. Furthermore, an established analogy is not exactly abrogated by a subsequent analogy. If the first analogy is based on the Qur'ān, or

Sunnah, then a conflicting analogy would presumably be erroneous. Besides, the two analogies can coexist and be counted as two *ijtihādī* opinions without the one necessarily abrogating the other. For the rule concerning *ijtihād* is that the *mujtahid* deserves a reward for his effort even if his *ijtihād* is incorrect. In short, *naskh* basically applies to binding proofs, and *qiyās* is not one of them.[10]

In his *Risālah*, Imām Shāfiʿī has maintained the view that *naskh* is not a form of annulment (*ilghā'*); it is rather a suspension or termination of one ruling by another. *Naskh* in this sense is a form of explanation (*bayān*) which does not entail a total rejection of the original ruling.[11] *Naskh* is explanatory in the sense that it tells us of the termination of a particular ruling, the manner and the time of its termination, whether the whole of a ruling or only a part of it is terminated, and of course, the new ruling which is to take its place. However, the majority of ulema do not accept the view that *naskh* is a form of *bayān*. The fact that *naskh* terminates and puts an end to a ruling differentiates it from *bayān*, and when a ruling is terminated, it cannot be explained.

There may be instances of conflict between two texts which, after scrutiny, may turn out to be apparent rather than real, and it may be possible to reconcile them and to eliminate the conflict. One of the two texts may be general (*ʿāmm*) and the other specific (*khāṣṣ*), in which case the rules of interpretation and *takhṣīṣ* (specification) must be applied so as to eliminate the conflict as far as possible. If the two texts cannot be so reconciled, then the one which is stronger in respect of authenticity (*thubūt*) is to be preferred. If, for example, there be a conflict between the Qur'ān and a solitary Ḥadith, the latter is weaker and must therefore give way to the Qur'ān. The solitary, or *Āḥād*, Ḥadīth may also be abrogated by the *Mutawātir*, the *Mashhūr*, or another *Āḥād*, which is clearer in meaning or which is supported by a stronger chain of narration (*isnād*). But if the two texts happen to be equal on all of these points, then the prohibitory text is to be given priority over the permissive. Furthermore, in all instances of conflict, it is essential to determine the time factor. If this can be determined, then the later in time abrogates the earlier. The chronological sequence between the two rulings can, however, only be established by means of reliable reports, not by rational argumentation or analogical reasoning.[12]

As a general rule, *naskh* is not applicable to the 'perspicuous' texts of the Qur'ān and Ḥadīth, known as *muḥkamāt*. A text of this nature is often worded in such a way as to preclude the possibility of repeal. There are also certain subjects to which abrogation does not apply. Included among these are provisions pertaining to the attributes of God, belief in the principles of the faith, and the doctrine of *tawḥīd* and the hereafter, which could not be subjected to abrogation. Another subject is the *Sharīʿah* of Islam itself, which is the last of the revealed laws and can never be abrogated in its entirety.[13] The ulema are also in agreement that rational matters and moral truths such as the virtue of doing justice or being good to one's parents, and vices such as the enormity of telling lies, are not changeable and are therefore not open to abrogation. Thus a vice cannot be turned into a virtue or a virtue into a vice by the application of *naskh*. Similarly the *nuṣūṣ* of the Qur'ān and *Sunnah* which relate the occurrence of certain events in the past are not open to abrogation. To give an example, the following Qur'ānic text is not amenable to the application of *naskh*: 'As for the Thamūd, they were destroyed by a terrible storm, whereas the ʿĀd were destroyed by a furious and violent wind' (al-Ḥāqqah, 69:5–6). To apply *naskh* to such reports would imply the attribution of lying to its source, which cannot be entertained.[14]

To summarise the foregoing: no abrogation can take place unless the following conditions are satisfied. First, that the text itself has not precluded the possibility of abrogation. An example of this is the Qur'ānic provision concerning persons who are convicted of slanderous accusation (*qadhf*) that they may never be admitted as witnesses (al-Nūr, 24:4). Similarly the Ḥadīth which proclaims that '*jihād* shall remain valid till the day of resurrection',

الجهاد ماضٍ إلى يوم القيامة

obviously precludes the possibility of abrogating the permanent validity of *jihād*.[15] Second, that the subject is open to the possibility of repeal. Thus the attributes of God and the principles of belief, moral virtues and rational truths, etc., are not open to abrogation. Third, that the abrogating text is of a later origin than the abrogated. Fourth, that the two texts are of equal strength in regard to authenticity (*thubūt*) and meaning (*dalālah*). Thus a textual ruling of the Qur'ān may be abrogated either by another Qur'ānic text of similar strength or by a *Mutawātir* Ḥadīth, and, according to the Ḥanafīs, even by a *Mashhūr* Ḥadīth, as the latter is almost as strong as the *Mutawātir*. By the same token, one *Mutawātir* Ḥadīth may abrogate another. However, according to the preferred (*rājiḥ*) view, neither the Qur'ān nor the *Mutawātir* Ḥadīth may be abrogated by a solitary Ḥadīth. According to Imām Shāfiʿī, however, the *Sunnah*, whether as *Mutawātir* or *Āḥād*, may not abrogate the Qur'ān.[16] Fifth, that the two texts are genuinely in conflict and can in no way be reconciled with one another. And lastly, that the two texts are separate and are not related to one another in the sense of one being the condition (*sharṭ*), qualification (*waṣf*) or exception (*istithnā'*) to the other. For when this is the case, the issue is likely to be one of specification (*takhṣīṣ*), or qualification (*taqyīd*) rather than abrogation.[17]

Types of *Naskh*

Abrogation may either be explicit (*ṣarīḥ*), or implicit (*ḍimnī*). In the case of explicit abrogation, the abrogating text clearly repeals one ruling and substitutes another in its place. The facts of abrogation, including the chronological order of the two rulings, the fact that they are genuinely in conflict, and the nature of each of the two rulings, and so forth, can be ascertained in the relevant texts. An example of this is the Ḥadīth which provides: 'I had forbidden you from visiting the graves. Nay, visit them, for they remind you of the hereafter.'[18]

كنت نهيتكم عن زيارة القبور ، الا فزوروها فانّها
تُذكِّر الآخرة

In another Ḥadīth the Prophet is reported to have said, 'I had forbidden you from storing away the sacrificial meat because of the large crowds. You may now store it as you wish.'[19]

كنت نهيتكم عن ادّخـار لحوم الاضاحي لأجل
الدّافة ، الا فادّخروها

The initial order not to store the sacrificial meat during the ᶜ*īd* festival (ᶜ*īd al-Aḍḥā*) was given in view of the large number of visitors who attended the festival in Madinah, where the Prophet desired that they should be provided with necessary foodstuffs. The restriction was later removed as the circumstances had changed. In both these examples, the text leaves no doubt as to the nature of the two rulings and all the other relevant facts of abrogation. An example of explicit abrogation in the Qur'ān is the passage in sūra al-Baqarah (2:142–144) with regard to the change in the direction of the *qiblah* from Jerusalem to the Kaᶜbah. The relevant text of the Qur'ān as to the direction of the *qiblah* before and after the new ruling is clear, and leaves no doubt with regard to the facts of abrogation and the nature of the change which was effected thereby.[20]

In the case of implicit abrogation, the abrogating text does not clarify all the relevant facts. Instead we have a situation where the Lawgiver introduces a ruling which is in conflict with a previous ruling and the two cannot be reconciled, while it remains somewhat doubtful whether the two rulings present a genuine case for abrogation. An example of implicit abrogation is the ruling in sūra al-Baqarah (2:180) which permitted bequests to one's parents and relatives. This was subsequently abrogated by another text (al-Nisā', 4:11) which entitled the legal heirs to specific shares in inheritance. Notwithstanding the fact that the two rulings are not diametrically opposed to one another and could both be implemented in certain cases,[21] the majority of ulema have held that the initial ruling which validated bequests to relatives has been abrogated by the rules of inheritance. They have held that the *āyah* of inheritance prescribes specific portions for legal heirs which can be properly implemented only if they were observed in their entirety, and that the Qur'ānic scheme of inheritance is precise and self-contained, and any outside interference is likely to upset the individual shares as well as the overall balance between them. Since bequest to legal heirs is seen as a principal source of such interference it is totally forbidden. This analysis is substantiated by the explicit ruling of a Ḥadīth in which the Prophet is reported to have said, 'God has assigned a portion to all who are entitled. Hence there shall be no bequest to legal heirs.'[22]

إن الله أعطى لكل ذي حق حقه ، فلا وصية لوارث

Implicit abrogation has been sub-divided into two types, namely total abrogation (*naskh kullī*) and partial abrogation (*naskh juz'ī*). In the case of the former, the whole of a particular *naṣṣ* is abrogated by another, and a new ruling is enacted to replace it. This may be illustrated by a reference to the two Qur'ānic texts concerning the waiting period (*ʿiddah*) of widows, which was initially prescribed to be one year but was subsequently changed to four months and ten days. The two texts are as follows:

1. Those of you who are about to die and leave widows should bequeath for their widows a year's maintenance and residence; but if they leave the residence, you are not responsible for what they do of themselves (al-Baqarah, 2:240).
2. Those of you who die and leave widows, the latter must observe a waiting period of four months and ten days; when they have fulfilled their term, you are not responsible for what they do of themselves (al-Baqarah, 2:234).

As can be seen, the provision concerning the waiting period of widows in the first *āyah* has been totally replaced by the new ruling in the second. There is no doubt on the point that both of these rulings are exclusively concerned with the same subject, namely the widows. Both *āyāt* require them to observe a waiting period, whose length varies in each, and only one must be observed, not both. The two passages are thus in conflict and the latter abrogates the former. But this is a case, as already noted, of an implicit *naskh*, in that the two *āyāt* do not expound, with complete clarity, all the facts of abrogation and it is not certain whether they are genuinely in conflict, for the term 'a year's maintenance and residence' in the first *āyah* does not recur in the second. There is, in fact, no reference to either maintenance or residence in the second *āyah*. This would, for example, introduce an element of doubt concerning whether the two *āyāt* are concerned with different subjects of maintenance and *ʿiddah* respectively. There is, in other words, a level of discrepancy which might make it possible to apply each of the two rulings to different situations. This is not to argue against the majority view which seems to be the settled law, but merely to explain why an abrogation of this type has been classified as implicit *naskh*.

Partial abrogation (*naskh juz'ī*) is a form of *naskh* in which one text is only partially abrogated by another, while the remaining part continues to be operative. An example of this is the Qur'ānic *āyah* of *qadhf* (slanderous accusation) which has been partially repealed by the *āyah* of imprecation (*liʿān*). The two texts are as follows:

1. Those who accuse chaste women [of adultery] and then fail to bring four witnesses to prove it shall be flogged with eighty lashes (al-Nūr, 24:4).
2. Those who accuse their spouses and have no witnesses, other than their own words, to support their claim, must take four solemn oaths in the name of God and testify that they are telling the truth (al-Nūr, 24:6).

The first *āyah* lays down the general rule that anyone, be it a spouse or otherwise, who accuses chaste women of *zinā* must produce four witnesses for proof. The second *āyah* provides that if the accuser happens to be a spouse who cannot provide four witnesses and yet insists on pursuing the charge of *zinā*, he may take four solemn oaths to take the place of four witnesses. This is to be followed, as the text continues, by a statement in which the husband invokes the curse of God upon himself if he tells a lie. The ruling of the first text has thus been repealed by the second text insofar as it concerns a married couple.[23]

It will be noted that the text of the Qur'ān has two distinctive features, namely, the words of the text, and the ruling, or the *ḥukm*, that it conveys. Reading and reciting the words of the Qur'ān, even if its ruling is abrogated, still commands spiritual merit. The words are still regarded as part of the Qur'ān and *ṣalah* can be performed by reciting them. It is on the basis of this distinction between the words and the rulings of the Qur'ān that *naskh* has once again been classified into three types. The first and the most typical variety of abrogation is referred to as *naskh al-ḥukm*, or *naskh* in which the ruling alone is abrogated while the words of the text are retained. All the examples which we have given so far of the incidence of *naskh* in the Qur'ān fall into this category. Thus the words of the Qur'ānic text concerning bequests to relatives (al-Baqarah, 2:180) and the one concerning the *ᶜiddah* of widows (al-Baqarah, 2:240) are still a part of the Qur'ān despite the fact that they have both been abrogated. We still recite them as such, but do not apply the law that they convey. The other two varieties of *naskh*, respectively referred to as *naskh al-tilāwah* (sometimes as *naskh al-qirā'ah*), that is, abrogation of the words of the text while the ruling is retained, and *naskh al-ḥukm wa al-tilāwah*, that is, abrogation of both the words and the ruling – are rather rare and the examples which we have are not supported by conclusive evidence. Having said this, however, we might add that, except for a minority of Muᶜtazilī scholars, the ulema are generally in agreement on the occurrence of abrogation in both these forms.[24] An example of *naskh al-tilāwah* is the passage which, according to a report attributed to ᶜUmar b. al-Khaṭṭāb, was a part of the Qur'ān, although the passage in question does not appear in the standard text. However the ruling conveyed by the passage in question still represents authoritative law. The reported version of this text provides: 'When a married man or a married woman commits *zinā*, their punishment shall be stoning as a retribution ordained by God.'[25]

الشيخ والشيخة إذا زنيا فارجموهما البتة نكالا
من الله

In the event where the words of the text, and the law that they convey, are both repealed, then the text in question is of little significance. According to a report which is attributed to the Prophet's widow, ᶜĀ'ishah, it had been revealed in the Qur'ān that ten clear suckings by a child, make marriage unlawful between that child and others who drank the same, woman's milk. Then it was abrogated and substituted by five suckings and it was then that the Messenger of God died. The initial ruling which required ten suckings was read into the text of the Qur'ān. The ruling was then repealed and the words in which it was conveyed were also omitted from the text. However since neither of these reports is established by *tawātur*, they are not included in the Qur'ān. The position now, according to the majority of ulema, is that either five clear suckings, or any amount which reaches the stomach, even if it be one large sucking, constitutes the grounds of prohibition.[26]

According to the majority (*jumhūr*) view, the Qur'ān and the *Sunnah* may be abrogated by themselves or by one another. In this sense, abrogation may be once again classified into the following varieties: (1) Abrogation of the Qur'ān by the Qur'ān, which has already been illustrated. (2) Abrogation of the *Sunnah* by the *Sunnah*. This too has been illustrated by the two *aḥādīth* which we quoted under the rubric of explicit abrogation. (3) Abrogation of the Qur'ān by *Sunnah*. An example of this is the *āyah* of bequest in sūra al-Baqarah (2:180) which has been abrogated by the Ḥadīth which provides that 'there shall be no bequest to an heir'. It is generally agreed that 'the Qur'ān itself does not abrogate the *āyah* of bequest and there remains little doubt that it has been abrogated by the *Sunnah*'.[27] (4) Abrogation of the *Sunnah* by the Qur'ān. An example of this is the initial ruling of the Prophet which determined the *qiblah* in the direction of Jerusalem. When the Prophet migrated to Madinah, he ordered the believers to pray in the direction of Jerusalem. This was later repealed by the Qur'ān (al-Baqarah, 2:144) which ordered the Muslims to turn their faces toward the holy mosque of the Kaᶜbah.[28] The Qur'ān, in other words, abrogated a practice that was initially authorised by the *Sunnah*.

The main exception to the foregoing classification of *naskh* is taken by Imām Shāfiᶜī, the majority of the Muᶜtazilah, and Aḥmad b. Ḥanbal (according to one of two variant reports), who have validated the first two types of abrogation, but have overruled the validity of the remaining two. In their view, abrogation of the Qur'ān by the *Sunnah* and vice versa is not valid.[29] This is the conclusion that al-Shāfiᶜī has drawn from his interpretation of a number of Qur'ānic *āyāt* where it is indicated that the Qur'ān can only be abrogated by the Qur'ān itself.[30] Thus we read in sūra al-Naḥl (16:101):

> And when We substitute one *āyah* in place of another *āyah* [*āyatan makāna āyatin*], and God knows best what He reveals.

This text, according to al-Shāfiᶜī, is self-evident on the point that an *āyah* of the Qur'ān can only be abrogated or replaced by another *āyah*. The fact that the *āyah* occurs twice in this text provides conclusive evidence that the Qur'ān may not be abrogated by the *Sunnah*. In another place, the Qur'ān reads:

> None of our revelations do We abrogate [*mā nansakh min āyatin*] or cause to be forgotten unless We substitute for them something better or similar (al-Baqarah, 2 : 106).

The text in this *āyah* is once again clear on the point that in the matter of *naskh*, the Qur'ān refers only to itself. The Qur'ān, in other words, is self-contained in regard to *naskh*, and this precludes the possibility of it being abrogated by the *Sunnah*. *Naskh* in the Qur'ān, according to al-Shāfiʿī, is a wholly internal phenomenon, and there is no evidence in the Qur'ān to suggest that it can be abrogated by the *Sunnah*. Indeed the Qur'ān asks the Prophet to declare that he himself cannot change any part of the Qur'ān. This is the purport of the text in sūra Yūnus (10:15) which provides: 'Say: it is not for me to change it of my own accord. I only follow what is revealed to me.' It is thus not within the Prophet's terms of reference to abrogate the Qur'ān at his own initiative. 'The *Sunnah* in principle', writes al-Shāfiʿī, 'follows, substantiates, and clarifies the Qur'ān; it does not seek to abrogate the Book of God'.[31] All this, al-Shāfiʿī adds, is reinforced in yet another passage in the Qur'ān where it is provided: 'God blots out or confirms what He pleases. With Him is the Mother of the Book' (al-Raʿd, 13:39). The reference here is again to *naskh* and the source in which it originates is the Mother of the Book, that, is the Qur'ān itself. The *Sunnah*, even the *Mutawātir Sunnah*, may not abrogate the Qur'ān. Al-Shāfiʿī is equally categorical on the other limb of this theory, namely that the Qur'ān does not abrogate the *Sunnah* either. Only the *Sunnah* can abrogate the *Sunnah*: *Mutawātir* by *Mutawātir* and *Āḥād* by *Āḥād*. *Mutawātir* may abrogate the *Āḥād*, but there is some disagreement on whether the *Āḥād* can abrogate the *Mutawātir*. According to the preferred view, which is also held by al-Shāfiʿī, the *Āḥād*, however, can abrogate the *Mutawātir*. To illustrate this, al-Shāfiʿī refers to the incident when the congregation of worshippers at the mosque of Qubā' were informed by a single person (*khabar al-wāḥid*) of the change of the direction of the *qiblah* from Jerusalem to the Kaʿbah; they acted upon it and turned their faces toward the Kaʿbah. The fact that Jerusalem was the *qiblah* had been established by continuous, or *mutawātir*, *Sunnah*, but the congregation of Companions accepted the solitary report as the abrogator of *Mutawātir*.[32]

Al-Shāfiʿī elaborates his doctrine further. If there existed any occasion for the *Sunnah* to abrogate the Qur'ān or vice versa, the Prophet would be the first to say so. Thus in all cases where such an abrogation is warranted, there is bound to be a *Sunnah* of the Prophet to that effect, in which case the matter automatically becomes a part of the *Sunnah*. The *Sunnah* in other words is self-contained, and covers all possible cases of conflict and abrogation of the Qur'ān by the *Sunnah* and vice versa. If any *Sunnah* is meant to be abrogated, the Prophet himself would do it by virtue of another *Sunnah*, hence there is no case for the abrogation of *Sunnah* by the Qur'ān.[33]

Al-Shāfiʿī considers it necessary for the abrogation of *Sunnah* that the Prophet should have informed the people specifically about it. If the Qur'ān were to abrogate the *Sunnah*, while the Prophet has not indicated such to be the case, then, to give an example, all the varieties of sale which the Prophet had banned prior to the revelation of the Qur'ānic *āyah* on the legality of sale (al-Baqarah, 2:275) would be rendered lawful with the revelation of this *āyah*. Similarly, the punishment of stoning for *zinā* which is authorised by the Prophet would be deemed abrogated by the variant ruling of one hundred lashes in sūra al-Nūr (24:2). In the case of theft, too, the Prophet did not punish anyone for theft below the value of one-quarter of a dinar, nor did he apply the prescribed punishment to the theft of unguarded (*ghayr muḥraz*) property. These would all be deemed abrogated following the revelation of the *āyah* in sūra al-Mā'idah (5:38) which prescribes mutilation of the hand for theft without any qualification whatsoever. If we were to open this process, it would be likely to give rise to unwarranted claims of conflict and a fear of departure from the *Sunnah*.[34]

Notwithstanding the strong case that al-Shāfiʿī has made in support of his doctrine, the majority opinion, which admits abrogation of the Qur'ān and *Sunnah* by one another is preferable, as it is based on the factual evidence of having actually taken place. Al-Ghazālī is representative of the majority opinion on this when he writes that identity of source (*tajānus*) is not necessary in *naskh*. The Qur'ān and *Sunnah* may abrogate one another as they issue both from the same provenance. While referring to al-Shāfiʿī's doctrine, al-Ghazālī comments: 'how can we sustain this in the face of the evidence that the Qur'ān never validated Jerusalem as the *qiblah*; it was validated by the *Sunnah*, but its abrogating text occurs in the Qur'ān? Likewise, the fasting of ʿĀshurā' was abrogated by the Qur'ānic provision concerning the fasting of Ramadan while the former was only established by the *Sunnah*. Furthermore, the Qur'ānic *āyah* which permitted conjugal intercourse at night-time in Ramadan (al-Baqarah, 2:178) abrogated the prohibition that the *Sunnah* had previously imposed on conjugal relations during Ramadan'.[35]

Abrogation, Specification (*Takhṣīṣ*) and Addition (*Taz'īd*)

Naskh and *takhṣīṣ* resemble one another in that both tend to qualify or specify an original ruling in some way. This is particularly true, perhaps, of partial *naskh*, which really amounts to qualification / specification rather than repeal. We have already noted al-Shāfiʿī's perception of *naskh* which draws close to the idea of the coexistence of two rulings and an explanation of one by the other. A certain amount of confusion has also arisen between *naskh* and *takhṣīṣ* due to conceptual differences between the Ḥanafīs and the majority of ulema regarding *naskh* in that they tend to view *naskh* differently from one another. These differences of perspective have, however, been treated more pertinently in our discussion of the *ʿĀmm* and the *Khāṣṣ*. In this section, we shall outline the basic differences between *naskh* and *takhṣīṣ* without attempting to expound the differences between the various schools on the subject.

Naskh and *takhṣīṣ* differ from one another in that there is no real conflict in *takhṣīṣ*. The two texts, namely the general text and the specifying text, in effect complement one another. This is not, however, the case with *naskh*, in which it is necessary that the two rulings are genuinely in conflict and that they could not coexist. Another difference between *naskh* and *takhṣīṣ* is that *naskh* can occur in respect of either a general or a specific ruling whereas *takhṣīṣ* can, by definition, occur in respect of a general ruling only.[36]

As already stated, *naskh* is basically confined to the Qur'ān and *Sunnah* and could only be effected by the explicit rulings of divine revelation. *Takhṣīṣ* on the other hand could also occur by means of rationality and circumstantial evidence. *Naskh*, in other words, can only occur by *sharʿ* whereas *takhṣīṣ* can occur by rationality (*ʿaql*), custom (*ʿurf*) and other rational proofs. It would follow from this that *takhṣīṣ* (i.e. the specification or qualification of a general text) is possible by means of speculative evidence such as *qiyās* and solitary Ḥadīth. But in the case of *naskh*, a definitive ruling, that is, a *qaṭʿī*, can only be abrogated by another *qaṭʿī* ruling. Abrogation, in other words, is basically not operative with regard to speculative rulings.[37]

As already stated, in *naskh* it is essential that the abrogator (*al-nāsikh*) be later in time than the ruling which it seeks to abrogate. There can be no *naskh* if this order is reversed, nor even when the two rulings are known to have been simultaneous. But this is not a requirement of *takhṣīṣ*. With regard to *takhṣīṣ*, the Ḥanafīs maintain that the *ʿĀmm* and the *Khāṣṣ* must in fact be either simultaneous or parallel in time. But according to the majority, the *ʿĀmm* and the *Khāṣṣ* can precede or succeed one another and they need not be in any particular chronological order.

Lastly, *naskh* does not apply to factual reports of events (*akhbār*) whereas *takhṣīṣ* could occur in regard to factual reports. Thus a news report may be specified or qualified, but cannot be abrogated. The closest concept to abrogation in regard to reports is that they can be denied.

Another issue which arises concerning *naskh* is whether a subsequent addition (*taz'īd*) to an existing text, which may be at variance with it, amounts to its abrogation. When new materials are added to an existing law, the added materials may fall into one of the following two categories: (1) The addition may be independent of the original text but relate to the same subject, such as adding a sixth *ṣalāh* to the existing five. Does this amount to the abrogation of the original ruling? The majority of ulema have answered this question in the negative, holding that the new addition does not overrule the existing law but merely adds a new element to it. (2) The new addition may not be independent of the original text in that it may be dealing with something that constitutes an integral part of the original ruling. A hypothetical example of this would be to add another unit (*rakʿah*), or an additional prostration (*sajdah*) to one or more of the existing obligatory prayers. Another example would be to add to the existing requirement of releasing a slave in expiation for breaking the fast, a new condition that the slave has to be a Muslim. Does this kind of addition amount to the abrogation of the existing law? The ulema have differed on this, but once again the majority have held the view that it does not amount to abrogation as it does not seek to overrule the original text. The Ḥanafīs have held, however, that such an addition does amount to abrogation. It is on this ground that the Ḥanafīs have considered the ruling of the *Āḥād* Ḥadīth on the admissibility of one witness plus a solemn oath by the claimant to be abrogating the Qur'ānic text which enacts two witnesses as standard legal proof (al-Baqarah, 2 : 282). The abrogation, however, does not occur, not because the Ḥanafīs consider the new addition to be immaterial, but because the *Āḥād* cannot repeal the *Mutawātir* of the Qur'ān.[38] The majority opinion does not regard this to be a case for abrogation. For the Qur'ānic text on the requirement of two witnesses does not preclude the possibility of proof by other methods. Since the original Qur'ānic text does not impose an obligatory command, it leaves open the possibility of recourse to alternative methods of proof.[39]

The Argument Against *Naskh*

As already stated, the ulema are not unamimous over the occurrence of *naskh* in the Qur'ān. While al-Suyūṭī has claimed, in his *Itqān fī ʿUlūm al-Qur'ān*, twenty-one instances of *naskh* in the Qur'ān, Shāh Walī Allāh (d. 1762) has only retained five of al-Suyūṭī's twenty-one cases as genuine, stating that the rest can all be reconciled.[40] Another scholar, Abū Muslim al-Iṣfahānī (d. 934) has, on the other hand, denied the incidence of abrogation in the Qur'ān altogether.[41] The majority of ulema have nevertheless acknowledged the incidence of *naskh* in the Qur'ān on the authority of the Qur'ān itself. This is the conclusion that the majority have drawn from the relevant Qur'ānic passages. However, it will be noted that the counter-argument is also based on the same Qur'ānic passages which have been quoted in support of *naskh*. The following two *āyāt* need to be quoted again:

> None of our revelations do We abrogate nor cause to be forgotten unless We substitute for them something better or similar [*mā nansakh min āyatin aw nunsihā na'ti bi-khayrin minhā aw mithliha*] (al-Baqarah, 2:106).

Elsewhere we read in sūra al-Naḥl (16:106):

> When We substitute one revelation for another, and God knows best what He reveals [*wa idhā baddalnā āyatan makāna āyatin wa'Llāhu a^clam bimā yunazzil*].

To some commentators, the word '*āyah*' in these passages refers, not to the text of the Qur'ān itself, but to previous scriptures including the Torah and the Gospel. An interpretation of this type would, of course, render the *āyah* under discussion irrelevant to the occurrence of *naskh* in the Qur'ān. Abū Muslim al-Iṣfahānī, a Mu^ctazilī scholar and author of a Qur'ān commentary (*Jāmi^c al-Ta'wīl*), has held the view that all instances of so-called abrogation in the Qur'ān are in effect no more than qualifications and *takhṣīṣ* of one text by another.[42] To al-Iṣfahānī, the word '*āyah*' in these passages means not a portion of the Qur'ānic text, but 'miracle'. To read this meaning in the first of the two passages quoted above would imply that God empowered each of His Messengers with miracles that none other possessed; that God provided each of His Messengers with superior miracles, one better than the other. That this is the correct meaning of the text is substantiated, al-Iṣfahānī adds, by the subsequent portion of the same passage (i.e. al-Baqarah, 2:106) which reads: 'Do you not know that God is all-powerful?' (*^calā kulli shay'in qadīr*). Thus this particular attribute of God relates more appropriately in this context to the subject of miracles rather than abrogation of one *āyah* by another. This interpretation finds further support in yet another portion of the same passage (i.e. 2:108) which provides in an address to the Muslim community: 'Would you want to question your Prophet as Moses was questioned before?' It is then explained that Moses was questioned by the Banī Isrā'īl regarding his miracles, not the abrogation as such.[43] The word '*āyah*', in the second passage (i.e. al-Naḥl, 16:101) too means 'miracle'. For after all, '*āyah*' literally means 'sign' and a miracle is a sign. Al-Iṣfahānī further argues: *Naskh* is equivalent to *ibṭāl*, that is, 'falsification' or rendering something invalid, and *ibṭāl* as such has no place in the Qur'ān. This is what we learn from the Qur'ān itself which reads in sūra Ḥā-Mīm (41:42): 'No falsehood can approach it [the Book] from any direction [*lā ya'tīhi al-bāṭil min bayn yadayhi wa lā min khalfih*].' In response to this, however, it is said that *naskh* is not identical with *ibṭāl*; that *naskh* for all intents and purposes means suspension of a textual ruling, while the words of the text are often retained and not nullified.[44]

Two other points that al-Iṣfahānī has added to his interpretation are as follows. Supposing that the passages under consideration do mean abrogation, even then they do not confirm the actual occurrence of *naskh* but merely the possibility of it, and there is a difference between the two. Lastly, al-Iṣfahānī maintains that all instances of conflict in the Qur'ān are apparent rather than real, and can be reconciled and removed. This, he adds, is only logical of the *Sharīᶜah*, which is meant to be for all times; this is just another way of saying that it is not open to abrogation.[45]

Having explained al-Iṣfahānī's refutation of the theory of *naskh*, it remains to be said that according to the majority of ulema, the occurrence of *naskh* in the Qur'ān is proven, although not in so many instances as has often been claimed. The proponents of *naskh* have stated that the incidence of *naskh* in the Qurān is proven, not only by the Qur'ān itself, but also by a conclusive *ijmāᶜ*. Anyone who opposes it is thus going against the dictates of *ijmāᶜ*.[46] In the face of the foregoing disagreements, it is admittedly difficult to see the existence of a conclusive *ijmāᶜ* on the point. But according to the rules of *ijmāᶜ*, once an *ijmāᶜ* is properly concluded, any subsequent differences of opinion would not invalidate it. Divergent views such as that of al-Iṣfahānī seem to have been treated in this light, and almost totally ignored.

In his book *The Islamic Theory of International Relations: New Directions For Islamic Methodology and Thought* (originally a doctoral dissertation), Abdul Hamid AbuSulayman is critical of the classical approach to *naskh* and calls for a fresh and comprehensive understanding 'of the technique of *naskh* [. . .] on a systematic and conceptual basis, not a legalistic one'.[47] The author is of the view that the classical exposition of *naskh* is unnecessarily restrictive as it tends to narrow down the 'rich Islamic and Qur'ānic experience', and also indulges, in some instances at least, in a measure of exaggeration and excess.[48]

The author maintains that abrogation was primarily an historical, rather than juridical, phenomenon and ought to have been read in that context. This may be part of the reason why the jurists have found it difficult to establish the validity of abrogation by the direct evidence of the Qur'an or *Sunnah*. The argument runs that the facts of *naskh* in regard to, for example, the *āyah* of the sword, as discussed below, were historical and were largely dictated by the prevailing pattern of relationship between Muslims and non-Muslims at the time. Now, instead of understanding *naskh* as a circumstance of history, the ulema turned it into a juridical doctrine of permanent validity. This classical concept of permanent abrogation is oblivious of the space-time element which, if taken into account, would have restricted the application of *naskh* to those circumstance alone.[49]

The broad sweep of *naskh* was, however, taken so far as to invalidate a major portion of the Qur'ān. This is precisely the case with regard to the *āyah* of the sword (*āyah al-sayf*) which reads, in the relevant part: 'And fight the polytheists all together as they fight you all together, and know that God is with those who keep their duty [to Him]' (al-Tawbah, 9:36). Influenced by the prevailing pattern of hostile relations with non-Muslims, 'some jurists took an extreme position in interpreting this *āyah*,' and claimed that it abrogated all preceeding *āyāt* pertaining to patience, tolerance and the right of others to self-determination.[50] Although scholars are not in agreement as to the exact number of *āyāt* that were abrogated as a result, Muṣṭafā Abū Zayd has found that the *āyah* of the sword abrogated no less than 140 *āyāt* in the holy Book.[51] Jurists who were inclined to stress the aggressive aspect of *jihād* could only do so by applying abrogation to a large number of Qur'ānic *āyāt*, and 'using abrogation in this manner has', AbuSulayman contests, 'indeed narrowed the Qur'ānic experience'[52] and undermined the egalitarian substance of its teachings. In many passages the Qur'ān calls for peace, compassion and forgiveness, and promotes a set of moral values such as moderation, humility, patience and tolerance whose scope could not be said to be confined to relations among Muslims alone.

The Muslim jurists of the second *hijrah* century, as al-Zuḥaylī informs us, considered war as the norm, rather than the exception, in relations with non-Muslims, and they were able to do so partly because of a certain exaggeration in the use and application of *naskh*. The reason behind this attitude was the need, which was then prevalent, to be in a state of constant readiness for battle in order to protect Islam.[53] Under such political circumstances, it is not difficult to understand how abrogation was utilised as a means by which to strengthen the morale of the Muslims in facing their enemies.[54] It is to be noted further that the position of the classical jurists which characterised war as the permanent pattern of relationship with non-Muslims, as al-Zuḥaylī points out, is not binding on anyone, and is not supported by the balance of evidence in the Qur'ān and *Sunnah*.[55]

It is therefore important, AbuSulayman tells us, 'to put the concept of *naskh* back in proper context' and confine its application only to clear cases, such as the change of *qiblah* from the direction of Jerusalem to the Kaᶜbah. As for the rest, the rules and teachings of Islam are valid and applicable in unlimited combinations as they meet the needs and benefits of mankind, in the light of the broader values and objectives that the Qur'ān and *Sunnah* have upheld.[56]

NOTES

1. Ghazālī, *Mustaṣfā*, I, 69; Āmidī, *Iḥkām*, III, 102ff; Hitu, *Wajīz*, p. 241.
2. Badrān, *Uṣūl*, p. 442.
3. Khallāf, *ʿIlm*, p. 222; Abū Zahrah, *Uṣūl*, p. 148.
4. Shāṭibī, *Muwāfaqāt*, III, 63; Badrān, *Uṣūl*, p. 447.
5. Tāj, *Siyāsah*, p. 14.
6. Badrān, *Uṣūl*, p. 458.
7. Āmidī, *Iḥkām*, III, 161; Tāj, *Siyāsah*, p. 28.
8. Khallāf, *ʿIlm*, p. 228.
9. Badrān, *Uṣūl*, p. 459.
10. Āmidī, *Iḥkām*, III, 163ff; Badrān, *Uṣūl*, p. 459.
11. Shāfiʿī, *Risālah*, p. 103, Abū Zahrah, *Uṣūl*, p. 148.
12. Ghazālī, *Mustaṣfā*, I, 83; Badrān, *Uṣūl*, p. 455.
13. Ghazālī, *Mustaṣfā*, I, 72.
14. Badrān, *Uṣūl*, p. 454; Hitu, *Wajīz*, p. 244.
15. Abū Dāwud, *Sunan*, II, 702, Ḥadith no. 2526; Abū Zahrah, *Uṣūl*, p. 150.
16. Shāfiʿī, *Risālah*, p. 54; Āmidī, *Iḥkām*, III, 146ff.
17. Hitu, *Wajīz*, p. 244; Khallāf, *ʿIlm*, p. 223.
18. Tabrīzī, *Mishkāt*, I, 552, Ḥadīth no. 1762; Muslim, *Ṣāḥīḥ*, p. 340.
19. Ghazālī, *Mustaṣfā*, I, 83. Āmidī, *Iḥkām*, III, 181.
20. Another instance of explicit *naskh* in the Qur'ān is the passage in sūra al-Anfāl (8:65–66) which encouraged the Muslims to fight the unbelievers. The passage reads as follows: 'If there be of you twenty steadfast persons, they shall overcome two hundred, and if there be one hundred of you, they shall overcome one thousand.' The subsequent *āyah* reviewed these figures as follows: 'Now Allah has lightened your burden [. . .] if there be of you one hundred steadfast persons, they shall overcome two hundred, and if there be of you one thousand, they shall overcome two thousand.'
21. Shāfiʿī (*Risālah*, p. 69) has observed concerning these *āyāt* that the abrogation of bequests to relatives by the *āyah* of inheritance is a probability only, but he adds that the ulema have held that the *āyah* of inheritance has abrogated the *āyah* of bequests. On the same page, Shāfiʿī quotes the Ḥadīth that 'there shall be no bequest to an heir'. It thus appears that in his view, the abrogation of bequest to legal heirs in the Qur'ān is a probability which has been confirmed and explained by this and other *aḥādīth* on the subject.
22. Shāfiʿī, *Risālah*, p. 69; Abū Dāwud, *Sunan*, II, 808, Ḥadīth no. 2864; Khallāf, *ʿIlm*, p. 224.
23. Shāfiʿī, *Risālah*, p. 72; Khallāf, *ʿIlm*, p. 227.
24. Āmidī, *Iḥkām*, III, 141.
25. The Arabic version reads *'al-Shaykhu wa'l-shaykhatu idhā zanayā farjumūhumā albattatas nakālan min Allāh'*. Both Ghazālī (*Mustaṣfā*, I, 80, and Āmidī, *Iḥkām* III, 141) have quoted it. ʿUmar b. al-Khaṭṭāb is quoted to have added: 'Had it not been for fear of people saying that ʿUmar made an addition to the Qur'ān, I would have added this to the text of the Qur'ān.'
26. Āmidī, *Iḥkām*, IV, 154; Ghazālī, *Mustaṣfā*, I, 80; Denffer, *ʿUlūm*, p. 108.
27. Hitu, *Wajīz*, p. 252. See also Qadri, *Islamic Jurisprudence*, p. 230.
28. Ibid.
29. Āmidī, *Iḥkām*, III, 153.
30. Shāfiʿī, *Risālah*, p. 54ff; Āmidī, *Iḥkām*, III, 156ff.
31. Shāfiʿī, *Risalāh*, p. 54.

32. Ibid., p. 177; Ghazālī, *Mustaṣfā*, I, 81.
33. Shāfiʿī, *Risālah*, p. 102.
34. Ibid., pp. 57–58. In raising the fear of departure from the *Sunnah*, Shāfiʿī was probably thinking of the doubts that would arise with regard to establishing the precise chronological order between the Qur'ān and *Sunnah* in all possible cases of conflict. Since the Qur'ān is generally authentic, any doubts of this nature are likely to undermine the *Sunnah* more than the Qur'ān.
35. Ghazālī, *Mustaṣfā*, I, 81; see also Āmidī, *Iḥkām*, III, 150ff.
36. Ghazālī, *Mustaṣfā*, I, 71; Badrān, *Uṣūl*, p. 452.
37. Āmidī, *Iḥkām*, III, 113; Badrān, *Uṣūl*, p. 453.
38. Āmidī, *Iḥkām*, III, 170; Hitu, *Wajīz*, p. 256.
39. Āmidī, *Iḥkām*, III, 175; Hitu, *Wajīz*, p. 257.
40. Ṣubḥī al-Ṣāliḥ (*Mabāḥith*, p. 280) records the view that only ten of al-Suyūṭī's twenty-one instances of *naskh* in the Qur'ān are genuine and that all the rest can be reconciled.
41. Abū Zahrah, *Uṣūl*, p. 155; Denffer, *ʿUlum*, p. 110.
42. Ṣubḥi al-Ṣāliḥ, *Mabāḥith*, p. 274.
43. Āmidī, *Iḥkām*, III, 120.
44. Ibid., III, 124.
45. Abū Zahrah, *Uṣūl*, p. 155; Badrān, *Uṣūl*, p. 448.
46. Al-Ghazālī, *Mustaṣfā*, I, 72.
47. AbuSulayman, *The Islamic Theory*, p. 84.
48. Ibid, p. 107.
49. Ibid, p. 73.
50. Ibid, p. 36.
51. Abū Zayd, *Al-Nāsikh wa al-Mansūkh*, I, 289 ff and II, 503 ff.
52. AbuSulayman, *The Islamic Theory*, p. 36.
53. Wahbah al-Zuḥaylī, *Āthār al-Ḥarb*, p. 130.
54. AbuSulayman, *The Islamic Theory*, p. 74.
55. Al-Zuḥaylī, *Āthār al-Ḥarb*, p. 135.
56. cf. AbuSulayman, *The Islamic Theory*, p. 107; cf. the review of his book by James Piscatori, in *Journal of the Institute of Muslim Minority Affairs*, 10.2 (July 1989), pp. 542–3.

CHAPTER EIGHT

Ijmāᶜ, or Consensus of Opinion

It must be noted at the outset that unlike the Qur'ān and *Sunnah*, *ijmāᶜ* does not directly partake in divine revelation. As a doctrine and proof of *Sharīᶜah*, *ijmāᶜ* is basically a rational proof. The theory of *ijmāᶜ* is also clear on the point that it is a binding proof. But it seems that the very nature of this high status that is accorded to *ijmāᶜ* has demanded that only an absolute and universal consensus would qualify although absolute consensus on the rational content of *ijmāᶜ* has often been difficult to obtain. It is only natural and reasonable to accept *ijmāᶜ* as a reality and a valid concept in a relative sense, but factual evidence falls short of establishing the universality of *ijmāᶜ*. The classical definition and the essential requirements of *ijmāᶜ*, as laid down by the ulema of *uṣūl*, are categorical on the point that nothing less than a universal consensus of the scholars of the Muslim community as a whole can be regarded as conclusive *ijmāᶜ*. There is thus no room whatsoever for disagreement, or *ikhtilāf*, within the concept of *ijmāᶜ*. The theory of *ijmāᶜ* is equally unreceptive to the idea of relativity or a preponderance of agreement within its ranks.

The notion of a universal *ijmāᶜ* was probably inspired by the ideal of the political unity of the *ummah*, and its unity in faith and *tawḥīd*, rather than total consensus on juridical matters. As evidence will show, *ijmāᶜ* on particular issues, especially on matters that are open to *ijtihād*, is extremely difficult to prove. Thus the gap between the theory and practice of *ijmāᶜ* remains a striking feature of this doctrine. A universal *ijmāᶜ* can only be said to exist, as al-Shāfiᶜī has observed, on the obligatory duties, that is, the five pillars of the faith, and other such matters on which the Qur'ān and the *Sunnah* are unambiguous and decisive. However, the weakness of such an observation becomes evident when one is reminded that *ijmāᶜ* is redundant in the face of a decisive ruling of the Qur'ān or the *Sunnah*.

The *Sharīᶜah* has often been considered as 'a diversity within unity'. This is true in a general sense, in that there is unity in the essentials and in the broad outlines of the *aḥkām*. But the same cannot be said of the detailed rulings of the jurists. It is admittedly true to say, again in a general sense, that the *ikhtilāf* of individual jurists, or of the various schools of law, are different manifestations of the same divine will and may therefore be regarded as an essential unity. But to expect universal consensus on *ijtihādī* matters is totally unrealistic, as many prominent ulema have recognised.

The gap between the theory and practice of *ijmāᶜ* is reflected in the difficulty that many jurists have acknowledged to exist over implementing its theoretical requirements. The absolute terms of the classical definition of *ijmāᶜ* have hardly been fulfilled by conclusive factual evidence that would eliminate all levels of *ikhtilāf*. *Ijmāᶜ* has often been claimed for rulings on which only a majority consensus had existed within or beyond a particular school. The proof and authenticity of *ijmāᶜ* has, on the other hand, not received the kind of attention that has been given to the authentication of Ḥadīth through a reliable *isnād*. The only form of *ijmāᶜ* which has been generally upheld is that of the Companions of the Prophet, which is partly due to their special status and not always due to their participation and consensus. With these introductory remarks, then, we may begin to examine the meaning and definition of *ijmāᶜ*, and then proceed to discuss some of the issues we have raised.

Ijmāᶜ is the verbal noun of the Arabic word *ajmaᶜa*, which has two meanings: to determine, and to agree upon something. To give an example of the former, the expression *ajma ᶜa fulān ᶜalā kadhā*, means 'so-and-so decided upon such-and-such'. This usage of *ajmaᶜa* is found both in the Qur'ān and in the Ḥadīth.[1] The other meaning of *ajmaᶜa* is 'unanimous agreement'. Hence the phrase *ajmaᶜa al-qawm ᶜalā kadhā* means 'the people reached a unanimous agreement on such-and-such'. The second meaning of *ijmāᶜ* often subsumes the first, in that whenever there is a unanimous agreement on something, there is also a decision on that matter.

Ijmāᶜ is defined as the unanimous agreement of the *mujtahidūn* of the Muslim community of any period following the demise of the Prophet Muḥammad on any matter.[2] In this definition, the reference to the *mujtahidūn* precludes the agreement of laymen from the purview of *ijmāᶜ*. Similarly, by reference to the *mujtahidūn* of any period, is meant a period in which there exist a number of *mujtahidūn* at the time an incident occurs. Hence it would be of no account if a *mujtahid* or a number of *mujtahidūn* become available only after the occurrence of an incident. The reference in the definition to any matter implies that *ijmāᶜ* applies to all juridical (*sharᶜī*), intellectual (*ᶜaqlī*), customary (*ᶜurfī*) and linguistic (*lughawī* matters.[3] Furthermore, *sharᶜī*, in this context is used in contradistinction to *ḥissī*, that is, matters which are perceptible to the senses and fall beyond the scope of *ijmāᶜ*. Some ulema have confined *ijmāᶜ* to religious, and others to *sharᶜī* matters, but the majority of ulema do not restrict *ijmāᶜ* to either. Although the majority of jurists consider dogmatics (*iᶜtiqādiyāt*) to fall within the ambit of *ijmāᶜ*, some have expressed the view that *ijmāᶜ* may not be invoked in support of such subjects as the existence of God or the truth of the prophethood of Muḥammad. The reason is that such beliefs precede *ijmāᶜ* itself. *Ijmāᶜ* derives its validity from the *nuṣūṣ* on the infallibility (*ᶜiṣmah*) of the *ummah*. These *nuṣūṣ*, in turn, take for granted the existence of God and the Prophethood of Muḥammad. Now if one attempts to cite *ijmāᶜ* in support of these dogmas, this would amount to circumlocution. To illustrate the point further, it may be said that the Qur'ān cannot be proved by the *Sunnah*, because the Qur'ān precedes the *Sunnah*.[4] Matters of a practical type which do not partake in the nature of *tashrīᶜ* (legislation) do not constitute the proper subject of *ijmāᶜ*. For example, the agreement of the Companions to send out troops to Syria or to Persia, or their agreement on setting up certain government departments, etc., did not constitute *ijmāᶜ*. For these were practical decisions which were valid in connection with particular circumstances and did not bind the succeeding generations of Muslims. *Ijmāᶜ* on a *sharᶜī* ruling, on the other hand, has a quality of permanence and its validity is not confined by a time limit.[5]

Although the theory refuses to impose any restriction on the subject-matter of *ijmāᶜ*, in actual terms the application of *ijmāᶜ* is bound to be subject to some reservations. For example, *ijmāᶜ* must be of a somewhat limited application in regard to rational and linguistic matters. To say that lying is evil, or that 'hand' also means 'power', need not be supported by *ijmāᶜ*. In actual terms, *ijmāᶜ* has always been selective in determining its own subject-matter. It was perhaps in view of the dynamic nature of *ijmāᶜ* and its infallibility that the ulema were persuaded not to impose any advance reservations on its scope.

It is clear from its definition that *ijmāᶜ* can only occur after the demise of the Prophet. For during his lifetime, the Prophet alone was the highest authority on *Sharīᶜah*, hence the agreement or disagreement of others did not affect the overriding authority of the Prophet. In all probability, *ijmāᶜ* occurred for the first time among the Companions in the city of Madinah. Following the demise of the Prophet, the Companions used to consult each other over the problems they encountered, and their collective agreement was accepted by the community. After the Companions, this leadership role passed on to the next generation, the Successors (*tābiᶜūn*) and then to the second generation of Successors. When these latter differed on a point, they naturally referred to the views and practices of the Companions and the Successors. In this way, a fertile ground was created for the development of the theory of *ijmāᶜ*.[6] The essence of *ijmāᶜ* lies in the natural growth of ideas. It begins with the personal *ijtihād* of individual jurists and culminates in the universal acceptance of a particular opinion over a period of time. Differences of opinion are tolerated until a consensus emerges, and in the process there is no room for compulsion or the imposition of ideas upon the community.

Ijmāᶜ plays a crucial role in the development of *Sharīᶜah*. The existing body of *fiqh* is the product of a long process of *ijtihād and ijmāᶜ*. Since *ijmāᶜ* reflects the natural evolution and acceptance of ideas in the life of the community, the basic notion of *ijmāᶜ* can never be expected to discontinue. The idea that *ijmāᶜ* came to a halt after the first three generations following the advent of Islam seems to be a by-product of the phenomenon known as the closure of the gate of *ijtihād*. Since *ijmāᶜ* originates in *ijtihād*, with the closure of the gate of *ijtihād*, it was expected that *ijmāᶜ* also came to a close. This is, however, no more than a superficial equation, as in all probability *ijmāᶜ* continued to play a role in consolidating and unifying the law after the supposed termination of *ijtihād*.[7]

Ijmāᶜ ensures the correct interpretation of the Qur'ān, the faithful understanding and transmission of the *Sunnah*, and the legitimate use of *ijtihād*. The question as to whether the law, as contained in the divine sources, has been properly interpreted is always open to a measure of uncertainty and doubt, especially in regard to the deduction of new rules by way of analogy and *ijtihād*. Only *ijmāᶜ* can put an end to doubt, and when it throws its weight behind a ruling, this becomes decisive and infallible. *Ijmāᶜ* has primarily been regarded as the instrument of conservatism and of preserving the heritage of the past. This is obvious enough in the sense that whatever is accepted by the entire Muslim community as true and correct must be accepted as such. However, *ijmāᶜ* is also an instrument of tolerance and of the evolution of ideas in such directions as may reflect the vision of the scholars in the light of the fresh educational and cultural achievements fo the community. According to one observer, 'clearly this principle (i.e. *ijmāᶜ*) provides Islam with a potential for freedom of movement and a capacity for evolution. It furnishes a desirable corrective against the dead letter of personal authority. It has proved itself, at least in the past, an outstanding factor in the adaptability of Islam.'[8]

Ijmāᶜ enhances the authority of rules which are of speculative origin. Speculative rules do not carry a binding force, but once an *ijmāᶜ* is held in their favour, they become definite and binding. Instances can be cited, for example, where the Companions have, by their *ijmāᶜ*, upheld the ruling of a solitary Ḥadīth. In such cases, the ruling in question is elevated into a binding rule of law. For example, the prohibition concerning unlawful conjunction, that is, simultaneous marriage to the close relatives of one's wife, is a definitive ruling which is based on *ijmāᶜ*, despite the fact that the basis of this *ijmāᶜ* is a solitary Ḥadīth – namely the Ḥadīth that prohibits simultaneous marriage to the maternal or paternal aunt of one's wife. Similarly, the grandmother is entitled to a share in inheritance, and this is a *qaṭᶜī* ruling of *ijmāᶜ* which is based on a solitary Ḥadīth. The Ḥadīth in question is reported by al-Mughīrah b. Shuᶜbah to the effect that the Prophet assigned to the grandmother the portion of one-sixth. *Ijmāᶜ* has also played a role in regard to *aḥādīth* that were not equally known to all the *mujtahidūn* especially during the period preceding the collection and compilation of Ḥadīth. It was through *ijmāᶜ* that some scholars were informed of the existence of certain *aḥādīth*.[9]

And lastly, *ijmāᶜ* represents authority. Once an *ijmāᶜ* is established it tends to become an authority in its own right, and its roots in the primary sources are gradually weakened or even lost. It then becomes common practice to quote the law without a reference to the relevant sources. It is partly due to the significance of *ijmāᶜ* that the incentive to quote the authority tends to weaken. This is according to Shāh Walī Allāh, one of the reasons which induced the jurists to recognise *ijmāᶜ* as the third source of the *Sharīᶜah*.[10]

Essential Requirements (*Arkān*) of *Ijmāᶜ*

Whenever an issue arises and attracts the attention of the *mujtahidūn* of the Muslim community at the time of its incidence, and they reach a unanimous agreement on its ruling, it is implied that the ruling so agreed upon is the correct and authoritative ruling of the *Sharīᶜah*, provided that the following conditions are fulfilled:

(1) That there are a number of *mujtahidūn* available at the time when the issue is encountered. For consensus can never exist unless there is a plurality of concurrent opinion. Should there be a situation where a plurality of *mujtahidūn* could not be obtained, or when there is only

a single *mujtahid* in the community, no *ijmāᶜ* could be expected to materialise.[11]

(2) According to the majority of ulema, unanimity is a prerequisite of *ijmāᶜ*. All the *mujtahidūn*, regardless of their locality, race, colour and school or following, must reach a consensus on a juridical opinion at the time an issue arises. The presence of a dissenting view, even on the part of a small minority, precludes the possibility of *ijmāᶜ*. If, for example, the *mujtahidūn* of Mecca and Madinah, or those of Iraq, or the *mujtahidūn* of the family of the Prophet, or the Sunnī ulema without the agreement of their Shīᶜī counterparts agree upon a ruling, no *ijmāᶜ* will materialise.

The majority of ulema maintain that lay opinion is not taken into account: in every field of learning, only the opinion of the learned is relevant to *ijmāᶜ*. Al-Āmidī, however, prefers the minority view, attributed to Abū Bakr al-Bāqillānī and others, to the effect that *ijmāᶜ* includes the agreement of both the laymen and the *mujtahidūn*, the reason being that *ᶜiṣmah*, which is the doctrinal basis of *ijmāᶜ*, is a grace of God bestowed on the whole of the community. It would therefore be improper to turn the property of the entire community into a privilege of the *mujtahidūn*. The majority view is, however, based on the analysis that the *mujtahidūn*, in their capacity as the constituents of *ijmāᶜ*, merely represent the community, and therefore no change is proposed in the original locus of *ᶜiṣmah*.[12]

(3) The agreement of the *mujtahidūn* must be demonstrated by their expressed opinion on a particular issue. This may be verbal or in writing, such as by giving a *fatwā* in either of these forms, or it may be actual, when, for example, a judge adjudicates the issue in question; or it may be that every *mujtahid* expresses an opinion, and after gathering their views, they are found to be in agreement. Similarly the *mujtahidūn* may give their views collectively when, for example, the *mujtahidūn* of the Muslim world assemble at the time an issue is encountered and reach a consensus over its ruling.

(4) As a corollary of the second condition above, *ijmāᶜ* consists of the agreement of all the *mujtahidūn*, and not a mere majority among them. For so long as a dissenting opinion exists, there is the possibility that one side is in error, and no *ijmāᶜ* can be envisaged in that situation, for *ijmāᶜ* is a decisive proof, which must be founded on certainty. However, according to Ibn Jarīr al-Ṭabarī, Abū Bakr al-Rāzī, one of the two views of Aḥmad ibn Ḥanbal and Shāh Walī Allāh, *ijmāᶜ* may be concluded by a majority opinion. But al-Āsmidī prefers the majority view on this point, which requires the participation of all *mujtahidūn*.[13]

In regard to the rules of *fiqh*, it is the *ijmāᶜ* of the *fuqahā'* alone which is taken into account.[14] The question naturally arises whether *fuqahā'* belonging to certain factions like the Khawārij, the Shīᶜah, or those who might have been charged with heresy and *bidᶜah* are qualified to participate in *ijmāᶜ*. According to the majority view, if a *faqīh* is known to have actively invited the people to *bidᶜah*, he is excluded from *ijmāᶜ*; otherwise he is included in the ranks of *ahl al-ijmāᶜ*.[15] The Ḥanafīs preclude a transgressor (*fāsiq*) and one who does not act upon his doctrine from being among the *ahl al-ijmāᶜ*, whereas the Shāfiᶜīs and some Mālikīs maintain that a mere transgression is no disqualification.[16] Some *fuqahā'* have held that *ijmāᶜ* is concluded only with the disappearance of the generation (*inqirāḍ al-ᶜaṣr*), that is, when the *mujtahidūn* who took part in it have all passed away. For if any of them is known to be alive, there would still be a possibility that he may change his view, in which case the *ijmāᶜ* would collapse. A corollary of this rule is that *ijmāᶜ* is retrospective, in that it only binds succeeding generations but not its own constituents.[17]

The majority of jurists, however, maintain that this is not a condition of *ijmāᶜ* and that *ijmāᶜ* not only binds the next generation but also its own participants, as it would only be reasonable to expect that if *ijmāᶜ* did not bind its participants, it should not bind anyone else either.[18] With regard to the tacit *ijmāᶜ* (for which see below), too, some jurists have held that it is concluded only after the death of its participants, so that it can be established that none of them have subsequently expressed an opinion. For when they break their silence they will no longer be regarded as silent participants, and may even turn a tacit *ijmāᶜ* into an explicit one.

The majority of ulema, nevertheless, refuse to place any importance on the 'disappearance of the generation', for in view of the overlapping of generations (*tadākhul al-aᶜṣār*), it is impossible to distinguish the end of one generation from the beginning of the next. Thus the period of the Companions cannot be clearly distinguished from that of the Successors, nor can any other period be so distinguished from its preceding or succeeding generations.[19] However, al-Ghazālī, to all intents and purposes, has resolved this question by stating that 'for the formation of *ijmāᶜ*, it is enough that agreement should have taken place, even if only for an instant'.[20]

When *ijmāᶜ* fulfills the foregoing requirements, it becomes binding (*wājib*) on everyone. Consequently, the *mujtahidūn* of a subsequent age are no longer at liberty to exercise fresh *ijtihād* over the same issue. For once it is concluded, *ijmāᶜ* is not open to amendment or abrogation (*naskh*). The rules of *naskh* are not relevant to *ijmāᶜ* in the sense that *ijmāᶜ* can neither repeal nor be repealed. This is the majority view, although some jurists have stated that the constituents of *ijmāᶜ* themselves are entitled to repeal their own *ijmāᶜ* and to enact another one in its place. But once an *ijmāᶜ* is finalised, especially when all of its constituents have passed away, no further *ijmāᶜ* may be concluded on the same subject. Should there be a second *ijmāᶜ* on the same point, it will be of no account.[21]

Proof (*Ḥujjīyyah*) of *Ijmāᶜ*

What proof is there that *ijmāᶜ* is a source of law? The ulema have sought to justify *ijmāᶜ* on the authority of the Qur'ān, the *Sunnah*, and reason. We shall presently discuss the *āyāt* and the *aḥādīth* that have been quoted in support of *ijmāᶜ*. It should be noted at the outset, however, that the ulema have on the whole maintained the impression that the textual evidence in support of *ijmāᶜ* does not amount to a conclusive proof. Having said this, one might add that both al-Ghazālī and al-Āmidī are of the view that when compared to the Qur'ān, the *Sunnah* provides a stronger argument in favour of *ijmāᶜ*.[22]

1. *Ijmāᶜ* in the Qur'ān:

The Qur'ān (al-Nisā', 4:59) is explicit on the requirement of obedience to God, to His Messenger, and 'those who are in charge of affairs', the *ūlū al-amr*.[23] It is also suggested that this *āyah* lends support to the infallibility of *ijmāᶜ*. According to al-Fakhr al-Rāzī, since God has commanded obedience to the *ūlū al-amr*, the judgement of the *ūlū al-amr* must therefore be immune from error. For God cannot command obedience to anyone who is liable to committing errors.[24] The word '*amr*' in this context is general and would thus include both secular and religious affairs. The former is discharged by the political rulers, whereas the latter is discharged by the ulema. According to a commentary attributed to Ibn ᶜAbbās, *ūlū al-amr* in this *āyah* refers to ulema, whereas other commentators have considered it to be a reference to the *umarā'*, that is, 'rulers and commanders'. The *ẓāhir* of the text includes both, and enjoins obedience to each in their respective spheres. Hence, when the *ūlū al-amr* in juridical matters, namely the *mujtahidūn*, reach a consensus on a ruling, it must be obeyed.[26]

Further support for this conclusion can be found elsewhere in sūra al-Nisā' (4:83) which once again confirms the authority of the *ūlū al-amr* next to the Prophet himself.[26]

The one *āyah* which is most frequently quoted in support of *ijmāᶜ* occurs in sūra al-Nisā' (4:115), which is as follows:

> And anyone who splits off from the Messenger after the guidance has become clear to him and follows a way other than that of the believers, We shall leave him in the path he has chosen, and land him in Hell. What an evil refuge!

The commentators observe that 'the way of the believers' in this *āyah* refers to their 'agreement and the way that they have chosen', in other words, to their consensus. Adherence to the way of the community is thus binding, while departure from it is forbidden. Departing from the believers' way has been approximated to disobeying the Prophet, both of which are forbidden. There are several points that the commentators have highlighted concerning this *āyah*. However, before elaborating further, a brief discussion of the other Qur'ānic passages which are quoted in support of consensus would be useful.

The Qur'ān is expressive of the dignified status that God has bestowed on the Muslim community. Thus we read in sūra Āl-ᶜImrān (3:109): 'You are the best community that has been raised for mankind. You enjoin right and forbid evil and you believe in God.' This *āyah* attests to some of the outstanding merits of the Muslim community. It is thus argued that had the community been capable of agreeing on an error, the Qur'ān would not have praised it in such terms. It is further noted that the contents of this *āyah* give some indication as to the meaning of the phrase 'the believers' way'.

On the same theme, we read in sūra al-Baqarah (2:143): 'Thus We have made you a middle nation [*ummatan wasaṭan*], that you may be witnesses over mankind.' Literally, *wasaṭ* means 'middle', implying justice and balance, qualities which merit recognition of the agreed decision of the community and the rectitude of its way. Furthermore, it is by virtue of uprightness that God has bestowed upon the Muslim community the merit of being a 'witness over mankind'.[27]

In yet another reference to the *ummah*, the Qur'ān proclaims in sūra al-Aᶜrāf (7:181): 'And of those We created are a nation who direct others with truth and dispense justice on its basis.' There are three other *āyāt* which need to be quoted. These are:

> Āl-ᶜImrān (3:102): 'Cling firmly together to God's rope and do not separate.'

This *āyah* obviously forbids separation (*tafarruq*). Since opposition to the *ijmāᶜ* is a form of *tafarruq*, it is therefore prohibited.[28]

> Al-Shūrā (42:10): 'And in whatever you differ, the judgement remains with God', 'which implicitly approves that in which the community is in agreement.'[29]
> Al-Nisā' (4:59): 'Then if you dispute over something, refer it to God and the Messenger.'

By implication (i.e., divergent implication – *mafhūm al-mukhālafah*), this *āyah* too upholds the authority of all that is agreed upon by the community.[30]

Having quoted all the foregoing *āyāt*, al-Ghazālī observes that 'all of these are apparent indications (*ẓawāhir*) none of which amounts to a clear *naṣṣ* on the subject of *ijmāᶜ*.' Al-Ghazālī adds that of all these, the *āyah* at 4:115 is closest to the point. For it renders adherence to the 'believers' way' an obligation. Al-Shāfiᶜī has also quoted it, and has drawn the conclusion that this *āyah* provides a clear authority for *ijmāᶜ*. According to him, following a way other than that of the believers is *ḥarām*, and following the believers' way is *wājib*.[31] But despite this, al-Ghazālī explains that the main theme of this *āyah* is a warning against disobedience to the Prophet and hostility against the believers. It requires the believers to give the Prophet active support and defend him against enemies. It is not enough for a believer merely to avoid causing hardship (*mashaqqa*) to the Prophet; he must actively help him and obey all his commands and prohibitions. This is the main theme of the *āyah*. The Prophet himself has not given it a specific interpretation to warrant a departure from its manifest (*ẓāhir*) meaning. The Prophet, in other words, has not made any reference to *ijmāᶜ* in this context. From this analysis, it would appear that al-Ghazālī does not agree with the conclusion that al-Shāfiᶜī has drawn from this *āyah*.

Jalāl al-Dīn al-Suyūṭī's interpretation of the same *āyah* is broadly in line with what al-Ghazālī had to say. There is no indication in al-Suyūṭī's *Tafsīr al-Jalālayn* to the effect that this *āyah* provides an explicit authority for *ijmāᶜ*.[32]

'Following a path other than that of the believers', according to both al-Suyūṭī and al-Shawkānī, means abandoning Islam. Al-Shawkānī adds: 'A number of ulema have drawn the conclusion that this *āyah* provides the authority for *ijmāᶜ*. But this is an unwarranted conclusion, as following a way other than that of the believers means unbelief, that is, renouncing Islam in favour of another religion.' Al-Shawkānī further suggests that the occasion of revelation (*sha'n al-nuzūl*) of this *āyah* relates to the context of apostasy. Specifically, it is reported that one Ṭuᶜmah b. Ubayraq had accused a Jew of a theft which Ṭuᶜmah had committed himself. As a result of the revelation of this *āyah*, the Jew was cleared of the charge but Ṭuᶜmah himself renounced Islam and fled to Mecca.[33]

Muḥammad ᶜAbduh and his disciple, Rashīd Riḍā have observed that the *āyah* under discussion was revealed concerning the 'way of the believers' during the lifetime of the Prophet, and its application must be confined to that period. For hostility toward the Prophet was only possible when he was alive. ᶜAbduh further remarks that to quote this *āyah* in support of *ijmāᶜ* leads to irrational conclusions, for it would amount to drawing a parallel between those who are threatened with the punishment of Hell and a *mujtahid* who differs with the opinion of others. A *mujtahid*, even when he takes an exception to the prevalent opinion, or to the path followed by other *mujtahidūn*, is still a Muslim, and even merits a reward for his efforts. ᶜAbduh concludes that the *sha'n al-nuzūl* of this *āyah* does not lend support to the conclusion that al-Shāfiᶜī has drawn from it.[34]

It is further suggested that the threat in the *āyah* under discussion is primarily concerned with the first part of the *āyah*, namely, disobeying the Prophet, and not necessarily with the second. Hence divergence from the believers' way is lawful in the absence of opposition to the Prophet. The validity of this critique is, however, disputed, as the *āyah* itself does not distinguish betweeen the two parts as such, and therefore the threat applies equally to both.[35]

Al-Āmidī discusses the Qur'ānic *āyāt* concerning *ijmāᶜ*, and concludes that they may give rise to a probability (*ẓann*) but they do not impart positive knowledge. If we assume that *ijmāᶜ* is a decisive proof, then establishing its authority on the basis of speculative evidence is not enough. Speculative evidence would suffice only if *ijmāᶜ* were deemed to be a speculative doctrine, which is not the case.[36]

2. The Sunnah on *Ijmāᶜ*

The Ḥadīth which is most frequently quoted in support of *ijmāᶜ* reads:

لا تجتمع أمتي على الضلالة

'My community shall never agree on an error.'[37] The last word in this Ḥadīth, namely *al-ḍalālah*, is rendered in some reports as *al-khaṭa'*. The jurists have used the two words interchangeably, but in the classical Ḥadīth collections this Ḥadīth has been recorded with the word *al-ḍalālah*.[38] Al-Ghazālī has pointed out that this Ḥadīth is not *mutawātir*, and as such, it is not an absolute authority like the Qur'ān. The Qur'ān on the other hand is *mutawātir* but contains no *naṣṣ* on *ijmāᶜ*. Having said this, however, al-Ghazālī adds that a number of prominent Companions have reported *aḥādīth* from the Prophet, which although different in their wording, are all in consonance on the theme of the infallibility of the community and its immunity from error.[39] Leading figures among the Companions such as ᶜUmar b. al-Khaṭṭāb, ᶜAbdullāh b. Masᶜūd, Anas b. Mālik. ᶜAbdullāh b. ᶜUmar, Abū Saᶜīd al-Khudrī, Abū Hurayrah, Ḥudhayfah and others have reported *aḥādīth* which include the following:

1. My community shall never agree upon an error (*al-khaṭa'*):

لا تجتمع أمتي على الخطأ

2. God will not let my community agree upon an error:

لم يكن الله ليجمع أمتي على الضلالة

3. I beseeched Almighty God not to bring my community to the point of agreeing on *ḍalālah* and He granted me this:

سألت الله تعالى ان لا يجمع أمتي على الضـلالـة
فأعطـانيهـا

4. Those who seek the joy of residing in Paradise will follow the community. For Satan can chase an individual but he stands farther away from two people:

من سره أن يسـكن بحبـوحـة الجنـة فليلزم
الجـماعـة ، ان الشيطان مـع الفـرد وهـو من
الاثنين أبعـد

5. The hand of God is with the community and (its safety) is not endangered by isolated oppositions:

يد الله مع الجماعة . ولا يبالي بشذوذ من شذ

6. Whoever leaves the community or separates himself from it by the length of a span is breaking his bond with Islam:

من خرج عن الجماعة أو فارق الجماعة قيد شبر
فقد خلع ربقة الاسلام من عنقه

7. A group of my *ummah* shall continue to remain on the right path. They will be the dominant force and will not be harmed by the opposition of opponents:

لا تزال طائفـة من أمتي على الحق ظاهـرين
لا يضرهم من خالفهم

8. Whoever separates himself from the community and dies, dies the death of ignorance (*jāhiliyyah*):

من فارق الجماعة ومات فميتته جاهلية

9. And finally, the well-known saying of ʿAbdullāh b. Masʿūd which is as follows: 'Whatever the Muslims deem to be good is good in the eyes of God.'[40]

ما رأه المسلمون حسناً فهو عند الله حسن

Having quoted these (and other) *aḥādīth*, both al-Ghazālī and al-Āmidī observe that their main theme and purport has not been opposed by the Companions, the Successors and others throughout the ages, and that everyone has agreed on their broad outline. The ulema have continued to rely on them in their exposition of the general and detailed rules of the *Sharīʿah*. In answer to the point that all these are solitary (*āḥād*) reports which do not amount to a definitive proof, the same authors observe that the main purport of these *aḥādīth* nevertheless conveys positive knowledge, and that the infallibility of the *ummah* is sustained by their collective weight.[41] The point may be illustrated by saying that we know the courage of ʿAlī, the generosity of Ḥātim, the erudition of al-Shāfiʿī in *fiqh*, and the esteem in which the Prophet held his Companions, despite the absence of *Mutawātir* reports on these subjects. Although the foregoing *aḥādīth* are all *Āḥād* and could be subjected to doubt if taken individually, their collective import may, nevertheless, not be denied.[42]

As to the question whether '*ḍalālah*' and '*khaṭa*'', in these *aḥādīth* (especially in the first four) could mean disbelief (*kufr*) and heresy (*bidʿah*) with the view that the Prophet might have meant that his community shall not fall into disbelief, it is observed that *khaṭa*' is general and could include *kufr* but that *ḍalālah* does not, for *ḍalālah* only means an error or erroneous conduct.[43] If *ḍalālah* meant disbelief, then the *aḥādīth* under discussion would fail to provide an authority for the infallibility of the *ummah*, but if it meant an error only, then they could provide such authority.[44]

It is further observed that the article '*lā*' in the Ḥadīth under discussion could either imply negation (*nafy*) or prohibition (*nahy*). If the latter, it would simply prohibit the people from deviation, and as such the Ḥadīth could not sustain the notion of infallibility for the *ummah*.[45] According to another observer, the manifest (*ẓāhir*) meaning of the *Ḥadīth* is that the *ummah* abstains from a collective agreement on an error. The Ḥadīth, in other words, precludes a general agreement on an error, but not the error itself. These are some of the doubts which have been expressed concerning the precise meaning of the Ḥadīth. They may or may not be correct, but so long as the Ḥadīth is open to such doubts, it cannot provide a decisive proof (*dalīl qaṭʿī*) for *ijmāʿ*.[46] Muḥammad ʿAbduh has observed that the Ḥadīth in question does not speak of *ijmāʿ* at all, nor does it sustain the notion of infallibility for the community. It is an exaggerated claim to read *ijmāᶜ* into this Ḥadīth regardless of whether reference is made to the agreement of the jurists or to that of the community at large.[47]

It is further suggested that some of the foregoing *aḥādīth* (nos. 4, 5 and 6 in particular) simply encourage fraternity and love among the members of the community, and, as such, do not envisage the notion of *ijmāᶜ* as a source of law. As for our Ḥadīth number seven, although al-Ghazālī quotes it, it is not relevant to *ijmāᶜ*, as it obviously means that a group of the *ummah* shall remain on the right path, not the *ummah* as a whole. The Shīᶜah Imāmiyyah have quoted this Ḥadīth in support of their doctrine of the *ijmāᶜ* of *ahl al-bayt*, which refers to the members of the family of the Prophet.[48]

The word '*ummah*' (or *jamāᶜah*) in the foregoing *aḥādīth* means, according to one view, the overwhelming majority of Muslims. This view is supported in a number of statements from the Companions. According to another view, *jamāᶜah* refers to the scholars of the community only. The masses, it is argued, look up to the scholars from whom they acquire knowledge of law and religion, and it is the latter whose consensus is contemplated in the relevant *aḥādīth*. According to yet another opinion, *ummah* (and *jamāᶜah*) refers only to the Companions, who are the founding fathers of the Muslim community. According to this interpretation, *ummah* and *jamāᶜah* in all the foregoing *aḥādīth* refer to the Companions only.[49]

And finally, *ummah* and *jamāᶜah* refer to the whole of the Muslim community and not to a particular section thereof. The grace of *ᶜiṣmah*, according to this view, is endowed on the whole of the community without any reservation or specification. This is the view of al-Shāfiᶜī, who wrote in his *Risālah*: 'And we know that the people at large cannot agree on an error or on what may contradict the *Sunnah* of the Prophet.'[50]

Having discussed the *aḥādīth* relating to *ijmāᶜ*, Aḥmad Ḥasan observes that they are inconclusive. All of them emphasise unity and integration. Some of them are predictive and others circumstantial: 'They may mean *ijmāᶜ*, or something else.' Hence the argument that they provide the authority for *ijmāᶜ* is 'definitely subjective'. The same author elaborates that:

a) There was no idea of *ijmāᶜ* as a doctrine of jurisprudence in the early period;
b) The jurists could not determine a definite meaning for '*ummah*' or '*jamāᶜah*'; and
c) *Aḥādīh* which convey a general meaning should not be restricted to a particular point of view.[51]

Notwithstanding the doubts and uncertainties in the *nuṣūṣ*, the majority of ulema have concluded that the consensus of all the *mujtahidūn* on a particular ruling is a sure indication that the word of truth has prevailed over their differences; that it is due to the strength of that truth that they have reached a consensus. This rational argument in support of *ijmāᶜ* has been further advanced to the effect that consensus upon a *sharᶜī* ruling is bound to be founded on sound *ijtihād*. In exercising *ijtihād*, the *mujtahid* is normally guided by certain rules and guidelines. *Ijtihād* often consists of an interpretation of the *naṣṣ*, or of a rational extension of its ruling. Even in the absence of a *naṣṣ*, *ijtihād* still observes both the letter and spirit of the sources which the *mujtahid* has mastered through his general knowledge. Since *ijtihād* is founded on sound authority in the first place, the unanimous agreement of all the *mujtahidūn* on a particular ruling indicates that there is clear authority in the *Sharīᶜah* to sustain their consensus. In the event of this authority being weak or speculative, we can only expect disagreement (*ikhtilāf*), which would automatically preclude consensus. *Ijmāᶜ*, in other words, accounts for its own authority.

Feasibility of *Ijmāᶜ*

A number of ulema, including the Muᶜtazilī leader Ibrāhīm al-Naẓẓām and some Shīᶜī ulema, have held that *ijmāᶜ* in the way defined by the *jumhūr* ulema is not feasible. To ascertain the consensus of the ulema on any matter which is not obvious is just as impossible as their unanimity at any given moment on what they utter and what they eat.[52] It may be possible to ascertain the broad outline of an agreement among the *mujtahidūn* on a particular matter, but to say that their consensus could be ascertained in such a way as to impart positive knowledge is not feasible. Since the *mujtahidūn* would normally be located in distant places, cities and continents, access to all of them and obtaining their views is beyond the bounds of practicality. Difficulties are also encountered in distinguishing a *mujtahid* from a non-*mujtahid*. Since it is the *mujtahidūn* whose consensus constitutes *ijmāᶜ*, one must be able to identify them with certainty. Apart from the absence of clear criteria concerning the attributes of a *mujtahid*, there are some among them who have not achieved fame. Even granting that they could be known and numbered, there is still no guarantee to ensure that the *mujtahid* who gives an opinion will not change it before an *ijmāᶜ* is reached. So long as this is possible, no *ijmāᶜ* can be realised, for it is a condition of *ijmāᶜ* that all the *mujtahidūn* be simultaneously in agreement.[53] It is mainly due to these reasons that al-Shāfiᶜī confines the occurrence of *ijmāᶜ* to the obligatory duties alone as he considers that on matters other than these, *ijmāʿ* is not a realistic proposition at all.[54]

It is due partly to their concern over the feasibility of *ijmāʿ* that according to the Ẓāhirīs and Imām Aḥmad ibn Ḥanbal *ijmāʿ* refers to the consensus of the Companions alone. Imām Mālik on the other hand confines *ijmāʿ* to the people of Madinah, and the Shīʿah Imāmiyyah recognise only the agreement of the members of the Prophet's family (*ahl al-bayt*). In Shīʿī jurisprudence, *ijmāʿ* is inextricably linked with the *Sunnah*. For the agreement of the *ahl al-bayt* (that is, their recognised Imams), automatically becomes an integral part of the *Sunnah*. 'In the Shīʿite view', as Muṭahharī explains, 'consensus goes back to the *Sunnah* of the Prophet [...]. Consensus is not genuinely binding in its own right, rather it is binding inasmuch as it is a means of discovering the *Sunnah*.'[55] In support of their argument that *ijmāʿ* is confined to the *ahl al-bayt*, the Shīʿī ulema have referred to the Qur'ān (al-Aḥzāb 33:33): 'God wishes to cleanse you, the people of the house [of the Prophet], of impurities.' The Shīʿī doctrine also relies on the Ḥadīth in which the Prophet is reported to have said, 'I am leaving among you two weighty things, which, if you hold by them, you will not go astray: The Book of God, and my family.'

إني تارك فيكم ثقلين ، فان تمسكتم بهما لن
تضلّوا كتاب الله وعترتي

The reference in this Ḥadīth, according to its Shīʿī interpreters, is to ʿAlī, Fāṭimah, Ḥasan and Ḥusayn. The Sunnīs have maintained, however, that the *āyah* in sūra al-Aḥzāb was revealed regarding the wives of the Prophet and that the context in which it was revealed is different. Similarly, while quoting the foregoing Ḥadīth, al-Āmidī observes: 'doubtlessly the *ahl al-bayt* enjoy a dignified status, but dignity and descent are not necessarily the criteria of one's ability to carry out *ijtihād*'.[56]

There is yet another argument to suggest that *ijmāʿ* is neither possible nor, in fact, necessary. Since *ijmāʿ* is founded on *ijtihād*, the *mujtahid* must rely on an indication (*dalīl*) in the sources which is either decisive (*qaṭʿī*) or speculative (*ẓannī*). If the former is the case, the community is bound to know of it, for a decisive indication in the *nuṣūṣ* could not remain hidden from the entire community. Hence there would be no need for *ijmāʿ* to substantiate the *naṣṣ* or to make it known to the people. Furthermore, when there is *qaṭʿī* indication, then that itself is the authority, in which case *ijmāʿ* would be redundant.[57] *Ijmāʿ*, in other words, can add nothing to the authority of a decisive *naṣṣ*. But if the indication in the *naṣṣ* happens to be speculative, then once again there will be no case for *ijmāᶜ*: a speculative indication can only give rise to *ikhtilāf*, not *ijmāᶜ*.[58]

According to a report, ᶜAbdullāh b. Aḥmad b. Ḥanbal quoted his father to have said: 'It is no more than a lie for any man to claim the existence of *ijmāᶜ*. Whoever claims *ijmāᶜ* is telling a lie.'[59] The *jumhūr* ulema, however, maintain that *ijmāᶜ* is possible and has occurred in the past, adding that those who deny it are only casting doubt on the possibility of something which has occurred. Note for example the *ijmāᶜ* of the Companions on the exclusion of the son's son from inheritance, when there is a son; and their *ijmāᶜ* on the rule that land in the conquered territories may not be distributed to the conquerers; or their ruling that consanguine brothers are counted as full brothers in the absence of the latter.[60] This last rule is based on a Ḥadīth in which the Prophet counted them both as brothers without distinguishing the one from the other.[61] The *ijmāᶜ* that is recorded on these issues became standard practice during the period of the first four caliphs, who often consulted the Companions and announced their collective decisions in public.[62]

ᶜAbd al-Wahhāb Khallāf is of the view that an *ijmāᶜ* in accordance with its classical definition is not feasible in modern times. Khallāf adds that it is unlikely that *ijmāᶜ* could be effectively utilised if it is left to Muslim individuals and communities without there being a measure of government intervention. But *ijmāᶜ* could be feasible if it were to be facilitated by the ruling authorities. The government in every Muslim country could, for example, specify certain conditions for attainment to the rank of *mujtahid*, and make this contingent upon obtaining a recognised certificate. This would enable every government to identify the *mujtahidūn* and to verify their views when the occasion so required. When the views of all the *mujtahidūn* throughout the Islamic lands concur upon a ruling concerning an issue, this becomes *ijmāᶜ*, and the ruling so arrived at becomes a binding *ḥukm* of the *Sharīᶜah* upon all the Muslims of the world.[63]

The question is once again asked whether the classical definition of *ijmāᶜ* has ever been fulfilled at any period following the demise of the Prophet. Khallāf answers this question in the negative, although some ulema maintain that the *ijmāᶜ* of the Companions did fulfil these requirements. Khallāf observes that anyone who scrutinises events during the period of the Companions will note that their *ijmāᶜ* consisted of the agreement of the learned among them who were present at the time when an issue was deliberated, and the ruling which followed was a collective decision of the *shūrā*. When the caliph Abū Bakr could not find the necessary guidance for settling a dispute in the Qur'ān or the *Sunnah*, he would convene the community leaders for consultation, and if they agreed on an opinion, he would act upon it. The community leaders so convened did not include everyone; many were, in fact, on duty in Mecca, Syria, the Yemen, etc. There is nothing in the reports to suggest that Abū Bakr postponed the settlement of disputes until a time when all the *mujtahidūn* of the age in different cities reached an agreement. He would instead act on the collective decision of those who were present. The practice of ᶜUmar b. al-Khaṭṭāb corresponded with that of his predecessor, and this is what the *fuqahā'* have referred to as *ijmāᶜ*. This form of *ijmāᶜ* was only practiced during the period of the Companions, and intermittently under the Umayyads in al-Andalus when in the second Islamic century they set up a council of ulema for consultation in legislative affairs (*tashrīᶜ*). References are found, in the works of some ulema of the Andalus, to the effect that so-and-so was the 'learned member' of the council.

With the exception of these periods in the history of Islam, no collective *ijmāᶜ* is known to have taken place on any juridical matter. The *mujtahidūn* were engaged in their juridical activities as individuals, whose views either agreed or disagreed with those of the other *mujtahidūn*. The most that a particular *mujtahid* was able to say on any particular matter was that 'no disagreement is known to exist on the *ḥukm* of this or that incident'.[64]

Types of *Ijmāᶜ*

From the viewpoint of the manner of its occurrence, *ijmāᶜ* is divided into two types:

a) Explicit *ijmāᶜ* (*al-ijmāᶜ al-ṣarīḥ*) in which every *mujtahid* expresses his opinion either verbally or by an action; and
b) Tacit *ijmāᶜ* (*al-ijmāᶜ al-sukūtī*) whereby some of the *mujtahidūn* of a particular age give an expressed opinion concerning an incident while the rest remain silent.

According to the *jumhūr* ulema, explicit *ijmāᶜ* is definitive and binding. Tacit *ijmāᶜ* is a presumptive *ijmāᶜ* which only creates a probability (*ẓann*) but does not preclude the possibility of fresh *ijtihād* on the same issue. Since tacit *ijmāᶜ* does not imply the definite agreement of all its participants, the ulema have differed over its authority as a proof. The majority of ulema, including al-Shāfiᶜī, have held that it is not a proof and that it does not amount to more than the view of some individual *mujtahidūn*. But the Ḥanafīs have considered tacit *ijmāᶜ* to be a proof provided it is established that the *mujtahid* who has remained silent had known of the opinion of other *mujtahidūn* but then, having had ample time to investigate and to express an opinion, still chose to remain silent. If it is not known that the silence was due to fear or *taqiyyah* (hiding one's true opinion), or wariness of inviting disfavour and ridicule, then the silence of a *mujtahid* on an occasion where he ought to express an opinion when there was nothing to stop him from doing so would be considered tantamount to agreeing with the existing opinion.[65]

The proponents of tacit *ijmāᶜ* have further pointed out that explicit agreement or open speech by all the *mujtahidūn* concerning an issue is neither customary nor possible. In every age, it is the usual practice that the leading ulema give an opinion which is often accepted by others. Suppose that the entire *ummah* gathered in one place and shouted all at once saying that, 'we agree on such-and-such'. Even if this were possible, it would still not impart positive knowledge. For some of them might have remained silent due to fear, uncertainty, or *taqiyyah*.[66]

Further, the Ḥanafīs draw a distinction between the 'concession' (*rukhṣah*) and 'strict rule' (*ᶜazīmah*), and consider tacit *ijmāᶜ* to be valid only with regard to the former. In order to establish a strict rule, *ijmāᶜ* must be definitely stated or expressed by an act. The Ḥanafīs are alone in validating tacit *ijmāᶜ*. The Ẓāhirīs refuse it altogether, while some Shāfiᶜīs like al-Juwaynī, al-Ghazālī and al-Āmidī allow it with certain reservations. 'It is *ijmāᶜ*', al-Ghazālī tells us, 'provided that the tacit agreement is accompanied by indications of approval on the part of those who are silent.'[67]

The majority opinion on this matter is considered to be preferable. For the silence of a *mujtahid* could be due to a variety of factors, and it would be arbitrary to lump them all together and say that silence definitely indicates consent. But despite the controversy it has aroused, tacit *ijmāᶜ* is by no means an exceptional case. On the contrary, it is suggested that most of what is known by the name of *ijmāᶜ* falls under this category.[68]

The next topic that needs to be taken up in this context is the 'Madinese consensus', or *ijmāᶜ ahl al-Madīnah*.

According to the Mālikī ulema, since Madinah was the centre of Islamic teaching, the 'abode of hijrah' (*dār al-hijrah*) and the place where most of the Companions resided, the consensus of its people is bound to command high authority. Although the majority of ulema have held that the Madinese *ijmāᶜ* is not a proof on its own, Imām Mālik held that it is. There is some disagreement among the disciples of Mālik as to the interpretation of the views of their Imām. Some of these disciples have observed that Imām Mālik had only meant that the *ijmāᶜ* of the people of Madinah is a proof 'from the viewpoint of narration and factual reporting' (*min jihah al-naql wa'l-riwāyah*) as they were closest to the sources of the *Sharī*ᶜ*ah*. Other Mālikī jurists have held that Mālik only meant the Madinese *ijmā*ᶜ to be preferable but not exclusive. There are still others who say that Mālik had in mind the *ijmā*ᶜ of the Companions alone. The proponents of the Madinese *ijmā*ᶜ have sought to substantiate their views with *aḥādīth* which include the following: 'Madinah is sacred, and throws out its dross as fire casts out the dross of metal,'

المدينة طيبة تنفى خبثها كما ينفي الكير خبث الحديد

and 'Islam will cling to Madinah as a serpent clings to its hole.'[69]

إن الاسلام ليأرز إلى المدينة كما تأرز الحية إلى جحرها

The majority of jurists, however, maintain that these *aḥādīth* merely speak of the dignity of Madinah and its people. Even if the *aḥādīth* are taken to rule out the presence of impurity in Madinah, they do not mean that the rest of the *ummah* is impure, and even less that the Madinese *ijmā*ᶜ alone is authoritative. Had the sacred character of a place been a valid criterion, then one might say that the consensus of the people of Mecca would command even greater authority, as Mecca is the most virtuous of cities (*afḍal al-bilād*) according to the *naṣṣ* of the Qur'ān. Furthermore, knowledge and competence in *ijtihād* are not confined to any particular place. This is the purport of the Ḥadīth in which the Prophet said: 'My Companions are like stars. Whomsoever of them that you follow will guide you to the right path.'

أصحابي كالنجوم بأيّهم أقتديتم أهتديتم

This Ḥadīth pays no attention whatsoever to the place where a Companion might have resided.[70] To this analysis, Ibn Ḥazm adds the point that there were, as we learn from the Qur'ān, profligates and transgressors (*fussāq wa'l-munāfiqūn*) in Madinah just like other cities. The Companions were knowledgeable in the teachings of the Prophet wherever they were, within or outside Madinah, and staying in Madinah by itself did not necessarily enhance their standing in respect of knowledge, or the ability to carry out *ijtihād*.[71]

Basis (*Sanad*) of *Ijmāᶜ*

According to the majority if ulema, *ijmāᶜ* must be founded in a textual authority or in *ijtihād*. Al-Āmidī points out that it is unlikely that the *ummah* might reach unanimity over something that has no foundation in the sources.[72] The ulema are in agreement that *ijmāᶜ* may be based on the Qur'ān or the *Sunnah*. There is, however, disagreement as to whether *ijmāᶜ* can be based on a ruling in the secondary proofs such as *qiyās* or *maṣlaḥah*.

There are three views on this point, the first of which is that *ijmāᶜ* may not be founded on *qiyās*, for the simple reason that *qiyās* itself is subject to a variety of doubts. Since the authority of *qiyās* as a proof is not a subject on which the ulema are in agreement, how then could *ijmāᶜ* be founded on it? It is further noted that the Companions did not reach a consensus on anything without the authority of the Qur'ān or the *Sunnah*. In all cases in which the Companions are known to have reached a consensus, at the root of it there has been some authority in the primary sources.[73]

The second view is that *qiyās* in all of its varieties may form the basis of consensus. For *qiyās* itself consists of an analogy to the *naṣṣ*. Relying on *qiyās* is therefore equivalent to relying on the *mass*, and when *ijmāᶜ* is based on a *qiyās*, it relies not on the personal views of the *mujtahidūn* but on the *naṣṣ* of the *Shariᶜah*.

The third view on this subject is that when the effective cause (*ᶜillah*) of *qiyās* is clearly stated in the *naṣṣ*, or when the *ᶜillah* is indisputably obvious, then *qiyās* may validly form the basis of *ijmāᶜ*. But when the *ᶜillah* of *qiyās* is hidden and no clear indication to it can be found in the *nuṣūṣ*, then it cannot form a sound foundation for *ijmāᶜ*. Abū Zahrah considers this to be a sound opinion: when the *ᶜillah* of *qiyās* is indicated in the *nuṣūṣ*, reliance on *qiyās* is tantamount to relying on the *naṣṣ* itself.[74]

Instances could be cited of *ijmāᶜ* which is founded upon analogy. To give an example, a father is entitled to guardianship over the person and property of his minor child. By *ijmāᶜ* this right is also established for the grandfather regarding his minor grandchild. This ruling of *ijmāᶜ* is founded upon an analogy between the father and grandfather. A similar example is given regarding the assignment of punishment for wine-drinking (*shurb*). This penalty is fixed at eighty lashes, and an *ijmāᶜ* has been claimed in its support. When the Companions were deliberating the issue, ᶜAlī b. Abī Ṭālib drew an analogy between *shurb* and slanderous accusation (*qadhf*). Since *shurb* can lead to *qadhf*, the pescribed penalty for the latter was, by analogy, assigned to the former. The alleged *ijmāᶜ* on this point has, however, been disputed in view of the fact that ᶜUmar b. al-Khaṭṭāb determined the *ḥadd* of *shurb* at forty lashes, a position which has been adopted by Aḥmad b. Ḥanbal. To claim an *ijmāᶜ* on this point is therefore unwarranted.[75]

Transmission of *Ijmāᶜ*

The issue to be examined here is the nature of the evidence by which the fact that a particular question has been determined by *ijmāᶜ* may be proved. From this perspective, *ijmāᶜ* is divided into two types, namely 'acquired' (*muḥaṣṣal*) and 'transmitted' (*manqūl*). The first is concluded with the direct participation of the *mujtahid* without the mediation of reporters or transmitters. The *mujtahid* thus gains direct knowledge of the opinions of other *mujtahidūn* when they all reach a consensus on a ruling. But transmitted *ijmāᶜ* is established by means of reports which may either be solitary (*āḥād*) or conclusive (*mutawātir*). In the case of transmission by *tawātur* there is no problem of proof, and *ijmāᶜ* which is transmitted by *tawātur* is proven in the same way as acquired *ijmāᶜ*. But there is disagreement regarding *ijmāᶜ* which is transmitted by way of solitary reports. Al-Ghazālī points out that a solitary report is not sufficient to prove *ijmāᶜ*, although some *fuqahā'* have held otherwise. The reason is that *ijmāᶜ* is a decisive proof whereas an *āḥād* report amounts to no more than speculative evidence; thus, it cannot establish *ijmāᶜ*.[76]

Al-Āmidī explains that a number of the ulema of the Shāfiᶜī, Ḥanafī and Ḥanbalī schools validate the proof of *ijmāᶜ* by means of solitary reports whereas another group of Ḥanafī and Shāfiᶜī ulema do not. All have nevertheless agreed that anything which is proved by means of a solitary report is speculative of proof (*thubūt*) even if definitive in respect of content (*matn*).[77]

Proof by means of *tawātur* can only be claimed for the *ijmāᶜ* of the Companions; no other *ijmāᶜ* is known to have been transmitted by *tawātur*. This is the main reason why the *fuqahā'* have differed in their views concerning any *ijmāᶜ* other than that of the Companions. A large number of the ulema of *uṣūl* have maintained that transmission through solitary reports amounts to speculative evidence only. When *ijmāᶜ* is based on such evidence, it loses its value and the *ḥukm* for which *ijmāᶜ* is claimed must be referred back to the source from which it was derived in the first place.[78]

Reform Proposals

The modern critics of *ijmāᶜ* consider that *ijmāᶜ* according to its classical definition fails to relate to the search for finding solutions to the problems of the community in modern times. *Ijmāᶜ* is hence retrospective and too slow a process to accommodate the problems of social change. These and other considerations concerning the relevance of *ijmāᶜ* to social realities have prompted a response from modern scholars. We have already discussed the view of ᶜAbd al-Wahhāb Khallāf in regard to the feasibility of *ijmāᶜ*. Khallāf, however, was not the first to criticise *ijmāᶜ*.

An early critique of *ijmāᶜ* was advanced by Shāh Walī Allāh Dihlawī (d. 1176/1762), who tried to bring *ijmāᶜ* closer to reality and came out in support of 'relativity' in the concept of *ijmāᶜ*. Dihlawī overruled the notion of universal consensus in favour of relative *ijmāᶜ*. Dihlawī is also critical of the interpretation that is given to the *aḥādīth* concerning *ijmāᶜ*. He argues that the Ḥadīth, 'My community shall never agree upon an error' did not envisage *ijmāᶜ* at all. Hence the correct meaning of this Ḥadīth may be determined in the light of another Ḥadīth which provides that 'a section of my community will continue to remain on the right path [. . .].' *Ijmāᶜ* in other words does not mean a universal agreement but only the consensus of a limited number of *mujtahidūn*. With regard to the other *aḥādīth* that are quoted in support of *ijmāᶜ*, Dihlawī maintains that the two principal aims of these *aḥādīth* are the political unity of the *ummah*, and the integrity of the *Sharīᶜah*. The same author maintains that *ijmāᶜ* can be justified on the basis of all such *aḥādīth* that protect the unity and integrity of the community. But he adds that *ijmāᶜ* has never been meant to consist of the universal agreement of every member of the community (or of every learned member of the community for that matter), as this is plainly impossible to achieve. It has neither happened in the past nor could it conceivably happen in the future. *Ijmāᶜ*, according to Shāh Walī Allāh, is the consensus of the ulema and men of authority in different towns and localities. In this sense, *ijmāᶜ* can be held anywhere at any time. The *ijmāᶜ* of the Companions during the caliphate of ᶜUmar b. al-Khaṭṭāb, and the *ijmāᶜ* that was concluded in Mecca and Madinah under the pious caliphs, are all examples of *ijmāᶜ* in its relative sense.[79]

Muḥammad Iqbāl is primarily concerned with the question of how to utilise the potentials of *ijmāᶜ* in the process of modern statutory legislation. He considers it an important doctrine, but one which has remained largely theoretical. 'It is strange,' Iqbāl writes, that this important notion 'rarely assumed the form of a permanent institution'. He then suggests that the transfer of the power of *ijtihād* 'from individual representatives of schools to a Muslim legislative assembly [. . .] is the only possible form *ijmāᶜ* can take in modern times'.[80] In such an assembly, the ulema should play a vital part, but it must also include in its ranks laymen who happen to possess a keen insight into affairs. Furthermore Iqbāl draws a distinction between the two functions of *ijmāᶜ*, namely:

> Discovering the law and implementing the law. The former function is related to the question of facts and the latter relates to the question of law. In the former case, as for instance, when the question arose whether the two small sūras known as 'Muᶜawwazataīn' formed part of the Qur'ān or not, and the Companions unanimously decided that they did, we are bound by their decision, obviously because the Companions alone were in a position to know the fact. In the latter case, the question is one of interpretation only, and I venture to think, on the authority of Karkhi, that later generations are not bound by the decision of the Companions.[81]

It is thus clear that Iqbāl retains the binding character of *ijmāᶜ* only insofar as it relates to points of fact, but not with regard to *ijmāᶜ* that is based on juridical *ijtihād*. This distinction between the factual and juridical *ijmāᶜ* will presumably not apply to the *ijmāᶜ* that Iqbāl has proposed: the collective decisions of the legislative assembly will naturally be binding on points of law.

Iqbāl's proposed reform has been fairly widely supported by other scholars. It is a basically sound proposal. But to relate this to the idea of a distinction between the factual and *ijtihādī ijmāᶜ* seems questionable. Apart from the difficulty that might be involved in distinguishing a factual from a juridical *ijmāᶜ* one can expect but little support for the view that the *ijmāᶜ* of the Companions on *ijtihādī* matters is not binding.

Iqbāl's views have, however, been criticised on other grounds. S.M. Yūsuf has observed that Iqbāl was mistaken in trying to convert *ijmāᶜ* into a modern legislative institution. Yūsuf argues that *ijtihād* and *ijmāᶜ* have never been the prerogatives of a political organisation, and any attempt to institutionalise *ijmāᶜ* is bound to alter the nature of *ijmāᶜ* and defeat its basic purpose. For *ijtihād* is a non-transferable right of every competent scholar, and a *mujtahid* is recognised by the community by virtue of his merits known over a period of time, not through election campaigns or awards of official certificates. The process of arriving at *ijmāᶜ* is entirely different from that of legislation in a modern state assembly. *Ijmāᶜ* passes through a natural process which resembles that of the 'survival of the fittest'. No attempt is made in this process to silence the opposition or to defeat the minority opinion. Opposition is tolerated until the truth emerges and prevails. *Ijmāᶜ* is a manifestation of the conscience of the community, and it is due mainly to the natural strength of *ijmāᶜ* and the absence of rigid organisation 'that no one is able to lay his hands on Islam; when anyone tries to hammer Islam, he ultimately finds to his chagrin that he has only been beating in the air'.[82]

Aḥmad Ḥasan finds some weaknesses in Yūsuf's criticism of Iqbāl, and observes that 'Dr Yūsuf has probably not understood Iqbāl's view correctly.' Ḥasan finds Iqbāl's view to the effect that *ijtihād* should be exercised collectively instead of being a preserve of the individual *mujtahidūn*, to be basically sound. '*Ijtihād* today cannot be exercised in isolation. Modern conditions demand that it should be exercised collectively. A *mujtahid* may be expert in Islamic learnings, but he cannot claim to be perfectly acquainted with the social conditions of a country and the diverse nature of its problems.'[83] Aḥmad Ḥasan goes on to point out that the legislative assembly is 'the right place' for the purpose of collective *ijtihād*, which would in turn provide an effective method of finding solutions to urgent problems.[84]

The late Shaykh of al-Azhar, Maḥmūd Shaltūt, observes that the conditions of a conclusive *ijmāᶜ*, especially the one which requires the agreement of all the *mujtahidūn* of the *ummah*, is no more than a theoretical proposition which is never expressed in reality. *Ijmāᶜ*, in reality, has often meant either the absence of disagreement (*ᶜadam al-ᶜilm bi'l-mukhālif*), or the agreement of the majority only (*ittifāq al-kathrah*). Both of these are acceptable propositons which may form the basis of general legislation. Shaltūt goes on to quote in support the Qur'ānic *āyah* in sūra al-Baqarah (2:286) that 'God does not assign to any soul that which falls beyond its capacity.' Shaltūt is not opposed to the institutionalisation of *ijmāᶜ* provided that this does not violate the freedom of opinion which must in all eventualities be granted to the constituents of *ijmāᶜ*. Consensus must never be subjected to a condition which subjugates freedom of opinion to the arbitrary exercise of political power. Shaltūt further adds that since the realisation of *maṣlaḥah* through consensus is the objective of *ijmāᶜ*, *maṣlaḥah* is bound to vary according to circumstances of time and place. Hence the *mujtahidūn* who participate in *ijmāᶜ*, and their successors, should all be able to take into consideration a change of circumstances and it should be possible for them to review a previous *ijmāᶜ* if this is deemed to be the only way to realise the *maṣlaḥah*. Should they arrive at a second *ijmāᶜ*, this will nullify and replace the first, and constitute a binding authority on all members of the community.[85]

Conclusion

Under their classical definitions, *ijmāᶜ* and *ijtihād* were both subject to conditions that virtually drove them into the realm of utopia. The unreality of these formulations is reflected in modern times in the experience of Muslim nations and their efforts to reform certain areas of the *Sharīᶜah* through the medium of statutory legislation. The juristic basis for some of the modern reforms introduced in the areas of marriage and divorce, for example, has been sought through novel interpretations of the relevant passages of the Qur'ān. Some of these reforms may rightly be regarded as instances of *ijtihād* in modern times. Yet in none of these instances do the statutory texts or their explanatory memoranda make an open reference to *ijtihād* or *ijmāᶜ*. The total absence of these terms in modern statutes is a sad reflection of the unreality that is encountered in the strict definitions of these concepts. The classical definitions of *ijtihād* and *ijmāᶜ* might, at one time, have served the purpose of discouraging excessive diversity which was felt to be threatening the very existence and integrity of the *Sharīᶜah*. But there is no compelling reason to justify the continued domination of a practice which was designed to bring *ijtihād* to a close. *Ijtihād* and *ijmāᶜ* were brought to a standstill, thanks to the extremely difficult conditions that were imposed on them, conditions which often ran counter to the enterprising and creative spirit that characterised the period of the pious caliphs and the early imams of jurisprudence.

Dr Yūsuf's criticism of Iqbāl's proposed reform is based on the dubious assumption that an elected legislative assembly will not reflect the collective conscience of the community and will unavoidably be used as an instrument of power politics. Although the cautious advice of this approach may be persuasive, the assumption behind it goes counter to the spirit of *maṣlaḥah* and of the theory of *ijmāᶜ* which endows the community with the divine trust of having the capacity and competence to make the right decisions. If one is to observe the basic message of the textual authority in support of the *ᶜiṣmah* of the community, then one must trust the community itself to elect only persons who will honour their collective conscience and their *maṣlaḥah*. In addition, Dr Yūsuf's critique of Iqbāl merely suggests that nothing should be done to relate *ijmāᶜ* to the realities of contemporary life. The critic is content with the idea of letting *ijmāᶜ* and *ijtihād* remain beyond the reach of the individuals and societies of today. On the contrary, the argument for taking a positive approach to *ijmāᶜ* is overwhelming. The gap between the theory and practice of *Sharīᶜah* law has grown to alarming proportions, and any attempt at prolonging it further will have to be exceedingly persuasive. While the taking of every precaution to safeguard the authentic spirit and natural strength of *ijmāᶜ* is fully justified, this should not necessarily mean total inertia. The main issue in institutionalising *ijmāᶜ*, as Shaltūt has rightly assessed, is that freedom of opinion should be vouchsafed the participants of *ijmāᶜ*. This is the essence of the challenge which has to be met, not through a *laissez-faire* attitude toward *ijtihād* and *ijmāᶜ*, but by nurturing judicious attitudes and by evolving correct methods and procedures to protect freedom of opinion. The consensus that is arrived at in this spirit will have kept a great deal, if not all, of the most valuable features of *ijmāᶜ*.

NOTES

1. In the Qur'ān the phrase *fajmaᶜū amrakum* which occurs in sūra Yūnus (10:71) means 'determine your plan'. Similarly *fajmaᶜū kaydakum* in sūra Ṭāhā (20:64), where the Prophet Noah addresses his estranged followers, means 'determine your trick'. The Ḥadīth *lā ṣiyāma liman lam yajmaᶜ al-ṣiyāma min al-layl* means that fasting is not valid unless it is determined (or intended) in advance; i.e. from the night before. For details see Āmidī, *Iḥkām*, I, 195; Shawkānī, *Irshād*, p. 70.

2. Amidī, *Iḥkām*, I, 196; Shawkānī, *Irshād*, p. 71. Abū Zahrah and ᶜAbd al-Wahhāb Khallāf's definition of *ijmāᶜ* differs with that of Āmidī and Shawkānī on one point, namely the subject matter of *ijmāᶜ*, which is confined to *sharᶜī* matters only (see Abū Zahrah, *Uṣūl*, p. 156 and Khallāf, *ᶜIlm*, p. 45).

3. Shawkānī, *Irshād*, p. 71.

4. According to one view, attributed to the Qāḍī ᶜAbd al-Jabbār, matters pertaining to warfare, agriculture, commerce, politics and administration are described as worldly affairs, and *ijmāᶜ* is no authority regarding them. One reason given in support of this view is that the Prophet himself precluded these matters from the scope of the *Sunnah* and the same rule is to be applied to *ijmāᶜ*. Āmidī, however, confirms the majority view when he adds (in his *Iḥkām*, I, 284) that these restrictions do not apply to *ijmāᶜ*.

5. Abū Zahrah, *Uṣūl*, p. 165.

6. Cf. Aghnides, *Muhammadan Theories*, pp. 37–38.

7. Cf. Aḥmad Ḥasan, *Early Development*, p. 160ff.

8. Goldziher, *Introduction*, p. 52.

9. Muslim, *Ṣaḥīḥ*, p. 212, Ḥadīth no. 817; Ibn Mājah, *Sunan*, II, 910, Ḥadīth no. 2724; Abū Zahrah, *Uṣūl*, pp. 159–161.

10. Shāh Walī Allāh, *Qurrah*, p. 40.

11. For details on the essential requirements of *ijmāᶜ* see Khallāf, *ᶜIlm*, p. 45ff; Shawkānī, *Irshād*, p. 71ff.

12. Āmidī, *Iḥkām*, I, 226. Bazdawī, however, distinguishes matters which do not require specialised knowledge from other matters, and suggests that no discrimination should be made between the layman and the jurists regarding the essentials of the faith. *Ijmāᶜ* is thus confined to the *mujtahidūn* only in regard to matters which require expert knowledge. See for details, Bazdawī, *Uṣūl*, III, 239.

13. Āmidī, *Iḥkām*, I, 235.

14. Shawkānī, *Irshād*, p. 71.

15. Abū Zahrah, *Uṣūl*, p. 162.

16. Āmidī, *Iḥkām*, I, 261; ᶜAbdur Rahīm, *Jurisprudence*, p. 122.

17. Abū Zahrah, *Uṣūl*, p. 164.

18. Shawkānī, *Irshād*, p. 71.

19. Āmidī, *Iḥkām*, I, 257; Ibn Ḥazm, *Iḥkām*, IV, 154.

20. Ghazālī, *Mustaṣfā*, I, 121.
21. Khallāf, *ᶜIlm*, pp. 46–47; Abū Zahrah, *Uṣūl*, p. 167.
22. Ghazālī, *Mustaṣfā*, I, 111; Āmidī, *Iḥkām*, I, 219.
23. The *āyah* (4:59) provides: 'O you who believe, obey God, and obey the Messenger, and those charged with authority among you.'
24. Rāzī, *Tafsīr*, III, 243.
25. Khallāf, *ᶜIlm*, p. 47.
26. The *āyah* (4:83) provides: 'If they would only refer it to the Messenger and those among them who hold command, those of them who investigate matters would have known about it.' (Irving's translation, p. 45.)
27. Āmidī, *Iḥkām*, I, 211.
28. Ibid., I, 217; Ghazālī, *Mustaṣfā*, I, 111.
29. Ghazālī, *Mustaṣfā*, I, 111.
30. Ibid.
31. Ibid.
32. Suyūṭī, *Tafsīr*, I, 87.
33. Shawkānī, *Fatḥ al-Qadīr*, I, 515; idem., *Irshād*, p. 75. For a good summary of Shawkānī's views on the subject see Ṣadr, *Ijmāᶜ*, pp. 30–40.
34. Rashīd Riḍā, *Tafsīr al-Manār*, V, 201. For a similar view see Ṣadr, *Ijmāᶜ*, p. 40.
35. Āmidī, *Iḥkām*, I, 205.
36. Ibid., I, 218.
37. Ibn Mājah, *Sunan*, II, 1303, Ḥadīth no. 3950. This and a number of other *aḥādīth* on *ijmāᶜ* have been quoted by both Ghazālī and Āmidī as shown in footnote 41 below.
38. Cf. Aḥmad Ḥasan, *Doctrine*, p. 60.
39. Ghazālī, *Mustaṣfā*, I, 111.
40. Āmidī considers this to be a Ḥadīth whose chain of narration goes back to the Prophet (see his *Iḥkām*, I, 214). Aḥmad Ḥasan points out that Muḥammad b. Ḥasan al-Shaybānī initially reported this as a Ḥadīth, but that later it was attributed to Ibn Masᶜūd (see his *Doctrine*, p. 37).
41. Ghazālī, *Mustaṣfā*, I, 111;Āmidī, *Iḥkām*, I, 220–221.
42. Ghazālī, *Mustaṣfā*, I, 112.
43. Ibid., I, 112: We find in the Qur'ān, for example, in an address to the Prophet Muḥammad: 'And He found thee wondering [*ḍāllan*] and gave thee guidance' (al-Ḍuḥā, 93:7). In another place the Qur'ān relates of Moses the following words: 'He said: I did it then [i.e. slayed the Egyptian] when I was in error' (al-Shuᶜarā', 26:20). In both these instances *ḍalāl* does not imply disbelief. Similarly the Arabic expression *ḍalla fulān ᶜan al-ṭarīq* (so-and-so lost his way) confirms the same meaning of *ḍalāl*.
44. Ibid.
45. Ṣadr, *Ijmāᶜ*, p. 43: An example of the 'lā of prohibition' is the Qur'ānic prohibition concerning adultery which reads *lā taqrabū al-zinā* (do not approach *zinā*). With a *lā* of prohibition the Ḥadīth would simply instruct the community not to agree upon an error.
46. Ṣadr. *Ijmāᶜ*, 43.
47. Riḍā, *Tafsīr al-Manār*, V, 205.
48. Ṣadr, *Ijmāᶜ*, pp. 44–45.
49. Cf. Ḥasan, *Doctrine*, p. 59.
50. Shāfiᶜī's *Risālah* (trans. Khadduri), p. 285.
51. Ḥasan, *Doctrine*, pp. 59–60.
52. Shawkānī, *Irshād*, p. 79; Khallāf, *ᶜIlm*, p. 48.
53. Khallāf, *ᶜIlm*, p. 49.
54. Shāfiᶜī, *Risālah*, p. 205; Abū Zahrah, *Uṣūl*, p. 158.

55. Āmidī, *Iḥkām*, I, 230. Muṭahharī, *Jurisprudence*, p. 20.
56. Āmidī, *Iḥkām*, I, 246ff.
57. Khallāf, *ᶜIlm*, p. 49.
58. Ibid., p. 49; Shawkānī, *Irshād*, p. 79.
59. Āmidī, *Iḥkām*, I, 198; Shawkānī, *Irshād*, p. 73.
60. Abū Zahrah, *Uṣūl*, p. 159.
61. Ibid., p. 165.
62. Ḥasan, *Doctrine*, p. 164.
63. Khallāf, *ᶜIlm*, pp. 49–50.
64. Ibid., p. 50.
65. Ibid., p. 51; Shawkānī, *Irshād*, p. 72.
66. Shawkānī, *Irshād*, p. 72, Abū Zahrah, *Uṣūl*, p. 163.
67. Ghazālī, *Mustaṣfā*, I, 121; *Encyclopedia of Islam* (New Edition) III, 1024.
68. Khallāf, *ᶜIlm*, p. 51.
69. Bukhārī, *Ṣaḥīḥ* (Istanbul edn.), II, 221; Muslim, *Saḥīḥ*, p. 17, Ḥadīth no. 38; Āmidī, *Iḥkām*, I, 243. Ibn Ḥazm discusses *ijmāᶜ ahl al-Madīnah* in some length, but cites none of the *aḥādīth* that are quoted by Āmidī and others. He merely points out that 'some of the *aḥādīth* which are quoted in support of the Mālikī doctrine are authentic (*ṣaḥīḥ*), while others are mere fabrications (*makdhūb*/ *mawḍūᶜ*) reported by one 'Muḥammad ibn Ḥasan ibn Zabālah' (*Iḥkām* IV, 154–155).
70. Āmidī, *Iḥkām*, I, 243ff.
71. Ibn Ḥazm, *Iḥkām*, IV, 155.
72. Āmidī, *Iḥkām*, I, 261.
73. Abū Zahrah, *Uṣūl*, pp. 165–166.
74. Ibid.
75. Ibid., pp. 166, 193.
76. Ghazālī, *Mustaṣfā*, I, 127; Ṣadr, *Ijmāᶜ*, pp. 97–98.
77. Āmidī, *Iḥkām*, I, 281.
78. Abū Zahrah, *Uṣūl*, pp. 167–68.
79. Shāh Walī Allāh, *Izālah*, I, 266.
80. Iqbal, *Reconstruction*, pp. 173, 174.
81. Ibid., p. 175. Iqbāl goes on to quote the Ḥanafī jurist Abū'l-Ḥasan al-Karkhī as saying: 'The *Sunnah* of the companions is binding in matters which cannot be cleared up by *qiyās*, but it is not so in matters which can be established by *qiyās*'. (No specific reference is given to al-Karkhī's work.)
82. Yūsuf, *Studies*, pp. 212–218.
83. Ḥasan, *Doctrine*, p. 244.
84. Ibid.
85. Shaltūt, *Islām*, pp. 558–559.

CHAPTER NINE

Qiyās (Analogical Deduction)

Literally, *qiyās* means measuring or ascertaining the length, weight, or quality of something, which is why scales are called *miqyās*. Thus the Arabic expression, *qāsat al-thawb bi'l-dhirāᶜ* means that 'the cloth was measured by the yardstick'.[1] *Qiyās* also means comparison, with a view to suggesting equality or similarity between two things. Thus the expression *Zayd yuqās ilā Khālid fī ᶜaqlihi wa nasabih* means that 'Zayd compares with Khālid in intelligence and descent'.[2] *Qiyās* thus suggests an equality or close similarity between two things, one of which is taken as the criterion for evaluating the other.

Technically, *qiyās* is the extension of a *Sharīᶜah* value from an original case, or *aṣl*, to a new case, because the latter has the same effective cause as the former. The original case is regulated by a given text, and *qiyās* seeks to extend the same textual ruling to the new case.[3] It is by virtue of the commonality of the effective cause, or *ᶜillah*, between the original case and the new case that the application of *qiyās* is justified.

A recourse to analogy is only warranted if the solution of a new case cannot be found in the Qur'ān, the *Sunnah* or a definite *ijmāᶜ*. For it would be futile to resort to *qiyās* if the new case could be resolved under a ruling of the existing law. It is only in matters which are not covered by the *nuṣūṣ* and *ijmāᶜ* that the law may be deduced from any of these sources through the application of analogical reasoning.[4]

In the usage of the *fuqahā'*, the word '*qiyās*' is sometimes used to denote a general principle. Thus one often comes across statements that this or that ruling is contrary to an established analogy, or to a general principle of the law without any reference to analogy as such.

Analogical deduction is different from interpretation in that the former is primarily concerned with the extension of the rationale of a given text to cases which may not fall within the terms of its language. *Qiyās* is thus a step beyond the scope of interpretation. The emphasis in *qiyās* is clearly placed on the identification of a common cause between two cases which is not indicated in the language of the text. Identifying the effective cause often involves intellectual exertion on the part of the jurist, who determines it by recourse not only to the semantics of a given text but also to his understanding of the general objectives of the law.

Since it is essentially an extension of the existing law, the jurists do not admit that extending the law by the process of analogy amounts to establishing a new law. *Qiyās* is a means of discovering, and perhaps of developing, the existing law. Although *qiyās* offers considerable potential for creativity and enrichment, it is basically designed to ensure conformity with the letter and the spirit of the Qur'ān and the *Sunnah*. In this sense, it is perhaps less than justified to call *qiyās* one of the sources (*maṣādir*) of the *Sharīʿah*; it is rather a proof (*ḥujjah*) or an evidence (*dalīl*) whose primary aim is to ensure consistency between revelation and reason in the development of the *Sharīʿah*. *Qiyās* is admittedly a rationalist doctrine, but it is one in which the use of personal opinion (*ra'y*) is subservient to the terms of the divine revelation. The main sphere for the operation of human judgement in *qiyās* is the identification of a common *ʿillah* between the original and the new case. Once the *ʿillah* is identified, the rules of analogy then necessitate that the ruling of the given text be followed without any interference or change. *Qiyās* cannot therefore be used as a means of altering the law of the text on grounds of either expediency or personal preference.

The jurist who resorts to *qiyās* takes it for granted that the rules of *Sharīʿah* follow certain objectives (*maqāṣid*) which are in harmony with reason. A rational approach to the discovery and identification of the objectives and intentions of the Lawgiver necessitates recourse to human intellect and judgment in the evaluation of the *aḥkām*. It is precisely on this ground, namely the propriety or otherwise of adopting an inquisitive approach to the injunctions of the Lawgiver, referred to as *taʿlīl*, that *qiyās* has come under attack by the Muʿtazilah, the Ẓāhirī, the Shīʿī and some Ḥanbalī ulema. Since an enquiry into the causes and objectives of divine injunctions often involves a measure of juristic speculation, the opponents of *qiyās* have questioned its essential validity. Their argument is that the law must be based on certainty, whereas *qiyās* is largely speculative and superfluous. If the two cases are identical and the law is clearly laid down in regard to one, there is no case for *qiyās*, as both will be covered by the same law. If they are different but bear a similarity to one another, then it is impossible to know whether the Lawgiver had intended the subsidiary case to be governed by the law of the original case. It is once again in recognition of this element of uncertainty in *qiyās* that the ulema of all the juristic schools have ranked *qiyās* as a 'speculative evidence'. With the exception, perhaps, of one variety of *qiyās*, namely where the *ᶜillah* of *qiyās* is clearly identified in the text, *qiyās* in general can never be as high an authority as the *naṣṣ* or a definite *ijmāᶜ*, for these are decisive evidences (*adillah qaṭᶜiyyah*), whereas *qiyās* in most cases only amounts to a probability. It is, in other words, merely probable, but not certain, that the result of *qiyās* is in conformity with the intentions of the Lawgiver. The propriety of *qiyās* is thus always to be measured by the degree of its proximity and harmony with the *nuṣūṣ*. In our discussion of the methodology of *qiyās* it will at once become obvious that the whole purpose of this methodology is to ensure that under no circumstances does analogical deduction operate independently of the *nuṣūṣ*. It would be useful to start by giving a few examples.

1) The Qur'ān (al-Jumuᶜah, 62:9) forbids selling or buying goods after the last call for Friday prayer until the end of the prayer. By analogy this prohibition is extended to all kinds of transactions, since the effective cause, that is, diversion from prayer, is common to all.[5]
2) The Prophet is reported to have said, 'The killer shall not inherit [from his victim].'

   لا يرث القاتل

   By analogy this ruling is extended to bequests, which would mean that the killer cannot benefit from the will of his victim either.[6]
3) According to a Ḥadīth, it is forbidden for a man to make an offer of betrothal to a woman who is already betrothed to another man unless the latter permits it or has totally abandoned his offer.

   لا يخطب الرجل على خطبة أخيه حتى ينكح أو يترك

   The *ᶜillah* of this rule is to obviate conflict and hostility among people. By analogy the same rule is extended to all other transactions in which the same *ᶜillah* is found to be operative.[7]

The majority of ulema have defined *qiyās* as the application to a new case (*farᶜ*), on which the law is silent, of the ruling (*ḥukm*) of an original case (*aṣl*) because of the effective cause (*ᶜillah*) which is in common to both.[8] The Ḥanafī definition of *qiyās* is substantially the same, albeit with a minor addition which is designed to preclude certain varieties of *qiyās* (such as *qiyās al-awlā* and *qiyās al-musāwī*, [q.v.]) from the scope of *qiyās*. The Ḥanafī jurist, Ṣadr al-Sharīʿah, in his *Tawḍīḥ*, as translated by Aghnides, defines *qiyās* as 'extending the (*Sharīʿah*) value from the original case over to the subsidiary (*farʿ*) by reason of an effective cause which is common to both cases and cannot be understood from the expression (concerning the original case) alone.'[9] The essential requirements of *qiyās* which are indicated in these definitions are as follows:

1) The original case, or *aṣl*, on which a ruling is given in the text and which analogy seeks to extend to a new case.
2) The new case (*farʿ*) on which a ruling is wanting.
3) The effective cause (*ʿillah*) which is an attribute (*waṣf*) of the *aṣl* and is found to be in common between the original and the new case.
4) The rule (*ḥukm*) governing the original case which is to be extended to the new case.[10] To illustrate these, we might adduce the example of the Qur'ān (al-Mā'idah, 5:90), which explicitly forbids wine drinking. If this prohibition is to be extended by analogy to narcotic drugs, the four pillars of analogy in this example would be:

aṣl	*farʿ*	*ʿillah*	*ḥukm*
wine drinking	taking drugs	the intoxicating effect	prohibition

Each of the four essentials (*arkān*) of analogy must, in turn, qualify a number of other conditions which are all designed to ensure propriety and accuracy in the application of *qiyās*. It is to these which we now turn.

1. Conditions Pertaining to the Original Case (*Aṣl*)

Aṣl has two meanings. Firstly, it refers to the source, such as the Qur'ān or the *Sunnah*, which reveals a particular ruling. The second meaning of *aṣl* is the subject-matter of that ruling. In the foregoing example of the prohibition of wine in the Qur'ān, the *aṣl* is both the Qur'ān, which is the source, and wine, which is the original case or the subject-matter of the prohibition. However, to all intents and purposes, the two meanings of *aṣl* are convergent. We tend to use *aṣl* to imply the source as well as the original case, for the latter constitutes the subject-matter of the former, and the one cannot be separated from the other.[11]

The ulema are in unanimous agreement that the Qur'ān and the *Sunnah* constitute the sources, or the *aṣl*, of *qiyās*. According to the majority of jurists, *qiyās* may also be founded on a rule that is established by *ijmāʿ*. For example, *ijmāʿ* validates guardianship over the property of minors, a rule which has been extended by analogy to authorise the compulsory guardianship (*wilāyah al-ijbār*) of minors in marriage.[12]

There is, however, some disagreement as to whether *ijmāʿ* constitutes a valid *aṣl* for *qiyās*. Those who dispute the validity of *ijmāᶜ* as a basis of analogical deduction argue that the rules of consensus do not require that there should be a basis (*sanad*) for *ijmāᶜ*. In other words, *ijmāᶜ* does not always explain its own justification or rationale. In the absence of such information, it is difficult to construct an analogy. In particular it would be difficult to identify the *ᶜillah*, and *qiyās* cannot be constructed without the *ᶜillah*.[13] But this view is based on the assumption that the *ᶜillah* of *qiyās* is always identified in the sources, which is not the case.

The *ᶜillah* may at times be specified in the sources, but when this is not so, it is for the *mujtahid* to identify it in the light of the objectives (*maqāṣid*) of the Lawgiver. The *mujtahid*, in other words, is faced with the same task whether he derives the *ᶜillah* from *ijmāᶜ* or from the *nuṣūṣ*. Furthermore, the majority view which validates the founding of analogy on *ijmāᶜ* maintains that consensus itself is a basis (*sanad*) and that the effective cause of a ruling which is based on consensus can be identified through *ijtihād*.[14]

According to the majority of ulema, one *qiyās* may not constitute the *aṣl* of another *qiyās*. This is explained in reference to the effective cause on which the second analogy is founded. If this is identical with the original *ᶜillah*, then the whole exercise would be superfluous. For instance, if it be admitted that the quality of edibility is the effective cause which would bring an article within the scope of usury (*ribā*) then it would justify an analogy to be drawn between wheat and rice. But an attempt to draw a second analogy between rice and edible oil for the purpose of extending the rules of *ribā* to the latter would be unnecessary, for it would be preferable to draw a direct analogy between wheat and edible oil, which would eliminate the intermediate analogy with the rice altogether.[15]

However, according to the prominent Mālikī jurist, Ibn Rushd (whose views are here representative of the Mālikī school) and some Ḥanbalī ulema, one *qiyās* may constitute the *aṣl* of another: when one *qiyās* is founded on another *qiyās*, the *farᶜ* of the second becomes an independent *aṣl* from which a different *ᶜillah* may be deduced. This process may continue *ad infinitum* with the only proviso being that in cases where an analogy can be founded in the Qur'ān, recourse may not be had to another *qiyās*.[16] But al-Ghazālī rejects the proposition of one *qiyās* forming the *aṣl* of another altogether. He compares this to the work of a person who tries to find pebbles on the beach that look alike. Finding one that resembles the original, he then throws away the original and tries to find one similar to the second, and so on. By the time he finds the tenth, it would not be surprising if it turned out to be totally different from the first in the series. Thus, for al-Ghazālī, *qiyās* founded on another *qiyās* is like speculation built upon speculation, and the further it continues along the line, the more real becomes the possibility of error.[1]

Having discussed Ibn Rushd's view at some length, however, Abū Zahrah observes that from a juristic viewpoint, one has little choice but to agree with it. This is reflected, for example, in modern judicial practice where court decisions are often based on the analogical extension of the effective cause (i.e. *ratio decidendi*) of an existing decision to a new case. The new decision may be based on the rationale of a previous case but may differ with it in some respect. In this event the new case is likely to constitute an authority in its own right. When, for example, the Cassation Court (*maḥkamah al-naqḍ*) in Egypt approves a judicial ruling, it becomes a point of reference in itself, and an analogy upon it is made whenever appropriate without further inquiry into its origin. What Abū Zahrah is saying is that the doctrine of *stare decisis*, which is partially adopted in some Islamic jurisdictions, takes for granted the validity of the idea that one *qiyās* may become the *aṣl* of another *qiyās*.[18]

According to the Syrian jurist Muṣṭafā al-Zarqā, the formula that one *qiyās* may be founded on another *qiyās* has in it the seeds of enrichment and resourcefulness. No unnecessary restrictions should therefore be imposed on *qiyās* and on its potential contribution to the *Sharīʿah*.[19]

II. Conditions Pertaining to the *Ḥukm*

A *ḥukm* is a ruling, such as a command or a prohibition, which is dispensed by the Qur'ān, the *Sunnah* or *ijmāʿ*, and analogy seeks its extension to a new case. In order to constitute the valid basis of an analogy, the *ḥukm* must fulfil the following conditions.

1) It must be a practical *sharʿī* ruling, for *qiyās* is only operative in regard to practical matters inasmuch as this is the case with *fiqh* as a whole. *Qiyās* can only be attempted when there is a *ḥukm* available in the sources. In the event where no *ḥukm* can be found in any of the three sources regarding a case, and its legality is determined with reference to a general maxim such as original freedom from liability (*al-barā'ah al-aṣliyyah*), no *ḥukm* could be said to exist. Original freedom from liability is not regarded as a *ḥukm sharʿī* and may not therefore form the basis of *qiyās*.[20]
2) The *ḥukm* must be operative, which means that it has not been abrogated. Similarly, the validity of *ḥukm* which is sought to be extended by analogy must not be the subject of disagreement and controversy.[21]
3) The *ḥukm* must be rational in the sense that the human intellect is capable of understanding the reason or the cause of its enactment, or

that the *ʿillah* is clearly given in the text itself. For example, the effective cause of prohibitions such as those issued against gambling and misappropriating the property of another is easily discernable. But when a *ḥukm* cannot be so understood, as in the case of the number of prostrations in *ṣalāh*, or the quantity of *zakāh*, etc., it may not form the basis of analogical deduction. Ritual performances, or *ʿibādāt*, on the whole, are not the proper subject of *qiyās* simply because their effective causes cannot be ascertained by the human intellect. Although the general purpose of *ʿibādāt* is often understandable, this is not sufficient for the purpose of analogy. Since the specific causes (*al-ʿilal al-juz'iyyah*) of *ʿibādāt* are only known to Almighty God, no analogy can be based upon them.

All the rational *aḥkām* (*al-aḥkām al-maʿqūlah*), that is, laws whose causes are perceivable by human intellect, constitute the proper basis of *qiyās*. According to Imām Abū Ḥanīfah, who represents the majority opinion, all the *nuṣūṣ* of *Sharīʿah* are rational and their causes can be ascertained except where it is indicated that they fall under the rubric of *ʿibādāt*. The Ẓāhirīs, and ʿUthmān al-Battī, a contemporary of Abū Ḥanīfah have, on the other hand, held that the effective causes of the *nuṣūṣ* cannot be ascertained without an indication in the *nuṣūṣ* themselves. This view clearly discourages enquiry into the causes of the rules of *Sharīʿah* and advises total conformity to them without any search for justification or rationale.[22] 'We do not deny,' writes Ibn Ḥazm, 'that God has assigned certain causes to some of His laws, but we say this only when there is a *naṣṣ* to confirm it.' He then goes on to quote a Ḥadīth of the Prophet to the effect that 'the greatest wrong-doer in Islam is one who asks about something, which is not forbidden, and it is then forbidden because of his questioning'.

إن أعظم المسلمين في المسلمين جرماً من سأل
عن شيء لم يحرم على المسلمين فحرم عليهم
من أجل مسألته

Ibn Ḥazm continues: we firmly deny that all the *aḥkām* of *Sharīʿah* can be explained and rationalised in terms of causes. Almighty God enacts a law as He wills. The question of 'how and why' does not and must not be applied to His will. Hence it is improper for anyone to enquire, in the absence of a clear text, into the causes of divine laws. Anyone who poses questions and searches for the causes of God's injunctions 'defies Almighty God and commits a transgression'.[23] For he would be acting contrary to the purport of the Qur'ān where God describes Himself, saying, 'He cannot be questioned for His acts, but they will be questioned for theirs' (al-Anbiyā', 21:21). It is thus known, Ibn Ḥazm concludes, that causes of any kind are nullified from the acts and words of God. For justification and *taʿlīl* is the work of one who is weak and compelled (*muḍṭarr*), and God is above all this.[24]

The issue of causation acquires a special significance in the context of divinely-ordained laws, simply because the revelation was discontinued with the demise of the Prophet, who is no longer present to explain and identify the causes of the revealed laws. The Muslim jurists, like other believing Muslims, have shown a natural reluctance to be too presumptuous in their efforts to identify the causes of the divine laws. But the issue does not pose itself in the same way regarding secular or man-made law. The norm in regard to modern laws is that they all have identifiable causes which can be ascertained with reasonable certainty. As such, analogical deduction in the context of modern law is a relatively easier proposition. But there are certain restrictions which discourage a liberal recourse to analogy even in modern law. For one thing, the operation of analogy in modern law is confined to civil law, as in the area of crimes the constitutional principle of legality discourages the analogical extension of the text. It should be further noted that owing to extensive reliance on statutory legislation, there is no crime and no punishment in the absence of a statutory text which clearly defines the offence or the penalty in question. Crimes and penalties are thus to be governed by the text of the law and not by the analogical extension of the text. It will thus be noted that owing to the prevalence of statutory legislation in modern legal systems the need for recourse to analogy has been proportionately diminished. This would in turn explain why *qiyās* tends to play a more prominent role in the *Sharīʿah* than in modern law.

But in *Sharīʿah* law too, as we shall later elaborate, there are restrictions on the operation of *qiyās* in regard to crimes and penalties. The *qāḍī*, as a result, may not draw analogies between, for example, wine-drinking and hashish owing to the similar effects that they might have on the human intellect. Nor may the crime of *zinā* be made the basis of analogy so as to apply its penalty to similar cases.[25]

4) The fourth requirement concerning the *ḥukm* is that it must not be confined to an exceptional situation or to a particular state of affairs. *Qiyās* is essentially designed to extend the normal, not the exceptional, rules of the law. Thus when the Prophet admitted the testimony of Khuzaymah alone to be equivalent to that of two witnesses, he did so by way of an exception. The precedent in this case is therefore not

extendable by analogy.[26] Some of the rulings of the Qur'ān which relate exclusively to the Prophet, such as polygamy beyond the maximum of four, or the prohibition in regard to marriage for the widows of the Prophet (al-Aḥzāb, 33:53) are similarly not extendable by analogy. The legal norms on these matters have elsewhere been laid down in the Qur'ān which enacts the minimum number of witnesses at two, the maximum for polygamy at four, and allow a widow to remarry after the expiry of the *ᶜiddah* waiting period.

5) And lastly, the law of the text must not represent a departure from the general rules of *qiyās* in the first place. For example, travelling during Ramadan is the cause of a concession which exonerates the traveller from the duty of fasting. The concession is an exception to the general rule which requires everyone to observe the fast. It may therefore not form the basis of an analogy in regard to other types of hardship. Similarly the concession granted in *wuḍū'* (ablution) in regard to wiping over boots represents a departure from the general rule which requires washing the feet. The exception in this case is not extendable by way of analogy to similar cases such as socks.

But according to the Shāfiᶜīs, when the *ᶜillah* of a ruling can be clearly identified, analogy may be based on it even if the ruling was exceptional in the first place. For example, the transaction of *ᶜarāyā*, or the sale of fresh dates on the tree in exchange for dry dates, is exceptionally permitted by a Ḥadīth notwithstanding the somewhat usurious nature of this transaction; the rules of *ribā* forbidding exchange of identical commodities of unequal quantity. The *ᶜillah* of this permissibility is to fulfill the need of the owner of unripe dates for the dried variety. By way of analogy, the Shāfiᶜīs have validated the exchange of grapes for raisins on the basis of a similar need. The Ḥanafīs have, however, disagreed, as the ruling of *ᶜarāyā* is exceptional in the first place.[27]

III. The New Case (*Farᶜ*)

The *farᶜ* is an incident or a case whose ruling is sought by recourse to analogy. The *farᶜ* must fulfill the following three conditions.

1) The new case must not be covered by the text or *ijmāᶜ*. For in the presence of a ruling in these sources, there will be no need for a recourse to *qiyās*. However, some Ḥanafī and Mālikī jurists have at times resorted to *qiyās* even in cases where a ruling could be found in the sources. But they have done so only where the ruling in question was of a speculative type, such as a solitary Ḥadīth. We shall have occasion to elaborate on this point later.

2) The effective cause of analogy must be applicable to the new case in the same way as to the original case. Should there be no uniformity, or substantial equality between them, the analogy is technically called *qiyās maᶜal-fāriq*, or '*qiyās* with a discrepancy', which is invalid. If, for example, the *ᶜillah* in the prohibition of wine is intoxication, then a beverage which only causes a lapse of memory would differ with wine in respect of the application of *ᶜillah*, and this would render the analogy invalid.[28]

   To give another example, according to the Ḥanafīs, a sane and adult woman is competent to conclude a contract of marriage on her own behalf. They have inferred this by an anology to the Qur'ānic ruling (al-Nisā', 4:6) which entitles her to enter business transactions at her own free will. The majority of jurists, however, disagree, as they consider the analogy in question to be *qiyās* with a discrepancy. Marriage differs from other transactions; business transactions are personal matters but marriage concerns the family and the social status of the parents and guardians. Hence an analogy between marriage and other transactions is unjustified.[29]

3) The application of *qiyās* to a new case must not result in altering the law of the text, for this would mean overruling the text by means of *qiyās* which is *ultra vires*. An example of this is the case of false accusation (*qadhf*) which by an express *naṣṣ* (sūra al-Nūr, 24:4) constitutes a permanent bar to the acceptance of one's testimony. Al-Shāfiᶜī has, however, drawn an analogy betwen false accusation and other grave sins (*kabā'ir*): a person who is punished for a grave sin may be heard as a witness after repentance. In the case of false accusation, too, repentance should remove the bar to the admission of testimony. To this the Ḥanafīs have replied that an analogy of this kind would overrule the law of the text which forever proscribes the testimony of a false accuser.[30]

   On a similar note, the validity of the contract of *salam* has been established in a Ḥadīth which defines it as the advance sale of an article to be delivered at a fixed date. But when the Shāfiᶜīs hold that such a contract is lawful even if no date is fixed for delivery, they are charged with introducing a change in the law of the text.[31]

IV. The Effective Cause (*ᶜIllah*)

This is perhaps the most important of all the requirements of *qiyās*. *ᶜIllah* has been variously defined by the ulema of *uṣūl*. According to the majority, it is an attribute of the *aṣl* which is constant and evident and bears a proper (*munāsib*) relationship to the law of the text (*ḥukm*). It may be a fact, a circumstance, or a consideration which the Lawgiver has contemplated in issuing a *ḥukm*. In the works of *uṣūl*, the *ʿillah* is alternatively referred to as *manāṭ al-ḥukm* (i.e. the cause of the *ḥukm*), the sign of the *ḥukm* (*amārah al-ḥukm*), and *sabab*.[32] Some ulema have attached numerous conditions to the *ʿillah*, but most of these are controversial and may be summarised in the following five.[33]

1) According to the majority of ulema, the *ʿillah* must be a constant attribute (*munḍabiṭ*) which is applicable to all cases without being affected by differences of persons, time, place and circumstances. The Mālikīs and the Ḥanbalīs, however, do not agree to this requirement as they maintain that the *ʿillah* need not be constant, and that it is sufficient if the *ʿillah* bears a proper or reasonable relationship to the *ḥukm*. The difference between the two views is that the majority distinguish the effective cause from the objective (*ḥikmah*) of the law and preclude the latter from the scope of the *ʿillah*.[34]

The *ʿillah* is constant if it applies to all cases regardless of circumstantial changes. To give an example, according to the rules of pre-emption (*shufʿ*) the joint, or the neighbouring, owner of a real property has priority in buying the property whenever his partner or his neighbour wishes to sell it. The *ʿillah* in pre-emption is joint ownership itself, whereas the *ḥikmah* of this rule is to protect the partner/neighbour against a possible harm that may arise from sale to a third party. Now the harm that the Lawgiver intends to prevent may materialise, or it may not. As such, the *ḥikmah* is not constant and may therefore not constitute the *ʿillah* of pre-emption. Hence the *ʿillah* in pre-emption is joint ownership itself, which unlike the *ḥikmah* is permanent and unchangeable, as it does not fluctuate with such changes in circumstances.

The majority view maintains that the rules of *Sharīʿah* are founded in their causes (*ʿilal*), not in their objectives (*ḥikam*). From this, it would follow that a *ḥukm sharʿī* is present whenever its *ʿillah* is present even if its *ḥikmah* is not, and a *ḥukm sharʿī* is absent in the absence of its *ʿillah* even if its *ḥikmah* is present. The jurist and the judge must therefore enforce the law whenever its *ʿillah* is known to exist regardless of its *ḥikmah*. Hence it would be a mistake for the judge to entitle to the right of pre-emption a person who is neither a partner nor a neighbouring owner on the mere assumption that he may be harmed by the sale of the property to a certain purchaser.[35]

The Mālikīs and the Ḥanbalīs, on the other hand, do not draw any distinction between the *ʿillah* and the *ḥikmah*. In their view, the *ḥikmah* aims at attracting an evident benefit or preventing an evident harm, and this is the ultimate objective of the law. When, for example, the law allows the sick not to observe the fast, the *ḥikmah* is the prevention of hardship to them. Likewise the *ḥikmah* of retaliation (*qiṣāṣ*) in deliberate homicide, or of the *ḥadd* penalty in theft, is to protect the lives and properties of the people. Since the realisation of benefit (*maṣlaḥah*) and prevention of harm (*mafsadah*) is the basic purpose of all the rules of *Sharīʿah*, it would be proper to base analogy on the *ḥikmah*.[36]

The Ḥanafīs and the Shāfiʿīs however maintain that the *ʿillah* must be both evident and constant. In their view the *ʿillah* secures the *ḥikmah* most of the time but not always. Their objection to the *ḥikmah* being the basis of analogy is that the *ḥikmah* of the law is often a hidden quality which cannot be detected by the senses, and this would in turn render the construction of analogy upon them unfeasible. The *ḥikmah* is also variable according to circumstances, and this adds further to the difficulty of basing analogy on it. The *ḥikmah*, in other words, is neither constant nor well-defined, and may not be relied upon as a basis of analogy.

To give an example, the permission granted to travellers to break the fast while travelling is to relieve them from hardship. This is the *ḥikmah* of this ruling. But since hardship is a hidden phenomenon and often varies according to persons and circumstances, it may not constitute the effective cause of an analogy. The concession is therefore attached to travelling itself which is the *ʿillah* regardless of the degree of hardship that it may cause to individual travellers.[37]

To give another example, the *ʿillah* in the prohibition of passing a red traffic light is the appearance of the red light itself. The *ḥikmah* is to prevent traffic irregularities and accidents. Anyone who passes a red light is committing an offence even if no accident is caused as a result. The *ʿillah* and *ḥikmah* can as such exist independently of one another, the latter being less easily ascertainable than the former. On a similar note, the *ʿillah* in awarding a law degree is passing one's final examinations and obtaining the necessary marks therein. The *ḥikmah* may be the acquisition of a certain standard of knowledge in the disciplines concerned. Now it is necessary that university degrees are awarded on a constant and reliable basis, which is passing the exams. The acquisition of legal knowledge often, but not always, goes hand in hand with the ability to pass exams, but this by itself is not as readily ascertainable as are the exam results.

2) As already stated, the effective cause on which analogy is based must also be evident (*ẓāhir*). Hidden phenomena such as intention, goodwill, consent, etc., which are not clearly ascertainable may not constitute the *ʿillah* of analogy. The general rule is that the *ʿillah* must

be definite and perceptible to the senses. For example, since the consent of parties to a contract is imperceptible in its nature, the law proceeds upon the act of offer and acceptance. Similarly the *ʿillah* in establishing the paternity of a child is matrimonial cohabitation (*qiyām firāsh al-zawjiyyah*), or acknowledgement of paternity (*iqrār*), both of which are external phenomena and are susceptible to evidence and proof. Since conception through conjugal relations between the spouses is not an obvious phenomenon, it may not form the *ʿillah* of paternity. On a similar note, the law adopts as the *ʿillah* of legal majority, not the attainment of intellectual maturity, but the completion of a certain age, which is evident and susceptible to proof.[38]

3) The third condition of *ʿillah* is that it must be a proper attribute (*al-waṣf al-munāsib*) in that it bears a proper and reasonable relationship to the law of the text (*ḥukm*). This relationship is *munāsib* when it serves to achieve the objective (*ḥikmah*) of the Lawgiver, which is to benefit the people and to protect them against harm. For example, killing is a proper ground on which to exclude an heir from inheritance. For the basis of succession is the tie of kinship which relates the heir to the deceased, and is severed and nullified by killing. Similarly, the intoxicating effect of wine is the proper cause of its prohibition. An attribute which does not bear a proper relationship to the *ḥukm* does not qualify as an *ʿillah*. To give an example, murder must be retaliated for, not because the perpetrator happens to be a Negro or an Arab, but because he has deliberately killed another. Similarly, wine is prohibited not because of its colour or taste but because it is an intoxicant.[39]

4) The *ʿillah* must be 'transient' (*mutaʿaddī*), that is, an objective quality which is transferable to other cases. For analogy cannot be constructed on a *ʿillah* which is confined to the original case only. As the Ḥanafīs explain, the very essence of *ʿillah*, as much as that of *qiyās* in general, is its capability of extension to new cases, which means, that the *ʿillah* must be a transferable attribute. Travelling, for example, is the *ʿillah* of a concession in connection with fasting. As such, it is an *ʿillah* which is confined to the *aṣl* and cannot be applied in the same way to other devotional acts (*ibādāt*). Similarly, if we were to confine the *ʿillah* in the prohibition of wine to that variety which is derived from grapes, we would be precluding all the other varieties of wine from the scope of the prohibition.

Transferability (*taʿdiyah*) of the effective cause is not, however, required by the Shāfiʿīs, who have validated *qiyās* on the basis of an *ʿillah* which is confined to the original case (i.e. *ʿillah qāṣirah*). The Shāfiʿīs (and the Ḥanafī jurist, Ibn al-Humām) have argued that *taᶜdiyah* is not a requirement of the *ᶜillah*: when the *ᶜillah* is confined to the original case, it is probable that the Lawgiver had intended it as such. The probability may not be ignored merely for lack of *taᶜdiyah*. It is a requirement which is intellectually conceived without due regard for the precise terms of the law itself. The Shāfiᶜīs have further argued that the utility of the *ᶜillah* is not to be sought solely in its transferability. There is thus no inherent objection to the possibility of an *ᶜillah* being confined to the original case. The ulema are, however, in agreement that the textually prescribed causes must be accepted as they are regardless as to whether they are inherently transient or not.

The requirement of *taᶜdiyah* would imply that the *ᶜillah* of analogy must be an abstract quality and not a concrete activity or object. To illustrate this, we may again refer to the foregoing examples. Travelling, which is a concession in connection with fasting, is a concrete activity, whereas intoxication is an abstract quality which is not confined in its application. Similarly in the Ḥadīth regarding usury (*ribā*), the *ᶜillah* of its ruling which prohibits quantitative excess in the sale of the six specified articles is the quality of such articles being saleable by the measurement of weight or capacity and not their particular species. The Ḥadīth thus provides that 'gold for gold, silver for silver, wheat for wheat, barley for barley, dates for dates and salt for salt must be equal for equal, hand to hand [. . .]' Transaction in these commodities must, in other words, be without excess on either side and delivery shall be immediate, otherwise the transaction would amount to usury, which is forbidden. The *ᶜillah* of this prohibition is none of the concrete objects that are specified but an attribute or a concept which applies to all, namely their saleability by capacity or weight.[40]

الـذهب بالـذهب والفضة بالفضة ، والبر بالبر
والشعير بالشعير والتمـر بالتمـر والملح بالملح مثلا
بمثل سواءً بسواء يداً بيد

5) And finally, the effective cause must not be an attribute which runs counter to, or seeks to alter, the law of the text. To illustrate this we may refer to the story of a judge, Imām Yaḥyā of al-Andalus, who was asked by an Abbasid ruler as to the penance (*kaffārah*) of having conjugal relations during daytime in Ramadan. The judge responded that the *kaffārah* in this case was sixty days of fasting. This answer was incorrect as it sought to introduce a change in the text of the Ḥadīth which enacted the *kaffārah* to be freeing a slave, or sixty days of fasting, or feeding sixty poor persons. The *fatwā* given by the judge

sought to change this order of priority on the dubious assumption that freeing a slave (or feeding sixty persons) was an easy matter for a ruler and he should therefore be required to observe the fasting only. The *ʿillah* of the penance in this case is held to be the breaking of the fast itself and not any disrespect to the sanctity of Ramadan, nor having sexual intercourse with one's wife, which might have occurred to the judge while formulating his *fatwā*.[41]

Our next discussion concerning the *ʿillah* relates to the question of how the *ʿillah* can be identified. Are there any methods which the jurist may utilise in his search for the correct cause/rationale of a given law?

Identification of the *ʿIllah*

The effective cause of a ruling may be clearly stated, or suggested by indications in the *naṣṣ*, or it may be determined by consensus. When the *ʿillah* is expressly identified in the text, there remains no room for disagreement. Differences of opinion arise only in cases where the *ʿillah* is not identified in the sources. An example of the *ʿillah* which is expressly stated in the text occurs in sūra al-Nisā' (4:43): 'O you believers! Do not approach *ṣalāh* while you are drunk.' This *āyah* was revealed prior to the general prohibition of wine-drinking in sūra al-Mā'idah (5:93), but it provides, nevertheless, a clear reference to intoxication, which is also confirmed by the Ḥadīth 'every intoxicant is *khamr* [wine] and every *khamr* is forbidden'.[42]

كل مسكر خمر وكل خمر حرام

In another place, the Qur'ān explains the effective cause of its ruling on the distribution of one-fifth of war booty to the poor and the needy 'so that wealth does not accumulate in the hands of the rich' (al-Ḥashr, 59:7).

Instances are also found in the Ḥadīth where the text itself identifies the rationale of its ruling. Thus the effective cause of asking for permission when entering a private dwelling is stated in the Ḥadīth which provides that 'permission is required because of viewing'.

انما جعل الإذن لأجل البصر

The *ʿillah* of asking for permission is thus to protect the privacy of the home against unsolicited viewing.[43] In these examples, the occurrence of certain Arabic expressions such as *kay-lā* (so as not to), *li-ajli* (because of), etc., are associated with the concept of ratiocination (*taʿlīl*) and provide definite indications as to the *ʿillah* of a given ruling.[44]

Alternatively, the text which indicates the *ʿillah* may be a manifest *naṣṣ* (*al-naṣṣ al-ẓāhir*) which is in the nature of a probability or an allusion (*al-īmā' wa'l-ishārah*). Indications of this type are also understood from the language of the text and the use of certain Arabic particles such as *li, fa, bi, anna* and *inna*, which are known to be associated with *taʿlīl*. For example, in the Qur'ānic text (al-Mā'idah, 5:38): 'as to the thieves, male and female, cut off [*fa'qṭaʿū*] their hands,' theft itself is the cause of the punishment. Instances of this type are also found in sūra al-Nūr (24:2 and 4) regarding the punishment of adultery and false accusation respectively. In sūra al-Nisā' (4:34) we find another example, as follows: 'As for women whose rebellion [*nushūz*] you fear, admonish them (*fa-ʿiẓūhunna*) and leave them alone in their beds, and physically punish them.' In this text, *nushūz* is the effective cause of the punishment.[345] The writers on *uṣūl* give numerous examples of instances where the Qur'ān provides an indication, however indirect, as to the *ʿillah* of its rulings.[46]

The text of a Ḥadīth may allude to the *ʿillah* of its ruling. There is, for example, a Ḥadīth which provides that the saliva of cats is clean 'for they are usually around you in the homes'.

إنها من الطوافين عليكم والطوافات

Their domesticity, in other words, is the effective cause of the concession. Thus by way of analogy, all domestic animals would be considered clean, unless it is indicated otherwise. And lastly, in the Ḥadīth which provides that 'the judge who is in a state of anger may not adjudicate,'

لا يقضي القاضي وهو غضبان

anger itself is the *ʿillah* of the prohibition.[47] By analogy, the Companions have extended the ruling of this Ḥadīth to anything which resembles anger in its effect such as extreme hunger and depression.[48]

Sometimes the word *sabab* is used as a substitute for *ʿillah*. Although *sabab* is synonymous with *ʿillah* and many writers have used them as such, nevertheless, *sabab* is normally reserved for devotional acts (*ibādāt*) whose rationale is not perceptible to the human intellect. The text may sometimes provide an indication as to its *sabab*. Thus we find in sūra al-Isrā' (17:78) which enjoins, 'Perform the *ṣalāh* from the decline of the sun [*li-dulūk al-shams*] until twilight at night,' the *sabab* (cause) of *ṣalāh* is the time when the *ṣalāh* is due. Since the cause of the ruling in this text is not discernable to human intellect, it is referred to as a *sabab* but not as an ᶜ*illah*. From this distinction, it would appear that every ᶜ*illah* is concurrently a *sabab*, but not every *sabab* is necessarily an ᶜ*illah*.[49]

Next, the effective cause of a ruling may be established by consensus. An example of this is the priority of germane over consanguine brothers in inheritance, the ᶜ*illah* for which is held to be the former's superior tie with the mother. This ruling of *ijmā*ᶜ has subsequently formed the basis of an analogy according to which the germane brother is also given priority over the consanguine brother in respect of guardianship (*wilāyah*). *Ijmā*ᶜ has also determined the ᶜ*illah* of the father's right of guardianship over the property of his minor child to be the minority of the child. Once again this right has, by analogy, been acknowledged for the grandfather.[50] No *ijmā*ᶜ can, however, be claimed to exist in regard to the ᶜ*illah* of the father's right of guardianship over the property of his minor daughter. While the majority of ulema consider the ᶜ*illah* in this case to be minority, for the Shāfiᶜīs, the ᶜ*illah* in *ijbār* is virginity. The right of *ijbār* thus terminates upon loss of virginity even if the girl is still a minor.[51]

When the ᶜ*illah* is neither stated nor alluded to in the text, then the only way to identify it is through *ijtihād*. The jurist thus takes into consideration the attributes of the original case, and only that attribute which is considered to be proper (*munāsib*) is identified as the ᶜ*illah*. For example, in the Ḥadīth referred to above concerning the penance of conjugal relations during daytime in Ramadan, it is not precisely known whether the ᶜ*illah* of the penance is the breaking of the fast (*ifṭār*), or sexual intercourse. Although intercourse with one's wife is lawful, it may be that in this context it is regarded as a form of contempt for the sanctity of Ramadan. But it is equally reasonable to say that intercourse in this context is no different to other forms of *ifṭār*, in which case it is the *ifṭār* itself that is the ᶜ*illah* of the penance.[52] The method of reasoning which the *mujtahid* employs in such cases is called *tanqīḥ al-manāṭ*, or isolating the ᶜ*illah*, which is to be distinguished from two other methods referred to as *takhrīj al-manāṭ* (extracting the ᶜ*illah*) and *taḥqīq al-manāṭ* (ascertaining the ᶜ*illah*) respectively. This process of enquiry is roughly equivalent to what is referred to by some ulema of *uṣūl* as *al-sidr wa'l-taqsīm*, or elimination of the improper and assignment of the proper ᶜ*illah* to the *ḥukm*.

Tanqīḥ al-manāṭ implies that a ruling may have more than one cause, and the *mujtahid* has to identify the one that is proper (*munāsib*), as was the case in the foregoing examples. Literally, *tanqīḥ* means 'purifying', whereas *manāṭ* is another word for ᶜ*illah*. Technically, *tanqīḥ al-manāṭ* means 'connecting the new case to the original case by eliminating the discrepancy between them' (*ilḥāq al-far*ᶜ *bi'l-aṣl bi-ilghā' al-fāriq*).[53]

Extracting the *ᶜillah*, or *takhrīj al-manāṭ*, is in fact the starting point in the enquiry concerning the identification of *ᶜillah*, and often precedes *tanqīḥ al-manāṭ*. In all areas where the text or *ijmāᶜ* does not identify the effective cause, the jurist extracts it by looking at the relevant causes via the process of *ijtihād*. He may identify more than one cause, in which case he has completed the step involved in *takhrīj al-manāṭ* and must move on to the next stage, which is to isolate the proper cause. To illustrate this, the prohibition of usury (*ribā*) in wheat and five other articles is laid down in the Ḥadīth. When the jurist seeks to draw an analogy between wheat and raisins – to determine for example whether one should apply the tax of one-tenth by analogy to raisins – the *ᶜillah* may be any of the following: that both of them sustain life, that they are edible, that they are both grown in the soil, or that they are sold by measure. Thus far the jurist has completed the first step, namely extracting the *ᶜillah*. But then he proceeds to eliminate some of these by recourse to *tanqīḥ al-manāṭ*. The first *ᶜillah* is eliminated because salt, which is one of the six articles, does not sustain life; the second is also eliminated because gold and silver are not edible; and so is the third as neither salt nor precious metals are grown in the soil. The *ᶜillah* is therefore the last attribute, which comprises all the specified items in the Ḥadīth of *ribā*. The difference between the two stages of reasoning is that in *takhrīj al-manāṭ* the jurist is dealing with a situation where the *ᶜillah* is not identified, whereas in *tanqīḥ al-manāṭ*, more than one cause has been identified and his task is to select the proper *ᶜillah*.[54]

Ascertaining the *ᶜillah*, or *taḥqīq al-manāṭ*, follows the two preceding stages of investigation in that it consists of ascertaining the presence of an *ᶜillah* in individual cases. For purposes of drawing an analogy between wine and a herbal drink, for example, the investigation which leads to the conclusion that the substance in question has the intoxicating quality in common with wine is in the nature of *taḥqīq al-manāṭ*. Similarly, in the case of drawing an analogy between a thief and a pickpocket, the investigation as to whether or not the latter falls under the definition of theft is in the nature of *taḥqīq al-manāṭ*.[55]

Varieties of *Qiyās*

From the viewpoint of the strength or weakness of the *ᶜillah*, the Shāfiᶜī jurists have divided *qiyās* into three types:

a) 'Analogy of the Superior' (*qiyās al-awlā*). The effective cause in this *qiyās* is more evident in the new case than the original case, which is why it is called *qiyās al-awlā*. For example, we may refer to the Qur'ānic text in sūra al-Isrā' (17:23) which provides regarding parents: 'say not to them *uff* [i.e. a single word of contempt] nor repel them, but address them in dignified terms'. By analogy it may be deduced that the prohibition against lashing or beating them is even more obvious than verbal abuse. Similarly, the penance (*kaffārah*) of erroneous killing is, by way of analogy, applicable to intentional killing as the transgression which invokes the *kaffārah* is even more evident in the latter. This is the Shāfiʿī view, but the Ḥanafīs do not consider the first example to be a variety of *qiyās* but a mere implication of the text (*dalālah al-naṣṣ*) which falls within the scope of interpretation rather than analogy. Likewise the Ḥanafīs do not require *kaffārah* for deliberate killing, a ruling which has been determined on grounds of interpretation rather than *qiyās*.[56]

b) 'Analogy of Equals' (*qiyās al-musāwī*). The *ʿillah* in this type of *qiyās* is equally effective in both the new and the original cases, as is the ruling which is deduced by analogy. We may illustrate this by reference to the Qur'ān (al-Nisā', 4:2) which forbids 'devouring the property of orphans'. By analogy, it is concluded that all other forms of destruction and mismanagement which lead to the loss of such property are equally forbidden. But this is once again regarded by the Ḥanafīs to fall within the scope of interpretation rather than analogy. To give another example, according to a Ḥadīth, a container which is licked by a dog must be washed seven times.

إذا ولغ الكلب في الانـاء فـاغسلـوه سـبـع
مرات . . .

The Shāfiʿīs extend the same ruling by analogy to a container which is licked by swine. The Ḥanafīs, however, do not allow this Ḥadīth in the first place.[57]

c) 'Analogy of the Inferior' (*qiyās al-adnā*). The effective cause in this form of *qiyās* is less clearly effective in the new case than the original case. Hence it is not quite so obvious whether the new case falls under the same ruling which applies to the original case. For example, the rules of *ribā* prohibit the exchange of wheat and of other specified commodities unless the two amounts are equal and delivery is immediate. By analogy this rule is extended to apples, since both wheat and apples are edible (according to Shāfiʿī) and measurable (according to Ḥanafī) jurists. But the *ʿillah* of this *qiyās* is weaker in regard to apples which, unlike wheat, are not a staple food.[57]

This type of *qiyās* is unanimously accepted as *qiyās* proper, but, as earlier stated, the Ḥanafīs and some Ẓāhirīs consider the first two varieties to fall within the meaning of the text. It would appear that the Ḥanafīs apply the term '*qiyās*' only to that type of deduction which involves a measure of *ijtihād*. The first two varieties are too direct for the Ḥanafīs to be considered as instances of *qiyās*.[58]

Qiyās has been further divided into two types, namely 'obvious analogy' (*qiyās jalī*) and 'hidden analogy' (*qiyās khafī*). This is mainly a Ḥanafī division. In the former, the equation between the *aṣl* and *far*ᶜ is obvious and the discrepancy between them is removed by clear evidence. An example of this is the equation the ulema have drawn between the male and the female slave with regard to the rules of manumission. Thus if two persons jointly own a slave and one of them sets the slave free to the extent of his own share, it is the duty of the Imām to pay the other part-owner his share and release the slave. This ruling is explicit regarding the male slave, but by an 'obvious analogy' the same rule is applied to the female slave. The discrepancy of gender in this case is of no consequence in regard to their manumission.[59]

The 'hidden analogy' (*qiyās khafī*) differs from the 'obvious' variety in that the removal of discrepancy between the *aṣl* and the *far*ᶜ is by means of a probability (*ẓann*). Shawkānī illustrates this with a reference to the two varieties of wine, namely *nabīdh*, and *khamr*. The former is obtained from dates and the latter from grapes. The rule of prohibition is analogically extended to *nabīdh* despite some discrepancy that might exist between the two.[60] Another example of *qiyās khafī* is the extension, by the majority of ulema (excepting the Ḥanafīs), of the prescribed penalty of *ẓinā* to sodomy, despite a measure of discrepancy that is known to exist between the two cases. And finally, the foregoing analysis would suggest that *qiyās khafī* and *qiyās al-adnā* are substantially concurrent.

Proof (*Ḥujjiyyah*) of *Qiyās*

Notwithstanding the absence of a clear authority for *qiyās* in the Qur'ān, the ulema of the four Sunnī schools and the Zaydī Shīᶜah have validated *qiyās* and have quoted several Qur'ānic passages in support of their views. Thus, a reference is made to sūra al-Nisā' (4:59) which reads, in an address to the believers: 'should you dispute over something, refer it to God and to the Messenger, if you do believe in God'.

The proponents of *qiyās* have reasoned that a dispute can only be referred to God and to the Prophet by following the signs and indications that we find in the Qur'ān and *Sunnah*. One way of achieving this is to identify the rationale of the *aḥkām* and apply them to disputed matters, and this is precisely what *qiyās* is all about.[61] The same line of reasoning has been advanced with regard to a text in sūra al-Nisā' (4:105) which proclaims: 'We have sent to you the Book with the Truth so that you may judge among people by means of what God has shown you.' A judgement may thus be based on the guidance that God has clearly given or on that which bears close similarity to it.[62] The Qur'ān often indicates the rationale of its laws either explicitly or by reference to its objectives. The rationale of retaliation, for example, is to protect life, and this is clearly stated in the text (al-Baqarah, 2:79). Likewise, the rationale of *zakāh* is to prevent the concentration of wealth in a few hands, which is clearly stated in the Qur'ān (al-Ḥashr, 59:7). Elsewhere in the Qur'ān, we read in a reference to the permissibility of *tayammum* (ablution with sand in the absence of water) that 'God does not intend to impose hardship on you' (al-Mā'idah, 5:6).

In all these instances, the Qur'ān provides clear indications which call for recourse to *qiyās*. In the absence of a clear ruling in the text, *qiyās* must still be utilised as a means of achieving the general objectives of the Lawgiver. It is thus concluded that the indication of causes and objectives, similitudes and contrasts, would be meaningless if they were not observed and followed as a guide for conduct in the determination of the *aḥkām*.[63]

The proponents of *qiyās* have further quoted, in support of their views, a verse in sūra al-Ḥashr (59:2) which enjoins: 'Consider, O you possessors of eyes!' 'Consideration' in this context means attention to similitudes and comparison between similar things. Two other *āyāt* which are variously quoted by the ulema occur in sūra al-Nāziᶜāt, that 'there is a lesson in this for one who fears' (79:26); and in Āl-ᶜImrān (3:13) which provides: 'in their narratives there was a lesson for those who possessed vision'.

There are two types of indication in the *Sunnah* to which the proponents of *qiyās* have referred:

1) *Qiyās* is a form of *ijtihād*, which is expressly validated in the Ḥadīth of Muᶜādh b. Jabal. It is reported that the Prophet asked Muᶜādh upon the latter's departure as judge to the Yemen, questions in answer to which Muᶜādh told the Prophet that he would resort to his own *ijtihād* in the event that he failed to find guidance in the Qur'ān and the *Sunnah*, and the Prophet was pleased with this reply. Since the Ḥadīth does not specify any form of reasoning in particular, analogical reasoning falls within the meaning of this Ḥadīth.[64]

لما أراد رسـول الله ان يبعث معاذ بن جبل إلى
الـيمـن قال له : كيف تقضي إذا عرض لك

القضاء ؟ قال : أقضي بكتاب الله ، فان لم أجد
فبسنة رسول الله ، فان لم أجد اجتهد رأيي ولا
آلـو . فضرب رسـول الله على صدره وقـال :
الحمد الله الذي وفق رسول رسول الله لما يرضي
رسول الله

2) The *Sunnah* provides evidence that the Prophet resorted to analogical reasoning on occasions when he did not receive a revelation on a particular matter. On one such occasion, a woman known as al-Khathʿamiyyah came to him and said that her father had died without performing the *ḥajj*. Would it benefit him if she performed the *ḥajj* on her father's behalf? The Prophet asked her: 'Supposing your father had a debt to pay and you paid it on his behalf, would this benefit him?' To this her reply was in the affirmative, and the Prophet said, 'The debt owed to God merits even greater consideration.'[65]

قـوله عليه الصلاة والسلام للخثعمية : أرأيت لو
كان على أبيك دين فقضيته أكان ينفعه ذلك ؟
قالت : نعم ، فقال لها : فدين الله أحق
بالقضاء

It is also reported that ʿUmar b. al-Khaṭṭāb asked the Prophet whether kissing vitiates the fast during Ramadan. The Prophet asked him in return: 'What if you gargle with water while fasting?' ʿUmar replied that this did not matter. The Prophet then told him that 'the answer to your first question is the same'.[66]

The Companions are said to have reached a consensus on the validity of *qiyās*. We find, for example, that the first Caliph, Abū Bakr, drew an analogy between father and grandfather in respect of their entitlements in inheritance. Similarly, ʿUmar ibn al-Khaṭṭāb is on record as having ordered Abū Mūsā al-Ashʿarī 'to ascertain the similitudes for purposes of analogy'.[67] Furthermore, the Companions pledged their fealty (*bayʿah*) to Abū Bakr on the strength of the analogy that ʿUmar drew between two forms of leadership: ʿUmar had asked the Companions, 'Will you not be satisfied, as regards worldly affairs, with the man with whom the Prophet was satisfied as regards religious affairs?' And they agreed with ʿUmar, notwithstanding the fact that the issue of succession was one of the utmost importance.[68] Again, when the Companions held a council to determine the punishment of wine-drinking, ᶜAlī b. Abī Ṭālib suggested that the penalty of false accusation should be applied to the wine drinker, reasoning by way of analogy, 'When a person gets drunk, he raves and when he raves, he accuses falsely.'[69] It is thus concluded that *qiyās* is validated by the Qur'ān, the *Sunnah*, and the *ijmā*ᶜ of the Companions.

The Argument Against *Qiyās*

This has been advanced mainly by the Ẓāhirī school, and some Muᶜtazilah, including their leader, Ibrāhīm al-Naẓẓām. The leading Ẓāhirī jurist, Ibn Ḥazm, is the most outspoken against *qiyās*. The main points of his argument may be summarised as follows:

1) The rules of the *Sharī*ᶜ*ah* are conveyed in the form of commands and prohibitions. There are also the intermediate categories of 'recommended' (*mandūb*) and 'reprehensible' (*makrūh*), which are essentially two varieties of *mubāḥ* (permissible). There are thus only three types of *aḥkām*: command, prohibition, and permissibility. Should there be no clear text in respect of any matter, then it would fall under the principle of *ibāḥah* (permissibility) which is established in the Qur'ān.[70] Commands and prohibitions are determined by the clear authority of the Qur'ān, the *Sunnah*, or *ijmā*ᶜ, in whose absence nothing else can determine an obligatory or a prohibitory injunction, and the matter would automatically fall under the category of *mubāḥ*. There is thus no room for analogy in the determination of the *aḥkām*.[71]

2) The supporters of analogy, according to Ibn Ḥazm, proceed on the assumption that the *Sharī*ᶜ*ah* fails to provide a *naṣṣ* for every matter, an assumption which is contrary to the explicit provisions of the Qur'ān. Ibn Ḥazm goes on to quote the following to this effect: 'We have neglected nothing in the Book' (al-Anᶜām, 6:89); and 'We revealed the Book as an explanation for everything' (al-Naḥl, 16:89). In yet another passage, we read in the Qur'ān: 'This day, I perfected your religion for you, and completed My favour upon you' (al-Mā'idah, 5:4).

   Since the *aḥkām* of the Lawgiver are all-inclusive and provide complete guidance for all events, our only duty is to discover and implement them. To consider *qiyās* as an additional proof would be tantamount to an acknowledgement that the Qur'ān fails to provide complete guidance.[72]

3) *Qiyās* derives its justification from an ᶜ*illah* which is common to both the original and the new case. The ᶜ*illah* is either indicated in the text, in which case the ruling is derived from the text itself and *qiyās* is

redundant; or alternatively, where the *ᶜillah* is not so indicated, there is no way of knowing it for certain. *Qiyās* therefore rests on conjecture, which must not be allowed to form the basis of a legal ruling. This is, according to Ibn Ḥazm, the purport of the Qur'ānic *āyah* (al-Najm, 53:28) which proclaims that 'conjecture avails nothing against the truth'. Identifying the *ᶜillah* in *qiyās* is an exercise in speculation, whereas the Qur'ān enjoins us to 'pursue not that of which you have no knowledge' (al-Isrā', 17:36).[73]

4) And lastly, Ibn Ḥazm holds that *qiyās* is clearly forbidden in the Qur'ān.[74] Thus we read in sūra al-Ḥujurāt (49:1): 'O you believers! Do not press forward before God and His Messenger, and fear God [. . .]', which means that the believers must avoid legislating on matters on which the Lawgiver has chosen to remain silent. The same point is conveyed in the Ḥadīth where the Prophet ordered the believers as follows:

> Ask me not about matters which I have not raised. Nations before you were faced with destruction because of excessive questioning and disputation with their prophets. When I command you to do something, do it to the extent that you can, and avoid what I have forbidden.[75]

دعوني ما تركتكم ، فانما هلك من كان قبلكم
بكثرة مسائلهم واختلافهم على نبيهم ، فإذا
أمرتكم بشيء فأتوا منه ما استطعتم ، وإذا
نهيتكم عن شيء فاجتنبوه

Thus in regard to matters on which the *naṣṣ* is silent, it is not proper for a Muslim to take the initiative in issuing a *ḥukm*, for he is ordered not to do so. *Qiyās* therefore violates the express terms of the Qur'ān and the *Sunnah*.

To sum up, Ibn Ḥazm's argument is based on two main points, one of which is that the *nuṣūṣ* of the Qur'ān and *Sunnah* provide for all events, and the other is that *qiyās* is an unnecessary addition to the *nuṣūṣ*. Regarding the first point, the majority of *ulema* hold the view that the *nuṣūṣ* do admittedly cover all events, either explicitly or through indirect indications. However, the Ẓāhirīs rely only on the explicit *nuṣūṣ* and not on these indirect indications. The majority, on the other hand, go beyond the confines of literalism and validate *qiyās* in the light of the general objectives of the *Sharīᶜah*. For the majority, *qiyās* is not an addition or a superimposition on the *nuṣūṣ*, but their logical extension. Hence the Ẓāhirī argument that *qiyās* violates the integrity of the *nuṣūṣ* is devoid of substance.[76]

With reference to some of the Qur'ānic passages that the opponents of *qiyās* have quoted, especially on the use of speculative evidence in law, it is contended that the *āyāt* in question forbid recourse to speculation (*ẓann*) in matters of belief only. As for the practical rules of *fiqh*, most of them partake in *ẓann*, and a great deal of the *nuṣūṣ* are themselves speculative in their purport and implication (*ẓannī al-dalālah*). But this does not necessarily mean that action upon them must be suspended. On the contrary, a measure of diversity and variation in the practical rules of *Sharīᶜah* is not only tolerated, but is considered to be a sign of the bounty of Almighty God, and the essence of flexibility in the *Sharīᶜah*.[77]

In principle, the Shīᶜah Imāmiyyah do not recognise the validity of *qiyās*, as they maintain that *qiyās* is pure conjecture which must be avoided. In addition, the Qur'ān, the *Sunnah* and the rulings of the Imāms, according to the Shīᶜī ulema, provide sufficient guidance for conduct, and any reference to analogy is unnecessary and unwarranted.[78] This is definitely the view of the Akhbārī branch of the Twelver Shīᶜah, whose refutation of *qiyās* closely resembles that of the Ẓāhirīs. But the Uṣūlī branch of the Shīᶜah validate action upon certain varieties of *qiyās*, namely *qiyās* whose *ᶜillah* is explicitly stated in the text (*qiyās manṣūṣ al-ᶜillah*), analogy of the superior (*qiyās al-awlā*) and obvious analogy (*qiyās jalī*). These varieties of *qiyās*, in their view, are not mere speculations; they either fall within the meaning of the text or else constitute a strong probability (*al-ẓann al-qawī*) which may be adopted as a guide for conduct. But they validate this through recourse to *ijtihād* and *ᶜaql* rather than *qiyās* per se.[79]

Qiyās in Penalties

The ulema of the various schools have discussed the application of *qiyās* to juridical, theological, linguistic, rational and customary matters, but the main question which needs to be discussed here is the application of analogy in regard to prescribed penalties (*ḥudūd*) and penances (*kaffārāt*).

The majority of ulema do not draw any distinction in this respect, and maintain the view that *qiyās* is applicable to *ḥudūd* and *kaffārāt* in the same way as it is to other rules of the *Sharīᶜah*. This is explained by reference to the Qur'ānic passages and the *aḥādīth* which are quoted in support of *qiyās*, which are all worded in absolute terms, none drawing any distinction in regard to penalties: and since the evidence in the sources does not impose any restriction on *qiyās*, it is therefore applicable in all spheres of the *Sharīᶜah*.[80] An example of *qiyās* in regard to the *ḥudūd* is the application of the punishment of theft to the *nabbāsh*, or thief who steals the shroud of the dead, as the common ʿ*illah* between them is taking away the property of another without his knowledge. A Ḥadīth has also been quoted in support of this ruling.[81] Similarly the majority of ulema (excluding the Ḥanafīs) have drawn an analogy between *zinā* and sodomy, and apply the *ḥadd* of the former by analogy to the latter.[82]

The Ḥanafīs are in agreement with the majority to the extent that *qiyās* may validly operate in regard to *ta*ʿ*zīr* penalties, but they have disagreed as to the application of *qiyās* in the prescribed penalties and *kaffārāt*. They would not, for example, approve of an analogy between abusive words (*sabb*) and false accusation (*qadhf*), nor would they extend the *ḥadd* of *zinā* by analogy to other sexual offences. These, according to the Ḥanafīs, may be penalised under *ta*ʿ*zīr* but not by analogy to the *ḥudūd*. The main reason that the Ḥanafīs have given is that *qiyās* is founded on the ʿ*illah*, whose identification in regard to the *ḥudūd* involves a measure of speculation and doubt. There is a Ḥadīth which provides: 'drop the *ḥudūd* in cases of doubt as far as possible. If there is a way out, then clear the way, for in penalties, if the Imām makes an error on the side of leniency, it is better than making an error on the side of severity'.[83]

إدرؤا الحدود عن المسلمين ما استطعتُم فان كان
له مخرج فتخلّوا سبيله ، فان الامام ان يخطیء في
العفو خير من ان يخطیء في العقوبة

It is thus concluded that any level of doubt in ascertaining the ʿ*illah* of *ḥadd* penalties must prevent their analogical extension to similar cases.[84]

As stated above, the majority validate the application of *qiyās* in regard to *kaffārāt*. Thus the analogy between the two forms of breaking the fast (*ifṭār*), namely deliberate eating during daytime in Ramadan, and breaking the fast by having sexual intercourse, would extend the *kaffārah* of the latter to the former. Similarly the majority have validated the analogy between deliberate killing and erroneous homicide for purposes of *kaffārah*. The Qur'ān only prescribes a *kaffārah* for erroneous killing, and this is extended by analogy to deliberate homicide. The common ʿ*illah* between them is the killing of another human being. If *kaffārah* is required in erroneous killing, then by way of a superior analogy (*qiyās al-awlā*) the ʿ*illah* is even more evident in the case of a deliberate killing. Both are therefore liable to the payment of *kaffārah*, which is releasing a slave, or two months of fasting, or feeding sixty persons. The Ḥanafīs are once again in disagreement with the majority, as they maintain that for purposes of analogy, the *kaffārah* resembles the *ḥadd*. Since doubt cannot be totally eliminated in the identification of their effective causes, *kaffārāt* may not be extended by means of analogy.[85]

Notwithstanding the fact that the jurists have disagreed on the application of *qiyās* in penalties, it will be noted that the ulema have on the whole discouraged recourse to *qiyās* in the field of criminal law. Consequently, there is very little actual *qiyās* to be found in this field. This is also the case in modern law, which discourages analogy in respect of penalties. The position is somewhat different in regard to civil transactions (*muᶜāmalāt*), in which *qiyās* is generally permitted.[86]

Conflicts between *Naṣṣ* and *Qiyās*

Since the *ᶜillah* in analogy is a general attribute which applies to all similar cases, there arises the possibility of *qiyās* coming into conflict with the *nuṣūṣ*. The question to be asked is how such a conflict should be removed. Responding to this question, the ulema have held two different views, which may be summarised as follows:

1) According to Imām Shāfiᶜī, Aḥmad b. Ḥanbal, and one view which is attributed to Abū Ḥanīfah, whenever there is a *naṣṣ* on a matter *qiyās* is absolutely redundant. *Qiyās* is only applicable when no explicit ruling could be found in the sources. Since recourse to *qiyās* in the presence of *naṣṣ* is *ultra vires* in the first place, the question of a conflict arising between the *naṣṣ* and *qiyās* is therefore of no relevance.[87]
2) The second view, which is mainly held by the Mālikīs, also precludes the possibility of a conflict between *qiyās* and a clear text, but does not dismiss the possibility of a conflict arising between a speculative text and *qiyās*. Analogy could, according to this view, come into conflict with the *ᶜĀmm* of the Qur'ān and the solitary Ḥadīth.

The Ḥanafīs have maintained that the *ᶜĀmm* is definitive in implication (*qaṭᶜī al-dalālah*), whereas *qiyās* is speculative. As a rule, a speculative item cannot qualify a definitive one, which would mean that *qiyās* does not specify the *ᶜĀmm* of the Qur'ān. The only situation where the Ḥanafīs envisage a conflict between *qiyās* and the *ᶜĀmm* of the Qur'ān is where the *ᶜillah* of *qiyās* is stated in a clear *naṣṣ*. For in this case, a conflict between the *ᶜĀmm* of the Qur'ān and *qiyās* would be that of one *qaṭᶜī* with another. However, for the most part *qiyās* is a speculative evidence, and as such may not specify the *ᶜĀmm* of the Qur'ān. But once the *ᶜĀmm* is specified, on whatever grounds, then it becomes speculative itself, at least in respect of that part which remains unspecified. After the first instance of specification (*takhṣīṣ*), in other words, the *ᶜĀmm* becomes speculative, and is then open to further specification by means of *qiyās*. For example, the word *bayᶜ* (sale) in the Qur'ānic text stating that 'God has permitted sale and prohibited usury' (al-Baqarah, 2:275) is *ᶜĀmm*, but has been qualified by solitary *aḥādīth* which prohibit certain types of sale. Once the text has been so specified, it remains open to further specification by means of *qiyās*.[88]

This was the Ḥanafīs' view of conflict between a general text and *qiyās*. But the Mālikīs who represent the majority view, consider the *ᶜĀmm* of the Qur'ān to be speculative in the first place. The possibility is therefore not ruled out, according to the majority, of a conflict arising between the *naṣṣ* and *qiyās*. In such an event, the majority would apply the rule that one speculative principle may be specified by another. Based on this analysis, *qiyās*, according to most of the jurists, may specify the *ᶜĀmm* of the Qur'ān and the *Sunnah*.[89]

As for conflict between *qiyās* and a solitary Ḥadīth, it is recorded that Imām Shāfiᶜī, Ibn Ḥanbal and Abū Ḥanīfah do not give priority to *qiyās* over such a Ḥadīth. An example of this is the vitiation of ablution (*wuḍū'*) by loud laughter during the performance of *ṣalāh*, which is the accepted rule of the Ḥanafī school despite its being contrary to *qiyās*. Since the rule here is based on the authority of a solitary Ḥadīth, the latter has been given priority over *qiyās*, for *qiyās* would only require vitiation of *ṣalāh*, not the *wuḍū'*.[90]

روى عن النبي صلى الله عليه وسلم انه أمر رجلاً
ضحك بالصلاة ان يعيد الوضوء والصلاة

Although the three Imāms are in agreement on the principle of giving priority to solitary Ḥadīth over *qiyās*, regarding this particular Ḥadīth, only the Ḥanafīs have upheld it. The majority, including Imām Shāfiᶜī, consider it to be *Mursal* and do not act on it.

Additionally, there are other views on the subject which merit brief attention. Abu'l Ḥusayn al-Baṣrī, for example, divides *qiyās* into four types, as follows:

1) *Qiyās* which is founded in a decisive *naṣṣ*, that is, when the original case and the effective cause are both stated in the *naṣṣ*. This type of *qiyās* takes priority over a solitary Ḥadīth.
2) *Qiyās* which is founded in speculative evidence, that is, when the *aṣl* is a speculative text and the *ᶜillah* is determined through logical deduction (*istinbāṭ*). This type of *qiyās* is inferior to a solitary Ḥadīth and the latter takes priority over it. Al-Baṣrī has claimed an *ijmāᶜ* on both one and two above.

3) *Qiyās* in which both the *aṣl* and the *ᶜillah* are founded in speculative *nuṣūṣ*, in which case it is no more than a speculative form of evidence and, should it conflict with a solitary Ḥadīth, the latter takes priority. On this point al-Baṣrī quotes Imām Shāfiᶜī in support of his own view.
4) *Qiyās* in which the *ᶜillah* is determined through *istinbāṭ* but whose *aṣl* is a clear text of the Qur'ān or *Mutawātir* Ḥadīth. This type of *qiyās* is stronger than two and three above, and the ulema have differed as to whether it should take priority over a solitary Ḥadīth.[91]

The Mālikīs, and some Ḥanbalī ulema, are of the view that in the event of a conflict between a solitary Ḥadīth and *qiyās*, if the latter can be substantiated by another principle or *aṣl* of the *Sharīᶜah*, then it will take priority over a solitary Ḥadīth. If for example the *ᶜillah* of *qiyās* is 'removal of hardship', which is substantiated by several texts, then it will add to the weight of *qiyās*, and the latter will take priority over a solitary Ḥadīth. For this kind of evidence is itself an indication that the Ḥadīth in question is weak in respect of authenticity.[92] Similarly, some Ḥanafīs have maintained that when a solitary Ḥadīth, which is in conflict with *qiyās*, is supported by another *qiyās*, then it must be given priority over the conflicting *qiyās*. This is also the view which Ibn al-ᶜArabī has attributed to Imām Mālik, who is quoted to the effect that whenever a solitary Ḥadīth is supported by another principle, then it must take priority over *qiyās*. But if no such support is forthcoming, then the solitary Ḥadīth must be abandoned. For example, the following Ḥadīth has been found to be in conflict with another principle: 'When a dog licks a container, wash it seven times, one of which should be with clean sand.'[93]

إذا ولغ الكلب في الاناء فاغسلوه سبع
مرات . . .

It is suggested that this solitary Ḥadīth is in conflict with the permissibility of eating the flesh of game which has been fetched by a hunting dog. The game is still lawful for consumption notwithstanding its having come into contact with the dog's saliva. There is, on the other hand, no other principle that could be quoted in support of either of the two rulings, so *qiyās* takes priority over the solitary Ḥadīth. Our second example is of a solitary Ḥadīth which is in conflict with one principle but stands in accord with another. This is the Ḥadīth of *ᶜarāyā*, which provides that 'the Prophet (upon whom be peace) permitted the sale of dates on the palm tree for its equivalent in dry dates'.

عن زيد بن ثابت ان رسول الله صلى الله
عليه وسلم رخص في العريّة

This is permitted despite its being in conflict with the rules of *ribā*. However the permissibility in this case is supported by the principle of *dafᶜ al-ḥaraj* 'removal of hardship' in that the transaction of *ᶜarāyā* was permitted in response to a need, and, as such, it takes priority over the *qiyās* which might bring it under the rules of *ribā*.[94]

NOTES

1. Āmidī, *Iḥkām*, III, 183.
2. Ghazālī, *Mustaṣfā*, II, 54.
3. Shawkānī, *Irshād*, p. 198.
4. Cf. Abdur Rahim, *Jurisprudence*, p. 137.
5. Khallāf, *ᶜIlm*, p. 52, Abdur Rahim, *Jurisprudence*, p. 138.
6. Ibn Qayyim, *Iᶜlām*, II, 242; Khallāf, *ᶜIlm*, p. 53.
7. Abū Dāwud, *Sunan* (Hasan's trans.). II, 556, Ḥadīth no. 2075; Tabrīzī, *Mishkāt*, II, 940, Ḥadīth no. 3144; Mūsā, *Aḥkām*, p. 45.
8. Āmidī, *Iḥkām*, III, 186.
9. ᶜUbaydullāh ibn Masᶜūd Ṣadr al-Sharīᶜah, *al-Tawḍīḥ fī Ḥall Ghawāmiḍ al-Tanqīḥ*, p. 444; Aghnides, *Muhammedan Theories*, p. 49.
10. Āmidī (*Iḥkām*, III, 193) is however of the view that the result of *qiyās*, that is the ruling which is to be applied to the new case (i.e. *ḥukm al-farᶜ*), should not be included in the essential requirements (*arkān*) of *qiyās*. For the *ḥukm* is only arrived at at the end of the process; it should therefore not be a *rukn*. Isnawī has on the other hand included the *ḥukm al-farᶜ* among the essentials of *qiyās*. The disagreement is perhaps mainly theoretical as the *ḥukm* of the new case is, for all intents and purposes, identical with the *ḥukm* of the original case. Cf. Zuhayr, *Uṣūl*, IV, 58–59.
11. Shawkānī, *Irshād*, pp. 204–205; Abū Zahrah, *Uṣūl*, p. 180.
12. Abū Zahrah, *Uṣūl*, p. 181.
13. Khallāf, *ᶜIlm*, p. 53, Shawkānī, *Irshād*, p. 210.
14. Abū Zahrah, *Uṣūl*, p. 128.
15. Ghazālī, *Mustaṣfā*, II, 87; Shawkānī, *Irshād*, p. 205.
16. Ibn Rushd, *Bidāyah*, I, 4–5: Abū Zahrah, *Uṣūl*, p. 183; Nour, '*Qiyās*', 29.
17. Ghazālī, *Mustaṣfā*, II, 87.
18. Cf. Abū Zahrah, *Uṣūl*, p. 184.
19. Since al-Zarqā's work is not available to me, my knowledge of his views is confined to the extent that he is quoted by Nour, '*Qiyās*', 29.
20. Shawkānī, *Irshād*, p. 205; Khuḍarī, *Uṣūl*, p. 295.
21. Āmidī, *Iḥkām*, III, 196–97.
22. Abū Zahrah, *Uṣūl*, p. 185; Khallāf, *ᶜIlm*, pp. 61–62.
23. Ibn Ḥazm, *Iḥkām*, VIII, 102; Muslim, *Ṣaḥīḥ Muslim*, 1, 423, Ḥadīth no, 1599.
24. Ibid., VIII, 103.
25. Shawkānī, *Irshād*, p. 222; Abū Zahrah, *Uṣūl*, p. 185.

26. The relevant Ḥadīth reads: 'If Khuzaymah testifies for anyone, that is sufficient as a proof.'
Ghazālī, *Mustaṣfā*, II, 88; Abū Dāwud, *Sunan*, III, 1024, Ḥadīth no. 3600.
27. Muslim, *Ṣaḥīḥ Muslim*, p. 247, Ḥadīth no. 920; Shaᶜbān, *Uṣūl*, p. 130.
28. Shawkānī, *Irshād*, p. 209.
29. Shaᶜbān, *Uṣūl*, p. 134.
30. Aghnides, *Muhammadan Theories*, p. 62.
31. Bukhārī, *Ṣaḥīḥ* (Istanbul edn.), III, 44 (*Kitāb al-Salam*, Ḥadīth no. 3); Sarakhsī (*Uṣūl*, p. 152) writes: The Prophet forbade the sale of an object which does not exist at the time of sale but permitted *salam* as an exception. *Salam* is valid on condition that the time of delivery is stipulated and that the parties are able to meet the conditions of their agreement. See also Abdur Rahim, *Jurisprudence*, p. 145.
32. Shawkānī, *Irshād*, p. 207; Abū Zahrah, *Uṣūl*, p. 188.
33. Note, for example, Shawkānī, (*Irshād*, p. 207–208) who has listed 24 conditions for the *ᶜillah* whereas the Mālikī jurist, Ibn Ḥājib has recorded only eleven.
34. Khallāf, *ᶜIlm*, 64; Abū Zahrah, *Uṣūl*, p. 188.
35. Shawkānī, *Irshād*, pp. 207–208; Khallāf, *ᶜIlm*, pp. 88–97.
36. Abū Zahrah, *Uṣūl*, p. 188.
37. Khallāf, *ᶜIlm*, p. 64.
38. Shawkānī, *Irshād*, p. 207, Abdur Rahim, *Jurisprudence*, p. 149; Abū Zahrah, *Uṣūl*, p. 189; Khallāf, *ᶜIlm*, p. 69.
39. Abū Zahrah, *Uṣūl*, p. 189; Khallāf, *ᶜIlm*, pp. 69–70.
40. Muslim, *Ṣaḥīḥ Muslim*, p. 252, Ḥadīth no. 949; Ghazālī, *Mustaṣfā*, II, 98; Khuḍarī, *Uṣūl*, p. 320; Abū Zahrah, *Uṣūl*, p. 190; Abdur Rahim, *Jurisprudence*, p. 151–2.
41. Abū Zahrah, *Uṣūl*, pp. 187, 190, 194.
42. Abū Dāwud, *Sunan*, III, 1043, Ḥadīth no. 3672.
43. Muslim, *Ṣaḥīḥ*, p. 375, Ḥadīth no. 1424; Ghazālī, Mustaṣfā, II, 74; Ibn Ḥazm, *Iḥkām*, VIII, 91; Abū Zahrah, *Uṣūl*, p. 193. There are also passages in the Qur'ān on the subject of *isti'dhān*, or asking permission before entering a private home. Note, for example, sūra al-Nūr (24:27) which enjoins: 'O you believers, do not enter houses other than your own unless you act politely and greet their occupants.'
44. Shawkānī lists a number of other expressions such as *li-allā, min ajli, laᶜallahu kadhā, bi-sabab kadhā*, etc. all of which are associated with the idea of explaining the causes (*Irshād*, p. 211).
45. Imām Mālik has by analogy extended the same penalties to a husband who ill-treats his wife. He must first be admonished; if he continues, he must continue paying the wife her maintenance but she is not required to obey him; finally he may be subjected to physical punishment. See Abū Zahrah, *Uṣūl*, p. 193.
46. Note, for example, sūra al-Baqarah (2:222) concerning conjugal relations with one's wife during her menstruation, which are to be avoided. The text indicates menstruation to be the *ᶜillah* of its ruling. Shawkānī, (*Irshād*, pp. 212–213) provides an exhaustive list of the particles of *taᶜlīl* with their illustrations from the Qur'ān and the Ḥadīth.
47. Abū Dāwud, *Sunan*, III, 1018, Ḥadīth no 3582; Ghazālī, Mustaṣfā, II, 75; Shawkānī, *Irshād*, pp. 210, 212.
48. Shaᶜbān, *Uṣūl*, p. 151.
49. Khallāf, *ᶜIlm*, pp. 67–68.
50. Shawkānī, *Irshād*, p. 210.
51. Nawawī, *Minhāj* (Howard's trans.), p. 284.
52. Ghazālī, *Mustaṣfā*, II, 54; Abū Zahrah, *Uṣūl*, p. 194; Khallāf, *ᶜIlm*, p. 78.
53. Shawkānī, *Irshād*, pp. 221–22; Abū Zahrah, *Uṣūl*, p. 194.
54. Ghazālī, *Mustaṣfā*, II, 55; Khallāf, *ᶜIlm*, p. 77.

55. Abū Zahrah, *Uṣūl*, p. 195; Khallāf, *ᶜIlm*, p. 78. For other examples see Shawkānī, *Irshād*, p. 222.
56. Muslim, *Ṣaḥīḥ Muslim*, p. 41, Ḥadīth no. 119; Ibn Ḥazm, *Iḥkām*, VII, 54–55; Abū Zahrah, *Uṣūl*, p. 195–196. Zuhayr, *Uṣūl*, IV, 44.
57. Ibid.
58. Zuhayr, *Uṣūl*, IV, 44–45; Nour, 'Qiyās', 24–45.
59. Shawkānī, *Irshād*, 222; Ibn Qayyim, *Iᶜlām*, I, 178; Zuhayr, *Uṣūl*, IV, 45.
60. Ibid.
61. Ibn Qayyim, *Iᶜlām*, I, 197; Abū Zahrah, *Uṣūl*, p. 175; Khallāf, *ᶜIlm*, p. 54.
62. Ghazālī, *Mustaṣfā*, II, 64; Shāṭibī, *Muwāfaqāt*, III, 217; Ibn Qayyim, *Iᶜlām*, I. 198.
63. Abū Zahrah, *Uṣūl*, p. 176.
64. Abū Dawūd, *Sunan* (Hasan's trans.) III, 109 (Ḥadīth 1038), Khallāf, *ᶜIlm*, p. 56.
65. Ghazālī, *Mustaṣfā*, II, 64; Shawkānī, *Irshād*, p. 212; Ibn Qayyim, *Iᶜlām*, I, 200.
66. Ibn Ḥazm, *Iḥkām*, VII, 100; Ibn Qayyim, *Iᶜlām*, I, 200; Khallāf, *ᶜIlm*, p. 57.
67. Ibn Ḥazm, *Iḥkām*, VII, 147; Abū Zahrah, *Uṣūl*, p. 177.
68. Ibn Ḥazm, *Iḥkām*, VII, 160; Ibn Qayyim, *Iᶜlām*, I. 182.
69. Shawkānī, *Irshād*, p. 223; Abū Zahrah, *Uṣūl*, p. 177.
70. Two of the Qur'ānic *āyāt* which validate *ibāḥah* are as follows: 'It is He who has created for you all things that are on earth' (al-Baqarah, 2:29); and 'O you believers! Make not unlawful the good things which God has made lawful to you' (al-Mā'idah, 5:90).
71. Ibn Ḥazm, *Iḥkām*, VIII, 3.
72. Ibid., VIII, 18.
73. Ibid., VIII, 9.
74. Ibid.
75. Ibid., VIII, 15.
76. Abū Zahrah, *Uṣūl*, pp. 179–80.
77. Khallāf, *ᶜIlm*, p. 79.
78. Mutahhari, *Jurisprudence*, p. 21.
79. For further details see Aṣghari, *Qiyās*, pp. 119, 139.
80. Zuhayr, *Uṣūl*, IV, 51; Abū Zahrah, *Uṣūl*, p. 205.
81. The following Ḥadīth is recorded in Abū Dāwud (*Sunan*, III, 1229, Ḥadīth no. 4395): 'The hand of one who rifles the grave should be amputated, as he has entered the house of the deceased.'
82. Shawkānī, *Irshād*, p. 222.
83. Tabrīzī, *Mishkāt*, II, 1061, Ḥadīth No. 3570; Abū Yūsuf, *Kitāb al-Kharāj*, p. 152; Ibn Qayyim, *Iᶜlām*, I, 209.
84. Abū Zahrah, *Uṣūl*, p. 205.
85. Zuhayr, *Uṣūl*, IV, 51.
86. Abū Zahrah, *Uṣūl*, p. 206.
87. Ibid., p. 200.
88. Ibid., pp. 201–202.
89. Ibid., p. 203.
90. Bukhārī, *Ṣaḥīḥ* (Istanbul edn.), I, 51 (*Kitāb al-Wuḍū'*, Ḥadīth no. 34); Khīn, *Athar*, p. 403.
91. Baṣrī, *Muᶜtamad*, II, 162–64.
92. Abū Zahrah, *Uṣūl*, p. 204.
93. Ibn Ḥazm, *Iḥkām*, VIII, 79; Abū Zahrah, *Uṣūl*, p. 205.
94. Abū Dāwud, *Sunan* (Hasan's trans.) II, 955, Ḥadīth 3355; Ibn Ḥazm, *Iḥkām*, VIII, 106; Zuhayr, *Uṣūl*, IV, 50–58; Abū Zahrah, *Uṣūl*, p. 205.

CHAPTER TEN

Revealed Laws Preceding the *Sharīʿah* of Islam

In principle, all divinely revealed laws emanate from one and the same source, namely, Almighty God, and as such they convey a basic message which is common to them all. The essence of belief in the oneness of God and the need for divine authority and guidance to regulate human conduct and the values of morality and justice constitute the common purpose and substance of all divine religions. This essential unity is confirmed in more than one place in the Qur'ān, which proclaims in an address to the Holy Prophet: 'He has established for you the same religion as that which He enjoined upon Noah, and We revealed to you that which We enjoined on Abraham, Moses and Jesus, namely, that you should remain steadfast in religion and be not divided therein' (al-Shūrā, 42:13). More specifically, in a reference to the Torah, the Qur'ān confirms its authority as a source of inspiration and guidance: 'We revealed the Torah in which there is guidance (*hudā*) and light; and prophets who submitted to God's will have judged the Jews by the standards thereof' (al-Mā'idah, 5:44). It is thus observed that Muḥammad, being one of the Prophets, is bound by the guidance that is found in the Torah. Further confirmation for the basic harmony of the divinely revealed laws can be found in the Qur'ānic *āyah* which, in a reference to the previous Prophets, directs the Prophet of Islam to follow their guidance: 'Those are the ones to whom God has given guidance, so follow their guidance [*hudāhum*]' (al-Anʿām 6:90). Basing themselves on these and similar proclamations in the Qur'ān, the ulema are unanimous to the effect that all the revealed religions are different manifestations of an essential unity.[1] This is, of course, not to say that there are no differences between them. Since each one of the revealed religions was addressed to different nations at different points of time, they each have their distinctive features which set them apart from the rest. In the area of *ḥalāl* and *ḥarām*, for example, the rules that are laid down by different religions are not identical. Similarly, in the sphere of devotional practices and the rituals of worship, they differ from one another even if the essence of worship is the same. The *Sharīᶜah* of Islam has retained many of the previous laws, while it has in the meantime abrogated or suspended others. For example, the law of retaliation (*qiṣāṣ*) and some of the *ḥadd* penalties which were prescribed in the Torah have also been prescribed in the Qur'ān.[2]

The general rule to be stated here is, however, that notwithstanding their validity in principle, laws that were revealed before the advent of Islam are not applicable to the Muslims. This is especially so with regard to the practical rules of *Sharīᶜah*, that is, the *aḥkām*, in which the *Sharīᶜah* of Islam is self-contained. The jurists are also in agreement to the effect that the laws of the previous religions are not to be sought in any source other than that of the *Sharīᶜah* of Islam itself. For the rules of other religions do not constitute a binding proof as far as the Muslims are concerned. The *Sharīᶜah*, in other words, is the exclusive source of all law for the Muslims.

In view of the ambivalent character of the evidence on this subject, however, the question has arisen as to the nature of the principle that is to be upheld: whether to regard the laws preceding the *Sharīᶜah* of Islam as valid unless they are specifically abrogated by the *Sharīᶜah*, or whether to regard them as basically nullified unless they are specifically upheld. In response to this, it is said that laws that were introduced in the previous scriptures but which are not upheld by the *Sharīᶜah*, and on which no ruling is found in the Qur'ān or the *Sunnah* are not, according to general agreement, applicable to the Muslims. The correct rule regarding the enforcement of the laws of the previous revelations is that they are not to be applied to the followers of Islam unless they are specifically upheld by the *Sharīᶜah*.[3]

Once again the question arises as to whether the foregoing statement is in harmony with the Qur'ānic proclamations that were quoted above. The general response given to this is that the Prophet of Islam was ordered to follow the previous revelations as a source of guidance only in regard to the essence of the faith, that is, belief in God and monotheism. It has thus been pointed out that the word *hudā* 'guidance' in the second *āyah*, and *hudāhum* 'their guidance' in the third *āyah* quoted above only mean *tawḥīd*, or belief in the oneness of God, which is undoubtedly the norm in the *Sharīᶜah* of Islam. Their guidance cannot be upheld *in toto* in the face of clear evidence that some of their laws have been abrogated.

The reference is therefore to that aspect of guidance which is in common between Islam and the previous religions, namely *tawḥīd*. It has been further suggested that the reference to 'Prophets' in the second *āyah* above is confined, as the text itself suggests, to the Prophets of Banū Isrā'īl, and the holy Prophet Muḥammad is not one of them.[4]

The Qur'ān on many occasions refers to the rules of previous revelations on specific issues, but the manner in which these references occur is not uniform. The Qur'ān alludes to such laws in the following three forms:

1. The Qur'ān (or the *Sunnah*) may refer to a ruling of the previous revelation and simultaneously make it obligatory on the Muslims, in which case there remains no doubt that the ruling so upheld becomes an integral part of the *Sharīʿah* of Islam. An example of this is the Qur'ānic text on the duty of fasting which provides: 'O believers, fasting is prescribed for you as it was prescribed for those who came before you' (al-Baqarah, 2:183). To give a similar example in the *Sunnah*, which confirms the ruling of a previous religion, we may refer to the Ḥadīth which makes sacrifice by slaughtering animals lawful for Muslims. The believers are thus instructed to 'Give sacrifice, for it is the tradition of your ancestor, Abraham, peace be upon him'.

ضحوا فأنّه سنة أبيكم ابراهيم عليه السلام

2. The Qur'ān or the *Sunnah* may refer to a ruling of the previous revelation but at the same time abrogate and suspend it, in which case the ruling in question is to be abandoned and discontinued. An example of this can be found in the Qur'ān where a reference is made to the prohibition of certain varieties of food to the Jews while at the same time the prohibitions are lifted from the Muslims. The text thus provides: 'And to the Jews We forbade every animal having claws and of oxen and sheep, We forbade the fat [. . .] Say: nothing is forbidden to eat except the dead carcass, spilled blood, and pork' (al-Anʿām, 16:146). The second portion of this text clearly removes the prohibitions that were imposed upon the Jews. For a similar example in the *Sunnah*, we may refer to the Ḥadīth concerning the legality of spoils of war where the Prophet has proclaimed: 'Taking booty has been made lawful to me, but it was not lawful to anyone before me.'[6]

أُحلّت لي الغنائم ولم تحل لأحد من قبلي

Likewise, the expiation (*kaffārah*) for sins was not acceptable under the Torah; and when a garment became unclean, the unclean portion had to be cut out according to the rules of Judaism. But these restrictions were lifted with the effect that the *Sharīʿah* of Islam validated expiation for sins, and clothes can be cleaned by merely washing them with clean water.[7]

3. The Qur'ān or the *Sunnah* may refer to a ruling of the previous revelation without clarifying the position as to whether it should be abandoned or upheld. Unlike the first two eventualities, on which there is little disagreement among jurists, the present situation has given rise to wider differences of opinion. To give an example, we read in the Qur'ān, in a reference to the law of retaliation which was enacted in the Torah: 'We ordained therein for them life for life, eye for eye, nose for nose, tooth for tooth and wounds equal for equal' (al-Mā'idah, 5:48). Here there is no clarification as to whether the same law has to be observed by the Muslims. In yet another passage in the same sūra the Qur'ān stresses the enormity of murder in the following terms: 'We ordained for the children of Israel that anyone who slew a person, unless it be for murder or mischief in the land, it would be as if he slew the whole of mankind' (al-Mā'idah, 5:35). Once again, this *āyah* narrates a law of the previous revelation but does not specify whether this also constitutes a part of the *Sharīʿah* of Islam.

The majority of Ḥanafī, Mālikī, Ḥanbalī and some Shāfiʿī jurists have held the view that the foregoing is a part of the *Sharīʿah* of Islam and the mere fact that the Qur'ān refers to it is sufficient to make the law of retaliation binding on the Muslims. For the Lawgiver spoke of the law of the Torah to the Muslims and there is nothing in the *Sharīʿah* of Islam either to abrogate it or to warrant a departure from it. This is the law of God which He spoke of to us that He might be obeyed. It is on the basis of this conclusion that the Ḥanafīs have validated the execution of a Muslim for murdering a non-Muslim (i.e. a *dhimmī*), and a man for murdering a woman, as they all fall within the meaning of the Qur'ānic phrase 'life for life'.[8] There are some variant opinions on this, but even those who disagree with the Ḥanafī approach to this issue subscribe to the same principle which they find enunciated elsewhere in the Qur'ān. In particular, two *āyāt* have been quoted, one of which proclaims, 'and the punishment of an evil is an evil like it' (al-Shūrā, 42:40); and the other that, 'Whoever acts aggressively against you, inflict injury on him according to the injury he has inflicted on you, and keep your duty to God [. . .]' (al-Baqarah, 2:194). It is thus concluded that these *āyāt* provide sufficient evidence in support of the law of retaliation even without any reference to previous revelations.

The majority of the Shāfiᶜīs, the Ashᶜarites, and the Muᶜtazilah have maintained the view that since Islam abrogated the previous laws, they are no longer applicable to the Muslims; and hence these laws do not constitute a part of the *Sharīᶜah* of Islam unless they are specifically validated and confirmed. They maintain that the *Sharīᶜah* norm regarding the laws of the previous religions is 'particularity' (*khuṣūṣ*), which means that they are followed only when specifically upheld; whereas the norm with regard to the *Sharīᶜah* itself is generality (*ᶜumūm*) in that it is generally applied as it has abrogated all the previous scriptures.[9] This restriction is necessitated in view of the fact that the previous religions have not been correctly transmitted to us and have undergone considerable distortion.[10] The proponents of this view have quoted in support the Qur'ānic text which declares, in a reference to different nations and communities: 'For every one of you We have ordained a divine law and an open road' (al-Mā'idah, 5:48). Thus it is suggested that every nation has a *Sharīᶜah* of its own, and therefore the laws that were revealed before Islam are not binding on this *ummah*. Further evidence for this view has been sought in the Ḥadīth of Muᶜādh b. Jabal which indicates only three sources for the *Sharīᶜah*, namely the Qur'ān, the *Sunnah* and *ijtihād*.[11] The fact that this Ḥadīth has made no reference to previous revelations must mean that they are not a source of law for the followers of Islam. This last point has, however, been disputed in that when Muᶜādh referred to the Qur'ān, it was sufficient, as the Qur'ān itself contains numerous references to other revealed scriptures. Furthermore it is well-known that the Prophet did not resort to the Torah and Injīl in order to find the rulings of particular issues, especially at times when he postponed matters in anticipation of divine revelation. This would obviously imply that the Prophet did not regard the previous laws as binding on his own community.[12]

The correct view is that of the majority, which maintains that the *Sharīᶜah* of Islam only abrogates rules which were disagreeable to its teachings. The Qur'ān, on the whole, confirms the Torah and the Injīl, and whenever a ruling of the previous scriptures is quoted without abrogation, it becomes an integral part of the *Sharīᶜah* of Islam.[13] And finally, it may be added, as Abū Zahrah has pointed out, that disagreement among jurists on the authority or otherwise of the previous revelations is of little practical consequence, as the *Sharīᶜah* of Islam is generally self-contained and its laws are clearly identified. With regard to retailiation, for example, notwithstanding the differences of opinion among the jurists as to the precise import of the Qur'ānic references to this subject, the issue is resolved, once and for all, by the *Sunnah* which contains clear instructions on retaliation and leaves no doubt that it is an integral part of the *Sharīᶜah* of Islam.[14]

NOTES

1. Abū Zahrah, *Uṣūl*, p. 241; Qāsim, *Uṣūl*, p. 173.
2. Abū Zahrah, Uṣūl, p. 242; Badrān *Uṣūl*, p. 237.
3. Badrān, *Uṣūl*, p. 234; Ismāʿīl, *Adillah*, p. 320.
4. Ghazālī, *Mustaṣfā*, I, 134; Abū Zahrah, *Uṣūl*, p. 242; Ismāʿīl, *Adillah*, p. 325.
5. Tabrīzī, *Mishkāt*, I, 466, Ḥadīth no. 1476; Badrān, *Uṣūl*, p. 235.
6. Muslim, *Ṣaḥīḥ*, p. 301, Ḥadīth no. 1137; Badrān, *Uṣūl*, p. 234.
7. Khallāf, *ʿIlm*, p. 93; Ismāʿīl, *Adillah*, p. 320.
8. Ibid., p. 94; Shaltūt, *Al-Islām*, p. 489; Badrān, *Uṣūl*, p. 235.
9. Shawkānī, *Irshād*, p. 240; Shaltūt, *Al-Islām*, p. 489; Badrān, *Uṣūl*, p. 236.
10. Abdur Rahim, *Jurisprudence*, p. 70.
11. Abū Dāwud, *Sunan* (Hasan's trans.), III, 1019. Ḥadīth no. 3585.
12. Ghazālī, *Mustaṣfā*, I, 133. The only exception which is cited in this connection is when the Prophet referred to the Torah on the stoning of Jews for adultery. But this was only to show, as Ghazālī explains, that stoning (*rajm*) was not against their religion, and not because the Prophet regarded the Torah as a source of law.
13. Khallāf, *ʿIlm*, p. 94.
14. Abū Zahrah, *Uṣūl*, p. 242.

CHAPTER ELEVEN

The *Fatwā* of a Companion

The Sunnī ulema are in agreement that the consensus (*ijmā*ʿ) of the Companions of the Prophet is a binding proof, and represents the most authoritative form of *ijmā*ʿ. The question arises, however, as to whether the saying or *fatwā* of a single Companion should also be recognised as a proof, and given precedence over evidences such as *qiyās* or the *fatwās* of other *mujtahidūn*. A number of leading jurists from various schools have answered this question in the affirmative, and have held the view that the *fatwā* of a Companion is a proof (*ḥujjah*) which must be followed. Their argument is that following the demise of the Prophet, the leadership of the Muslim community fell upon their shoulders, and a number of learned Companions, with their intimate knowledge of the Qur'ān and the teachings of the Prophet were able to formulate *fatwās* and issue decisions on a wide range of issues. The direct access to the Prophet that the Companions enjoyed during his lifetime, and their knowledge of the problems and circumstances surrounding the revelation of the Qur'ān, known as the *asbāb al-nuzūl*, put them in a unique position to formulate *ijtihād* and to issue *fatwā*s on the problems that they encountered. Some ulema and transmitters of Ḥadīth have even equated the *fatwā* of a Companion with the *Sunnah* of the Prophet. The most learned Companions, especially the four Rightly-Guided Caliphs, are particularly noted for their contributions and the impact they made in the determination of the detailed rules of *fiqh* regarding the issues that confronted them.[1] This is perhaps attested by the fact that the views of the Companions were occasionally upheld and confirmed by the Qur'ān. Reference may be made in this context to the Qur'ānic *āyah* which was revealed concerning the treatment that was to be accorded to the prisoners of war following the battle of Badr. This *āyah* (al-Anfāl, 8:67) is known to have confirmed the view which ʿUmar b. al-Khaṭṭāb had earlier expressed on the issue.[2] The question arises, nevertheless, as to whether the *fatwā* of a Companion should be regarded as a proof of *Sharīʿah* or a mere *ijtihād*, which may or may not be accepted by the subsequent generations of *mujtahidūn* and the rest of the community as a whole. No uniform response has been given to this question, but before we attempt to explore the different responses which the ulema have given, it will be useful to identify who exactly a Companion is.

According to the majority (*jumhūr*) of ulema, anyone who met the Prophet, while believing in him, even for a moment and died as a believer, is a Companion (*ṣaḥābī*) regardless of whether he or she narrated any Ḥadīth from the Prophet or not. Others have held that the very word *ṣaḥābī*, which derives from *ṣuḥbah*, that is 'companionship', implies continuity of contact with the Prophet and narration of Ḥadīth from him. It is thus maintained that one or the other of these criteria, namely prolonged company, or frequent narration of Ḥadīth, must be fulfilled in order to qualify a person as a *ṣaḥābī*.[3] Some observers have made a reference to custom (*ʿurf*) in determining the duration of contact with the Prophet which may qualify a Companion. This criterion would, in turn, overrule some of the variant views to the effect that a *ṣaḥābī* is a person who has kept the company of the Prophet for specified periods such as one or two years, or that he participated with the Prophet in at least one of the battles.[4] But notwithstanding the literal implications of the word *ṣaḥābī*, the majority view is to be preferred, namely that continuity or duration of contact with the Prophet is not a requirement. Some ulema have held that the encounter with the Prophet must have occurred at a time when the person had attained the age of majority, but this too is a weak opinion as it would exclude many who met the Prophet and narrated Ḥadīth from him and attained majority only after his death. Similarly, actual eye-witnessing is not required, as there were persons among the Companions like Ibn Umm Maktūm, who were blind but were still regarded as *ṣaḥābī*.

The fact of being a Companion may be established by means of continuous testimony, or *tawātur*, which is the case with regard to the most prominent Companions such as the *Khulafāʾ Rāshidūn* and many others. To be a *ṣaḥābī* may even be established by a reputation which falls short of amounting to *tawātur*. Similarly, it may be established by the affirmation of another well-known Companion. According to some ulema, including al-Bāqillānī, we may also accept the Companion's own affirmation in evidence, as they are all deemed to be upright (*ʿudūl*), and this precludes the attribution of lying to them. There is, however, a difference of opinion on this point. The preferred view is that reference should be made to corroborating evidence, which may affirm or refute a person's claim concerning himself. This precaution is taken with a view to preventing false allegations and the admittance of self-styled individuals into the ranks of the Companions.[5]

The saying of a Companion, referred to both as *qawl al-ṣaḥābī*, and *fatwā al-ṣaḥābī*, normally means an opinion that the Companion had arrived at by way of *ijtihād*. It may be a saying, a considered opinion (*fatwā*), or a judicial decision that the Companion had taken on a matter in the absence of a ruling in the Qur'ān, *Sunnah* and *ijmāᶜ*. For in the face of a ruling in these sources, the *fatwā* of a Companion would not be the first authority on that matter. If the *fatwā* is related to the Qur'ān and *Sunnah*, then it must be on a point that is not self-evident in the source. There would, in other words, be a gap in our understanding of the matter at issue had the Companion not expressed an opinion on it.[6]

As stated earlier, there is no disagreement among the jurists that the saying of a Companion is a proof which commands obedience when it is not opposed by other Companions. Rulings on which the Companions are known to be in agreement are binding. An example of this is the grandmother's share of one-sixth in inheritance on which the Companions have agreed, and it represents their authoritative *ijmāᶜ*. The ulema are, however, in disagreement with regard to rulings which are based in opinion (*ra'y*) and *ijtihād*, and in regard to matters on which the Companions differed among themselves.[7]

There is general agreement among the ulema of *uṣūl* on the point that the ruling of one Companion is not a binding proof over another, regardless as to whether the ruling in question was issued by one of the caliphs, a judge, or a leading *mujtahid* among their number. For the Companions were themselves allowed to disagree with one another in matters of *ijtihād*. Had the ruling of one Companion been a proof over another, disagreement among them would not have been tolerated. But as already noted, the ulema of *uṣūl* have differed as to whether the ruling of a Companion constitutes a proof as regards the Successors (*tābiᶜūn*) and the succeeding generations of *mujtahidūn*.[8] There are three views on this, which may be summarised as follows:

1. That the *fatwā* of a Companion is a proof absolutely, and takes priority over *qiyās* regardless of whether it is in agreement with the *qiyās* in question or otherwise. This is the view of Imām Mālik, one of the two views of Imām Shāfiᶜī, one of the two views of Imām Aḥmad b. Ḥanbal and of some Ḥanafī jurists. The proponents of this view have referred to the Qur'ānic text which provides in a reference to the Companions: 'the first and foremost among the Emigrants and Helpers and those who followed them in good deeds, God is well-

pleased with them, as they are with Him' (al-Tawbah, 9:100). In this text, God has praised 'those who followed the Companions'. It is suggested that this manner of praise for those who followed the opinion and judgment of the Companions warrants the conclusion that everyone should do the same . The *fatwā* of a *ṣaḥābī*, in other words, is a proof of *Sharīʿah*. Another Qur'ānic *āyah* which is quoted by the proponents of this view also occurs in the form of a commendation, as it reads in an address to the Companions: 'You are the best community that has been raised for mankind; you enjoin right and you forbid evil' (Āl-ʿImrān, 3:109). Their active and rigorous involvement in the propagation of Islam under the leadership of the Prophet is the main feature of the *amr bi'l-maʿrūf* (enjoining right) which the Companions pursued. The Qur'ān praises them as 'the best community' and as such their example commands authority and respect.[9]

It has, however, been suggested that the Qur'ānic references to the Companions are all in the plural, which would imply that their individual views do not necessarily constitute a proof. But in response to this, it is argued that the *Sharīʿah* establishes their uprightness (*ʿadālah*) as individuals, and those who follow them in good deeds have been praised because they followed their opinion and judgment both as individuals and groups. It is further pointed out that those who followed the Companions are praised because they followed the personal opinion of the Companions and not because the latter themselves followed the Qur'ān and *Sunnah*. For if this were to be the case, then the Qur'ānic praise would be of no special significance as it would apply to everyone who followed the Qur'ān and *Sunnah*, whether a Companion or otherwise. If there is any point, in other words, in praising those who followed the Companions, then it must be because they followed the personal views of the Companions. It is thus concluded that following the *fatwā* of Companions is obligatory, otherwise the Qur'ān would not praise those who followed it in such terms.[10]

The proponents of this view have also referred to several *aḥādīth*, one of which provides: 'My Companions are like stars; whoever you follow will lead you to the right path.'

أصحابي كالنجوم بأيّهم أقتديتم أهتديتم

Another Ḥadīth which is also quoted frequently in this context reads: 'Honour my Companions, for they are the best among you, and then those who follow them and then the next generation, and then lying will proliferate after that [. . .]'[11]

اكـرمـوا أصحـابي فانهم خيارکم ، ثم الـذين
يلونهم ، ثم الذين يلونهم ثم يظهر الكذب

It is thus argued that according to these *aḥādīth*, following the way of the Companions is equated with correct guidance, which would imply that their sayings, teachings and *fatwās* constitute a proof that commands adherence.

It is, however, contended that these *aḥādīth* refer to the dignified status of the Companions in general, and are not categorical to the effect that their decisions must be followed. In addition, since these *aḥādīth* are conveyed in absolute terms in that they identify all the Companions as a source of guidance, it is possible that the Prophet had meant only those who transmitted the Ḥadīth and disseminated the Prophetic teachings, in which case the reference would be to the authority of the Prophet himself. The Companions in this sense would be viewed as mere transmitters and propagators of the *Sunnah* of the Prophet.[12]

Furthermore, the foregoing references to the Companions, as al-Ghazālī points out, are in the nature of praise, which indicates their piety and propriety of conduct in the eyes of God, but does not render adherence to their views an obligation. Al-Ghazālī also quotes a number of other *aḥādīth* in which the Prophet praises individual Companions by name, all of which consist of commendation and praise; they do not necessarily man that the saying of that Companion is a binding proof (*ḥujjah*).[13]

2. The second view is that the *ijtihād* of a Companion is not a proof and does not bind the succeeding generations of *mujtahidūn* or any one else. This view is held by the Ashᶜarites, the Muᶜtazilah, Imām Aḥmad b. Ḥanbal (according to one of his two views), and the Ḥanafī jurist Abū al-Ḥasan al-Karkhī.[14] The proponents of this view have quoted in support the Qur'ānic *āyah* (al-Ḥashr, 59:2) which provides: 'Consider, O you who have vision.' It is argued that this *āyah* makes *ijtihād* the obligation of everyone who is competent to exercise it, and makes no distinction over whether the *mujtahid* is a Companion or anyone else. What is obligatory is *ijtihād* itself, not adhering to the *ijtihād* of anyone in particular. This *āyah* also indicates that the *mujtahid* must rely directly on the sources and not imitate anyone, including the Companions. The proponents of this view also refer to the *ijmāᶜ* of the Companions, referred to above, to the effect that the views of one *mujtahid* among them did not bind the rest of the Companions.[15]

Al-Ghazālī and al-Āmidī both consider this to be the preferred view, saying that those who have held otherwise have resorted to evidence which is generally weak. Al-Shawkānī has also held that the *fatwā* of a Companion is not a proof, as he explains that the *ummah* is required to follow the Qur'ān and *Sunnah*. The *Sharīᶜah* only renders the *Sunnah* of the Prophet binding on the believers, and no other individual, whether a Companion or otherwise, has been accorded a status similar to that of the Prophet.[16] Abū Zahrah has, however, criticised al-Shawkānī's conclusion, and explains that when we say that the saying of a Companion is an authoritative proof, it does not mean that we create a rival to the Prophet. On the contrary, the Companions were most diligent in observing the Qur'ān and *Sunnah*, and it is because of this and their closeness to the Prophet that their *fatwā* carries greater authority than that of the generality of other *mujtahidūn*.[17]

3. The third view, which is attributed to Abū Ḥanīfah, is that the ruling of the Companion is a proof when it is in conflict with *qiyās* but not when it agrees with *qiyās* . The explanation for this is that when the ruling of a *ṣaḥābī* conflicts with *qiyās*, it is usually for a reason, and the fact that the Companion has given a ruling against it is an indication of the weakness of the *qiyās*; hence the view of the Companion is to be preferred. In the event where the ruling of the Companion agrees with *qiyās*, it merely concurs with a proof on which the *qiyās* is founded in the first place. The ruling of the Companion is therefore not a separate authority.[18]

There is yet another view which maintains that only the rulings of the four Rightly-Guided Caliphs command authority. This view quotes in support the Ḥadīth in which the Prophet ordered the believers, 'You are to follow my *Sunnah* and the *Sunnah* of the *Khulafā' Rāshidūn* after me'.

عليكم بسنتي وسنة الخلفاء الراشدين من بعدي

This is even further narrowed down, according to another Ḥadīth, to include the first two caliphs only. The Ḥadīth in question reads: 'Among those who succeed me, follow Abū Bakr and ᶜUmar'.

أقتدوا بالذي من بعدي أبي بكر وعمر

The authenticity of this second Ḥadīth has, however, been called into question, and in any case, it is suggested that the purpose of these *aḥādīth* is merely to praise the loyalty and devotion of these luminaries to Islam, and to commend their excellence of conduct.[19]

Imām Shāfiʿī is on record as having stated that he follows the *fatwā* of a Companion in the absence of a ruling in the Qur'ān, *Sunnah* and *ijmāʿ*. Al-Shāfiʿī's view on this point is, however, somewhat ambivalent, which is perhaps why it has been variously interpreted by the jurists. In a conversation with al-Rabīʿ, al-Shāfiʿī has stated: 'We find that the ulema have sometimes followed the *fatwā* of a Companion and have abandoned it at other times; and even those who have followed it are not consistent in doing so.' At this point the interlocutor asks the Imām, 'What should I turn to, then?' To this al-Shāfiʿī replies: 'I follow the ruling of the Companion when I find nothing in the Qur'ān, *Sunnah* or *ijmāʿ*, or anything which carries through the implications of these sources.' Al-Shāfiʿī has further stated that he prefers the rulings of the first three caliphs over those of the other Companions, but that when the Companions are in disagreement, we should look into their reasons and also try to ascertain the view which might have been adopted by the majority of the Companions. Furthermore, when the ruling of the Companion is in agreement with *qiyās*, then that *qiyās*, according to al-Shāfiʿī, is given priority over a variant *qiyās* which is not so supported.[20]

Imām Abū Ḥanīfah is also on record as having said, 'When I find nothing in the Book of God and the *Sunnah* of the Prophet, I resort to the saying of the Companions. I may follow the ruling which appeals to me and abandon that which does not, but I do not abandon their views altogether and do not give preference to others over them.' It thus appears that Abū Ḥanīfah would give priority to the ruling of a Companion over *qiyās*, and although he does not consider it a binding proof, it is obvious that he regards the *fatwā* of a *ṣaḥābī* to be preferable to the *ijtihād* of others.[21]

Imām Aḥmad ibn Ḥanbal has distinguished the *fatwās* of Companions into two types, one being a *fatwā* which is not opposed by any other Companion, or where no variant *ijtihād* has been advanced on the same point. Ibn Ḥanbal regards this variety of *fatwā* as authoritative. An example of this is the admissibility of the testimony of slaves, on which the Imām has followed the *fatwā* of the Companion, Anas b. Mālik. Ibn Ḥanbal is quoted to the effect that he had not known of anyone who rejected the testimony of a slave; it is therefore admissible. The second variety of *fatwā* that Ibn Ḥanbal distinguishes is one on which the Companions disagreed, and issued two or three different rulings concerning the same problem. In this situation, Imām Ibn Ḥanbal considers them all to be valid and equally authoritative, unless it is known that the *Khulafā' Rāshidūn* adopted one in preference to the others, in which case the Imām would do likewise. An example of such disagreement is the case of the allotment of a share in inheritance to germane brothers in the presence of the father's father. According to Abū Bakr, the father's father in this case is accounted like the father who would in turn exclude the germane brothers altogether. Zayd b. Thābit, on the other hand, counted the father's father as one of the brothers and would give him a minimum of one-third, whereas ʿAlī b. Abī Ṭālib counted the father's father as one of the brothers whose entitlement must not be less than one-sixth. Imām Ibn Ḥanbal is reported to have accepted all the three views as equally valid, for they each reflect the light and guidance that their authors received from the Prophet, and they all merit priority over the *ijtihād* of others.[22]

The Ḥanbalī scholar Ibn Qayyim al-Jawziyyah quotes Imām al-Shāfiʿī as having said, 'It is better for us to follow the *ra'y* of a Companion rather than our own opinion,' Ibn al-Qayyim accepts this without reservation, and produces evidence in its support. He then continues to explain that the *fatwā* of a Companion may fall into any of six categories. Firstly, it may be based on what the Companion might have heard from the Prophet. Ibn al-Qayyim explains that the Companions knew more about the teachings of the Prophet than what has come down to us in the form of Ḥadīth narrated by the Companions. Note, for example, that Abū Bakr al-Ṣiddīq transmitted no more than one hundred *aḥādīth* from the Prophet notwithstanding the fact that he was deeply knowledgeable of the *Sunnah* and was closely associated with the Prophet not only after the Prophetic mission began, but even before. Secondly, the *fatwā* of a Companion may be based on what he might have heard from a fellow Companion, Thirdly, it may be based on his own understanding of the Qur'ān in such a way that the matter would not be obvious to us had the Companion not issued a *fatwā* on it. Fourthly, the Companion may have based his view on the collective agreement of the Companions, although we have received it through one Companion only. Fifthly, the *fatwā* of a Companion may be based on the learned opinion and general knowledge that he acquired through long experience. And sixthly, the *fatwā* of a Companion may be based on an understanding of his which is not a result of direct observation but of information that he received indirectly, and it is possible that his opinion is incorrect, in which case his *fatwā* is not a proof and need not be followed by others.[23]

And lastly, it will be noted that Imām Mālik has not only upheld the *fatwās* of Companions but has almost equated it with the *Sunnah* of the Prophet. This is borne out by the fact, as already stated in our discussion of the *Sunnah*, that in his *Muwaṭṭa'*, he has recorded over 1,700 *aḥādīth*, of which over half are the sayings and *fatwās* of Companions.

On a similar note, Abū Zahrah has reached the conclusion that the four

Imāms of Jurisprudence have all, in principle, upheld and followed the *fatwās* of Companions and all considered them to be authoritative, although some of their followers have held views which differ with those of their leading Imāms. The author then quotes al-Shawkānī at some length to the effect that the *fatwā* of a Companion is not a proof. Having quoted al-Shawkānī, Abū Zahrah refutes his view by saying that it is 'not free of exaggeration'. (We have already given a brief outline of Abū Zahrah's critique of al-Shawkānī.) Abū Zahrah then quotes Ibn al-Qayyim's view on this matter which we have already discussed, and supports it to the effect that the *fatwā* of a Companion is authoritative. But it is obvious from the tenor of his discussion and the nature of the subject as a whole that the *fatwā* of a Companion is a speculative proof only.[24] Although the leading Imāms of jurisprudence are in agreement on the point that the *fatwā* of a Companion is authoritative, none has categorically stated that it is a binding proof. Nonetheless, the four leading Imāms consider the *fatwā* of a Companion to be a persuasive source of guidance in that it carries a measure of authority which merits careful consideration, and commands priority over the *ijtihād* of other *mujtahidūn*.

NOTES

1. Khallāf, *ᶜIlm*, p. 94; Mahmassānī, *Falsafah*, p. 98; Ismāᶜīl, *Adillah*, p. 281.
2. Ghazālī, *Mustaṣfā*, I, 136.
3. Shawkānī, *Irshād*, p. 70.
4. Ismāᶜīl, *Adillah*, p. 282.
5. Shawkānī, *Irshād*, p. 71; Ismāᶜīl, *Adillah*, p. 283.
6. Cf. Ismāᶜīl, *Adillah*, pp. 284–85.
7. Khallāf, *ᶜIlm*, p. 95.
8. Āmidī, *Iḥkām*, IV, 149; Shawkānī, *Irshād*, p. 243.
9. Abū Zahrah, *Uṣūl*, p. 168; Zuhayr, *Uṣūl*, IV, 192.
10. Ismāᶜīl, *Adillah*, pp. 291–92.
11. Tabrīzī, *Mishkāt*, III, 1695, Ḥadīth no. 6001 and 6003; Ghazālī, *Mustaṣfā*, I, 136; Āmidī, *Iḥkām*, IV, 152.
12. Zuhayr, *Uṣūl*, IV, 192; Ismāᶜīl, *Adillah*, p. 287.
13. Ghazālī, *Mustaṣfā*, I, 136–37.
14. Ismāᶜīl, *Adillah*, p. 294; Zuhayr, *Uṣūl*, IV, 193.
15. Ghazālī, *Mustaṣfā*, I, 135; Āmidī, *Iḥkām*, IV, 149.
16. Shawkānī, *Irshād*, p. 214.
17. Abū Zahrah, *Uṣūl*, p. 172; Ismāᶜīl, *Adillah*, p. 299.
18. Zuhayr, *Uṣūl*, IV, 194; Ismāᶜīl, *Adillah*, p. 301.
19. Ibn Mājah, *Sunan*, I, 37, Ḥadīth no. 97; Ghazālī, *Mustaṣfā*, I, 135; Āmidī, *Iḥkām*, IV, 152.

20. Shāfiʿī, *Risālah*, p. 261; Shawkānī, *Irshād*, p. 243; Abū Zahrah, *Uṣūl*, p.170.
21. Abū Zahrah, *Uṣūl*, p.170.
22. Abū Zahrah, *Ibn Ḥanbal*, p. 287; Ismāʿīl, *Adillah*, pp. 295–96.
23. Ibn Qayyim, *Iʿlām*, II, 191ff; Abū Zahrah, *Uṣūl*, pp. 169–70.
24 Abū Zahrah, *Uṣūl*, p.172.

CHAPTER TWELVE

Istiḥsān, or Equity in Islamic Law

The title I have chosen for this chapter draws an obvious parallel between equity and *istiḥsān* which should be explained, for although they bear a close similarity to one another, the two are not identical. 'Equity' is a Western legal concept which is grounded in the idea of fairness and conscience, and derives legitimacy from a belief in natural rights or justice beyond positive law.[1] *Istiḥsān* in Islamic law, and equity in Western law, are both inspired by the principle of fairness and conscience, and both authorise departure from a rule of positive law when its enforcement leads to unfair results. The main difference between them is, however, to be sought in the overall reliance of equity on the concept of natural law, and of *istiḥsān* on the underlying values and principles of the *Sharīʿah*. But this difference need not be overemphasised if one bears in mind the convergence of values between the *Sharīʿah* and natural law. Notwithstanding their different approaches to the question of right and wrong, for example, the values upheld by natural law and the divine law of Islam are substantially concurrent. Briefly, both assume that right and wrong are not a matter of relative convenience for the individual, but derive from an eternally valid standard which is ultimately independent of human cognizance and adherence. But natural law differs with the divine law in its assumption that right and wrong are inherent in nature.[2] From an Islamic perspective, right and wrong are determined, not by reference to the 'nature of things', but because God has determined them as such. The *Sharīʿah* is an embodiment of the will of God, the Lord of the universe and the supreme arbiter of values. If equity is defined as a law of nature superior to all other legal rules, written or otherwise, then this is obviously not what is meant by *istiḥsān*. For *istiḥsān* does not recognise the superiority of any other law over the divine revelation, and the solutions which it offers are for the most part based on principles which are upheld in the divine law. Unlike equity, which is founded in the recognition of a superior law, *istiḥsān* does not seek to constitute an independent authority beyond the *Sharīᶜah*. *Istiḥsān*, in other words, is an integral part of the *Sharīᶜah*, and differs with equity in that the latter recognises a natural law apart from, and essentially superior to, positive law.[3]

While discussing the general theory of *istiḥsān*, this chapter also draws attention to two main issues concerning this subject. One of these is whether or not *istiḥsān* is a form of analogical reasoning: is it to be regarded as a variety of *qiyās* or does it merit to stand as a principle of equity in its own right? The other issue to be raised is the controversy over the validity of *istiḥsān*, which started with al-Shāfiᶜī's unambiguous rejection of this principle. A glance at the existing literature shows how the ulema are preoccupied with the polemics over *istiḥsān* and have differed on almost every aspect of the subject. I shall therefore start with a general characterisation of *istiḥsān*, and then discuss the authority which is quoted in its support. This will be followed by a brief account of the related concepts, *ra'y* and *qiyās*. The discussion will end with an account of the controversy over *istiḥsān* and a conclusion where I have tried to see the issues in a fresh light with a view to developing a perspective on *istiḥsān*.

Istiḥsān is an important branch of *ijtihād*, and has played a prominent role in the adaptation of Islamic law to the changing needs of society. It has provided Islamic law with the necessary means with which to encourage flexibility and growth. Notwithstanding a measure of juristic technicality which seems to have been injected into an originally simple idea, *istiḥsān* remains basically flexible, and can be used for a variety of purposes, as will later be discussed. Yet because of its essential flexibility, the jurists have discouraged an over-reliance on *istiḥsān* lest it result in the suspension of the injunctions of the *Sharīᶜah* and become a means of circumventing its general principles. *Istiḥsān* has thus become the subject of much controversy among our jurists. Whereas the Ḥanafī, Mālikī and Ḥanbalī jurists have validated *istiḥsān* as a subsidiary source of law, the Shāfiᶜī, Ẓāhirī and Shīᶜī ulema have rejected it altogether and refused to give it any credence in their formulation of the legal theory of *uṣūl al-fiqh*.[4]

Istiḥsān literally means 'to approve, or to deem something preferable'. It is a derivation from *ḥasuna*, which means being good or beautiful. In its juristic sense, *istiḥsān* is a method of exercising personal opinion in order to avoid any rigidity and unfairness that might result from the literal enforcement of the existing law. 'Juristic preference' is a fitting description of *istiḥsān*, as it involves setting aside an established analogy in favour of an alternative ruling which serves the ideals of justice and public interest in a better way.

Enforcing the existing law may prove to be detrimental in certain situations, and a departure from it may be the only way of attaining a fair solution to a particular problem. The jurist who resorts to *istiḥsān* may find the law to be either too general, or too specific and inflexible. In both cases, *istiḥsān* may offer a means of avoiding hardship and generating a solution which is harmonious with the higher objectives of the *Sharīᶜah*. It has been suggested that the ruling of the second caliph, ᶜUmar b. al-Khaṭṭāb, not to enforce the *ḥadd* penalty of the amputation of the hand for theft during a widespread famine, and the ban which he imposed on the sale of slave-mothers (*ummahāt al-awlād*), and marriage with *kitābīyahs* in certain cases were all instances of *istiḥsān*.[5] For ᶜUmar set aside the established law in these cases on grounds of public interest, equity and justice.[6]

The Ḥanafī jurist al-Sarakhsī (d. 483/1090), considers *istiḥsān* to be a method of seeking facility and ease in legal injunctions. It involves a departure from *qiyās* in favour of a ruling which dispels hardship and brings about ease to the people. 'Avoidance of hardship (*rafᶜ al-ḥaraj*)' al-Sarakhsī adds, 'is a cardinal principle of religion which is enunciated in the Qur'ān, where we read, in an address to the believers, that 'God intends facility for you, and He does not want to put you in hardship' (al-Baqarah 2:185). Al-Sarakhsī substantiates this further by quoting the Ḥadīth that reads: 'The best of your religion is that which brings ease to the people.'[7]

خير دينكم أيسره.

Al-Khuḍarī has rightly explained that in their search for solutions to problems, the Companions and Successors resorted in the first place to the Qur'ān and the normative example of the Prophet. But when they found no answer in these sources, they exercised their personal opinion (*ra'y*) which they formulated in the light of the general principles and objectives of the *Sharīᶜah*. This is illustrated, for example, in the judgement of ᶜUmar ibn al-Khaṭṭāb in the case of Muḥammad ibn Salamah. The caliph was approached by Ibn Salamah's neighbour who asked for permission to extend a water canal through Ibn Salamah's property, and he was granted the request on the ground that no harm was likely to accrue to Ibn Salamah, whereas extending a water canal was to the manifest benefit of his neighbour.[8]

It thus appears that *istiḥsān* is essentially a form of *ra'y* which gives preference to the best of the various solutions that may exist for a particular problem. In this sense, *istiḥsān* is an integral part of Islamic jurisprudence and indeed of many other areas of human knowledge. Hence it is not surprising to note Imām Mālik's observation that '*istiḥsān* represents nine-tenth of human knowledge'. While quoting this view, Abū Zahrah adds that when Mālik made this remark, he was apparently including the broad concept of *maṣlaḥah* within the purview of *istiḥsān*. 'For it is *maṣlaḥah* which accounts for the larger part of the nine-tenth.'[9]

Evidence suggests that the Companions and Successors were not literalists who would seek a specific authority in the revealed sources for every legal opinion (*fatwā*) they issued. On the contrary, their rulings were often based on their understanding of the general spirit and purpose of the *Sharīᶜah*, and not necessarily on the narrow and literal meaning of its principles. *Istiḥsān* has been formulated in this spirit; it is the antidote to literalism and takes a broad view of the law which must serve, not frustrate, the ideals of fairness and justice.

To give an example, oral testimony is the standard form of evidence in Islamic law on which a consensus (*ijmāᶜ*) can be claimed to exist. This normally requires two upright (*ᶜadl*) witnesses unless the law provides otherwise (the proof of *zinā*, for instance, requires four witnesses). The number of witnesses required in these cases is prescribed in the Qur'ān, but the rule that testimony should be given orally is determined by consensus. Muslim jurists have insisted on oral testimony and have given it priority over other methods of proof, including confession and documentary evidence. In their view, the direct and personal testimony of a witness who speaks before the judge with no intermediary is the most reliable means of discovering the truth. The question arises, however, whether one should still insist on oral testimony at a time when other methods such as photography, sound recording, laboratory analyses, etc. offer at least equally, if not more, reliable methods of establishing facts. Here we have, I think, a case for a recourse to *istiḥsān* which would give preference to these new and often more reliable means of proof. It would mean departing from the established rules of evidence in favour of an alternative ruling which is justified in light of the new circumstances. The rationale of this *istiḥsān* would be that the law requires evidence in order to establish the truth, and not the oral testimony for its own sake. If this is the real spirit of the law, then recourse to *istiḥsān* would seem to offer a better way to uphold that spirit.

The jurists are not in agreement on a precise definition for *istiḥsān*. The Ḥanafīs have, on the whole, adopted Abu'l-Ḥasan al-Karkhī's (d. 340/947) definition, which they consider accurate and comprehensive. *Istiḥsān* is accordingly a principle which authorises departure from an established precedent in favour of a different ruling for a reason stronger than the one which is obtained in that precedent. While quoting this, al-Sarakhsī adds that the precedent which is set aside by *istiḥsān* normally consists of an established analogy which may be abandoned in favour of a superior proof, that is, the Qur'ān, the *Sunnah*, necessity (*ḍarūrah*), or a stronger *qiyās*.[10]

The Ḥanbalī definition of *istiḥsān* also seeks to relate *istiḥsān* closely to the Qur'ān and the *Sunnah*. Thus according to Ibn Taymiyyah, *istiḥsān* is the abandonment of one legal norm (*ḥukm*) for another which is considered better on the basis of the Qur'ān, *Sunnah*, or consensus.[11]

Notwithstanding the fact that the Mālikī jurists lay greater emphasis on *istiṣlāḥ* (consideration of public interest) and are not significantly concerned with *istiḥsān*, they have in principle validated *istiḥsān*. But the Māliks view *istiḥsān* as a broad doctrine, somewhat similar to *istiṣlāḥ*, which is less stringently confined to the Qur'ān and Sunnah than the Ḥanafīs and Ḥanbalis have. Thus according to Ibn al-ᶜArabī, '*istiḥsān* is to abandon exceptionally what is required by the law because applying the existing law would lead to a departure from some of its own objectives.' Ibn al-ᶜArabī points out that the essence of *istiḥsān* is to act on 'the stronger of two indications (*dalīlayn*)'. Whereas the majority of ulema would hold to *qiyās* when it was attacked on grounds of rigidity, Mālik and Abū Ḥanīfah departed from *qiyās*, or specified the general in *qiyās*, on grounds of *maṣlaḥah* and other indications.[12]

There are certain differences in the terms of these definitions which will hopefully become clearer as our discussion proceeds. But it appears that departure from an existing precedent on grounds of more compelling reasons is a feature of *istiḥsān* which is common to all the foregoing definitions. According to Abū Zahrah, the Ḥanafīs have adopted al-Karkhī's definition, as it embraces the essense of *istiḥsān* in all of its various forms. The essence of *istiḥsān*, Abū Zahrah adds, is to formulate a decision which sets aside an established analogy for a reason that justifies such a departure and seeks to uphold a higher value of the *Sharīᶜah*.[13] The departure to an alternative ruling in *istiḥsān* may be from an apparent analogy (*qiyās jalī*) to a hidden analogy (*qiyās khafī*), or to a ruling which is given in the *naṣṣ* (i.e. the Qur'ān or the *Sunnah*), consensus, custom, or public interest.

There is no direct authority for *istiḥsān* either in the Qur'ān or in the *Sunnah*, but the jurists have quoted both in their arguments for it. The opponents of *istiḥsān* have, on the other hand, argued that *istiḥsān* amounts to a deviation from the principles of the *Sharīᶜah*. It is an idle exercise in human preferences which only detracts from our duty to rely exclusively on divine revelation. Both sides have quoted the Qur'ān and the *Sunnah* in support of their arguments. They were able to do so partly because the Qur'ānic *āyāt* which they have quoted are on the whole open to various interpretations.

The Ḥanafī jurists have mainly quoted two Qur'ānic *āyahs*, both of which employ a derivation of the root word *ḥasuna*, and enjoin the believers to follow the best of what they hear and receive. They are as follows:

1. And give good tidings to those of my servants who listen to the word and follow the best of it [*aḥsanahu*]. Those are the ones God has guided and endowed with understanding (al-Zumar, 39:18);
2. And follow the best [*aḥsan*] of what has been sent down to you from your Lord (al-Zumar, 39:55).

Qawl (lit. 'word' or 'speech') in the first *āyah* could either mean the word of God, or any other speech. If it means the former, which is more likely, then the question arises as to whether one should distinguish between the words of God which are *aḥsan* (the best) as opposed to those which are merely *ḥasan* (good). Some commentators have suggested that the reference here is to a higher course of conduct. The Qur'ān, in other words, distinguishes a superior course of conduct from that which may be considered as ordinary. Punishing the wrong-doer, for example, is the normal course enjoined by the *Sharīᶜah*, but forgiveness may at times be preferable (*aḥsan*) and would thus represent the higher course of conduct. The basic concept of *istiḥsān*, in other words, can be seen in the Qur'ān, although not in its technical form which the ulema of jurisprudence have developed.[14]

The following two *aḥādīth* have also been quoted in support of *istiḥsān*:

1. 'What the Muslims deem to be good is good in the sight of God'[15];

ما رأه المسلمون حسناً فهو عند الله حسن

2. 'No harm shall be inflicted or reciprocated in Islam.'[16]

لا ضرر ولا ضرار في الاسلام

The critics of *istiḥsān* have argued, however, that none of the foregoing provide a definite authority in support of this doctrine. Regarding the first of the two *āyahs*, for example, Āmidī points out that it merely praises those who follow the best of what they hear. There is no indication in this *āyah* to render adherence to the 'best speech' an obligation. Nor does the second *āyah* bind one to a search for the best in the revelation: if there is an injunction in the revealed sources, it would bind the individual regardless of whether it is the best of the revelation or otherwise.[17] As for the Tradition, 'what the Muslims deem good is good in the sight of God', both al-Ghazālī and al-Āmidī have observed that, if anything, this would provide the authority for consensus (*ijmā*ʿ). There is nothing in this Tradition to suggest, and indeed it would be arbitrary to say, that what a Muslim individual deems good is also good in the sight of God.[18]

The critics of *istiḥsān* have further suggested that this doctrine was initially introduced by Ḥanafī jurists in response to certain urgent situations. The Ḥanafīs then tried to justify themselves by quoting the Qur'ān and the Ḥadīth *ex-post facto*. The Qur'ānic foundation of *istiḥsān*, in other words, is weak, and no explicit authority for it can be found in the *Sunnah* either.[19]

The historical origins of *istiḥsān* are somewhat uncertain too. While Goldziher has suggested that Abū Ḥanīfah was the first to introduce and use the term in its juristic sense, Joseph Schacht has attributed the origin of *istiḥsān* to Abū Ḥanīfah's disciple, Abū Yūsuf. Fazlur Rahman has confirmed the former view, which he thinks is substantiated by the fact that al-Shaybānī, another disciple of Abū Ḥanīfah, in a number of cases attributed *istiḥsān* to Abū Ḥanīfah himself.[20]

Ra'y, *Qiyās* and *Istiḥsān*

Istiḥsān is closely related to both *ra'y* and analogical reasoning. As already stated, *istiḥsān* usually involves a departure from *qiyās* in the first place, and then the departure in question often means giving preference to one *qiyās* over another. Broadly speaking, *qiyās* is the logical extension of an original ruling of the Qur'ān, the *Sunnah* (or even *ijmā*ʿ) to a similar case for which no direct ruling can be found in these sources. *Qiyās* in this way extends the *ratio legis* of the divine revelation through the exercise of human reasoning. There is, in other words, a rationalist component to *qiyās*, which consists, in the most part, of a recourse to personal opinion (*ra'y*). This is also true of *istiḥsān*, which relies even more heavily on *ra'y*. It is this rationalist tendency verging on personal opinion in both *qiyās* and *istiḥsān* which has been the main target of criticism by al-Shāfiʿī and others. Hence the controversy over the validity of *istiḥsān* is essentially similar to that encountered with regard to *qiyās*.[21] However, because of its closer identity with the Qur'ān and the *Sunnah*, *qiyās* has gained wider acceptance as a principle of jurisprudence. But even so, *qiyās* and *istiḥsān* are both considered to be expressive of rationalist tendencies in a system of law which must keep a close identity with its origins in divine revelation. In the centre of this controversy lies the question of the validity or otherwise of recourse to personal opinion (*ra'y*) in the development of the *Sharīᶜah*.

From an historical vantage point, it will be noted that in their recourse to personal opinion, the Companions were careful not to exercise *ra'y* at the expense of the *Sunnah*. This concern over possible violation of the *Sunnah* was greater in those days when the Ḥadīth had not yet been compiled nor consolidated. With the territorial expansion of the Islamic domain under the Umayyads, and the dispersal of jurists and Companions who were learned in the Ḥadīth, direct access to them became increasingly difficult. Fear of isolating the *Sunnah* led the jurists to lay down certain rules which restricted free recourse to *ra'y*. In order to be valid, the jurists ruled, *ra'y* must derive its authority from the *Sharīᶜah* principles which are enunciated in the Qur'ān and the *Sunnah*. This was the genesis of *qiyās*, which was initially a disciplined form of *ra'y*. However, the exercise of this relatively liberal form of *ra'y* during the formative stages of jurisprudence had already led to considerable disagreement among the *fuqahā'*. Those who called for a close adherence to the Ḥadīth, namely the *Ahl al-Ḥadīth*, mainly resided in the holy cities of Makkah and Madinah. The *Ahl al-Ḥadīth* regarded the *Sunnah* to be supplementary to the Qur'ān. They insisted on strict adherence to the *Sunnah* which, in their view, was a basic requirement of the faith. Acceptance of the faith, they argued, must be on a dogmatic basis without referring to the rationale or causes (*taᶜlīl*) of its ordinances. They were, in other words, literalists who denied the *mujtahid* the liberty to resort to the basic rationale of the *Sharīᶜah* rules. Whenever they failed to find an explicit authority in the sources concerning a problem, they chose to remain silent and avoid recourse to *ra'y*. This they considered to be the essence of piety and unquestioning submission to God.[22]

The *fuqahā'* of Iraq, on the other hand, resorted more liberally to personal opinion, which is why they are known as *Ahl al-Ra'y*. In their view, the *Sharīᶜah* was in harmony with the dictates of reason. Hence they had little hesitation to refer, in their search for solutions to legal problems, both to the letter and the spirit of the *Sharīᶜah* ordinances. The *Ahl al-Ra'y* are thus known for their frequent resort to analogical reasoning and *istiḥsān*.

As will be shown in the following pages, *istiḥsān* reflects an attempt on the part of the *fuqahā'* at regulating the free exercise of *ra'y* in matters of law and religion. Any restrictions imposed on *istiḥsān*, such as the one that sought to turn *istiḥsān* into a technical formula, were basically designed to tilt the balance in the continuous debate over the use of *ra'y* versus literalism in favour of the latter. Yet those who saw *istiḥsān* as a predominantly rationalist doctrine had reservations over subjecting it to restrictions that eroded its rationalist content and rendered *istiḥsān* a mere subdivision of *qiyās*.

Although the classical theory of *uṣūl al-fiqh* tacitly recognised that in some cases analogical reasoning might entail injustice and that it was then permissible to resort to *istiḥsān*, this was, however, not to be regarded as 'giving human reason a sovereign role'. *Istiḥsān* and *maṣlaḥah* were to be applied strictly in the absence of a specific ruling in the Qur'ān or the *Sunnah*.[23]

Qiyās Jalī, *Qiyās Khafī* and *Istiḥsān*

Qiyās jalī, or 'obvious analogy', is a straightforward *qiyās* which is easily intelligible to the mind. An oft-quoted example of this is the analogy between wine and another intoxicant, say a herbal drink, both of which have in common the effective cause (*ᶜillah*) of being intoxicating. Hence the prohibition concerning wine is analogically extended to the intoxicant in question. But *qiyās khafī*, or 'hidden analogy', is a more subtle form of analogy in the sense that it is not obvious to the naked eye but is intelligible only through reflection and deeper thought. *Qiyās khafī*, which is also called *istiḥsān* or *qiyās mustaḥsan* (preferred *qiyās*) is stronger and more effective in repelling hardship than *qiyās jalī*, presumably because it is arrived at not through superficial observation of similitudes, but through deeper reflection and analysis.

According to the majority of jurists, *istiḥsān* consists of a departure from *qiyās jalī* to *qiyās khafī*. When the jurist is faced with a problem for which no ruling can be found in the definitive text (*naṣṣ*), he may search for a precedent and try to find a solution by means of analogy. His search for alternatives may reveal two different solutions, one of which is based on an obvious analogy and the other on a hidden analogy. If there is a conflict between the two, then the former must be rejected in favour of the latter. For the hidden analogy is considered to be more effective and therefore preferable to the obvious analogy. This is one form of *istiḥsān*. But there is another type of *istiḥsān* which mainly consists of making an exception to a general rule of the existing law when the jurist is convinced that justice and equity will be better served by making such an exception. The jurist might have reached this decision as a result of his personal *ijtihād*, or the exception may have already been authorised by any of the following: *naṣṣ*, *ijmāᶜ*, approved custom, necessity (*ḍarūrah*), or considerations of public interest (*maṣlaḥah*).[24] These will be illustrated in the examples that follow. The examples chosen will also show more clearly the role that *istiḥsān* has played in the development of *fiqh*.

1) To give an example of *istiḥsān* which consists of a departure from *qiyās jalī* to *qiyās khafī*, it may be noted that under Ḥanafī law, the *waqf* (charitable endowment) of cultivated land includes the transfer of all the ancillary rights (the so-called 'easements') which are attached to the property, such as the right of water (*ḥaqq al-shurb*), right of passage (*ḥaqq al-murūr*) and the right of flow (*ḥaqq al-masīl*), even if these are not explicitly mentioned in the instrument of *waqf*. This ruling is based on *qiyās khafī* (or *istiḥsān*), as I shall presently explain. It is a rule of the Islamic law of contract, including the contract of sale, that the object of contract must be clearly identified in detail. What is not specified in the contract, in other words, is not included therein. Now if we draw a direct analogy (i.e. *qiyās jalī*) between sale and *waqf* – as both involve the transfer of ownership – we must conclude that the attached rights can only be included in the *waqf* if they are explicitly identified. It is, however, argued that such an analogy would lead to inequitable results: the *waqf* of cultivated lands, without its ancillary rights, would frustrate the basic purpose of *waqf*, which is to facilitate the use of the property for charitable purposes. To avoid hardship, a recourse to an alternative analogy, namely, to *qiyās khafī*, is therefore warranted. The hidden analogy in this case is to draw a parallel, not with the contract of sale, but with the contract of lease (*ijārah*). For both of these involve a transfer of usufruct (*intifāʿ*). Since usufruct is the essential purpose of *ijārah*, this contract is valid, on the authority of a Ḥadīth, even without a clear reference to the usufruct. This alternative analogy with *ijārah* would enable us to say that *waqf* can be validly concluded even if it does not specify the attached rights to the property in detail.

To give another example, supposing A buys a house in a single transaction from B and C at a price of 40,000 pounds payable in instalments. A pays the first instalment of 2,000 pounds to B assuming that B will hand over C's portion to him. But before this happens, B loses the 2,000 and the question arises as to who should suffer the loss. By applying *qiyās jalī*, B and C should share the loss. For B received the money on behalf of the partnership and not for himself alone. Their position in sharing the loss, in other words, is analogous to their status as partners in the first place. But by applying *istiḥsān*, only B, who received the money, suffers the loss. For C, although a partner, was basically under no obligation to obtain his portion of the 2,000 from B. It was only his right/privilege, and he would be at the liberty to waive it. C's portion of the 2,000 pounds would consequently become a part of the remainder of the price (or the debt) that A owed to both.

Only B is therefore to suffer the loss. The solution is based on the subtle analogy that one who is under no obligation should not have to pay any compensation either.[25]

2) The second variety of *istiḥsān* consists of making an exception to a general rule of the existing law, which is why some writers have called this type 'exceptional *istiḥsān*' (*istiḥsān istithnā'ī*), as opposed to 'analogical *istiḥsān*' (*istiḥsān qiyāsī*) – the latter consisting of a departure from one *qiyās* to another.[26] Of these two, exceptional *istiḥsān* is considered to be the stronger, for it derives support from another recognised source, especially when this is the Qur'ān or the *Sunnah*. The scholars of various schools are generally in agreement on the validity of the *istiḥsān* for which authority can be found in the primary sources, but they have disputed *istiḥsān* which is based on *qiyās khafī* alone. In fact the whole controversy over *istiḥsān* focuses on this latter form of *istiḥsān*.[27] But more to the point, the authority for an exceptional *istiḥsān* may be given either in the *naṣṣ*, or in one of the other recognised proofs, namely consensus (*ijmāᶜ*), necessity (*ḍarūrah*), custom (*ᶜurf*, or *ᶜādah*), and public interest (*maṣlaḥah*). We shall illustrate each of these separately, as follows:

2.1 An example of the exceptional *istiḥsān* which is based in the *naṣṣ* of the Qur'ān is its ruling on bequests to relatives: 'It is prescribed that when death approaches any of you, if he leaves any assets, that he makes a bequest to parents and relatives' (al-Baqarah 2: 180).

This Qur'ānic provision represents an exception to a general principle of the *Sharīᶜah*, namely that a bequest is basically not valid: since bequest regulates the division of the estate after the death of the testator, the latter is not allowed to accelerate this process. A bequest made during the lifetime of the testator is thus tantamount to interference in the rights of the heirs after the testator's death, which is unlawful. However, the Qur'ān permits bequest as an exception to the general rule, that is by way of an exceptional *istiḥsān*. It sets aside the general principle in favour of an exception which contemplates a fair distribution of wealth in the family, especially in cases where a relative is destitute and yet is excluded from inheritance in the presence of other heirs.[28]

2.2 Exceptional *istiḥsān* which is based on the *Sunnah* may be illustrated with reference to the contract of *ijārah* (lease or hire). According to a general rule of the *Sharīᶜah* law of contract, an object which does not exist at the time of contract may not be sold. However, *ijārah* has been validated despite its being the sale of the usufruct (i.e. in exchange for rent) which is usually non-existent at the moment the contract is concluded. Analogy would thus invalidate *ijārah*, but *istiḥsān* exceptionally validates it on the authority of the *Sunnah* (and *ijmāᶜ*), proofs which are stronger than analogy and which justify a departure from it.[29]

Similarly, the option of cancellation (*khiyār al-sharṭ*) represents an exceptional *istiḥsān* which is authorised by the *Sunnah*. It is employed when a person buys an object on condition that he may revoke the contract within the next three days or so. This kind of stipulation amounts to a departure from the general rule of the *Sharīᶜah* law of contract, which is that a contract becomes binding upon its conclusion. An exception to this rule has, however, been made, by way of *istiḥsān*, which is based on the Ḥadīth: 'When you agree on the terms of a sale, you may say: it is not binding and I have an option for three days.'[30]

قولـه عليه الصـلاة والسـلام : إذا بايعت فقل
لا خلابـة ولـي الخيار ثلاثة أيام

2.3 To illustrate exceptional *istiḥsān* which is authorised by *ijmāᶜ*, we may refer to *istiṣnāᶜ*, or the contract for manufacture of goods. Recourse to this form of *istiḥsān* is made when someone places an order with a craftsman for certain goods to be made at a price which is determined at the time of the contract. *Istiḥsān* validates this transaction despite the fact that the object of the contract is non-existent at the time the order is placed. This form of *istiḥsān* closely resembles the one which is authorised by custom, as will later be discussed.[31]

2.4 An example of exceptional *istiḥsān* which is based on necessity (*ḍarūrah*) is the method adopted for the purification of polluted wells. If a well, or a pond for that matter, is contaminated by impure substances, its water may not be used for ablution. It will be noted, however, that the water in the well cannot be purified by removing that part which is impure – and it cannot be poured out either, for it is in continuous contact with the water which flows into the well. The solution has been found through *istiḥsān*, which provides that contaminated wells can be purified by removing a certain number, say a hundred, buckets of water from the well (the exact number is determined with reference to the type and intensity of pollution). *Istiḥsān* in this case is validated by reason of necessity and prevention of hardship to the people.[32]

In a similar vein, strict analogy requires that witnesses, in order to be admissible, must in all cases be *ᶜadl*, that is, upright and irreproachable. For judicial decisions must be founded on truth, and this is faciliated by the testimony of just witnesses. However if the *qāḍī* happens to be in a place where *ᶜadl* witnesses cannot be found, then it is his duty, by virtue of *istiḥsān*, to admit witnesses who are not totally reliable so that the rights of the people may be protected.[33] Similarly with regard to the *qāḍī*, the general rule requires that he be a *mujtahid*, but a non-*mujtahid* may be appointed as *qāḍī* where no *mujtahid* can be found for this office.

2.5 To illustrate exceptional *istiḥsān* which is authorised by custom, we may refer to the *waqf* of moveable goods. Since *waqf*, by definition, is the endowment of property on a permanent basis, and moveable goods are subject to destruction and loss, they are therefore not to be assigned in *waqf*. This general rule has, however, been set aside by the Ḥanafī jurists, who have validated the *waqf* of moveables such as books, tools and weapons on grounds of its acceptance by popular custom.[34] Similarly, a strict analogy would require that the object of sale be accurately defined and quantified. However, popular custom has departed from this rule in the case of entry to public baths where the users are charged a fixed price without any agreement on the amount of water they use or the duration of their stay.[35] Another example is *bayᶜ al-taᶜāṭī*, or sale by way of 'give and take', where the general rule that offer and acceptance must be verbally expressed is not applied owing to customary practice.

2.6 And finally, to illustrate *istiḥsān* which is founded on considerations of public interest (*maṣlaḥah*), we may refer to the responsibility of a trustee (*amīn*) for the loss of goods which he receives in his custody. The general rule here is that the trustee is not responsible for loss or damage to such property unless it can be attributed to his personal fault or negligence (*taqṣīr*). Hence a tailor, a shoemaker or a craftsman is not accountable for the loss of goods in his custody should they be stolen, or destroyed by fire. But the jurists, including Abū Yūsuf and al-Shaybānī, have set aside the general rule in this case and have held, by way of *istiḥsān*, the trustee to be responsible for such losses, unless the loss in question is caused by a calamity, such as fire or flood, which is totally beyond his control. This *istiḥsān* has been justified on grounds of public interest so that trustees and tradesmen may exercise greater care in safeguarding people's property.[36]

The Ḥanafī – Shāfiʿī Controversy Over *Istiḥsān*

Al-Shāfiʿī has raised serious objections against *istiḥsān*, which he considers to be a form of pleasure-seeking (*taladhdhudh wa–hawā*) and 'arbitrary law-making in religion'.[37] A Muslim must obey God and His Messenger at all times, and follow injunctions which are enshrined in the clear texts (*nuṣūṣ*). Should there arise any problem or difference of opinion, they must be resolved with reference to the Qur'ān and the *Sunnah*. In support of this, al-Shāfiʿī quotes the Qur'ānic *naṣṣ* in sūra al-Nisā' (4:59): 'Should you dispute over a matter among yourselves, refer it to God and His Messenger, if you do believe in God and the Last Day.'

Al-Shāfiʿī continues on the same page: Anyone who rules or gives a *fatwā* on the basis of a *naṣṣ* or on the basis of *ijtihād* which relies on an analogy to the *naṣṣ* has fulfilled his duty and has complied with the command of the Lawgiver. But anyone who prefers that which neither God nor His Messenger has commanded or approved, his preference will be acceptable neither to God nor to the Prophet. *Istiḥsān* involves, according to al-Shafiʿī, personal opinion, discretion and the inclination of the individual jurist, an exercise which is not in harmony with the Qur'ānic *āyah* which reads: 'Does man think that he will be left without guidance [*an yutraka sudā*]?' (al-Qiyāmah, 75:36).

Commentators are in agreement that '*sudā*' in this *āyah* means a state of lawlessness in which the individual is not subject to any rules, commands or prohibitions. With this meaning in mind, Imām Shāfiʿī observes: if every judge and every *muftī* ruled according to their own inclinations, one can imagine that self-indulgence and chaos would afflict the life of the community. Unlike *qiyās*, whose propriety can be tested by the methodology to which it must conform, *istiḥsān* is not regulated as such. Since *istiḥsān* consists neither of *naṣṣ* nor of an analogy to *naṣṣ*, it is *ultra vires* and must therefore be avoided.[38]

In response to this critique, the Ḥanafīs have asserted that *istiḥsān* is not an arbitrary exercise in personal preference. It is a form of *qiyās* (viz., *qiyās khafī*), and is no less authoritative than *qiyās*. Thus it is implied that, contrary to allegations by the Shāfiʿī jurists, *istiḥsān* is not an independent source of law, but a branch of *qiyās* which has a firm grounding in the *Sharīʿah*. If this argument is accepted, it would imply that *istiḥsān* must be subjected to the same rules which are applicable to *qiyās*, and would therefore lose its status as a juristic principle in its own right. The scope and flexibility of *istiḥsān* would consequently be restricted as it would mean changing *istiḥsān* from a predominantly equitable doctrine into a form of analogical reasoning. This would confine *istiḥsān* only to matters on which a parallel ruling could be found in the primary sources. Having said this, however, it is doubtful whether *istiḥsān* is really just another form of *qiyās*.

Aḥmad Ḥasan has observed that *istiḥsān* is more general than *qiyās khafī*, as the former embraces a wider scope and can apply to matters beyond the confines of the latter.[39] Aghnides has similarly held that *istiḥsān* is a new principle which goes beyond the scope of *qiyās*, whether or not this is openly admitted to be the case:

> Abū Hanifah and his earliest disciples did not consider *istiḥsān* as a kind of *qiyās* [. . .] nor did he use the word in any technical sense. Had that been the case, like so many of his views, it would probably have been placed on record. The fact is that he used the word *istiḥsān* in its usual meaning, namely, that of abandoning *qiyās* for an opinion thought to be more subservient to the social interest.[40]

Aghnides goes on to suggest that when the Shāfiʿī jurists attacked *istiḥsān* on the grounds that it meant a setting aside of the revealed texts, the disciples of Abū Ḥanīfah felt themselves forced to show that such was not the case. Hence they put forward the contention that *istiḥsān* was nothing but another kind of *qiyās*. According to another observer, the attempt to bring *istiḥsān* within the sphere of *qiyās* is unjustified. For 'it really lies outside of this narrow sphere and must therefore be recognised as a special form of deduction'.[41]

Al-Ghazālī has criticized *istiḥsān* on different grounds. He has observed that the jurists of the Shāfiʿī school have recognised the validity of *istiḥsān* which is based on an indication (*dalīl*) from the Qur'ān or *Sunnah*. When there exists a *dalīl* of this kind, then the case at hand would be governed not by *istiḥsān* but directly by the provision of the Qur'ān or *Sunnah* itself.[42] Furthermore al-Ghazālī is critical of Abū Ḥanīfah for his departure, in a number of cases, from a sound Ḥadīth in favour of *qiyās or istiḥsān*.[43] And finally, al-Ghazālī rejects *istiḥsān* which is based on popular custom, for custom by itself is not a source of law. He observes that approved customs are often justified with reference, not to *istiḥsān*, but to other proofs. While referring to the example of entry to a public bath for a fixed price without quantifying the consumption of water, al-Ghazālī asks: 'How is it known that the community adopted this practice by virtue of *istiḥsān*? Is it not true that this was the custom during the time of the Prophet, in which case it becomes a tacitly approved *Sunnah* (*Sunnah taqrīriyyah*) so as to prevent hardship to the people?'[44]

Another Shāfiʿī jurist, al-Āmidī, has stated that notwithstanding his explicit denunciation of *istiḥsān*, al-Shāfiʿī himself resorted to *istiḥsān*. Al-Shāfiʿī has been quoted to have used a derivation of *istiḥsān* on several occasions including the ruling in which he said, 'I approve (*astaḥsinu*) *mutᶜah* (gift of consolation) at the level of 30 dirhams'; and 'I approve (*astaḥsinu*) the proof of pre-emption (*shufᶜ*) to be three days' (following the date when the sale of the property in question came to the knowledge of the claimant). Al-Āmidī thus draws the conclusion that 'there is no disagreement on the essence of *istiḥsān* between the two schools,'[45] which obviously means that their differences amount to no more than splitting hairs over words.

The Mālikī jurist al-Shāṭibī has held that *istiḥsān* does not mean the pursuit of one's desires; on the contrary, a jurist who understands *istiḥsān* has a profound understanding of the intention of the Lawgiver. When the jurist discovers that a strict application of analogy to a new problem leads to loss of *maṣlaḥah* and possibly to an evil (*mafsadah*) then he must set aside *qiyās* and resort to *istiḥsān*.[46]

While discussing the controversy over *istiḥsān*, another observer, Shaykh al-Khuḍarī, writes that anyone who is familiar with the works of the ulema of jurisprudence would agree that Abū Ḥanīfah and his disciples are not alone in their reliance on *istiḥsān*. All jurists have resorted to *istiḥsān* in one form or another, and a reader of the various juristic schools of thought is bound to come across opinions which are founded in it.[47]

This view finds further support from Yūsuf Mūsā, who has tersely observed that juristic differences over *istiḥsān* essentially amount to no more than arguments over words. For the *fuqahā'* of every major school have invariably resorted to *istiḥsān* in one form or another.[48]

If this is accepted, then one naturally wonders as to the causes that might explain the controversy in question. Al-Taftāzānī has observed that neither of the two sides of the controversy over *istiḥsān* have understood one another, and that the whole debate is due to a misunderstanding. Those who argue in favour of *istiḥsān* have perceived this principle differently to those who have argued against it. Had *istiḥsān* been properly understood, al-Taftāzānī adds, its basic validity would never have been disputed.[49]

Al-Taftāzānī's assessment has been widely endorsed by modern writers on the subject, including Khallāf, Abū Zahrah and Yūsuf Mūsā. In Khallāf's opinion, the essential validity of *istiḥsān* is undeniable, for it enables a departure from the apparent or the general rule of law to a variant ruling which warrants such a departure. Every judge and jurist must consider the circumstances of an individual case, and occasionally decide not to apply a certain rule, or to make an exception, as he considers this to be required by *maṣlaḥah* and justice.[50] And lastly, Abū Zahrah observes that, 'One exception apart, none of al-Shāfiᶜī's criticisms are relevant to the Ḥanafī conception of *istiḥsān*'. The one exception that may bear out some of al-Shāfiʿī's criticisms is *istiḥsān* which is authorised by custom. For custom is not a recognised source of law and is, in any case, not sufficiently authoritative to warrant a departure from *qiyās*.[51]

Conclusion

The attempt at linking *istiḥsān* with *qiyās* has involved tortuous reasoning which somehow remains less than convincing. One way to resolve some of the juristic differences on this issue may be to go back to the origin of *istiḥsān* and recapture the meaning that was given to it by Abū Ḥanīfah and the early ulema of jurisprudence. On this point there is evidence to suggest that Abu- Ḥanīfah (d. 150/767) did not conceive of *istiḥsān* as an analogical form of reasoning. About half a century later, when al-Shāfiʿī wrote his *Risālah* and *Kitāb al-Umm*, there was still little sign of a link between *istiḥsān* and *qiyās*. Al-Shāfiʿī is, in fact, completely silent on this point. Had al-Shāfiʿī (d. 204/820) known that *istiḥsān* was a variety of *qiyās*, one can imagine that he might have softened his stand with regard to it. Originally *istiḥsān* was conceived in a wider and relatively simple form which was close to its literal meaning and free of the complexities that were subsequently woven into it. One is here reminded of Imām Mālik's characteristic statement which designates *istiḥsān* as nine-tenth of human knowledge, a statement which grasps the true essence of *istiḥsān* as a method of finding better and more equitable alternatives to existing problems both within and beyond the confines of analogical reasoning. *Istiḥsān* is basically antithetic to *qiyās* and not a part of it. It enables the jurist to escape from strict conformity to the rules of *qiyās* when such conformity is likely to lead to unfair results. *Istiḥsān* was originally formulated, not as another variety of *qiyās*, but as a doctrine which liberated the jurist from the strait-jacket of *qiyās*, especially where conformity to *qiyās* clashed with the higher objectives of the *Sharīʿah*.

It is well to remember that much of the juristic controversy over *istiḥsān* has developed under the pressure of conformity to the strict requirements of the legal theory once it was finally formulated by al-Shāfiʿī and gradually accepted by others. The thrust of al-Shāfʿī's effort in formulating the legal theory of the *uṣūl* was to define the role of reason vis-à-vis the revelation. Al-Shāfiʿī confined the scope of human reasoning in law to analogy alone. In his well-known statement concerning *ijtihād* and *qiyās*, especially where he considered the two to be synonymous, one hardly fails to notice the attempt at confining the use of human reasoning to *qiyās* alone:

> On all matters touching the life of a Muslim there is either a binding decision or an indication as to the right answer. If there is a decision, it should be followed; if there is no indication as to the right answer, it should be sought by *ijtihād*, and *ijtihād* is *qiyās*.[52]

In this statement, al-Shāfiʿī reflected the dominant mood of his time. From that point onward, any injection of rationalist principles into the legal theory of the *uṣūl* had to seek justification through *qiyās*, which was the only channel through which a measure of support could be obtained for *istiḥsān*. In order to justify *istiḥsān* within the confines of the legal theory, it was initially equated with *qiyās* and eventually came to be designated as a sub-division of it.

The next issue over which the *fuqahā'* have disagreed is whether an *istiḥsān* which is founded in the Qur'ān, *Sunnah*, or *ijmāʿ* should be called *istiḥsān* at all. In cases where a Ḥadīth authorises departure from an existing analogy in favour of an alternative ruling, then all that one needs to authorise the departure in question is the Ḥadīth itself. It would therefore seem redundant to apply the word *istiḥsān* to this form of departure from the rules of *qiyās*. Whenever a ruling can be found in the Qur'ān (or the *Sunnah*), the jurist is obliged to follow it and should, basically, have no choice of resorting to *qiyās* or to *istiḥsān*. If the Qur'ān provides the choice of an alternative ruling which seems preferable, then the alternative in question is still a Qur'ānic rule, not *istiḥsān*.

It would appear that the *fuqahā'* initially used the term *istiḥsān* close to its literal sense, which is to 'prefer' or to deem something preferable. The literal meaning of *istiḥsān* was naturally free of the restrictions which were later evolved by the *fuqahā'*. A measure of confusion between the literal and technical meanings of *istiḥsān* probably existed ever since it acquired a technical meaning in the usage of the jurists. This distinction between the literal and juristic meanings of *istiḥsān* might help explain why some ulema have applied *istiḥsān* to the rulings of the Qur'ān, the *Sunnah*, and *ijmāʿ*. When we say that the Qur'ān, by way of *istiḥsān*, permitted bequests to be made during the lifetime of the testator, we are surely not using *istiḥsān* in its technical/juristic sense – that is, giving preference to one *qiyās* over another or making an exception to an existing legal norm – but merely saying that the Qur'ān preferred one of the two conceivable solutions in that particular case. When the Qur'ān authorises bequests, then one might say that it has established a legal norm in its own right regardless as to whether it can be described as an exception to another norm or not. To regard this Qur'ānic ruling as an *istiḥsān* can only be true if *istiḥsān* is used in its literal sense. For as a principle of jurisprudence, *istiḥsān* can add nothing to the authority of the Qur'ān and the *Sunnah*. Although one might be able to find the genesis of *istiḥsān* in the Qur'ān, this would have nothing to do with the notion of constructing *istiḥsān* as an alternative to, or a technique of escape from, *qiyās*. Furthermore, to read *istiḥsān* into the lines of the Qur'ān would seem superfluous in the face of the legal theory of the *uṣūl* that there is no room for rationalist doctrines such as *istiḥsān* in the event that a ruling can be found in the *nuṣūṣ*.

Notwithstanding the fact that many observers have considered Abu'l-Ḥasan al-Karkhī's definition to be the most acceptable, my enquiry leads to the conclusion that the Mālikī approach to *istiḥsān* and Ibn al-ᶜArabī's definition of it, is wider in scope and probably closest to the original conception of *istiḥsān*, for it does not seek to establish a link between *istiḥsān* and *qiyās*.

Istiḥsān has undoubtedly played a significant role in the development of Islamic law, a role which is sometimes ranked even higher than that of *qiyās*. Notwithstanding a measure of reticence on the part of the ulema to highlight the role of *istiḥsān*, it in reality features most prominently in bridging the gap between law and social realities by enabling the jurist to pay individual attention to circumstances and the peculiarities of particular problems. But for reasons which have already been explained, the *fuqahā'* have exercised restraint in the use of *istiḥsān*, which, as a result, has not been utilised to the maximum of its potential. Hence, it is not surprising to note that a certain gap between theory and practice has developed in Islamic Law.[53] The potentials of *istiḥsān* could hardly be translated into reality unless *istiḥsān* is stripped of its unwarranted accretions. The only consideration that needs to be closely observed in *istiḥsān* is whether there exists a more compelling reason to warrant a departure from an existing law. The reason which justifies resort to *istiḥsān* must not only be valid in *Sharīᶜah* but must serve a higher objective of it and must therefore be given preference over the existing law which is deemed unfair. Since *istiḥsān* enables a choice between alternative solutions, it contemplates the relative merits and demerits of each of the alternatives. The existing law is always the base to which an alternative is devised through *istiḥsān*. In this sense, *istiḥsān* offers considerable potential for innovation and for imaginative solutions to legal problems. The question in *istiḥsān* is not merely to find a solution to a particular problem but to find a better solution to the one which already exists. It therefore calls for a higher level of analysis and refinement which must in essence transcend the existing law and analogy.

The potential for new alternatives in *istiḥsān* would thus be considerably restricted if it were to be subjected to the requirements of *qiyās*. The two are essentially designed for different purposes and each must be allowed to function in its best capacity. Analogy essentially extends the logic of the Qur'ān and the *Sunnah*, whereas *istiḥsān* is designed to tackle the irregularities of *qiyās*. Thus it would seem methodologically incorrect to amalgamate the two into a single formula.

Istiḥsān has admittedly not played a noticeable role in the legal and judicial practices of our times. It has, as it were, remained in the realm of controversy, which may partly be explained by the dominance of the phenomenon of *taqlīd* in shaping the attitude of lawyers and judges towards *istiḥsān*. Only the rulings of the jurists of the past have been upheld on *istiḥsān*, and even this has not been totally free of hesitation. Muslim rulers and judges have made little or no use of *istiḥsān* either in developing the existing law or in the day-to-day administration of justice. This is patently unjustified, especially in view of the eminent suitability of *istiḥsān* in the search for fair and equitable solutions.

Istiḥsān can best be used as a method by which to improve the existing law, to strip it of impractical and undesirable elements and to refine it by means of making necessary exceptions. *Istiḥsān*, in other words, generally operates within the confines of the legal *status quo* and does not seek a radical change in the existing law, although it has considerable potential to effect innovation and refinement.

Judges and lawyers are generally reluctant to depart from the existing law, or to make exceptions to it, even in the face of evidence to the effect that a departure would be in the interests of fairness and justice. Their reluctance is often due to the reticence in the law as to precisely what role the judge has to play in such a situation. Judges are normally expected to enforce the law at all costs, and often have little choice in the matter regardless of the circumstances or results. Alternatively, it may be that the judges are, in fact, doing this – departing from the law when it seems patently unfair – without openly acknowledging what they are doing. In any case, it would seem advisable if the legislature explicitly authorised the judge to resort to *istiḥsān* when he considers this to be the only way of achieving a fair solution in a case under consideration. In this way, *istiḥsān* would hopefully find a place in the day-to-day administration of justice and would consequently encourage flexibility and fairness in law and judicial practice. Judicial decisions would, in turn, influence legislation and contribute towards attaining a more refined and equitable legal order. A clear and well-defined role for *istiḥsān* would hopefully mark a new opening in the evolutionary process of Islamic law.

NOTES

1. Osborn's *Concise Law Dictionary*, at p. 124, defines equity as follows: 'Primarily fairness or natural justice. A fresh body of rules by the side of the original law, founded on

distinct principles, and claiming to supersede the law in virtue of a superior sanctity inherent in those principles. Equity is the body of rules formulated and administered by the Court of Chancery to supplement the rules and procedure of the Common Law.'

2. See for a discussion Kerr's *Islamic Reform*, p. 57.

3. See for a discussion John Makdisi, 'Legal Logic,' p. 90.

4. For details see Ṣābūnī, *Madkhal*, p. 119ff.

5. *Umm al-walad* is a female slave who has borne a child to her master, and who is consequently free at his death. A *kitābīyah* is a woman who is a follower of a revealed religion, namely Christianity and Judaism.

6. Cf. Aḥmad Ḥasan, *Early Development*, p. 145.

7. Sarakhsī, *Mabsūṭ*, X, 145; Ibn Ḥanbal, *Musnad*, V, 22.

8. Khuḍarī, *Tārīkh*, p. 199.

9. Abū Zahrah, *Uṣūl*, p. 207, and 215. Imām Mālik's characterisation of *istiḥsān* also appears in Shāṭibī, *Muwāfaqāt* (ed. Dirāz), IV, 208.

10. Sarakhsī, *Mabsūṭ*, X, 145.

11. Ibn Taymiyyah, *Mas'alah al-istiḥsān*, p. 446.

12. '*Al-istiḥsān huwa tark muqtaḍā al-dalīl 'alā ṭarīq al istithnā' wa'l-tarakhkhuṣ li-muᶜāraḍah mā yūᶜāraḍ bihī fī baᶜd muqtaḍāyātih.*' See Ibn al-ᶜArabī, *Ahkām al-Qur'ān*, II, 57. A discussion of Ibn al-ᶜArabī's definition also appears in Shāṭibī, *Muwāfaqāt*, (ed. Dirāz), IV, 208.

13. Abū Zahrah, *Uṣūl*, p. 207.

14. Yūsuf Ali's commentary to *The Holy Qur'ān*, p. 1241 at f.n. 4269.

15. Āmidī (*Iḥkām*, I, 214) considers this to be a Ḥadīth but it is more likely to be a saying of the prominent companion, ᶜAbd Allāh ibn Masᶜūd; see also Shāṭibī, *Iᶜtiṣām*, II, 319.

16. Ibn Mājah, *Sunan*, II, 784, Ḥadīth no. 2340; Shāṭibī, *Muwāfaqāt* (ed. Dirāz), III, 17; Khuḍarī, *Tārīkh*, p. 199.

17. Āmidī, *Iḥkām*, IV, 159.

18. Ibid., p. 160; Ghazālī, *Mustaṣfā*, I, 138.

19. Ahmad Hasan, 'The Principle of Istiḥsān', p. 347.

20. Fazlur Rahman, *Islamic Methodology*, p. 32.

21. See further on *qiyās* Kamali, 'Qiyās (Analogy)' in *The Encyclopedia of Religion* XII, 128ff.

22. Khuḍarī, *Tārīkh*, p. 200ff.

23. Coulson, *Conflicts*, pp. 6–7.

24. Shaᶜbān, *Uṣūl*, p. 100.

25. Khallāf, *ᶜIlm*, p. 82; al-Nabhānī, *Muqaddimah*, p. 67.

26. Note the use of these terms e.g., in Ṣābūnī, *Madkhal*, p. 123.

27. Thus the Mālikī jurist Ibn al-Ḥājib classifies *istiḥsān* into three categories of accepted (*maqbūl*), rejected (*mardūd*) and uncertain (*mutaraddid*), adding that *istiḥsān* which is based on stronger grounds is acceptable to all. But *istiḥsān* which can find no support in the *naṣṣ*, *ijmāᶜ* or *qiyās* is generally disputed. See Ibn al-Ḥājib, *Mukhtaṣar*, II, 485.

28. Cf. Ṣābūnī, *Madkhal*, p. 123.

29. Cf. Mūsā, *Madkhal*, p. 197; Khallāf, *ᶜIlm*, p. 82. For *aḥādīth* which validate various types of *ijārah* (land, labour, animals, etc.) see Ibn Rushd, *Bidayāh*, II, 220–221.

30. *Ṣaḥīḥ al-Bukhārī* (trans. Khan), III, 575, Ḥadīth no. 893; Ṣābūnī, *Madkhal*, pp. 123–24.

31. See Abū Zahrah, *Uṣūl*, p. 211.

32. Ibid., pp. 211–12.

33. Cf. Ṣābūnī, *Madkhal*, p. 124.

34. Ibid.
35. Shāṭibī, *Iᶜtiṣām*, II, 318.
36. Ṣābūnī, *Madkhal*, p. 125.
37. Shāfiᶜī, *Kitāb al-Umm*, 'Kitāb Ibṭāl al-Istiḥsān', VII, 271.
38. Ibid., VII, 272.
39. Ahmad Hasan, 'The Principle of Istiḥsān', p.352.
40. Aghnides, *Muhammadan Theories*, p. 73.
41. Paret, 'Istiḥsān and Istiṣlāḥ', *Encyclopedia of Islam*, new ed., IV, 256.
42. Ghazālī, *Mustaṣfā*, I. 137.
43. Ghazālī criticises Abū Ḥanīfah's ruling, for example, with regard to implementing the punishment of *zinā* on the testimony of four witnesses each of whom point at a different corner of the room where *zinā* is alleged to have taken place. This is a case, according to Ghazālī, of doubt (*shubha*) in the proof of *zinā* which would prevent the enforcement of the *ḥadd* penalty. For according to a a Ḥadīth, *ḥudūd* are to be dropped in all cases of doubt. Abū Ḥanīfah's ruling is based on *istiḥsān*, apparently on the grounds that disbelieving the Muslims (*takdhīb al-muslimīn*) is reprehensible. Ghazālī regards Abū Ḥanīfah's ruling as whimsical and a form of *istiḥsān* which should not be followed (*Mustaṣfā*, I, 139).
44. Ibid., II, 138.
45. Āmidī, *Iḥkām*, IV, 157.
46. Shāṭibī, *Muwāfaqāt* (ed. Dirāz), IV, 206.
47. Khuḍarī, *Tārīkh*, p. 201.
48. Mūsā, *Madkhal*, p.198.
49. Taftāzānī, *Talwīḥ*, p. 82. It is not certain whether Taftāzānī was a Ḥanafī or a Shāfiᶜī. In a bibliographical note on Taftāzānī, it is stated that he is sometimes considered a Ḥanafī and sometimes a Shāfiᶜī. See *al-Mawsūᶜah al-Fiqhiyyah*, I, 344.
50. Khallāf, *ᶜIlm*, p. 83; Mūsā, *Madkhal*, p. 197.
51. Abū Zahrah, *Uṣūl*, p. 215.
52. Shāfiᶜī, *Risālah*, p. 206.
53. Joseph Schacht has devoted a chapter to the subject, entitled 'Theory and Practice' where he elaborates on how the gap between the law and social realities has widened: *An Introduction*, pp. 76–86.

CHAPTER THIRTEEN

Maṣlaḥah Mursalah (Considerations of Public Interest)

Literally, *maṣlaḥah* means 'benefit' or 'interest'. When it is qualified as *maṣlaḥah mursalah*, however, it refers to unrestricted public interest in the sense of its not having been regulated by the Law giver insofar as no textual authority can be found on its validity or otherwise.[1] It is synonymous with *istiṣlāḥ*, and is occasionally referred to as *maṣlaḥah muṭlaqah* on account of its being undefined by the established rules of the *Sharīᶜah*. For al-Ghazālī, *maṣlaḥah* consists of considerations which secure a benefit or prevent a harm but which are, simultaneously, harmonious with the objectives (*maqāṣid*) of the *Sharīᶜah*. These objectives, the same author adds, consist of protecting the five 'essential values', namely religion, life, intellect, lineage and property. Any measure which secures these values falls within the scope of *maṣlaḥah*, and anything which violates them is *mafsadah* ('evil'), and preventing the latter is also *maṣlaḥah*.[2] More technically, *maṣlaḥah mursalah* is defined as a consideration which is proper and harmonious (*waṣf munāsib mulā'im*) with the objectives of the Lawgiver; it secures a benefit or prevents a harm; and the *Sharīᶜah* provides no indication as to its validity or otherwise.[3] The Companions, for example, decided to issue currency, to establish prisons, and to impose tax (*kharāj*) on agricultural lands in the conquered territories despite the fact that no textual authority could be found in favour of this.[4]

The ulema are in agreement that *istiṣlāḥ* is not a proof in respect of devotional matters (*ᶜibādāt*) and the specific injunctions of the *Sharīᶜah* (*muqaddarāt*). Thus the *nuṣūṣ* regarding the prescribed penalties (*ḥudūd*) and penances (*kaffārāt*), the fixed entitlements in inheritance (*farā'iḍ*), the specified periods of *ᶜiddah* which the divorced women must observe, and such other *aḥkām* which are clear and decisive fall outside the scope of *istiṣlāḥ*. Since the precise values and causes of *ᶜibādāt* cannot be ascertained by the human intellect, *ijtihād*, be it in the form of *istiṣlāḥ*, juristic preference (*istiḥsān*) or *qiyās*, does not apply to them. Furthermore, with regard to *ᶜibādāt* and other clear injunctions, the believer is duty-bound to follow them as they are. But outside these areas, the majority of ulema have validated reliance on *istiṣlāḥ* as a proof of *Sharīᶜah* in its own right.[5]

Istiṣlāḥ derives its validity from the norm that the basic purpose of legislation (*tashrīᶜ*) in Islam is to secure the welfare of the people by promoting their benefit or by protecting them against harm. The ways and means which bring benefit to the people are virtually endless. The *maṣāliḥ* (pl. of *maṣlaḥah*), in other words, can neither be enumerated nor predicted in advance as they change according to time and circumstance.[6] To enact a law may be beneficial at one time and harmful at another; and even at one and the same time, it may be beneficial under certain conditions, but prove to be harmful in other circumstances. The ruler and the *mujtahid* must therefore be able to act in pursuit of the *maṣāliḥ* as and when these present themselves.[7]

The majority of ulema maintain that *istiṣlāḥ* is a proper ground for legislation. When the *maṣlaḥah* is identified and the *mujtahid* does not find an explicit ruling in the *nuṣūṣ*, he must act in its pursuit by taking the necessary steps to secure it. This is justified by saying that God's purpose in revealing the *Sharīᶜah* is to promote man's welfare and to prevent corruption in the earth. This is, as al-Shāṭibī points out, the purport of the Qur'ānic *āyah* in Sūra al-Anbiyā' (21:107) where the purpose of the prophethood of Muḥammad is described in the following terms: 'We have not sent you but as a mercy for all creatures.' In another passage, the Qur'ān describes itself, saying: 'O mankind, a direction has come to you from your Lord, a healing for the ailments in your hearts [. . .]' (Yūnus, 10:75). The message here transcends all barriers that divide humanity; none must stand in the way of seeking mercy and beneficience for human beings. Elsewhere, God describes His purpose in the relevation of religion, saying that it is not within His intentions to make religion a means of imposing hardship (al-Ḥajj, 22:78). This is confirmed elsewhere in sūra al-Mā'idah (5:6) where we read, in more general terms, that 'God never intends to impose hardship upon people.'[8]

These are some of the Qur'ānic objectives which grasp the essence of *maṣlaḥah*; they are permanent in character and would be frustrated if they were to be subjected to the kind of restrictions that the opponents of *maṣlaḥah* have proposed. We shall discuss the views of the opponents of *maṣlaḥah* in fuller detail; suffice it here to point out that the argument they have advanced amounts to a proposition that the general objectives of the Qur'ān can only be implemented, in regard to particular cases, if there is another *naṣṣ* available in their support. This would seem to amount to an unwarranted restriction on the general objectives of the Lawgiver as these are expounded in the Qur'ān.

The ulema have quoted a number of *aḥādīth* which authorise acting upon *maṣlaḥah*, although none is in the nature of a clear *naṣṣ* on the subject. Particular attention is given, in this context, to the Ḥadīth which provides that 'No harm shall be inflicted or reciprocated in Islam'.[9]

لا ضرر ولا ضرار في الاسلام

The substance of this Ḥadīth is upheld in a number of other *aḥādīth*, and it is argued that this Ḥadīth encompasses the essence of *maṣlaḥah* in all of its varieties.[10] Najm al-Din al-Ṭūfī, a Ḥanbalī jurist (d. 716 A.H.), has gone so far as to maintain, as we shall further elaborate, that this Ḥadīth provides a decisive *naṣṣ* on *istiṣlāḥ*. The widow of the Prophet, ʿĀ'ishah, is reported to have said that 'the Prophet only chose the easier of two alternatives, so long as it did not amount to a sin'.[11]

إنه ما خير بين أمرين الا اختار أيسرهما ما لم
يكن اثماً

According to another Ḥadīth, the Prophet is reported to have said that 'Muslims are bound by their stipulations unless it be a condition which turns a *ḥarām* into *ḥalāl* or a *ḥalāl* into a *ḥarām*.'[12]

المسلمون على شروطهم إلا شرطاً أحلّ حراماً أو
حرّم حلالاً

This would seem to be granting Muslims the liberty to pursue their benefits and to commit themselves to that effect provided that this does not amount to a violation of the explicit commands and prohibitions of the *Sharīʿah*. In yet another Ḥadīth, the Prophet is quoted to have said: 'God loves to see that His concessions (*rukhaṣ*) are observed, just as He loves to see that His strict laws (*ʿazā'im*) are obeyed.'[13]

إن الله يحب أن تؤتى رخصه كما يحب ان تؤتى
عزائمه

This would confirm the doctrine that no unnecessary rigour in the enforcement of the *aḥkām* is recommended, and that the Muslims should avail themselves of the flexibility and concessions that the Lawgiver has granted them and utilise them in pursuit of their *maṣāliḥ*. The rigorous approach that the Ẓāhirī ulema have taken in regard to *maṣlaḥah*, as will later be discussed, tends to oppose the purport of this Ḥadīth.

Technically, however, the concept of *maṣlaḥah mursalah* does not apply to the rulings of the Prophet. When there is a Prophetic ruling in favour of a *maṣlaḥah*, it becomes part of the established law, and hence no longer a *maṣlaḥah mursalah*. Historically, the notion of *maṣlaḥah mursalah* originated in the practice of the Companions. This is, of course, not to say that the Prophet did not rule in favour of *maṣlaḥah*, but merely to point out that as a principle of jurisprudence, *maṣlaḥah mursalah* does not apply to the rulings of the *Sunnah*.

The practice of the Companions, the Successors and the leading *mujtahidūn* of the past tends to suggest that they enacted laws and took measures in pursuance of *maṣlaḥah* despite the lack of textual authority to validate it. The Caliph Abū Bakr, for example, collected and compiled the scattered records of the Qur'ān in a single volume; he also waged war on those who refused to pay the *zakāh*; and he nominated ʿUmar to succeed him.[14] Similarly, ʿUmar b. al-Khaṭṭāb held his officials accountable for the wealth they had accumulated in abuse of public office and expropriated such wealth. He also poured away milk to which water had been added as a punishment to deter dishonesty in trade. Furthermore, ʿUmar b. al-Khaṭṭāb suspended the execution of the prescribed punishment for theft in a year of famine, and approved of the views of the Companions to execute a group of criminals for the murder of one person.[15] These decisions were taken despite the clear ruling of the Qur'ān concerning retaliation (*qiṣāṣ*), which is 'life for life' and the Qur'ānic text on the amputation of the hand, which is not qualified in any way whatsoever. But the Caliph ʿUmar's decision concerning *qiṣāṣ* was based on the rationale that the lives of the people would be exposed to aggression if participants in murder were exempted from *qiṣāṣ*. Public interest thus dictated the application of *qiṣāṣ* for all who took part in murdering a single individual. Furthermore, the third Caliph, ʿUthmān, distributed the authenticated Qur'ān and destroyed all the variant versions of the text. He also validated the right to inheritance of a woman whose husband had divorced her in order to be disinherited. The fourth

Caliph, ᶜAlī, is also on record as having held craftsmen and traders responsible for the loss of goods that were placed in their custody. This he considered to be for the *maṣlaḥah* of the people so that traders should take greater care in safeguarding people's property.[16] In a similar vein, the ulema of the various schools have validated the interdiction of the ignorant physician, the clowning *muftī*, and the bankrupt trickster, on grounds of preventing harm to the people. The Mālikīs have also authorised detention and *taᶜzīr* for want of evidence of a person who is accused of a crime.[17] In all these instances, the ulema have aimed at securing the *maṣlaḥah mursalah* by following a *Sharīᶜah*-oriented policy (*siyāsah sharᶜiyyah*), which is largely concurrent with the dictates of *maṣlaḥah*. As Ibn al-Qayyim has observed, '*siyāsah sharᶜiyyah* comprises all measures that bring the people close to wellbeing (*ṣalāḥ*) and move them further away from corruption (*fasād*), even if no authority is found for them in divine revelation and the *Sunnah* of the Prophet.'[18]

The main support for *istiṣlāḥ* as a proof and basis of legislation (*tashrīᶜ*) comes from Imām Mālik, who has given the following reasons in its favour:

1) The Companions have validated it and have formulated the rules of *Sharīᶜah* on its basis.
2) When the *maṣlaḥah* is compatible with the objectives of the Lawgiver (*maqaṣīd al-shāriᶜ*) or falls within the genus or category of what the Lawgiver has expressly validated, it must be upheld. For neglecting it under such circumstances is tantamount to neglecting the objectives of the Lawgiver, which is to be avoided. Hence *maṣlaḥah* as such is a norm of the *Sharīᶜah* in its own right; it is by no means extraneous to the *Sharīᶜah* but an integral part of it.
3) When *maṣlaḥah* is of the genus of the approved *maṣāliḥ* and is not upheld, the likely result would be to inflict hardship on the people, which must be prevented.[19]

Types of *Maṣlaḥah*

The *maṣāliḥ* in general are divided into three types, namely, the 'essentials' (*ḍarūriyyāt*), the 'complementary' (*ḥājiyyāt*), and the 'embellishments' (*taḥsīniyyāt*). The *Sharīᶜah* in all of its parts aims at the realisation of one or the other of these *maṣāliḥ*. The 'essential' *maṣāliḥ* are those on which the lives of people depend, and whose neglect leads to total disruption and chaos. They consist of the five essential values (*al-ḍarūriyyāt al-khamsah*) namely religion, life, intellect, lineage and property. These must not only be promoted but also protected against any real or unexpected threat which undermines their safety. To uphold the faith would thus require observance of the prescribed forms of *ᶜibādāt*, whereas the safety of life and intellect is secured by obtaining lawful means of sustenance as well as the enforcement of penalties which the *Sharīᶜah* has provided so as to protect them against destruction and loss.[20]

The *ḥājiyyāt* are on the whole supplementary to the five essential values, and refer to interests whose neglect leads to hardship in the life of the community although not to its collapse. Thus in the area of a *ᶜibādāt* the concessions (*rukhaṣ*) that the *Sharīᶜah* has granted to the sick and to the traveller, permitting them not to observe the fast, and to shorten the *ṣalāh*, are aimed at preventing hardship. Similarly, the basic permissibility (*ibāḥah*) regarding the enjoyment of victuals and hunting is complementary to the main objectives of protecting life and intellect.[21]

The 'embellishments' (*taḥsīniyyat*, also known as *kamāliyyāt*) denote interests whose realisation lead to improvement and the attainment of that which is desirable. Thus the observance of cleanliness in personal appearance and *ᶜibādāt*, moral virtues, avoiding extravagance in consumption, and moderation in the enforcement of penalties fall within the scope of *taḥsīniyyāt*.

It will be noted that the unrestricted *maṣlaḥah* does not represent a specific category of its own in the foregoing classification, for the obvious reason that it could fall into any of the three types of *maṣāliḥ*. Should it be the case that the realisation of *maṣlaḥah mursalah* is *sine qua non* to an essential *maṣlaḥah*, then the former becomes a part of the latter. Likewise, if *maṣlaḥah mursalah* happens to be a means to attaining one of the second classes of *maṣāliḥ*, then it would itself fall into that category, and so on. Furthermore, we may briefly add here the point which al-Shāṭibī has discussed at some length, that the *maṣāliḥ* are all relative (*nisbī, iḍāfī*), and as such, all the varieties of *maṣlaḥah*, including the essential *maṣāliḥ*, partake in a measure of hardship and even *mafsadah*. Since there is no absolute *maṣlaḥah* as such, the determination of value in any type of *maṣlaḥah* is based on the preponderance of benefit that accrues from it, provided that the benefit in question is in harmony with the objectives of the Lawgiver.[22]

From the viewpoint of the availability or otherwise of a textual authority in its favour, *maṣlaḥah* is further divided into three types. First, there is *maṣlaḥah* which the Lawgiver has expressly upheld and enacted a law for its realisation. This is called *al-maṣlaḥah al-muᶜtabarah*, or accredited *maṣlaḥah*, such as protecting life by enacting the law of retaliation (*qiṣāṣ*), or defending the right of ownership by penalising the thief, or protecting the dignity and honour of the individual by penalising adultery and false accusation. The Lawgiver has, in other words, upheld that each of these offences constitutes a proper ground (*waṣf munāsib*) for the punishment in question. The validity of *maṣlaḥah* in these cases is definitive and no longer open to debate. The ulema are in agreement that promoting and protecting such values constitutes a proper ground for legislation. The fact that the Lawgiver has upheld them is tantamount to His permission and approval of all measures, including legislation, that aim at their realisation.[23]

But the *maṣāliḥ* that have been validated after the divine revelation came to an end fall under the second class, namely the *maṣlaḥah mursalah*. Although this too consists of a proper attribute (*waṣf munāsib*) to justify the necessary legislation, but since the Lawgiver has neither upheld nor nullified it, it constitutes *maṣlaḥah* of the second rank. For example, in recent times, the *maṣlaḥah* which prompted legislation in many Muslim countries providing that the claim of marriage, or of ownership in real property, can only be proved by means of an official document has not been explicitly validated by the *Sharīʿah*. The law on these points has thus upheld the unrestricted *maṣlaḥah*; more specifically it is designed to prevent a *mafsadah*, which is the prevalence of perjury (*shahādah al-zūr*) in the proof of these claims.[24]

The third variety of *maṣlaḥah* is the discredited *maṣlaḥah*, or *maṣlaḥah mulghā*, which the Lawgiver has nullified either explicitly or by an indication that could be found in the *Sharīʿah*. The ulema are in agreement that legislation in the pursuance of such interests is invalid and no judicial decree may be issued in their favour. An example of this would be an attempt to give the son and the daughter an equal share in inheritance on the assumption that this will secure a public interest. But since there is a clear *naṣṣ* in the Qur'ān (al-Nisā', 4:11) which assigns to the son double the portion of the daughter, the apparent *maṣlaḥah* in this case is clearly nullified (*mulghā*).[25]

To summarise: when the *Sharīʿah* provides an indication, whether direct or implicit, on the validity of a *maṣlaḥah*, it falls under the accredited *maṣāliḥ*. The opposite of this is *maṣlaḥah mulghā*, which is overruled by a similar indication in the sources. The unrestricted *maṣlaḥah* applies to all other cases which are neither validated nor nullified by the *Sharīʿah*.

Conditions (*Shurūṭ*) of *Maṣlaḥah Mursalah*

The following conditions must be fulfilled in order to validate reliance on *maṣlaḥah mursalah*. These conditions are designed so as to ensure that *maṣlaḥah* does not become an instrument of arbitrary desire or individual bias in legislation.

1) The *maṣlaḥah* must be genuine (*ḥaqīqiyyah*), as opposed to a specious *maṣlaḥah* (*maṣlaḥah wahmiyyah*), which is not a proper ground for legislation. A mere suspicion or specious conjecture (*tawahhum*) that a certain legislation will be beneficial without ascertaining the necessary balance between its possible benefits and harms is not sufficient. There must, in other words, be a reasonable probability that the benefits of enacting a *ḥukm* in the pursuance of *maṣlaḥah* outweigh the harms that might accrue from it. An example of a specious *maṣlaḥah*, according to Khallāf, would be to abolish the husband's right of *ṭalāq* by vesting it entirely in a court of law.[26]

   Genuine *maṣāliḥ* are those which contemplate the protection of the five essential values noted above. Protecting the faith, for example, necessitates the prevention of sedition (*fitnah*) and of the propagation of heresy. It also means safeguarding freedom of belief in accordance with the Qur'ānic principle that 'there shall be no compulsion in religion' (al-Baqarah, 2:256). Similarly, safeguarding the right to live includes protecting the means which facilitate an honourable life such as the freedom to work, freedom of speech, and freedom to travel. Protecting the intellect (*ᶜaql*) necessitates the promotion of learning and safeguards against calamities which corrupt the individual and make him a burden to society. Furthermore, safeguarding the purity of lineage (*nasl*) entails protection of the family and creation of a favourable environment for the care and custody of children. And lastly, the protection of property requires defending the right of ownership. It also means facilitating fair trade and the lawful exchange of goods and services in the community.[27]

2) The second condition is that the *maṣlaḥah* must be general (*kulliyyah*) in that it secures benefit, or prevents harm, to the people as a whole and not to a particular person or group of persons. This means that enacting a *ḥukm* on grounds of *istiṣlāḥ* must contemplate a benefit yielded to the largest possible number of people. It is not *maṣlaḥah* if it secures the interest of a few individuals regardless of their social and political status. The whole concept of *maṣlaḥah* derives its validity from the idea that it secures the welfare of the people at large.[28]

3) Lastly, the *maṣlaḥah* must not be in conflict with a principle or value which is upheld by the *naṣṣ* or *ijmāᶜ*. Hence the argument, for example, that *maṣlaḥah* in modern times would require the legalisation of usury (*ribā*) on account of the change in the circumstances in which it is practiced, comes into conflict with the clear *naṣṣ* of the Qur'ān. The view that *ribā* in the way it is practiced in modern banking does not fall under the Qur'ānic prohibition, as Abū Zahrah

points out, violates the *naṣṣ* and therefore negates the whole concept of *maṣlaḥah*.[29]

Imām Mālik has added two other conditions to the foregoing, one of which is that the *maṣlaḥah* must be rational (*maᶜqūlah*) and acceptable to people of sound intellect. The other condition is that it must prevent or remove hardship from the people, which is the express purpose of the Qurānic *āyah* in sūra al-Mā'idah (5:6) quoted above.[30]

Furthermore, according to al-Ghazālī, *maṣlaḥah*, in order to be valid, must be essential (*al-maṣlaḥah al-ḍarūriyyah*). To illustrate this, al-Ghazālī gives the example of when unbelievers in the battlefield take a group of Muslims as hostages. If the situation is such that the safety of all the Muslims and their victory necessitates the death of the hostages, then al-Ghazālī permits this in the name of *al-maṣlaḥah al-ḍarūriyyah*.[31] However the weakness of al-Ghazālī's argument appears to be that the intended *maṣlaḥah* in this example entails the killing of innocent Muslims, and the *Sharīᶜah* provides no indication to validate this.[32]

Al-Ṭūfī's View of *Maṣlaḥah Mursalah*

Whereas the majority of jurists do not allow recourse to *istiṣlāḥ* in the presence of a textual ruling, a prominent Ḥanbalī jurist, Najm al-Dīn al-Ṭūfī, stands out for his view which authorises recourse to *maṣlaḥah* with or without the existence of *naṣṣ*. In a treatise entitled *al-Maṣāliḥ al-Mursalah*, which is a commentary on the Ḥadīth that 'no harm shall be inflicted or reciprocated in Islam', al-Ṭūfī argues that this Ḥadīth provides a clear *naṣṣ* in favour of *maṣlaḥah*. It enshrines the first and most important principle of *Sharīᶜah* and enables *maṣlaḥah* to take precedence over all other considerations. Al-Ṭūfī precludes devotional matters, and specific injunctions such as the prescribed penalties, from the scope of *maṣlaḥah*. In regard to these matters, the law can only be established by the *naṣṣ* and *ijmāᶜ*. If the *naṣṣ* and *ijmāᶜ* endorse one another on *ᶜibādāt*, the proof is decisive and must be followed. Should there be a conflict of authority between the *naṣṣ* and *ijmāᶜ*, but it is possible to reconcile them without interfering with the integrity of either, this should be done. But if this is not possible, then *ijmāᶜ* should take priority over other indications.[33]

As for transactions and temporal affairs (*aḥkām al-muᶜāmalāt wa al-siyāsiyyāt al-dunyawiyyah*), al-Ṭūfī maintains that if the text and other proofs of *Sharīᶜah* happen to conform to the *maṣlaḥah* of the people in a particular case, they should be applied forthwith, but if they oppose it, then *maṣlaḥah* should take precedence over them. The conflict is really not between the *naṣṣ* and *maṣlaḥah*, but between one *naṣṣ* and another, the latter being the Ḥadīth of *la ḍarar wa la ḍirār fi'l-Islam.*[34] One must therefore not fail to act upon that text which materialises the *maṣlaḥah.* This process would amount to restricting the application of one *naṣṣ* by reason of another *naṣṣ* and not to a suspension or abrogation thereof. It is a process of specification (*takhṣīṣ*) and explanation (*bayān*), just as the *Sunnah* is sometimes given preference over the Qur'ān by way of clarifying the text of the Qur'ān.[35]

In the areas of transactions and governmental affairs, al-Ṭūfī adds, *maṣlaḥah* constitutes the goal whereas the other proofs are like the means; the end must take precedence over the means. The rules of *Sharīᶜah* on these matters have been enacted in order to secure the *maṣāliḥ* of the people, and therefore when there is a conflict between a *maṣlaḥah* and *naṣṣ*, the Ḥadīth *la ḍarar wa la ḍirār* clearly dictates that the former must take priority.[36] In short, al-Ṭūfī's doctrine, as Mahmassānī has observed, amounts to saying after each ruling of the text, 'Provided public interest does not require otherwise.'[37]

Differences between *Istiṣlāḥ*, Analogy, and *Istiḥsān*

In his effort to determine the *sharᶜī* ruling on a particular issue, the jurist must refer to the Qur'ān, the *Sunnah* and *ijmāᶜ*. In the absence of any ruling in these sources, he must attempt *qiyās* by identifying a common *ᶜillah* between a ruling of the text and the issue for which a solution is wanting. However, if the solution arrived at through *qiyās* leads to hardship or unfair results, he may depart from it in favour of an alternative analogy in which the *ᶜillah*, although less obvious, is conducive to obtaining a preferable solution. The alternative analogy is a preferable *qiyās*, or *istiḥsān*. In the event, however, that no analogy can be applied, the jurist may resort to *maṣlaḥah mursalah* and formulate a ruling which, in his opinion, serves a useful purpose or prevents a harm that may otherwise ensue.[38]

It thus appears that *maṣlaḥah mursalah* and *qiyās* have a feature in common in that both are applicable to cases on which there is no clear ruling available in the *nuṣūṣ* or *ijmāᶜ*. They also resemble one another in the sense that the benefit that is secured by recourse to them is based on a probability, or *ẓann*, either in the form of a *ᶜillah* in the case of *qiyās*, or of a rational consideration which secures a benefit in the case of *maṣlaḥah mursalah*. However, *qiyās* and *maṣlaḥah* differ from one another in certain respects. The benefit which is secured by *qiyās* is founded on an indication from the Lawgiver, and a specific *ᶜillah* is identified to justify the analogy to the *naṣṣ*. But the benefit which is sought through *maṣlaḥah mursalah* has no specific basis in the established law, whether in favour or against. *Maṣlaḥah mursalah* in other words stands on its own justification, whereas *qiyās* is the extension of a ruling which already exists.

This explanation would also serve to clarify the main difference between *maṣlaḥah* and *istiḥsān*. A ruling which is based on *maṣlaḥah mursalah* is original in the sense that it does not follow, or represent a departure from, an existing precedent. As for *istiḥsān*, it only applies to cases on which there is a precedent available (usually in the form of *qiyās*), but *istiḥsān* seeks a departure from it in favour of an alternative ruling. This alternative may take the form of a hidden analogy (*qiyās khafī*), or of an exception to a ruling of the existing law, each representing a variation of *istiḥsān*.[39]

The Polemics over *Maṣlaḥah*

The main point in the argument advanced by the opponents of *istiṣlāḥ* is that the *Sharīᶜah* takes full cognizance of all the *maṣāliḥ*; it is all-inclusive and there is no *maṣlaḥah* outside the *Sharīᶜah* itself. This is the view of the Ẓāhirīs and some Shāfiᶜīs like al-Āmidī, and the Mālikī jurist Ibn al-Ḥājib, who do not recognise *maṣlaḥah* as a proof in its own right. They maintain that the *maṣāliḥ* are all exclusively contained in the *nuṣūṣ*. When the *Sharīᶜah* is totally silent on a matter, it is a sure sign that the *maṣlaḥah* in question is no more than a specious *maṣlaḥah* (*maṣlaḥah wahmiyyah*) which is not a valid ground for legislation.[40]

The Ḥanafīs and most Shāfiᶜīs have on the other hand adopted a relatively more flexible stance, maintaining that the *maṣāliḥ* are either validated in the explicit *nuṣūṣ*, or indicated in the rationale (*ᶜillah*) of a given text, or even in the general objectives of the Lawgiver. Only in the presence of a textual indication can *maṣlaḥah* constitute a valid ground for legislation. The identification of the causes (*ᶜilal*) and objectives, according to this view, entails the kind of enquiry into the *ᶜillah* that would be required in *qiyās*. The main difference between this view and that of the Ẓāhirīs is that it validates *maṣlaḥah* on the basis of the rationale and the objective of the *Sharīᶜah* even in the absence of a specific *naṣṣ*. Both these views are founded in the argument that if *maṣlaḥah* is not guided by the values upheld in the *nuṣūṣ* there is a danger of confusing *maṣlaḥah* with arbitrary desires, which might lead to corruption and *mafsadah*. Experience has shown that this has frequently occurred at the behest of rulers and governors who have justified their personal wishes in the name of *maṣlaḥah*. The way to avoid this is indicated in the Qur'ān, in sūra al-Qiyāmah (75 : 36) where we read: 'Does man think that he has been left without guidance?' The *maṣlaḥah* must therefore be guided by the values that the Lawgiver has upheld. Hence there is no *maṣlaḥah* unless it is corroborated by an indication in the *Sharīʿah*.[41] While commenting on *istiḥsān*, Imām Ghazālī writes: "We know that the *maṣāliḥ* must always follow the *sharʿī* indications; *istiḥsān* is not guided by such indications and therefore amounts to no more than a whimsical opinion". As for *maṣlaḥah mursalah*, al-Ghazālī maintains that when it is not approved by the Lawgiver, it is like *istiḥsān*.[42] Al-Ghazālī recognises the 'accredited' *maṣlaḥah*, that is, when the *maṣlaḥah* is indicated in the *naṣṣ*. He also approves of *maṣlaḥah mursalah* when it is based in definite necessity, that is, *maṣlaḥah ḍarūriyyah*. In the absence of a definite necessity, al-Ghazālī maintains that *maṣlaḥah* is not valid. Consequently, al-Ghazālī does not approve of the remaining two classes of the *maṣāliḥ*, namely the complementary (*ḥājiyyāt*), and the embellishments (*tahsīniyyāt*).[43] By making the stipulation that the *maṣlaḥah*, in order to be valid, must be founded in definite necessity, however, al-Ghazālī is no longer speaking of *maṣlaḥah mursalah*, but of necessity (*ḍarūrah*), which is a different matter altogether and governed by a different set of rules.[44] It thus appears that this view only validates the type of *maṣlaḥah* which is referred to as *maṣlaḥah muʿtabarah*.

The opponents of *istiṣlāḥ* further add that to accept *istiṣlāḥ* as an independent proof of *Sharīʿah* would lead to disparity, even chaos, in the *aḥkām*. The *ḥalāl* and *ḥarām* would be held to be applicable in some places or to some persons and not to others. This would not only violate the permanent and timeless validity of the *Sharīʿah* but would open the door to corruption.[45]

As already stated, the Ḥanafīs and the Shāfiʿīs do not accept *istiṣlāḥ* as an independent proof. Al-Shāfiʿī approves of *maṣlaḥah* only within the general scope of *qiyās*; whereas Abū Ḥanīfah validates it as a variety of *istiḥsān*. This would explain why the Shāfiʿīs and the Ḥanafīs are both silent on the conditions of *maṣlaḥah*, as they treat the subject under *qiyās* and *istiḥsān* respectively. They have explained their position as follows: should there be an authority for *maṣlaḥah* in the *nuṣūṣ*, that is, if *maṣlaḥah* is one of the accredited *maṣāliḥ*, then it will automatically fall within the scope of *qiyās*. In the event where no such authority could be found in the *nuṣūṣ*, it is *maṣlaḥah mulghā* and is of no account. But it would be incorrect to say that there is a category of *maṣlaḥah* beyond the scope of the *naṣṣ* and analogy to the *naṣṣ*. To maintain that *maṣlaḥah mursalah* is a proof would amount to saying that the *nuṣūṣ* of the Qur'ān and the *Sunnah* are incomplete.[46]

The opponents of *istiṣlāḥ* have further argued that the Lawgiver has validated certain *maṣāliḥ* and overruled others. In between there remains the *maṣlaḥah mursalah* which belongs to neither. It is therefore equally open to the possibility of being regarded as valid (*muᶜtabarah*) or invalid (*mulghā*). Since there is no certainty as to their validity, no legislation may be based on it, for law must be founded in certainty, not doubt.

In response to this, it is argued that the Lawgiver has proscribed certain *maṣāliḥ* not because there is no benefit in them but mainly because of their conflict with other and superior *maṣāliḥ*, or because they lead to greater evil. None of these considerations would apply to *maṣlaḥah mursalah*, for the benefit in it outweighs its possible harm. It should be borne in mind that the *maṣāliḥ* which the Lawgiver has expressly overruled (i.e. *maṣāliḥ mulghā*) are few compared to those which are upheld. When we have a case of *maṣāliḥ mursalah* on which no clear authority may be found in the sources, and they appear to be beneficial, they are more likely to belong to the part which is more extensive and preponderant (*kathīr al-ghālib*), not to that which is limited and rare (*qalīl al-nādir*).[47]

The Ẓāhirīs do not admit speculative evidence of any kind as a proof of *Sharīᶜah*. They have invalidated even *qiyās*, let alone *maṣlaḥah*, on the grounds that *qiyās* partakes in speculation. The rules of *Sharīᶜah* must be founded in certainty, and this is only true of the clear injunctions of the Qur'ān, *Sunnah* and *ijmāᶜ*. Anything other than these is mere speculation, which should be renounced.[48] As for the reports that the Companions issued *fatwās* on the basis of their own *ra'y* which might have partaken in *maṣlaḥah*, Ibn Ḥazm is categorical in saying that 'these reports do not bind anyone'.[49] Thus it would follow that the Ẓāhirīs do not accept *maṣlaḥah mursalah*, which they consider to be founded in personal opinion (*ra'y*).[50]

The Mālikīs and the Ḥanbalīs have, on the other hand, held that *maṣlaḥah mursalah* is authoritative and that all that is needed to validate action upon it is to fulfil the conditions which ensure its propriety. When these conditions are met, *maṣlaḥah* becomes an integral part of the objectives of the Lawgiver even in the absence of a particular *naṣṣ*. Aḥmad b. Ḥanbal and his disciples are known to have based many of their *fatwās* on *maṣlaḥah*, which they have upheld as a proof of *Sharīᶜah* and an instrument of protecting the faith, securing justice, and preventing *mafsadah*. They have thus validated the death penalty for spies whose activity violates the *maṣlaḥah* of the Muslim community. The Ḥanbalīs have also validated, on grounds of *maṣlaḥah*, the death penalty for propagators of heresy when protecting the *maṣlaḥah* of the community requires this. But in all this, the Ḥanbalīs, like the Mālikīs, insist that the necessary conditions of *maṣlaḥah* must be fulfilled. *Maṣlaḥah* must pursue the valid objectives of the *Sharīʿah* and the dictates of sound intellect, acting upon which fulfils a useful purpose, or serves to prevent harm to the people.[51] Some of the more far-reaching instances of *maṣlaḥah* in the Mālikī doctrine may be summarised as follows:

1) Imām Mālik validated the pledging of *bayʿah* (oath of allegiance) to the *mafḍūl*, that is the lesser of the two qualified candidates for the office of the Imām, so as to prevent disorder and chaos afflicting the life of the community.[52]
2) When the Public Treasury (*bayt al-māl*) runs out of funds, the Imām may levy additional taxes on the wealthy so as to meet the urgent needs of the government without which injustice and sedition (*fitnah*) may become rampant.[53]
3) In the event where all the means of earning a lawful living are made inaccessible to a Muslim, he is in a situation where he cannot escape to another place, and the only way for him to earn a living is to engage in unlawful occupations; he may do so but only to the extent that is necessary.[54]

Conclusion

Despite their different approaches to *maṣlaḥah*, the leading ulema of the four Sunnī schools are in agreement, in principle, that all genuine *maṣāliḥ* which do not conflict with the objectives (*maqāṣid*) of the Lawgiver must be upheld. This is the conclusion that both Khallāf and Abū Zahrah have drawn from their investigations.[55] The Shāfiʿī and Ḥanafī approach to *maṣlaḥah* is essentially the same as that of the Mālikī and Ḥanbalī schools, with the only difference being that the former have attempted to establish a common ground between *maṣlaḥah* and the *qiyās* which has an identifiable *ʿillah*. Some Mālikī jurists, including Shihāb al-Dīn al-Qarāfī have observed that all the jurists are essentially in agreement over the concept and validity of *maṣlaḥah mursalah*. They only differ on points of procedure: while some would adopt it directly, others would do so by bringing the *maṣlaḥah* within the purview of *qiyās*.[56] But Imām Mālik's concept of *maṣlaḥah* is the most far-reaching of the four Sunnī schools. Since *maṣlaḥah* must always be harmonious with the objectives of the Lawgiver, it is a norm by itself. *Maṣlaḥah mursalah* as such specifies the general (*ʿĀmm*) of the Qur'ān, just as the *ʿĀmm* of the Qur'ān may be specified by *qiyās*. In the event of conflict between a genuine *maṣlaḥah* and a solitary Ḥadīth, the former takes priority over the latter.[57]

The changing conditions of life never cease to generate new interests. If legislation were to be confined to the values which the Lawgiver has expressly decreed, the *Sharīʿah* would inevitably fall short of meeting the *maṣāliḥ* of the community. To close the door of *maṣlaḥah* would be tantamount to enforcing stagnation and unnecessary restriction on the capacity of the *Sharīʿah* to accommodate social change. ʿAbd al-Wahhāb Khallāf is right in his assessment that any claim to the effect that the *nuṣūṣ* of the *Sharīʿah* are all-inclusive and cater for all eventualities is simply not true. The same author goes on to say: 'There is no doubt that some of the *maṣāliḥ* have neither been upheld nor indicated by the *Sharīʿah* in specific terms.'[58]

As for the concern that the opponents of *maṣlaḥah mursalah* have expressed that validating this doctrine would enable arbitrary and self-seeking interests to find their way under the banner of *maṣlaḥah*, they only need to be reminded that a careful observance of the conditions that are attached to *maṣlaḥah* will ensure that only the genuine interests of the people which are in harmony with the objectives of the *Sharīʿah* would qualify. This concern is admittedly valid, but one which cannot be confined to *maṣlaḥah* alone. Arbitrariness and the pursuit of self-seeking interests have never been totally eliminated in any society, under any legal system. It is a permanent threat which must be carefully checked and minimised to the extent that this is possible. But this very purpose will be defeated if legislation on grounds of *istiṣlāḥ* were to be denied validity. To combat the evil of an arbitrary indulgence which waves the banner of *maṣlaḥah* would surely have greater prospects of success if the *mujtahid* and the Imām were to be able to enact the necessary legislation on grounds of preventing harm to society. Consequently the argument that the opponents of *maṣlaḥah* have advanced would appear to be specious and self-defeating.

NOTES

1. Khallāf, *ʿIlm*, p. 84; Badrān *Uṣūl*, p. 209.
2. Ghazālī, *Mustaṣfā*, I, 139–140.
3. Badrān, *Uṣūl*, p. 210; Ṣābūnī, *Madkhal*, p. 131.
4. Khallāf, *ʿIlm*, p. 84.
5. Badrān, *Uṣūl*, p. 210; Ṣābūnī, *Madkhal*, p. 134.
6. Shāṭibī, *Muwāfaqāt*, II, 2–3; Ṣābūnī, *Madkhal*, p. 133.
7. Khallāf, *ʿIlm*, p. 84; Badrān, *Uṣūl*, p. 211.
8. Cf. Shāṭibī, *Muwāfaqāt*, II, 3; Muṣṭafā Zayd, *Maṣlaḥah*, p. 25.
9. Ibn Mājah, *Sunan*, Ḥadīth no 2340.
10. Khallāf, *ʿIlm*, p. 90; Abū Zahrah, *Uṣūl*, p. 222.
11. Muslim, *Ṣaḥīḥ Muslim*, p. 412, Ḥadīth no. 1546.
12. Abū Dāwud, *Sunan* (Hasan's trans.), III, 1020, Ḥadīth no 3587.

13. Ibn al-Qayyim, *Iᶜlām*, II, 242; Muṣṭafā Zayd, *Maṣlaḥah*, p. 120.
14. Shāṭibī, *Iᶜtiṣām*, II, 287; Khallāf, *ᶜIlm*, p. 86.
15. Ibn al-Qayyim, *Iᶜlām*, I, 185; Abū Zahrah, *Uṣūl*, pp. 222–223; Muṣṭafā Zayd, *Maṣlaḥah*, p. 52.
16. Shāṭibī, *Iᶜtiṣām*, II, 292, 302; Ibn al-Qayyim, *Iᶜlām*, I, 182; Abū Zahrah, *Uṣūl*, p. 223.
17. Shāṭibī, *Iᶜtiṣām*, II, 293, Khallāf, *ᶜIlm*, p. 86; Abū Zahrah, *Uṣūl*, p. 223.
18. Ibn al-Qayyim, *Ṭuruq*, p. 16.
19. Shāṭibī, *Iᶜtiṣām*, II, 282–287; Abū Zahrah, *Uṣūl*, p. 223.
20. Shāṭibī, *Muwāfaqāt*, II, 3–5; Badrān, *Uṣūl*, p. 208.
21. Shāṭibī, *Muwāfaqāt*, Ibid., II, 5; Muṣṭafā Zayd, *Maṣlaḥah*, pp. 54–55.
22. Ibid., II, 27ff.
23. Khallāf, *ᶜIlm*, p. 84; Badrān, *Uṣūl*, pp. 209–10.
24. Khallāf, *ᶜIlm*, p. 85; Badrān, *Uṣūl*, p. 215.
25. Badrān, *Uṣūl*, p. 209.
26. Khallāf, *ᶜIlm*, p. 86.
27. Abū Zahrah, *Uṣūl*, p. 220.
28. Khallāf, *ᶜIlm*, p. 87; Badrān, *Uṣūl*, p. 214.
29. Abū Zahrah, *Uṣūl*, p. 219; Badrān, *Uṣūl*, p. 215.
30. Shāṭibī, *Iᶜtiṣām*, II, 307–14; Muṣṭafā Zayd, *Maṣlaḥah*, p. 51.
31. Ghazālī, *Mustaṣfā*, I, 141.
32. Badrān, *Uṣūl*, pp. 215–16.
33. Ṭūfī, *Maṣāliḥ*, p. 139.
34. Ibid., p. 141; Muṣṭafā Zayd, *Maṣlaḥah*, pp. 238–240. This book is entirely devoted to an exposition of Ṭūfī's doctrine of *Maṣlaḥah*.
35. Cf. Muṣṭafā Zayd, *Maṣlaḥah*, p. 121; Abū Zahrah, *Uṣūl*, p. 223. A discussion of Ṭūfi''s doctrine can also be found in Kerr, *Islamic Reform*, p. 97ff.
36. Ṭūfī, *Maṣāliḥ*, p. 141; Muṣṭafā Zayd, *Maṣlaḥah*, p. 131–132.
37. Mahmassānī, *Falsafah al-Tashrīᶜ*, p. 117. This author also quotes Shaykh Muṣṭafā al-Ghalayīnī in support of his own view.
38. Cf. Ṣābūnī, *Madkhal*, pp. 134–35.
39. Cf. Badrān, *Uṣūl*, pp. 216–217; Ṣābūnī, *Madkhal*, p. 135.
40. Khallāf, *ᶜIlm*, p. 88; Badrān, *Uṣūl*, p. 213.
41. Abū Zahrah, *Uṣūl*, pp. 221, 224; Khallāf, *ᶜIlm*, p. 88; Badrān, *Uṣūl*, p. 213.
42. Ghazālī, *Mustaṣfā*, I, 138.
43. Ibid., I, 139–140.
44. Cf. Badrān, *Uṣūl*, p. 211.
45. Khallāf, *ᶜIlm*, p. 88.
46. Abū Zahrah, *Uṣūl*, p. 222; Muṣṭafā Zayd, *Maṣlaḥah*, p. 61; Badrān. *Uṣūl*, p. 213.
47. Badrān, *Uṣūl*, p. 214.
48. Ibn Ḥazm, *Iḥkām*, V, 55–56.
49. Ibid., VI, 40.
50. Cf. Muṣṭafā Zayd, *Maṣlaḥah*, p. 62.
51. Ibid., p. 60.
52. Shāṭibī, *Iᶜtiṣām*, II, 303.
53. Ibid., II, 295.
54. Ibid., II, 300.
55. Abū Zahrah, *Uṣūl*, p. 224; Khallāf, *ᶜIlm*, p. 85.
56. Qarāfī, *Furūq*, II, 188; Abū Zahrah, *Uṣūl*, p. 225.
57. Abū Zahrah, *Uṣūl*, p. 225.
58. Khallāf, *ᶜIlm*, p. 88.

CHAPTER FOURTEEN

ᶜUrf (Custom)

As a noun derived from its Arabic root *ᶜarafa* (to know), *ᶜurf* literally means 'that which is known'. In its primary sense, it is the known as opposed to the unknown, the familiar and customary as opposed to the unfamiliar and strange. *ᶜUrf* and *ᶜādah* are largely synonymous, and the majority of ulema have used them as such. Some observers have, however, distinguished the two, holding that *ᶜādah* means repetition or recurrent practice, and can be used with regard to both individuals and groups. We refer, for example, to the habits of individuals as their personal *ᶜādah*. But *ᶜurf* is not used in this capacity: we do not refer to the personal habits of individuals as their *ᶜurf*. It is the collective practice of a large number of people that is normally denoted by *ᶜurf*. The habits of a few or even a substantial minority within a group do not constitute *ᶜurf*.[1]

ᶜUrf is defined as 'recurring practices which are acceptable to people of sound nature.' This definition is clear on the point that custom, in order to constitute a valid basis for legal decisions, must be sound and reasonable. Hence recurring practices among some people in which there is no benefit or which partake in prejudice and corruption are excluded from the definition of *ᶜurf*.[2] *ᶜUrf* and its derivative, *maᶜrūf*, occur in the Qur'ān, and it is the latter of the two which occurs more frequently. *Maᶜrūf*, which literally means 'known' is, in its Qur'ānic usage, equated with good, while its opposite, the *munkar*, or 'strange', is equated with evil. It is mainly in this sense that *ᶜurf* and *maᶜrūf* seem to have been used in the Qur'ān. The commentators have generally interpreted *maᶜrūf* in the Qur'ān as denoting faith in God and His Messenger, and adherence to God's injunctions. Thus the standard commentary on the Qur'ānic phrase *ta'murūna bi al-maᶜrūf wa tanhawna ᶜan al-munkar* (Āl-ᶜImrān, 3:110) given by the exegetes is that 'you enjoin belief in God and in His

Messenger and enforce His laws, and you forbid disbelief and indulgence in the *ḥarām*.'[3] The same interpretation is given to the term '*ᶜurf*' in the text which occurs in sūra al-Aᶜrāf (7:199): 'Keep to forgiveness, enjoin *ᶜurf [wa'mur bi'l-ᶜurf]* and turn away from the ignorant.' According to the exegetes, *ᶜurf* in this context means fear of God and the observance of His commands and prohibitions. But occasionally, *maᶜrūf* in the Qur'ān occurs in the sense of good conduct, kindness and justice, especially when the term is applied to a particular situation. It is only when *ᶜurf* or *maᶜrūf* is ordered generally without reference to a particular matter, situation or problem that it carries the meaning of adhering to God's injunctions. The reason for the position taken by the exegetes becomes apparent if one bears in mind Islam's perspective on good and evil (*ḥusn wa-qubḥ*) which are, in principle, determined by divine revelation. Hence when God ordered the promotion of *maᶜrūf*, He could not have meant the good which reason or custom decrees to be such, but what He enjoins.[4] This would also explain why *ᶜurf* in the sense of custom is not given prominence in the legal theory of the *uṣūl al-fiqh*, although it carries some authority, as we shall presently explain.

Custom which does not contravene the principles of *Sharīᶜah* is valid and authoritative; it must be observed and upheld by a court of law. According to a legal maxim which is recorded by the Shāfiᶜī jurist al-Suyūṭī, in his well-known work, *al-Ashbāh wa al-Naẓā'ir*, 'What is proven by *ᶜurf* is like that which is proven by a *sharᶜī* proof.' This legal maxim is also recorded by the Ḥanafī jurist al-Sarakhsī, and was subsequently adopted in the Ottoman *Majallah* which provides that custom, whether general or specific, is enforceable and constitutes a basis of judicial decisions.[5] The ulema have generally accepted *ᶜurf* as a valid criterion for purposes of interpreting the Qur'ān. To give an example, the Qur'ānic commentators have referred to *ᶜurf* in determining the precise amount of maintenance that a husband must provide for his wife. This is the subject of sūra al-Ṭalāq (65:7) which provides: 'Let those who possess means pay according to their means.' In this *āyah*, the Qur'ān does not specify the exact amount of maintenance, which is to be determined by reference to custom. Similarly, in regard to the maintenance of children, the Qur'ān only specifies that this is the duty of the father, but leaves the quantum of maintenance to be determined by reference to custom (*bi'l-maᶜrūf*) (al-Baqarah, 2:233). The *Sharīᶜah* has, in principle, accredited approved custom as a valid ground in the determination of its rules relating to *ḥalāl* and *ḥarām*. This is in turn reflected in the practice of the *fuqahā'*, who have adopted *ᶜurf*, whether general or specific, as a valid criterion in the determination of the *aḥkām* of *Sharīᶜah*.[6] The rules of *fiqh* which are based in juristic opinion (*ra'y*) or in speculative analogy and *ijtihād* have often been formulated in the light of prevailing custom; it is therefore permissible to depart from them if the custom on which they were founded changes in the course of time. The *ijtihādī* rules of *fiqh* are, for the most part, changeable with changes of time and circumstance. To deny social change due recognition in the determination of the rules of *fiqh* would amount to exposing the people to hardship, which the *Sharīᶜah* forbids. Sometimes even the same *mujtahid* has changed his previous *ijtihād* with a view to bringing it into harmony with the prevailing custom. It is well-known, for example, that Imām al-Shāfiᶜī laid the foundations of his school in Iraq, but that when he went to Egypt, he changed some of his earlier views owing to the different customs he encountered in Egyptian society.[7]

Customs which were prevalent during the lifetime of the Prophet and were not expressly overruled by him are held to have received his tacit approval and become part of what is known as *Sunnah taqrīriyyah*. Pre-Islamic Arabian custom which was thus approved by the Prophet was later upheld by the Companions, who often referred to it through statements such as 'we used to do such-and-such while the Prophet was alive'.[8] Islam has thus retained many pre-Islamic Arabian customs while it has at the same time overruled the oppressive and corrupt practices of that society. Islam also attempted to amend and regulate some of the Arab customary laws with a view to bringing them into line with the principles of the *Sharīᶜah*. The reverse of this is also true in the sense that pre-Islamic customs of Arabia influenced the *Sharīᶜah* in its formative stages of development. Even in the area of the verbal and actual *Sunnah*, there are instances where Arabian custom has been upheld and incorporated within the *Sunnah* of the Prophet. An example of this is the rulings of the *Sunnah* concerning the liability of the kinsmen of an offender (i.e. the *ᶜāqilah*) for the payment of blood money, or *diyah*. Similarly, the *Sunnah* which regulates certain transactions such as mortgage (*rahn*), advance sale (*salam*) and the requirement of equality (*kafā'ah*) in marriage have their roots in the pre-Islamic custom of the Arabs. There are also vestiges of pre-Islamic custom in the area of inheritance, such as the significance that the rules of inheritance attach to the male line of relationship, known as the *ᶜaṣabah*. As for the post-Islamic custom of Arabian society, Imām Mālik has gone so far as to equate the *ᶜamal ahl al-Madīnah*, that is the customary practice of the people of Madinah, with *ijmāᶜ*. This type of *ᶜamal* (lit. 'practice') constitutes a source of law in the absence of an explicit ruling in the Qur'ān and *Sunnah*. Custom has also found its way into the *Sharīᶜah* through juristic preference (*istiḥsān*) and considerations of public interest (*maṣlaḥah*). And of course, *ijmāᶜ* itself has to a large extent served as a vehicle of assimilating customary rules which were in harmony with the *Sharīʿah*, or were based in necessity (*ḍarūrah*), into the general body of the *Sharīʿah*.[9]

Conditions of Valid *ʿUrf*

In addition to being reasonable and acceptable to people of sound nature, *ʿurf*, in order to be authoritative, must fulfil the following requirements.

1) *ʿUrf* must represent a common and recurrent phenomenon. The practice of a few individuals or of a limited number of people within a large community will not be authoritative, nor would a usage of this nature be upheld as the basis of a judicial decision in *Sharīʿah* courts. The substance of this condition is incorporated in the *Majallah al-Aḥkām al-ʿAdliyyah* where it is provided that 'effect is only given to custom which is of regular occurrence' (Art. 14). To give an example, when a person buys a house or a car, the question as to what is to be included in either of these is largely determined by custom, if this is not otherwise specified in the terms of the agreement. More specifically, one would need to refer to the common practice among estate agents or car dealers respectively. But if no custom could be established as such, or there are disparate practices of various sorts, no custom could be said to exist and no judicial order may be based on it. Custom, in order to be upheld, must not only be consistent but also dominant in the sense that it is observed in all or most of the cases to which it can apply. If it is observed only in some cases but not in others, it is not authoritative. Similarly, if there are two distinct customary practices on one and the same matter, the one which is dominant is to be upheld. If, for example, a sale is concluded in a city where two or three currencies are commonly accepted and the contract in question does not specify any, the one which is the more dominant and common will be deemed to apply.[10]
2) Custom must also be in existence at the time a transaction is concluded. In contracts and commercial transactions, effect is given only to customs which are prevalent at the time the transaction is concluded, and not to customs of subsequent origin. This condition is particularly relevant to the interpretation of documents, which are to be understood in the light of the custom that prevailed at the time they were written. Consequently, a rule of custom which is prevalent at the time the interpretation is attempted will not be relevant if it only became prevalent after the document was concluded. For it is generally assumed that documents which are not self-evident and require

clarification can only convey concepts that were common at the time they were written.[11]

3) Custom must not contravene the clear stipulation of an agreement. The general rule is that contractual agreements prevail over custom, and recourse to custom is only valid in the absence of an agreement. Since contractual agreements are stronger than custom, should there arise a conflict between them it will normally be determined in favour of the former. If for example the prevailing custom in regard to the provision of dower (*mahr*) in marriage requires the payment of one-half at the time of the conclusion of the contract and the remainder at a later date, but the contract clearly stipulates the prompt payment of the whole of the dower, the rule of custom would be of no account in the face of this stipulation. For custom is only to be invoked when no clear text can be found to determine the terms of a particular dispute; and whenever a clear text is in existence, recourse to custom will be out of the question. To give another example: the costs of formal registration in the sale of real property are customarily payable by the purchaser. But if there is a stipulation in the contract that specifically requires the vendor to bear those costs, then the custom will be of no account and the purchaser will not be required to pay the costs of registration.[12]

4) Lastly, custom must not violate the *naṣṣ*, that is, the definitive principle of the law. The opposition of custom to *naṣṣ* may either be absolute or partial. If it is the former, there is no doubt that custom must be set aside. Examples of such conflicts are encountered in the bedouin practice of disinheriting the female heirs, or the practice of usury (*ribā*) and wine-drinking. The fact that these are widely practiced is of no consequence, as in each case there is a prohibitory *naṣṣ*, or a command which always takes priority, and no concession or allowance is made for the practice in question. But if the conflict between custom and text is not absolute in that the custom opposes only certain aspects of the text, then custom is allowed to act as a limiting factor on the text. The contract of *istiṣnāᶜ*, that is, the order for the manufacture of goods at an agreed price, may serve as an example here. According to a Ḥadīth, 'the Prophet prohibited the sale of non-existing objects but he permitted *salam* (i.e. advance sale in which the price is determined but delivery postponed)'.[13]

نهى عن بيع ما ليس عند الانسان ورخص في
السلم

This Ḥadīth is general in that it applies to all varieties of sale in which the object of sale is not present at the time of contract. *Salam* was exceptionally permitted as it was deemed to be of benefit to the people. The general prohibition in this Ḥadīth would equally apply to *istiṣnāᶜ* as in this case too the object of sale is non-existent at the time of contract. But since *istiṣnāᶜ* was commonly practiced among people of all ages, the *fuqahā'* have validated it on grounds of general custom. The conflict between *istiṣnāᶜ* and the ruling of the Ḥadīth is not absolute, because the Ḥadīth has explicitly validated *salam*. If realisation of benefit to the people was the main ground of the concession that has been granted in respect of *salam*, then *istiṣnāᶜ* presents a similar case. Consequently the custom concerning *istiṣnāᶜ* is allowed to operate as a limiting factor on the textual ruling of the Ḥadīth in that the Ḥadīth is qualified by the custom concerning *istiṣnāᶜ*.

Another example where a general text is qualified by custom is when a person is appointed to act as agent (*wakīl*) for another in respect of concluding a particular contract such as sale or marriage. The agent's power to conclude the contract, although not limited by the terms of his appointment, is nevertheless qualified by the prevalent custom. In the matter of sale, for example, the expected price which represents the fair market price would be upheld, and the currency of the locality would be accepted in exchange.

According to a Ḥadīth, the Prophet is said to have forbidden conditional sale, that is, sale with conditions that may not be in agreement with the nature of this contract. An example of this would be when A sells his car to B for 10,000 dollars on condition that B sells his house to A for 50,000 dollars. The Ḥadīth quoted to this effect provides that the Prophet 'forbade sale coupled with a condition'.

إن النبي ﷺ نهى عن بيع وشرط

However, the majority of Ḥanafī and Mālikī jurists have validated conditions which are accepted by the people at large and which represent standard custom. Here again the general prohibition is retained, but only conditions that are adopted by *ᶜurf* are upheld; the general terms of the Ḥadīth are, in other words, qualified by custom.[14]

It would be useful in this connection to distinguish *ᶜurf* from *ijmāᶜ*, for they have much in common with one another, which is why they are sometimes confused. But despite their similarities, there are substantial differences between *ᶜurf* and *ijmāᶜ* which may be summarised as follows:

1) *ᶜUrf* materialises by the agreement of all, or the dominant majority of, the people and its existence is not affected by the exception or

disagreement of a few individuals. *Ijmāᶜ* on the other hand requires, for its conclusion, the consensus of all the *mujtahidūn* of the period or the generation in which it materialises. Disagreement and dissension has no place in *ijmāᶜ*, and any level of disagreement among the *mujtahidūn* invalidates *ijmāᶜ*.

2) Custom does not depend on the agreement of the *mujtahidūn*, but must be accepted by the majority of the people, including the *mujtahidūn*. The laymen have, on the other hand, no say in *ijmāᶜ* on juridical matters, which require the participation only of the learned members of the community.
3) The rules of *ᶜurf* are changeable, and a custom may in course of time give way to another custom or may simply disappear with a change of circumstances. But this is not the case with *ijmāᶜ*. Once an *ijmāᶜ* is concluded, it precludes fresh *ijtihād* on the same issue and is not open to abrogation or amendments. *ᶜUrf* on the other hand leaves open the possibility of fresh *ijtihād*, and a ruling of *ijtihād* which is founded in *ᶜurf* may be changed even if the *ᶜurf* in which it originates does not.
4) Lastly, *ᶜurf* requires an element of continuity in that it can only materialise if it exists over a period of time. *Ijmāᶜ* can, on the other hand, come into existence whenever the *mujtahidūn* reach a unanimous agreement which, in principle, requires no continuity for its conclusion.[15]

Types of Custom

Custom is initially divided into two types, namely verbal (*qawlī*) and actual (*fiᶜlī*). Verbal *ᶜurf* consists of the general agreement of the people on the usage and meaning of words deployed for purposes other than their literal meaning. As a result of such agreement, the customary meaning tends to become dominant and the original or literal meaning is reduced to the status of an exception. There are many examples in the Qur'ān and *Sunnah* of words which have been used for a meaning other than their literal one, which were as a result commonly accepted by popular usage. Words such as *ṣalāh, zakāh* and *ḥajj* have been used in the Qur'ān for purposes other than their literal meanings, and this usage eventually became dominant to the extent that the literal meaning of these words was consigned to obscurity. The verbal custom concerning the use of these words thus originated in the Qur'ān and was subsequently accepted by popular custom. We also find instances of divergences between the literal and the customary meanings of words in the Qur'ān where the literal meaning is applied regardless of the customary meaning. The word *walad*, for example, is used in the Qur'ān in its literal sense, that is 'offspring' whether a son or daughter (note sūra al-Nisā', 4:11), but in its popular usage *walad* is used for sons only.

Another example is *laḥm*, that is, meat, which in its Qur'ānic usage includes fish, but in its customary usage is applied only to meat other than fish. Whenever words of this nature, that is, words which have acquired a different meaning in customary usage, occur in contracts, oaths and commercial transactions, their customary meaning will prevail. For example, when a person takes an oath that he will never 'set foot' in so-and-so's house, what is meant by this expression is the customary meaning, namely, actually entering the house. In this sense, the person will have broken the oath if he enters the house while never 'setting foot', such as by entering the house while mounted. But if he only technically sets his foot in the house without entering it, he will not be liable to expiation (*kaffārah*) for breaking his oath.[16] For this would not amount to what is customarily meant by 'setting foot' in the house.

Actual *ᶜurf* consists of commonly recurrent practices which are accepted by the people. An example of actual *ᶜurf* is the give-and-take sale, or *bayᶜ al-taᶜāṭī*, which is normally concluded without utterances of offer and acceptance. Similarly, customary rules regarding the payment of dower in marriage may require a certain amount to be paid at the time of contract and the rest at a later date. The validity of this type of custom is endorsed by the legal maxim which reads: 'What is accepted by *ᶜurf* is tantamount to a stipulated agreement (*al-maᶜrūf ᶜurfan ka'l-mashrūṭ sharṭan*).' Consequently, actual *ᶜurf* is to be upheld and applied in the absence of an agreement to the contrary.

ᶜUrf, whether actual or verbal, is once again divided into the two types of general and special: *al-ᶜurf al-ᶜāmm* and *al-ᶜurf al-khāṣṣ* respectively. A general *ᶜurf* is one which is prevalent everywhere and on which the people agree regardless of the passage of time. A typical example of this is *bayᶜ al-taᶜāṭī* to which reference has already been made. Similarly, the customary practice of charging a fixed price for entry to public baths is another example of general *ᶜurf*, which is anomalous to the strict requirements of sale (as it entails consuming an unknown quantity of water) but the people have accepted it and it is therefore valid. It will be further noted that in their formulation of the doctrine of *istiḥsān*, the Ḥanafī jurists have validated departure from a ruling of *qiyās* in favour of general *ᶜurf*. This has already been elaborated in the separate chapter on *istiḥsān*.[17]

"Special custom" is *ᶜurf* which is prevalent in a particular locality, profession or trade. By its very nature, it is not a requirement of this type of *ᶜurf* that it be accepted by people everywhere. According to the preferred view of the Ḥanafī school, special *ᶜurf* does not qualify the general provisions of the *naṣṣ*, although some Ḥanafī jurists have held otherwise. Consequently, this type of *ᶜurf* is entirely ignored when it is found to be in conflict with the *naṣṣ*. The general rule to be stated here is that the *aḥkām* of *Sharīᶜah* pertaining to the authority of *ᶜurf* only contemplate the provisions of general *ᶜurf*. A ruling of *qiyās*, especially *qiyās* whose effective cause is not expressly stated in the *naṣṣ*, that is, *qiyās ghayr manṣūṣ al-ᶜillah*, may be abandoned in favour of a general *ᶜurf*, but will prevail if it conflicts with special *ᶜurf*. A number of prominent ulema have, however, given the *fatwā* that special *ᶜurf* should command the same authority as general *ᶜurf* in this respect. The reason why general *ᶜurf* is given priority over *qiyās* is that the former is indicative of the people's need, whose disregard may amount to an imposition of hardship on them. Some Ḥanafī jurists like Ibn al-Humām have taught that *ᶜurf* in this situation commands an authority equivalent to that of *ijmāᶜ*, and that as such it must be given priority over *qiyās*. It is perhaps relevant here to add that Abū Ḥanīfah's disciple, al-Shaybānī, validated the sale of honeybees and silkworms as this was commonly practiced during his time despite the analogical ruling that Abū Ḥanīfah had given against it on the grounds that they did not amount to a valuable commodity (*māl*). Furthermore, the ulema have recorded the view that since *ᶜurf* is given priority over *qiyās* despite the fact that *qiyās* originates in the *nuṣūṣ* of the Qur'ān and *Sunnah*, it will *a fortiori* be preferred over considerations of public interest (*maṣlaḥah*) which are not rooted in the *nuṣūṣ*. Having said this, however, it would seem that cases of conflict between general *ᶜurf* and *maṣlaḥah* would be rather rare. For *ᶜurf* by definition must be sound and reasonable, considerations which tend to bring *ᶜurf* close to *maṣlaḥah*. For after all, *ᶜurf* and *maṣlaḥah* each in their respective capacities serve as a means for the realisation of public welfare and the prevention of hardship to people.

And lastly, from the viewpoint of its conformity or otherwise with the *Sharīᶜah*, custom is once again divided into the two types of approved or valid custom (*al-ᶜurf al-ṣaḥīḥ*) and disapproved custom (*al-ᶜurf al-fāsid*). As is indicated in the terms of these expressions, the approved *ᶜurf* is one which is observed by the people at large without there being any indication in the *Sharīᶜah* that it contravenes any of its principles. The disapproved custom is also practiced by the people but there is evidence to show that it is repugnant to the principles of *Sharīᶜah*. We have already referred to the bedouin practice of disinheriting female relatives, and the prevalence of *ribā*, which although commonly practiced are both in clear violation of the *Sharīᶜah*, and as such represent examples of *al-ᶜurf al-fāsid*.[18]

Proof (*Ḥujjiyyah*) of *ᶜUrf*

Although the ulema have attempted to locate textual authority for *ᶜurf* in the Qur'ān, their attempt has not been free of difficulties. To begin with, reference is usually made to the Qur'ānic text in sūra al-Ḥajj (22:78) which provides: 'God has not laid upon you any hardship in religion.' This is obviously not a direct authority on the subject, but it is argued that ignoring the prevailing *ᶜurf* which does not conflict with the *nuṣūṣ* of *Sharīᶜah* is likely to lead to inflicting hardship on the people, which must be avoided. The next *āyah* which is quoted in support of *ᶜurf* occurs in sūra al-Aᶜrāf (7:199), but although this has a direct reference to *ᶜurf*, difficulties have been encountered in identifying it as its main authority. This *āyah*, to which a reference has already been made, enjoins the Prophet to 'keep to forgiveness, and enjoin *ᶜurf*, and turn away from the ignorant'. According to the Mālikī jurist Shihāb al-Dīn al-Qarāfī, this *āyah* is explicit and provides a clear authority for *ᶜurf*. According to this view *ᶜurf* is clearly upheld in the Qur'ān as a proof of *Sharīᶜah* and an integral part of it.[19] The generality of ulema, however, maintain the view that the reference to *ᶜurf* in this *āyah* is to the literal meaning of the word, that is, to the familiar and good, and not to custom as such. But then it is added: bearing in mind that approved custom is normally upheld by people of sound nature and intellect, the Qur'ānic concept of '*ᶜurf*' comes close to the technical meaning of this word. The literal or the Qur'ānic meaning of *ᶜurf*, in other words, corroborates its technical meaning and the two usages of the word are in essential harmony with one another. The commentators, however, further add that since the word '*ᶜurf*' in this *āyah* can mean many things, including 'profession of the faith', 'that which the people consider good', and of course 'that which is familiar and known', as well as *ᶜurf* in the sense of custom, it cannot be quoted as textual authority for custom as such.[20] Among the indirect evidence in support of *ᶜurf* the ulema have also quoted the following saying of the prominent Companion, ᶜAbd Allāh b. Masᶜūd, that 'what the Muslims deem to be good is good in the sight of God'.

ما رآه المسلمون حسناً فهو حسن عند الله

Although many scholars have considered this to be a Ḥadīth from the Prophet, it is more likely, as al-Shāṭibī points out, to be a saying of ᶜAbd Allāh b. Masᶜūd.[21] The critics have, however, suggested that this saying/Ḥadīth refers to the approval of '*al-muslimūn*', that is, all the Muslims, whereas *ᶜurf* varies from place to place, and the approval of all Muslims in its favour cannot be taken for granted. In response to this, it has been further suggested that '*muslimūn*' in this context only denotes those among them who possess sound intellect and judgement, and not necessarily every individual member of the Muslim community.[22]

The upshot of this whole debate over the authoritativeness of ᶜ*urf* seems to be that notwithstanding the significant role that it has played in the development of the *Sharīᶜah*, it is not an independent proof in its own right. The reluctance of the ulema in recognising ᶜ*urf* as a proof has been partly due to the circumstantial character of the principle, in that it is changeable upon changes of conditions of time and place. This would mean that the rules of *fiqh* which have at one time been formulated in the light of the prevailing custom would be liable to change when the same custom is no longer prevalent. The differential *fatwās* that the later ulema of different schools have occasionally given in opposition to those of their predecessors on the same issues are reflective of the change of custom on which the *fatwā* was founded in the first place. In addition, since custom is basically unstable it is often difficult to ascertain its precise terms. These terms may not be self-evident, and the frequent absence of written records and documents might add to the difficulty of verification.[23]

The issue has perhaps become even more complex in modern times. Owing to a variety of new factors, modern societies have experienced a disintegration of their traditional patterns of social organisation. The accelerated pace of social change in modern times is likely to further undermine the stability of social customs and organisations. The increased mobility of the individual in terms of socio-economic status, massive urbanisation and the unprecedented shift of populations to major urban centres, and so forth, tend to interfere with the stability and continuity of ᶜ*urf*.

Another factor which merits attention in this context is the development of statutory legislation as an instrument of government in modern times. The attempt to codify the law into self-contained statutes has to some extent reduced the need to rely on social custom as the basis of decision-making. But even so, it would be far from accurate to say that custom has ceased to play an important role both as a source of law and a basis of judicial decision-making. This is perhaps evident from the general reference to custom as a supplementary source of law in the civil codes of many Islamic countries of today. The typical style of reference to custom in such statutes appears to be that custom is authoritative in the absence of a provision in the statute concerning a particular dispute.

The *fuqahā'* of the later ages (*muta'akhkhirūn*) are on record as having changed the rulings of the earlier jurists which were based in custom owing to subsequent changes in the custom itself. The examples which are given below will show that the jurists have on the whole accepted ᶜ*urf* not only as a valid basis of *ijtihād* but also as the key indicator of the need for legal reform:

1) Under the rules of *fiqh*, a man who causes harm to another by giving him false information is not responsible for the damage he has caused. The rule of *fiqh* that applies to such cases is that the *mubāshir*, that is, the one who acted directly, is responsible for the losses. However owing to the spread of dishonesty and corruption, the later *fuqahā'* have validated a departure from this rule in favour of holding the false reporter responsible for the losses caused.[24]
2) According to Imām Abū Ḥanīfah, when the *qāḍī* personally trusts the reliability of a witness who testifies before him, there is no need for recourse to cross-examination or *tazkiyah*. This ruling is based on the Ḥadīth which provides that 'Muslims are *ʿudūl* [i.e. upright and trustworthy] in relationship to one another'.

المسلمون عدول بعضهم على بعض

Abū Ḥanīfah's ruling was obviously deemed appropriate for the time in which it was formulated. But experience in later times aroused concern over dishonesty and lying by witnesses. It was consequently considered necessary to take precautions so as to prevent perjury, and the ulema reached the opinion that *tazkiyah* should be applied as a standard practice to all witnesses. Abū Ḥanīfah's disciples are reported to have given a *fatwā* in favour of making *tazkiyah* a regular judicial practice. Consequently *tazkiyah* was held to be a condition for admitting the testimony of witnesses, and a ruling was formulated to the effect that no testimony without *tazkiyah* may constitute the basis of a court decision.[25]
3) According to the accepted rule of the Ḥanafī school, which is attributed to Abū Ḥanīfah himself, no-one was allowed to charge any fees for teaching the Qur'ān, or the principles of the faith. For teaching these subjects was held to be a form of worship (*ʿibādah*) and no reward for it was to be expected from anyone other than God. But subsequent experience showed that some people were reluctant to teach the Qur'ān, and an incentive by way of remuneration was considered necessary in order to encourage the teaching of Islam. Consequently the *fuqahā'* gave a *fatwā* in favour of charging fees for teaching the Qur'ān.[26]
4) Among the rules of *fiqh* which have tended to 'change with the change of custom', there is one concerning the determination of the age by which a missing person (*mafqūd*) is to be declared dead. According to the generally accepted view, the missing person must not be declared dead until he reaches the age at which his contemporaries would normally be expected to die. Consequently the jurists of the Ḥanafī-

school have variously determined this age at seventy, ninety and one hundred, and their respective rulings have taken into consideration the changes of experience and conditions that prevailed at the time the new rulings were formulated.[27]

5) And lastly, in the area of transactions, the concept of *al-ghabn al-fāḥish*, that is, radical discrepancy between the market price of a commodity and the actual price charged to the customer, is determined with reference to *ᶜurf*. To ascertain what margin of discrepancy in a particular transaction amounts to *al-ghabn al-fāḥish* is determined by reference to the practice among tradesmen and people who are engaged in similar transactions. Since these practices are liable to change, the changes are in turn reflected in the determination of what might amount to *al-ghabn al-fāḥish*.[28]

NOTES

1. Badrān, *Uṣūl*, p. 224; Ziadeh, 'ᶜUrf and Law', p. 60; Ismāᶜīl, *Adillah*, p. 389.
2. Mahmassānī, *Falsafah* (Ziadeh's trans.), p. 132; Ismāᶜīl, *Adillah*, p. 388; Badrān, *Uṣūl*, p. 224.
3. Ṭabarī, *Tafsīr*, (Būlāq 1323–29), IV, 30; Ziadeh, 'ᶜUrf and Law', pp. 60–61; Ismāᶜīl, *Adillah*, p. 401.
4. Cf. Ziadeh, 'ᶜUrf and Law', p. 62.
5. *The Mejelle* (Tyser's trans.) (Art. 36); Abū Zahrah, *Uṣūl*, p. 216; Mahmassānī, *Falsafah*, p. 132.
6. Ṣābūni, *Madkhal*, p. 138; Ismāᶜīl, *Adillah*, p. 403.
7. Abū Zahrah, *Uṣūl*, p. 217; Aghnides, *Muhammedan Theories*, p. 82.
8. Ziadeh, 'ᶜUrf and Law', p. 62; Abdul Rahim, *Jurisprudence*, p. 137; Mahmassānī, *Falsafah*, p. 132.
9. Mahmassānī, *Falsafah*, p. 132; Ṣābūnī, *Madkhal*, p. 143; Badrān, *Uṣūl*, p. 242.
10. Mahmassānī, *Falsafah*, pp. 133–134; Ṣābūnī, *Madkhal*, pp. 139–140; Ismāᶜīl, *Adillah*, pp. 398–399.
11. Mahmassānī, *Falsafah*, p. 134; Ṣābūnī, *Madkhal*, p. 143.
12. Ismāᶜīl, *Adillah*, p. 400.
13. Bukhārī, *Ṣaḥīḥ*, III, 44 (*Kitāb al-Salam*, Ḥadīth nos. 1–3); Badrān, *Uṣūl*, p. 121.
14. Shawkānī, *Irshād*, p. 161; Abū Zahrah, *Uṣūl*, p. 217; Badrān, *Uṣūl*, p. 230.
15. Badrān, *Uṣūl*, p. 225; Ismāᶜīl, *Adillah*, p. 291.
16. Ismāᶜīl, *Adillah*, pp. 392–393; Ṣābūnī, *Madkhal*, p. 137; Badrān, *Uṣūl*, p. 226.
17. Abū Zahrah, *Uṣūl*, p. 217; Ṣābūnī, *Madkhal*, p. 138; Aghnides, *Muhammedan Theories*, p. 81.
18. Badrān, *Uṣūl*, p. 231; Ismāᶜīl, *Adillah*, p. 393.
19. Qarāfī, *Furūq*, II, 85; Ṣābūnī, *Madkhal*, p. 143; Badrān, *Uṣūl*, p. 226.
20. Ṭabarī, *Tafsīr*, IV, 30; Ismāᶜīl, *Adillah*, pp. 401–402; Ziadeh, 'ᶜUrf and Law', pp. 61–62.
21. Shāṭibī, *Iᶜtiṣām*, II, 319. Mahmassānī (*Falsafah*, p. 77) has also reached the conclusion that this is the saying of ᶜAbd Allāh b. Masᶜūd. But Āmidī (*Iḥkām*, I, 214) has quoted it as a Ḥadīth.

22. Cf. Ismāʿīl, *Adillah*, p. 402.
23. Cf. Badrān, *Uṣūl*, p. 233.
24. Abū Zahrah, *Uṣūl*, p. 218.
25. Bayhaqī, *al-Sunan al-Kubrā*, X, 155–56; Abū Zahrah, *Uṣūl*, p. 219; Ṣābūnī, *Madkhal*, pp. 144–45.
26. Abū Zahrah, *Uṣūl*, p. 219.
27. Ṣābūnī, *Madkhal*, p. 145.
28. Ibid.

CHAPTER FIFTEEN

Istiṣḥāb (Presumption of Continuity)

Literally, *istiṣḥāb* means 'escorting' or 'companionship'. Technically, *istiṣḥāb* denotes a rational proof which may be employed in the absence of other indications; specifically, those facts, or rules of law and reason, whose existence or non-existence had been proven in the past, and which are presumed to remain so for lack of evidence to establish any change. The technical meaning of *istiṣḥāb* relates to its literal meaning in the sense that the past 'accompanies' the present without any interruption or change.[1] *Istiṣḥāb* is validated by the Shāfiʿī school, the Ḥanbalīs, the Ẓāhirīs and the Shīʿah Imāmiyyah, but the Ḥanafīs, the Mālikīs and the *mutakallimūn*, including Abū al-Ḥusayn al-Baṣrī do not consider it a proof in its own right. The opponents of *istiṣḥāb* are of the view that establishing the existence of a fact in the past is no proof of its continued existence. The continued existence of the original state is still in need of proof in the same way as the claim which seeks to establish that the original condition has changed.[2]

For the Shāfiʿīs and the Ḥanbalīs, *istiṣḥāb* denotes 'continuation of that which is proven and the negation of that which had not existed'. *Istiṣḥāb*, in other words, presumes the continuation of both the positive and the negative until the contrary is established by evidence. In its positive sense, *istiṣḥāb* requires, for example, that once a contract of sale (or of marriage for that matter), is concluded, it is presumed to remain in force until there is a change. Thus the ownership of the purchaser, and the marital status of the spouses, are presumed to continue until a transfer of ownership, or dissolution of marriage, can be established by evidence. Since both of these contracts are permanently valid under the *Sharīʿah* and do not admit of any time limits it is reasonable to presume their continuity until there is evidence to the contrary. A mere possibility that the property in question might have been sold, or that the marriage might have been dissolved, is not enough to rebut the presumption of *istiṣḥāb*.[3] However, if the law only validates a contract on a temporary basis, such as lease and hire (*ijārah*), then *istiṣḥāb* cannot presume its continuity on a permanent basis. The contract will continue to operate within the specified period and terminate when the period expires.

Istiṣḥāb also presumes the continuation of the negative. For example, A purchases a hunting dog from B with the proviso that it has been trained to hunt, but then A claims that the dog is untrained. A's claim will be acceptable under *istiṣḥāb* unless there is evidence to the contrary. For *istiṣḥāb* maintains the natural state of things, which in the case of animals is the absence of training.[4]

Presumption of continuity under *istiṣḥāb* is different from the continued validity of a rule of law in a particular case. The false accuser, for example, may never be admitted as a witness, a rule which is laid down in a clear Qur'ānic text (al-Nūr, 24:5). The permanent validity of the *ḥukm* in this case is established by the legal text, which is in no need of any presumption. *Istiṣḥāb* only applies when no other evidence (*dalīl*) is available, which is obviously not the case when there is a clear text that could be invoked.[5]

Since *istiṣḥāb* consists of a probability, namely the presumed continuity of the *status quo ante*, it is not a strong ground for the deduction of the rules of *Sharīᶜah*. Hence when *istiṣḥāb* comes into conflict with another proof, the latter takes priority. As it is, *istiṣḥāb* is the last ground of *fatwā*: when the jurist is asked about the ruling of a particular case, he must first search for a solution in the Qur'ān, the *Sunnah*, consensus of opinion, and *qiyās*. If a solution is still wanting, he may resort to *istiṣḥāb* in either its positive or negative capacities. Should there be doubt over the non-existence of something, it will be presumed to exist, but if the doubt is in the proof of something, the presumption will be that it is not proven. In the case of a missing person, for example, the nature of the situation is such that no other proof of *Sharīᶜah* could be employed to determine the question of his life or death. Since the main feature of the doubt concerning a missing person is the possibility of his death, *istiṣḥāb* will presume that he is still alive. But in the event of an unsubstantiated claim when, for example, A claims that B owes him a sum of money, the doubt here is concerned with the proof over the existence of a debt, which will be presumed unproven.[6]

With regard to the determination of the rules of law that may be applicable to a particular issue, the presumption of *istiṣḥāb* is also guided by the general norms of the *Sharīᶜah*. The legal norm concerning foods, drinks, and clothes, for example, is permissibility (*ibāḥah*). When a question arises as to the legality of a particular kind of beverage or food, and there is no other evidence to determine its value, recourse may be had to *istiṣḥāb*, which will presume that it is permissible. But when the norm in regard to something is prohibition, such as cohabitation between members of the opposite sex, the presumption will be one of prohibition, unless there is evidence to prove its legality.

Istiṣḥāb is supported by both *sharʿī* and rational (*ʿaqlī*) evidences. Reason tells us that in God's order of creation and in popular custom, it is normal to expect that pledges, contracts and laws will probably continue to remain operative until the contrary is established by evidence. It is equally normal to expect that things which had not existed will probably remain so until the contrary is proved. When reasonable men (*ʿuqalāʾ*) and men who comply with the accepted norms of society (*ahl al-ʿurf*) have known of the existence or non-existence of something, as al-Āmidī observes, from that point onwards they tend to formulate their judgements on the basis of what they know, until they are assured by their own observation or evidence that there is a change.[7] Reason also tells us not to accept claims, unsubstantiated by evidence, that suggest a change in a *status quo* which is otherwise expected to continue. Hence a mere claim that a just person (*ʿādil*) has become a profligate (*fāsiq*) will be of no account, and the person will be presumed to be *ʿādil* until the contrary is established. Similarly, when a student is admitted and registered for a degree course his status as a student remains unchanged until there is evidence to suggest that this is no longer the case. But until then there is no need for him to prove his status every week or every month.[8]

To presume the continuity of something which might have been present or absent in the past, as al-Āmidī points out, is equivalent to a *ẓann* which is valid evidence in juridical (*sharʿī*) matters, and action upon it is justified.[9] The rules of *Sharīʿah* continue to remain valid until there is a change in the law or in the subject to which it is applied. The Law, for example, has forbidden the consumption of wine, a ruling which will remain in force until there is a state of emergency or the wine loses its intoxicating quality, such as by being changed into vinegar.

Varieties of *Istiṣḥāb*

From the viewpoint of the nature of the conditions that are presumed to continue, *istiṣḥāb* is divided into four types, as follows:

1) Presumption of original absence (*istiṣḥāb al-ʿadam al-aṣlī*), which means that a fact or rule of law which had not existed in the past is presumed to be non-existent until the contrary is proved. Thus a child

and an uneducated person are presumed to remain so until there is a change in their status, for example by attaining majority, or obtaining educational qualifications respectively. Similarly if A, who is a trading partner to B, claims that he has made no profit, the presumption of absence will be in A's favour unless B can prove otherwise. Another area which is determined by the presumption of original absence is the original freedom from liability, or the presumption of innocence, which will be separately discussed later.[10]

2) Presumption of original presence (*istiṣḥāb al-wujūd al-aṣlī*). This variety of *istiṣḥāb* takes for granted the presence or existence of that which is indicated by the law or reason. For example, when A is known to be indebted to B, A is presumed such until it is proved that he has paid the debt or was acquitted of it. Provided that B's loan to A is proven in the first place as a fact, this is sufficient to give rise to the presumption of its continuity and B need not prove the continuity of the loan in question every day of the month. Similarly, under the presumption of original presence, the purchaser is presumed liable to pay the purchase price by virtue of the presence of the contract of sale until it is proved that he has paid it. By the same token, a husband is liable to pay his wife the dower (*mahr*) by virtue of the existence of a valid marriage contract. In all these instances, *istiṣḥāb* presumes the presence of a liability or a right until an indication to the contrary is found. The ulema are in agreement on the validity of this type of *istiṣḥāb*, which must prevail until the contrary is proved.[11]

3) *Istiṣḥāb al-ḥukm*, or *istiṣḥāb* which presumes the continuity of the general rules and principles of the law. As earlier stated, *istiṣḥāb* is not only concerned with presumption of facts but also with the established rules and principles of the law. *Istiṣḥāb* thus takes for granted the continued validity of the provisions of the *Sharīᶜah* in regard to permissibility and prohibition (*ḥalāl* and *ḥarām*). When there is a ruling in the law, whether prohibitory or permissive, it will be presumed to continue until the contrary is proved. But when there is no such ruling available, recourse will be had to the principle of *ibāḥah*, which is the general norm of *Sharīᶜah* law concerning a matter that is deemed beneficial and free of evil consequences. Hence when the law is silent on a matter and it is not repugnant to reason it will be presumed to be permissible. This is the majority view, although some Muᶜtazilah have held a variant opinion, which is that the general norm in *Sharīᶜah* is prohibition unless there is an indication to the contrary. The principle of permissibility (*ibāḥah*) originates in the Qur'ān, in particular those of its passages which subjugate the earth and its resources to the welfare of man. Thus we read in sūra al-Baqarah

(2:29): 'It is He who has created for you all that is in the earth,' and in sūra al-Jāthiyah (45:13) that 'God has subjugated to you all that is in the heavens and in the earth.' These Qur'ānic declarations take for granted that man should be able to utilise the resources of the world around him to his advantage, which is another way of saying that he is generally permitted to act in the direction of securing his benefits unless he has been expressly prohibited. Hence all objects, legal acts, contracts and exchange of goods and services which are beneficial to human beings are lawful on grounds of original *ibāḥah*.[12] But when the legal norm in regard to something is prohibition, then *istiṣḥāb* presumes its continuity until there is evidence to suggest that it is no longer prohibited.

4) *Istiṣḥāb al-waṣf*, or continuity of attributes, such as presuming clean water (purity being an attribute) to remain so until the contrary is established to be the case (for example, through a change in its colour or taste). Similarly, when a person makes an ablution to perform the *ṣalāh*, the attribute of ritual purity (*ṭahārah*) is presumed to continue until it is vitiated. A mere doubt that it might have been vitiated is not sufficient to nullify *ṭahārah*. By the same token, a guarantor (*kafīl* – *kafālah* being a juridical attribute) remains responsible for the debt of which he is guarantor until he or the debtor pays it or when the creditor acquits him from payment.[13]

The jurists are in agreement on the validity, in principle, of the first three types of *istiṣḥāb*, although they have differed in their detailed implementation, as we shall presently discuss. As for the fourth type of *istiṣḥāb*, which relates to the attributes, whether new or well-established, it is a subject on which the jurists have disagreed. The Shāfiʿī and the Ḥanbalī schools have upheld it absolutely, whereas the Ḥanafī and Mālikī schools accept it with reservations. The case of the missing person is discussed under this variety of *istiṣḥāb*, as the question is mainly concerned with the continuity of his life – life being the attribute. Since the missing person (*mafqūd*) was alive at the time when he disappeared, he is presumed to be alive unless there is proof that he has died. He is therefore entitled, under the Shāfiʿī and Ḥanbalī doctrines, to inherit from a relative who dies while he is still a missing person. But no-one is entitled to inherit from him for the obvious reason that he is presumed alive. Yet under the Ḥanafī and Mālikī law, the missing person neither inherits from others nor can others inherit from him. The Ḥanafīs and Mālikīs accept *istiṣḥāb al-waṣf* only as a means of defence, that is, to defend the continued existence of an attribute, but not as a means of proving new rights and new attributes. *Istiṣḥāb* can therefore not be used as a means of acquiring new rights for the missing person, but can be used so as to protect all of his existing rights. To use a common expression, *istiṣḥāb* can only be used as a shield, not as a sword. If, for example, the missing person had owned property at the time of his disappearance, he continues to be the owner. Similarly his marital rights are presumed to continue, just as he remains responsible to discharge his obligations until his death is established by evidence or by a judicial decree. But for as long as he remains a missing person, he will not be given a share in inheritance or bequest, although a share will be reserved for him until the facts of his life or death are established. If he is declared dead, the reserved share will be distributed among the other heirs on the assumption that he was dead at the time of the death of his relative. Upon declaration of his death his own estate will be distributed among his heirs as of the time the court declares him dead. This is the position under the Ḥanafī and Mālikī schools, which maintain that although the *mafqūd* is presumed to be alive, this is only a presumption, not a fact, and may therefore not be used as a basis for the creation of new rights.[14] The question may arise: why can his heirs not inherit from the *mafqūd*? If nothing is certain, perhaps his heirs could be assigned their shares, or the shares may be reserved in their names until the facts are known. In response to this, the Ḥanafīs invoke the principle of "original absence", which means here that a right to inheritance is originally absent and will be presumed so until there is positive proof that it has materialised.[15]

The Shāfiʿīs and the Ḥanbalīs have, on the other hand, validated *istiṣḥāb* in both its defensive (*li-dafʿ*) and affirmative (*li-kasb*) capacities, that is, both as a shield and as a sword. Hence the *mafqūd* is presumed to be alive in the same way as he was at the time of his disappearance right up to the time when he is declared dead. The *mafqūd* is not only entitled to retain all his rights but can acquire new rights such as gifts, inheritance and bequests.[16]

It thus appears that the jurists are in disagreement, not necessarily on the principle, but on the detailed application of *istiṣḥāb*. The Ḥanafīs and Mālikīs who accept *istiṣḥāb* on a restricted basis have argued that the existence of something in the past cannot prove that it continues to exist. They have further pointed out that an over-reliance on *istiṣḥāb* is likely to open the door to uncertainty, even conflict, in the determination of *aḥkām*. The main area of juristic disagreement in this connection is the identification of what exactly the original state which is presumed to continue by means of *istiṣḥāb* might be. This is a question which permeates the application of *istiṣḥāb* in its various capacities, which is, perhaps, why the Ḥanbalī scholar Ibn al-Qayyim is critical of over-reliance on *istiṣḥāb* and of those who have employed it more extensively than they should.[17] The following illustrations, which are given in the context of legal maxims that originate in *istiṣḥāb*, also serve to show how the ulema have differed on the application of this doctrine to various issues. Some of the well-known legal maxims which are founded in *istiṣḥāb* may be outlined as follows:

1) Certainty may not be disproved by doubt (*al-yaqīn la yazūl bi'l-shakk*). For example, when someone is known to be sane, he will be presumed such until it is established that he has become insane. The presumption can only be set aside with certainty, not by a mere doubt. Similarly, when a person eats in the early morning during Ramadan while in doubt as to the possibility that he might have eaten after dawn, his fast remains intact and no belated performance (*qaḍā'*) is necessary by way of compensation. To identify the two elements of the maxim under discussion, namely the certainty and doubt in this example, night represents certainty whereas daybreak is the state of doubt, and the former prevails over the latter. However, the same rule would lead us to a totally different result if it were applied to the situation of a person who ends his fast late in the day in Ramadan while in doubt as to the occurrence of sunset. In this case, his fast is vitiated and a belated performance would be required in compensation. For the certainty which prevails here is the daytime which is presumed to continue, while the onset of night is in doubt. To say that certainty prevails over doubt in this case means that the fast has been terminated during the day, which is held to be the prevailing state of certainty.[18]

To illustrate some of the difficulties that are encountered in the implementation of the maxim under discussion, we may give in example the case of a person who repudiates his wife by *ṭalāq* but is in doubt as to the precise terms of his pronouncement: whether it amounted to a single or a triple *ṭalāq*. According to the majority of jurists, only a single *ṭalāq* takes place, which means that the husband is still entitled to revocation (*rijᶜah*) and may resume normal marital relations. Imām Mālik has, on the other hand, held that a triple *ṭalāq* takes place, which would preclude the right to revocation. The difference between the majority opinion and that of Imām Mālik arises from the variant interpretations that they give to the question of certainty and doubt. The majority view presumes the marriage to be the state of certainty which would continue until its dissolution is established by evidence. The doubt in this case is the pronouncement of *ṭalāq*. The doubtful *ṭalāq*, according to the majority, may not be allowed to disprove a certain fact. The marriage is certain and the *ṭalāq* is doubtful, hence the former is presumed to continue.

Imām Mālik, on the other hand, considers the occurrence of a divorce to be the certainty in this case. What is in doubt is the husband's right to the revocation of the *ṭalāq*. As for determining the precise number of *ṭalāqs*, which is crucial to the question of revocation, Imām Mālik holds that the right to revocation cannot be established by a mere doubt. Hence the husband has no right to revocation, which means that the divorce is final.[19]

While the majority of jurists consider marriage to be the certain factor in this case, for Imām Mālik it is the actual pronouncement of *ṭalāq*, regardless of the form it might have taken, which represents the state of certainty and the basis on which *istiṣḥāb* must operate. While commenting on these differences, both Ibn al-Qayyim and Abū Zahrah have considered the majority decision to be preferable. The marriage in this case must therefore not be allowed to be disproved by a doubtful *ṭalāq*.[20]

To give yet another example: when a man repudiates one of his two wives, but is not certain as to which one, according to the Mālikīs the certain fact is that a *ṭalāq* has been pronounced, while the uncertainty in this case is the identity of the divorcee. Both are divorced, on grounds of *istiṣḥāb*, which establishes that certainty must prevail over doubt. For the majority of ulema, however, the certain fact is that the man has two wives, in other words, the existence of a valid marriage in respect of both. The doubt concerning the identity of the divorcee must not be allowed to disprove the state of certainty, namely the marriage. Hence neither of the two are divorced.[21] Once again the juristic disagreement in this case arises from the differential perception of the ulema as to identifying the state of certainty on which the rules of *istiṣḥāb* must operate.

2) Presumption of generality until the general is subjected to limitation is another maxim that originates in *istiṣḥāb*. The general (*ᶜāmm*) must therefore remain *ᶜāmm* in its application until it is qualified in some way.

Just as a general text remains general until it is specified, so is the validity of that text, which is presumed to continue until it is abrogated. This would mean that a legal text remains valid and must be implemented as such unless it is abrogated or replaced by another text.[22] While discussing the maxim under discussion, al-Shawkānī records the variant view which is held by some ulema to the effect that the rule of law in these situations is established through the interpretation of words and not by the application of *istiṣḥāb*.[23] To say that a text is general or specified, or that a text remains valid and has not been abrogated, is thus determined on grounds of interpretation of words and not by the application of *istiṣḥāb*. For example, the

Qur'ānic rule which assigns to the male a double share of the female in inheritance (al-Nisā, 4:11) is general and would have remained so if it were not qualified by the Ḥadīth that 'the killer does not inherit'.[24]

لا يرث القاتل

Similarly, the ruling of the *Sunnah* concerning the direction of the *qiblah* remained in force until it was abrogated by the Qur'ānic injunction in Sūra al-Baqarah (2:144), which changed the *qiblah* from Jerusalem to the Kaᶜbah. This is all obvious so far, and perhaps al-Shawkānī is right in saying that there is no need for a recourse to *istiṣḥāb* in these cases. What *istiṣḥāb* might tell us in this context may be that in the event where there is doubt as to whether the general in the law has been qualified by some other enactment, or when there is doubt as to whether the law on a certain point has been abrogated or not, *istiṣḥāb* would presume the absence of specification and abrogation until the contrary is established by evidence.

3) Presumption of original freedom from liability (*barā'ah al-dhimmah al-aṣliyyah*), which means freedom from obligations until the contrary is proved. No person may, therefore, be compelled to perform any obligation unless the law requires so. For example, no-one is required to perform the *ḥajj* pilgrimage more than once in his lifetime, or to perform a sixth *ṣalāh* in one day, because the *Sharīᶜah* imposes no such liability. Similarly, no-one is liable to punishment until his guilt is established through lawful evidence.[25] However, the detailed implementation of this principle too has given rise to disagreement between the Shāfiᶜī and Ḥanafī jurists. To give an example, A claims that B owes him fifty dollars and B denies it. The question may arise as to whether a settlement (*ṣulḥ*) after denial is lawful in this case. The Ḥanafīs have answered this in the affirmative, but the Shāfiᶜīs have held that a settlement after denial is not permissible. The Shāfiᶜīs argue that since prior to the settlement B denied the claim, the principle of original freedom from liability would thus apply to him, which means that he would bear no liability at all. As such it would be unlawful for A to take anything from B. The settlement is therefore null and void. The Ḥanafīs have argued, on the other hand, that B's non-liability after the claim is not inviolable. The claim, in other words, interferes with the operation of the principle under discussion. B can no longer be definitely held to be free of liability; this being so, a settlement is permissible in the interests of preventing hostility between the parties.[26]

4) Permissibility is the original state of things (*al-aṣl fī al-ashyā'*

al-ibāḥah). We have already discussed the principle of *ibāḥah*, which is a branch of the doctrine of *istiṣḥāb*. To recapitulate, all matters which the *Sharīʿah* has not regulated to the contrary remain permissible. They will be presumed so unless the contrary is proved to be the case. The one exception to the application of *ibāḥāh* is relationships between members of the opposite sex, where the basic norm is prohibition unless it is legalised by marriage. The Ḥanbalīs have given *ibāḥah* greater prominence, in that they validate it as a basis of commitment (*iltizām*) unless there is a text to the contrary. Under the Ḥanbalī doctrine, the norm in *ʿibādāt* is that they are void (*bāṭil*) unless there is an explicit command to validate them. But the norm in regard to transactions and contracts is that they are valid unless there is a *naṣṣ* to the contrary.[27] To give an example, under the Ḥanbalī doctrine of *ibāḥah*, prospective spouses are at liberty to enter stipulations in their marriage contract, including a condition that the husband must remain monogamous. The Ḥanbalīs are alone in their ruling on this point, as the majority of jurists have considered such a condition to amount to a superimposition on the legality of polygamy in the *Sharīʿah*. The provisions of the *Sharīʿah* must, according to the majority, not be circumvented in this way. The Lawgiver has permitted polygamy and it is not for the individual to overrule it. The Ḥanbalīs have argued, on the other hand, that the objectives of the Lawgiver in regard to marriage are satisfied by monogamy. As it is, polygamy is a permissibility, not a requirement, and there is no *naṣṣ* to indicate that the spouses could not stipulate against it. The stipulation is therefore valid and the spouses are committed to abide by it.

Conclusion

Istiṣḥāb is not an independent proof or a method of juristic deduction in its own right, but mainly functions as a means of implementing an existing indication (*dalīl*) whose validity and continued relevance are established by the rules of *istiṣḥāb*. This might explain why the ulema have regarded *istiṣḥāb* as the last ground of *fatwā*, one which does not command priority over other indications. The Mālikīs have relied very little on it as they are known for their extensive reliance on other proofs, both revealed and rational, in the development of the rules of *Sharīʿah*; so much so that they have had little use for *istiṣḥāb*. This is also true of the Ḥanafī school of law, which has only rarely invoked *istiṣḥāb* as a ground for the determination of legal rules. *Istiṣḥāb* is applicable either in the absence of other proofs or as a means of establishing the relevance of applying an existing proof. It is interesting to note in this connection the fact that *istiṣḥāb* is more extensively applied by those who are particularly strict in their acceptance of other rational proofs. Thus we find that the opponents of *qiyās*, such as the Ẓāhirīs and the Akhbārī branch of the Shīʿah Imāmiyyah, have relied on it most and have determined the *aḥkām* on its basis in almost all instances where the majority have applied *qiyās*. Similarly the Shāfiʿīs who reject *istiḥsān* have relied more frequently on *istiṣḥāb* than the Ḥanafīs and the Mālikīs. In almost all cases where the Ḥanafīs and Mālikīs have applied *istiḥsān* or custom (*ʿurf*), the Shāfiʿīs have resorted to *istiṣḥāb*.[28]

Istiṣḥāb is often described as a principle of evidence, as it is mainly concerned with the establishment or rebuttal of facts, and as such it is of greater relevance to the rules of evidence. The application of *istiṣḥāb* to penalties and to criminal law in general is to some extent restricted by the fact that these areas are mainly governed by the definitive rules of *Sharīʿah* or statutory legislation. The jurists have on the whole advised caution in the application of penalties on the basis of presumptive evidence only. Having said this, however, the principle of the original absence of liability is undoubtedly an important feature of *istiṣḥāb* which is widely upheld not only in the field of criminal law but also in constitutional law and civil litigations generally. This is perhaps equally true of the principle of *ibāḥah*, which is an essential component of the principle of legality, also known as the principle of the rule of law. This feature of *istiṣḥāb* is once again in harmony with the modern concept of legality in that permissibility is the norm in areas where the law imposes no prohibition.

I shall end this chapter by summarising a reformist opinion concerning *istiṣḥāb*. In his booklet entitled *Tajdīd Uṣūl al-Fiqh al-Islāmī*, Ḥasan Turābī highlights the significance of *istiṣḥāb* and calls for a fresh approach to be taken toward this doctrine. The author explains that *istiṣḥāb* has the potential of incorporating within its scope the concept of natural justice and the approved customs and mores of society.

According to Turābī, *istiṣḥāb* derives its basic validity from the belief that Islam did not aim at establishing a new life on earth in all of its dimensions and details, nor did it aim at nullifying and replacing all the mores and customs of Arabian society. The Prophet did not take an attitude of opposition to everything that he encountered, but accepted and allowed the bulk of the existing social values and sought to reverse or replace only those which were oppressive and unacceptable. We also find in the Qur'ān references to *amr bi al-ʿurf*, or acting in accordance with the prevailing custom unless it has been specifically nullified or amended by the *Sharīʿah* of Islam.

Similarly when the Qur'ān calls for the implementation of justice, beneficience (*iḥsān*) and fairness in the determination of disputes, it refers, among other things, to the basic principles of justice that are upheld by humanity at large and the good conscience of decent individuals. Life on earth is thus a cumulative construct of moral and religious teachings, aided and abetted by enlightened human nature which seeks to rectify what it deems to be wrong, unjust and undesirable. The *Sharīᶜah* has also left many things unregulated, and when this is the case human action may in regard to them be guided by good conscience and the general teachings of divine revelation. This is the substance, as Turābī explains, of the juridical doctrine of *istiṣḥāb*. In its material part *istiṣḥāb* declares permissibility to be the basic norm in *Sharīᶜah*; that people are deemed to be free of liability unless the law has determined otherwise; and that human beings may utilise everything in the earth for their benefit unless they are forbidden by the law. It thus appears that *istiṣḥāb*, as a proof of *Sharīᶜah*, merits greater prominence and recognition than we find to be the case in the classical formulations of this doctrine.[29]

NOTES

1. Shawkānī, *Irshād*, p. 237; Āmidī, *Iḥkām*, IV, 127; Ibn al-Qayyim, *Iᶜlām*, I, 294.
2. Shawkānī, Irshād, p. 237; Abū Zahrah, *Uṣūl*, p. 234; Mahmassānī, *Falsafah* (Ziadeh's trans.) p. 95.
3. Ibn al-Qayyim, *Iᶜlām*, I, 294; Badrān, *Uṣūl*, p. 218; Abū Zahrah, *Uṣūl*, p. 234.
4. Badrān, *Uṣūl*, p. 218.
5. Ibid.
6. Shawkānī, *Irshād*, p. 237; Abū Zahrah, *Uṣūl*, p. 235.
7. Āmidī, *Iḥkām*, IV, 128; Badrān, *Uṣūl*, p.221
8. Cf. Abū Zahrah, *Uṣūl*, p. 235.
9. Āmidī, *Iḥkām*, IV, 127.
10. Shawkānī, *Irshād*, p. 238; Badrān, *Uṣūl*, p. 219; Abū Zahrah, *Uṣūl*, p. 236.
11. Khallāf, *ᶜIlm*, p. 92.
12. Abū Zahrah, *Uṣūl*, p. 236; Khallāf, *ᶜIlm*, p.92; Badrān, *Uṣūl*, p. 219; Khuḍarī, *Uṣūl*, pp. 354–55.
13. Ibn al-Qayyim, *Iᶜlām*, I, 295; Badrān, *Uṣūl*, p. 219.
14. Shawkānī, *Irshād*, p. 238; Abū Zahrah, *Uṣūl*, p. 237; Badrān, *Uṣūl*, p. 223; Coulson, *Succession*, p. 198ff.
15. Zuhayr, *Uṣūl*, IV, 180.
16. Shawkānī, *Irshād*, p.237.
17. Ibn al-Qayyim, *Iᶜlām*, I, 294.
18. Badrān, *Uṣūl*, pp. 220–221.
19. Ibn al-Qayyim, *Iᶜlām*, I, 296; Abū Zahrah, *Uṣūl*, p. 238.
20. Ibid.
21. Abū Zahrah, *Uṣūl*, p. 239.
22. Khuḍarī, *Uṣūl*, p. 356; Mahmassānī, *Falsafah*, p.90.
23. Shawkānī, *Irshād*, p. 238.

24. Ibn Mājah, *Sunan*, II, 913, Ḥadīth no. 2735; al-Dārimī, *Sunan* (*Kitāb al-Farā'iḍ*), II, 384.

25. Shawkānī, *Irshād*, p. 238; Mahmassānī, *Falsafah*, p. 90. The principle of original freedom from liability appears in al-Suyūṭī's *al-Ashbāh wa al-Naẓā'ir* and in the *Majallah al-Aḥkām al-ᶜAdliyyah* (Art. 8).

26. Zuhayr, *Uṣūl*, IV, 180–181.

27. Ibn al-Qayyim, *Iᶜlām*, I, 300.

28. Cf. Abū Zahrah, *Uṣūl*, p. 241.

29. Turābī, *Tajdīd*, pp. 27–28.

CHAPTER SIXTEEN

Sadd al-Dharāʾiᶜ (Blocking the Means)

Dharīᶜah (pl. *dharāʾiᶜ*) is a word synonymous with *wasīlah*, which signifies the means to obtaining a certain end, while *sadd* literally means 'blocking'. *Sadd al-dharāʾiᶜ* thus implies blocking the means to an expected end which is likely to materialise if the means towards it is not obstructed. Blocking the means must necessarily be understood to imply blocking the means to evil, not to something good. Although the literal meaning of *sadd al-dharāʾiᶜ* might suggest otherwise, in its juridical application, the concept of *sadd al-dharāʾiᶜ* also extends to 'opening the means to beneficience'. But as a doctrine of jurisprudence, it is the former meaning, that is, blocking the means to evil, which characterises *sadd al-dharāʾiᶜ*. The latter meaning of this expression is not particularly highlighted in the classical expositions of this doctrine, presumably because opening the means to beneficence is the true purpose and function of the *Sharīᶜah* as a whole and as such is not peculiar to *sadd al-dharāʾiᶜ*.

When the means and the end are both directed toward beneficience and *maṣlaḥah* and are not explicitly regulated by a clear injunction (*naṣṣ*), the matter is likely to fall within the ambit of *qiyās*, *maṣlaḥah*, or *istiḥsān*, etc. Similarly, when both the means and the end are directed towards evil, the issue is likely to be governed by the general rules of *Sharīᶜah*, and a recourse to *sadd al-dharāʾiᶜ* would seem out of place. Based on this analysis, it would appear that as a principle of jurisprudence, *sadd al-dharāʾiᶜ* applies when there is a discrepancy between the means and the end on the good-neutral-evil scale of values. A typical case for the application of *sadd al-dharāʾiᶜ* would thus arise when a lawful means is expected to lead to an unlawful result, or when a lawful means which normally leads to a lawful result is used to procure an unlawful end.

Both the means and the end may be good or evil, physical or moral, and they may be visible or otherwise, and the two need not necessarily be present simultaneously. For example, *khalwah* or illicit privacy between members of the opposite sexes, is unlawful because it constitutes a means to *zinā* whether or not it actually leads to it. All sexual overtures which are expected to lead to *zinā* are similarly forbidden by virtue of the certainty or likelihood that the conduct in question would lead to *zinā*. *Dharīᶜah* may also consist of the omission of a certain conduct such as trade and commercial transactions during the time of the Friday congregational prayer. The means which obstruct the said prayer, in other words, must be blocked, that is, by abandoning trade at the specified time.

The whole concept of *sadd al-dharā'i*ᶜ is founded in the idea of preventing an evil before it actually materialises. It is therefore not always necessary that the result should actually obtain. It is rather the objective expectation that a means is likely to lead to an evil result which renders the means in question unlawful even without the realisation of the expected result. This is the case in both the examples given above: *khalwah* is thus unlawful even without actually leading to *zinā*, and trading during the time of the Friday prayer is unlawful whether or not it actually hinders the latter. Furthermore, since *sadd al-dharā'i*ᶜ basically contemplates preventing an evil before its occurrence, the question of intention to procure a particular result cannot be a reliable basis for assessing the means that leads to that result. Abū Zahrah has aptly observed that the nature and value of the means is determined by looking at the purpose that it pursues regardless as to whether the latter is intended or otherwise. When a particular act is deemed to lead to a certain result, whether good or evil, it is held to be the means toward that end. The question of the intention of the perpetrator is, as such, not relevant to the objective determination of the value of the means. It is rather the expected result which determines the value of the means. If the result is expected to be good and praiseworthy, so will be the means towards it, and if it is expected to be blameworthy the same will apply to the means regardless of the intention of the perpetrator, or the actual realisation of the result itself. This is, for example, borne out by the Qur'ānic text which forbids the Muslims from insulting idol-worshippers, notwithstanding the inherent enormity of idol-worshipping or the actual intention behind it. The text thus proceeds: 'And insult not the associators lest they [in return] insult God out of spite and ignorance' (al-Anᶜām; 6:108). The means to an evil is thus obstructed by putting a ban on insulting idol-worshippers, a conduct which might have been otherwise permissible and even praiseworthy, as it would mean denunciation of falsehood and firmness of faith on the part of the believer. Thus a means which is intrinsically praiseworthy leads to an evil result, and acquires the value of the latter. Furthermore, the prohibition in this example is founded on the likelihood that the associators would insult God as a result. It is, in other words, the expected result which is taken into account. Whether the latter actually materialises or not is beside the point: insulting the idols and their worshippers is thus forbidden regardless of the actual result that such conduct may lead to. Similarly, the question of intending whether or not to bring about a particular result is irrelevant to the prohibition under discussion. Insulting idol-worshippers is thus forbidden even when a Muslim does not intend to bring about the expected result, that is, an insult to God; his intention may be good or bad, in either case, insulting the idols and their worshippers is forbidden as it is, on an objective basis, most likely to invoke the expected result.[1]

The doctrine of *sadd al-dharā'iᶜ* contemplates the basic objectives of the Lawgiver. Hence the general rule regarding the value of the means in relationship to the end is that the former acquires the value of the latter. Al-Shāṭibī has aptly observed that the Lawgiver has legalised certain forms of conduct and prohibited others in accordance with the benefit or harm that they lead to. When a particular act or form of conduct brings about a result which is contrary to the objectives of the Lawgiver, then the latter would be held to prevail over the former.[2] If the means, in other words, violate the basic purpose of the *Sharīᶜah*, then they must be blocked. The laws of *Sharīᶜah* are for the most part distinguishable in regard to their objectives (*maqāṣid*), and the means which procure or obstruct those objectives. The means are generally viewed in the light of the ends they are expected to obtain, and it is logically the latter which prevail over the former in that the means follow their ends, not vice versa. Normally the means to *wājib* become *wājib* and the means to *ḥarām* become *ḥarām*. Means may at times lead to both a good and an evil in which case, if the evil (*mafsadah*) is either equal to or greater than the benefit (*maṣlaḥah*), the former will prevail over the latter. This is according to the general principle that 'preventing an evil takes priority over securing a benefit'.[3] *Sadd al-dharā'iᶜ* thus becomes a principle of jurisprudence and a method of deducing the juridical ruling (*ḥukm sharᶜī*) of a certain issue or type of conduct which may not have been regulated in the existing law but whose ruling can be deduced through the application of this principle.

In addition to the Qur'ānic *āyah* (al-Anᶜām, 6:108) on the prohibition of insulting idols as referred to above, the ulema have quoted in authority for *sadd al-dharāʾiᶜ* the Qur'ānic passage in sūra al-Baqarah (2: 104), as follows: 'O believers! Address not the Prophet by the word *rāᶜinā*, but address him respectfully and listen to him.' The reason for this prohibition was that the word '*rāᶜinā*', being a homonym, had two meanings, one of which was 'please look at us or attend to us', while with a slight twist the same word would mean 'our shepherd'. The Jews used to insult the Prophet with it, and in order to block the means to such abuse, the Muslims were forbidden from using that form of address to the Prophet despite their good intentions and the fact that the word under discussion was not inherently abusive.[4]

Authority is also found for the principle of *sadd al-dharāʾiᶜ* in the *Sunnah*, especially the ruling in which the Prophet forbade a creditor from taking a gift from his debtor lest it became a means to usury and the gift a substitute to *ribā*. The Prophet also forbade the killing of hypocrites (*al-munāfiqūn*) and people who were known to have betrayed the Muslim community during battles. It was feared that killing such people would become a means to evil, namely, of giving rise to a rumour that 'Muḥammad kills his own Companions',[5] which would, in turn, provide the enemy with an excuse to undermine the unity of the Muslim community. Consequently the Prophet put a ban on killing the *munāfiqūn*. On a similar note, the Prophet suspended enforcement of the *ḥadd* penalty for theft during battles so as to avoid defection to enemy forces. It was for this reason, namely to block the means to an evil, that the army commanders were ordered not to enforce the prescribed penalties during military engagements.[6]

The leading Companions are also known to have entitled to inheritance the divorced woman whom her husband had irrevocably divorced during his death illness in order to exclude her from inheritance. This was forbidden by the Companions so that a divorce of this kind would not become a means to abuse. It is also reported that during the time of the caliph ᶜUmar b. al-Khaṭṭāb, one of his officials, Ḥudhayfah, married a Jewish women in al-Madā'in. The caliph wrote to him saying that he should divorce her. Ḥudhayfah then asked the caliph if the marriage was unlawful. To this the caliph replied that it was not, but that his example might be followed by others who might be lured by the beauty of the women of *ahl al-dhimmah*. The caliph thus forbade something which the Qur'ān had declared lawful so as to block the means to an evil as he perceived it at the time. It might be interesting to add here that Ibn Qayyim al-Jawziyyah records at least seventy-seven instances and rulings of the learned Companions and the subsequent generations of ulema in which they resorted to *sadd al-dharā'iᶜ* so as to block the means that led to evil.[7]

The ulema are, however, in disagreement over the validity of *sadd al-dharā'iᶜ*. The Ḥanafī and Shāfiᶜī jurists do not recognise it as a principle of jurisprudence in its own right, on the grounds that the necessary ruling regarding the means can be derived by recourse to other principles such as *qiyās*, and the Ḥanafī doctrines of *istiḥsān* and *ᶜurf*. But the Mālikī and Ḥanbalī jurists have validated *sadd al-dharā'iᶜ* as a proof of *Sharīᶜah* in its own right. Despite the different approaches that the ulema have taken to this doctrine, the Mālikī jurist al-Shāṭibī has reached the conclusion that the ulema of various schools are essentially in agreement over the conceptual validity of *sadd al-dharā'iᶜ* but have differed in its detailed application. Their differences relate mainly to the grounds which may be held to constitute the means to something else, and also to the extent to which the concept of *sadd al-dharā'iᶜ* can be validly applied.[8] Abū Zahrah has reached essentially the same conclusion by observing that the Shāfiᶜī and Ḥanafī jurists are for the most part in agreement with their Mālikī and Ḥanbalī counterparts, and that they differ only in regard to some issues.[9] The following classification of *sadd al-dharā'iᶜ* may cast light on the consensus, as well as some of the areas which the ulema are in disagreement, over the application of this doctrine. It is perhaps well to remember at this point that notwithstanding the application of *sadd al-dharā'iᶜ* in respect of opening the means to beneficience (*maṣlaḥah*), it is usually the prevention of evil (*mafsadah*) that acquires greater prominence in the discussion of this principle.

From the viewpoint of the degree of probability or otherwise that a means is expected to lead to an evil end, the ulema of *uṣūl* have divided the *dharā'iᶜ* into four types.

1) Means which definitely lead to evil, such as digging a deep pit next to the entrance door to a public place which is not lit at night, so that anyone who enters the door is very likely to fall into it. Based on the near-certainty of the expected result of injuring others, the means which leads to that result are equally forbidden. The ulema of all schools are, in principle, unanimous on the prohibition of this type of *dharīᶜah* and a consensus (*ijmāᶜ*) is said to have been reached on this point.[10] Having said this, however, it should be added that the jurists have envisaged two possible eventualities. Firstly, the *dharīᶜah* may consist of an unlawful act of transgression in the first place, as was the case in the foregoing example, in which case the perpetrator is held to be responsible for any loss or damage that might be caused, as by digging a pit in a place where he has no right or authority to do so. Secondly, the *dharīᶜah* may consist of an act which is basically lawful,

in which case the ulema have disagreed over the question of responsibility. If, for example, someone digs a water well in his own house but so close to the wall of his neighbour that the wall collapses as a result, the act here is held to be basically lawful as it consists of the exercise of the right of ownership, which is said to be irreconcilable with the idea of liability for damages. According to a variant view, however, the perpetrator is liable for damages. This ruling draws support from the principle, already referred to, that preventing an evil takes priority over securing a benefit.[11]

2) The second type of means is that which is most likely (i.e. on the basis of *al-ẓann al-ghālib*) to lead to evil and is rarely, if ever, expected to lead to a benefit. An example of this would be selling weapons during warfare or selling grapes to a wine maker. Although al-Shāṭibī has noted that these transactions are invalid according to the consensus (*ijmāᶜ*) of the ulema, both Abū Zahrah and Badrān have noted that it is only the Mālikī and Ḥanbalī ulema who have considered these transactions to be forbidden (*ḥarām*), as they are most likely to lead to evil notwithstanding the absence of certain knowledge that this will always be the case. In their opinion, a dominant probability or *ẓann* is generally accepted as a valid basis for the *aḥkām* of *Sharīᶜah*. Consequently when there is a strong likelihood that means would lead to an evil, the means may be declared forbidden on the basis of this probability alone.[12]

3) The third of the four types of means under discussion is that which frequently leads to evil, but in which there is no certainty, nor even a dominant probability, that this will always be the case. An example of this would be a sale which is used as a means to procuring usury (*ribā*). These types of sales, generally known as *buyūᶜ al-ājāl* (deferred sales), in which either the delivery of the object of sale, or the payment of its price, is deferred to a later date, would all tend to fall under this category of means. If, for example, A sells a garment for ten rials to B with the price being payable in six months' time, and A then buys the same garment from B for eight rials with the price being payable immediately, this transaction in effect amounts to a loan of eight rials to B on which he pays an interest of two rials after six months. There is a dominant probability that this sale would lead to *ribā* although there is an element of uncertainty that it may not, which is why the ulema have disagreed as to the validity or otherwise of this type of transaction. Imām Mālik and Aḥmad b. Ḥanbal have held that the means which are likely to lead to usury are unlawful (*ḥarām*) and must be obstructed. They have acknowledged the possibility that a deferred sale may not actually lead to *ribā*; they also take cognizance of the

basic norm in regard to sale, which is legality, and yet they have ruled, on grounds of caution (*iḥtiyāṭ*), that sales which are likely to lead to *ribā* are unlawful. The mere possibility that *ribā* may not actually materialise is of no account, and although sale is generally lawful, this basic legality is of no consequence if it is expected to procure an evil. Furthermore, to prevent the latter must be given priority over any possible benefit that the sale in question might entail.

The Imāms Abū Ḥanīfah and al-Shāfiʿī have, on the other hand, ruled that unless it definitely leads to evil, the basic legality of sale must be held to prevail. Sale is basically lawful in all of its varieties, deferred or otherwise, and in the absence of either positive knowledge (*ʿilm*) or of a dominant *ẓann* that a sale would lead to *ribā*, a mere frequency of occurrence should not be allowed to override the original legality of sale. The preferred view, however, is that of the Mālikī and Ḥanbalī schools, for there is evidence in the *Sunnah* to the effect that original permissibility may be overruled in the face of a likelihood (or customary practice), even without definite evidence, that it might open the way to evil.[13]

The ulema have similarly differed over the validity or otherwise of a marriage that is concluded with the intention of merely satisfying one's sexual desire without a life-long commitment. Imām Mālik considers this to be invalid (*bāṭil*), as acts, according to this view, are to be judged by the intention behind them, and since the norm in marriage is permanence, the absence of an intention to that effect vitiates the *nikāḥ*. The main thrust of this view is to prevent the likely abuse to which the marriage in question is likely to lead. Imām Shāfiʿī has on the other hand held that the *nikāḥ* is valid so long as there is nothing in the contract to vitiate it. The *Sharīʿah*, according to this view, cannot operate on the hidden intentions of people but only on tangible facts that are susceptible to proof. Whether the *nikāḥ* in this case is a means to abuse is a matter for the conscience of the individual, and not the positive application of the law.[14] The difference here is one of perspective. Whereas the Shāfiʿī and Ḥanafī view is based on the apparent validity of a contract, the Mālikī and Ḥanbalī view takes into consideration the objective of a contract and the necessary caution that must be taken in order to prevent an evil.[15] The ulema are, on the other hand, all in agreement on the prohibition of illicit privacy (*khalwah*) which is founded in the likelihood, though not amounting to positive proof, that it might lead to adultery.[16]

Another, similar instance in which the jurists have invoked the principle of *sadd al-dharāʾiʿ* is the ruling, disputed by some, that close relatives may neither act as witnesses nor as judges in each other's disputes. Likewise, a judge may not adjudicate a dispute on the basis of his personal knowledge of facts without the formal presentation of evidence, lest it lead to prejudice in favour or against one of the parties. The principle involved here is that such activities might constitute the means to an evil end, namely miscarriage of justice, and are therefore to be avoided. The Ḥanafīs on the other hand maintain, particularly in reference to adjudication on the basis of personal knowledge, that it is lawful. Some ulema have also held the view that testimony by a relative may in fact facilitate justice and may not lead to evil, especially if relations testify against each other, which is why the ulema of various schools have allowed the testimony of father or son, or of spouses, against one another, but not in favour.[17] The jurists have thus disagreed over the application of *sadd al-dharā'iᶜ* to particular issues and the extent to which it may be validly applied to different situations.

4) The last of the four varieties of means are those which are rarely expected to lead to evil and are most likely to lead to a benefit. An example of this would be to dig a water well in a place which is not likely to cause injury or harm to anyone, or speaking a word of truth to a tyrannical ruler, or growing certain varieties of fruits, such as grapes, on one's own property. In all of these, as in many other matters, there is a possibility that a *mafsadah* might be caused as a result. In the case of growing grapes, for example, it is possible that the fruit may be fermented into wine, but a mere possibility of this kind is overlooked in view of the stronger likelihood of the benefit that it would otherwise achieve. The ulema are generally in agreement on the permissibility of this type of means. The basic norm in regard to acts and transactions that would fall under this category of means is permissibility, and no one may be prevented from attempting them on account of the mere possibility that they may lead to a *mafsadah*. On a similar note, no-one may be prevented from giving testimony in judicial disputes, nor may anyone be obstructed from telling the truth to a tyrannical ruler because of a mere possibility that this might give rise to a *mafsadah*.[18]

The foregoing discussion of *sadd al-dharā'iᶜ* has primarily been concerned with means which led to an unlawful end. There was, in other words, no attempt to change the *ḥarām* into *ḥalāl*: whenever there was a likelihood that a lawful means led to an unlawful end, the means itself became unlawful. But the application of *sadd al-dharā'iᶜ* also covers the eventuality where a *ḥarām* may be turned into *ḥalāl* or *mubāḥ* if this is likely to prevent a greater evil. A lesser evil is, in other words, tolerated in order to prevent a greater one. To give an example: it is permissible to seek the release of Muslim prisoners of war in exchange for the payment of a monetary ransom. To give money to the warring enemy is basically unlawful as it adds strength to the enemy, which is generally harmful. But it is permitted here as it achieves the freedom of Muslim prisoners, which would in turn add to the strength of the Muslim forces. This ruling is based in the principle of *sadd al-dharā'i*ᶜ, and consists of opening, rather than blocking, the means to the desired benefit. On a similar note, it is permissible for the Muslim community to pay the enemy so as to prevent the latter from inflicting harm on the Muslims, but only when the Muslim community is otherwise powerless to defend itself. Furthermore, the ulema have generally held that giving bribes is permissible if it is the only way to prevent oppression, and the victim is otherwise unable to defend himself. To this the Ḥanbalī and Mālikī jurists have added the proviso that giving bribes is only permissible as a means of defending one's proven rights but not if the right in question is disputed.[19]

Notwithstanding the essential validity of *sadd al-dharā'i*ᶜ as a principle of *Sharī*ᶜ*ah*, over-reliance on it is not recommended. The ulema have cautioned that an excessive use of this principle may render the lawful (*mubāḥ*) or even the praiseworthy (*mandūb*) and the obligatory (*wājib*) unlawful, which should not be encouraged. An example of this would be when an upright person refuses to take custody of the property of the orphan, or of *waqf* property, for the pious motive of avoiding the possibility of incurring a sin. A refusal of this nature would seem to over-emphasise the significance of the means that might lead to evil. With regard to the guardianship of the property of orphans, the Qur'ān offers some guidance in that it permits mixing their property with that of the guardian as a matter of trust, a conclusion which is drawn from the text where we read in a reference to the orphans: 'If you mix their affairs with yours, they are your brethren, but God knows the wrong-doer from the upright' (al-Baqarah, 2:220).

While discussing the ulema's caution against over-reliance on *sadd al-dharā'i*ᶜ, Abū Zahrah quotes the renowned Mālikī jurist Ibn al-ᶜArabī, to the effect that the application of this principle should be regulated so as to ensure propriety and moderation in its use. Abū Zahrah then concurs with Ibn al-ᶜArabī to the effect that if an evil is to be prevented by blocking the means towards it, one must ascertain that the evil in question is *manṣūṣ* ᶜ*alayh*, that is, one which has been ruled upon as such in the Qur'ān or the *Sunnah*. Similarly, when a benefit is to be facilitated by opening the means towards it, the propriety of the benefit must be sustainable by analogy to a *ḥālal manṣūṣ* (that which has been declared lawful in the *naṣṣ*). But Abū Zahrah is careful to add that these conditions remain in the nature of an opinion and are not required in the accepted Mālikī exposition of this doctrine.[20]

And finally, with regard to the guardianship of property and trust in the foregoing example, it is suggested that the harm which is likely to arise from refusal by an upright person to undertake it is likely to be greater than that which might arise from undertaking it. If the orphans were to be neglected for fear of opening the means to misuse of trust, or if no-one gave testimony for fear of indulging in lying, then surely this would itself become a means to greater evil and should therefore be avoided.

We might end our discussion of *sadd al-dharā'iʿ* by distinguishing the means from the preliminary (*muqaddimah*), although the two can at times coincide and overlap. Briefly, a 'preliminary' consists of something which is necessary for obtaining the result that it contemplates, in the sense that the latter cannot materialise without the former. For instance, ablution (*wuḍū'*) is a preliminary to *ṣalāh* and the latter cannot be performed without the former. But a means to something does not stand in the same relationship to its end. Although the means is normally expected to lead to the end it contemplates, the latter may also be obtained through some other means. The end, in other words, is not exclusively dependent on the means. To give an example: travelling in order to commit a theft is a preliminary to the theft that it contemplates but not a means to it. Travelling which might consist of riding a train in a certain direction is basically neutral and cannot, on an objective basis, be said to constitute a means to theft. But *taḥlīl*, that is, an intervening marriage concluded in order to legalise remarriage between a divorced couple, is a means to the proposed marriage but not a preliminary to it, as the latter is not exclusively dependent on *taḥlīl* and can, for example, follow a normal intervening marriage. Similarly, seductive overtures between members of the opposite sexes are a means, but not a preliminary, to adultery, as the latter can materialise even without such overtures. Sexual overtures can only constitute a preliminary to *zinā* when they actually lead to it.

The other difference to note between the means and the preliminary for our purposes, is, as already indicated, that the former is usually evaluated and declared unlawful on an objective basis even without the realisation of its expected end. The preliminary to an act, on the other hand, is of little value without the actual occurrence of the act of which it becomes a part. The relationship between preliminary and its result is subjective in the sense that it can only be evaluated in the light of the completed or the intended result. Walking in the direction of a mosque to perform the Friday prayers, for example, can only acquire the value of the *wājib* if it actually leads to the performance of the prayers, not otherwise.[21]

NOTES

1. Cf. Abū Zahrah, *Uṣūl*, p. 228.
2. Shāṭibī, *Muwāfaqāt* (Dirāz edition), IV, 194.
3. Ibid., IV, 195; Badrān, *Uṣūl*, p. 242.
4. Cf. Abū Zahrah, *Uṣūl*, p. 228; Ismāʿīl, *Adillah*, p. 197.
5. Shāṭibī, *Muwāfaqāt*, IV, 62; Shalabī, *Fiqh*, p. 187.
6. Abū Zahrah, *Uṣūl*, p. 229; Shalabī, *Fiqh*, p.187; Ismāʿīl, *Adillah*, p. 200.
7. Ibn Qayyim al-Jawziyyah, *Iʿlām*, III, 122 ff; Shalabī, *Fiqh*, p. 188.
8. Shāṭibī, *Muwāfaqāt*, IV, 201.
9. Abū Zahrah, *Uṣūl*, pp. 227–228.
10. Abū Zahrah, *Uṣūl*, p. 228; Badrān, *Uṣūl*, p. 243.
11. Abū Zahrah, *Uṣūl*, p. 230; Badrān, *Uṣūl*, p. 243.
12. Abū Zahrah, *Uṣūl*, p. 231; Badrān, *Uṣūl*, p. 244.
13. Shāṭibī, *Muwāfaqāt*, IV, 200; Badrān, *Uṣūl*, p. 244; Abū Zahrah, *Uṣūl*, p. 232.
14. Ismāʿīl, *Adillah*, p. 175.
15. Abū Zahrah, *Uṣūl*, p. 231.
16. Badrān, *Uṣūl*, p. 245.
17. Shalabī, *Fiqh*, p. 186; Badrān, *Uṣūl*, p. 244; Ismāʿīl, *Adillah*, p. 211.
18. Shāṭibī, *Muwāfaqāt*, II, 249; Badrān, *Uṣūl*, p. 245; Abū Zahrah, *Uṣūl*, p. 230.
19. Abū Zahrah, *Uṣūl*, p. 232.
20. Ibid., p. 233.
21. Cf. Badrān, *Uṣūl*, pp. 245–246; Ismāʿīl, *Adillah*, p. 171.

CHAPTER SEVENTEEN

Ḥukm Sharʿī (Law or Value of *Sharīʿah*)

The ulema of *uṣūl* define *ḥukm sharʿī* as a locution or communication from the Lawgiver concerning the conduct of the *mukallaf* (person in full possession of his faculties) which consists of a demand, an option or an enactment. A demand (*ṭalab*, or *iqtiḍā'*) is usually communicated in the form of either a command or a prohibition. The former demands that the *mukallaf* do something, whereas the latter requires him to avoid doing something. A demand may either be binding, which leaves the *mukallaf* with no choice but to conform, or may not be binding. When a demand to do or not to do something is established by definitive proof (*dalīl qaṭʿī*) it is referred to as *wājib* or *ḥarām* respectively. Such is the majority view, but according to the Ḥanafī jurists, if the text which conveys such a demand is not definitive in its meaning (*dalālah*) or authenticity (*thubūt*), it is *wājib*, but if it is definitive in both respects, it is *farḍ*. As for the demand to avoid doing something, the Ḥanafīs maintain that if it is based on definitive proof in terms of both meaning and authenticity, it is *ḥarām*, otherwise it is *makrūh taḥrīmī*. When a demand is not utterly emphatic and leaves the individual with an element of choice it is known as *mandūb* (recommended). The option (*takhyīr*), on the other hand, is a variety of *ḥukm sharʿī* which leaves the individual at liberty either to do or to avoid doing something. A *ḥukm* of this kind is commonly known as *mubāḥ* (permissible). An enactment, or *waḍʿ*, is neither a demand nor an option, but an objective exposition of the law which enacts something as a cause (*sabab*) or a condition (*sharṭ*) of obtaining something else; or it may be conveyed in the form of a hindrance (*māniʿ*) that might operate as an obstacle against obtaining it.[1]

To give some examples, the Qur'ānic command which addresses the believers to 'fulfil your contracts' (al-Mā'idah, 5:1) is a speech of the Lawgiver addressed to the *mukallaf* which consists of a particular demand. A demand addressed to the *mukallaf* which conveys a prohibition may be illustrated by reference to the Qur'ānic text which provides: 'O you believers, let not some people ridicule others, for it is possible that the latter are better than the former [. . .]' (al-Ḥujurāt, 49:11). To illustrate a *ḥukm* which conveys an option, we refer to the Qur'ānic text which permits the believers to 'hunt when you have come out of the state of *iḥrām*' (sacred state entered into for the purpose of performing the *ḥajj* pilgrimage) (al-Mā'idah, 5:2). Another Qur'ānic text which consists of an option occurs in sūra al-Baqarah (2:229) which provides: 'If you fear that they [i.e. the spouses] would be unable to observe the limits set by God, then there would be no sin on them if she gives a consideration for her freedom.' The married couple are thus given the choice to incur a divorce by mutual consent, known as *khulᶜ*, if they so wish, but they are under no obligation if they do not. Another form of option which occurs in the Qur'ān may be illustrated with reference to the expiation (*kaffārah*) of erroneous killing. The perpetrator has here been given the choice either to set a slave free, or feed sixty destitutes, or fast for two consecutive months (al-Nisā', 4:92). The following Ḥadīth also conveys a *ḥukm* in which the individual is given a choice. The Ḥadīth reads: 'If any of you sees something evil, he should set it right by his hand; if he is unable to do so, then by his tongue; and if he is unable to do even that, then within his heart – but this is the weakest form of faith.'[2]

من رأى منكم منكراً فليغيره بيده فان لم يستطع
فبلسانه ، فان لم يستطع فبقلبه وذلك أضعف
الايمان

Here the choice is given according to the ability of the *mukallaf* and the circumstances which might influence his decision. Lastly, to illustrate a *ḥukm* which consists of an enactment (*waḍᶜ*) we may refer to the Ḥadīth which provides that 'the killer does not inherit'.[3]

لا يرث القاتل

This is a speech of the Lawgiver concerning the conduct of the *mukallaf* which is neither a demand nor an option but an objective ruling of the law that envisages a certain eventuality.

The ulema of *uṣūl* have differed with the *fuqahā'* in regard to the identification of *ḥukm sharʿī*. To refer back to the first example where we quoted the Qur'ān concerning the fulfilment of contracts; according to the ulema of *uṣūl*, the text itself, that is, the demand which is conveyed in the text, represents the *ḥukm sharʿī*. However, according to the *fuqahā'*, it is the effect of that demand, namely the obligation (*wujūb*) that it conveys which embodies the *ḥukm sharʿī*. To give another example, the Qur'ānic prohibition which provides in an address to the believers: 'Do not approach adultery' (al-Isrā', 17:32), is itself the embodiment of the *ḥukm sharʿī*, according to the ulema of *uṣūl*. But according to the *fuqahā'*, it is the effect of the demand in this *āyah*, namely the prohibition (*taḥrīm*) which represents the *ḥukm sharʿī*. Similarly, the Qur'ānic text in respect of the permissibility of hunting which we earlier quoted is itself the embodiment of the *ḥukm sharʿī* according to the ulema of *uṣūl*, but it is the effect of that text, namely the permissibility (*ibāḥah*) which is the *ḥukm* according to the *fuqahā'*. Having explained this difference of perspective between the ulema of *uṣūl* and the *fuqahā'*, it will be noted, however, that it is of no practical consequence concerning the rulings of the *Sharīʿah*, in that the two aspects of *ḥukm* that they highlight are to all intents and purposes concurrent.[4]

Ḥukm sharʿī is divided into the two main varieties of *al-ḥukm al-taklīfī* (defining law) and *al-ḥukm al-waḍʿī* (declaratory law). The former consists of a demand or an option, whereas the latter consists of an enactment only. 'Defining Law' is a fitting description of *al-ḥukm al-taklīfī*, as it mainly defines the extent of man's liberty of action. *Al-ḥukm al-waḍʿī* is rendered 'declaratory law', as this type of *ḥukm* mainly declares the legal relationship between the cause (*sabab*) and its effect (*musabbab*) or between the condition (*sharṭ*) and its object (*mashrūṭ*)[5]. Defining law may thus be described as a locution or communication from the Lawgiver which demands the *mukallaf* to do something or forbids him from doing something, or gives him an option between the two. This type of *ḥukm* occurs in the well-known five categories of *wājib* (obligatory), *mandūb* (recommended), *ḥarām* (forbidden), *makrūh* (abominable) and *mubāḥ* (permissible). Declaratory law is also subdivided into the five categories of *sabab* (cause), *sharṭ* (condition), *māniʿ* (hindrance), *ʿazīmah* (strict law) as opposed to *rukhṣah* (concessionary law), and *ṣaḥīḥ* (valid) as opposed to *bāṭil* (null and void).[6] We shall discuss the defining law and its various sub-divisions first.

I. Defining Law (*al-Ḥukm al-Taklīfī*)

As stated above, 'defining law' is a locution or communication from the Lawgiver addressed to the *mukallaf* which consists of a demand or of an option; it occurs in the five varieties of *wājib, mandūb, ḥarām, makrūh* and *mubāḥ*. We shall discuss each of these separately, as follows.

I.1 The Obligatory (*Wājib, Farḍ)*

For the majority of ulema, *wājib* and *farḍ* are synonymous, and both convey an imperative and binding demand of the Lawgiver addressed to the *mukallaf* in respect of doing something. Acting upon something *wājib* leads to reward, while omitting it leads to punishment in this world or in the hereafter. The Ḥanafīs have, however, drawn a distinction between *wājib* and *farḍ*. An act is thus obligatory in the first degree, that is, *farḍ*, when the command to do it is conveyed in a clear and definitive text of the Qur'ān or *Sunnah*. But if the command to do something is established in a speculative (*ẓannī*) authority, such as an *Āḥād* Ḥadīth, the act would be obligatory in the second degree (*wājib*). The obligatory commands to perform the *ṣalāh*, the *ḥajj*, and to obey one's parents are thus classified under *farḍ*, as they are each established in a definitive text of the Qur'ān. But the obligation to recite sūra al-Fātiḥah in *ṣalāh*, or to perform *ṣalāt al-witr*, that is, the three units of prayers which conclude the late evening prayers (*ṣalāt al-ʿishā'*), are on the other hand classified under *wājib*, as they are both established in the authority of Ḥadīth whose authenticity is not completely free of doubt. A Muslim is bound to do acts which are obligatory either in the first or in the second degree; if he does them, he secures reward and spiritual merit, but if he wilfully neglects them, he makes himself liable to punishment. The difference between the two classes of obligations, according to the vast majority of the jurists, including the Ḥanafīs, is that the person who refuses to believe in the binding nature of a command which is established by definitive proof becomes an unbeliever, but not if he disputes the authority of an obligatory command of the second degree, although he becomes a transgressor. Thus to neglect one's obligation to support one's wife, children and poor parents amounts to a sin but not to infidelity.[7]

Another consequence of the distinction between *farḍ* and *wājib* is that when the former is neglected in an act required by the *Sharīʿah*, the act as a whole becomes null and void (*bāṭil*). If, for example, a person leaves out the bowing (*rukūʿ*) or prostration (*sajdah*) in obligatory prayers, the whole of the prayer becomes null and void. But if he leaves out the recitation of al-Fātiḥah, the *ṣalāh* is basically valid, albeit deficient. This is the Ḥanafī view, but according to the majority the *ṣalāh* is null and void in both cases. However, the difference between the Ḥanafīs and the majority in this respect is regarded as one of form rather than substance, in that the consequences of their disagreement are on the whole negligible.[8] Al-Ghazālī is representative of the majority opinion, including that of the Shāfiʿīs, when he writes: 'As far as we are concerned, there is no difference between *farḍ* and *wājib*; the two terms are synonymous. According to the Ḥanafīs, *farḍ* is based on definitive authority but *wājib* is founded in speculative proof. Once again, we do not deny the division of *wājib* into definitive and speculative (*maqṭūʿ wa-maẓnūn*) and there is no objection to the use of different expressions once their meaning is clear.'[9]

Wājib is sub-divided into at least three varieties, the first of which is the division of *wājib* into personal (*ʿaynī*) and collective (*kafā'ī*). *Wājib ʿaynī* is addressed to every individual *sui juris* and cannot, in principle, be performed for or on behalf of another person. Examples of *wājib* (or *farḍ*) *ʿaynī* are *ṣalāh, ḥajj, zakāh*, fulfilment of contracts and obedience to one's parents. *Wājib kafā'ī* consists of obligations that are addressed to the community as a whole. If only some members of the community perform them, the law is satisfied and the rest of the community is absolved of it. For example, the duty to participate in *jihād* (holy struggle), funeral prayers, the *ḥisbah*, (promotion of good and prevention of evil), building hospitals, extinguishing fires, giving testimony and serving as a judge, etc., are all collective obligations of the community, and are thus *wājib* (or *farḍ*) *kafā'ī*. Thus when a person dies leaving no property to meet the cost of his burial, it is the *wājib kafā'ī* of the community to provide it and to give him a decent burial. Only some members of the community may actually contribute toward the costs, but the duty is nevertheless discharged from the whole of the community. The merit (*thawāb*), however, only attaches to those who have actually taken part in discharging the *wājib kafā'ī* duty.

The collective obligation sometimes changes into a personal obligation. This is, for example, the case with regard to *jihād*, which is a *wājib kafā'ī*, although when the enemy attacks and besieges a locality it becomes the personal duty of every resident to defend it. Similarly, when there is only one *mujtahid* in a city, it becomes his personal duty to carry out *ijtihād*.[10]

Wājib is also divided into *wājib muwaqqat*, that is, *wājib* which is contingent on a time-limit, and *wājib muṭlaq*, that is, 'absolute *wājib*', which is free of such a limitation. Fasting and the obligatory *ṣalāh* are examples of contingent *wājib*, as they must each be observed within specified time limits. But performing the *ḥajj* or the payment of an expiation (*kaffārah*) are not subject to such restrictions and are therefore absolute *wājib*. Provided that one performs the *ḥajj* once during one's lifetime and pays the *kaffārah* at any time before one dies, the duty is discharged.[11] Furthermore, the absolute *wājib* is called absolute because there is no time-limit on its performance and it may be fulfilled every time whenever the occasion arises. This is, for example, the case regarding one's duty to obey one's parents, or the obligation to carry out *ḥisbah*, namely, to promote good and to prevent of evil as and when the occasion arises.

A consequence of this division is that *wājib muwaqqat* materialises only when the time is due for it; it may neither be hastened nor delayed, but within the given time limits the *mukallaf* has a measure of flexibility. Furthermore, to fulfil a contingent *wājib* it is necessary that the *mukallaf* have the intention (*niyyah*) specifically to discharge it.[12]

Lastly, the *wājib* is divided into quantified *wājib* (*wājib muḥaddad*) and unquantified *wājib* (*wājib ghayr muḥaddad*). An example of the former is *ṣalāh, zakāh*, payment of the price (*thaman*) by the purchaser in a sale transaction, and payment of rent in accordance with the terms of a tenancy agreement, all of which are quantified. Similarly, enforcement of the prescribed penalties (*ḥudūd*) falls under the rubic of *wājib muḥaddad* in the sense that the *ḥadd* penalties are all specified in terms of quantity. The unquantified *wājib* may be illustrated by reference to one's duty to support one's close relatives, charity to the poor, feeding the hungry, paying a dower (*mahr*) to one's wife, the length of standing (*qiyām*), bowing and prostration in *ṣalāh*, wiping the head in ablution (*wuḍū'*) and quantifying the *taᶜzīr* penalties for offences which are punishable but in regard to which the Lawgiver has not quantified the punishment. (It is for the judge to quantify the punishment in light of the individual circumstances of the offender and the offence.) Consequently, the *mukallaf*, be it the individual believer, the *qāḍī* or the imām, enjoys the flexibility to determine the quantitative aspect of the unquantified *wājib* himself.[13]

A consequence of this division is that if the quantified *wājib* is not discharged within the given time-limit, it constitutes a liability on the person (*dhimmah*) of the individual, as in the case of unpaid *zakāh* or an unpaid debt. Failure to discharge a *wājib ghayr muḥaddad*, on the other hand, does not result in a personal liability.

A question arises with regard to the value of the excessive portion in the supererogation of quantified *wājib*. The question is whether an over-fulfilment of this type becomes a part of the *wājib* itself. There are two main views on this, one of which maintains that excessive performance in quantified *wājib* also becomes a part of the *wājib*. But the preferred view is that any addition to the minimal requirement becomes *mandūb* only. For no punishment can be imposed for a failure to perform anything in addition to the minimum required.[14]

It would be inaccurate to say that a means to a *wājib* is also a *wājib*, or that a necessary ingredient of *wājib* is also *wājib* in every case. For such a view would tend to ignore the personal capacity of the *mukallaf*, especially if the latter is unable to do what is required to be done: in the event, for example, when the Friday congregational prayer cannot be held for lack of a large number of people in a locality. It would be more accurate to say that when the means to *wājib* consist of an act which is within the capacity of the *mukallaf* then that act is also *wājib*.[15]

The distinction between *wājib* and *mandūb* is, broadly speaking, based on the idea that ignoring the *wājib* entails punishment (*ʿiqāb*) while ignoring the *mandūb* does not. The distinction between *ḥarām* and *makrūh* is based on a similar criterion: if doing something is punishable, it is *ḥarām*, otherwise it is *makrūh*. This is generally correct, but one must add the proviso that punishment is not a necessary requirement of a binding obligation, or *wujūb*. In addition, as Imām Ghazālī points out, the element of punishment, whether in this world or in the hereafter, is not a certainty. Whereas in its positive sense the *wājib* is normally enforceable in this world and might also lead to a tangible advantage or reward, the spiritual punishment for its neglect is, however, awaited and postponed to the hereafter. Hence the invocation of punishment is not a necessary requirement of *wājib*. When God Almighty renders an act obligatory upon people without mentioning a punishment for its omission, the act which is so demanded is still *wājib*.[16]

I.2 *Mandūb* (Recommended)

Mandūb denotes a demand of the Lawgiver which asks the *mukallaf* to do something which is, however, not binding on the latter. To comply with the demand earns the *mukallaf* spiritual reward (*thawāb*) but no punishment is inflicted for failure to perform. Creating a charitable endowment (*waqf*), for example, giving alms to the poor, fasting on days outside Ramadan, attending the sick, etc., are duties of this kind. *Mandūb* is variously known as *Sunnah*, *mustaḥabb* and *nafl*, which are all here synonymous and covered by the same definition.[17] If it is an act which the Prophet has done at one time but omitted at other times, it is called *Sunnah*. There are two types of *Sunnah*, namely *Sunnah mu'akkadah* (the emphatic *Sunnah*, also known as *Sunnah al-hudā*), and *Sunnah ghayr mu'akkadah*, or supererogatory *Sunnah*. The call to congregational prayers (i.e. the *adhān*), attending congregational prayers, and gargling as a part of the ablution (*wuḍū'*) are examples of the former, whereas non-obligatory charity, and supererogatory prayers preceding the obligatory *ṣalāh* in early and late afternoon (i.e. *ẓuhr*, and *ʿaṣr*) are examples of supererogatory *Sunnah*. Performing the emphatic *Sunnah* leads to spiritual reward from Almighty God while its neglect is merely blameworthy but not punishable. However, if the entire population of a locality agree to abandon the emphatic *Sunnah*, they are to be fought for contempt of the *Sunnah*. To perform the supererogatory *Sunnah*, on the other hand, leads to spiritual reward while neglecting it is not blameworthy. There is a third variety of *Sunnah* known as *Sunnah al-zawā'id*, which mainly refers to the acts and conduct performed by the Prophet as a human being, such as his style of dress and choice of food, etc., whose omission is neither abominable nor blameworthy.[18]

Mandūb often occurs in the Qur'ān in the form of a command which is then accompanied by indications to suggest that the command is only intended to convey a recommendation. An example of this is the Qur'ānic command which requires that giving and taking of period loans must be set down in writing (al-Baqarah, 2:282). But the subsequent portion of the same passage provides that 'if any of you deposits something with another, then let the trustee [faithfully] discharge his trust'. This passage implies that if the creditor trusts the debtor, they may forego the requirement of documentation. Another example of a command which only denotes a recommendation is the Qur'ānic provision regarding slaves, where the text provides, 'and if any of your slaves seek their release from you in writing, set them free [*fa-kātibūhum*] if you know any good in them' (al-Nūr, 24:3). The last portion of this text indicates an element of choice which renders the command therein *mandūb*. But in the absence of such accompanying evidence in the text itself, the Qur'ānic command is sometimes evaluated into *mandūb* by reference to the general principles of the *Sharī*ᶜ*ah*.

Sometimes the *mandūb* is conveyed in persuasive language rather than as a command *per se*. An example of this is the Ḥadīth which provides: 'Whoever makes an ablution for the Friday prayers, it is good, but if he takes a bath, it is better – [*afḍal*].'[19]

من توضأ يوم الجمعة فبها ونعمت ، ومن
اغتسل فالغسل أفضل

A question arises in this connection as to whether the *mandūb* remains a *mandūb* once it has been started, or becomes obligatory of continuation until it is completed. The Ḥanafīs have held that once the *mandūb* is commenced, it turns into an obligation and must be completed. For example, when a person starts a supererogatory fast, according to this view, it is obligatory that he complete it, and failure to do so renders him liable to the duty of belated performance (*qaḍā'*). But according to the Shāfiᶜīs, whose view here is generally preferred, the *mandūb* is never turned into *wājib* and always remains as *mandūb*, thereby leaving the person who has started it with the choice of discontinuing it whenever he wishes. There is thus no duty of belated performance (*qaḍā'*) on account of failure to complete a *mandūb*.[20]

I.3 *Ḥarām* (Forbidden)

According to the majority of ulema, *ḥarām* (also known as *maḥẓūr*) is a binding demand of the Lawgiver in respect of abandoning something, which may be founded in a definitive or a speculative proof. Committing the *ḥarām* is punishable and omitting it is rewarded. But according to the Ḥanafīs, *ḥarām* is a binding demand to abandon something which is established in definitive proof; if the demand is founded in speculative evidence, it constitutes a *makrūh taḥrīmī*, but not *ḥarām*. The former resembles the latter in that committing both is punished and omitting them is rewarded. But the two differ from one another insofar as the wilful denial of the *ḥarām* leads to infidelity, which is not the case with regard to *makrūh taḥrīmī*.[21]

The textual evidence for *ḥarām* occurs in a variety of forms, which may be summarised as follows:

Firstly, the text may clearly use the word *ḥarām* or any of its derivatives. For example, the Qur'anic text which provides, 'forbidden to you [*ḥurrimat ʿalaykum*] are the dead carcass, blood and pork' (al-Mā'idah, 5:3); and 'God permitted sale but prohibited [*ḥarrama*] usury' (al-Baqarah, 2:275). Similarly, the Ḥadīth which provides, 'everything belonging to a Muslim is forbidden [*ḥarām*] to his fellow Muslims: his blood, his property and his honour'.[22]

كل المسلم على المسلم حرام ، دمه وماله
وعرضه

Secondly, *ḥarām* may be conveyed in other prohibitory terms which require the avoidance of a certain form of conduct. For example, there is the Qur'ānic text which provides, 'slay not [*la taqtulū*] the life that God has made sacrosanct, save in the course of justice' (al-Mā'idah, 5:90); and 'devour not [*lā ta'kulū*] one another's property in defiance of the law' (al-Baqarah, 2:188).

Thirdly, *ḥarām* may be communicated in the form of a command to avoid a certain form of conduct. For example: there is the Qur'ānic text which provides that wine-drinking and gambling are works of the devil and then orders the believers to 'avoid it [*fa-jtanibūh*]' (al-Mā'idah, 5:90).

Fourthly, *ḥarām* may be communicated through expressions such as 'it is not permissible' or 'it is unlawful' in a context which is indicative of total prohibition. For example, the Qur'ānic text which proclaims that 'it is not permissible for you [*lā yaḥillu lakum*] to inherit women against their will' (al-Nisā', 4:19), or the Ḥadīth which provides 'it is unlawful [*la yaḥillu*] for a Muslim to take the property of another Muslim without his consent'.[23]

لا يحل مال امرىء مسلم إلا بطيب عن نفسه

Fifthly, *ḥarām* is also identified by the enactment of a punishment for a certain form of conduct. There are many instances of this in the Qur'ān and *Sunnah*. The *ḥudūd* penalties are the most obvious examples of this variety of *ḥarām*. As is implied by its name, the *ḥadd* penalty is specific in reference to both the quantity of punishment and the type of conduct which it penalises. Alternatively, the text which communicates *taḥrīm* may only consist of an emphatic condemnation of a certain act without specifying a penalty for it as such. Thus the Qur'ān prohibits devouring the property of orphans by denouncing it in the following terms: 'Those who eat up the property of orphans swallow fire into their own bodies; they will soon be enduring a blazing fire' (al-Nisā', 4:10).

Ḥarām is divided into two types: (a) *ḥarām li-dhātih* or 'that which is forbidden for its own sake', such as theft, murder, adultery, marrying a close relative and performing *ṣalāh* without an ablution, all of which are forbidden for their inherent enormity; and (b) *ḥarām li-ghayrih*, or 'that which is forbidden because of something else'. An act may be originally lawful but has been made unlawful owing to the presence of certain circumstances. For example: a marriage which is contracted for the sole purpose of *taḥlīl*, that is, in order to legalise another intended marriage, performing *ṣalāh* in stolen clothes, and making an offer of betrothal to a woman who is already betrothed to another man. In each of these examples, the act involved is originally lawful but has become *ḥarām* owing to the attending circumstances. A consequence of this distinction between the two varieties of *ḥarām* is that *ḥarām li-dhātih*, such as marriage to one's sister or the sale of dead carcasses, is null and void *ab initio* (*bāṭil*), whereas violating a prohibition which is imposed owing to an extraneous factor is *fāsid* (irregular) but not *bāṭil*, and as such may fulfil its intended legal purpose. A marriage which is contracted for the purpose of *taḥlīl* is clearly forbidden, but it validly takes place nevertheless. Similarly, a contract of sale which is concluded at the time of the Friday prayer is *ḥarām li-ghayrih* and is forbidden. But according to the majority of ulema the sale takes place nevertheless; with the exception of the Ḥanbalīs and Ẓāhirīs, who regard such a sale as *bāṭil*.[24]

Another consequence of this distinction is that *ḥarām li-dhātih* is not permissible save in cases of dire necessity (*ḍarūrah*) of a kind which threatens the safety of the 'five principles' of life, religion, intellect, lineage and property. In this way, uttering a word of infidelity, or drinking wine, is only permitted when it saves life. *Ḥarām li-ghayrih*, on the other hand, is permissible not only in cases of absolute necessity but also when it prevents hardship. Thus a physician is permitted to look at the private parts of a patient even in the case of illnesses which do not constitute an immediate threat to life.[25]

Another criterion for distinguishing the two varieties of *ḥarām* that some ulema have mentioned is that *ḥarām li-ghayrih* consists of an act which leads to *ḥarām li-dhātih*. In this way, looking at the private parts of another person is forbidden because it can lead to *zinā*, which is *ḥarām* by itself. Similarly, marrying two sisters simultaneously is *ḥarām* because it leads to the severance of ties of kinship (*qaṭʿ al-arḥām*), which is *ḥarām* by itself.[26]

I.4 *Makrūh* (Abominable)

Makrūh is a demand of the Lawgiver which requires the *mukallaf* to avoid something, but not in strictly prohibitory terms. *Makrūh* is the opposite of *mandūb*, which means that neglecting the *mandūb* amounts to *makrūh*. Since *makrūh* does not constitute a binding law, we merely say that omitting something which is *makrūh* is preferable to committing it. The perpetrator of something *makrūh* is not liable to punishment, and according to the majority of ulema, he does not incur moral blame either. The Ḥanafīs are in agreement with the majority view in respect of only one of the two varieties of *makrūh*, namely *makrūh tanzīhī*, but not in regard to *makrūh taḥrīmī*. The latter, according to the Ḥanafīs, entails moral blame but no punishment. The ulema are all in agreement that anyone who avoids the *makrūh* merits praise and gains closeness to God.[27]

The textual authority for *makrūh* may consist of a reference to something which is specifically identified as *makrūh*, or may be so identified by words that may convey an equivalent meaning. There is a Ḥadīth, for example, in which the Prophet discouraged any prayers at midday until the decline of the sun, with the exception of Friday. The actual word used in the Ḥadīth is that the Prophet disliked [*kariha al-nabī*] prayers at that particular time.[28]

كره النبي الصلاة نصف النهار حتى تزول
الشمس إلا يوم الجمعة

An equivalent term to *makrūh* occurs, for example, in the Ḥadīth which reads: 'The most abominable of permissible things [*abghaḍ al-ḥalāl*] in the sight of God is divorce.'[29]

أبغض الحلال الى الله الطلاق

Makrūh may also be conveyed in the form of a prohibition but in language that indicates only reprehensibility. An example of this is the Qur'ānic text which provides, in an address directed to the believers, 'Ask not about things which, if made clear to you, would trouble you, but if you ask about them when the Qur'ān is being revealed, then they will be explained to you' (al-Mā'idah, 5:101). An example of this style of communication in the Ḥadīth is as follows: 'Leave that of which you are doubtful in favour of that which you do not doubt [. . .]'[30]

دع ما يريبك إلى ما لا يريبك . . .

Makrūh is the lowest degree of prohibition (*taḥrīm*), and in this sense is used as a convenient category for matters which fall in the grey areas between *ḥalāl* and *ḥarām*, that is, matters which are definitely discouraged but where the evidence to establish them as *ḥarām* is less than certain.[31]

As already noted, the Ḥanafīs have divided *makrūh* into the two types of *makrūh tanzīhī* and *makrūh taḥrīmī*. The former is considered abominable for purposes of keeping pure such as avoiding raw onion and garlic just before going to congregational prayers, or neglecting *ṣalāt al-nafl*, that is, supererogatory prayers preceding, for example, the *ṣalāt al-ẓuhr* (early afternoon prayers). This kind of *makrūh* is nearer to *mubāḥ* than to *ḥarām*. Its commission is not punished but its omission is rewarded. The Ḥanafī description of *makrūh tanzīhī* is the same as that which the majority of ulema have given to *makrūh* in general. The majority of ulema have characterised the value of *makrūh* to be that 'committing it is not punishable but omitting it is praiseworthy'. *Makrūh taḥrīmī*, or 'abominable to the degree of prohibition' is, on the other hand, nearer to *ḥarām*. An act is *ḥarām* when its prohibition is decreed in definitive terms, otherwise it is *makrūh taḥrīmī*. An example of *makrūh taḥrīmī* is the wearing of gold jewellery and silk garments for men, which are forbidden by an *Āḥād* (solitary) Ḥadīth. While referring to these two items, the Ḥadīth provides: 'These are forbidden [*ḥarām*] to the men of my community but are lawful [*ḥalāl*] to their women.'[32]

هذان حرامان لرجال أمتي حلالان لنسائهم

Similarly, it is *makrūh taḥrīmī* for a person to offer to buy something for which another person has already made an offer. There is a Ḥadīth which forbids this kind of purchase in the same way as it forbids making an offer of engagement to a woman who is already betrothed to another man:[33]

لا يبيع الرجل على بيع أخيه ولا يخطب على
خطبة أخيه إلا ان يأذن له

Since both of the foregoing *aḥādīth* are *Āḥād* whose authenticity is not devoid of doubt, the prohibition therein is reduced from *ḥarām* to *makrūh taḥrīmī.*

The difference between the Ḥanafīs and the majority of ulema relates to the nature of the evidence on which the *makrūh* is founded. When a prohibition is conveyed in an imperative demand of the Lawgiver but there is some doubt over its authenticity or meaning, the majority of ulema classify it as *ḥarām*, whereas the Ḥanafīs classify it as *makrūh taḥrīmī.* The Ḥanafī position in regard to the division of *makrūh* into these two types is essentially similar to their approach in regard to drawing a distinction between *farḍ* and *wājib.*[34]

I.5 *Mubāḥ* (Permissible)

Mubāḥ (also referred to as *ḥalāl* and *jā'iz*) is defined as communication from the Lawgiver concerning the conduct of the *mukallaf* which gives him the option to do or not to do something. The Lawgiver's communication may be in the form of a clear *naṣṣ* such as the Qur'ānic text which provides, in a reference to foodstuffs, that 'this day all things good and pure have been made lawful (*uḥilla*) to you [. . .]' (al-Mā'idaḥ, 5:6). Alternatively the text may state that the *mukallaf* will not incur a sin, blame or liability if he wishes to act in a certain way. Concerning the permissibility of betrothal, for example, the Qur'ān provides, 'there is no blame on you [*lā junāḥa ʿalaykum*] if you make an offer of betrothal to a woman [. . .]' (al-Baqarah, 2:235). Similarly, committing a sinful act out of sheer necessity is permissible on the authority of the Qur'ān, which provides, 'If someone is compelled by necessity without wilful disobedience or transgression, then he is guiltless [*falā ithma ʿalayh*]' (al-Baqarah, 2:173).[35]

Sometimes a command in the Qur'ān may only amount to permissibility when the nature of the conduct in question or other relevant evidence indicates that such is the case. An example of this is the text which orders worshippers to 'scatter in the earth' once they have completed the Friday prayers (al-Jumuʿah, 62:10). Although the believers have been ordered to 'scatter in the earth', the nature of this command and the type of activity to which it relates suggest that it conveys permissibility only.

In the event where the law provides no ruling to specify the value of a certain form of conduct, then according to the doctrine of *istiṣḥāb al-aṣl* (presumption of continuity), permissibility (*ibāḥah*) remains the original state which is presumed to continue. The authority for this presumption is found in the Qur'ānic text which provides, in an address to mankind, that God Almighty 'has created everything in the earth for your benefit' (al-Baqarah, 2:29). By implication, it is understood that the benefit in question cannot materialise unless 'everything in the earth' is made *mubāḥ* for mankind to use and to utilise in the first place.

Mubāḥ has been divided into three types. The first is *mubāḥ* which does not entail any harm to the individual whether he acts upon it or not, such as eating, hunting or walking in the fresh air. The second type of *mubāḥ* is that whose commission does not harm the individual although it is essentially forbidden. Included in this category are the prohibited acts which the Lawgiver has made permissible on account of necessity, such as uttering words of unbelief under duress, or eating the flesh of a dead carcass to save one's life. The third variety of *mubāḥ* is not really *mubāḥ per se*; it is included under *mubāḥ* for lack of a better alternative. This category of *mubāḥ* consists of things which were practiced at one time but were then prohibited with the proviso that those who indulged in them before the prohibition are exonerated. The Qur'ān thus prohibits marriage with certain relatives, and the text then continues to make an exception for such marriages that might have occurred in the past (al-Nisā', 4:22). Similarly, wine-drinking was not prohibited until the Prophet's migration to Madinah, and fell under the category of *mubāḥ* until the revelation of the *āyah* in sūra al-Mā'idah (5:90) which imposed a total ban on it.[36]

It would be incorrect, as al-Ghazālī explains, to apply the term '*mubāḥ*' to the acts of a child, an insane person, or an animal, nor would it be correct to call the acts of God *mubāḥ*. Acts and events which took place prior to the advent of Islam are not to be called *mubāḥ* either. 'As far as we are concerned, our position regarding them is one of abandonment [*tark*]', which obviously means that such activities are not to be evaluated at all. *Mubāḥ* proper, al-Ghazālī adds, is established in the express permission of Almighty God which renders the commission or omission of an act permissible either in religious terms or in respect of a possible benefit or harm that may accrue from it in this world.[37]

The ulema of *uṣūl* definitely consider *mubāḥ* to be a *ḥukm sharʿī*, although including it under *al-ḥukm al-taklīfī* is on the basis of mere probability as there is basically no liability [*taklīf*] in *mubāḥ* as one of the five varieties of defining law. The Ḥanafīs have only differed with the majority with regard to the sub-divisions of *wājib* and *makrūh* as already explained, but not with regard to *mubāḥ*.

Bearing in mind the two sub-divisions of *wājib* and *makrūh* that the Ḥanafīs have added to *al-ḥukm al-taklīfī*, the Ḥanafīs thus classify the latter into seven types, whereas the majority divide it into five varieties only.

II. Declaratory Law (*al-Ḥukm al-Waḍʿī*)

'Declaratory law' is defined as communication from the Lawgiver which enacts something into a cause (*sabab*), a condition (*sharṭ*) or a hindrance (*mániʿ*) to something else. This may be illustrated by reference to the Qur'ānic text regarding the punishment of adultery, which enacts the act of adultery itself as the cause of its punishment (al-Baqarah, 2 : 24). An example of the declaratory law which consists of a condition is the Qur'ānic text on the pilgrimage of *ḥajj*: 'Pilgrimage is a duty owed to God by people who can manage to make the journey' (Āl-ʿImrān, 3 : 97). Both of the foregoing texts, in fact, consist of a defining law and a declaratory law side by side. The defining law in the first text is the ruling that the adulterer must be punished with a hundred lashes, and in the second text it is the duty of the *ḥajj* pilgrimage itself. The declaratory law in the first text is the cause, which is the act of adultery – the affect being the punishment, and in the second, it is the condition which must be present if the law of the text is to be implemented. The second of the two texts thus enacts the ability of the individual to make the journey into a condition for performing the pilgrimage. A more explicit example of a declaratory law is the Ḥadīth which provides that 'there is no *nikāḥ* without two witnesses'.[38]

لا نكاح الا بشاهدين

The presence of two witnesses is thus rendered a condition for a valid marriage. And lastly, an example of a declaratory law consisting of a hindrance is the Ḥadīth which provides that 'there shall be no bequest to an heir',[39]

لا وصية لوارث

which obviously enacts the tie of kinship between the testator and the legatee into a hindrance to bequest. Similarly, the Ḥadīth which lays down the rule that 'the killer shall not inherit',

لا يرث القاتل

renders killing a hindrance to inheritance.[40]

To execute the defining law is normally within the capacity of the *mukallaf*. The demands, for example, addressed to the *mukallaf* concerning prayers and *zakāh* are both within his means. Declaratory law may, on the other hand, be within or beyond the capacity of the *mukallaf*. For instance, the arrival of a particular time of day which is the cause (*sabab*) of *ṣalāh* is beyond the means and capacity of the worshipper.[41]

The function of declaratory law is explanatory in relation to defining law, in that the former explains the component elements of the latter. Declaratory law thus informs us whether certain facts or events are the cause, condition or hindrance in relationship to defining law. It is, for example, by means of declaratory law that we know offer and acceptance in a contract of sale to be the cause of the buyer's ownership, that divorce causes the extinction of marital rights and obligations, and that the death of a person is the cause of the right of the heir to his inheritance. Similarly, it is by means of a declaratory law that we know intellectual maturity to be the condition of voluntary disposition of property in gift (*hibah*) and charitable endowment (*waqf*).[42]

The basic notion of dividing the rules of *Sharīʿah* into *taklīfī* and *waḍʿī* is also applicable to modern western law. When we read, in the Rent Act for example, a clause which requires the tenant to pay the rent in accordance with the tenancy contract, it is a *ḥukm taklīfī* which consists of a command. Similarly, when there is a clause which requires the tenant not to use the premises for commercial purposes, it is a demand consisting of a prohibition. And if there be a clause to the effect that the tenant may sublet the property, it is an option which the tenant may or may not wish to exercise. Needless to say, any aspect of such provisions may be subjected to certain conditions or hindrances as the contracting parties may wish to stipulate.[43]

As noted above, declaratory law is divided into five varieties. The first three of these, namely cause, condition and hindrance, have already been discussed to some extent. Two other varieties which are added to these are the *ʿazīmah* (strict law) as opposed to *rukhṣah* (concessionary law), and valid (*ṣaḥīḥ*) as opposed to invalid (*bāṭil*). To include the first three under *al-ḥukm al-waḍʿī* is obvious from the very definition of the latter. But classifying the last two divisions, that is, *ʿazimah-rukhṣah* and *ṣaḥīḥ-bāṭil*, under *al-ḥukm al-waḍʿī* may need a brief explanation. It is well to point out in this connection that almost every concession that the Lawgiver has granted to the individual is based on certain causes which must be present if the concession is to be utilised. The Lawgiver, for example, enacts travelling, illness or removal of hardship into the cause of a concession in regard to, say, fasting or *ṣalāh*. In classifying *ṣaḥīḥ* and *bāṭil* as sub-divisions of declaratory law, it will be further noted that a *ḥukm* is valid when the conditions of its validity are fulfilled, and is invalid if these conditions are not met. In short, since the last two divisions are basically concerned with causes and conditions, they are included under the class of declaratory law.[44]

We shall now proceed to discuss each of the five varieties of *al-ḥukm al-waḍʿī* separately.

II.1 Cause (*Sabab*)

A *sabab* is defined as an attribute which is evident and constant [*waṣf ẓāhir wa-munḍabaṭ*] and which the Lawgiver has identified as the indicator of a *ḥukm* in such a way that its presence necessitates the presence of the *ḥukm* and its absence means that the *ḥukm* is also absent. A *sabab* may be an act which is within the power of the *mukallaf*, such as murder and theft in their status as the causes of retaliation (*qiṣāṣ*) and a *ḥadd* penalty respectively. Alternatively, the *sabab* may be beyond the control of the *mukallaf*, such as minority being the cause of guardianship over the person and property of a minor. When the *sabab* is present, whether it is within or beyond the control of the *mukallaf*, its effect (i.e. the *musabbab*) is automatically present even if the *mukallaf* had not intended it to be. For example, when a man divorces his wife by a revocable *ṭalāq*, he is entitled to resume marital relations with her even if he openly denies himself that right. Similarly, when a man enters into a contract of marriage, he is obligated to provide dower and maintenance for his wife even if he explicitly stipulates the opposite in their contract. For once the Lawgiver identifies something as a cause, the effect of that cause comes about by virtue of the Lawgiver's decree regardless of whether the *mukallaf* intended it to be so or not.[45]

II.2 Condition (*Sharṭ*)

A *sharṭ* is defined as an evident and constant attribute whose absence necessitates the absence of the *ḥukm* but whose presence does not automatically bring about its object (*mashrūṭ*). For example, the presence of a valid marriage is a precondition of divorce, but it does not mean that when there is a valid marriage, it must lead to divorce. Similarly, the ablution (*wuḍū'*) is a necessary condition of *ṣalāh*, but the presence of *wuḍū'* does not necessitate *ṣalāh*.

A condition normally complements the cause and gives it its full effect. Killing is, for example, the cause of retaliation; however, this is on condition that it is deliberate and hostile. The contract of marriage legalises/causes sexual enjoyment between the spouses; however, this is on condition that two witnesses testify to the marriage. The legal consequences of a contract are not fully realised without the fulfilment of its necessary conditions.

A condition may be laid down by the Lawgiver, or by the *mukallaf*. Whenever the former enacts a condition, it is referred to as *sharṭ sharᶜī*, or 'legal condition', but if it is a condition which is stipulated by the *mukallaf*, it is referred to *sharṭ jaᶜlī*, or 'improvised condition'. An example of the former is witnesses in a marriage contract, and of the latter, the case when spouses stipulate in their marriage contract the condition that they will reside in a particular locality.

Sharṭ also differs with *rukn* (pillar, essential requirement) in that the latter partakes in the essence of a thing. This would mean that the law, or *ḥukm*, could not exist in the absence of its *rukn*. When the whole or even a part of the *rukn* is absent, the *ḥukm* collapses completely, with the result that the latter becomes null and void (*bāṭil*). A *sharṭ*, on the other hand, does not partake in the essence of a *ḥukm*, although it is a complementary part of it. Bowing and prostration (*rukūᶜ* and *sajdah*), for example, are each an essential requirement (*rukn*) of *ṣalāh* and partake in the very essence of *ṣalāh*, but ablution is a condition of *ṣalāh* as it is an attribute whose absence disrupts the *ṣalāh* but which does not partake in its essence.[46]

II.3 Hindrance (*Mūniᶜ*)

A *māniᶜ* is defined as an act or an attribute whose presence either nullifies the *ḥukm* or the cause of the *ḥukm*. In either case, the result is the same, namely that the presence of the *māniᶜ* means the absence of the *ḥukm*. For example, difference of religion, and killing, are both obstacles to inheritance between a legal heir and his deceased relative, despite the fact that there may exist a valid tie of kinship (*qarābah*) between them: when the obstacle is present, the *ḥukm*, which is inheritance, is absent.

From the viewpoint of its effect on the cause (*sabab*) or on the *ḥukm* itself, the *māniᶜ* is divided into two types. First, the *māniᶜ* which affects the cause in the sense that its presence nullifies the cause. An example of this is the indebtedness of a person who is liable to the payment of *zakāh*. The fact of his being in debt hinders the cause of *zakāh*, which is ownership of property. A person who is in debt to the extent of insolvency is no longer considered, for purposes of *zakāh*, to be owning any property at all. Thus when the cause is nullified, the *ḥukm* itself, which is the duty to pay *zakāh*, is also nullified. Secondly, there is the hindrance which affects the *ḥukm*. The presence of this type of hindrance nullifies the *ḥukm* directly, even if the cause and the condition are both present. An example of this is paternity, which hinders retaliation: if a father kills his son, he is not liable to retaliation although he may be punished otherwise. Paternity thus hinders retaliation according to the majority of ulema (except Imām Mālik) despite the presence of the cause of retaliation, which is killing, and its condition, which is hostility and the intention to kill. Imām Mālik has held, on the other hand, that the father may be retaliated against for the deliberate killing of his offspring.[47]

II.4 Strict Law (*ʿAzīmah*) and Concessionary Law (*Rukhṣah*)

A law, or *ḥukm*, is an *ʿazīmah* when it is in its primary and unabated rigour without reference to any attenuating circumstances which may soften its original force or even entirely suspend it. It is, in other words, a law as the Lawgiver had intended it in the first place. For example, *ṣalāh*, *zakāh*, the *ḥajj*, *jihād*, etc., which God has enjoined upon all competent individuals, are classified under *ʿazīmah*. A law, or *ḥukm*, is a *rukhṣah*, by contrast, when it is considered in conjunction with attenuating circumstances. Whereas *ʿazīmah* is the law in its normal state, *rukhṣah* embodies the exceptions, if any, that the Lawgiver has granted with a view to bringing facility and ease in difficult circumstances. Thus the law which grants a concession to travellers to break the fast during Ramadan is an exception to the norm that requires everyone to fast. The concessionary law in this case is valid only for the duration of travelling, after which the *ʿazīmah* must be complied with again. Similarly, if a Muslim is compelled to renounce his faith, he is permitted to do so even though the strict law would require him to persist in his faith until death. The excuse in this case is founded in the right of the person to life, and is clearly granted in the Qur'ān (al-Naḥl, 16:106), which allows the utterance of words of infidelity under duress. Strict law may consist of either commands or prohibitions. Thus the prohibition of murder, theft, adultery, wine-drinking, etc., are all instances of *ʿazīmah* in the Qur'ān.[48]

ʿAzīmah is a command of the Lawgiver which binds the *mukallaf*, while *rukhṣah* embodies a concession in respect of that command. The two are interrelated in that *rukhṣah* can only exist when there is *ʿazīmah* in the first place. God Almighty has not made, for example, fasting in the month of Shawwāl (the month following Ramadan) obligatory upon Muslims. This is not a concession, as there exists no obligation in the first place. Similarly, the normal state of *ibāḥah* regarding foods and drinks is not *rukhṣah*, whereas the permission to eat prohibited meat in certain circumstances is *rukhṣah*. It would also be incorrect to call the permissibility of *tayammum* (i.e. dry ablution with clean earth or sand) in the absence of water a *rukhṣah*: when there is no water it is not possible to make an ablution proper *wuḍū'* in the first place. But *tayammum* is a *rukhṣah* if it is a substitute for *wuḍū'* when the weather is extremely cold. The point is that in *rukhṣah* the individual must be able to take an alternative course of action.[49]

Rukhṣah occurs in any of four varieties. Firstly, in the form of permitting a prohibited act on grounds of necessity, such as eating the flesh of a carcass, and drinking wine at the point of starvation or extreme thirst. Secondly, *rukhṣah* may occur in the form of omitting a *wājib* when conformity to that *wājib* causes hardship, such as the concession granted to the traveller to shorten the quadruple *ṣalāh*, or not to observe the fasting of Ramadan. Thirdly, in the area of transactions, *rukhṣah* occurs in the form of validating contracts which would normally be disallowed. For example, lease and hire (*ijārah*), advance sale (*salam*) and order for the manufacture of goods (*istiṣnāᶜ*) are all anomalous, as the object of contract therein is non-existent at the time of contract, but they have been exceptionally permitted in order to accommodate the public need for such transactions. And lastly, *rukhṣah* occurs in the form of concessions to the Muslim *ummah* from certain rigorous laws which were imposed under previous revelations. For example, *zakāh* to the extent of one-quarter of one's property, the impermissibility of *ṣalāh* outside a mosque, and the illegality of taking booty (i.e. *ghanīmah*), which were imposed on people under previous religions, have been removed by the *Sharīᶜah* of Islam.[50]

II.5 Valid, Irregular and Void (*Ṣaḥīḥ, Fāsid, Bāṭil*)

These are *Sharīᶜah* values which describe and evaluate legal acts incurred by the *mukallaf*. To evaluate an act according to these criteria depends on whether or not the act in question fulfils the essential requirements (*arkān*) and conditions (*shurūṭ*) that the *Sharīᶜah* has laid down for it, as well as to ensure that there exist no obstacles to hinder its proper conclusion. For example, *ṣalāh* is a *sharᶜī* act and is evaluated as valid when it fulfils all the essential requirements and conditions that the *Sharīᶜah* has provided in this regard. Conversely, *ṣalāh* becomes void when any of its essential requirements and conditions are lacking. Similarly, a contract is described as valid when it fulfils all of its necessary requirements, and where there is nothing to hinder its conclusion; otherwise it is void. When *ṣalāh* is performed according to its requirements, it fulfils the *wājib*, otherwise, the *wājib* remains unfulfilled. A valid contract gives rise to all of its legal consequences whereas a void contract fails to satisfy its legal purpose.

The ulema are in agreement to the effect that acts of devotion (*ᶜibādāt*) can either be valid or void, in the sense that there is no intermediate category in between. Legal acts are valid when they fulfil all the requirements pertaining to the essential requirements (*arkān*), causes, conditions and hindrances, and are void when any of these is lacking or deficient. An act of devotion which is void is non-existent *ab initio* and of no consequence whatsoever. The majority of ulema have maintained a similar view with regard to transactions, namely, that a transaction is valid when it is complete in all respects. Only a valid contract of sale, for example, can give rise to its legal consequences, namely, to transfer ownership of the object of sale to the buyer and to establish the vendor's ownership over its price (*thaman*). A contract is void when it is deficient in respect of any of its requirements, although the Ḥanafīs are in disagreement with the majority over the precise nature of this deficiency. The majority of ulema maintain that invalidity is a monolithic concept in that there are no shades and degrees of invalidity. An act or transaction is either valid or void, and there is nothing in between. According to this view, *fāsid* and *bāṭil* are two words with the same meaning, whether in reference to devotional matters or to civil transactions. Likewise, to the majority it makes no difference whether the deficiency in a contract affects an essential element (*rukn*) such as the sale of a dead carcass, or a condition, such as sale for an unspecified price; both are void and non-existent *ab initio*.

The Ḥanafīs have, however, distinguished an intermediate category between the valid and void, namely the *fāsid*. When the deficiency in a contract affects an essential requirement (*rukn*), the contract is null and void and fulfils no legal purpose. If, however, the deficiency in a contract only affects a condition, the contract is *fāsid* but not void. A *fāsid* contract, although deficient in some respects, is still a contract and produces some of its legal consequences, but not all. Thus a *fāsid* contract of sale establishes the purchaser's ownership over the object of sale when he has taken possession thereof, but does not entitle the purchaser to the usufruct (*intifāʿ*). Similarly, in the case of an irregular contract of marriage, such as one without witnesses, the spouses or the *qāḍī* must either remove the deficiency or dissolve the marriage, even if the marriage has been consummated. If the deficiency is known before consummation, the consummation is unlawful. But the wife is still entitled to the dower (*mahr*) and must observe the waiting period of *ʿiddah* upon dissolution of marriage. The offspring of a *fāsid* marriage is legitimate, but the wife is not entitled to maintenance, and no right of inheritance between the spouses can proceed from such a marriage.

The Ḥanafīs describe the *fāsid* as something which is essentially lawful (*mashrūʿ*) but is deficient in respect of an attribute (*waṣf*) as opposed to the *bāṭil* which is unlawful (*ghayr mashrūʿ*) on account of its deficiency in regard to both essence (*aṣl*) and attribute. The Ḥanafī approach to the *fāsid* is also grounded in the idea that the deficiency which affects the attribute but not the essence of a transaction can often be removed and rectified. If, for example, a contract of sale is concluded without assigning a specified price, it is possible to specify the price (*thaman*) after the conclusion of the contract and thus rectify the irregularity at a later opportunity, that is, as soon as it is known to exist or as soon as possible.[51]

III. The Pillars (*Arkān*) of *Ḥukm Sharʿī*

The *ḥukm sharʿī*, that is, the law or value of *Sharīʿah*, consists of three essential components. First of all, the *ḥukm* must have been authorised by the *ḥākim*, that is, the Lawgiver; it must also have a subject matter which is referred to as *maḥkūm fīh*; and then an audience, namely the *maḥkūm ʿalayh*, who must be capable of understanding or at least of receiving the *ḥukm*. We shall treat each of these under a separate heading, as follows.

III.1 The Lawgiver (*Ḥākim*)

The ulema are unanimous to the effect that the source of all law in Islam is God Most High, whose will and command is known to the *mukallaf* either directly through divine revelation, or indirectly by means of inference, deduction and *ijtihād*. The Qur'ān repeatedly tells us that 'The prerogative of command belongs to God alone' (Āl-ʿImrān, 6:57). Law and justice in the Muslim community must derive their validity and substance from the principles and values that the Lawgiver has sanctioned. This is the purport of the Qur'ānic text in sūra al-Mā'idah (5:45 and 5:49) which declares to be unbelievers those who refuse to accept the authority of the divine law. Even the Prophet does not partake in the prerogative of command, as his command, or that of the ruler, the imām, the master or the father for that matter, does not constitute binding authority in its own right; instead, obedience to such individuals is founded in the command of the Lawgiver. Neither is human intellect, or *ʿaql*, alone, a source of law in its own right.[52]

The ulema are in disagreement, however, as to the way in which the will or the *ḥukm* of the Lawgiver regarding the conduct of the *mukallaf* is to be known and identified. Can we know it by means of our intellectual faculty without the aid and mediation of messengers and scriptures, or is the human intellect incapable of ascertaining the law without divine guidance? A similar question arises concerning harmony and concordance between reason and revelation, in that when the human intellect determines that something is good (*ḥasan*) or evil (*qabīḥ*), is it imperative that the *ḥukm* of the Lawgiver should be identical with the dictates of reason? In response to these questions, the ulema have advanced three different views, which are as follows:

Firstly, the Ashʿarites, namely the followers of Abu'l-Ḥasan al-Ashʿarī (d. 324 A.H.), maintain that it is not possible for human intellect to determine what is good and evil in the conduct of the *mukallaf*, or to identify the *ḥukm* of the Lawgiver concerning the conduct of the *mukallaf*, without the aid of divine guidance. For human reasoning and judgment are liable to err. While an act may be evaluated by one person as good, another person might say the opposite. We normally say, for example, that honesty is good, but when it is likely to cause the death of an innocent person in the hands of a tyrant, it may be regarded as evil. It is therefore not for the human intellect to determine the values of things, and we cannot say that what the *ʿaql* deems to be good is necessarily good in the sight of God, or that what it considers evil is also evil in His sight. The Ashʿarites thus maintain that right and wrong are not determined by reference to the nature of things, or our perception thereof, but are determined as such by God. When the Lawgiver permits or demands an act, we know that it is right/good, and when He forbids an act, it is certain that the act in question is wrong/evil. Hence the criterion of right and wrong is *sharʿ*, not *ʿaql*. According to this view, which is held by the majority of ulema, what the law commands is good and what it forbids is evil. This view is in accord with what is known as the principle of the rule of law (also known as the principle of legality) which establishes that a man is not required to do something or to avoid doing it unless the law has been communicated to him in advance. No-one is either rewarded for an act or punished for an omission unless he knows its status by means of a clear communication. Thus when a person happens to be living in total isolation and has never received the message of the Lawgiver, he is not a *mukallaf* and deserves neither reward nor punishment. This view quotes in support the Qur'ānic proclamation: 'And We never punish until We send a messenger' (al-Isrā', 17:15), which indicates that reward and punishment are based on the revealed law, not the human intellect. Elsewhere in the Qur'ān, we also read, in a reference to the purpose of divine revelation, '[. . .] so that after the coming of messengers, mankind would have no plea against God' (al-Nisā', 4:165). In yet another place the Qur'ān affirms that punishment is imposed only after the people are duly warned but not before: in a reference to the disbelievers, the Qur'ān thus proclaims: 'Had We inflicted on them a penalty before this [revelation] they would have said: Our Lord! If only you had sent us a messenger, we would have followed your signs [. . .]' (Ṭā-Hā, 20:134).

The Ashᶜarites maintain the view that the commands of the Lawgiver relate to the conduct of the *mukallaf* only after the advent of Islam and that prior to this event there is no basis for obligation. Infidelity (*kufr*) is not *ḥarām*, nor is faith (*lymān*) *wājib* before the revelation actually declares it so.[53]

Secondly, the Muᶜtazilah, that is, the followers of Ibrāhīm al-Naẓẓām, have held the view that human intellect can identify the law of God regarding the conduct of the *mukallaf* even without the mediation of scriptures and messengers. The *sharᶜ* only removes the curtain from what the *ᶜaql* could itself perceive, and in essence the former is identical with the latter. The intellect (*ᶜaql*) can identify the good and evil in human conduct by reference to its benefit and harm. God's law concerning the conduct of the *mukallaf* is not only identifiable by the human intellect but is also identical with the dictates of the human intellect. God only asks the *mukallaf* to do what is beneficial and forbids him from doing what is harmful. Whatever the *ᶜaql* sees as good or right, is also good in the sight of God, and vice versa. A person who acts against the requirement of reason may therefore be punished and one who acts in harmony with it may be rewarded. In this way, a person who has received no communication from the Lawgiver can still be considered a *mukallaf* and be held responsible on the basis of reason, and his punishment or reward can be determined accordingly. The Muᶜtazilah assert that it is impossible for God to command something which is inherently evil or to prohibit something that is intrinsically good, which obviously means that *sharᶜ* and *ᶜaql* are always in agreement with one another.[54]

Al-Ghazālī is critical of the Muᶜtazilī view for its propensity to turn the determination of good and evil into a totally relative proposition. When an act is agreeable to one person and disagreeable to another, it is good from the viewpoint of the former and evil from that of the latter. Such a relativistic and circumstantial approach to good and evil is totally unacceptable. The *Sharīᶜah* does not and cannot operate on this basis. Instead, the *Sharīᶜah* evaluates the acts and conduct of the *mukallaf* on an objective plane regardless of whether they agree or disagree with particular interests. When the Lawgiver commands an act, or when He praises it, it is praiseworthy and good in all cases.[55] Al-Shawkānī is also critical of the Muᶜtazilī view, and highlights some of its weaknesses by saying that certain areas of human conduct are not amenable to rational evaluation. It is true that *ᶜaql* can determine the value, say, of truth and falsehood, as truth is beneficial and lying is harmful. *ᶜAql* can also discern the value of saving the life of a drowning or of a starving man, yet it cannot determine the virtue of fasting on the last day of Ramadan or the enormity of fasting on the day which follows it. The good and evil in this case can only be determined by *sharʿ*, not by *ʿaql*.[56] Most of the *ʿibādāt*, including *ṣalāh* and the pilgrimage of *ḥajj*, fall under this category. The human intellect may be able to perceive a value in them only because of a benevolence and grace (*luṭf*) therein which prevents obscenity and corruption; but *ʿaql* alone is unable to assess the precise value of *ʿibādāt*.[57]

The Muʿtazilī approach to the question of right and wrong embodies a utilitarian approach to jurisprudence in the sense that a good law is that which brings the greatest benefit to the largest number. Right and wrong are evaluated from the viewpoint of the benefit and harm that they entail to the person who acts upon it and to others. Acts which do not relate to this context are simply regarded as of no consequence; they are branded as *ʿabath*, that is, totally 'in vain'.

Thirdly, the Māturīdīs, namely the followers of Abū Manṣūr al-Māturīdī (d.333 A.H.) have suggested a middle course, which is adopted by the Ḥanafīs and considered to be the most acceptable. According to this view, right and wrong in the conduct of the *mukallaf* can indeed be ascertained and evaluated by the human intellect. But this does not necessarily mean that the law of God in regard to such conduct is always identical with the dictates of *ʿaql*, for human intellect is liable to error. The knowledge of right and wrong must therefore be based on divine communication. This view basically combines the two foregoing opinions, but tends to lean more toward the Ashʿarites in that the responsibility of the *mukallaf* is to be determined not with reference to the dictates of human reason but on the basis of the law as the Lawgiver has communicated it. *ʿAql* is capable of discerning good and evil, but this evaluation does not constitute the basis of reward and punishment; which is a matter which is solely determined by the Lawgiver. Whatever the Lawgiver has commanded is right, and merits reward, and whatever He has forbidden is wrong and its perpetrator is liable to punishment. This view also agrees with that of the Muʿtazilah to the extent of its recognition that the inherent values of things are discernible by human intellect which can perceive and detect values in the nature of things. The Māturīdīs, however, differ with the Muʿtazilah in that they hold that no reward or punishment can be granted on the basis of *ʿaql* alone.[58]

III.2 The Subject-Matter of *Ḥukm* (*al-Maḥkūm Fīh*)

Maḥkūm fīh denotes the acts, rights and obligations of the *mukallaf* which constitute the subject-matter of a command, prohibition or permissibility. When the ruling of the Lawgiver occurs in the forms of either *wājib* or *mandūb*, in either case the individual is required to act in some way. Similarly, when the *ḥukm* of the Lawgiver consists of a prohibition (*taḥrīm*) or abomination (*karāhah*), it is once again concerned with the conduct of the *mukallaf*. In sum, all commands and prohibitions are concerned with the acts and conduct of the *mukallaf*.

When the demand of the Lawgiver occurs in the form of a defining law (*al-ḥukm al-taklīfī*) such as fasting, *jihād*, and the payment of *zakāh*, etc., the subject-matter of the *ḥukm* is the act of the *mukallaf*. Similarly, when the demand of the Lawgiver occurs in the form of declaratory law (*al-ḥukm al-waḍʿī*), such as ablution (*wuḍū'*) being a condition of *ṣalāh*, or sale which is the cause (*sabab*) of ownership, or killing which is a hindrance (*māniʿ*) to inheritance, the subject-matter of *ḥukm* in all these consists of the act of the *mukallaf*. Occasionally, the *maḥkūm fīh* does not consist of the conduct of the individual, but even then it is related to it. For example, the arrival of Ramadan which is the cause (*sabab*) of fasting is not an act of the individual, but is related to the latter in the sense that the effect (*musabbab*) of that cause, namely the fasting, consists of the act of the *mukallaf*.[59] In order to constitute the subject-matter of a *ḥukm*, the conduct which the individual is required to do, or avoid doing, must fulfil the following three conditions.

Firstly, the individual must know the nature of the conduct so that he can perform what is required of him or refrain from that which is forbidden.[60] An ambivalent text or a locution which does not impart this knowledge cannot constitute the basis of either a command or a prohibition. The ambivalent (*mujmal*) text of the Qur'ān concerning *ṣalāh*, *zakāh* and *ḥajj*, for example, did not obligate anyone until these matters were explained and clarified by the Prophet. The manner in which these obligations were to be discharged was also explained in precise terms. Furthermore, the ulema are in agreement to the effect that the necessary instruction or explanations must not be delayed and must be given in time when they are needed, otherwise they would fail to provide the basis of obligation (*taklīf*).

When we say that the individual must know the nature of the act he is required to do, it means that it should be possible for him to obtain such knowledge. Hence when a person is in full possession of his capacities and it is possible for him to learn the law, he is presumed to know his legal obligations. The law is therefore applied to him, and his ignorance of the rules of *Sharīʿah* is no excuse. For if actual knowledge by the individual were to be a requirement of the law, it would be very difficult to prove such knowledge in all cases of violation. It is therefore sufficient to ensure that the individual can acquire knowledge of the *Sharīʿah* either directly or by asking those who have such knowledge.

Secondly, the act which the individual is required to do must be within his capability, or, in the case of a prohibition, be within his capability to avoid. No law may thus demand something which is beyond the capacity of the individual. The principle here is clearly stated in the Qur'ān, which declares that 'God does not obligate a living soul beyond the limits of his capacity' (al-Baqarah, 2:256) and that 'God puts no burden on any person beyond what He has given him' (al-Ṭalāq, 65:7).

An act may be conceptually unfeasible, such as asking a person to be awake and asleep at the same time, or asking him to do and not to do something simultaneously. Likewise, an act may be physically impossible, such as ordering a person to fly without the necessary means. No-one may be required to do the impossible, and it makes no difference whether the act is impossible by its nature or whether it is beyond the capacity of the individual in view of his particular conditions.[61]

A corollary of this rule is that no person may be obligated to act on behalf of another person or to stop another competent individual from acting. For this would be tantamount to asking a person to do the impossible. No-one may therefore be legally obligated to pay the *zakāh* on behalf of his brother, or to perform the *ṣalāh* on behalf of his father, or to prevent his neighbour from committing theft. All that one *mukallaf* may be lawfully expected to do in such situations is to give good advice (*naṣīḥah*) as a part of his general duty to promote good and to prevent evil to the extent that this is possible for him as a law-abiding citizen.

Similarly, no-one may be obligated to do or not to do something in regard to which he has no choice, such as asking someone to act against his natural and biological functions. Thus when we read in the Ḥadīth a command asking the Muslims to 'avoid anger [*la taghḍab*]', although the manifest (*ẓāhir*) terms of this Ḥadīth demand avoidance of a natural phenomenon, what it really means is that the adverse consequences of uncontrolled anger which might lead to taking the law into one's own hands must be avoided. To give another example, the Qur'ān orders the believers 'not to despair over matters that have passed you by, nor to exult over the favours that are bestowed upon you' (al-Ḥadīd, 57:23). Pleasure and despair are natural phenomena, and as such they are basically beyond the individual's control. What is really meant here is that one should avoid the consequences of despair such as violence against oneself or another person, and ensure that joy and happiness do not lead to arrogance and contemptuous behaviour.

There is, of course, some hardship involved in all obligations. The kind of hardship that people can tolerate without prejudice or injury is not the aim. It is intolerable hardship which the *Sharīʿah* does not impose. The *Sharīʿah*, for instance, forbids continuous fasting (*ṣawm al-wiṣāl*), or staying up all night for worship. Furthermore, the *Sharīʿah* has granted certain concessions with a view to preventing hardship to individuals, and it is strongly recommended that they be utilised. This is the purport of the reminder contained in the Ḥadīth that 'God loves to see that His concessions are taken advantage of, just as He hates to see the commission of a sin.'[62]

إن الله يحب أن تؤتى رخصه كما يكره ان تؤتى معصيته

In yet another Ḥadīth we read an address to the believers, who are asked: 'fulfil your duties to the extent of your ability',[63]

خذوا من الأعمال ما تطيقون

which obviously means that legal obligations are only operative within the limits of one's capacity.

A *ḥukm sharʿī* may sometimes impose unusual hardship on the individual, such as the fulfilment of certain collective obligations like *jihād* (holy struggle) and *ḥisbah*, that is, promotion of good and prevention of evil, under adverse conditions. *Jihād* which requires the sacrifice of one's life is undoubtedly onerous in the extreme. But it is deemed necessary and warranted in view of the values that are upheld and defended thereby.[64]

And lastly, the demand to act or not to act must originate in an authoritative source which can command the obedience of the *mukallaf*. This would mean that the *ḥukm* must emanate from God or His messenger. It is mainly due to this requirement that the proof or evidence in which the law is founded must be identified and explained. Consequently, we find that in their juristic expositions, the *fuqahā'* normally explain the evidential basis (*ḥujjiyyah*) of the rules of *Sharīʿah* that they expound, especially rules which are aimed at regulating the conduct of the *mukallaf*.[65]

The next topic which needs to be discussed under the subject-matter of *ḥukm* is the division of rights into the two categories of *ḥaqq Allāh* and *ḥaqq al-ʿabd*.

The acts of the *mukallaf* may consist of either a Right of God (*ḥaqq Allāh*) or a Right of Man (*ḥaqq al-ʿabd*), or of a combination of both. The Right of God is called so not because it is of any benefit to God, but because it is beneficial to the community at large and not merely to a particular individual. It is, in other words, a public right and differs from the Right of Man, or private right, in that its enforcement is a duty of the state. The enforcement of a private right, on the other hand, is up to the person whose right has been infringed, who may or may not wish to demand its enforcement.[66] The ulema have further classified these rights under four main categories, which are as follows.

Firstly, acts which exclusively consist of the Right of God, such as acts of devotion and worship, including *ṣalāh* and *jihād*, which are the pillars of religion and are necessary for the establishment of an Islamic order. These, which are often referred to as *ḥuqūq Allāh al-khāliṣah*, or 'pure Rights of God', occur in eight varieties:

a) Rights of God which consist exclusively of worship, such as professing the faith (*īmān*), *ṣalāh*, *zakāh*, the pilgrimage and *jihād*.
b) Rights which consist of both worship and financial liability (*ma'ūnah*), such as charity given on the occasion of *ʿīd al-fiṭr*, marking the end of Ramadan.
c) Rights in which financial liability is greater than worship, like the tithe that is levied on agricultural crops.
d) Rights of God which consist of financial liability but have a propensity toward punishment, such as the imposition of *kharāj* tax on land in the conquered territories.
e) Rights which consist of punishment only, like the *ḥudūd*, that is, the prescribed penalties for theft and adultery, and so forth.
f) Rights which consist of minor punishment (*ʿuqūbah qāṣirah*), such as excluding the murderer from the inheritance of his victim. This is called *ʿuqūbah qāṣirah* on account of the fact that it inflicts only a financial loss.
g) 'Punishments which lean toward worship', such as the penances (*kaffārāt*).
h) Exclusive rights, in the sense that they consist of rights alone and are not necessarily addressed to the *mukallaf*, such as the community right to mineral wealth or to the spoils of war (*ghanā'im*).[67]

Secondly, acts which exclusively consist of the rights of men, such as the right to enforce a contract, or the right to compensation for loss, the purchaser's right to own the object he has purchased, the vendor's right to own the price paid to him, the right of pre-emption (*shufʿ*), and so on. To enforce such rights is entirely at the option of the individual concerned; he may demand them or waive them, even without any consideration.

Thirdly, acts in which the rights of the community and those of individuals are combined, while of the two the former preponderate. The right to punish a slanderer (*qādhif*) belongs, according to the Ḥanafīs, to this class, by reason of the attack made on the honour of one of its members. Since the Right of God is dominant in *qadhf*, the victim of this offence (i.e. the *maqdhūf*) cannot exonerate the offender from punishment. The Shāfiʿīs have, however, held the contrary view by saying that *qadhf* is an exclusive Right of Man and that the person so defamed is entitled to exonerate the defamer. All acts which aim at protecting human life, intellect and property, fall under this category. To implement consultation (*shūrā*) in public affairs is one example, or the right of the individual in respect of *bayʿah* in electing the head of state. According to the Mālikī jurist al-Qarāfī, all rights in Islam partake in the Right of God in the exclusive sense that there is no right whatsoever without the *ḥaqq Allāh* constituting a part thereof. Thus when a person buys a house, he exercises his private right insofar as it benefits him, but the transaction partakes in the Right of God insofar as the buyer is liable to pay the purchase price. The basic criterion of distinction between the Right of God and the Right of Man is whether it can be exempted by the individual or not. Thus the vendor is able to exonerate the purchaser from paying the price, and a wife is able to exonerate her husband from paying her a dower (*mahr*), but the individual cannot exonerate anyone from obligatory prayers, or from the payment of *zakāh*.[68]

Fourthly, there are matters in which public and private rights are combined but where the latter preponderate. Retaliation (*qiṣāṣ*), and blood-money (*diyah*) of any kind, whether for life or for grievous injury, fall under this category of rights. The community is entitled to punish such violations, but the right of the heirs in retaliation and in *diyah* for erroneous killing, and the right of the victim in respect of *diyah* for injuries, is preponderant in view of the grievance and loss that they suffer as a result. The guardian (*walī*) of the deceased, in the case of *qiṣāṣ*, is entitled to pardon the offender or to accept a compensation from him. But the state, which represents the community, is still entitled to punish the offender through a *taʿzīr* punishment even if he is pardoned by the relatives of the deceased.[69]

III.3 Legal Capacity (*Ahliyyah*)

Being the last of the three pillars (*arkān*) of *ḥukm sharʿī* this section is exclusively concerned with the legal capacity of the *maḥkūm ʿalayh*, that is, the person to whom the *ḥukm* is addressed, and it looks into the question of whether he is capable of understanding the demand that is addressed to him and whether he comprehends the grounds of his responsibility (*taklīf*). Since the possession of the mental faculty of *ʿaql* is the basic criterion of *taklīf*, the law concerns itself with the circumstances that affect the sanity and capacity of the individual, such as minority, insanity, duress, intoxication, interdiction (*ḥajr*) and mistake.

Legal capacity is primarily divided into two types: capacity to receive or inhere rights and obligations, referred to as *ahliyyah al-wujūb*, and capacity for the active exercise of rights and obligations, which is referred to as *ahliyyah al-adā'*. The former may be described as 'receptive legal capacity', and the latter as 'active legal capacity'.[70]

Every person is endowed with legal capacity of one kind or another. Receptive legal capacity is the ability of the individual to receive rights and obligations on a limited scale, whereas active legal capacity enables him to fulfil rights and discharge obligations, to effect valid acts and transactions, and to bear full responsibility toward God and his fellow human beings. The criterion of the existence of receptive legal capacity is life itself, whereas the criterion of active legal capacity is maturity of intellect. Receptive legal capacity is vested in every human being, competent or otherwise. An insane person, a foetus in the womb, a minor and a foolish person (*safīh*), whether in good health or in illness: all possess legal capacity by virtue of their dignity as human beings.[71]

Active legal capacity is only acquired upon attaining a certain level of intellectual maturity and competence. Only a person who understands his acts and his words is competent to conclude a contract, discharge an obligation, or be punished for violating the law. Active legal capacity, which is the basis of responsibility (*taklīf*), is founded in the capacity of the mind to understand and to discern. But since intelligence and discernment are hidden qualities which are not readily apparent to the senses, the law has linked personal responsibility with the attainment of the age of majority (*bulūgh*), which is an obvious phenomenon and can be established by factual evidence. However, it is the intellectual faculty of the individual rather than age as such which determines his legal capacity. This is why an adult who is insane, or an adult of any age who is asleep, is not held responsible for his conduct. The principle here is clearly stated in the Ḥadīth which provides: 'The pen is lifted from three persons: the one who is asleep until he wakes, the child until he attains puberty, and the insane person until he regains sanity.'[72]

رُفع القلم عن ثلاثة : عن النائم حتى
يستيقظ وعن الصبي حتى يحتلم وعن
المجنون حتى يعقل

Receptive legal capacity may either be 'deficient' or 'complete'. The receptive legal capacity of a child in the womb is incomplete in the sense that it can only receive certain rights, such as inheritance and bequest, but cannot bear any obligation toward others. Receptive legal capacity is complete when a person can both have rights and bear obligations. This type of legal capacity is acquired by every human being as of the moment of birth. During its infancy and later stages of childhood, a child is capable of discharging, albeit through his guardian, certain obligations in respect, for example, of maintenance, liability for loss (*ḍamān*), and payment for services rendered to him.

As for the active legal capacity, three possible situations are envisaged. First, a person may be totally lacking of active legal capacity, as in the case of a child during infancy or an insane person of any age. Since neither is endowed with the faculty of intellect, no legal consequences accrue from their words and acts. When a child or a madman kills someone or destroys the property of another person, they can only be held liable with reference to their property, but not to their persons. They cannot be subjected, for example, to retaliation, or to any other type of punishment.

Second, a person may be partially lacking in active legal capacity. Thus a discerning child (*al-ṣabī al-mumayyiz*), that is, a child between seven and fifteen years of age, or an idiot (*maʿtūh*) who is neither insane nor totally lacking in intellect but whose intellect is defective and weak, possess a legal capacity which is deficient. Both of them possess an active legal capacity which is incomplete and partial.[73] The discerning child and the idiot are capable only of concluding acts and transactions that are totally to their benefit, such as accepting a gift or charity, even without the permission of their guardians. But if the transaction in question is totally disadvantageous to them, such as giving a gift or making a will, or pronouncing a divorce, these are not valid at all even if their guardians happen to approve of them. As for transactions which partake in both benefit and loss, they are valid but only with the permission of the guardian (*walī*), otherwise they are null and void.

Thirdly, active legal capacity is complete upon the attainment of intellectual maturity. Hence every major person who has acquired this ability is presumed to possess active legal capacity unless there is evidence to show that he or she is deficient of intellect or insane.

Persons who are fully competent may sometimes be put under interdiction (*ḥajr*) with a view to protecting the rights of others. A person may be interdicted by means of a judicial order which might restrict his powers to conclude certain transactions. A debtor may thus be interdicted so that the rights of his creditors may be protected.

A person in his death-illness (*maraḍ al-mawt*) is also deficient of legal capacity, as severe illness and fear of imminent death affect the physical and mental faculties of the individual. But ordinary illness and other conditions which do not impair the intellectual capacity of a person have no bearing on his active legal capacity. This is partly why Imām Abū Ḥanīfah has differed with the majority of jurists by holding the view that foolishness (*safāhah*), indebtedness and carelessness (*ghaflah*), do not affect the active legal capacity of a person. Abū Ḥanīfah refuses to accept these as proper grounds of interdiction, as in his view the benefit of interdiction in these cases is far outweighed by its possible harm.[74]

NOTES

1. Ghazālī, *Mustaṣfā*, I, 42; Shawkānī, *Irshād*, p. 6; Khallāf, *ʿIlm*, p. 100.
2. Muslim, *Ṣaḥīḥ Muslim*, p. 16, Ḥadīth no. 34.
3. Shāfiʿī, *Risālah*, p. 80; Ibn Mājah, *Sunan*, II, 913, Ḥadīth no. 2735.
4. Khallāf, *ʿIlm*, 100; Khuḍarī, *Uṣūl*, p. 18; Abū ʿĪd, *Mabāḥith*, p. 58.
5. Cf. Abdur Rahim, *Jurisprudence*, p. 193, for the use of English terminology.
6. Khallāf, *ʿIlm*, p. 101; Qāsim, *Uṣūl*, p. 213.
7. Abū ʿĪd, *Mabāḥith*, p. 63; Qāsim, *Uṣūl*, p. 216; Abdur Rahim, *Jurisprudence*, p. 197.
8. Abū Zahrah, *Uṣūl*, pp. 23–24; Abū ʿĪd, *Mabāḥith*, p. 63.
9. Ghazālī, *Mustaṣfā*, I. 42.
10. Khallāf, *ʿIlm*, p. 109; Qāsim, *Uṣūl*, p. 218; Abū ʿĪd, *Mabāḥith*, p. 69.
11. The Muʿtazilah have held the view that a flexibility of this kind negates the whole concept of *wujūb*, as in their view *wājib* precludes the element of choice altogether. But the majority of ulema refute this by saying that there is no necessary contradiction in dividing the *wājib* into *wājib muwaqqat* and *wājib muṭlaq*. For details see Ghazālī, *Mustaṣfā*, I, 43–44.
12. Khuḍarī, *Uṣūl*, p. 33; Khallāf, *ʿIlm*. p. 108.
13. Ghazālī, *Mustaṣfā*, I, 47; Khallāf, *ʿIlm*, p. 110; Abū Zahrah, *Uṣūl*, p. 35; Khuḍarī, *Uṣūl*, p. 42.
14. Ghazālī, *Mustaṣfā*, I, 47.
15. Ibid., I, 46; Abū Zahrah, *Uṣūl*, p. 23.
16. Ghazālī, *Mustaṣfā*, I, 42.
17. Ibid., I, 42; Khallāf, *ʿIlm*, p. 112; Abdur Rahim, *Jurisprudence*, p. 197.
18. Abū ʿĪd, *Mabāḥith*, p. 71; Khuḍarī, *Uṣūl*, p. 46.
19. Tabrīzī, *Mishkāt*, I, 168, Ḥadīth no. 540.
20. Ghazālī, *Mustaṣfā*, I, 48; Abū ʿĪd, *Mabāḥith*, pp. 72–74; Qāsim, *Uṣūl*, p. 322.
21. Qāsim, *Uṣūl*, p. 225; Aghnides, *Muhammedan Theories*, p. 89; Abdur Rahim, *Jurisprudence*, p. 198.
22. Muslim, *Ṣaḥīḥ Muslim*, p. 473, Ḥadīth no. 1775.
23. Bayhaqī, *al-Sunan al-Kubrā*, III, 10.
24. Khallāf, *ʿIlm*, p. 113; Abū Zahrah, *Uṣūl*, p. 34; Abū ʿĪd, *Mabāḥith*, p. 70ff.
25. Abū Zahrah, *Uṣūl*, p. 35; Qāsim, *Uṣūl*, p. 226 ff.
26. Abū Zahrah, *Uṣūl*, p. 34.
27. Khallāf, *ʿIlm*, p. 114; Abū Zahrah, *Uṣūl*, p. 36.
28. Tabrīzī, *Mishkāt* I, 330, Ḥadīth no. 1047.

29. Ibid., II, 978, Ḥadīth no. 3280; Abū ʿĪd, *Mabāḥith*, p. 80.
30. Tabrīzī, *Mishkāt*, II, 845, Ḥadīth no. 2773.
31. Qāsim, *Uṣūl*, p. 225.
32. Abū Dāwud, *Sunan*, III, 1133, Ḥadīth no. 4046.
33. Abū Dāwud, Sunan, II, 556, Ḥadīth no. 2075.
34. Abū ʿĪd, *Mabāḥith*, pp. 80–82; Khallāf, *ʿIlm*, p. 116; Aghnides, *Muhammedan Theories*, p. 89.
35. Ghazālī, *Mustaṣfā*, I, 42; Khallāf, *ʿIlm*, p. 115; Abdur Rahim, *Jurisprudence*, p. 198.
36. Abū ʿīd, *Mabāḥith*, pp. 84–88.
37. Ghazālī, *Mustaṣfā*, I, 42.
38. Abū Dāwud, *Sunan*, II, 557, Ḥadīth no. 2078.
39. Abū Dāwud, *Sunan*, II, 808; Ḥadīth no. 2864.
40. Shāfiʿī, *Risālah*, p. 80; Ibn Mājah, *Sunan*, II, 913, Ḥadīth no. 2735.
41. Khallāf, *ʿIlm*, p. 102; Abū ʿĪd, *Mabāḥith*, p. 60.
42. Abdur Rahim, *Jurisprudence*, pp. 61–62.
43. Cf. Khallāf, *ʿIlm*, p. 104.
44. Qāsim, *Uṣūl*, p. 228; Abū ʿĪd, *Mabāḥith*, p. 105.
45. Shawkānī, *Irshād*, p. 6; Khallāf, *ʿIlm*; p. 118; Abū ʿId, *Mabāḥith*, p. 92.
46. Khallāf, *ʿIlm*, p. 118; Abū ʿĪd, *Mabāḥith*, pp. 96–99; Qāsim, *Uṣūl*, p. 231.
47. Khallāf, *ʿIlm*, p. 120; Abū ʿĪd, *Mabāḥith*, p. 101.
48. Aghnides, *Muhammedan Theories*, p. 85ff; Abū ʿĪd, *Mabāḥith*, p. 104.
49. Ghazālī, *Mustaṣfā*, I, 62–63.
50. Abū Zahrah, *Uṣūl*, p. 50; Abū ʿĪd, *Mabāḥith*, pp. 106–112.
51. Abū Zahrah, *Uṣūl*, pp. 51–52; Abū ʿĪd, *Mabāḥith*, pp. 103–104; Qāsim, *Uṣūl*, pp. 236–238.
52. Ghazālī, *Mustaṣfā*, I, 53; Abū Zahrah, *Uṣūl*, p. 54.
53. Shawkānī, *Irshād*, p. 7. Abū Zahrah, *Uṣūl*, p. 57ff; Khallāf, *ʿIlm*, p. 97.
54. Ghazālī, *Mustaṣfā*, I, 36; Khallāf, *ʿIlm*, p. 98; Abū ʿĪd, *Mabāḥith*, p. 121.
55. Ghazālī, *Mustaṣfā*, I, 136.
56. Shawkānī, *Irshād*, p. 7.
57. Ghazālī, *Mustaṣfā*, I, 36.
58. Abū Zahrah *Uṣūl*, p. 56; Khallāf, *ʿIlm*, p. 99; Abū ʿĪd, *Mabāḥith*, p. 123; Qāsim, *Uṣūl*, pp. 239–243.
59. Khallāf, *ʿIlm*, p. 128; Abū Zahrah, *Uṣūl*, p. 249.
60. Knowledge in this context means understanding the nature of a command or a prohibition by the individual to the extent that he can act upon it. It does not mean affirmation of the mind (*taṣdīq*). For if this were to be a requirement, the unbelievers would have been excluded from the meaning of *mukallaf*, which they are not. See Shawkānī, *Irshād*, p. 11.
61. Shawkānī, *Irshād*, p. 11; Khallāf, *ʿIlm*, p. 128ff; Abū Zahrah, *Uṣūl*, 250ff.
62. Ibn Ḥanbal, *Musnad*, II, 108.
63. Muslim, *Ṣaḥīḥ Muslim*, p. 104,. Ḥadīth no. 378.
64. Cf. Abū ʿĪd, *Mabāḥith*, p. 139.
65. Abdur Rahim, *Jurisprudence*, p. 202; Abū Zahrah, *Uṣūl*, p. 256ff.
66. Khallāf, *ʿIlm*, p. 128; AbūʿĪd, *Mabāḥith*, p. 128.
67. Abū Sinnah, '*Naẓariyyah al-Ḥaqq*', p. 179; Abū ʿĪd, *Mabāḥith*, p. 141ff.
68. Ibid., p. 181.
69. Abū Zahrah, *Uṣūl*, p. 257; Abū ʿĪd, *Mabāḥith*, p. 145.
70. Cf. Abdur Rahim, *Jurisprudence*, p. 217.
71. Khallāf, *ʿIlm*, p. 136.

72. Tabrīzī, *Mishkāt*, II, 980, Ḥadīth no. 3287.

73. An idiot (*maʿtūh*) is a person who is markedly defective of understanding. A foolish and reckless person (*safīh*) is also regarded as being of defective legal capacity, in a lesser degree than the *maʿtūh*. Cf. Abdur Rahim, *Jurisprudence*, p. 240.

74. Khallāf, *ʿIlm*, p. 140; Abdur Rahim, *Jurisprudence*, p. 220.

CHAPTER EIGHTEEN

Conflict of Evidences

Conflict (*taʿāruḍ*) occurs when each of two evidences of equal strength requires the opposite of the other. This would mean that if one of them affirms something, the other would negate it at the same time and place. A conflict is thus not expected to arise between two evidences of unequal strength, as in this case the stronger of the two evidences would naturally prevail. Thus a genuine conflict cannot arise between a definitive (*qaṭʿī*) and a speculative (*ẓannī*) evidence, nor could there be a conflict between the *naṣṣ* and *ijmāʿ*, nor between *ijmāʿ* and *qiyās*, as some of these are stronger than others and would prevail over them. A conflict may, however, be encountered between two texts of the Qur'ān, or between two rulings of Ḥadīth, or between a Qur'ānic *āyah* and a *Mutawātir* Ḥadīth, or between two non-*Mutawātir* Ḥadīths, or between two rulings of *qiyās*. When there is a conflict between two Qur'ānic *āyāt*, or between one Ḥadīth and a pair of *aḥādīth*, or between one *qiyās* and a pair of analogies, it is a case of conflict between equals, because strength does not consist in number and consequently a single *āyah*, Ḥadīth or *qiyās* is not necessarily set aside to make room for the pair. The strength of two conflicting evidences is determined by reference to the evidence itself or to the extraneous/additional factors which might tip the balance in favour of the one over the other. For example, of the two conflicting solitary or *Āḥād* Ḥadīths, the one which is narrated by a *faqīh* is considered to be stronger than that which is narrated by a non-*faqīh*.[1]

Conflict can only arise between two evidences which cannot be reconciled, in the sense that the subject-matter of one cannot be distinguished from the other, nor can they be so distinguished in respect of the time of their application. There are, for example, three different rulings in the Qur'ān on wine-drinking, but since they were each revealed one after the other, not simultaneously, there is consequently no case of conflict between them. Similarly, if investigation reveals that each of two apparently conflicting rules can be applied to the same issue under a different set of circumstances, then once again there will be no conflict.

A genuine conflict can arise between two speculative (*ẓannī*) evidences, but not between definitive (*qaṭʿī*) proofs. In this way, all cases of conflict between the definitive rulings of the Qur'ān and *Sunnah* are deemed to be instances of apparent, not genuine, conflict. Furthermore, the ulema have maintained the view that a genuine conflict between two *āyāt* or two *aḥādīth*, or between an *āyah* and a Ḥadīth, does not arise; whenever a conflict is observed between these proofs, it is deemed to be only apparent (*ẓāhirī*), and lacking in reality and substance. For the all-pervasive wisdom of the Lawgiver cannot countenance the enactment of contradictory laws. It is only the *mujtahid* who is deemed unable to envision the purpose and intention of the Lawgiver in its entirety who may therefore find cases of apparent conflict in the divinely-revealed law. Only in cases of evident abrogation (*naskh*), which are largely identified and determined by the Prophet himself, could it be said that a genuine conflict had existed between the rulings of divine revelation.[2] When there is a case of apparent conflict between the rulings of the *nuṣūṣ*, one must try to discover the objective of the Lawgiver and remove the conflict in the light of that objective. Indeed, the rules of reconciliation and preference proceed on the assumption that no genuine conflict can exist in the divine laws; hence it becomes necessary to reconcile them or to prefer one to the other. This would mean that either both or at least one of the evidences at issue can be retained and implemented. The *mujtahid* must therefore try to reconcile them as far as possible, but if he reaches the conclusion that they cannot be reconciled, then he must attempt to prefer one over the other. If the attempt at reconciliation and preference fails, then one must ascertain whether recourse can be had to abrogation, which should be considered as the last resort. But when abrogation also fails to offer a way out of the problem, then action must be suspended altogether and both of the conflicting texts are abandoned.[3]

A case of conflict between the *nuṣūṣ* and *ijmāʿ*, or between two rulings of the latter, is inconceivable for the obvious reason that no *ijmāʿ* can be concluded which is contrary to the Qur'ān and *Sunnah* in the first place. Should a conflict arise between two analogies or proofs other than the *nuṣūṣ* and *ijmāʿ*, and neither can be given preference over the other and they cannot be reconciled, both must be suspended. Abrogation in this case does not offer an alternative course of action. For abrogation is basically confined to the definitive rulings of the Qur'ān and *Sunnah*; it is irrelevant to *ijmā*ᶜ and can be of little help in cases of conflict between speculative evidences.

Among the many instances of abrogation which the ulema have identified in the Qur'ān, we may refer to only two; but in both cases a closer analysis will show that the conflict at issue is not genuine. Our first illustration is concerned with the precise duration of the waiting period (*ᶜiddah*) of widows. According to one of the two *āyāt* on this subject (al-Baqarah, 2:234), the widow must observe a *ᶜiddah* of four months and ten days following the death of her husband. This *āyah* consists of a general provision which applies to every widow regardless as to whether she is pregnant at the time her husband dies or not. But elsewhere in the Qur'ān, there is another ruling concerning the *ᶜiddah* of pregnant women. This *āyah* (al-Ṭalāq, 65:4) also conveys a general ruling to the effect that the *ᶜiddah* of pregnant women continues until the delivery of the child. This ruling also applies to a pregnant widow, who must wait until the termination of her pregnancy. Thus a pregnant woman whose husband dies and who gives birth to a child on the same day would have completed her *ᶜiddah* according to the second of the two rulings, whereas she must, under the first ruling, still wait for four months and ten days. The two texts thus appear to be in conflict regarding the *ᶜiddah* of a pregnant widow.

For a second illustration of an apparent conflict in the Qur'ān, we refer to the two texts concerning the validity of making a bequest to one's relatives. This is explicitly permitted in sūra al-Baqarah (2:180) which provides: 'It is prescribed when death approaches any of you, if he leaves any assets, that he makes a bequest to his parents and relatives.' This ruling is deemed to have been abrogated by another text (al-Nisā', 4:11) which prescribes for each of the close relatives a share in inheritance. This share is obviously determined, not by the will of the testator, but by the will of God. The two texts thus appear to be in conflict; however the conflict is not genuine as they can be reconciled, and both can be implemented under different circumstances. The first of the two rulings may, for example, be reserved for a situation where the parents of the testator are barred from inheritance by a disability such as difference of religion. Since the parents in this case would be excluded from the scope of the second *āyah*, the conflict would consequently not arise and there would be no case for abrogation. The same approach can be taken regarding the foregoing *āyāt* on the waiting period of widows. Whereas the first of the two texts prescribed the *ᶜiddah* of widows to be four months and ten days, the second enacted the *ᶜiddah* of pregnant women until the termination of pregnancy. The two texts could be reconciled if widows were to observe whichever of the two periods were the longer. If the pregnant widow delivers her child before the expiry of four months and ten days following the death of her husband, then she should wait until this period expires. But if she waits four months and ten days and has still not delivered the child, then her ᶜ*iddah* should continue until the birth of the child. Thus the apparent conflict between the *āyāt* under discussion is removed by recourse to specification (*takhṣīṣ*): the second *āyah* in this case specifies the general ruling of the first insofar as it concerns pregnant widows.[4]

To reconcile two evidences both of which are general (ᶜ*Āmm*), one may distinguish the scope and subject-matter of their application from one another by recourse to allegorical interpretation (*ta'wīl*). Supposing there were two conflicting orders on *ṣalāh*, one providing that '*ṣalāh* is obligatory on my *ummah*' and the other that '*ṣalāh* is not obligatory on my *ummah*.' To reconcile these two, one may assume the first to have contemplated the adult and competent members of the community and the second the minors and lunatics. If this is not possible, then the two rulings may be distinguished in regard to the times of their respective application, or they might be assumed to have each envisaged a different set of circumstances. It is possible that one or both of the two rulings are in the nature of a manifest (*Ẓāhir*) provision and may thus be open to *ta'wīl*. The *Ẓāhir* may be given an interpretation other than that of its obvious meaning so as to avoid a clash. This may be illustrated by the two apparently conflicting Ḥadīths on the subject of testimony. In the first of the two reports, the Prophet is quoted to have addressed an audience as follows: 'Should I inform you who makes the best of witnesses?' To this, the audience responded, 'Yes O Messenger of God', and the Prophet said, 'It is one who gives testimony before he is requested to do so.'[5]

الا أخبركم بخير الشهود ؟ قالوا بلى
يا رسول الله : قال الذي يأتي بشهادته قبل أن
يُسألها

However, according to another Ḥadīth, the Prophet said, 'The best generation is the one in which I live, then the generation after that and then the next one, but after that there will be people who will give testimony although they are not invited to give it.'[6]

خير القرون قرني ثم الذين يلونهم ، ثم الذين
يلونهم ، ثم إن بعدهم قوماً يشهدون ولا
يستشهدون

Thus the first Ḥadīth recommends something which the second seems to be discouraging. The best form of testimony under the first Ḥadīth is unsolicited testimony, whereas this is frowned upon in the second. Since neither of the two Ḥadīth have specified a particular context, it is suggested by way of *ta'wīl* that the first Ḥadīth contemplates the Rights of God (*ḥuqūq Allāh*) whereas the second Ḥadīth contemplates the Rights of Men (*ḥuqūq al-ᶜibād*). In this way, the apparent conflict between the two texts is removed through an allegorical interpretation.[7]

Allegorical interpretations may offer a solution even in cases where two conflicting orders are both specific (*Khāṣṣ*). Recourse to *ta'wīl* in this case would once again serve the purpose of distinguishing the subject-matter and scope of each of the two conflicting orders. For example, if Aḥmad issues two orders to his employee, one of which tells the latter to 'pay 1000 dinars to Zayd' and the other tells him 'do not pay 1000 dinars to Zayd', then if circumstances would so permit, the first order may be assumed to have contemplated normal relations between Zayd and Aḥmad while the second had envisaged a hostile situation between the two parties.[8]

In the event where one of the two conflicting rulings is general (*ᶜĀmm*) and the other specific (*Khāṣṣ*), they can be reconciled by excepting the latter from the scope of the former through a procedure which is known as *takhṣīṣ al-ᶜĀmm*, that is, 'specifying a part of the general'. This would once again mean that each of the two rulings applied separately from one another to a different subject-matter, and both can remain operative. Similarly, a text may be absolute in its wording and appear to be in conflict with another text. They could be reconciled and the conflict between them removed if one of them is so interpreted as to limit and qualify the absolute terms of the other. Examples to illustrate these and other methods of interpretation can be found in the separate chapter of this work devoted to the rules of interpretation.

Should the attempt at reconciliation fail, the next step in resolving a conflict, as stated above, is to give preference to one over the other. Investigation may reveal that one of the two texts is supported by stronger evidence, in which case we are basically dealing with two texts of unequal strength. To prefer the one over the other in this case may even amount to a form of clarification or explanation of one by the other. Inequality in strength may be in content (*matn*) or in proof of authenticity (*riwāyah*). The former is concerned with the clarity or otherwise of the language of the text, and the latter with the historical reliability of the transmitters. Preference on the basis of content would require that the literal is preferred to the metaphorical, the clear (*Ṣarīḥ*) to the implicit (*Kināyah*), the explicit meaning (*ᶜibārah al-naṣṣ*) to the allusive meaning (*ishārah al-naṣṣ*), and the latter is preferred to the inferred meaning of the text (*dalālah al-naṣṣ*). Similarly, words which convey greater clarity are to be preferred to those which are less clear. Thus the *Muḥkam* (perspicuous) will be preferred to the *Mufassar* (unequivocal), the latter to the *Naṣṣ* (explicit) and the *Naṣṣ* to the *Ẓahīr* (manifest). Among unclear words, the *Khafī* (obscure) takes priority over the *Mushkil* (difficult), the latter over the *Mujmal* (ambivalent) and the *Mujmal* over the *Mutashābih* (intricate), in an order of priority which again has been stated elsewhere under the rules of interpretation.

Inequality in respect of transmission is mainly concerned with the Ḥadīth: when, for example, the *Mutawātir* is compared to the *Mashhūr*, the former is preferred to the latter. Similarly the *Mashhūr* takes priority over the solitary (*Āḥād*) Ḥadīth, and the report of a transmitter who is *faqīh* is preferred to the report of a transmitter who is not. Reports by persons who are known to be retentive of memory take priority over those which are transmitted by persons whose retentiveness is uncertain. On a similar note, *aḥādīth* that are transmitted by leading Companions are given preference to those transmitted by Companions who are less well known for their prominence and continuity of contact with the Prophet. The Ḥanafīs also consider the action of the transmitter upon his own narration to be a supportive factor which adds to the strength of a Ḥadīth. The Mālikīs on the other hand prefer a Ḥadīth that is in agreement with the practice of the people of Madinah over one which is not. Similarly, the report of a transmitter who is directly involved in an incident is preferable to other reports. Thus with the Ḥadīth which is reported by the Prophet's wife Maymūnah, to the effect that the Prophet married her while both of them were *ḥalāl*, that is outside the sacred state of *iḥrām* for the *ḥajj* ceremonies; this report is preferred to that of Ibn ʿAbbās to the effect that the Prophet married Maymūnah while he was in the sacred state of *iḥrām*.[9] In this way, a Ḥadīth which is supported by a more reliable chain of transmission is preferred to a Ḥadīth which is weak in its proof of authenticity.

At times the *mujtahid* may be confronted with a situation where each of the two conflicting Ḥadīths is stronger in respect of some of these factors but weaker in regard to others, in which case it is for the *mujtahid* to assess and determine the overall strength or weakness of the Ḥadīth according to his own *ijtihād*.

The ulema of Ḥadīth are in agreement that a Ḥadīth which is reported by all the six imāms of Ḥadīth, namely al-Bukhārī, Muslim, Abū Dāwūd, al-Nasā'ī, al-Tirmidhī, and Ibn Mājah, takes priority over that which might have been reported only by some and not all of these authorities. Among *aḥādīth* which are not reported by all the six authorities, those which are reported by the first two are preferred, and if one of the two conflicting Ḥadīth is reported by al-Bukhārī and the other by Muslim, the former is preferred to the latter.[10]

According to another rule of preference, affirmative evidence takes priority over the negative. This may be illustrated by the two rulings of Ḥadīth concerning the right of a slave—woman to a divorce upon her release from slavery. It is reported that a slave woman by the name of Barīrah was owned by ᶜĀ'ishah and was married to another slave, Mughīth. ᶜĀ'ishah set her free, and she wanted to be separated from Mughīth, who was still a slave. The case was brought to the attention of the Prophet, who gave Barīrah the choice either to remain married to Mughīth or be separated. But a second report on the same subject informs us that Barīrah's husband was a free man when she was emancipated. The two reports are thus conflicting with regard to the status of the husband. But since it is known for certain that Mughīth was originally a slave, and there is no dispute over this, the report which negates this original state is therfore ignored in view of the general rule that the affirmative, that is, the evidence which affirms continuation of the original state, takes priority over that which negates it. The jurists have consequently held that when a slave-woman is set free while married to a slave, she will have the choice of repudiating or retaining the marriage. If the husband is a free man, she will have no such choice according to Mālik, Shāfiᶜī, and the majority of scholars. Abū Ḥanīfah, however, maintains that she will have the option even when her husband is a free man.[11]

Another rule of preference which may be mentioned briefly is that prohibition takes priority over permissibility. Thus if there are two conflicting rules of equal strength on the same issue, one prohibitory and the other permissive, the former will take priority over the latter. Having said this, however, it is possible that the *mujtahid* may depart from this rule and instead apply that which brings ease in preference to the one that entails hardship.[12]

If the attempt at reconciling two conflicting texts, or at preferring one over the other, have both failed, recourse may be had to abrogation. This would necessitate an enquiry into the occasions of revelation (*asbāb al-nuzūl*), the relevant materials in the *Sunnah*, and the chronological order between the two texts. If this also proves unfeasible, then action must be suspended on both and the *mujtahid* may resort to inferior evidences in order to determine the ruling for the issue. Thus if the conflict happens to be between two rulings of the Qur'ān, he may depart from both and determine the matter with reference to the *Sunnah*. Should there be a conflict between two rulings of the *Sunnah*, then the *mujtahid* may refer, in a descending order, to the *fatwā* of Companions, and failing that the issue may be determined on grounds of *qiyās*. However, if the *mujtahid* fails to find a ruling in any of the lower categories of proofs, then he may resort to the general norms of *Sharīʿah* that may be applicable to the case. These may be illustrated in the following example. A conflict is encountered between the two rulings of Qur'ān concerning the recitation of the portions of the Qur'ān in congregational prayers. The question which needs to be answered is, whether in a congregational *ṣalāh*, the congregation member, that is the *muqtadī*, is required to recite the sūra al-Fātiḥah after the imām, or whether he should remain silent. Two conflicting answers can be derived for this question from the Qur'ān. The first of the two *āyāt* under discussion provides: 'And when the Qur'ān is being read, listen to it attentively and pay heed, so that you may receive mercy' (al-Aʿrāf, 7:204). It would appear that the *muqtadī*, according to this *āyah*, should remain silent when the imām recites the Qur'ān. However, according to another *āyah*, everyone, that is both the imām and the *muqtadī*, is ordered to 'read whatever is easy for you of the Qur'ān' (al-Muzammil, 73:20). Although neither of the two texts make a particular reference to *ṣalāh*, they appear nevertheless to be in conflict with regard to the position of the *muqtadī*. There is no additional evidence available to enable the preference of one to the other; action is therefore suspended on both and the issue is determined with reference to the *Sunnah*. It is thus reported that on one occasion when the Prophet led the *ṣalāh*, he asked the members of the congregation whether they recited the Qur'ān with him, and having heard their answers, he instructed them not to recite the Qur'ān behind the imām. But there still remains a measure of inconsistency even in the *aḥādīth* that are reported on this point, which would explain why the jurists have also differed on it: Abū Ḥanīfah, Mālik, Ibn Ḥanbal, and al-Shāfiʿī (according to his former view which he revised later) have held that it is not necessary to recite al-Fātiḥah behind the imām in those prayers in which he recites the Qur'ān aloud, but that when the imām recites quietly, the worshippers should recite al-Fātiḥah. The later Ḥanafī jurists have, however, held the view that it is not necessary for the worshipper to recite the Qur'ān behind the imām in either case.[13]

In the event where an issue cannot be determined by reference to the *Sunnah*, the *mujtahid* may resort to the *fatwā* of a Companion, and failing that, to *qiyās*. There is, for example, an apparent conflict between the two reports concerning the way that the Prophet performed the *ṣalāt al-kusūf*, that is, prayer offered on the occasion of a solar eclipse. According to one of the reports, the Prophet offered two units (i.e. two *rakʿahs*) of *ṣalāh*, each consisting of two bowings (*rukūʿ*) and two prostrations (*sajdah*). But according to another report, each of the two units contained four bowings and four prostrations. There is yet another report to the effect that each of the two *rakʿahs* contained three bowings and three prostrations.[14] The conflicting contents of these reports can neither be reconciled nor given preference one over the other. Hence action is suspended on all and the matter is determined on grounds of *qiyās*. In this case, since *ṣalāt al-kusūf* is a variety of *ṣalāh*, the normal rules of *ṣalāh* are applied to it. Since all obligatory *ṣalāh*, without any variation, contains one bowing and two prostrations, this is also by way of analogy extended to *ṣalāt al-kusūf*.[15]

In the event of a conflict occurring between two analogies, if they cannot be reconciled with one another, then one of them must be given preference. *The qiyās* whose effective cause (*ʿillah*) is stated in an explicit text is to be preferred to the one whose *ʿillah* has been derived through inference (*istinbāṭ*). Similarly, a *qiyās* whose *ʿillah* is founded in an allusive text (*ishārah al-naṣṣ*) takes priority over *qiyās* whose *ʿillah* is merely a proper or reasonable attribute which is derived through inference and *ijtihād*. When the *ʿillah* of *qiyās* is explicitly stated in the *naṣṣ* or when the result of *qiyās* is upheld by *ijmāʿ*, no conflict is expected to arise. In the unlikely event when the *mujtahid* constructs an analogy on the basis of an inferred effective cause (*ʿillah mustanbaṭah*) while the *ʿillah* is explicitly stated in the *naṣṣ*, and he reaches a divergent result, it is put down to his ignorance of the *naṣṣ*, and the result that he has reached will be ignored.[16]

A conflict may well arise between two analogies which are both founded on an inferred *ʿillah*, since this type of *ʿillah* involves a measure of speculative reasoning and *ijtihād*. Two *mujtahids* may thus arrive at different conclusions with regard to the identification of an *ʿillah*. This is, for example, the case regarding the *ʿillah* of compulsory guardianship (*wilāyah al-ijbār*) in the marriage of a minor girl. Imām Abū Ḥanīfah considers the *ʿillah* of the guardian's power of *ijbār* in marriage to be the minority of the ward, whereas Imām Shāfiʿī considers the *ʿillah* to be her virginity. This difference of *ijtihād* would in turn give rise to analogies whose results diverge from one another depending on which of the two effective causes they are based on. However, differences of this nature are tolerated and neither of the two Imāms have attempted to discourage diversity in *ijtihād*. In the event where neither of the two conflicting analogies can be preferred to the other, it is for the *mujtahid* to choose the one that seems good to him even if there is no basis for such preference other than his own personal opinion.[17]

If none of the foregoing methods can be applied in order to determine the ruling of an issue, then the *mujtahid* may base his decision on the original norms of the *Sharīʿah*. This would be done on the assumption that no specific indication could be found in the *Sharīʿah* on the case. An example of this is to determine the ruling of the *Sharīʿah* that might have to be applied to a hermaphrodite whose gender, whether male or female, cannot be determined and where neither side could be preferred to the other. A recourse to the original norms in this case means that the issue remains where it was in the first place. Since neither of the two possibilities can be preferred to the other, action will be based on one side or the other, not because of any evidence to warrant such a preference but as a precautionary measure when the circumstances may indicate such a course of action. Thus in some situations, in the distribution of shares in inheritance, for example, the hermaphrodite will be presumed a male, while he will be presumed a female in other situations as considerations of caution and prevention of possible harm to him may suggest.[18]

In making such decisions, it is essential that the *mujtahid* does not act against the general principles and spirit of the *Sharīʿah*. When he weighs the merits and demerits of conflicting evidences he must never lose sight of the basic objectives of the Lawgiver.

NOTES

1. Badrān, *Uṣūl*, p. 461; Khuḍarī, *Uṣūl*, p. 359; Aghnides, *Muhammedan Theories*, p. 66.
2. Ghazālī, *Mustaṣfā*, II, 126; *Khallāf*, *ʿIlm*, p. 230.
3. Khallāf, *ʿIlm*, p. 229; Khuḍarī, *Uṣūl*, p. 359.
4. Abū Zahrah, *Uṣūl*, p. 245; Badrān, *Uṣūl*, p. 467; Khallāf, *ʿIlm*, p. 231.
5. Muslim, *Ṣaḥīḥ*, p. 281, Ḥadīth no. 1059; Badrān, *Uṣūl*, p. 465.
6. Tabrīzī, *Mishkāt*, III, 1695, Ḥadīth no. 6001.
7. Badrān, *Uṣūl*, pp. 466.
8. Cf. Khuḍarī, *Uṣūl*, p. 361.
9. Abū Dāwud, *Sunan*, II, 486–87, Ḥadīth nos. 1839 and 1840; Ghazālī, *Mustaṣfā*, II, 128; Khuḍarī, *Uṣūl*, p. 367.
10. Abū Zahrah, *Uṣūl*, p. 246.
11. Abū Dāwud, *Sunan*, II, 601–602, Ḥadīth nos. 2223–7 and footnote no. 1548; Badrān, *Uṣūl*, p. 465; Khuḍarī, *Uṣūl*, p. 363.
12. Khallāf, *ʿIlm*, p. 232; Badrān, *Uṣūl*, p. 470; Khuḍarī, *Uṣūl*, p. 367.
13. Abū Dāwud, *Sunan*, II, 211, Ḥadīth no. 825 and footnote no. 373; Badrān, *Uṣūl*, pp.468–69; Khuḍarī, *Uṣūl*, p. 359.
14. Abū Dāwud, *Sunan*, I, 304, Ḥadīth nos. 1173–7.
15. Badrān, *Uṣūl*, p. 469.
16. Khallāf, *ʿIlm*, p. 232; Badrān, *Uṣūl*, p. 470.
17. Abū Zahrah, *Uṣūl*, pp. 247–48; Khuḍarī, *Uṣūl*, p. 360.
18. Badrān, *Uṣūl*, pp. 469–70.

CHAPTER NINETEEN

Ijtihād, or Personal Reasoning

Ijtihād is the most important source of Islamic law next to the Qur'ān and the *Sunnah*. The main difference between *ijtihād* and the revealed sources of the *Sharīʿah* lies in the fact that *ijtihād* is a continuous process of development whereas divine revelation and Prophetic legislation discontinued upon the demise of the Prophet. In this sense, *ijtihād* continues to be the main instrument of interpreting the divine message and relating it to the changing conditions of the Muslim community in its aspirations to attain justice, salvation and truth.

Since *ijtihād* derives its validity from divine revelation, its propriety is measured by its harmony with the Qur'ān and the *Sunnah*. The sources of Islamic law are therefore essentially monolithic, and the commonly accepted division of the roots of jurisprudence into the primary and secondary is somewhat formal rather than real. The essential unity of the *Sharīʿah* lies in the degree of harmony that is achieved between revelation and reason. *Ijtihād* is the principal instrument of maintaining this harmony. The various sources of Islamic law that feature next to the Qur'ān and the *Sunnah* are all manifestations of *ijtihād*, albeit with differences that are largely procedural in character. In this way, consensus of opinion, analogy, juristic preference, considerations of public interest (*maṣlaḥah*), etc., are all inter-related not only under the main heading of *ijtihād*, but via it to the Qur'ān and the *Sunnah*.[1] It is partly due to the formalistic character of these sub-divisions that they are often found to be overlapping and concurrent. Thus a ruling of *ijmāʿ* is often based on analogy, *maṣlaḥah* or *istiḥsān*, and so on, despite its being designated as *ijmāʿ*. Similarly, *qiyās* and *istiḥsān* are closely related to one another in the sense that one of the two main varieties of *istiḥsān* consists of a selection between two analogies on the same issue. The difference between *maṣlaḥah* and *istiḥsān* is largely procedural, for they are essentially the same, the one being reflective of the Mālikī and the other of the Ḥanafī approach to *ijtihād*. It is thus evident that all the non-revealed proofs of *Sharīʿah* are an embodiment of the single phenomenon of *ijtihād*.

Being a derivation from the root word *jahada*, *ijtihād* literally means striving, or self-exertion in any activity which entails a measure of hardship. It would thus be in order to use *jahada* in respect of one who carries a heavy load, but not so if he carries only a trivial weight. Juridically, however, *ijtihād* mainly consists not of physical, but of intellectual exertion on the part of the jurist. *Ijtihād* is defined as the total expenditure of effort made by a jurist in order to infer, with a degree of probability, the rules of *Sharīʿah* from their detailed evidence in the sources.[2] Some ulema have defined *ijtihād* as the application by a jurist of all his faculties either in inferring the rules of *Sharīʿah* from their sources, or in implementing such rules and applying them to particular issues.[3] *Ijtihād* essentially consists of an inference (*istinbāṭ*) that amounts to a probability (*ẓann*), thereby excluding the extraction of a ruling from a clear text. It also excludes the discovery of a *ḥukm* by asking a learned person or by consulting the relevant literature without the exercise of one's own opinion and judgement. Thus a person who knows the rules of *Sharīʿah* in detail but is unable to exercise his judgement in the inference of the *aḥkām* direct from their sources is not a *mujtahid*. *Ijtihād*, in other words, consists of the formulation of an opinion in regard to a *ḥukm sharʿī*. The presence of an element of speculation in *ijtihād* implies that the result arrived at is probably correct, while the possibility of its being erroneous is not excluded. *Ẓann* in this context is distinguished from *ʿilm*, which implies positive knowledge. Since the decisive rules of *Sharīʿah* impart positive knowledge, they are excluded from the scope of *ijtihād*.[4] Essential to the meaning of *ijtihād* is also the concept that the endeavour of the jurist involves a total expenditure of effort in such a manner that the jurist feels an inability to exert himself further. If the jurist has failed to discover the evidence which he was capable of discovering, his opinion is void.[5] And lastly, the definition of *ijtihād* is explicit on the point that only a jurist (*faqīh*) may practice *ijtihād*. This is explained by the requirements of *ijtihād*, namely the qualifications that must be fulfilled for attainment to the rank of *mujtahid*. When these requirements are met, it is inevitable that the *mujtahid* must also be a *faqīh*. Thus the definition of *ijtihād* precludes self-exertion by a layman in the inference of *aḥkām*.[6]

The subject of *ijtihād* must be a question of *Sharīʿah*; more specifically, *ijtihād* is concerned with the practical rules of *Sharīʿah* which usually regulate the conduct of those to whom they apply (i.e. the *mukallaf*). This would preclude from the scope of *ijtihād* purely intellectual (*ʿaqlī*) and customary (*ʿurfī*) issues, or matters that are perceptible to the senses (*ḥissī*) and do not involve the inference of a *ḥukm sharʿī* from the evidence present in the sources. Thus *ijtihād* may not be exercised in regard to such issues as the createdness of the universe, the existence of a Creator, the sending of prophets, and so forth, because there is only one correct view in regard to these matters, and any one who differs from it is wrong. Similarly, one may not exercise *ijtihād* on matters such as the obligatory status of the pillars of the faith, or the prohibition of murder, theft, and adultery. For these are evident truths of the *Sharīʿah* which are determined in the explicit statements of the text.[7]

The detailed evidences found in the Qur'ān and the *Sunnah* are divided into four types, as follows.

1) Evidence which is decisive both in respect of authenticity and meaning.
2) Evidence which is authentic but speculative in meaning.
3) That which is of doubtful authenticity, but definite in meaning.
4) Evidence which is speculative in respect both of authenticity and meaning.

Ijtihād does not apply to the first of the foregoing categories, such as the clear *nuṣūṣ* concerning the prescribed penalties (*ḥudūd*). But *ijtihād* can validly operate in regard to any of the remaining three types of evidence, as the following illustrations will show:

1) An example of *ijtihād* concerning evidence which is definite of proof but speculative of meaning is the Qur'ānic text in sūra al-Baqarah (2 : 228): 'The divorced women must observe three courses (*qurū'*) upon themselves.' There is no doubt concerning the authenticity of this text, as the Qur'ān is authentic throughout. However its meaning, in particular the precise meaning of the word *qurū'*, is open to speculation. *Qurū'* is a homonym meaning both 'menstruations' and 'the clean periods between menstruations'. Whereas Imām Abū Ḥanīfah and Ibn Ḥanbal have adopted the former, Imām Shāfiʿī and Mālik have adopted the latter meaning, and their respective *ijtihād* leads them to correspondingly different results.[8]
2) *Ijtihād* in regard to the second variety of evidence relates mainly to Ḥadīth material, which may have a definitive meaning but whose authenticity is open to doubt. To give an example, the Ḥadīth which provides in regard to *zakāh* on camels that 'a goat is to be levied on every five camels'[9]

من كل خمس شاة

has a clear meaning, which is why the jurists are in agreement that there is no *zakāh* on less than five camels. But since this is a solitary Ḥadīth, its authenticity remains speculative. *Ijtihād* concerning this Ḥadīth may take the form of an investigation into the authenticity of its transmission and the reliability of its narrators, matters on which the jurists are not unanimous due to the different criteria that they apply.

This would in turn lead them to different conclusions. Should the differences of *ijtihād* and the rulings so arrived at be conflicting to the point that no reliance can be placed on any, they are all to be abandoned and no obligation may be established on their basis.[10]

3) To give an example of *ijtihād* concerning evidence that is speculative in both authenticity and meaning, we may refer to the Ḥadīth which provides: 'There is no *ṣalāh* [*lā ṣalāta*] without the recitation of sūra al-Fātiḥah.'[11]

لا صلاة إلا بفاتحة الكتاب

Being a solitary Ḥadīth, its authenticity is not proven with certainty. Similarly it is open to different interpretations in the sense that it could mean either that *ṣalāh* without the *Fātiḥah* is invalid, or that it is merely incomplete. The Ḥanafīs have held the latter, whereas the Shāfiʿīs have adopted the former meaning of the Ḥadīth.

And finally with regard to such matters on which no evidence can be found in the *nuṣūṣ* or *ijmāʿ*, *ijtihād* may take the form of analogical deduction, juristic preference (*istiḥsān*), or the consideration of public interest (*maṣlaḥah*), and so on.

The Value (*Ḥukm*) of *Ijtihād*

Legal theory in all of its parts derives its validity from the revealed sources. It is partly for this reason and partly for the reason of man's duty to worship his Creator that the practice of *ijtihād* is a religious duty. The ulema are in agreement that *ijtihād* is the collective obligation (*farḍ kafā'ī*) of all qualified jurists in the event where an issue arises but no urgency is encountered over its ruling. The duty remains unfulfilled until it is performed by at least one *mujtahid*. If a question is addressed to two *mujtahids*, or to two judges for that matter, and one of them exerts himself to formulate a response, the other is absolved of his duty. But *ijtihād* becomes a personal obligation (*wājib* or *farḍ ʿaynī*) of the qualified *mujtahid* in urgent cases, that is, when there is fear that the cause of justice or truth may be lost if *ijtihād* is not immediately attempted. This is particularly the case when no other qualified person can be found to attempt *ijtihād*. With regard to the *mujtahid* himself, *ijtihād* is a *wājib ʿaynī*: he must practice *ijtihād* in order to find the ruling for an issue that affects him personally. This is so because imitation (*taqlīd*) is forbidden to a *mujtahid* who is capable of deducing the *ḥukm* directly from the sources. Should there be no urgency over *ijtihād*, or in the event where other *mujtahids* are available, then the duty remains as a *farḍ kafāʾī* only. Furthermore, *ijtihād* is recommended (*mandūb*) in all cases where no particular issue has been referred to the *mujtahid*, or when it is attempted in the absence of an issue by way of theoretical construction at the initiative of the jurist himself. And finally *ijtihād* is forbidden (*ḥarām*) when it contradicts the decisive rules of the Qur'ān, the *Sunnah* and a definite *ijmāʿ*.[12]

The ulema of *uṣūl* are in agreement that the *mujtahid* is bound by the result of his own *ijtihād*. Once he has deduced the ruling on a particular issue which is founded in his true conviction and belief, he may not imitate other *mujtahids* on that matter regardless as to whether they agree with him or otherwise. For the *mujtahid*, the conclusion that he reaches is tantamount to a divine command which he must observe. It is therefore unlawful for him to abandon it or to follow anyone else in respect of it. But if he had not rendered his own *ijtihād* on an issue which is not urgent, and he has time to investigate, then according to some ulema he may imitate other *mujtahids*. However, the preferred view is that he must avoid *taqlīd*, even of one who might be more learned than him. Only a *ʿāmmī* (layman) who is incapable of *ijtihād* is allowed to follow the opinion of others.[13] This is considered to be the purport of the Qur'ānic command, addressed to all those who have the capacity and knowledge, to exert themselves in the cause of justice and truth (al-Ḥashr, 59:2). Elsewhere we read in the Qur'ān (Muḥammad, 47: 24): 'Will they not meditate on the Qur'ān, or do they have locks on their hearts?'

The same conclusion is sustained in another Qur'ānic passage, in sūra al-Nisā' (4:59) where the text requires the judgement of all disputes to be referred to God and to His Messenger. These and many similar *āyāt* in the Qur'ān lend support to the conclusion that it is the duty of the learned to study and investigate the Qur'ān and the teachings of the Prophet. The correct meaning of the manifest directives (*ẓawāhir*) of the Qur'ān is also understood from the practice of the Companions who used to investigate matters, and each would formulate their own *ijtihād*, in which case they would not imitate anyone else.[14] The *mujtahid* is thus the authority (*ḥujjah*) for himself. His is the duty to provide guidance to those who do not know, but he himself must remain in close contact with the sources. This is also the purport of another Qur'ānic *āyāh* which enjoins those who do not possess knowledge: 'Then ask those who have knowledge (*ahl al-dhikr*) if you yourselves do not know' (al-Naḥl, 16: 43). Thus only those who do not know may seek guidance from others, not those who have the ability and knowledge to deduce the correct answer themselves. The *ahl al-dhikr* in this *āyah* refers to the ulema, regardless as to whether they actually know the correct ruling of an issue or not, provided they have the capacity to investigate and find out.[15]

When a *mujtahid* exerts himself and derives the ruling of a particular issue on the basis of probability, but after a period of time changes his opinion on the same issue, he may set aside or change his initial ruling if this would only affect him personally. For example, when he enters a contract of marriage with a woman without the consent of her guardian (*walī*) and later changes his opinion on the validity of such a marriage, he must annul the *nikāḥ*. But if his *ijtihād* affects others when, for example, he acts as a judge and issues a decision on the basis of his own *ijtihād*, and then changes his views, he may not, according to the majority of ulema, set aside his earlier decision. For if one ruling of *ijtihād* could be set aside by another, then the latter must be equally subject to reversal, and this would lead to uncertainty and loss of credibility in the *aḥkām*.[16] It is reported that ᶜUmar b. al-Khaṭṭāb adjudicated a case, known as Ḥajariyyah, in which the deceased, a woman, was survived by her husband, mother, two consanguine and two uterine brothers. ᶜUmar b. al-Khaṭṭāb entitled all the brothers to a share in one-third of the estate, but was told by one of the parties that the previous year, he (ᶜUmar) had not entitled all the brothers to share the portion of one-third. To this the caliph replied, 'That was my decision then, but today I have decided it differently.' Thus the Caliph ᶜUmar upheld both his decisions and did not allow his latter decision to affect the validity of the former.[17] Similarly, the decision of one judge may not be set aside by another merely because the latter happens to have a different opinion on the matter. It is reported that a man whose case was adjudicated by ᶜAlī and Zayd informed ᶜUmar b. al-Khaṭṭāb of their decision, to which the latter replied that he would have ruled differently if he were the judge. To this the man replied, 'Then why don't you, as you are the Caliph?' ᶜUmar b. al-Khaṭṭāb replied that had it been a matter of applying the Qur'ān or the *Sunnah*, he would have intervened, but since the decision was based in *ra'y*, they were all equal in this respect.[18] Since in matters of juristic opinion no-one can be certain that a particular view is wrong, the view that has already been embodied in a judicial decree has a greater claim to validity than the opposite view. The position is, however, different if the initial decision is found to be in violation of the law, in which case it must be set aside. This is the purport of the ruling of ᶜUmar ibn al-Khaṭṭāb which he conveyed in his well-known letter to Abū Mūsā al-Ashᶜarī as follows: 'After giving a judgment, if upon reconsideration you arrive at a different opinion, do not let the judgment stand in the way of retraction. For justice may not be disregarded, and you are to know that it is better to retract than to persist in injustice.'[19]

The precedent of the Companions on this issue has led to the formulation of a legal maxim which provides that '*ijtihād* may not be overruled by its equivalent' (*al-ijtihād lā yunqaḍ bi-mithlih*). Consequently, unless the judge and the *mujtahid* is convinced that his previous *ijtihād* was erroneous, he must not attempt to reverse it. Thus a judicial decision which is based on the personal opinion and *ijtihād* of a particular judge-cum-*mujtahid* is irreversible on the basis of a mere difference of opinion by another judge. It is further suggested that the issuing judge himself may change his initial decision which was based on *ijtihād* in a subsequent case if he is convinced that this is a preferable course to take. But the credibility of judicial decisions is a factor that would discourage the issuing judge to change his initial decision unless it proves to have been manifestly oppressive.

The Proof (*Ḥujjiyyah*) of *Ijtihād*

Ijtihād is validated by the Qur'ān, the *Sunnah* and the dictates of reason (*ᶜaql*). Of the first two, the *Sunnah* is more specific in validating *ijtihād*. The Ḥadīth of Muᶜādh b. Jabal,[20] as al-Ghazālī points out, provides a clear authority for *ijtihād*. The same author adds: The claim that this Ḥadīth is *mursal* (i.e. a Ḥadīth whose chain of narration is broken at the point when the name of the Companion who heard it from the Prophet is not mentioned) is of no account. For the *ummah* has accepted it and has consistently relied on it; no further dispute over its authenticity is therefore warranted.[21] According to another Ḥadīth, 'When a judge exercises *ijtihād* and gives a right judgement, he will have two rewards, but if he errs in his judgment, he will still have earned one reward.'[22]

الحاكم إذا اجتهد فأصاب فله أجران وان
اجتهد فاخطأ فله أجر

This Ḥadīth implies that regardless of its results, *ijtihād* never partakes in sin. When the necessary requirements of *ijtihād* are present, the result is always meritorious and never blameworthy.[23] In another Ḥadīth, the Prophet is reported to have said: 'Strive and endeavour (*ijtahidū*), for everyone is ordained to accomplish that which he is created for.'[24]

اجتهدوا فكل ميسر لما خلق له

There is also the Ḥadīth which reads: 'When God favours one of His servants, He enables him to acquire knowledge (*tafaqquh*) in religion.'[25]

من يرد الله به خيراً يفقهه في الدين

The ulema of *uṣūl* have also quoted in this connection two other *aḥādīth*, one of which makes the pursuit of knowledge an obligation of every Muslim, man or woman,

طلب العلم فريضة على كل مسلم
ومسلمة

and the other declares the Ulema to be the successors of the Prophets.[26]

العلماء ورثة الأنبياء

The relevance of the last two *aḥādīth* to *ijtihād* is borne out by the fact that *ijtihād* is the main instrument of creativity and knowledge in Islam.

The numerous Qur'ānic *āyāt* that relate to *ijtihād* are all in the nature of probabilities (*ẓawāhir*). All the Qur'ānic *āyāt* which the ulema have quoted in support of *qiyās* (see page 217) can also be quoted in support of *ijtihād*. In addition, we read, in sūra al-Tawbah (9:122): 'Let a contingent from each division of them devote themselves to the study of religion [*li-yatafaqqahū fi'l-dīn*] and warn their people [. . .]' Devotion to the study of religion is the essence of *ijtihād*, which should be a continuous feature of the life of the community. Although the pursuit of knowledge is a duty of every individual, attaining *tafaqquh*, or 'erudition in religious disciplines', is necessary for those who guide the community and warn them against deviation and ignorance. On a similar note, we read in sūra al-ᶜAnkabūt (29:69): 'And those who strive [*wa'l-ladhīna jāhadū*] in Our cause, We will certainly guide them in Our paths.' It is interesting that in this *āyah* the word *subulanā* ('Our paths') occurs in the plural form, which might suggest that there are numerous paths toward the truth, which are all open to those who exert themselves in its pursuit. Furthermore, we read in sūra al-Nisā' (4:59): 'If you dispute over something, then refer it to God and to the Messenger.' The implementation of this *āyah* would necessitate knowledge of the Qur'ān, the *Sunnah* and the objectives (*maqāṣid*) of the Lawgiver on whose basis disputed matters could be adjudicated and resolved.

The Companions practiced *ijtihād*, and their consensus is claimed in support of it.[27] In their search for solutions to disputed matters, they would base their judgement on the Qur'ān and the *Sunnah*, but if they failed to find the necessary guidance therein, they would resort to *ijtihād*. The fact that the Companions resorted to *ijtihād* in the absence of a *naṣṣ* is established by continuous testimony (*tawātur*).[28]

The rational argument in support of *ijtihād* is to be sought in the fact that while the *nuṣūṣ* of *Sharīᶜah* are limited, new experiences in the life of the community continue to give rise to new problems. It is therefore imperative for the learned members of the community to attempt to find solutions to such problems through *ijtihād*.[29]

Conditions (*Shurūṭ*) of *Ijtihād*

The *mujtahid* must be a Muslim and a competent person of sound mind who has attained a level of intellectual competence which enables him to form an independent judgment. In his capacity as a successor to the Prophet, the *mujtahid* performs a religious duty, and his verdict is a proof (*ḥujjah*) to those who follow him; he must therefore be a Muslim, and be knowledgeable in the various disciplines of religious learning. A person who fails to meet one or more of the requirements of *ijtihād* is disqualified and may not exercise *ijtihād*. The requirements which are discussed below contemplate *ijtihād* in its unrestricted form, often referred to as *ijtihād fī'l-sharᶜ*, as opposed to the varieties of *ijtihād* that are confined to a particular school, or to particular issues within the confines of a given *madhhab*.

The earliest complete account of the qualifications of a *mujtahid* is given in Abū'l-Ḥusayn al-Baṣrī's (d. 436/1044) *al-Muᶜtamad fī Uṣūl al-Fiqh*. The broad outline of al-Baṣrī's exposition was later accepted, with minor changes, by al-Shīrāzī (d. 467/1083), al-Ghazālī (d. 505/111) and al-Āmidī (d. 632/1234). This does not mean that the requirements of *ijtihād* received no attention from the ulema who lived before al-Baṣrī. But it was from then onwards that they were consistently adopted by the ulema of *uṣūl* and became a standard feature of *ijtihād*.[30] These requirements are as follows:

(a) Knowledge of Arabic to the extent that enables the scholar to enjoy a correct understanding of the Qur'ān and the *Sunnah*. A complete command and erudition in Arabic is not a requirement, but the *mujtahid* must know the nuances of the language and be able to comprehend the sources accurately and deduce the *aḥkām* from them with a high level of competence.[31] Al-Shāṭibī, however, lays greater emphasis on the knowledge of Arabic: a person who possesses only an average knowledge of Arabic cannot aim at the highest level of attainment in *ijtihād*. The language of the Qur'ān and the *Sunnah* is the key to their comprehension and the *ijtihād* of anyone who is deficient in this respect is unacceptable. The same author adds: Since the opinion of the *mujtahid* is a proof (*ḥujjah*) for a layman, this degree of authority necessitates direct access to the sources and full competence in Arabic.[32]

The *mujtahid* must also be knowledgeable in the Qur'ān and the *Sunnah*, the Makkī and the Madinese contents of the Qur'ān, the occasions of its revelation (*asbāb al-nuzūl*) and the incidences of abrogation therein. More specifically, he must have a full grasp of the legal contents, or the *āyāt al-aḥkām*, but not necessarily of the narratives and parables of the Qur'ān and its passages relating to the hereafter.[33] According to some ulema, including al-Ghazālī, Ibn al-ᶜArabī, and Abū Bakr al-Rāzī, the legal *āyāt* of the Qur'ān which the *mujtahid* must know amount to about five hundred. Al-Shawkānī, however, observes that a specification of this kind cannot be definitive. For a *mujtahid* may infer a legal rule from the narratives and parables that are found in the Qur'ān. The knowledge of *āyāt al-aḥkām* includes knowledge of the related commentaries (*tafāsīr*) with special reference to the *Sunnah* and the views of the Companions. Al-Qurṭubī's *Tafsīr al-Qurṭubī*, and the *Aḥkām al-Qur'ān* of Abū Bakr ᶜAlī al-Jaṣṣāṣ, are particularly recommended.[34]

Next, the *mujtahid* must possess an adequate knowledge of the *Sunnah*, especially that part of it which relates to the subject of his *ijtihād*. This is the view of those who admit the divisibility (*tajzi'ah*) of *ijtihād* (for which see below), but if *ijtihād* is deemed to be indivisible, then the *mujtahid* must be knowledgeable of the *Sunnah* as a whole, especially with reference to the *aḥkām* texts, often referred to as *aḥādīth al-aḥkām*. He must know the incidences of abrogation in the *Sunnah*, the general and the specific, (*ᶜāmm* and *khāṣṣ*), the absolute and the qualified (*muṭlaq* and *muqayyad*), and the reliability or otherwise of the narrators of Ḥadīth. It is not necessary to commit to memory the *aḥādīth al-aḥkām* or the names of their narrators, but he must know where to find the *aḥādīth* when he needs to refer to them, and be able to distinguish the reliable from the weak and the authentic from the spurious.[35] Imām Ghazālī points out that an adequate familiarity with the *aḥādīth al-aḥkām* such as those found in *Sunan Abī Dāwud*, *Sunan al-Bayhaqī*, or the *Musnad* of Ibn Ḥanbal would suffice. According to another view, which is attributed to Aḥmad b. Ḥanbal, the *aḥādīth al-aḥkām* are likely to number in the region of 1,200.[36]

The *mujtahid* must also know the substance of the *furū*ᶜ works and the points on which there is an *ijmā*ᶜ. He should be able to verify the consensus of the Companions, the Successors, and the leading Imāms and *mujtahidūn* of the past so that he is guarded against the possibility of issuing an opinion contrary to such an *ijmā*ᶜ. It would be rare, al-Shawkānī observes, for anyone who has attained the rank of a *mujtahid* not to be aware of the issues on which there is a conclusive *ijmā*ᶜ. By implication, the *mujtahid* must also be aware of the opposing views, as it is said, 'the most learned of people is also one who is most knowledgeable of the differences among people'.[37]

In their expositions of the qualifications of a *mujtahid*, the ulema of *uṣūl* place a special emphasis on the knowledge of *qiyās*. The Qur'ān and the *Sunnah*, on the whole, do not completely specify the law as it might be stated in a juristic manual, but contain general rulings and indications as to the causes of such rulings. The *mujtahid* is thus enabled to have recourse to analogical deduction in order to discover the ruling for an unprecedented case. An adequate knowledge of the rules and procedures of *qiyās* is thus essential for the *mujtahid*. Imām Shāfiᶜī has gone so far as to equate *ijtihād* with *qiyās* . Analogy, in other words, is the main bastion of *ijtihād*, even if the two are not identical. Al-Ghazālī has observed that notwithstanding the claim by some ulema that *qiyās* and *ijtihād* are identical and coextensive, *ijtihād* is wider than *qiyās* as it comprises methods of reasoning other than analogy.[38]

Furthermore, the *mujtahid* should know the objectives (*maqāṣid*) of the *Sharīᶜah*, which consist of the *maṣāliḥ* (considerations of public interest). The most important *maṣāliḥ* are those which the Lawgiver has Himself identified and which must be given priority over others. Thus the protection of the 'Five Principles', namely of life, religion, intellect, lineage and property, are the recognised objectives of the Lawgiver. These are the essentials (*ḍarūriyyāt*) of the *maṣāliḥ* and as such they are distinguished from the complementary (*ḥājiyyāt*) and the embellishments (*taḥsīniyyāt*). The *mujtahid* must also know the general maxims of *fiqh* such as the removal of hardship (*raf*ᶜ *al-ḥaraj*), that certainty must prevail over doubt, and other such principles which are designed to prevent rigidity in the *aḥkām*. He must be able to distinguish the genuine *maṣāliḥ* from those which might be inspired by whimsical desires, and be able to achieve a correct balance between values.[39]

Al-Shāṭibī summarises all the foregoing requirements of *ijtihād* under two main headings, one of which is the adequate grasp of the objectives of the *Sharīᶜah*, while the other is the knowledge of the sources and the methods of deduction. The first of these is fundamental, and the second serves as an instrument of achieving the first.[40]

It is further suggested in this connection that the *mujtahid* must be capable of distinguishing strength and weakness in reasoning and evidence. This requirement has prompted some ulema to say that the *mujtahid* should have a knowledge of logic (*manṭiq*). But this is not strictly a requirement. For logic as a discipline had not even developed during the time of the Companions, but this did not detract from their ability to practice *ijtihād*.[41]

And finally, the *mujtahid* must be an upright (*ᶜādil*) person who refrains from committing sins and whose judgement the people can trust. His sincerity must be beyond question and untainted with self-seeking interests. For *ijtihād* is a sacred trust, and anyone who is tainted with heresy and self-indulgence is unworthy of it.[42] These are the conditions of independent *ijtihād*, but a *mujtahid* on particular issues need only know all the relevant information concerning those issues and may, at least according to those who admit the 'divisibility' of *ijtihād*, practice *ijtihād* in respect of them. His lack of knowledge in matters unrelated to the issues concerned does not prejudice his competence for *ijtihād*.[43]

Some observers have suggested that the practice of *ijtihād* was abandoned partly because the qualifications required for its practice were made 'so immaculate and rigorous and were set so high that they were humanly impossible of fulfilment'.[44] This is, however, an implausible supposition which has been advanced mainly by the proponents of *taqlīd* with a view to discouraging the practice of *ijtihād*. As for the actual conditions, Abdur Rahim (with many others) has aptly observed that 'the qualifications required of a *mujtahid* would seem to be extremely moderate, and there can be no warrant for supposing that men of the present day are unfitted to acquire such qualifications'.[45] There is little evidence to prove that fulfilling the necessary conditions of *ijtihād* was beyond the reach of the ulema of later periods. On the contrary, as one observer has pointed out, 'the total knowledge required on the part of the jurist enabled many to undertake *ijtihād* in one area of the law or another'.[46] Their task was further facilitated by the legal theory, in particular the Ḥadīth which absolved the *mujtahid* who committed an error from the charge of sin, and even entitled him to a spiritual reward. Furthermore, the recognition in the legal theory of the divisibility of *ijtihād*, as we shall presently discuss, enabled the specialist in particular areas of the *Sharīᶜah* to practice *ijtihād* even if he was not equally knowledgeable in all of its other disciplines.

Divisibility of *Ijtihād*

The question to be discussed here is whether a person who is learned on a particular subject is qualified to practice *ijtihād* in that area, or whether he is required to qualify as a full *mujtahid* first in order to be able to carry out any *ijtihād* at all. The majority of ulema have held the view that once a person has fulfilled the necessary conditions of *ijtihād* he is qualified to practice it in all areas of the *Sharīʿah*. According to this view, the intellectual ability and competence of a *mujtahid* cannot be divided into compartments. *Ijtihād*, in other words, is indivisible, and we cannot say that a person is a *mujtahid* in the area of matrimonial law and an imitator (*muqallid*) in regard to devotional matters (*ʿibādāt*) or vice-versa. To say this would be tantamount to a contradiction in terms, as *ijtihād* and *taqlīd* cannot be combined in one and the same person.[47] The majority view is based on the analysis that *ijtihād* for the most part consists of formulating an opinion, or *ẓann*, concerning a rule of the *Sharīʿah*. A *ẓann* of this type occurs only to a fully qualified *mujtahid* who has attained the necessary level of intellectual competence. It is further argued that all the branches of the *Sharīʿah* are interrelated, and ignorance in one may lead to an error or misjudgment in another. The majority view is further supported by the argument that once a person has attained the rank of *mujtahid* he is no longer permitted to follow others in matters where he can exercise *ijtihād* himself.[48] Among the majority there are some ulema who have allowed an exception to the indivisibility of *ijtihād*. This is the area of inheritance, which is considered to be self-contained as a discipline of *Sharīʿah* law and independent of the knowledge of the other branches. Hence a jurist who is only knowledgeable in this field may practice *ijtihād* in isolation from the other branches of *Fiqh*.[49]

Some Mālikī, Ḥanbalī and Ẓāhirī ulema have, however, held the view that *ijtihād* is divisible. Hence when a person is learned in a particular area of the *Sharīʿah* he may practice *ijtihād* in that area only. This would in no way violate any of the accepted principles of *ijtihād*. There is similarly no objection, according to this view, to the possibility of a person being both a *mujtahid* and a *muqallid* at the same time. Thus a *mujtahid* may confine the scope of his *ijtihād* to the area of his specialisation. This has, in fact, been the case with many of the prominent Imāms who have, on occasions, admitted their lack of knowledge in regard to particular issues. Imām Mālik is said to have admitted in regard to thirty-six issues at least that he did not know the right answer. But in spite of this, there is no doubt concerning Mālik's competence as a fully-fledged *mujtahid*.[50]

The view that *ijtihād* is divisible is supported by a number of prominent ulema, including Abū'l-Ḥusayn al-Baṣrī, al-Ghazālī, Ibn al-Humām, Ibn Taymiyyah, his disciple Ibn al-Qayyim, and al-Shawkānī. Al-Ghazālī thus observes that a person may be particularly learned in *qiyās* and be able to practice *ijtihād* in the form of analogy even if he is not an expert on Ḥadīth. According to the proponents of this view, if knowledge of all the disciplines of *Sharīᶜah* were to be a requirement, most ulema would fail to meet it and it would impose a heavy restriction on *ijtihād*. Al-Shawkānī, Badrān, and al-Kassāb have all observed that this is the preferable of the two views.[51] One might add here that in modern times, in view of the sheer bulk of information and the more rapid pace of its growth, specialisation in any major area of knowledge would seem to hold the key to originality and creative *ijtihād*. Divisibility of *ijtihād* would thus seem to be in greater harmony with the conditions of research in modern times. By way of a postscript, one might also remark that the classification of *mujtahids* into various ranks, such as *mujtahids* in a particular school or on particular issues, takes for granted the idea that *ijtihād* is divisible.

Procedure of *Ijtihād*

Since *ijtihād* occurs in a variety of forms, such as *qiyās*, *istiḥsān*, *maṣlaḥah mursalah*, and so on, each of these is regulated by its own rules. There is, in other words, no uniform procedure for *ijtihād* as such. The ulema have nevertheless suggested that in practicing *ijtihād*, the jurist must first of all look at the *nuṣūṣ* of the Qur'ān and the Ḥadīth, which must be given priority over all other evidences. Should there be no *naṣṣ* on the matter, then he may resort to the manifest text (*ẓāhir*) of the Qur'ān and Ḥadīth and interpret it while applying the rules pertaining to the general (*ᶜāmm*) and specific (*khāṣṣ*), the absolute and the qualified, and so forth, as the case may be. Should there be no manifest text on the subject in the Qur'ān and the verbal *Sunnah*, the *mujtahid* may resort to the actual (*fiᶜlī*) and tacitly approved (*taqrīrī*) *Sunnah*. Failing this, he must find out if there is a ruling of *ijmāᶜ* or *qiyās* available on the problem in the works of the renowned jurists. In the absence of any guidance in these works, he may attempt an original *ijtihād* along the lines of *qiyās*. This would entail a recourse to the Qur'ān, the Ḥadīth, or *ijmāᶜ* for a precedent that has a *ᶜillah* identical to that of the *farᶜ* (i.e. the case for which a solution is wanting). When this is identified, he is to apply the principles of *qiyās* in order to deduce the necessary ruling. In the absence of a textual basis on which an analogy could be founded, the *mujtahid* may resort to any of the recognised methods of *ijtihād* such as *istiḥsān*, *maṣlaḥah mursalah*, *istiṣḥāb*, etc, and derive a solution while applying the rules that ensure the proper implementation of these doctrines.[52]

The foregoing procedure has essentially been formulated by al-Shāfiʿī, who is noted to have observed the following. When an incident occurs, the *mujtahid* must first check the *nuṣūṣ* of the Qur'ān, but if he finds none, he must refer to *Mutawātir* Ḥadīths and then to solitary Ḥadīths. If the necessary guidance is still not forthcoming, he should postpone recourse to *qiyās* until he has looked into the manifest (*ẓāhir*) text of the Qur'ān. If he finds a manifest text which is general, he will need to find out if it can be specified by means of Ḥadīth or *qiyās*. But if he finds nothing that would specify the manifest text, he may apply the latter as it stands. Should he fail to find a manifest text in the Qur'ān or the *Sunnah*, he must look into the *madhāhib*. If he finds a consensus among them, he applies it, otherwise he resorts to *qiyās*, but in doing so, he must pay more attention to the general principles of the *Sharīʿah* than to its subsidiary detail. If he does not find this possible, and all else fails, then he may apply the principle of original absence of liability (*al-barā'ah al-aṣliyyah*). All this must be in full cognisance of the rules that apply to the conflict of evidences (*al-taʿāruḍ bayn al-adillah*), which means that the *mujtahid* should know the methods deployed in reconciling such conflicts, or even eliminating one in favour of the other, should this prove to be necessary. The ruling so arrived at may be that the matter is obligatory (*wājib*), forbidden (*ḥarām*), reprehensible (*makrūh*), or recommended (*mandūb*).[53]

From the viewpoint of the procedure that it employs, *ijtihād* may occur in any of the following four varieties. Firstly, there is the form of a juridical analogy (*qiyās*) which is founded on an effective cause (*ʿillah*). The second variety of *ijtihād* consists of a probability (*ẓann*) without the presence of any *ʿillah*, such as practicing *ijtihād* in regard to ascertaining the time of *ṣalāh* or the direction of the *qiblah*. The third type of *ijtihād* consists of the interpretation of the source materials and the deduction of *aḥkām* from an existing evidence. This type of *ijtihād* is called *ijtihād bayānī*, or 'explanatory *ijtihād*', which takes priority over 'analogical *ijtihād*', or *ijtihād qiyās*. The fourth variety of *ijtihād*, referred to as *ijtihād istiṣlāḥī*, is based on *maṣlaḥah* and seeks to deduce the *aḥkām* in pursuance of the spirit and purpose of the *Sharīʿah*, which may take the form of *istiṣlāḥ*, juristic preference (*istiḥsān*), the obstruction of means (*sadd al-dharā'iʿ*), or some other technique. Imām Shāfiʿī accepts only the first type, namely analogical *ijtihād*, but for the majority of ulema, *ijtihād* is not confined to *qiyās* and may take the form of any of the foregoing varieties.[54]

The *Ijtihād* of the Prophet and his Companions

The question to be discussed here is whether all the rulings of the Prophet should be regarded as having been divinely inspired or whether they also partake in *ijtihād*. The ulema are generally in agreement that the Prophet practiced *ijtihād* in temporal and military affairs, but they have differed as to whether his rulings in *sharʿī* matters could properly fall under the rubric of *ijtihād*. According to the Ashʿarīs, the Muʿtazilah, Ibn Ḥazm al-Ẓāhirī and some Ḥanbalī and Shāfiʿī ulema, the Qur'ān provides clear evidence that every speech of the Prophet partakes in *waḥy*. A specific reference is thus made to sūra al-Najm (53:3) which provides: 'He says nothing of his own desire, it is nothing other than revelation [*waḥy*] sent down to him.' This *āyah* is quite categorical on the point that the Prophet is guided by divine revelation and that all his utterances are to be seen in this light. This would mean that all the rulings of the Prophet consist of divine revelation and that none would occur in the form of *ijtihād*.[55]

The majority of ulema have, however, held that the Prophet in fact practiced *ijtihād* just as he was allowed to do so. This, it is said, is borne out by the numerous *āyāt* of the Qur'ān where the Prophet is invited, along with the rest of the believers, to meditate on the Qur'ān and to study and think about the created world. As for the *āyah* in sūra al-Najm quoted above, the majority of ulema have held that the reference here is to the Qur'ān itself, and not to every word that the Prophet uttered. That this is so is borne out by the use of the pronoun 'it' (*huwa*) in this *āyah*, which refers to the Qur'ān itself. The majority view adds that the occasion for the revelation (*sha'n al-nuzūl*) of this *āyah* supports this interpretation. (The *āyah* was revealed in refutation of the unbelievers who claimed that the Qur'ān was the work of the Prophet himself and not the speech of God.) Besides, the Prophet often resorted to reasoning by way of analogy and *ijtihād*,and did not postpone all matters until the reception of divine revelation.[56]

The minority view on this subject overrules the claim of the practice of *ijtihād* by the Prophet and maintains that if it were true that the Prophet practiced *ijtihād*, then disagreeing with his views would be permissible. For it is a characteristic of *ijtihād* to allow disagreement and opposition. Opposing the Prophet is, however, clearly forbidden, and obedience to him is a Qur'ānic duty upon every Muslim (al-Nisā', 4:14 and 58).

There is yet a third opinion on this point which, owing to the conflicting nature of the evidence, advises total suspension. This view is attributed to al-Shāfiʿī and upheld by al-Bāqillānī and al-Ghazālī. Al-Shawkānī, however, rejects it by saying that the Qur'ān gives us clear indications not only to the effect that *ijtihād* was permissible for the

Prophet but also that he was capable of making errors.[57] Nonetheless, the ulema who have maintained this view add that such an error is not sustained, meaning that any error the Prophet might have made was rectified by the Prophet himself or through subsequent revelation.[58] Thus we find passages in the Qur'ān which reproach the Prophet for his errors. To give an example, a text in sūra al-Anfal (8:67) provides: 'It is not proper for the Prophet to take prisoners [of war] until he has subdued everyone in the earth.' This *āyah* was revealed concerning the captives of the battle of Badr. It is reported that seventy persons from the enemy side were taken prisoner in the battle. The Prophet first consulted Abū Bakr, who suggested that they should be released against a ransom, whereas ʿUmar b. al-Khaṭṭāb held the view that they should be killed. The Prophet approved of Abū Bakr's view but then the *āyah* was revealed which disapproved of taking ransom from the captives. Elsewhere, in sūra al-Tawbah (9:43), in an address to the Prophet, the text provides: 'God granted you pardon, but why did you permit them to do so before it became clear to you who was telling the truth?' This *āyah* was revealed concerning the exemption that the Prophet granted, prior to investigating the matter, to those who did not participate in the battle of Tabūk. These and similar passages in the Qur'ān indicate that the Prophet had on occasions acted on his own *ijtihād*. For had he acted in pursuance of a divine command, there would have been no occasion for a reprimand, or the granting of divine pardon for his mistakes.[59]

The majority view that the Prophet resorted to *ijtihād* finds further support in the *Sunnah*. Thus, according to one Ḥadīth, the Prophet is reported to have said, 'When I do not receive a revelation (*waḥy*) I adjudicate among you on the basis of my opinion (*ra'y*).'[60]

انما أقضي بينكم برأيي فيما لم ينزل عليّ فيه
وحي

The next point to be raised in this connection is whether *ijtihād* was lawful for the Companions during the lifetime of the Prophet. Once again the majority of ulema have held that it was, regardless as to whether it took place in the presence of the Prophet or in his absence. The ulema have, however, differed over the details. Ibn Ḥazm held that such an *ijtihād* is valid in matters other than the *ḥalāl* and *ḥarām*, whereas al-Āmidī and Ibn al-Ḥājib have observed that it is only speculative and does not establish a definitive ruling. There are still others who have held that *ijtihād* was lawful for the Companions only if it took place in the presence of the Prophet, with his permission, or if the Prophet had approved of it in some way. Those who invalidate *ijtihād* for the Companions during the lifetime of the Prophet maintain that the Companions had access to the Prophet in order to obtain the necessary authority, which would be decisive and final. If one is able to obtain a decisive ruling on a juridical matter, *ijtihād* which is merely a speculative exercise is unlawful.[61] This view is, however, considered to be weak as it takes for granted ready access to the Prophet; it also discounts the possibility that certain decisions had to be made by the Companions without delay. The correct view is therefore that of the majority, which is supported by the fact that the Companions did, on numerous occasions, practice *ijtihād* both in the presence of the Prophet and in his absence. The Ḥadīth of Muᶜādh b. Jabal is quoted as clear authority to the effect that the Prophet authorised Muᶜādh to resort to *ijtihād* in his absence (i.e. in the Yemen). [62] Numerous other names are quoted, including those of Abū Bakr, Saᶜd b. Muᶜādh, ᶜAmr b. al-ᶜĀṣ and Abū Mūsā al-Ashᶜarī, who have delivered *ijtihād* in the absence of the Prophet.[63] It is also reported in a Ḥadīth that when the Prophet authorised ᶜAmr b. al-ᶜĀṣ to adjudicate in some disputes, he asked the Prophet, 'Shall I render *ijtihād* while you are present?' To this the Prophet replied, 'Yes. If you are right in your judgement, you earn two rewards, but if you err, only one.' It is similarly reported that Saᶜd b. Muᶜādh rendered a judgment concerning the Jews of Banū Qurayẓah in the presence of the Prophet, and that he approved of it.[64]

Truth and Fallacy of *Ijtihād*

The jurists have differed as to whether every *mujtahid* can be assumed to be right in his conclusions, or whether only one of several solutions to a particular problem may be regarded as true to the exclusion of all others. At the root of this question lies the uncertainty over the unity or plurality of truth in *ijtihād*. Has Almighty God predetermined a specific solution to every issue, which alone may be regarded as right? If the answer to this is in the affirmative then it will follow that there is only one correct solution to any juridical problem and that all others are erroneous. This would in turn beg the question of whether it is at all possible for the *mujtahid* to commit a sin by rendering an erroneous *ijtihād*. In the face of the Ḥadīth which promises a spiritual reward to every *mujtahid* regardless of the accuracy of his conclusions, plus the fact that he is performing a sacred duty – is it theoretically possible for a *mujtahid* to commit a sin?

The ulema are in agreement that in regard to the essentials of dogma, such as the oneness of God (*tawḥīd*), His attributes, the truth of the prophethood of Muḥammad, the hereafter, and so on, there is only one truth and anyone, whether a *mujtahid* or otherwise, who takes a different view automatically renounces Islam.[65]

With regard to juridical or *sharʿī* matters, the majority of ulema, including the Ashʿarīs and the Muʿtazilah, recognise two types:

1) Juridical matters which are determined by a clear and definitive text, such as the obligatoriness of *ṣalāh* and other pillars of the faith, the prohibition of theft, adultery, and so on. In regard to these matters, once again, there is only one truth with which the *mujtahid* may not differ. Anyone who takes an exception to it commits a sin, and according to some, even heresy and disbelief.
2) *Sharʿī* matters on which no decisive ruling is found in the sources. There is much disagreement on this. The Ashʿarīs and the Muʿtazilah have held the view that *ijtihād* in regard to such matters is always meritorious and partakes in truth regardless of the nature of its results. But according to the four leading imāms and many other ulema, only one of the several opposing views on a particular issue may be said to be correct. For it is impossible to say that one and the same thing at the same time regarding the same person could be both lawful and unlawful.[66] This view has quoted in support the Qur'ānic text where in reference to the two judgements of David and Solomon on one and the same issue, God validated only one. The text runs:

> And when David and Solomon both passed judgement on the field where some people's sheep had strayed to pasture there at night, We acted as Witnesses for their decision. We made Solomon understand it. To each We gave discretion and knowledge [. . .] (al-Anbiya', 21:78–79).

Had there been more than one correct solution to a juridical problem, then this *āyah* would have upheld the judgements both of David and Solomon. It is thus suggested that this *āyah* confirms the unitary character of truth in *ijtihād*. Furthermore, when one looks at the practice of the Companions, it will be obvious that not only did they admit the possibility of error in their own judgements but that they also criticised one another. If all of them were to be right in their *ijtihād*, there would be no point in their criticising one another or in admitting the possibility of error in their own *ijtihād*. To give an example, the Caliph Abū Bakr is reported to have said in regard to the issue of *kalālah* (i.e. when the deceased leaves no parent or child to inherit him): 'I decided the question of *kalālah* according to my opinion. If it is correct, it is an inspiration from God; if it is wrong, then the error is mine and Satan's.'[67] It is further reported that when ʿUmar b. al-Khaṭṭāb adjudicated a case, one of the parties to the dispute who was present at the time said, 'By God this is the truth.' To this the caliph replied that he did not know whether he had attained the truth, but that he had spared no effort in striving to do so.[68]

The *aḥādīth* and the practice of the Companions on *ijtihād* clearly entertain the possibility of error in *ijtihād*. A *mujtahid* may be right or may have erred, but in either case, his effort is commendable and worthy of reward.

The opposite view, which is a minority opinion, maintains that there is no pre-determined truth in regard to *ijtihādī* matters. Almighty God has not determined one particular solution as truth to the exclusion of all others. The result of *ijtihād* may thus vary and several verdicts may be regarded as truth on their merit. This view quotes in support the same Qur'ānic text, quoted above, which in its latter part refers to David and Solomon with the words: 'To each We gave discretion and knowledge.' Had either of them committed an error, God would not have praised them thus. It is hence implied that both were right, and that every *mujtahid* attains the truth in his own way. It is further argued that had there been only one truth in regard to a particular issue, the *mujtahid* would not have been bound by the result of his own *ijtihād*. His duty to follow his own *ijtihād* to the exclusion of anyone else's suggests that every *mujtahid* attains the truth.[69] This view seeks further support in the rule of *Sharīʿah* which authorises the Imām or the *mujtahid* to appoint as judge another *mujtahid* who may differ with him in *ijtihād*. This was, for example, the case when Abū Bakr appointed Zayd b. Thābit as a judge while it was common knowledge among the Companions that Zayd had differed with Abū Bakr on many issues. Had a difference of opinion in *ijtihādī* matters amounted to divergence from truth and indulgence in error, Abū Bakr would not have appointed Zayd to judicial office. And lastly, the proponents of this view have referred to the Ḥadīth which reads: 'My Companions are like stars; any one of them that you follow will lead you to the right path.'

أصحابي كالنجوم بأيّهم أقتديتم أهتديتم

Had there been any substance to the idea that truth is unitary, the Prophet would have specified adherence only to those of his Companions who attained to it.[70]

These differences may be resolved, as the majority of ulema suggest, in the light of the celebrated Ḥadīth, which we quote again: 'When a judge renders *ijtihād* and gives a right judgement, he will have two rewards, but if he errs, he will still have earned one reward.' This Ḥadīth clearly shows that the *mujtahid* is either right (*muṣīb*), or in error (*mukhṭi'*), that some *mujtahidūn* attain the truth while others do not; but that sin attaches to neither as they are both rewarded for their efforts. Hence anyone who maintains that there are as many truths as there are *mujtahids* is clearly out of line with the purport of this Ḥadīth. If every *mujtahid* were supposed to be right, then the division of *mujtahids* into two types in this Ḥadīth would have no meaning.[71]

Classification and Restrictions

In their drive to impose restrictions on *ijtihād*, the ulema of *uṣūl* of the fifth/eleventh century and the subsequent period classified *ijtihād* into several categories. Initially it was divided into two types: firstly, *ijtihād* which aims at deducing the law from the evidence in the sources, often referred to as 'independent *ijtihād*'; and secondly, *ijtihād* which is concerned mainly with the elaboration and implementation of the law within the confines of a particular school, known as 'limited *ijtihād*'. During the first two and a half centuries of Islam, there was never any attempt at denying a scholar the right to find his own solutions to legal problems. It was only at a later period that the question of who was qualified to practice *ijtihād* was raised. From about the middle of the third/ninth century, the idea began to gain currency that only the great scholars of the past had enjoyed the right to practice *ijtihād*.[72] This was the beginning of what came to be known as the 'closure of the gate of *ijtihād*'. Before the fifth/eleventh century, no trace may be found of any attempt to classify *ijtihād* into categories of excellence. Al-Ghazālī (d. 505/1111) was the first to divide *ijtihād* into two categories, as noted above.[73] This division was later developed into five, and eventually into seven classes. While representing the prevailing opinion of his time, al-Ghazālī admitted that independent *mujtahids* were already extinct.[74] About two centuries later, the number of the ranks of *mujtahidūn* reached five, and by the tenth/sixteenth century seven ranks were distinguished, while from the sixth/twelfth century onwards jurists are said to belong to only the last two categories on the scale of seven.[75] This is as follows:

1) Full *Mujtahid* (*mujtahid fi'l-sharᶜ*). This rank is assigned to those who fulfilled all the requirements of *ijtihād*. They deduced the *aḥkām* from the evidence in the sources, and in so doing were not restricted by the rules of a particular *madhhab*. The learned among the Companions, and the leading jurists of the succeeding generation, like Saᶜīd b. al-Musayyib and Ibrāhīm al-Nakhaᶜī, the leading Imāms of the four schools, the leading Imāms of the Shīᶜah Muḥammad al-Bāqir and his son Jaᶜfar al-Ṣādiq, al-Awzāᶜī and many others were identified as independent *mujtahids*. It is by the authority of these that consensus of opinion, analogy, juristic preference, *maṣlaḥah mursalah*, etc., were formulated and established as the secondary proofs of *Sharīᶜah*.[76]

Although Abū Yūsuf and al-Shaybānī are usually subsumed under the second rank, Abū Zahrah, who has written extensively on the lives and works of the leading ulema, regards them as full *mujtahids*. The criteria of distinguishing the first from the second class of *mujtahidūn* is originality and independent thought. If this is deemed to be the case the mere fact that a *mujtahid* has concurred with the opinion of another is immaterial in the determination of his rank. For many of the leading *mujtahids* are known to have concurred with the views of other ulema. For example, it is known that Abū Ḥanīfah on many occasions agreed with and followed the views of his teacher, Ibrāhīm al-Nakhaʿī, but this was only because he was convinced of the accuracy of his reasoning, and not out of imitation for its own sake.[77] The question arises whether this type of *ijtihād* is still open or came to an end with the so-called closure of the gate of *ijtihād*. With the exception of the Ḥanbalīs who maintain that *ijtihād* in all of its forms remains open, the ulema of the other three schools have on the whole acceded to the view that independent *ijtihād* has discontinued.[78] Another related question that has been extensively debated by the ulema is whether the idea of the total extinction of *mujtahids* at any given period or generation is at all acceptable from the viewpoint of doctrine. Could the *Sharīʿah* entertain such a possibility and maintain its own continuation, both at the same time? The majority of the ulema of *uṣūl*, including al-Āmidī, Ibn al-Ḥājib, Ibn al-Humām, Ibn al-Subkī, and Zakarīyā al-Anṣārī have answered this question in the affirmative, whereas the Ḥanbalīs have held otherwise. The Ḥanbalīs have argued that *ijtihād* is an obligatory duty of the Muslim community whose total abandonment would amount to an agreement on deviation/error, which is precluded by the Ḥadīth which states that 'My community shall never agree on an error.'[79]

لا تجتمع أمتي على الضلالة

To say that *ijtihād* is a *wājib*, whether *ʿaynī* or *kafāʾī*, takes it for granted that it may never be discontinued. This is also the implication of another Ḥadīth which provides that 'a section of my *ummah* will continue to be on the right path; they will be the dominant force and they will not be vanquished till the Day of Resurrection.'[80]

لا تزال طائفة من أمتي على الحق ظاهرين حتى
تقوم الساعة

Since the successful pursuit of truth is not possible without knowledge, the survival of *mujtahidūn* in any given age (*ᶜaṣr*) is therefore sustained by this Ḥadīth. Furthermore, according to some ulema, the duty to perform *ijtihād* is not fulfilled by means of limited *ijtihād* or by practising the delivery of *fatwā* alone. According to the Ḥanbalīs, the claim that *ijtihād* has discontinued is to be utterly rejected. *Ijtihād* is not only open, but no period may be without a *mujtahid*. The Shīᶜah Imāmiyyah have held the same view. The Shīᶜah, however, follow their recognised Imāms, in whose absence they may exercise *ijtihād* on condition that they adhere, both in principle and in detail, to the rulings of the Imāms. In the absence of any ruling by the Imāms, the Shīᶜah recognise *ᶜaql* as a proof following the Qur'ān, the *Sunnah*, and the rulings of their Imāms.[81] And finally, it may be said that the notion of the discontinuation of *ijtihād* would appear to be in conflict with some of the important doctrines of *Sharīᶜah*. The theory of *ijmāᶜ*, for example, and the elaborate procedures relating to *qiyās* all proceed on the assumption that they are the living proofs of the law and contemplate the existence of *mujtahidūn* in every age.[82]

2) *Mujtahids* within the School. These are jurists who expounded the law within the confines of a particular school while adhering to the principles laid down by their Imāms. Among the prominent names that feature in this category are Zufar b. al-Hudhayl, Ḥasan b. Ziyād in the Ḥanafī school; Ismāᶜīl b. Yaḥyā al-Muzanī, ᶜUthmān Taqī al-Dīn b. al-Ṣalāḥ and Jalāl al-Dīn al-Suyūṭī in the Shāfiᶜī; Ibn ᶜAbd al-Barr and Abū Bakr b. al-ᶜArabī in the Mālikī, and Ibn Taymiyyah and his disciple Ibn Qayyim al-Jawziyyah in the Ḥanbalī schools. It is observed that although these ulema all followed the doctrines of their respective schools, nevertheless they did not consider themselves bound to follow their masters in the implementation of the general principles or in arguments concerning particular issues. This is borne out by the fact that they have held opinions that were opposed to those of their leading Imāms.[83]

3) *Mujtahids* on Particular Issues. These are jurists who were competent to elucidate and apply the law in particular cases which were not settled by the jurists of the first and second ranks. They did not oppose the leading *mujtahidūn* and generally followed the established principles of their schools. Their main pre-occupation was to elaborate the law on fresh points which were not clearly determined by the higher authorities. Scholars like Abū'l-Ḥasan al-Karkhī and Abū Jaᶜfar al-Ṭaḥāwī in the Ḥanafī school, Abū al-Faḍl al-Marwazī and Abū Isḥāq al-Shīrāzī in the Shāfiᶜī, Abū Bakr al-Abhārī in the Mālikī and ᶜAmr b. Ḥusayn al-Khiraqī in the Ḥanbalī schools have been placed in this category.

All the preceding three classes were designated as *mujtahids*, but the remaining four classes of ulema, as described below have been classified as imitators.[84]

4) The so-called *aṣḥāb al-takhrīj*, who did not deduce the *aḥkām* but were well conversant in the doctrine and were able to indicate which view was preferable in cases of ambiguity, or regarding suitability to prevailing conditions.[85]
5) The *aṣḥāb al-tarjīḥ* are those who were competent to make comparisons and distinguish the correct (*ṣaḥīḥ*) and the preferred (*rājiḥ, arjaḥ*) and the agreed upon (*muftā bihā*) views from the weak ones. Authors like ʿAlā' al-Dīn al-Kāsānī and Burhān al-Dīn al-Marghinānī of the Ḥanafī school, Muḥyī al-Dīn al-Nawawī of the Shāfiʿī, Ibn Rushd al-Qurṭubī of the Mālikī and Muwaffaq al-Dīn ibn Qudāmah of the Ḥanbalī schools and their equals have been placed in this category.[86]
6) The so-called *aṣḥāb al-taṣḥīḥ*: those who could distinguish between the manifest (*ẓāhir al-riwāyah*) and the rare and obscure (*al-nawādir*) views of the schools of their following. Textbook writers whose works are in use in the various *madhāhib* are said to fall into this category.[87]

   It will be noted here that the previous three categories are somewhat overlapping and could be unified under one category to comprise all those who drew comparisons and evaluated the strengths and weaknesses of the existing views.
7) And finally the *muqallidūn*, or the 'imitators', who lack the abilities of the above and comprise all who do not fall in any of the preceding classes. It is said concerning them that, 'They do not distinguish between the lean and the fat, right and left, but get together whatever they find, like the one who gathers wood in the dark of the night.'[88]

While referring to this classification, Aghnides is probably right in observing that 'It implies a gratuitous assumption that the latter *mujtahids* could not show greater independence of thought.'[89] The restrictions that were imposed on *ijtihād* and the ensuing phenomenon of the 'closing of its gate' are, in the most part, an historical development which could find little if any support in the legal theory of *ijtihād*. Similarly, the notion that the ulema, at around the beginning of the fourth century, reached such an immutable consensus of opinion that further *ijtihād* was unnecessary is ill-conceived and untenable.[90] The mendacity of such a claim is attested by the rejection on the part of numerous ulema, including those of the Ḥanbalī and the Shīʿah Imāmiyyah, of the validity of such a consensus.

Authors throughout the Muslim world have begun to criticise *taqlīd* and advocate the continued validity of *ijtihād* as a divinely prescribed legal principle. A number of most prominent ulema, including Shāh Walī Allāh, Muḥammad b. Ismāʿīl al-Ṣanʿānī, Muḥammad bin ʿAli al-Shawkānī and Ibn ʿAlī al-Sanūsī led the call for the revival of *ijtihād*.[91] The nineteenth century Salafiyyah movement in Egypt advocated the renovation of Islam in the light of modern conditions and the total rejection of *taqlīd*.

Al-Shawkānī (d.1255/1839) vehemently denies the claim that independent *mujtahidūn* have become extinct, a claim which smacks of 'crass ignorance and is utterly to be rejected'. The same author goes on to name a number of prominent ulema who have achieved the highest rank of erudition in *Sharīʿah*. Among the Shāfiʿīs, for example, at least six such ulema can be named who have fulfilled, in an uninterrupted chain of scholarship, all the requirements of *ijtihād*. These are ʿIzz al-Dīn ibn ʿAbd al-Salām and his disciple, Ibn Daqīq al-ʿĪd, then the latter's disciple Muḥammad ibn Sayyid al-Nās, then his disciple Zayn al-Dīn al-ʿIrāqī, his disciple Ibn Ḥajar al-ʿAsqalānī, and his disciple, Jalāl al-Dīn al-Suyūṭī. That they were all full *mujtahids* is attested by the calibre of their works and the significant contributions they have made to the *Sharīʿah*. The first two of these are particularly prominent. In his well-recognised juristic work. *Al-Baḥr al-Muḥīṭ*, Muḥammad b. ʿAbd Allāh al-Zarkashī has acknowledged that they had both attained the rank of *mujtahid*. 'It is utter nonsense' writes al-Shawkānī, 'to say that God Almighty bestowed the capacity for knowledge and *ijtihād* on the bygone generations of ulema but denied it to the later generations.' What the proponents of *taqlīd* are saying to us is that we must know the Qur'ān and the *Sunnah* through the words of other men while we still have the guidance in our hands. 'Praise be to God, this is the greatest lie (*buhtānun ʿaẓīm*) and there is no reason in the world to vindicate it.[92]

Iqbal Lahori considers the alleged closure of the gate of *ijtihād* to be 'a pure fiction' suggested partly by the crystallisation of legal thought in Islam, and partly by that intellectual laziness which, especially in periods of spiritual decay, turns great thinkers into idols. Iqbal continues: if some of the later doctors have upheld this fiction, 'modern Islam is not bound by this voluntary surrender of intellectual independence'.[93]

Abū Zahrah is equally critical of the alleged closure of the door of *ijtihād*. How could anyone be right in closing the door that God Almighty has opened for the exertion of the human intellect? Anyone who has advanced this claim could surely have no convincing argument to prove it. Abū Zahrah continues: the fact that *ijtihād* has not been actively pursued has had the chilling effect of moving the people further away from the sources of the *Sharīʿah*. The tide of *taqlīd* has carried some so far as to say that there is no further need to interpret the Qur'ān and Ḥadīth now that the door of *ijtihād* is closed. In Abū Zahrah's phrase, 'nothing is further from the truth – and we seek refuge in God from such excesses'.[94]

Conclusion

The conditions under which *ijtihād* was formerly practiced by the ulema of the early periods are no longer what they were. For one thing, the prevalence of statutory legislation as the main instrument of government in modern times has led to the imposition of further restrictions on *ijtihād*. The fact that the law of the land in the majority of Islamic countries has been confined to the statute book, and the parallel development whereby the role of interpreting the statute has also been assigned to the courts of law, has had, all in all, a discouraging effect on *ijtihād*. The *mujtahid* is given no recognised status, nor is he required to play a definite role in legislation or the administration of justice in the courts. This is confirmed by the fact that many modern constitutions in Islamic countries are totally silent on *ijtihād*. It was this total neglect of *ijtihād* which prompted Iqbal to propose, in his well-known work *The Reconstruction of Religious Thought in Islam*, that the only way to utilise both *ijmāᶜ* and *ijtihād* (which he refers to as the 'principle of movement') into the fabric of modern government is to institutionalise *ijtihād* by making it an integral feature of the legislative function of the state (p. 174).

Essentially the same view has been put forward by al-Ṭamāwī, who points out that *ijtihād* by individuals in the manner that was practiced by the *fuqahā'* of the past is no longer suitable to modern conditions. The revival of *ijtihād* in our times would necessitate efforts which the government must undertake. Since education is the business and responsibility of modern governments, it should be possible to provide the necessary education and training that a *mujtahid* would need to possess, and to make attainment to this rank dependent on special qualifications. Al-Ṭamāwī further recommends the setting up of a council of qualified *mujtahids* to advise in the preparation and approval of statutory law so as to ensure its harmony with *Sharīᶜah* principles.[95]

This is, of course, not to say that the traditional forms of learning in the *Sharīᶜah* disciplines, or of the practice of *ijtihād*, are obsolete. On the contrary, the contribution that the ulema and scholars can make, in their individual capacities, to the incessant search for better solutions and more refined alternatives should never be underestimated. It is further hoped that, for its part, government will also play a positive role in preserving the best heritage of the traditional modes of learning, and encourage the ulema to enhance their contribution to law and development. The universities and legal professions in many Islamic countries are currently committed to the training of lawyers and barristers in the modern law stream. To initiate a comprehensive and well-defined programme of education for prospective *mujtahids*, which would combine training in both the traditional and modern legal disciplines, would not seem to be beyond the combined capabilities of universities and legal professions possessed of long-standing experience in Islamic legal education.

Furthermore, in a *Sharīʿah*-oriented government it would seem desirable that the range of selection to senior advisory, educational and judicial posts would include the qualified *mujtahidūn*. This would hopefully provide the basis for healthy competition and incentives for high performance among the candidates, and help to create a definite role for them in the various spheres of government.

NOTES

1. Amin Islahi (*Islamic Law*, p. 109) has thus aptly stated that: 'There are three prominent and fundamental sources of Islamic Law: the Holy Qur'ān, the Sunnah of the holy Prophet (p.b.u.h.) and *ijtihād*.'
2. Āmidī, *Iḥkām*, IV,162; Shawkānī, *Irshād*, p. 250; Khuḍarī, *Uṣūl*, p. 367.
3. Abū Zahrah, *Uṣūl*, p. 301.
4. Shawkānī, *Irshād*, p. 250; Zuhayr, *Uṣūl*, IV, 223–25; Badrān, *Uṣūl*, p. 471.
5. Ghazālī, *Mustaṣfā*, II, 102; Āmidī, *Iḥkām*, IV, 162.
6. Shawkānī, *Irshād*, p. 250.
7. Ibid., p. 252; Zuhayr, *Uṣūl*, IV, 225; Aghnides, *Muhammedan Theories*, p. 91; Badrān, *Uṣūl*, p. 471.
8. Kassāb, *Aḍwā'*, p. 29; Badrān, *Uṣūl*, p. 473.
9. Abū Dāwud, *Sunan* (Hasan's trans.), II, 407, Ḥadīth no. 1562.
10. Kassāb, *Aḍwā'*, p. 30; Badrān, *Uṣūl*, p.474.
11. Abū Dāwud, *Sunan* (Hasan's trans.), I, 209, Ḥadīth, no. 819.
12. Shawkānī, *Irshād*, p. 253; Khuḍarī, *Uṣūl*, p. 368; Zuhayr, *Uṣūl*, IV, 227.
13. Ghazālī, *Mustaṣfā*, II, 121; Āmidī, *Iḥkām* IV, 204; Kassāb, *Aḍwā'*, p. 119.
14. Āmidī, *Iḥkām*, IV, 14; Khuḍarī, *Uṣūl*, p. 380.
15. Āmidī, *Iḥkām*, IV, 206; Kassāb, *Aḍwā'*, p. 121.
16. Āmidī, *Iḥkām*, IV, 14; Khuḍarī, *Uṣūl*, p. 380.
17. Ibn al-Qayyim, *Iʿlām*, I, 177; Kassāb, *Aḍwā'*, p. 108; Badrān, *Uṣūl*, p. 485.
18. Ibid.
19. Ghazālī, *Mustaṣfā*, II, 120; Āmidī, *Iḥkām*, IV, 184; Ibn al-Qayyim, *Iʿlām*, I, 71–72; Mahmassānī, *Falsafah* (Ziadeh's trans.), p. 97.
20. Abū Dāwud, *Sunan* (Hasan's trans.), III, 1019, Ḥadīth no. 3585. The full version of this Ḥadīth appears at page 218.
21. Ghazālī, *Mustaṣfā*, II, 63–64.

22. Abū Dāwud, *Sunan*, III, 1013, Ḥadīth no.3567.
23. Ghazālī, *Mustaṣfā*, II, 105; Āmidī, *Iḥkām*, IV, 186.
24. Bukhārī, *Ṣaḥīḥ* (Istanbul ed.), VI, 84; Āmidī, *Iḥkām*, IV, 209.
25. Ibid., I, 25–26.
26. Ibn Mājah, *Sunan*, I, 81, Ḥadīth no. 224; Āmidī, *Iḥkām*, IV, 230, 234; Shāṭibī, *Muwāfaqāt*, IV, 140.
27. Ibn al-Qayyim, *Iᶜlām*, I, 176; Mahmassānī, *Falsafah*, p. 95; Kassāb, *Aḍwā'*, p. 19.
28. Ghazālī, *Mustaṣfā*, II, 106; Ibn al-Qayyim, *Iᶜlām*, I, 176; Kassāb, *Aḍwā'*, p. 19.
29. Cf. Kassāb, *Aḍwā'*, p. 20.
30. Cf. Hallaq, *The Gate*, pp. 14–17.
31. Ghazālī, *Mustaṣfā*, II, 102; Abū Zahrah, *Uṣūl*, p. 302.
32. Shāṭibī, *Muwāfaqāt*, IV, 60.
33. Ghazālī, *Mustaṣfā*, II, 101.
34. Shawkānī, *Irshād*, pp. 250–51; Abū Zahrah, *Uṣūl*, p. 304; Zuhayr, *Uṣūl*, IV, 226.
35. Shawkānī, *Irshād*, p. 251ff; Abū Zahrah, *Uṣūl*, p. 304.
36. Ghazālī, *Mustaṣfā*, II, 101; Shawkānī, *Irshād*, p. 251.
37. Shawkānī, *Irshād*, p. 251; Ghazālī, *Mustaṣfā*, II, 101; Abū Zahrah, *Uṣūl*, p. 305.
38. Ghazālī, *Mustaṣfā*, II, 54; Shawkānī, *Irshād*, p. 252; Abū Zahrah, *Uṣūl*, p. 306.
39. Shawkānī, *Irshād*, p. 252; Abū Zahrah, *Uṣūl*, p. 307; Badrān, *Uṣūl*, p. 208.
40. Shāṭibī, *Muwāfaqāt*, IV, 56; Abū Zahrah, *Uṣūl*, p. 307.
41. Abū Zahrah, *Uṣūl*, pp. 308–309; Ghazālī, (*Mustaṣfā*, II, 103), considers a knowledge of Arabic, Ḥadīth and *uṣūl al-fiqh* to be essential to *ijtihād*. However the requirement concerning the knowledge of *Uṣūl* would seem to be repetitive in view of the separate conditions that the *mujtahid* must fulfil, such as the knowledge of *qiyās* and other such requirements, which fall under the subject of *Uṣūl*.
42. Ghazālī, *Mustaṣfā*, II, 101; Shawkānī, *Irshād*, p. 252.
43. Ghazālī, *Mustaṣfā*, II, 102–103; Kassāb, *Aḍwā'*, p. 38.
44. Cf. Fazlur Rahman, *Islam*, p. 78.
45. Abdur Rahim, *Jurisprudence*, p. 174.
46. Hallaq, *The Gate*, p.14.
47. Shawkānī, *Irshād*, p. 254; Abū Zahrah, *Uṣūl*, p. 318; Badrān, *Uṣūl* p. 486.
48. Āmidī, *Iḥkām*, IV, 204; Shawkānī, *Irshād*, p. 255.
49. Kassāb, *Aḍwā'*, p. 96.
50. Shawkānī, *Irshād*, p. 255; Abū Zahrah, *Uṣūl*, p. 318; Badrān, *Uṣūl*, p. 486.
51. Ghazālī, *Mustaṣfā*, II, 103; Shawkānī, *Irshād*, p. 255; Badrān, *Uṣūl*, p. 486.
52. Shirāzī, *Lumaᶜ*, pp. 83–84.
53. Shāfiᶜī, *Risālah*, pp. 261–62; Shawkānī, *Irshād*, p. 258.
54. Kassāb, *Aḍwā'*, p. 24; Hallaq, *The Gate*, p. 12.
55. Shawkānī, *Irshād*, p. 255.
56. Ibid. p. 256; Zuhayr, *Uṣūl*, IV, 227.
57. Shawkānī, *Irshād*, p. 256; Ghazālī, *Mustaṣfā*, II, 104.
58. Kassāb, *Aḍwā'*, p. 61.
59. Shawkānī, *Irshād*, p. 256; Ghazālī, *Mustaṣfā*, II, 104; Kassāb, *Aḍwā'*, p. 61.
60. Abū Dāwud, *Sunan* (Hasan's trans.), III, 1017, Ḥadīth no. 3578; Kassāb, *Aḍwā'*, p.58. For other *aḥādīth* on this point see Shawkānī, *Irshād*, p. 256.
61. Shawkānī, *Irshād*, p. 257; Zuhayr, *Uṣūl*, IV, 234.
62. Ghazālī, *Mustaṣfā*, II, 104.
63. Shawkānī, *Irshād*, p.257; Zuhayr, *Uṣūl*, IV, 237.
64. Shawkānī, *Irshād*, p. 257; Kassāb, *Aḍwā'*, p. 80. Ghazālī has however expressed some reservations as to the validity of *ijtihād* in the presence of the Prophet, as he considers

that unless the Prophet granted permission, *ijtihād* in his presence would be discourteous (*Mustaṣfā*, II, 104).

65. Shawkānī, *Irshād*, p. 259.

66. Ibid., pp. 260–61; Zuhayr, *Uṣūl*, IV, 238.

67. Āmidī, *Iḥkām*, IV, 187; Ibn al-Qayyim, *Iᶜlām*, I, 177.

68. Āmidī, *Iḥkām*, IV, 187.

69. Shawkānī, *Irshād*, p. 262; Zuhayr, *Uṣūl*, IV, 239; Kassāb, *Aḍwā'*, pp. 102–103.

70. Shawkānī, *Irshād*, p. 262; Āmidī, *Iḥkām* IV, 152; Zuhayr, *Uṣūl*, IV, 241.

71. Shawkānī, *Irshād*, p. 261.

72. Cf. Schacht, 'Idjtihād', *Encyclopedia of Islam*, IV, 1029.

73. Hallaq, *The Gate*, p. 18.

74. While quoting Ghazālī's statement, Shawkānī (*Irshād*, p. 253) considers it of questionable validity and adds that Ghazālī almost contradicted himself when he said that he did not follow Shāfiᶜī in all of his opinions.

75. A more detailed account of the historical developments concerning the classification of *ijtihād* can be found in Hallaq, *The Gate*, p. 84ff.

76. Abū Zahrah, *Uṣūl*, p. 310; Kassāb, *Aḍwā'*, p. 38; Abdur Rahim, *Jurisprudence*, pp. 182–83.

77. Ibid.

78. While stating the position of the three Sunni schools on the point, Abū Zahrah (*Uṣūl*, p. 311) adds that this is not definite as, for example, some Ḥanafīs have considered Kamāl al-Dīn ibn al-Humām as a *mujtahid* of the first class.

79. Muslim, *Ṣaḥīḥ*, p. 290, Ḥadīth no. 1095; Shawkānī, *Irshād*, p. 253; Ghazālī, *Mustaṣfā*, I, 111.

80. Ibid.

81. Abū Zahrah, *Uṣūl*, p. 312; Kassāb, *Aḍwā'*, p. 112.

82. Cf. Abdur Rahim, *Jurisprudence*, p. 174.

83. Abū Zahrah, *Uṣūl*, p. 312; Kassāb, *Aḍwā'*, p. 39; Abdur Rahim, *Jurisprudence*, p. 183.

84. Abū Zahrah, *Uṣūl*, p. 314; Kassāb, *Aḍwā'*, p. 40; Aghnides, *Muhammedan Theories*, p. 95; *Mawsūᶜah Jamāl*, I, 253 and VII, 387.

85. Abū Zahrah, *Uṣūl*, p. 315; Kassāb, *Aḍwā'*, p. 40; Aghnides, *Muhammedan Theories*, p. 96.

86. Ibid.

87. Ibid.

88. Abū Zahrah, *Uṣūl*, p. 316.

89. Aghnides, *Muhammedan Theories*, p. 96.

90. Cf. Weiss, 'Interpretation', p. 208.

91. Further details on developments in the Ḥijāz and in the Indian subcontinent can be found in Fazlur Rahman, *Islam*, p. 197 ff; Enayat, *Modern Islamic Political Thought*, p. 63 ff.

92. Shawkānī, *Irshād*, p. 254.

93. Iqbāl, *Reconstruction*, p. 178.

94. Abū Zahrah, *Uṣūl*, p. 318.

95. Ṭamawī, *Al-Sulutāt*, p. 307.

Bibliography

Abū Sinnah, Aḥmad Fahmī. 'Naẓariyyah al-Ḥaqq', in Muḥammad Tawfīq ʿUwayḍah, ed., *al-Fiqh al-Islāmī Asās al-Tashrīʿ*. Cairo: Maṭābiʿ al-Ahrām, 1391/1971.

Aghnides, Nicolas P. *Muhammadan Theories of Finance*. New York: Longmans Green & Co., 1916. Reprint, Lahore: Premier Book House, 1957.

Al-Āmidī, Sayf al-Dīn ʿAlī b. Muḥammad. *al-Iḥkām fī Uṣūl al-Aḥkām*. 4 vols. ed. ʿAbd al-Razzāq ʿAfīfī, 2nd edn. Beirut: al-Maktab al-Islāmī, 1402/1982.

Al-Anṣārī, Abū Yaḥyā Zakarīyā. *Ghāyah al-Wuṣūl ilā Lubāb al-Uṣūl*. Cairo: ʿĪsā al-Bābī al-Ḥalabī, n.d.

Ibn al-ʿArabī, Abū Bakr b. ʿAbd Allāh. *Aḥkām al-Qur'ān*. Cairo: Maṭbaʿah Dār al-Saʿādah, 1330 A.H.

Aṣgharī, Sayyid Moḥammad. *Qiyās wa sayr-e Takwīn-e ān dar Ḥuqūq-e Islām*. n.p., 1361/1982.

Azami, Muhammad Mustafa. *Studies in Hadith Methodology and Literature*. Indianapolis: American Trust Publications, 1977.

Badrān, Abū al-ʿAynayn Badrān. *Uṣūl al-Fiqh al-Islāmī*. Alexandria: Mu'assasah Shabāb al-Jāmiʿah, 1404/1984.

——. *Bayān al-Nuṣūṣ al-Tashrīʿiyyah: Ṭuruquh wa-Anwāʿuh*. Alexandria: Mu'assasah Shabāb al-Jāmiʿah, 1402/1982.

Al-Baṣrī, Abu'l-Ḥusayn Muḥammad b. ʿAlī. *al-Muʿtamad fī Uṣūl al-Fiqh*, ed. Shaykh Khalīl al-Mays. Beirut: Dār al-Kutub al-ʿIlmiyyah, 1403/1483.

Al-Bayhaqī, Abū Bakr Aḥmad b. al-Ḥusayn. *al-Sunan al-Kubrā*. 10 vols. Beirut: Dār al-Fikr, n.d.

Al-Bukhārī, Muḥammad b. Ismāʿīl. *Ṣaḥīḥ al-Bukhārī*. Istanbul: al-Maktabah al-Islāmiyyah. 8 vol., 1981.

——. *Ṣaḥīḥ al-Bukhārī*. Eng. trans. Muhammad Muhsin Khan. 9 vols. Lahore: Qazi Publications, 1979.

Al-Bukhārī, ᶜAlā' al-Dīn ᶜAbd al-ᶜAzīz. *Kashf al-Asrār ᶜAlā Uṣūl al-Bazdawī*. Istanbul, 1307 A.H.

Coulson, Noel, J. *Conflicts and Tensions in Islamic Jurisprudence*. Chicago & London: University of Chicago Press, 1969.

Curson, L.B. *Jurisprudence*. Plymouth: Macdonald & Evans, 1979.

Al-Dārimī. Muḥammad. *Sunan al-Dārimī*. 2 vol. Beirut: Dār al-Kutub al-ᶜIlmiyyah. n.d.

Abū Dāwud al-Sijistānī. *Sunan Abū Dāwud*. Eng. trans. Ahmad Hasan. 3 vols. Lahore: Ashraf Press, 1984.

Denffer, Ahmad von. *ᶜUlūm al-Qur'ān: An Introduction to the Sciences of the Qur'ān*. Leicester: The Islamic Foundation, 1983.

Dias, R.W. *Jurisprudence*. 4th edn. London: Butterworths, 1976.

Dīn, Hārūn. *al-Nafaqah wa'l-Shiqāq wa-Taᶜaddud al-Zawjāt*. Kuala Lumpur: Maṭbaᶜah Waṭan, 1405/1985.

Encyclopedia of Islam. New edn. Leiden: E.J. Brill, 1965 – continuing.

Enayat, Hamid. *Modern Islamic Political Thought*. London: Macmillan Press Ltd., 1982.

Al-Ghazālī, Abū Ḥāmid Muḥammad. *al-Mustaṣfā min ᶜIlm al-Uṣūl*. Cairo: Al-Maktabah al-Tijāriyyah. 2 vols. 1356/1937.

Gilani, Riaz ul-Hasan. *The Reconstruction of Religious Thought in Islam*. Lahore: Rippon Press, 1977.

Goldziher, Ignaz. *Introduction to Islamic Theology and Law*. Trans. Andras and Ruth Hamori. Princeton (New Jersey): Princeton University Press, 1981.

Guraya, Muhammad Yusuf. *Origins of Islamic Jurisprudence* (with special reference to the *Muwaṭṭa'* of Imām Mālik). Lahore: Sh. Muhammad Ashraf, 1985.

Ibn al-Ḥājib, Jamāl al-Dīn Abū ᶜAmr. *Mukhtaṣar al-Muntahā*. Constantinople: al-Maktabah al-Islāmiyyah, 1310. A.H.

Hallaq, Wael B. 'The Gate of Ijtihad: A Study in Islamic Legal History'. PhD dissertation (University of Washington).

Ibn Ḥanbal, Aḥmad. *Musnad al-Imām Aḥmad ibn Ḥanbal*. 6 vols, Beirut: Dār al-Fikr, n.d.

Hasan, Ahmad. *The Early Development of Islamic Jurisprudence*. Islamabad: Islamic Research Institute, 1970.

——. *The Doctrine of Ijmāᶜ in Islam*. Islamabad: Islamic Research Institute, 1976.

——. 'The Principle of Istiḥsān in Islamic Jurisprudence', *Islamic Studies* 16 (1977), 347–363.

——. 'Rationality of Islamic Legal Injunctions: The Problem of Valuation (*Taᶜlīl*)', *Islamic Studies* 13 (1974), 95–110.

Ibn Ḥazm, Abū Muḥammad ᶜAlī b. Aḥmad. *al-Iḥkām fī Uṣūl al-Aḥkām*. Ed. Aḥmad Muḥammad Shākir. 4 vols. Beirut: Dār al-Āfāq al-Jadīda, 1400/1980.

Hitu, Huḥammad Ḥasan. *al-Wajīz fī Uṣūl al-Tashrīᶜ al-Islāmī*. 2nd edn., Beirut: Mu'assasah al-Risālah, 1405/1984.

Hughes, Thomas Patrick. *A Dictionary of Islam*. London 1885. Rev. edn., Lahore: The Book House, n.d.

Iqbal, Muhammad, *The Reconstruction of Religious Thought in Islam*. Lahore: Sh. Muhammad Ashraf. rept. 1982.

Islahi, Amin Ahsan. *Islamic Law, Concept and Codification*. Eng. trans. S.A. Rauf. Lahore: Islamic Publications Ltd. 1979.

Ismāᶜīl, ᶜAbd al-Ḥamīd Abū al-Makārim. *al-Adillah al-Mukhtalaf fīhā Atharuhā fī al-Fiqh al-Islāmī*. Cairo: Dār al-Muslim, n.d.

Al-Isnāwī, Jamāl al-Dīn Abū Muḥammad ᶜAbd al-Raḥīm. *al-Tamhīd fī Takhrīj al-Furūᶜ ᶜala'l-Uṣūl*, ed., Muḥammad Ḥasan Hitu, 3rd edn., Beirut: Mu'assasah al-Risālah, 1404/1984.

——. *Nihāyah al-Sūl fī Sharḥ Minhāj al-Wuṣūl ilā ᶜIlm al-Uṣūl*. 3 vols. Cairo: Maṭbaᶜah al-Tawfīq, n.d.

Kamali, Mohammad Hashim. 'The Citizen and State in Islamic Law', *Sharīᶜah Law Journal* 3 (April 1986) 15–47. Published by the International Islamic University, Selangor, Malaysia.

——. 'Qiyās (Analogy)', *The Encyclopedia of Religion*. New York: The Macmillan Publishing Company, 1987, XII, 128 ff.

Kassāb, al-Sayyid ᶜAbd al-Laṭīf. *Aḍwā' Ḥawl Qaḍiyyah al-Ijtihād fī al-Sharīᶜah al-Islāmiyyah*. Cairo: Dār al-Tawfīq, 1404/1984.

Kerr, Malcolm H. *Islamic Reform*. Berkeley: University of California Press, 1961.

Khadduri, Majid. *Islamic Jurisprudence: Al-Shāfiᶜīs Risālah*. Baltimore: Johns Hopkins Press, 1961. Reprint, Cambridge: The Islamic Texts Society, 1987.

Khallāf, ᶜAbd al-Wahhāb. *ᶜIlm Uṣūl al-Fiqh*, 12th edn., Kuwait: Dār al-Qalam, 1398/1978.

——. *Maṣādir al-Tashrīᶜ al-Islāmī fīma lā Naṣṣa fīh*. Kuwait: Dār al-Qalam, 1398/1978.

Al-Khaṭīb, Muḥammad al-Sharbīnī. *Mughnī al-Muḥtāj ilā Maᶜrifah Maᶜānī Alfāẓ al-Minhāj*. Cairo: Muṣṭafā al-Bābī al-Ḥalabī, 1377/1958.

Al-Khīn, Muṣṭafā Saᶜīd. *Athar al-Ikhtilāf fi'l-Qawā'id al-Uṣūliyyah fī Ikhtilāf al-Fuqahā'*. 3rd edn., Beirut: Mu'assasah al-Risālah, 1402/1982.

Al-Khuḍarī, Shaykh Muḥammad. *Uṣūl al-Fiqh*. 7th edn., Cairo: Dār al-Fikr, 1401/1981.

——. *Tārīkh al-Tashrīᶜ al-Islāmī.* 7th edn., Beirut: Dār al-Fikr, 1401/1981.

Mahmassānī, Subḥī Rajab. *Falsafah al-Tashrīᶜ fi'l-Islām: The Philosophy of Jurisprudence in Islam.* Trans. Farhat J. Ziadeh. Leiden: E.J. Brill, 1961.

Ibn Mājah, Muḥammad b. Yazīd al-Qazwīnī. *Sunan Ibn Mājah.* Istanbul: Çağrı Yayınları, 2 vols. 1401/1981.

Makdisi, John. 'Legal Logic and Equity in Islamic Law'. *American Journal of Comparative Law*, 33 (1985), 63–92.

Al-Marghinānī, Burhān al-Dīn. *Hidāya.* Eng. trans. Hamilton. Lahore: Premier Book House, 1982.

Al-Mawsūᶜah al-Fiqhiyyah. Published by the Ministry of Awqāf, Kuwait: Maṭbaᶜah al-Mawsūᶜah, 1400/1980.

Mawsūᶜah al-Fiqh al-Islāmī. Originally *Mawsūᶜah Jamāl ᶜAbd al-Nāṣir*). Cairo: al-Majlis al-Aᶜlā li'l-Shu'ūn al-Islāmiyyah, 1391 A.H.

Mūsā, Muḥammad Yūsuf. *Aḥkām al-Aḥwāl al-Shakhṣiyyah.* Cairo: Dār al-Kitāb al- ᶜArabī, 1376/1956.

——. *al-Madkhal li-Dirāsah al-Fiqh al-Islāmī.* 2nd edn., Cairo: Dār al-Fikr al-ᶜArabī, 1373/1953.

Muslim. Abū al-Ḥusayn ibn al-Ḥajjāj al-Nīshābūrī. *Mukhtaṣar Ṣaḥīḥ Muslim.* ed., Muḥammad al-Albānī. 4th edn., Beirut: al-Maktab al-Islāmī, 1402/1982.

Muṭahharī, Morteẓā. *Jurisprudence and its Principles.* Trans. Mohammad Salman Tawheedi. New York (Elmhurst): Tahrike Tarsile Qur'ān Inc., *c.* 1982.

Al-Nabhān, Muḥammad Fārūq. *al-Madkhal li'l-Tashrīᶜ al-Islāmī: Nisha'atuh, Adwāruh al-Tārīkhiyyah, Mustaqbaluh*, 2nd edn., Beirut: Dār al-Qalam, 1981.

Al-Nawawī, Muḥyī al-Dīn Abū Zakarīya Yaḥyā ibn Sharaf. *Minhāj al-Ṭālibīn.* Eng. trans. E.C. Howard. Lahore: Law Publishing Company, n.d.

Nour, Alhaji A.M. 'Qiyas as a Source of Islamic Law', *Journal of Islamic and Comparative Law*, 5 (1974), 18–51.

Osborn, P.G. *A Concise Law Dictionary.* 5th edn., London: Sweet & Maxwell, 1964.

Paret. R. 'Istiḥsān and Istiṣlāḥ', *Encyclopedia of Islam*, New Edition. Leiden: E.J. Brill, 1965, continuing.

Qadri, Anwar Ahmad. *Islamic Jurisprudence in the Modern World.* 2nd edn., Lahore: Shaikh Muhammad Ashraf, 1981.

Al-Qaṭṭān, Mannāᶜ Khalīl. *al-Tashrīᶜ wa'l-Fiqh fī'l-Islām, Tārīkhān wa Manhājan.* 4th edn., Beirut: Mu'assasah al-Risālah, 1405/1985.

Al-Qarāfī, Shihāb al-Dīn. *Kitāb al-Furūq*. Cairo: Dār al-Kutub al-ʿArabiyyah, 1346 A.H.

Ibn Qayyim al-Jawziyyah, ʿAbd Allāh Muḥammad b. Abū Bakr. *al-Ṭuruq al-Ḥukmiyyah fi'l-Siyāsah al-Shariʿiyyah*. Cairo: Al-Mu'assasah al-ʿArabiyyah li'l-Ṭibāʿah, 1380/1961.

——. *Iʿlām al-Muwaqqiʿīn ʿan Rabb al-ʿĀlamīn*. ed. Muḥammad Munīr al-Dimashqī. Cairo: Idārah al-Ṭibāʿ ah al-Munīriyyah. 4 vols., n.d.

The Qur'ān, Text, Translation and Commentary by Abdullah Yusuf Ali. Jedda: Islamic Education Centre, 1984. Reprint by the Muslim Converts Association of Singapore, n.d.

The Qur'ān, The First American Version, Translation and Commentary by Thomas B. Irving. Brattleboro (Vermont): Amana Books, 1985.

Al-Qurṭubī, Abū ʿAbd Allāh Muḥammad b. Aḥmad. *al-Jāmiʿ li-Aḥkām al-Qur'ān* (also known as *Tafsīr al-Qurṭubī*). 3rd edn. Cairo: Dār al-Kutub al- ʿArabiyyah, 1387/1967.

Al-Qurṭubī, Muḥammad b. Aḥmad b. Rushd. *Bidāyah al-Mujtahid*. Cairo: Musṭafā al-Bābī al-Ḥalabī, 1401/1981.

Rahim, Abdur. *Principles of Muhammadan Jurisprudence*. London: Luzac and Co. 1911.

Rahman, Fazlur. *Islamic Methodology in History*. Karachi: Islamic Research Institute, 1965.

——. *Islam*. 2nd edn., Chicago and London: University of Chicago Press, 1979.

Al-Rāzī, Fakhr al-Dīn b. ʿUmar. *al-Tafsīr al-Kabīr* (also known as *Mafātīḥ al-Ghayb*). Beirut: Dār al-Fikr, 1398/1978.

Riḍā, Muḥammad Rashīd. *Tafsīr al-Qur'ān al-ʿAẓīm* (also known as *Tafsīr al-Manār*). 4th edn., Cairo: Maṭbaʿah al-Manār, 1373 A.H.

Al-Ṣābūnī, ʿAbd al-Raḥmān. *Muḥāḍarāt fi'l-Sharīʿah al-Islāmiyyah*, n.p. 1392/1972.

Al-Ṣābūnī, ʿAbd al-Raḥmān, Khalīfah Bābakr and Maḥmūd Tanṭāwī. *al-Madkhal al-Fiqhī wa-Tārīkh al-Tashrīʿ al-Islāmī*. Cairo: Maktabah Wahbah, 1402/1982.

Al-Ṣadr, Muḥammad Ṣādiq. *al-Ijmāʿ fi'l-Tashrīʿ al-Islāmī*. Beirut: Manshūrāt ʿUwaydāt: 1969.

Al-Ṣāliḥ, Ṣubḥī, *Mabāḥith fī ʿUlūm al-Qur'ān*. 15th edn., Beirut: Dār al-ʿIlm li al-Malāyīn, 1983.

Al-Sarakhsī, Shams al-Dīn Muḥammad. *Uṣūl al-Sarakhsī*. Ed. Abu'l-Wafā al-Afghānī. Cairo: Maṭbaʿah Dār al-Kitāb al-ʿArabī. 1372 A.H.

——. *al-Mabsūṭ*. 30 vols. Cairo: Maṭbaʿah al-Saʿādah, 1324 A.H.

Schacht, Joseph. *An Introduction to Islamic Law*. Oxford: Clarendon Press, 1964, rept. 1979.

Sha^c^bān, Zakī al-Dīn. 'Manhaj al-Qur'ān fī Bayān al-Ahkām', in ed., Muḥammad Tawfīq ^c^Uwayḍah, *Al-Fiqh al-Islāmī Asās al-Tashrī^c^*. Cairo: Maṭābi^c^ al-Ahrām, 1391/1971, pp. 11–65.

——. *Uṣūl al-Fiqh al-Islāmī*. 2nd edn., Beirut: Dār al-Kitāb, 1971.

Shabir, Mohammad. *The Authority and Authenticity of Hadith As a Source of Islamic Law*. New Delhi: Kitab Bhavan, 1982.

Shāfi^c^ī, Muḥammad b. Idrīs. *Kitāb al-Umm*. 7 vols. Cairo: Dār al-Sha^c^b, 1321, A.H.

——. *al-Risālah*. Ed. Muḥammad Sayyid Kīlānī, 2nd edn., Cairo: Muṣṭafā al-Bābī al-Ḥalabī, 1403/1983.

Shāh Walī Allāh, *Izālah al-Khafā' ^c^an Khilāfah al-Khulafā'*. Karachi: Bareilly, 1286/1869.

——. *Qurrah al-^c^Aynayn fī Tafḍīl al-Shaykhayn*, Delhi, 1310/1931.

Shalabī, Muḥammad Muṣṭafā. *al-Fiqh al-Islāmī bayn al-Mithāliyyah wa al-Wāqi^c^iyyah*. Beirut: Al-Dār al-Jāmi^c^iyyah, 1982.

Shaltūt, Maḥmūd. *al-Islām, ^c^Aqīdah wa-Sharī^c^ah*. Kuwait: Maṭābi^c^ Dār al-Qalam, *c.* 1966.

Al-Shāṭibī, Abū Isḥāq Ibrāhīm. *al-Muwāfaqāt fī Uṣūl al-Aḥkām*. Ed. Muḥammad Ḥasanayn Makhlūf. Cairo: Al-Maṭba^c^ah al-Salafiyyah, 1341 A.H.

——. *al-Muwāfaqāt fī Uṣūl al-Sharī^c^ah*. Ed. Shaykh ^c^Abd Allāh Dirāz. Cairo: Al-Maktabah al-Tijāriyyah al-Kubrā, n.d.

——. *al-I^c^tiṣām*. Cairo: Maṭbā^c^ah al-Manār, 1332/1914.

——. *Fatḥ al-Qadīr*. 3rd edn., Cairo: Dār al-Fikr, 1393/1973.

Al-Shīrāzī, Abū Isḥāq. *al-Luma^c^ fī Uṣūl al-Fiqh*. Cairo: Dār al-Rā'id al-^c^Arabī, 1970.

Al-Sibā^c^ī, Muṣṭafā Ḥusnī. *al-Sunnah wa Makānatuhā fi'l-Tashrī^c^ al-Islāmī*. 3rd edn., Beirut, 1402/1982.

Al-Sijistānī, Abū Dāwud. *Sunan*. Eng. trans. Ahmad Hasan. 3 vols. Lahore: Ashraf Press, 1984.

Al-Suyūṭī, Jalāl al-Dīn, and al-Maḥallī, Jalāl al-Dīn. *Tafsīr al-Qur'ān al-^c^Aẓīm* (also known as *Tafsīr al-Jalālayn*). Cairo: Dār al-Fikr, 1401/1981.

Ṭabarī, Abū Ja^c^far Muḥammad b. Jarīr. *Jāmi^c^ al-Bayān ^c^an Ta'wīl Āyī al-Qur'ān*. Cairo: Dār al-Ma^c^ārif, 1374 A.H.

Al-Tabrīzī, Muḥammad b. ^c^Abd Allāh al-Khaṭīb. *Mishkāt al-Maṣābīh*. Ed. Muḥammad al-Dīn al-Albānī. 2nd edn., Beirut: al-Maktab al-Islāmī, 3 vols. 1399/1979.

Taftāzānī, Sa^c^d al-Dīn Mas^c^ūd b. ^c^Umar. *al-Talwīḥ ^c^Ala'l-Tawḍīḥ*. On the margin of ^c^Ubayd Allāh b. Mas^c^ūd Ṣadr al-Sharī^c^ah, *al-Tawḍīh fī Ḥall Ghawāmiḍ al-Tanqīḥ*. Cairo: ^c^Īsā al-Bābī al-Ḥalabī, 1327/1957.

Tāj, ʿAbd al-Raḥmān. *al-Siyāsah al-Sharʿiyyah*. Cairo: Maṭbaʿah Dār al-Ta'līf, 1373/1953.

Ibn Taymiyyah, Taqī al-Dīn. *Mas'alah al-Istiḥsān*. Trans. and ed. George Makdisi as 'Ibn Taymiyyah's Manuscript on Istihsan', in G. Makdisi, ed., *Arabic and Islamic Studies in Honour of Hamilton A.R. Gibb*. Leiden: E.J. Brill, 1965.

Al-Ṭamāwī, Sulaymān Muḥammad. *al-Suluṭāt al-Thalāth fi'l-Dasātīr al-ʿArabiyyah wa fi'l-Fikr al-Siyāsī al-Islāmī*. 2nd edn. Cairo: Dār al-Fikr al-ʿArabī, 1973.

Al-Ṭūfī, Najm al-Dīn. *Al-Maṣāliḥ al-Mursalah*. This treatise of about 40 pages appears in the Appendix to ʿAbd al-Wahhāb Khallal, *Masādir al-Tashriʿ al-Islāmī fi-mā la-Naṣṣa fīh*, Kuwait: Matabiʿ Dar al-Qalam, 1970.

Weiss, Bernard. 'Interpretation in Islamic Law: The Theory of Ijtihad', *The American Journal of Comparative Law*, 26 (1978), 199–212.

Abū Yūsuf, Yaʿqūb b. Ibrāhīm. *Kitāb al-Kharāj*. 2nd edn., Cairo: Al-Maṭbaʿah al-Salafiyyah, 1352 A.H.

Yusuf, S.M. *Studies in Islamic History and Culture*. Lahore: Sh. Muhammad Ashraf, 1970.

Abū Zahrah, Muḥammad. *Uṣūl al-Fiqh*. Cairo: Dār al-Fikr al-ʿArabī, 1377/1958.

——. *Ibn Ḥanbal*. Cairo: Dār al-Fikr al-ʿArabī, 1367/1947.

Zayd, Muṣṭafā. *al-Maṣlaḥah fi'l-Tashriʿ al-Islāmī wa-Najm al-Dīn al-Ṭūfī*. 2nd ed., Cairo: Dār al-Fikr al-ʿArabī, 1384/1964.

Zaydān, ʿAbd al-Karīm. *al-Fard wa'l-Dawlah fi'l-Sharīʿah al-Islāmiyyah*. 2nd ed., Gary (Indiana): International Islamic Federation of Student Organizations, 1390/1970.

Zuhayr, Muḥammad Abū al-Nūr. *Uṣūl al-Fiqh*. 4 vols. Cairo: Dār al-Ṭibāʿah al-Muḥammadiyyah, *c*. 1372/1952.

Glossary

ʿadl: justice, upright and just.
ʿadālah: justice, uprightness of character.
adillah (pl. of *dalīl*): proofs, evidences, indications.
āḥād: solitary Ḥadīth, report by a single person or by odd individuals.
aḥādīth (pl. of Ḥadīth): narratives and reports of the deeds and sayings of the Prophet.
aḥkām (pl. of *ḥukm*): laws, values and ordinances.
ahliyyah: legal capacity.
ahliyyah al-adā': active legal capacity which can incur rights as well as obligations.
ahliyyah al-wujūb: receptive legal capacity which is good for receiving but cannot incur obligations.
ʿamal: act, practice, precedent.
ʿāmm: general, unspecified.
amr (pl. *awāmir, umūr*): command, matter, affair.
ʿaql: intellect, rationality, reason.
arkān (pl. of *rukn*): pillars, essential requirements.
aṣl: root, origin, source.
athar: lit. impact, trace, vestige; also deeds and precedents of the Companions of the Prophet.
āyah (pl. *āyāt*): lit. sign, indication; a section of the Qur'ānic text often referred to as a 'verse'.
ʿazīmah: strict or unmodified law which remains in its original rigour due to the absence of mitigating factors.
bāṭil: null and void.
bayān: explanation, clarification.
dalālah: meaning, implication.
dalālah al-naṣṣ: inferred or implied meaning of a given text.
dalīl: proof, indication, evidence.
faqīh (pl. *fuqahā'*): jurist, one who is learned in *fiqh*.

*far*ᶜ: lit. a branch or a sub-division, and (in the context of *qiyās*) a new case.
farḍ: obligatory, obligation.
farḍ ᶜayn: personal obligation.
farḍ kafā'ī: collective obligation.
fāsid: corrupt, void; deficient (as opposed to *bāṭil*, which is null and void).
*furū*ᶜ (pl. of *far*ᶜ): branches or subsidiaries, such as in *furū*ᶜ *al-fiqh*, that is, the 'branches of *fiqh*', as opposed to its roots and sources (*uṣūl al-fiqh*).
ḥadd (pl. *ḥudūd*): lit. limit, prescribed penalty.
ḥajj: the once-in-a-lifetime obligation of pilgrimage to the holy Kaᶜbah.
ḥaqīqī: real, original, literal (as opposed to metaphorical).
ḥaqq Allāh: Right of God, or public right.
ḥaqq al-ᶜabd (also *ḥaqq al-ādamī*): Right of Man, or private right.
hijrah: The Prophet's migration from Makkah to Madīnah, signifying the beginning of the Islamic calendar.
ḥirābah: highway robbery (see p.22).
ḥisbah: lit. computation or checking, but commonly used in reference to what is known as *amr bi'l maᶜrūf wa-nahy ᶜan al-munkar*, that is, 'promotion of good and prevention of evil'.
ḥujjiyyah: producing the necessary proof/authority to validate a rule or concept.
ḥukm (pl. *aḥkām*) as in *ḥukm sharᶜī*: law, value, or ruling of Sharīᶜah.
al-ḥukm al-taklīfī: defining law, law which defines rights and obligations.
al-ḥukm al-waḍᶜī: declaratory law, that is, law which regulates the proper implementation of *al-ḥukm al-taklīfī*, such as by expounding the conditions, exceptions and qualifications thereof.
ᶜibārah al-naṣṣ: explicit meaning of a given text which is borne out by its words.
ᶜiddah: the waiting period following dissolution of marriage by death or divorce.
ifṭār: breaking the fast.
*ijmā*ᶜ: consensus of opinion.
ijtihād: lit. 'exertion', and technically the effort a jurist makes in order to deduce the law, which is not self-evident, from its sources.
ikhtilāf: juristic disagreement.
ᶜillah: effective cause, or *ratio legis*, of a particular ruling.
iqtiḍā' al-naṣṣ: the required meaning of a given text.
ishārah al-naṣṣ: an alluded meaning that can be detected in a given text.
ᶜiṣmah: infallibility, immunity from making errors.

istiḥsān: to deem something good, juristic preference.
istiṣḥāb: presumption of continuity, or presuming continuation of the *status quo ante*.
istiṣlāḥ: consideration of public interest.
istinbāṭ: inference, deducing a somewhat hidden meaning from a given text.
jihād: holy struggle.
jumhūr: dominant majority.
kaffārah (pl. *kaffārāt*): penance, expiation.
kalām: lit. speech, but often used as abbreviation for *ᶜilm al- kalām*, that is, 'theology' and dogmatics.
karāhah (or *karāhiyyah*): abhorrence, abomination.
khabar: news, report; also a synonym for Ḥadīth.
khafī: hidden, obscure; also refers to a category of unclear words.
khāṣṣ: specific, a word or a text which conveys a specific meaning.
al-Khulafā' al-Rāshidūn: the rightly guided Caliphs; the first Four Caliphs of Islam.
Kitābiyah: female follower of a non-Islamic revelation.
madhhab (pl. *madhāhib*): juristic/theological school.
mafqūd: a missing person of unknown whereabouts.
mafhūm al-mukhālafah: divergent meaning, an interpretation which diverges from the obvious meaning of a given text.
majāzī: metaphorical, figurative.
makrūh: abominable, reprehensible.
mandūb: commendable.
māniᶜ: hindrance, obstacle.
mansūkh: abrogated, repealed.
maqāṣid: (pl. of *maqṣūd*): goals and objectives.
mashhūr: well-known, widespread.
maṣlaḥah: considerations of public interest.
mawḍūᶜ (pl. *mawḍūᶜāt*): fabricated, forged.
mubāḥ: permissible.
mufassar: explained, clarified.
muḥārabah: highway robbery.
mukallaf: a competent person who is in full possession of his faculties.
mukhtaṣar: abridgement, summary, esp. of juristic manuals composed for mnemonic and teaching purposes.
muḥkam: perspicuous, a word or a text conveying a firm and unequivocal meaning.
mujmal: ambivalent, ambiguous, referring to a category of unclear words.
munāsib: appropriate, in harmony with the basic purpose of the law.

muqayyad: confined, qualified.
mursal: 'discontinued' or 'disconnected' Ḥadīth, esp. at the level of a Companion.
mushkil: difficult; also refers to a category of unclear words.
mushtarak: homonym, a word or phrase imparting more than one meaning.
musnad: Ḥadith with a continuous chain of transmitters.
mutashābih: intricate, unintelligible, referring to a word or a text whose meaning is totally unclear.
muṭlaq: absolute, unqualified.
nahy: prohibition.
naqlī: transmitted, as e.g., in 'transmitted proofs' which are to be distinguished from 'rational proofs'.
nāsikh: the abrogator, as opposed to the *mansūkh* (abrogated).
naskh: abrogation, repeal.
naṣṣ: a clear injunction, an explicit textual ruling.
nikāḥ: marriage contract.
nuṣūṣ (pl. of *naṣṣ*): clear textual rulings.
qadhf: slanderous accusation.
qādhif: slanderous accuser.
qāḍī: judge.
qaṭʿī: definitive, decisive, free of speculative content.
qiṣāṣ: just retaliation.
rajm: stoning to death.
riwāyah: narration, transmission.
rukhṣah: concession or concessionary law, that is, law which is modified due to the presence of mitigating factors.
rukn: pillar, essential ingredient.
sabab (pl. *asbāb*): cause, means of obtaining something.
ṣaḥīḥ: valid, authentic.
ṣalāh: obligatory prayers.
sanad: basis, proof, authority.
sharṭ (pl. *shurūṭ*): condition.
shūrā: consultation.
shurb: wine-drinking.
taḥlīl: an intervening marriage contracted for the sole purpose of legalising remarriage between a divorced couple.
taḥrīm: prohibition, or rendering something into *ḥarām*.
taʿdiyah: transferrability.
taʿlīl: ratiocination, search for the effective cause of a ruling.
ta'wīl: allegorical interpretation.
taʿzīr: deterrence, discretionary penalty determined by the *qāḍī*.

takhṣīṣ: specifying the general.
taklīf: liability, obligation.
ṭalāq: divorce initiated by the husband.
taqiyyah: concealment of one's views to escape persecution.
taqlīd: imitation, following the views and opinions of others.
tashrīᶜ: legislation.
tawātur: continuous recurrence, continuous testimony.
tayammum: ablution with clean sand/earth in the event no water may be found.
tazkiyah: compurgation, testing the reliability of a witness, cross-examination.
ṯhaman: the purchase price.
ūlū al-amr: persons in authority and in charge of community affairs.
ummah: The Faith-community of Islam.
uṣūl al-Qānūn: modern jurisprudence.
waḥy: divine revelation.
wājib: obligatory, often synonymous with *farḍ*.
wājib ᶜaynī: personal obligation.
wājib kafāʾī: collective obligation of the entire community.
walī: guardian.
waqf: charitable endowment.
waṣf (pl. *awṣāf*): quality, attribute, adjective.
wilāyah (also *walāyah*): authority, guardianship (of minors and lunatics).
wuḍūʾ: ablution with clear water.
wujūb: obligation, rendering something obligatory.
ẓann: speculation, doubt, conjecture.
ẓannī: speculative, doubtful.
ẓāhir: manifest, apparent.
zinā: adultery, fornication.

Index